Breach of Fid
- Discipline
- Tort Damages

incompetence & Lack of communication
- discipline
- civil liability
- malpractice
- breach of fid.

Fraud
- tort of misrepresentation
- negligent misrepresentation
→ criminal or civil
Discipline

ineffective counsel

malpractice

Discipline

335 - 346

367 - 380

1.13
3.3 = Disclosure?
4.1

Traversing the Ethical Minefield

Traversing the Ethical Minefield

Problems, Law, and Professional Responsibility

Susan R. Martyn

Stoepler Professor of Law and Values
University of Toledo College of Law

Lawrence J. Fox

Partner, Drinker Biddle & Reath
Lecturer, Adjunct Professor, University of Pennsylvania Law School

1185 Avenue of the Americas, New York, NY 10036
www.aspenpublishers.com

A Wolters Kluwer Company
www.aspenpublishers.com

Printed in the United States of America.

1 2 3 4 5 6 7 8 9 0

0-7355-3345-8

Library of Congress Cataloging-in-Publication Data

Martyn, Susan R., 1947—
Traversing the ethical minefield : problems, law, and professional responsibility / Susan R. Martyn, Lawrence J. Fox.
p. cm.
Includes index.
ISBN 0-7355-3345-8
1. Legal ethics—United States. 2. Attorney and client—United States.
I. Fox, Lawrence J., 1943—II. Title.

KF306.M37 2004
174'.3'0973—dc22 2003063577

About Aspen Publishers

Aspen Publishers, headquartered in New York City, is a leading information provider for attorneys, business professionals, and law students. Written by preeminent authorities, our products consist of analytical and practical information covering both U.S. and international topics. We publish in the full range of formats, including updated manuals, books, periodicals, CDs, and online products.

Our proprietary content is complemented by 2,500 legal databases, containing over 11 million documents, available through our Loislaw division. Aspen Publishers also offers a wide range of topical legal and business databases linked to Loislaw's primary material. Our mission is to provide accurate, timely, and authoritative content in easily accessible formats, supported by unmatched customer care.

To order any Aspen Publishers title, go to *www.aspenpublishers.com* or call 1-800-638-8437.

To reinstate your manual update service, call 1-800-638-8437.

For more information on Loislaw products, go to *www.loislaw.com* or call 1-800-364-2512.

For Customer Care issues, e-mail *CustomerCare@aspenpublishers.com*; call 1-800-234-1660; or fax 1-800-901-9075.

Aspen Publishers
A Wolters Kluwer Company

For Peter, Angela, and Sarah
For Paulette, Tony, and Emily

Summary of Contents

Contents

PART II: LAWYERS AND CLIENTS: FIDUCIARY DUTY

Preface

This book represents a unique collaboration between a law professor with extensive academic experience (Susan Martyn) and a long-time practitioner who has dealt with most of the issues in this book (Larry Fox). We suspect that our casebook is unlike many you have encountered so far in law school, and therefore we begin your study by introducing you to our pedagogical goals as well as several distinctive features of the book you are about to use.

Overall, we intend these materials to accomplish four goals. First, we seek to engage you in a fascinating and dynamic subject. Second, we expect to teach you the rapidly expanding law governing lawyers. Third, we want to remind you of the need to pay careful attention to facts and context. Fourth, we invite you to recognize good lawyering, or the need to develop practical ethical judgment, a task that often may require lawyers to do more than simply comply with the law. To achieve these goals, we provide you with a combination of short problems, professional code provisions, interesting cases, short stories, and a series of continuing notes that introduce and develop repeating themes in the material.

The Problems

The short problems that introduce each section of the book ask you to evaluate the actions of a hypothetical law firm, Martyn & Fox. Each set of problems is followed by citations to the relevant professional code provisions and sections of the Restatement of the Law Governing Lawyers found in your rules supplement. You should prepare for each class by formulating answers to the problems after considering these provisions along with the relevant cases and other materials in the book.

As you address the dilemmas faced by Martyn & Fox, you will discover that the firm is capable of great inconsistency. At times, the lawyers at Martyn & Fox may seem wise and capable. On other occasions, you will wonder at their fallibility. In many situations, you may identify with their confusion and angst. Most often, the firm can be rescued from disaster by sage advice.

We intend these problems to promote all of our pedagogical goals, so you should expect to approach them on several levels. First, we hope they will engage you in interesting issues faced by modern lawyers. Second, we want them to motivate you to study the relevant provisions in various lawyer codes, the Restatement of the Law Governing Lawyers, and the cases and other materials that explain and construe them. Third, we anticipate that the relative brevity of each problem will lead you to conclude that the answer "depends on" additional facts that might change the advice you offer Martyn & Fox. Indeed, issues of professional responsibility often require careful attention to facts as well as law. We invite you to articulate your assumptions and to anticipate how additional facts might change your answer. For example, does it matter whether Martyn & Fox is a two- or two-hundred-person law firm? Whether it focuses primarily on litigation or transactional work? Whether its practice is located in a rural area or a major city? Whether the lawyer is a partner or an associate? Whether Martyn & Fox's client is an individual or an entity? How much Martyn & Fox's client can pay?

Finally, once you get into the law that governs the situation described in a problem, you will discover occasions when Martyn & Fox has a range of options. In these instances, you should identify the discretion ceded to the lawyer's individual moral conscience and articulate how you believe that discretion should be exercised. Here, we hope to assist you in developing practical ethical judgment as well as learning the law.

The Cases

Most people new to this subject are surprised at the vast array of cases that explain and expand on the professional code provisions and other remedies that make up the law governing lawyers. We offer you a rich assortment of these cases, emphasizing those decided in the past decade. Each of the 59 cases in this book has been edited for clarity. We use ellipses or brackets to indicate omissions from the court's opinion, but omitted citations and footnotes are not identified.

The Short Stories

The short stories in this book offer you the opportunity to engage in a difficult issue of legal ethics from the viewpoint of the lawyers confronting the situation. Larry wrote each story as a chapter in his book, *Legal Tender: A Lawyer's Guide to Handling Professional Dilemmas.* We have included these vignettes to offer you a break from traditional law study and an alternative way to learn some substantive law. Primarily, however, we intend these excerpts to show you the human face of some of the legal issues raised in the story. The extended detail of the story will enable you to understand more fully the context in which the lawyer must make a practical ethical judgment.

The Continuing Notes

Unlike the note material in most casebooks, the notes in this book are short essays organized around five general themes. These notes provide transitions between various topics in the materials, further explanation of a case or series of cases, and an opportunity to explore a topic at an accessible but more advanced level. They also serve as occasions to connect and integrate the basic ideas and themes that the courts have woven throughout the law governing lawyers.

The first set of continuing notes, entitled **Lawyers' Roles**, makes explicit the often-unnoticed roles lawyers assume when they represent clients, with particular emphasis on the balance of power in the professional relationship. Five notes on this theme appear throughout the book:

In these notes we identify various client-lawyer relationships and examine the legal risks created by each of these roles. We consider both philosophical issues, such as whether a lawyer who serves a client also can serve the interest of justice, and personal matters, such as the effect of various client-lawyer relationships on the personal and professional happiness and success of the lawyer. We hope these notes prod you to think about why some of the lawyers who became the subject of cases in this book got into trouble, as well as encourage you to consider the kind of lawyer you want to be.

The second series of continuing notes, entitled **The Law Governing Lawyers**, encompasses seven notes:

Here, we explore the fiduciary obligations lawyers assume when they say "yes," or agree to represent clients, and the remedies provided by the cases and materials when these obligations are ignored. We emphasize the difference and connections between professional discipline and the other legal consequences that can flow from lawyer malfeasance, such as disqualification, malpractice, ineffective assistance of counsel, and fee forfeiture. We also consider empirical studies of lawyers' work, which indicate how these legal consequences influence lawyer behavior in practice.

In the third group of notes, entitled **The Limits of the Law**, seven notes explain when lawyers may or must say "no" to clients, because of some external legal control that imposes a limit on the lawyer's advocacy.

In these notes, we explore the vast law of fraud, the ever-expanding criminal law, federal and state statutes concerning conflict of interest, procedural sanctions, and the impact of the Constitution on the regulation of lawyer conduct. Each of these bodies of general law has been read into the professional codes to create an explicit boundary beyond which lawyers tread only at great risk both to themselves and to their clients.

The fourth series of continuing notes, entitled **Practice Pointers**, offers you practical advice about how to avoid or mitigate the legal consequences raised by the problems, cases, and other materials. Here we showcase six topics:

The final set of notes, entitled **Lawyers and Other Professionals**, examines whether the courts treat lawyers and other professionals consistently. Here we identify issues that confront a variety of professionals, including:

This series of notes will enable you to compare the duties and obligations of lawyers with those of other professionals, such as health care providers, design professionals, accountants, clergy, and mental health professionals.

The Combination

Overall, we intend the problems, rules, cases, stories, and continuing notes in this book to serve as a guide to identifying, understanding, and avoiding the minefields and mistakes that the lawyers in these materials have confronted. We also hope you enjoy this study as much as we have enjoyed preparing it.

Susan Martyn and Larry Fox

February 2004

Acknowledgments

We could not have completed this casebook without the accumulated wisdom of hundreds of lawyers who have taught and refined our understanding of these issues. In particular, we thank our colleagues who served as reporters and advisors to the American Law Institute's Restatement (Third) of The Law Governing Lawyers and those who served with us on the ABA Ethics 2000 Commission. We also are indebted to many at the ABA Center for Professional Responsibility, who provided us with research data and information about recent developments exactly when we needed it.

The two of us first met in 1987 in a windowless conference room at the American Law Institute during a meeting of the advisors to the Restatement of the Law Governing Lawyers. These meetings clearly are an acquired taste. The Reporters to Restatement projects circulate a draft weeks before each meeting, then sit on a raised dais facing a semicircle of 25 or 30 judges, professors, and lawyers to defend each section, comment, and example line by line, usually for several days at a time. Only the good will and good humor of the participants can make such a process bearable, and we soon found that we were providing large doses of both for each other. From our 13-year sojourn with the ALI, a broad friendship developed that also took us into new adventures, including CLE programs and the ABA's Ethics 2000 project in which we both served as Commissioners to undertake a stem-to-stern review of the ABA Model Rules of Professional Conduct.

For us, nothing has been quite like our work on this volume. After Larry returned from a stay in Ithaca, Susan learned of the problems he had developed for his Professional Responsibility course at Cornell Law School and decided they could form the backbone of a casebook. Susan selected and edited the cases, organized the materials, and wrote the continuing notes in the book while teaching the materials to students at Toledo and Marquette. Larry contributed several chapters of short stories from his previously published book, *Legal Tender*, and provided often irreverent but helpful editorial critiques, which more than occasionally led to another conversation that benefited us both. In short, we could not have completed this book without each other, and we both feel free to blame the other for the flaws that remain.

The faculties and students at four law schools—Cornell, Marquette, the University of Pennsylvania, and the University of Toledo—contributed to these materials by consulting, arguing, and correcting many of our mistakes. Thanks also to Professors James Henderson, Richard Pearson, and John Siliciano, who inspired us with their continuing notes in *The Torts Process*. Others across the country also commented on and helped us formulate our ideas. Special thanks to Henry Bourguignon, James Caruso, David Caylor, Roger Cramton, Susan Daicoff, Stuart Green, Geoffrey Hazard, Barbara and Charles Hicks, Jack Kircher, Margaret Love, Judith Maute, Nancy Moore, Ellyn Rosen, Jack Sahl, Jack Sammons, Becky Stretch,

William Van Alstyne, and Brad Wendel. We also received able research assistance from Melinda Campbell, Karin Clarkston, Sajid Khan, Sarah Martyn, Stacy Roberts, Cheryl Slotterbeck, and Florence Vincent.

Our ideas never would have taken shape without the capable, cheerful, and knowledgeable assistance of Linda Whalen and Bea Cucinotta.

Susan would not have had the time to devote to this project without a sabbatical leave granted by the University of Toledo and the assistance of the Eugene N. Balk Fund, which provided the funds to carry out most of the research in the continuing notes. Larry never would have been able to develop the problems if it were not for the invitation from Charles Wolfram to escape practice and teach at the Cornell Law School.

Finally, our thanks to the following for permission to reproduce all or portions of their work:

American Bar Association, Formal Opinions 92-368, 93-379, 94-389. Reprinted by permission of the American Bar Association. Copies of ABA Ethics opinions are available from Service Center, American Bar Association, 650 North Lake Shore Drive, Chicago, IL 60600, 1-800-285-2221.

American Bar Association, *Legal Tender: A Lawyer's Guide to Handling Professional Dilemmas* by Lawrence J. Fox, pp. 122-125, 133-140, 157-166, 184-188. Reprinted by permission.

American Law Institute, *Implementing a Conflicts Control System* by Susan R. Martyn, in 40 The Practical Lawyer 15-24 (1994).

Cardozo Law Review, *Why Lawyers are Unhappy* by Martin E.P. Seligman, Paul R. Verkuil & Terry H. Kang, 23 Cardozo L. Rev. 33-53 (2001).

Matthew Bender & Co., a member of the LexisNexis Group, *Understanding Lawyers' Ethics* by Monroe H. Freedman & Abbe Smith, pp. 8, 51, 53-54, 60, 69-70, 79, 80 (2d ed. 2002). Reprinted with permission, © 2002, Matthew Bender & Co., a member of the LexisNexis Group. All rights reserved.

Nebraska Law Review, *In Defense of Client-Lawyer Confidentiality . . . And its Exceptions . . .* by Susan R. Martyn, 81 Neb. L. Rev. 1320-1350 (2003).

New York State Bar Association, Ethics Opinion 736, *Mediation, Matrimonial Matters* (2002), by the New York State Bar Association Committee on Professional Ethics.

Oxford University Press and Deborah L. Rhode, *In the Interests of Justice: Reforming the Legal Profession* © by Deborah L. Rhode, pp. 49-50, 53-58, 64-67, 77, and 79 (2000). Used by permission of Oxford University Press, Inc.

The University of Chicago Press and James Boyd White, *The Edge of Meaning*, pp. 223-226, 250-251 (2001).

Utah State Bar Association, Utah Ethics Advisory Opinion 99-04, by the Utah State Bar Association Ethics Advisory Opinion Committee (1999).

Traversing the Ethical Minefield

Part I

Introduction

Chapter 1

Lawyers, Role, and Law

A. Lawyers and Role

Problems

1-1. Should Martyn & Fox file a claim on behalf of a client after the statute of limitations has expired? What if we are fairly sure the opposing party will not be represented?

1-2. Based on nothing Martyn & Fox has said, the other side in a negotiation incorrectly believes that the property can be subdivided into ten lots. Should Martyn & Fox close the deal without correcting the mistake?

1-3. Should Martyn & Fox advise its client to sign an agreement in a divorce case that settles property division and child support where the opposing lawyer mistakenly believes that alimony can later be negotiated, but we know that the law will bar such a later claim? What if the opposing lawyer is a best friend and has not handled many divorces?

1-4. Should Martyn & Fox tell a client the chances of her getting caught doing something illegal (e.g., hiding a document requested by the other side in discovery or failing to pay parking tickets)?

Consider: Model Rules Preamble and Scope
Restatement of the Law Governing Lawyers §1

Monroe H. Freedman & Abbe Smith

Understanding Lawyers' Ethics

pp. 8, 51, 53-54, 60, 69-70, 79, 80 (2d ed., LexisNexis 2002)

. . . In expressing the distinctive feature of ethics in the legal profession, we would identify the client not as "this other person, over whom I have power," but as "this other person whom I have the power to help." In that view, the central concern of lawyers' ethics is not (as Professor Schaffer says, quoting Plato) how my client "can be made as good as possible."* Rather, it is how far we can ethically go — or

* *See* Thomas Shaffer, *Legal Ethics and the Good Client*, 36 Cath. U. L. Rev. 319, 320 (1987).

how far we should be required to go — to achieve for our clients full and equal rights under law.

Put otherwise, Professor Shaffer thinks of lawyers' ethics as being rooted in moral philosophy, while we think of lawyers' ethics as being rooted in the moral values that are expressed in the Bill of Rights. . . .

Can you be a good lawyer and a good person at the same time? The question implies that serving your clients competently and zealously will require you to violate your personal morality in at least some instances.

At the heart of that issue is whether it is the lawyer or the client who should make the moral decisions that come up in the course of the representation. As it is frequently put: Is the lawyer just a "hired gun," or must the lawyer "obey his own conscience, not that of his client?". . .

. . . In an article that has been widely cited with approval,[6] [Professor Richard] Wasserstrom recalls John Dean's list of those involved in the Watergate coverup. Dean placed an asterisk next to the names of each of the lawyers on the list, because he had been struck by the fact that so many of those implicated were lawyers. Wasserstrom concludes that the involvement of lawyers in Watergate was "natural, if not unavoidable," the "likely if not inevitable consequence of their legal acculturation." Indeed, on the basis of Wasserstrom's analysis the only matter of wonder is why so many of those on John Dean's list were *not* lawyers. What could possibly have corrupted the non-lawyers to such a degree as to have led them into the uniquely amoral and immoral world of the lawyers? "For at best," Wasserstrom asserts, "the lawyer's world is a simplified moral world; often it is an amoral one; and more than occasionally perhaps, an overtly immoral one."

Wasserstrom considers "role-differentiated behavior" to be the root of the problem. As he says, the "nature of role-differentiated behavior . . . often makes it both appropriate and desirable for the person in a particular role to put to one side considerations of various sorts — and especially various moral considerations — that would otherwise be relevant if not decisive."

Illustrative of how Wasserstrom thinks lawyers should make moral considerations relevant is his suggestion that a lawyer should refuse to advise a wealthy client of a tax loophole provided by the legislature for only a few wealthy taxpayers. If that case were to be generalized, it would mean that the legal profession can properly regard itself as an oligarchy, whose duty is to nullify decisions made by the people's duly elected representatives? . . .

Nevertheless, Wasserstrom suggests that lawyers should "see themselves less as subject to role-differentiated behavior and more as subject to the demands of *the* moral point of view." Is it really that simple? Is there a single point of view that can be identified as "the" moral one? . . .

In day-to-day practice, the most common instances of a moral or immoral conduct by lawyers are those occasions in which we preempt our clients' moral judgments. That occurs in two ways. Most often lawyers assume that the client wants her to maximize his material or tactical position in every way that is legally permissible, regardless of non-legal considerations. That is, lawyers tend to assume the worst regarding the client's desires, and act accordingly. Much less frequently, we believe, a lawyer will decide that a particular course of conduct is morally preferable, even though not required legally, and will follow that course on the client's behalf without

6. Richard Wasserstrom, *Lawyers as Professionals: Some Moral Issues*, 5 ABA Human Rights 1 (1975).

consultation. In either event, the lawyer fails in her responsibility to maximize the client's autonomy by providing the client with the fullest advice and counsel, legal and moral, so that the client can make the most informed choice possible. . . .

One of the essential values of a just society is respect for the dignity of each member of that society. Essential to each individual's dignity is the free exercise of his autonomy. Toward that end, each person is entitled to know his rights with respect to society and other individuals, and to decide whether to seek fulfillment of those rights through the due processes of law.

The lawyer, by virtue of her training and skills, has a legal and practical monopoly over access to the legal system and knowledge about the law. The lawyer's advice and assistance are often indispensable, therefore, to the effective exercise of individual autonomy.

Accordingly, the attorney acts both professionally and morally in assisting clients to maximize their autonomy, that is, by counseling clients candidly and fully regarding the clients' legal rights and moral responsibilities as the lawyer perceives them, and by assisting clients to carry out their lawful decisions. Further, the attorney acts unprofessionally and immorally by depriving clients of their autonomy, that is, by denying them information regarding their legal rights, by otherwise preempting their moral decisions, or by depriving them of the ability to carry out their lawful decisions.

Until the lawyer-client relationship is contracted, however — until, that is, the lawyer chooses to induce another to rely upon her professional knowledge and skills — the lawyer ordinarily acts entirely within the scope of her own autonomy. Barring extraordinary circumstances, therefore, the attorney is free to exercise her personal judgment as to whether to represent a particular client. Since a moral choice is implicated in such a decision, however, others are entitled to judge and to criticize, on moral grounds, a lawyer's decision to represent a particular client or cause. . . .

Closely related to the concept of client autonomy is the lawyer's obligation to give "entire devotion to the interest of the client, warm zeal in the maintenance and defense of his rights and the exertion of [the lawyer's] utmost learning ability."[1] This ethic of zeal is a "traditional aspiration" that was already established in Abraham Lincoln's day, and zealousness continues today to be "*the* fundamental principle of the law of lawyering," and "the dominant standard of lawyerly excellence."

Client autonomy refers to the client's right to decide what her own interests are. Zealousness refers to the dedication with which the lawyer furthers the client's interests. The ethic of zeal is, therefore, pervasive in lawyers' professional responsibilities, because it infuses all of the lawyer's other ethical obligations with "entire devotion to the interest of the client." . .

The obligation of "entire devotion to the interest of the client [and] warm zeal in the maintenance and defense of his rights" is not limited to the role of the lawyer as advocate in the courtroom. . . . It is important to remember, however, that any lawyer who counsels a client, negotiates on a client's behalf, or drafts a legal document for a client must do so with an actual or potential adversary in mind. When a contract is negotiated, there is a party on the other side. A contract, a will, or a form submitted to a government agency may well be read at some later date with an adversary's eye, and could become the subject of litigation. The advice given to a client and acted upon today may strengthen or weaken the client's position in litigation next year. In short, it is not just the advocate in the courtroom who functions

1. ABA Canons of Prof. Ethics 15 (1908).

in an adversary system, and it is not just the client currently in litigation who may both require and be entitled to "warm zeal in the maintenance and defense of his rights."

Deborah L. Rhode

In the Interests of Justice: Reforming the Legal Profession

pp. 49-79 (Oxford University Press 2000)

The Advocate's Role in the Adversary System

My first legal case was almost my last. It brought home Dostoevski's definition of an advocate as "a conscience for hire." And it made me wonder about putting mine on the market.

The insight came when I was interning at the Washington, D.C., public defender's office after my first year in law school. Two of the office's juvenile clients had stomped an elderly "wino" to death, just for the fun of it. They confessed to my supervising attorney and to the arresting officer; indeed, they appeared somewhat proud of their accomplishment. However, the police committed a number of constitutional and procedural violations in obtaining the confession and other inculpating evidence. My supervisor was able to get the case dismissed on what the public would consider a "technicality." He also was proud of his accomplishment. The clients were jubilant and unrepentant. I had no doubt that the office would see them again. Nor did I doubt that I was utterly unsuited to be a criminal defense lawyer. I wasn't sure I was ready to be a lawyer at all.

Now, with the benefit of a quarter century's hindsight, I think both my supervisor and I were right. He was providing an essential and ethically defensible safeguard for constitutional values. And I was right to feel morally troubled by the consequences. I had assisted a process that sent the wrong messages to guilty clients: some lives are cheap; a gifted lawyer can get you off.

This is one of the "hard cases" in legal ethics. Its moral tensions arise from deeply rooted conflicts in America's commitments to both individual rights and social responsibilities. This conflict plays out in many law-related contexts, and legal ethics is no exception. When lawyers straddle these cultural contradictions, the public both demands and condemns their divided loyalties. Defense of disempowered clients and unpopular causes earns lawyers their greatest respect but also their sharpest criticism. The clash between lawyers' responsibilities as officers of the court and advocates of client interests creates the most fundamental dilemmas of legal ethics. All too often, the bar has resolved this conflict by permitting overrepresentation of those who can afford it and underrepresentation of everyone else. The result is to privilege the profession's interests at the expense of the public's. . . .

The Premises of Partisanship

The standard ethical justifications for the advocate's role rest on two major premises. The first assumption, drawing on utilitarian reasoning, is that an adversarial clash between opposing advocates is the best way of discovering truth. The second assumption, based on individual rights, is that morally neutral partisanship is the most effective means of protecting human freedom and dignity. Both claims unravel at several key points.

The truth-based rationale for the advocate's role assumes that the "right" result is most likely to occur through competitive presentations of relevant law and facts. As a report by the Joint Conference of the American Bar Association and the Association of American Law Schools emphasized, only when a decision-maker "has had the benefit of intelligent and vigorous advocacy on both sides" can society have confidence in the decision. This faith in partisan process is part of a broader worldview that underpins America's basic social and economic institutions. Robert Kutak, chair of the ABA commission that drafted the Model Rules of Professional Conduct, observed that our commitment to the advocate's role in an adversarial framework reflects "the same deep-seated values we place on competition" in other contexts.

A second defense of neutral partisanship involves the protection of rights and the relationships necessary to safeguard those rights. Here again, the priority we give to personal liberties is rooted in more general cultural commitments. In a highly legalistic society, preservation of personal dignity and autonomy requires preservation of access to law. According to bar leaders, individual freedom would be severely compromised if the profession began screening cases on the basis of their moral merit. The result would be an "oligarchy of lawyers," in which "saints [would] have a monopoly on lawsuits," and lawyers would have a monopoly on determining who qualified for sainthood. The legal profession has no special claim to righteousness and no public accountability for their view of justice. By what right should they "play God" by foreclosing legal assistance or imposing "their own views about the path of virtue upon their clients"?

If advocates assumed such authority, bar leaders further claim that ethical professionals would refuse to assist those clients most in need of ethical counseling. And if advocates were held morally accountable for their clients' conduct, less legal representation would be available for those most vulnerable to popular prejudice and governmental repression. Our history provides ample illustrations of the social and economic penalties directed at attorneys with unpopular clients. It was difficult enough to find lawyers for accused communists in the McCarthy era and for political activists in the early southern civil rights campaign. Those difficulties would have been far greater without the principle that legal representation is not an endorsement of client conduct.

These rights-based justifications of neutral partisanship assume special force in criminal cases. Individuals whose lives, liberty, and reputation are at risk deserve an advocate without competing loyalties to the state. Ensuring effective representation serves not only to avoid unjust outcomes but also to affirm community values and to express our respect for individual rights. Guilt or innocence should be determined in open court with due process of law, not in the privacy of an attorney's office. The consequences of an alternative model are readily apparent in many totalitarian countries. Where defense lawyers' role is to "serve justice," rather than their clients, what passes for "justice" does not commend itself for export. Often the roles of counsel for the defendant and the state are functionally identical and the price is paid in innocent lives. A case in point involves China's celebrated prosecution of the Gang of Four following the Cultural Revolution of the 1960s. The attorney appointed to defend Mao Tse-tung's widow chose not to honor his client's request to assert her innocence or to conduct any investigations, present any witnesses, or challenge the government's case. According to the lawyer, such advocacy was unnecessary because "the police and the prosecutors worked on the case a very long time and the evidence they found which wasn't true they threw away."

This country has had similar experiences when the crime has been especially heinous or the accused has been a member of a particularly unpopular group. To take only the most obvious example, for most of this nation's history, southern blacks accused of an offense against a white victim stood little chance of anything approximating zealous advocacy or a fair trial. Despite substantial progress, racial and ethnic bias in legal proceedings remains common, as most Americans and virtually every bar task force agree. The risk of abuse is significant in other contexts as well. Perjury, fabrication of evidence, and suppression of exculpatory material by law enforcement officials remain pervasive problems. Such abuses were present in some two-thirds of the sixty-odd cases involving defendants facing the death penalty who recently have been exonerated by DNA evidence. . . .

Although these rationales for zealous advocacy have considerable force, they fall short of justifying current partisanship principles. A threshold weakness is the bar's overreliance on criminal defense as an all-purpose paradigm for the lawyer's role. Only a small amount of legal work involves either criminal proceedings or civil matters that raise similar concerns of individual freedom and governmental power. An advocacy role designed to ensure the presumption of innocence and deter prosecutorial abuse is not necessarily transferable to other legal landscapes. Bar rhetoric that casts the lawyer as a "champion against a hostile world" seems out of touch with most daily practice. The vast majority of legal work assists corporate and wealthy individual clients in a system that is scarcely hostile to their interests. When a Wall Street firm representing a Fortune 500 corporation squares off against understaffed regulators or a victim of unsafe practices, the balance of power is not what bar metaphors imply.

A similar problem arises with traditional truth-based justifications for neutral partisanship. Their underlying premise, that accurate results will emerge from competitive partisan presentations before disinterested tribunals, depends on factual assumptions that seldom hold in daily practice. Most legal representation never receives oversight from an impartial decision maker. Many disputes never reach the point of formal legal complaint, and of those that do, over 90 percent settle before trial. Moreover, even cases that end up in court seldom resemble the bar's idealized model of adversarial processes. That model presupposes adversaries with roughly equal incentives, resources, capabilities, and access to relevant information. But those conditions are more the exception than the rule in a society that tolerates vast disparities in wealth, high litigation costs, and grossly inadequate access to legal assistance. As a majority of surveyed judges agreed, a mismatch in attorneys' skills can distort outcomes; a mismatch in client resources compounds the problem. In law, as in life, the haves generally come out ahead. . . .

For similar reasons, the bar's traditional rights-based justifications offer inadequate support for prevailing adversarial practices. Such justifications implicitly assume that clients are entitled to assistance in whatever the law permits. This assumption confuses legal and moral rights. Some conduct that is socially indefensible may remain lawful because adequate prohibitions appear unenforceable or because decision-making bodies are too uninformed or compromised by special interests to impose effective regulation. An ethic of undivided client loyalty in these contexts has encouraged lawyers' assistance in some of the most socially costly enterprises in recent memory, the distribution of asbestos and Dalkon Shields, the suppression of health information about cigarettes, and the financially irresponsible ventures of savings and loan associations.

Defenders of neutral partisanship typically respond that protection of client rights is ethically justifiable despite such consequences because individual liberty and autonomy are of paramount value in a free society. Moral philosophers generally make no such mistake. As David Luban notes, this standard justification for zealous advocacy blurs an important distinction between the "desirability of people acting autonomously and the desirability of their autonomous acts." It is, for example, morally desirable for clients to make their own decisions about whether to attempt to defeat a needy opponent's valid claim through a legal technicality; it is not morally desirable for them actually to do so. Autonomy does not have intrinsic value; its importance derives from the values it fosters, such as individual initiative and responsibility. If a particular client objective does little to promote those values, or does so only at much greater cost to third parties, then the ethical justification for zealous advocacy is less convincing. . . .

Professional Interests and Partisan Practices

Whatever their inadequacies in serving the public interest, prevailing adversarial practices have been reasonably effective in serving professional interests. They permit all the justice that money can buy or a client who can afford it, and they impose few responsibilities on those who cannot. . . .

The Price of Partisanship

Yet these financial and psychological comforts come at a price. The avoidance of ethical responsibility is ultimately corrosive for lawyers, clients, and the legal framework on which they depend. For many practitioners, the neutral partisan role undermines the very commitments that led them to become lawyers. . . . The submersion of self into a role too often leaves the advocate alienated from his own moral convictions. When professional action becomes detached from ordinary moral experience, the lawyer's ethical sensitivity erodes. The agnosticism that neutral partisanship encourages can readily spill over into other areas of life and undercut a lawyer's sense of moral identify. . . .

Neither lawyers' nor clients' long-term interests are served by eroding the institutional frameworks on which an effective rule of law depends. Taken to its logical extreme, a professional role that gives primary allegiance to client concerns can undermine the legal order. Yale law professor Robert Gordon gives an example: "[T]ake any simple case of compliance counseling; suppose the legal rule is clear, yet the chance of detecting violations low, the penalties small in relation to the gains from non compliance, or the terrorizing of regulators into settlement by a deluge of paper predictably easy. The mass of lawyers who advise and then assist with noncompliance in such a situation could, in the vigorous pursuit of their clients' interests, effectively nullify the laws.". . .

The bar has similar responsibilities concerning core cultural values. Norms like good faith, honesty, and fair dealing are essential for efficient markets and effective regulatory systems. These values depend on some shared restraint in the pursuit of short-term client interests. Legal processes present frequent opportunities for obstruction, obfuscation, and overreaching. An advocacy role that imposes few practical constraints on such behavior erodes expectations of trust and cooperation. These expectations are common goods on which clients as a group ultimately depend. In the short term, free riders can profit by violating norms that others respect. But these values cannot survive if deviance becomes a routine and acceptable part of the advocate's repertoire. Over the long run, a single-minded pursuit of clients' individual self-interests is likely to prove self-defeating for clients as a group. . . .

An Alternative Framework

An alternative framework for the advocate's role needs to be ethically justifiable in principle and consistently reinforced in practice. At its most basic level, such a framework would require lawyers to accept personal responsibility for the moral consequences of their professional actions. Attorneys should make decisions as advocates in the same way that morally reflective individuals make any ethical decision. Lawyers' conduct should be justifiable under consistent, disinterested, and generalizable principles. These moral principles can, of course, recognize the distinctive needs of lawyers' occupational role. . . .

However, unlike the bar's prevailing approach, this alternative framework would require lawyers to assess their obligations in light of all the societal interests at issue in particular practice contexts. . . . Respect for law is a fundamental value, particularly among those sworn to uphold it. Adherence to generally accepted rules also serves as a check against the decision maker's own bias or self-interest. But attorneys may confront cases in which the applicable rules are so indeterminate or inadequate that reference to broader moral principles is necessary.

Most ethical dilemmas arise in areas where the governing standards already leave significant room for discretion. Individual attorneys can decide whether to accept or withdraw from representation and whether to pursue certain tactics. In resolving such questions, lawyers need to consider the social context of their choices. They cannot simply rely on some idealized model of adversarial and legislative processes. Rather, lawyers must assess their action against a realistic backdrop, in which wealth, power, and information are unequally distributed, not all interests are adequately represented, and most matters will never reach a neutral tribunal. The less confidence that attorneys have in the justice system's capacity to deliver justice in a particular case, the greater their own responsibility to attempt some corrective.

. . . At one end of the spectrum are those who believe that lawyers have responsibilities to pursue substantive justice and that such responsibilities may sometimes authorize noncompliance with formal legal requirements. In defending this position, William Simon analogizes to the decisions of judges or juries when they nullify a law. Our system accepts their refusal to enforce an outmoded statute or to convict a guilty defendant when necessary to avoid serious injustice. In Simon's view, we should grant lawyers similar discretion to disregard legal rules that appear plainly wrong and that compromise fundamental values. Under his analysis, rules that irrationally withhold minimal welfare support might justify such noncompliance. At the other end of the spectrum are ethics experts who deny that the equities for clients should define the responsibilities for attorneys. According to Harvard law professor Andrew Kaufman, "Being on the wrong side of the entitlement line does not seem to me to give the welfare mother any moral claim to the lawyer's assistance." Geoffrey Hazard similarly argues that the appropriateness of lawyers' strategies in divorce cases should not "turn on the underlying merits." From these commentators' perspective, respect for formal rules is essential for effective legal processes. If these rules result in substantial injustice, a lawyer should work publicly for their reform, not subvert them privately for particular clients.

An intermediate position, and the one most compatible with the contextual ethical framework proposed here, seeks ways of advancing justice without violating formal prohibitions. Lawyers taking this position may pursue a result that is morally but not substantively justified as long as they refrain from illegal conduct such as knowing presentation of perjury or preparation of fraudulent documents. . . .

. . . [T]he aim of this alternative framework is for lawyers to make the merits matter and to assess them from a moral as well as a legal vantage. Not all poor clients would be entitled to unqualified advocacy. But neither would factors like poverty be irrelevant if they affect the justice of a particular claim. Of course, in a profession as large and diverse as the American bar, different lawyers will make different judgments about what is in fact just. Although such judgments should be defensible under accepted ethical principles, their application will necessarily reflect individuals' own experiences and commitments. . . . But the framework proposed here does not demand that lawyers reach the same results in hard cases. It demands rather that lawyers recognize that such cases *are* hard and that they call for contextual moral judgments. . . .

Lawyers' Roles: *The Client-Lawyer Relationship*

Close your eyes and try to imagine yourself as the lawyer for a potential client. You meet this prospective client for the first time. First, do you envision an individual or an organizational client? Second, how do you decide whether to undertake this representation? Is your primary concern whether and how much the client can pay? Or are you equally or exclusively concerned about the effect of this legal representation upon society as a whole? Third, assuming you decide to handle the matter, think of what you will do for the client. Do you see yourself as a legal technician who will execute the client's instructions? Or are you more comfortable imagining yourself as a guardian of the rule of law whose job it is to explain the legal realities of the situation to the client? Will you talk to the client about the moral as well as the legal implications of the client's chosen course of action? Finally, imagine the place where this meeting occurs and what it conveys about the answers to these questions. Are you meeting in your office? Your client's office or home? A courtroom? Where are you sitting or standing? Across from the client at your desk? At the client's desk? Alongside the client?

In this series of notes entitled "Lawyer's Roles," we will examine these questions, focusing on the way lawyers articulate their own sense of role in relation both to clients and the legal system. Professors Freedman, Smith, and Rhode understand lawyers' ethics as a function of the social role a lawyer assumes in representing a client. They all believe that the lawyer professional codes should foster a distinct model of the client-lawyer relationship. As you assess the law governing lawyers, you will find it helpful to inquire whether each rule and policy advances a model of law practice that you wish to follow.

Professors Freedman and Smith endorse what has been labeled the "dominant" or the adversary ethic. This view emphasizes that lawyers have fiduciary duties to represent clients zealously, motivated by and focused on the client's values and goals. Legal rights exist to protect human autonomy, which is essential to human dignity. Lawyers do the right thing by serving what is essentially human in others. Justice is defined in terms of the legal rights granted to citizens. The legal system protects and reinforces the individual decisions that people are best able to make for themselves, rather than any competing version of social welfare or outcome.

To a philosopher, this view is "relentlessly deontological" that is, focused on the duties of lawyers in relation to clients, rather than on any particular outcome those relationships create.[1] The lawyer's morality depends primarily on her role as an advocate, which in turn requires two primary virtues. The lawyer must be simultaneously both neutral (because her client's interests should prevail), and partisan (to promote those interests). Amoral advocacy becomes the guiding norm of the adversary ethic.[2]

Professor Rhode criticizes the neutral partisanship this role seems to require. She argues instead for a public interest ethic that would require lawyers to be subject to personal moral responsibility for the results of their actions. Although she agrees with Professors Freedman and Smith that deontological or rights-based justifications have special force in criminal cases where individuals can be overwhelmed by governmental power, she questions why lawyers should apply the same ethic to powerful interests like wealthy individuals and large corporations. She also defines justice in terms of distributive fairness rather than individual rights, meaning that lawyers should consider the social harm they help clients foist on unrepresented persons or interests.

A philosopher might label Professor Rhode's view teleological or utilitarian, that is, focused on the ultimate goal or consequences of individual client-lawyer relationships. According to this view, lawyers should assess the consequences of each legal representation and hold themselves personally accountable for the outcome. Lawyers who adopt this view will envision their social role as connected to some larger conception of the public interest. This lawyer ultimately will need to accept personal moral responsibility for distributive fairness, or "justice in the long run."[3]

Commentators have characterized these two views in a number of colorful ways.[4] A lawyer who adopts some form of the dominant or adversarial ethic has been labeled "client-centered," as well as called an "amoral instrument," "hired gun," "plumber," "puppet," or "prostitute." This lawyer can overidentify with clients and can lack the independent judgment necessary to provide proper legal advice. The other extreme has been called "directive," "traditional," "authoritarian," or "parentalist."[5] Expert lawyers, familiar with the legal system, presume they know what is best and act as authorities in all aspects of the relationship. These lawyers can underidentify with clients and can assume a judgelike perspective, ignoring fiduciary duties that demand advice and advocacy.

Lawyers as Instruments

Instrumental lawyers tend to focus on providing individual client representation and adversarial advocacy. Some pride themselves in representing almost any client who

---

1. Timothy P. Terrell, *Turmoil at the Normative Core of Lawyering: Uncomfortable Lessons from the "Metaethics" of Legal Ethics*, 49 Emory L.J. 87 (2000); Stephen L. Pepper, *The Lawyer's Amoral Ethical Role: A Defense, a Problem, and Some Possibilities*, 1986 Am. Bar Found. Research J. 613.
2. *See* David Luban, *Lawyers and Justice: An Ethical Study*, at xx (Princeton U. Press 1988).
3. *See* William H. Simon, *The Practice of Justice; A Theory of Lawyers' Ethics* 53-76 (Harvard U. Press 1998).
4. *See* James E. Moliterno, *Ethics of the Lawyer's Work* 129-130 (2d ed., West 2003); Symposium, *Client Counseling and Moral Responsibility*, 30 Pepp. L. Rev. 591 (2003).
5. Professors Shaffer and Cochran divide this category into two parts. They call the first the lawyer as "Godfather," where the lawyer controls the representation and seeks client victory, and the second the lawyer as "guru" where the lawyer controls the representation and seeks client goodness. Thomas L. Shaffer & Robert F. Cochran, Jr., *Lawyers, Clients, and Moral Responsibility* 7-9, 32-39 (West 1994).

seeks their assistance, on the theory that every point of view deserves legal representation. Others, like Professors Freedman and Smith, prefer to exercise moral judgment about which clients to represent, because they are not willing to devote their legal skills to advocate every point of view.

Once they agree to take on a representation, instrumental lawyers rightly recognize fiduciary duties of competence, communication, confidentiality, and loyalty to clients.[6] At the same time, their preference for client autonomy may tempt them to suppress their own moral judgment and cede all authority to the client in the process. Single-minded loyalty to a client then becomes transformed into a narrow-minded unquestioning devotion to that client's will. The client's value system controls the representation, and the lawyer escapes any moral accountability for the outcome or means used.

Lawyers who prefer an instrumental view of their role see only one limit to client advocacy: the bounds of the law and the legal system itself. Yet these legal bounds may be unclear to an instrumental lawyer, when law itself is viewed as a malleable means to pursue the client's desires.[7] If the legal system exists to promote individual welfare, then law can be viewed primarily as a process that provides clients with a means to challenge or take advantage of the existing order.[8] It follows that, if the client has an arguable legal right, the lawyer should or must pursue it. Instrumental lawyers view the social fabric as relatively strong, capable of withstanding most challenges to the existing limits of the law or other majoritarian interests.

At the same time, however, focusing primarily or exclusively on client interests may cause instrumental lawyers to lose opportunities to explain a legal or moral boundary to clients or even to discover a client's true intention. Worse, these lawyers can become blind to a clear legal limit that may subject the client and the lawyer to severe sanctions. The result may be serious harm to others as well as the client and the lawyer.

Professor Wasserstrom warns that assuming such role-differentiated behavior also may transform a lawyer's entire personality. Lawyers who see their role in instrumental terms, for example, may be unrelenting and unwilling to compromise, even when the client seeks settlement. Lawyers who live an amoral professional life may be tempted to assume an amoral personal existence as well. Such lawyers also may incorporate those qualities deemed essential to accomplishing their task, such as competitive, aggressive, ruthless, and pragmatic behavior rather than cooperative, accommodating, compassionate, and principled action.[9]

Lawyers as Directors

Directive lawyers tend to focus on their roles as officers of the legal system and members of a profession. Some pride themselves in taking on any client, because they care little or not at all about the client's goals or viewpoint. Others, accustomed

---

6. David A. Binder, Paul Bergman & Susan C. Price, *Lawyers as Counselors: A Client-Centered Approach* 16-24 (West 1991).

7. Of course, this statement vastly oversimplifies the complexity of various philosophies of law, which may shape any lawyer's practice. *See* Gerald B. Wetlaufer, *Systems of Belief in Modern American Law: A View from Century's End*, 49 Am. U. L. Rev. 1 (1999).

8. Professor Wetlaufer includes some legal realists and the proponents of contemporary critical theory in this category and describes these lawyers as generally skeptical about the fairness and legitimacy of the existing order, the possibility of the rule of law, the use of reason, and the use of language to convey stable and determinate meaning. *Id.* at 61-62.

9. Richard Wasserstrom, *Lawyers as Professionals: Some Moral Issues,* 5 Human Rights 1 (1975).

to relying on their own judgment, tend to lean on their own personal values in deciding which clients to represent. This may mean, for example, that the client's willingness to pursue a particular legal goal, or the client's ability to pay become dominant factors in determining whether to take on a matter.

Once they agree to take on a representation, directive lawyers nod to basic fiduciary duties, but also regard themselves as legal experts who should determine how to handle the matter with little client consultation. Their preference for legal solutions may tempt them to underidentify with clients, whom they see as lacking the lawyer's experience and judgment or as too emotionally close to the matter to consider the short and long-term consequences of their decisions. The lawyer's legal expertise then can generalize and transform into a moral judgment about the proper outcome for a client. Here, the lawyer cedes little authority to the client and the lawyer's values control the representation.

Lawyers who believe they know more than their clients also may find it relatively easy to impose limits on client advocacy. The lawyer's own view of the law and its limits often are seen as an objective datum not subject to argument or modification. Directive lawyers can see the legal system as a means to promote social order and stability, and the law as the categorization of principles that shape client expectations.[10] They are apt to see law as necessary to preserving a relatively thin social fabric that easily could unravel without constant tending by lawyers.

It follows that lawyers should seek the best legal solution to a client matter by pigeonholing client interests into preexisting legal categories. At the same time, focusing on legal outcomes means that the lawyer can lose an opportunity to challenge a legal rule or apply it in a different context. More extreme is the tendency of some directive lawyers to limit client advocacy by imposing their own social agenda on the client's matter. Even worse, knowing what is best may be confused with preferring a lawyer's own personal agenda (often a monetary goal) over the client's interests. The client then becomes an object to be used to pursue the lawyer's goals, rather than a subject who deserves individual respect. If this occurs, lawyers who believe they know best can become blind to basic fiduciary duty, which requires them to consult and obey client instructions.

Like the instrumental lawyer, the directive lawyer may assume personality characteristics that permeate the lawyer's life. Directive lawyers who define their role as conciliatory, for example, may pressure a client to settle or compromise when the client wishes to vindicate an important right. Such lawyers also can be judgmental, controlling, even patronizing and overbearing in their professional and personal life. They also may be impatient and have trouble listening to others. Directive lawyers may share the pragmatism of instrumental lawyers, but they often will prefer tangible legal standards to less clearly articulated individual facts or emotional feelings.

Lawyers as Collaborators

The problems with both of these models point to a golden mean that most lawyers adopt most of the time. The lawyer who heeds both fiduciary duty and the limits of the law but steers clear of the instrumental and directive extremes can be character-

10. Professor Wetlaufer attributes this view to those he calls "Team Faithful" because of their faith in the fairness and legitimacy of the existing social order. He includes legal formalists, natural law proponents, positivists, as well as the legal process and law and economics schools of thought in this group. Wetlaufer, *supra* note 7, at 61-63, 72.

ized as a "collaborator,"[11] "translator,"[12] "wise counselor,"[13] teacher,"[14] "statesman,"[15] or "friend."[16] Collaborative lawyers create enough professional distance to offer objective advice, but foster a relationship that enables the client to articulate the ends and means of the representation. Clients are seen as best able to make decisions for themselves, but need the expertise and perspective of lawyers to consider fully both their own interests as well as the effect of their decisions on others.

Philosophically, this model of the client-lawyer relationship acknowledges both a deontological and a utilitarian view, but also can rely on a relational ethic of care.[17] Collaborative lawyers adopt a deontological viewpoint because they respect and see it as their duty to promote the individual autonomy of each client. Collaborative lawyers also care about the utilitarian legal and nonlegal consequences of a client representation, both for the client and those that the client might affect. Beyond professional duties and client rights, many collaborative lawyers also exhibit character traits such as empathy and compassion in order to discern the client's full scope of interests. In deciding how to proceed, this means that the lawyer weighs heavily the significant obligation to favor the client's interests as articulated by the client.

To enable clients to articulate their interests, collaborative lawyers believe that they should join with clients in the representation, but neither dominate nor be dominated by a client's values. The relationship itself is participatory,[18] deliberative, or collaborative. At the same time, collaborative lawyers care about integrating personal and professional morality, which may lead them to question or even challenge the goals of the representation as well as the client's values. Lawyer and client might even be characterized as friends, who "wrestle with and resolve the moral issues" in the representation.[19] Individual clients should be respected as subjects not treated as objects, but entity clients may be more objectified.

Lawyers as collaborators recognize the law itself as more than formless process, but less than categorical command. They understand that many legal norms are definitive and apply to shape the matter in question. At the same time, they appreciate the fact that applicable legal norms may conflict and that law must be applied to individual circumstances. Overall, they view law as deeply embedded with moral norms that address some of the most significant issues in human existence. They understand and value the contribution of these norms to the social welfare, but remain willing to challenge existing majoritarian interests when they do not respect

---

11. Robert F. Cochran, Jr., John M. A. DiPippa & Martha M. Peteres, *The Counselor-at-Law: A Collaborative Approach to Client Interviewing and Counseling* (Lexis 1999).
12. Clark D. Cunningham, *The Lawyer as Translator, Representation as Text: Towards an Ethnography of Legal Discourse,* 77 Cornell L. Rev. 1298 (1992).
13. Lon L. Fuller & John D. Randall, *Professional Responsibility: Report of the Joint Conference of the American Bar Association and the Association of American Law School,* 44 ABA J. 1159, 1161 (1958).
14. William F. May, *Beleaguered Rulers: The Public Obligation of the Professional* (Westminster John Knox 2001).
15. Anthony T. Kronman, *The Lost Lawyer: Failing Ideals of the Legal Profession* (Harvard 1993).
16. Shaffer & Cochran, *supra* note 5, at 44-54; Stephen R. Morris, *The Lawyer as Friend: An Aristotelian Inquiry,* 26 J. Legal Prof. 55 (2002). Some commentators have used this appellation to describe the instrumental lawyer. *See, e.g.,* Charles H. Fried, *The Lawyer as Friend,* 85 Yale L.J. 1060 (1976), which has been criticized by a number of commentators. *See, e.g.,* Charles J. Ogletree, Jr., *Beyond Justifications: Seeking Motivations to Sustain Public Defenders,* 106 Harv. L. Rev. 1239 (1993); Edward A. Dauer & Arthur A. Leff, *Correspondence, The Lawyer as Friend,* 86 Yale L.J. 573 (1977).
17. *See* Stephen Ellmann, *The Ethic of Care as an Ethic for Lawyers,* 81 Geo. L.J. 2665 (1993).
18. Douglas E. Rosenthal, *Lawyer and Client: Who's in Charge?* (Russell Sage Found. 1974).
19. Shaffer & Cochran, *supra* note 5, at 42-54.

the individual rights of a client. Overall, collaborative lawyers seek to act as translators of the moral norms of the law to their clients as well as translators of their client's moral interests back to the legal system.[20]

Collaborative lawyers believe that they assume joint moral accountability with their clients for the representation. They feel free to express their own moral and legal judgment, but remain subject to the client's final determination of which interests to pursue, within the limits of the law. They attempt to steer clear of directive thinking by focusing on fiduciary duty to their clients, and they try to avoid instrumental thinking by being aware of the limits of the law and refusing to exclude their own personal values from a professional representation.

In practice, individual lawyers may tend toward one of these points of view and also tend to impose that view on the client. Perhaps more common are the lawyers who borrow from all three models, just as many morally reflective persons rely on a combination of deontological, utilitarian, and relational moral theories to assess right and wrong. As you study the materials in this book, consider how the lawyers involved characterized their roles. If a lawyer ended up in trouble, think about whether that lawyer's view of his role contributed to the problem. Consider also whether one point of view may be more helpful in some representations, such as litigation or transactional practice, or with some clients, such as individuals or entities. As you assess what the lawyers in these cases and materials did well or poorly, you may be able to begin to formulate your own concept of the kind relationship you want to establish with your clients.

B. Lawyers and Law

Every other course you take in law school is designed to improve your ability to assist your clients in achieving their goals, by articulating their interests, asserting their rights, and defending their positions. Only in this course are you provided with the tools to recognize your own obligations and professional responsibilities, the limitations on your own conduct, as well as your rights as a lawyer, an officer of the legal system and a citizen.

Our experience indicates that many legally educated professionals (practicing lawyers and academics) are less than fully aware of some of the most crucial concepts covered in this course. Our purpose is to ensure that this will not be the case for you. As we examine the law governing lawyers, we will encounter two very interesting dimensions. First, this is a typical law school class, which examines the lawyer codes, such as the American Bar Association's Model Rules of Professional Conduct, as well as the application of general law (constitutional, criminal, and civil) to lawyer conduct. Second, the "ethics" in legal ethics indicates that both this course and the law governing lawyers addresses moral questions, questions of what is right and wrong.

■ The Law Governing Lawyers: *Sources of Law*

In this series of notes entitled "The Law Governing Lawyers," we consider the response of lawyers to the remedies and sanctions embedded in the various strands of law that taken as a whole constitute the law governing lawyers. Professional

20. Cunningham, *supra* note 12.

responsibility or legal ethics is the study of what is required for a lawyer to provide a professional service to another. The client simultaneously empowers the lawyer to act and becomes subject to the lawyer's power, which is a function of the lawyer's specialized knowledge and ability to access the legal system. The law governing lawyers regulates this relationship and also creates obligations to the legal system that act as limits on a lawyer's conduct on behalf of a client.

Sources of Law

The law that governs the conduct and shapes the behavior of lawyers shares one unifying factor: the lawyer's work. Two vast bodies of law, the lawyer codes and the application of general law to lawyers together constitute the law governing lawyers. This is the meaning behind the title of a recent Restatement on the subject, which brings together the lawyer codes and other constitutional, statutory, and decisional law that has been applied to lawyer conduct.[1] Although each body of law carries different legal consequences, they have developed in parallel paths and cross-fertilized each other over the past century.

Unlike any other professional group, lawyers are subject to licensure and control by the judicial rather than the legislative branch of government.[2] Courts have claimed the power to license and regulate lawyers for several centuries, including the prerogative to admit and discipline lawyers, to promulgate official lawyer codes, to define the practice of law, and to levy monetary assessments to fund bar admission and discipline.[3]

Once a lawyer is admitted to practice, a lawyer code applies to that lawyer's conduct and becomes the primary source of the lawyer's duties.[4] In the past century, the American Bar Association has promulgated and recommended various model professional codes to the highest court in each jurisdiction.[5] Each state and federal court in turn has enacted its own version of an official lawyer code, usually in the form of court rules. Violation of a lawyer code provision subjects a lawyer to professional discipline, with sanctions ranging from private or public reprimand, to fines, suspensions, or even permanent disbarment from legal practice.[6] Disciplinary proceedings usually are administrative in nature, require a high burden of proof (clear and convincing evidence), and allow for an appeal to the highest state court.[7]

The idea of a lawyer code originated in the work of Retired Judge George Sharswood, who began an annual series of lectures on legal ethics at the University of Pennsylvania Law School in the mid-nineteenth century.[8] The later publication

---

1. *Restatement (Third) The Law Governing Lawyers* (2000).
2. Nearly every professional group has adopted some kind of Professional Code. A compendium of these Professional Codes can be found in *Codes of Professional Responsibility: Ethics Standards in Business, Health, and Law* (Rena A. Gorlin, ed., BNA 1999). In most professions, violation of these standards results in loss of membership in a private professional organization, although some groups also notify official licensure boards. For lawyers, violation of a professional code adopted by a state or federal court subjects the lawyer to professional discipline.
3. Charles W. Wolfram, *Modern Legal Ethics* 22-25 (West 1986).
4. Bar admission authorities appointed by the highest state courts also refer to the lawyer codes in considering the fitness of an applicant to practice law.
5. The American Bar Association is a private organization of lawyers. At any given time, one third to more than one half of licensed U.S. lawyers are members.
6. *See, e.g., ABA Standards for Imposing Lawyer Sanctions* (1986).
7. *See, e.g., ABA Model Rules for Lawyer Disciplinary Enforcement* (1996).
8. George Sharswood, *An Essay on Professional Ethics* (5th ed., T & J. W. Johnson & Co. 1884). Sharswood's essays were influenced by David Hoffman's "Resolutions in Regard to Professional Deportment" in *A Course of Legal Study Addressed to Students and the Profession Generally* 752-775 (2d ed. 1836).

of his essays influenced the development of the first professional code, promulgated by the ABA in 1908. This document, called the Canons of Professional Ethics ("Canons"), consisted of largely aspirational paragraphs, and was soon widely adopted by nearly every jurisdiction in this country. The ABA Model Code of Professional Responsibility ("Model Code," or "CPR") superseded the Canons in 1969. Nearly every jurisdiction (except California) soon followed the ABA's recommendation, replacing the Canons with the Model Code. The Model Code retained the aspirational language of the Canons in statements called Ethical Considerations, and added black letter mandatory standards, called Disciplinary Rules.

In 1983, the ABA recommended that the Model Rules of Professional Conduct ("Model Rules") replace its Model Code. The Model Rules significantly expanded the provisions of the Model Code and changed its structure to mirror other Uniform Codes: black letter rules followed by comments. To date, approximately 45 jurisdictions have adopted some version of the Model Rules, often adding their own amendments. In 1997, the ABA established the Ethics 2000 Commission to update and recommend changes to the Model Rules. The ABA adopted these revisions in 2002, which has prodded most jurisdictions to study and update their own professional codes.

These various lawyer codes evolved in a slow two-hundred-year process from an application of general legal and moral concepts found in other bodies of law, such as constitutional law, the law of agency, contracts, property, torts, civil procedure, and evidence.[9] Courts have applied these general legal principles to lawyer conduct, addressing issues beyond professional discipline, such as fiduciary duties, the formation of a client-lawyer relationship, fee arrangements, malpractice liability for professional errors, and the attorney-client privilege. This application of general law to lawyers has created multiple remedies apart from, and in addition to, professional discipline, such as civil liability, disqualification, and fee forfeiture.

Legal Remedies and Sanctions

These various strands of the law governing lawyers create a vast minefield for lawyers to confront in their daily practice. Professional discipline, which can be imposed for violation of a lawyer code, is probably the most serious consequence a lawyer may suffer, because it involves both the potential loss of a license to practice as well as a loss of professional reputation.[10] In addition, professional disciplinary systems are becoming increasingly well funded and staffed, which increases the number of lawyers disciplined each year.

When lawyers are unsure about the meaning or applicability of a lawyer code provision, they can ask a local, state, or national bar association for an ethics opinion.[11] Opinions are written by volunteer members of an ethics committee, who issue both informal opinions addressed to a discrete circumstance or lawyer, and formal opinions addressed more broadly to many similarly situated lawyers. Unless written by an official disciplinary agency, ethics opinions are advisory, that is, not

9. For example, Judge Sharswood referred to tort law in describing duties of care owed by lawyers to clients, Sharswood, *supra* note 8, at 76-78; agency law in describing conflicts of interest and fees, *Id.* at 110, 149; and the evidentiary attorney-client privilege in discussing duties of confidentiality. *Id.* at 85-86.
10. *Restatement (Third) The Law Governing Lawyers* §5 (2000).
11. *See* Peter A. Joy, *Making Ethics Opinions Meaningful: Towards More Effective Regulation of Lawyer's Conduct*, 15 Geo. J. Legal Ethics 313 (2002).

binding on courts. However, courts that subsequently disagree with an ethics opinion rarely discipline a lawyer for following the committee's advice.[12]

Beyond discipline, lawyers increasingly worry about other consequences, such as the threat of a malpractice suit, or the problem of collecting a legal fee. In the past half-century, courts have recognized a number of additional judicial remedies that create new pitfalls for lawyers. Lawyers who violate procedural rules (such as Federal Rule of Civil Procedure 11 or 26) can be sanctioned, usually in the form of a monetary fine. Moreover, judges now exercise their power to "fire" lawyers representing clients by disqualifying them if the lawyer's conduct threatens to taint a trial process, or enjoining them from continuing representation outside of court. Courts also dismiss claims and defenses, grant new trials, deny the admission of evidence, exercise their contempt power, and order fee forfeiture.[13]

The parallel development and influence of the lawyer codes and general civil and criminal law applied to lawyers can result in multiple legal consequences for the same conduct. For example, because the lawyer codes incorporate some general legal obligations (such as competence or confidentiality) as well as some general legal prohibitions (against fraud or frivolous lawsuits), lawyers who are professionally disciplined also may suffer criminal or civil accountability for the same conduct.[14] In a similar manner, courts applying general law to lawyers sometimes rely on the lawyer codes to establish a lawyer's standard of care or other boundaries of acceptable conduct. This explains the general rule that violation of a lawyer code provision may be "evidence of breach of the applicable standard of conduct" in a civil suit or motion to disqualify.[15]

Your Study of the Law Governing Lawyers

As you analyze the rest of the problems in this book, the law governing lawyers should enable you to give the lawyers in Martyn & Fox solid legal advice, both about past events and future plans. In preparing your answers to these problems, notice whether a question asks you about professional discipline or other remedies. If it asks only about professional discipline, then the answer should be found in a lawyer code. The fact that most jurisdictions have enacted some form of the ABA Model Rules of Professional Conduct makes the most recent version of the Model Rules the focus of our study in this course.

Most of the problems in this book will ask more generally whether a lawyer "may" or "should" take a specific action. In that case, you should refer both to the relevant lawyer code sections and to the general law applied to lawyers, including

---

12. *See, e.g.,* Morrell v. St., 575 P.2d 1200 (Alaska 1978).

13. *Restatement (Third) The Law Governing Lawyers* §6 (2000).

14. *E.g.,* In re Halverson, 998 P.2d 833 (Wash. 2000) (lawyer who had sexual relationship with client suspended from practice for six months, five years after he settled a civil suit by the client for a "substantial sum"); People v. Sichta, 948 P.2d 1018 (Colo. 1998) (lawyer convicted of security and wire fraud disbarred); Dodrill v. Exec. Dir., Comm. on Prof. Conduct, 824 S.W.2d 383 (Ark. 1992) (lawyer who filed repeated frivolous complaints and motions in bankruptcy court violated FRCP 11, held in criminal contempt and suspended for one year); In re Perl, 407 N.W.2d 678 (Minn. 1987); Gilchrist v. Perl, 387 N.W.2d 412 (Minn. 1986) (lawyer who employed opposing party's adjuster on other matters suspended from practice for one year and forfeited some or all of $705,000 fee to 128 plaintiffs in Dalcon Shield litigation); In re Conway, 301 N.W.2d 253 (Wis. 1981); Ennis v. Ennis, 276 N.W.2d 341 (Wis. App. 1979) (lawyer who represented wife in divorce against husband who was a former client disqualified from further representation, denied fee award and publicly reprimanded).

15. Model R. Prof. Conduct, Preamble and Scope ¶20; *Restatement (Third) The Law Governing Lawyers* §52(2) (2000).

the cases and other materials that follow each set of problems as well as the applicable sections of the Restatement of the Law Governing Lawyers ("RLGL").[16] When you move beyond the lawyer codes, remember that you are examining other legal remedies that might exist, or other consequences that may befall an errant lawyer or law firm, such as civil or criminal liability, litigation sanctions, fee forfeiture or judicial disqualification.

In seeking legal answers to the problems confronting Martyn & Fox, you will discover that the law governing lawyers, like all law, often embodies moral judgments. As the first four problems in this chapter demonstrated, you also will realize that the law in this course, unlike much of the law you study in law school, directly addresses your own personal concept of what it means to be a lawyer in modern society. In traversing the law governing lawyers and the choices of the lawyers involved in these materials, try to identify the moral discretion inherent in the rules and answers you articulate. At the same time, you should feel free to question the moral choices that Martyn & Fox lawyers contemplate, as well as the rules that govern their conduct.

Ultimately, the stories of lawyers that run throughout this book should help you consider whether you wish to follow their examples. We see the law governing lawyers as a map that will help you understand your professional responsibilities and avoid the ethical minefields that await you in law practice. At the same time, we see the "ethics" in legal ethics as an integral part of the lawyer's practical moral wisdom that is essential to make modern law practice meaningful. We hope that as you study the law governing lawyers your explorations also will help you map out the kind of lawyer you want to be.

16. This usage parallels the use of the term "may" in the Multistate Professional Responsibility Examination, where "may" "asks whether the conduct referred to or described in the question is professionally appropriate in that it:

a. would not subject the lawyer . . . to discipline; and
b. is not inconsistent with the Preamble, Comments or text of the ABA Model Rules of Professional Conduct. . . ; and
c. is not inconsistent with generally accepted principles of the law of lawyering."

Chapter 2

Judicial and Professional Regulation of Lawyers

This chapter focuses on two aspects of the inherent power of the judicial branch of government to regulate the practice of law: admission to practice and professional discipline. The last note in Chapter 1 indicated that lawyers are subject to licensure and control by the judicial rather than the legislative branch of government. In some states, constitutions explicitly grant the judicial branch this power to regulate lawyers. In most jurisdictions, courts have claimed an inherent power to license and regulate lawyers that is implied from the constitutional recognition of the separation of powers because lawyers are necessary to ensure the proper administration of justice.

Few give a second thought to the special power that a law license provides. Yet, only lawyers can file complaints on behalf of clients, an awesome power that triggers, with no more than the act of the lawyer, the machinery of the system of justice to assign a number and a judge, to start time limits running that require the response of others and ultimately to adjudicate the claim, whether for damages, an injunction, incarceration or even execution of a defendant. Similarly, only lawyers can serve discovery requests requiring others to gather thousands or even millions of documents, answer intrusive interrogatories, or respond to requests for admissions. Equally significant is the power of lawyers to force both parties and party representatives, simply by filing a notice of deposition, to sit for hours or days of testimony under oath in a lawyer's office and to force these witnesses to bring documents with them.

Beyond litigation, only lawyers can provide the legal opinions that a corporation is duly formed, that stock is properly issued and non-assessable, that corporate action is duly authorized, that security interests have been perfected, and the multiple other legal opinions that must be issued every day to permit transactions to be consummated and the wheels of commerce to turn smoothly.

The fact that lawyers exercise all these powers—and others—regularly should not lessen our appreciation of the fact that a law license grants them exclusively to members of our profession.

A. Bar Admission

Problem

2-1. Martyn & Fox represent Mary Moore, who is about to graduate from law school.

(*a*) Will Moore be denied admission to the bar because she included as text, without attribution, seven direct quotations, three from cases and four from law review articles in a seminar paper in law school?

(*b*) What if Moore pled guilty to drunk driving five years ago and again last year?

(*c*) What if Moore believes in Aryan supremacy and has announced plans to become General Counsel to the KKK White Council?

Consider: Model Rule 8.1
Model Code DR 1-101

In re Application of Converse

602 N.W.2d 500 (Neb. 1999)

PER CURIAM.

Paul Raymond Converse appeals a decision of the Nebraska State Bar Commission (Commission) denying his request to take the July 1998 Nebraska bar examination. Converse claims that the decision of the Commission should be reversed because the Commission rested its denial of Converse's application, at least in part, upon conduct protected by the First Amendment to the U.S. Constitution and, in the alternative, that Converse's conduct did not constitute sufficient cause under Nebraska law for denying his application on the ground of deficient moral character. For the reasons that follow, we affirm the decision of the Commission....

The evidence at the Commission hearing revealed that as part of the application process, Converse was required to request that the dean of his law school submit a form certifying completion of Converse's law school studies. That form contained a question asking, "Is there anything concerning this applicant about which the Bar Examiners should further inquire regarding the applicant's moral character of fitness to practice law?" The question was answered, "Yes," and the dean also noted, "Additional information will be provided upon request." The Commission followed up on this notation by conducting an investigation which ultimately revealed certain facts regarding Converse.

After the completion of his first semester at the University of South Dakota (USD) Law School, Converse sent a letter to then assistant dean Diane May regarding certain issues not relevant to this appeal that he had had with the law school during fall classes, closing that letter with the phrase, "Hope you get a full body tan in Costa Rica." Subsequent to that note, Converse had several more encounters with May, beginning with his writing letters to May about receiving grades lower than what he believed he had earned in an appellate advocacy class.

After he received a grade he believed to be unjustified by his performance in the appellate advocacy course, Converse wrote letters to May and to the USD law school dean, Barry

Vickrey, requesting assistance with an appeal of that grade. In addition to writing letters to Vickrey and May, Converse also sent a letter to the South Dakota Supreme Court regarding the appellate advocacy course professor's characterization of his arguments, with indications that carbon copies of the letter were sent to two well-known federal court of appeals judges.... Despite all such correspondence, Converse testified at the hearing that no formal appeal of the grievance was ever filed. Converse's grade was never adjusted.

The evidence showed that following the grade "appeal," Converse prepared a memorandum and submitted it to his classmates, urging them to recall an "incident" in which yet another professor lashed out at him in class, and to be cognizant of the image that incident casts "on [that professor's] core professionalism" prior to completing class evaluations. Converse also wrote a letter to a newspaper in South Dakota, the Sioux Falls Argus Leader, regarding a proposed fee increase at the USD law school. Converse immediately began investigating the salaries of USD law professors and posted a list of selected professors' salaries on the student bulletin board, as well as writing a letter that accused Vickrey of trying to pull a "fast one."

Converse's next altercation at the USD law school involved a photograph of a nude female's backside that he displayed in his study carrel in the USD law library. The picture was removed by a law librarian. In response to the removal of this photograph, Converse contacted the American Civil Liberties Union (ACLU) and received a letter indicating that his photograph might be a protected expression under the First Amendment. Once again, Converse went to the student newspaper to alert the student body of the actions of the law school authorities, accusing them of unconstitutional censorship.

Converse redisplayed the photograph once it was returned by the law librarians. Vickrey received several complaints about the photograph from other students, classifying Converse's behavior as "unprofessional and inappropriate." Upon Converse's redisplay of the photograph, Vickrey sent him a memorandum explaining that the picture would not be removed only because Vickrey did not want to involve the school in controversy during final examinations. Converse testified that he redisplayed the photograph in order to force the alleged constitutional issue.

The evidence also revealed that Converse filed an ethics complaint with the North Dakota Bar Association regarding certain correspondence between Vickrey and a retired justice of the North Dakota Supreme Court. The complaint was dismissed. Converse went to the USD student newspaper, claiming that a letter from a retired North Dakota justice to the ACLU, in response to questions from Vickrey, was a violation of professional ethics (apparently Model Rules of Professional Conduct Rule 4.2 (1999), which precludes a lawyer from discussing matters with opposing parties the lawyer knows to be represented by counsel). In addition to going to the press, Converse also contacted the president of USD referring to Vickrey as an "incompetent" and requesting that Vickrey be fired. In addition to this incident, Converse reported his suspicions about USD's student health insurance policy to the student newspaper under the title of "Law Student Suspects Health Insurance Fraud," as well as in a separate article alleging that USD had suppressed an investigation of its insurance carrier.

The Commission also heard testimony regarding Converse's attempt to obtain an internship with the U.S. Attorney's office in South Dakota. Converse arranged for the internship on his own, only to have his request subsequently rejected by the law school. Upon receiving his denial, Converse sent a complaint to all of USD's law school faculty members. Vickrey testified that Converse's internship was rejected because he failed to comply with the law school's procedures regarding internships. Converse then contacted the chairperson of the law school committee of the South Dakota State Bar Association with his complaint, expressly referring to Vickrey as being "arrogant." There is no indication of a response from the chairperson in the record.

The issue next considered by the Commission was that of various litigation threatened by Converse. Converse indicated that he would "likely" be filing a lawsuit against Vickrey for violations of his First Amendment rights. Converse was also involved in a dispute with other law students, in which he threatened to file a lawsuit and warned the students that all lawsuits in which they were involved would need to be reported to proper authorities when they applied to take a bar examination. Further, Converse posted signs on the bulletin board at the law school denouncing a professor, in response to the way in which Converse's parking appeal was handled, and then went to the student newspaper to criticize the process and those involved in that appeal.

One of the final issues addressed by the Commission in its hearing was that of a T-shirt Converse produced and marketed on which a nude caricature of Vickrey is shown sitting astride what appears to be a large hot dog. The cartoon on the shirt also contains the phrase "Astride the Peter Principle," which Converse claims connotes the principle that Vickrey had been promoted past his level of competence; however, Converse admits that the T-shirt could be construed to have certain sexual overtones. Converse admitted that the creation of this T-shirt would not be acceptable behavior for a lawyer.

In response to not being allowed to post signs and fliers at the law school, Converse sent a memo to all law students in which he noted to his fellow students that his "Deanie on a Weanie" T-shirts were in stock. In that same memo, Converse included a note to his schoolmates:

> So far 4 causes of action have arisen, courtesy Tricky Vickrey. [He then listed what he believed the causes of action to be.] When you pass the SD Bar, if you want to earn some atty [sic] fees, get hold of me and we can go for one of these. I've kept evidence, of course.

Vickrey asked Converse not to wear his T-shirt to his graduation ceremony, and Converse decided that "it would be a better choice in [his] life not to go to that commencement." Converse acknowledges that Vickrey's request was made in a civil manner.

The evidence also revealed that prior to law school, Converse, in his capacity as a landlord, sued a tenant for nonpayment of rent and referred to the tenant as a "fucking welfare bitch." At the hearing, in response to questioning from the Commission, Converse testified at great length as to how he tends to personally attack individuals when he finds himself embroiled in a controversy.

After the Commission notified Converse on December 18, 1998, that he would not be allowed to sit for the Nebraska bar examination, Converse appealed the adverse determination to this court pursuant to Neb. Ct. R. for Adm. of Attys. 15 (rev. 1996)....

Under rule 15, this court will consider the appeal of an applicant from a final adverse ruling of the Commission de novo on the record made at the hearing before the Commission....

Converse first assigns as error that the Commission's determination should not stand because it is based in large part upon speech that is protected by the First Amendment. Thus, the threshold question we must answer is whether conduct arguably protected by the First Amendment can be considered by the Commission during an investigation into an applicant's moral character and fitness to practice law. We answer this question in the affirmative.

There are four U.S. Supreme Court cases that provide particular guidance with respect to this issue. In Konigsberg v. State Bar, 366 U.S. 36 (1961), the bar applicant argued that when the California bar commission forced him to either answer questions about his affiliation with the Communist Party or to face the repercussions of not being certified as possessing the required moral character to sit for the bar, the commission violated his First Amendment rights. The Supreme Court disagreed, pointing out that "regulatory statutes, not intended to control the content of speech but incidentally limiting its unfettered exercise, have not been regarded as the type of law the First or Fourteenth Amendment [forbids] . . . when they have been found justified by subordinating valid governmental interests." . . . The Court balanced the effect of allowing such questions against the need for the state to do a complete inquiry into the character of an applicant and concluded that questions about membership would not chill association to the extent of harm caused by striking down the screening process. *Id.* The Court held that requiring the applicant to answer the questions was not an infringement of the applicant's First Amendments rights.

In 1971, the Court was once again confronted with the issue and decided a trilogy of cases concerning the bar admissions procedures of various states. *See* Baird v. St. Bar of Ariz., 401 U.S. 1 (1971); In re Stolar, 401 U.S. 23 (1971); Law Students Research Council v. Wadmond, 401 U.S. 154 (1971). . . .

Converse conceded at oral argument that the Commission's decision cannot be based solely on an applicant's exercise of First Amendment freedoms but that it is proper for the Commission to go behind the exercise of those freedoms and consider an applicant's moral character. That is exactly what was done by the Commission in the instant case. An investigation of Converse's moral character is not a proceeding in which the applicant is being prosecuted for conduct arguably protected by the First Amendment, but, rather, "an investigation of the conduct of [an applicant] for the purpose of determining whether he shall be [admitted]." *See* In re Doss, 12 N.E.2d 659, 660 (Ill. 1937). Converse's reliance upon cases where a judgment was invalidated at least in part because it was based on conduct protected by the First Amendment is therefore misplaced.

Were we to adopt the position asserted by Converse in this case, the Commission would be limited to conducting only cursory investigations of an applicant's moral character and past conduct. Justice Potter Stewart, writing for the majority in Law Students Research Council v. Wadmond, *supra*, noted that the implications of such an attack on a bar screening process are that no screening process would be constitutionally permissible beyond academic examination and an extremely minimal check for serious, concrete character deficiencies. "The principal means of policing the Bar would then be the deterrent and punitive effects of such post-admission sanctions as contempt, disbarment, malpractice suits, and criminal prosecutions." . . .

We conclude that the Commission properly considered Converse's conduct as it reflects upon his moral character, even if such conduct might have been protected by the First Amendment. . . .

Converse next contends that the Commission violated his due process rights by not making him aware of all of the "charges" against him in these proceedings. . . .

By alleging that he has not been made fully aware of the "charges" against him, Converse has confused this inquiry into his moral character with a trial....

There is no question that "[a] state can require high standards of qualification, such as good moral character or proficiency in its law, before it admits an applicant to the bar...." Schware v. Bd. of Bar Examiners, 353 U.S. 232, 239 (1957). The Court has also stated that it must be "kept clearly in mind ... that an applicant for admission to the bar bears the burden of proof of 'good moral character' a requirement whose validity is not, nor could well be, drawn in question here." Konigsberg v. St. Bar, 366 U.S. 36, 40-41 (1961). "If at the conclusion of the proceedings the evidence of good character and that of bad character are found in even balance, the State may refuse admission...."

Burden of Proof

The legal reality is that this court, and only this court, is vested with the power to admit persons to the practice of law in this state and to fix qualifications for admission to the Nebraska bar. ... With that in mind, we commence our analysis with the standards for moral character required for admission to the Nebraska bar as set out in our rules governing the admission of attorneys. Neb. Ct. R. for Adm. of Attys. 3 (rev. 1998) governs this situation, which provides in pertinent part:

> An attorney should be one whose record of conduct justifies the trust of clients, adversaries, courts, and others with respect to the professional duties owed to them. A record manifesting a significant deficiency by an applicant in one or more of the following essential eligibility requirements for the practice of law may constitute a basis for denial of admission. In addition to the admission requirements otherwise established by these Rules, the essential eligibility requirements for admission to the practice of law in Nebraska are:
>
> (a) The ability to conduct oneself with a high degree of honesty, integrity, and trustworthiness in all professional relationships and with respect to all legal obligations; ...
>
> (c) The ability to conduct oneself with respect for and in accordance with the law and the Code of Professional Responsibility; ...
>
> (j) The ability to conduct oneself professionally and in a manner that engenders respect for the law and the profession.

Under rule 3, Converse must prove that his past conduct is in conformity with the standards set forth by this court, and the record in this case compels the conclusion that he has failed to do so.

We considered an appeal of a similarly situated bar applicant in In re Appeal of Lane, 544 N.W.2d 367 (Neb. 1996). *Lane* involved an individual seeking readmission to the Nebraska bar whose past included confrontations with law school faculty, the use of strong and profane language with fellow students at his bar review course, the use of intimidating and rude conduct directed at a security guard at the place where he was taking his bar review course, and some controversial interactions with females. We held that, taken together, "these incidents show that Lane is prone to turbulence, intemperance, and irresponsibility, characteristics which are not acceptable in one who would be a counselor and advocate in the legal system," and we upheld the denial of his application.

We explained in ... *Lane* that the "requisite restraint in dealing with others is obligatory conduct for attorneys because 'the efficient and orderly administration of justice cannot be successfully carried on if we allow attorneys to engage in unwarranted attacks on the court [or] opposing counsel.... Furthermore, "'an attorney who exhibits [a] lack of civility, good manners and common courtesy ... tarnishes the ... image of ... the bar....'" ... We held in ... *Lane* that "abusive, disruptive, hostile, intemperate, intimidating, irresponsible, threatening, or turbulent behavior is a proper basis for the denial of admission to the bar." Expanding on this holding, we stated:

> Care with words and respect for courts and one's adversaries is a necessity, not because lawyers and judges are without fault, but because trial by combat long ago proved unsatisfactory. . . .
>
> The profession's insistence that counsel show restraint, self-discipline and a sense of reality in dealing with courts, other counsel, witnesses and adversaries is more than insistence on good manners. It is based on the knowledge that civilized, rational behavior is essential if the judicial system is to perform its function. Absent this, any judicial proceeding is likely to degenerate into [a] verbal free-for-all. . . . Habitual unreasonable reaction to adverse rulings . . . is conduct of a type not to be permitted of a lawyer when acting as a lawyer. What cannot be permitted in lawyers, cannot be tolerated in those applying for admission as lawyers. . . .

The evidence in this case shows that Converse's numerous disputes and personal attacks indicate a "pattern and a way of life which appear to be [Converse's] normal reaction to opposition and disappointment." *See Lane*. The totality of the evidence clearly establishes that Converse possesses an inclination to personally attack those with whom he has disputes. Such inclinations "are not acceptable in one who would be a counselor and advocate in the legal system."

In addition to Converse's tendency to personally attack those individuals with whom he has disputes, his pattern of behavior indicates an additional tendency to do so in arenas other than those specifically established within the legal system. This tendency is best exemplified by observing Converse's conduct in situations where there were avenues through which Converse could have and should have handled his disputes, but instead chose to mount personal attacks on those with whom he had disputes through letters and barrages in the media.

One such incident occurred when Converse received the below average grade in the appellate advocacy course, and he wrote letters to various individuals regarding his arguments. Converse testified that he wrote letters to members of the South Dakota Supreme Court, Judge Richard Posner, Judge Alex Kozinski, and others, but filed no formal appeal. Moreover, upon return of the nude photograph, Converse testified that he redisplayed the photograph to force the issue with the university, but chose not to pursue any action regarding the alleged violation of his rights. There was also the incident regarding Converse's internship with the U.S. Attorney's office, where Converse went outside established procedures, arranged for the internship on his own, and then complained to all faculty and to members of the South Dakota bar when his request was denied for not complying with established procedures. Finally, there was Converse's production and marketing of the T-shirt containing a nude depiction of Vickrey on a hot dog as a result of the ongoing tension between Vickrey and himself. Converse is 48 years old, and his actions cannot be excused as isolated instances of youthful indiscretions.

Taken together with the other incidents previously discussed, the evidence clearly shows that Converse is prone to turbulence, intemperance, and irresponsibility; characteristics which are not acceptable in one seeking admission to the Nebraska bar. . . . In light of Converse's admission that such conduct would be inappropriate were he already an attorney, we reiterate that we will not tolerate conduct by those applying for admission to the bar that would not be tolerated were that person already an attorney. Furthermore, Converse has consistently exhibited a tendency to cause disruption and then go to some arena outside the field of law to settle the dispute, often to an arena not specifically designed for dispute resolution. . . .

The record before us reflects that the Commission conducted such an inquiry and, at the conclusion thereof, correctly determined that Converse possessed a moral character inconsistent with one "dedicated to the peaceful and reasoned settlement of disputes," *see* 401 U.S. at 166, but, rather, more consistent with someone who wishes to go outside the field of law and settle disputes by mounting personal attacks and portraying himself as the victim and his opponent as the aggressor. Such disruptive, hostile, intemperate, threatening, and turbulent conduct certainly reflects negatively upon those character traits the applicant must prove prior to being admitted to the Nebraska bar, such as honesty, integrity, reliability, and trustworthiness.

The result might have been different if Converse had exhibited only a "single incident of rudeness or lack of professional courtesy," *see* In re Snyder, 472 U.S. 634, 647 (1985), but such is simply not the case. The record clearly establishes that he seeks to resolve disputes not in a peaceful manner, but by personally attacking those who oppose him in any way and then resorting to arenas outside the field of law to publicly humiliate and intimidate those opponents. Such a pattern of behavior is incompatible with what we have required to be obligatory conduct for attorneys, as well as for applicants to the bar.

Converse has exhibited a clear lack of self-restraint and lack of judgment, and our de novo review of the record leads us to independently conclude that Converse has exhibited such a pattern of acting in a hostile and disruptive manner as to render him unfit for the practice of law in Nebraska. We conclude that the Commission's determination to deny Converse's application was correct. . . .

Lawyers and Other Professionals: *Professional Licensure*

In this series of notes entitled "Lawyers and Other Professionals," we will examine the legal restraints on various groups of professionals, comparing the law governing lawyers with the vast body of law that regulates other professionals, such as health care providers, accountants, design professionals, and mental health practitioners (psychiatrists, psychologists, and counselors).

Professionals control and influence nearly every aspect of modern life. Indeed, much of the law governing professional behavior assumes that "professionals" are somehow distinct from others and should be treated in a specialized manner.[1] Most commentators agree that three features identify a professional. Professionals (a) "profess" a body of knowledge, (b) on behalf of someone else, (c) subject to the standards of that group of colleagues.[2] Professionals are distinguished from technicians by their level of knowledge and required study and their internal professional standards designed to serve the public.[3]

1. *See* William J. Curran, *Symposium on Professional Negligence*, 12 Vand. L. Rev. 535 (1959) (surveying the liability of physicians, pharmacists, architects, engineers, teachers, lawyers, abstracters, accountants, funeral directors, and insurance agents).

2. William F. May, *Beleaguered Rulers: The Public Obligation of the Professional* 7 (Westminster John Knox Press 2001).

3. This may explain why courts addressing the issue of whether a defendant is a professional now generally agree that nurses qualify, but are less sure about social workers, teachers, and funeral directors. *See* Frank J. Cavico & Nancy M. Cavico, *The Nursing Profession in the 1990's: Negligence and Malpractice Liability*, 43 Clev. St. L. Rev. 557 (1995); Michael J. Polelle, *Who's on First, and What's a Professional?*, 33 U.S.F. L. Rev. 205 (1999). *See also* Steven Mark Levy, *Liability of the Art Expert for Professional Malpractice*, 1991 Wis. L. Rev. 595.

All professionals are subject to direct governmental regulation through state licensing requirements. Lawyers, however, are the only professionally licensed group regulated by the judicial branch of government. All other professionals are licensed by the legislative branch, which often creates an administrative agency to manage professional licensure according to statutory criteria. For other professionals, this means that citizens theoretically have access through their elected representatives to creating and changing the criteria for licensure. For lawyers, such change occurs only when those in the judicial branch are convinced that change should occur. Typically this change has been initiated by bar groups, such as the American Bar Association or state and local bars. In other words, the regulated group, lawyers, directly rather than indirectly dominates the process and determines the content of the regulations.

Becoming a Licensed Professional

Most state licensure provisions require that a person who seeks a professional license satisfy at least three criteria:[4]

1. Age;
2. Education and/or experience; and
3. Examination.

In addition, some professions in some jurisdictions add a fourth requirement discussed in *Converse* that applies to all lawyers: good moral character.[5] Further, unlike other professionals, lawyers also are required to take an oath.

Converse illustrates that bar applicants bear the burden of proving the requisite character and fitness and typifies the focus of courts on factors that predict future ability to practice. In fact, some courts specifically refer to professional code requirements that govern the conduct of licensed lawyers in deciding whether an applicant has the requisite character and fitness to practice law.[6]

To facilitate consideration of character, applicants are required to complete a lengthy questionnaire that canvasses relevant topics. For example, concerns about the ability to act honestly may be evidenced by a criminal record, academic misconduct, or neglect of professional or financial obligations.[7] Bar examiners treat any lack of candor in the bar admission application itself as equally serious.[8] The ability to act in accordance with law can be tested by looking at a prior criminal record as well as use (or abuse) of the legal process.[9] The ability to act professionally in a

---

4. For descriptions of federal and state professional licensing requirements, *see Professional and Occupational Licensing Directory* (David P. Bianco, ed., 2d ed., Gale Research Inc. 1996).

5. *E.g.*, Ga. Code §43-3-6 (CPAs); 225 Ill. C. S. §25/11 (dentists); 32 Me. R. S. §13732 (pharmacists); N.J. Stat. §45:11-26 (nurses); 59 Okla. Stat. §46.24 (Architects); 26 Vt. Stat. §1391 (physicians).

6. *E.g.*, In re Mustafa, 631 A.2d 45 (D.C. App. 1993) (because applicant's conduct by a lawyer would have resulted in disbarment for at least five years, applicant should wait for a similar period of time from proven misconduct before good moral character can be established).

7. *E.g.*, In re Application of Chapman, 630 N.E.2d 322 (Ohio 1994) (consent decree in civil action by state attorney general against bar applicant alleging deceptive and unconscionable sales practices in connection with a business demonstrated recent pattern of highly questionable and outright illegal behavior that justified rejection of bar applicant; renewed application that would demonstrate substantial change in applicant's conduct may allow for admission at a later date).

8. *E.g.*, Radtke v. Bd. of Bar Examiners, 601 N.W.2d 642 (Wis. 1999) (lawyer who misstated material fact on his bar application about his earlier plagiarism did not satisfy character and fitness requirement).

9. *E.g.*, In re Prager, 661 N.E.2d 84 (Mass. 1996) (sixteen years of marijuana use, international smuggling, and living as a fugitive not outweighed by seven years of a credible work history, successful completion of probation, and law school; applicant could reapply in five years).

manner that engenders respect for law and the profession may be evidenced by letters of reference, reports of law school administrators, or by a history of treated or untreated drug or alcohol dependence or mental illness.[10]

Converse also illustrates how courts respond when confronted with a free speech and association challenge. In the first two decades following World War II, a series of cases raised the issue of whether Communist Party membership could be used as a ground to deny an applicant's bar admission. In the first case, the Supreme Court held that Communist Party membership prior to World War II could not be used as the basis to infer moral unfitness to practice law because such past membership had no rational connection to evil purposes or illegal conduct.[11] Subsequent decisions held that the states were free, however, to inquire about current Communist Party membership, and could deny bar admission to an applicant who refused to answer, because of the state's interest "in having lawyers who are devoted to the law in its broadest sense, including ... its procedures for orderly change."[12] The net result of these cases is that bar admissions officials may ask about specific associations, as long as membership in that group indicates a shared belief specifically contrary to a lawyer's ability to represent clients in this country's legal and political institutions.[13] On the other hand, a question that asks candidates to list memberships in all organizations during law school is not rationally related to fitness to practice and sweeps too broadly into First Amendment freedoms.[14]

These cases were relied on by the court in *Converse* and also shaped the analysis of the Illinois Bar's Committee on Character and Fitness in the case of bar applicant Matthew Hale, which "has crystallized the debate over the free speech rights of attorneys in a way that has not occurred since the McCarthy era's loyalty oath cases."[15] Hale readily admitted that he headed an organization called the World Church of the Creator, which did not believe in violence, but called for white racial supremacy and the use of political power to provide for the deportation of all other races, including Jews, blacks and other "mud races" so that the United States could then become a "white race" only country. He claimed he would follow the law until he could change it by peaceable means.

An initial inquiry panel found that Hale, unlike the applicants in *Baird* and *Stolar*, was not denied admission *solely* because of his beliefs, but because he was "actively involved in inciting racial hatred and ... had dedicated his life to destroying equal rights under law."[16] Eventually, a hearing panel focused on Hale's conduct, rather than his beliefs, denying him admission because he had admitted he would follow the Rules of Professional Conduct "only when he felt like it." They

10. *E.g.*, In re Covington, 50 P.3d 233 (Or. 2002) (three years of sobriety not enough time to establish that applicant's past abuse of drugs and alcohol would not recur); Frasher v. W. Va. Bd. of Law Examiners, 408 S.E.2d 675 (W. Va. 1991) (applicant established sufficient evidence of rehabilitation given his candor following two possession of marijuana convictions and five traffic offenses, which ended seven years before applicant sought admission).

11. Schware v. Bd. of Bar Examiners of N.M., 353 U.S. 232, 246-247 (1957).

12. Konigberg v. St. Bar of Cal., 366 U.S. 36, 52 (1961); In re Anastaplo, 366 U.S. 82, 90 (1961).

13. Law Students Civ. Rights Research Council, Inc. v. Wadmond, 401 U.S. 154 (1971) (upholding an inquiry into whether the applicant specifically intended to further an organization's advocacy of violent overthrow of the government while a member of the organization).

14. Baird v. St. Bar of Ariz., 401 U.S. 1 (1971) (overturning a general inquiry not connected to knowing membership); In re Stolar, 401 U.S. 23 (1971).

15. W. Bradley Wendel, *Free Speech for Lawyers*, 28 Hastings Const. L.Q. 305, 314 (2001).

16. In re Hale (Comm. on Character and Fitness, 3d App. Dist. of S. Ct. of Ill., Inquiry Panel 1998).

held that he was "absolutely entitled to his beliefs, but at the same time the public and the bar are entitled to be treated fairly and decently by attorneys."[17]

Two other licensure provisions, citizenship and residency requirements, also have been the subject of constitutional attack in the past quarter century. The Supreme Court invalidated citizenship requirements for lawyers on equal protection grounds in 1973, because the state could not prove a compelling interest that would overcome the strict scrutiny required by the Fourteenth Amendment to protect resident aliens.[18] The Court explained that lawyers, while "officers of the court," are not state officers in any political sense, simply "by virtue of being lawyers."[19] The Court subsequently has relied on this precedent to overturn citizenship requirements for notaries public,[20] engineers,[21] and real estate brokers.[22] At the same time, citizenship requirements designed to serve political rather than economic functions have been upheld, such as citizenship requirements for probation officers,[23] state police,[24] and public school teachers.[25]

The Supreme Court also has invalidated residency requirements in cases involving lawyers in three situations. In Piper v. New Hampshire,[26] the Court held that the practice of law was a "privilege" under article IV, §2 of the Constitution and prohibited states from imposing residency requirements because they violated the Privileges and Immunities Clause intended to create a national economic union. It also rejected all of the state's justifications for its refusal to admit nonresidents, concluding that the state could require lawyers to be familiar with local law, obey the jurisdiction's professional codes, participate in *pro bono* work, or be available to appear in court, but could not use residency as a surrogate for such restrictions.

In Barnard v. Thorstenn, the Court invalidated similar residency requirements in the Virgin Islands, despite its geographic isolation.[27] In Supreme Court of Virginia v. Friedman, the Court struck down a residency requirement imposed as a condition of admission on motion.[28] The same principles were applied to federal court residency requirements in Frazier v. Heebe, where the Court exercised its inherent power to invalidate a local district court residency requirement.[29] Similar

17. In re Hale (Comm. on Character and Fitness, 3d App. Dist. of S. Ct. of Ill., Hearing Panel 1999). The Illinois Supreme Court refused to hear the case on appeal, but one justice dissented, characterizing Hale's conduct as "open advocacy of racially obnoxious belief." In re Hale, 723 N.E.2d 206 (Ill. 1999), *cert. denied sub nom.* Hale v. Comm. on Character and Fitness of the Ill. Bar, 530 U.S. 1261 (2000).

Prof. Wendel points out that the Illinois Panel could have reached the same result by focusing on Hale's failure to disclose several arrests, disciplinary actions and protective orders against him. Wendel, *supra* note 15, at 323 n.65. Since this denial of admission, Hale has been arrested for soliciting the murder of a federal judge. Matt O'Connor, *Hale Held in Plot to Kill Judge; Professed Racist Grabbed by FBI Before Hearing*, Chicago Tribune 1 (Jan. 9, 2003).

18. In re Griffiths, 413 U.S. 717 (1973).
19. *Id.* at 729.
20. Bernal v. Fainter, 467 U.S. 216 (1984).
21. Examining Bd. of Engineers, Architects & Surveyors v. Flores, 426 U.S. 522 (1976).
22. Ind. Real Estate Commn. v. Satoskar, 417 U.S. 938 (1973).
23. Cabell v. Chavez-Salido, 454 U.S. 452 (1982).
24. Foley v. Connelie, 483 U.S. 291 (1978).
25. Quintero de Quintero v. Aponte-Roque, 974 F.2d 226 (1st Cir. 1992).
26. 470 U.S. 274 (1985).
27. 489 U.S. 546 (1989).
28. 487 U.S. 59 (1988).
29. 482 U.S. 641 (1987).

residency requirements have been overturned in cases involving engineers,[30] pharmacists,[31] real estate brokers,[32] and construction workers.[33]

The net result of these decisions is that states remain free to impose admission requirements on residents and nonresidents alike, as long as the prerequisites do not favor resident lawyers. The basic criteria of age, education, examination, character, and oath for lawyers therefore continue as the five hurdles to granting professional licensure. So, for example, the Third Circuit has upheld New Jersey's requirement that both resident and nonresident lawyers maintain a local bona fide office and attend continuing legal education courses.[34] Several courts also have upheld similar prerequisites to *pro hac vice* admissions (to represent a client in that particular matter).[35]

Losing a Professional License

Once a person qualifies for a professional license, that person becomes subject to the law governing that profession, including state licensure statutes, which may or may not include professional codes. The professional codes that govern lawyer behavior are embodied in official court rules adopted by the highest state court. Professionals other than lawyers are subject to professional discipline for violating relevant statutory or administrative standards. They also may lose membership in a private professional association if they violate that group's professional standards.

Common grounds for discipline in other professions generally parallel those found in lawyer codes: incompetence, conviction of a crime, or other "unprofessional conduct."[36] Some states add specific offenses relevant to a particular practice, such as unlawful sale of drugs, impairment due to substance abuse, commission of child abuse or neglect, or failure to report an adverse malpractice judgment or settlement to the licensing agency.[37]

Occasionally, lawyers and other professionals have challenged broad disciplinary rules as being void for vagueness. Courts have generally upheld these provisions, including competency standards,[38] prohibitions against sexual abuse[39] "habitual

---

30. Tetra Technologies Inc. v. Harter, 823 F. Supp. 1116 (S.D.N.Y. 1993).
31. National Pharms. Inc. v. De Melecio, 51 F. Supp. 2d 45 (D.P.R. 1999).
32. Baker v. MacLay Properties Co., 648 So. 2d 888 (La. 1995).
33. A.L. Blades & Sons v. Yerusalim, 121 F.3d 865 (3d Cir. 1997).
34. Tolchin v. S. Ct. of N.J., 111 F.3d 1099 (3d Cir.), *cert. denied*, 522 U.S. 977 (1997).
35. *See, e.g.,* Paciulan v. George, 229 F.3d 1226 (9th Cir. 2000) (residents not admitted to the bar not allowed to appear *pro hac vice*); Mowrer v. Warner-Lambert Co., 1998 U.S. Dist. LEXIS 12746 (E.D. Pa. 1998) (local counsel of record required for *pro hac vice* admission); Parnell v. S. Ct. of Appeals, 926 F. Supp. 570 (N.D. W. Va. 1996) (lawyer admitted in the state must maintain office in the state to qualify as "responsible local attorney" to support another lawyer's *pro hac vice* admission).
36. Barry R. Furrow et al., *Health Law* 82 (2d ed., West 2000).
37. *Id.* at 82-83.
38. *E.g.,* Braun v. Bd. of Dental Examiners, 702 A.2d 124 (Vt. 1997) (statute that prohibits delegating "diagnosis, treatment planning and prescription" to persons other than licensed dentists not void for vagueness); Rathle v. Grote, 584 F. Supp. 1128 (M.D. Ala. 1984) (statute that prohibited "practicing medicine ... in such a manner as to endanger the health of the patients of the practitioner" not void for vagueness).
39. *E.g.,* Haley v. Medical Disc. Bd., 818 P.2d 1062 (Wash. 1991) (statute that prohibits "the commission of an act of moral turpitude, dishonesty or corruption relating to the practice of person's profession, whether the act constitutes a crime or not" not void for vagueness as applied to physician who had a sexual relationship with a former patient who was a minor); Adams v. Tex. St. Bd. of Chiropractic Examiners, 744 S.W.2d 648 (Tex. App. 1988) (statute that prohibits "grossly unprofessional conduct or dishonorable conduct likely to deceive or defraud the public" not void for vagueness as applied to chiropractor who engaged in sexual misconduct with patients).

intemperance,"[40] as well as statutory definitions of practice such as "nurse midwifery."[41] Lawyers have been equally unsuccessful in challenging lawyer code provisions such as Model Rule 8.4(d) (conduct prejudicial to the administration of justice)[42] and Code of Professional Responsibility provisions that prohibited "clearly excessive fees."[43] Judges also have been unsuccessful in challenging their discipline for "conduct prejudicial to the administration of justice that brings the judicial office into disrepute,"[44] as well as "habitual intemperance."[45]

Both medicine and law have developed national practitioner databases to ensure that a practitioner's discipline in one jurisdiction will be reported to another. For physicians and dentists, Congress created the National Practitioner Data Bank, which has provided this information to hospitals and state licensing boards since 1990.[46] Hospitals are required to report adverse actions regarding institutional privileges; licensure agencies are required to report most disciplinary outcomes; and insurers must report adverse settlements or judgments over $10,000.[47] Consumers, however, are not allowed access to the information.[48] For lawyers, the American Bar Association has created a similar National Lawyer Regulatory Data Bank, which provides reciprocal discipline information to disciplinary and bar admission officials. Unlike the National Practitioner Data Base, the Data Bank for lawyers includes no information about malpractice judgments. Like the physician data base, the lawyer data bank is available only to officials charged with bar admissions and discipline and may not be used by others.[49]

Finally, like lawyers, other professionals have relied on the Americans with Disabilities Act to force accommodations in both admission and discipline such as those discussed in *Busch*. Consistent with *Busch*, courts have found a judicial

40. Colo. St. Bd. of Med. Examiners v. Hoffner, 832 P.2d 1062 (Colo. 1992).
41. St. v. Kimpel, 665 So. 2d 990 (Ala. Crim. App. 1995); People v. Rosburg, 805 P.2d 432 (Colo. 1991) ("midwife" not unconstitutionally vague).
42. Fla. Bar v. Zamft, 814 So. 2d 385 (Fla. 2002) (ex parte communication with a judge by a lawyer who did not represent either party in the matter); In re Stanbury, 561 N.W.2d 507 (Minn. 1997) (refusing to pay a law-related judgment and make payment on a court filing fee); In re Stuhff, 837 P.2d 853 (Nev. 1992) (intentionally interfering with sentencing of a criminal defendant by filing a disciplinary complaint against a judge just before the sentencing hearing); In re Haws, 801 P.2d 818 (Or. 1990) (failure to respond to bankruptcy trustee's inquiry and disciplinary complaint); St. ex rel. Neb. Bar Assn. v. Kirshen, 441 N.W.2d 161 (Neb. 1989) (failing to respond to bar complaint and properly supervise office staff); In re Jones, 534 A.2d 336 (D.C. App. 1987) (failure to respond to inquiries of bar counsel).
43. Atty. Grievance Commn. v. Korotki, 569 A.2d 1224 (Md. 1990); In re Kennedy, 472 A.2d 1317 (Del. 1984).
44. Fletcher v. Commn. on Jud. Performance, 968 P.2d 958 (1998) (multiple instances of, inter alia, improper comments about counsel, improper use of staff for campaign purposes, and alteration of orders); In re Lowery, 999 S.W.2d 639 (Tex. 1998) (persistent use of profane and rude language, threats to arrest persons without authority to do so); Miss. Commn. on Jud. Performance v. Russell, 691 So. 2d 929 (Miss. 1997) (releasing prisoners in excess of authority and jurisdiction); Matter of Young, 522 N.E.2d 386 (Ind. 1988) (visiting an adult bookstore, charged with public indecency and committing a battery on a police officer); Complaint Concerning Douglas, 370 S.E.2d 325 (W. Va. 1988) (remand to consider lawyer's inappropriate and vexatious statements); In re Kirby, 354 N.W.2d 410 (Minn. 1984) (intemperate use of alcohol and failing to treat attorneys with respect); In re Judge #491, 287 S.E.2d 2 (Ga. 1982) (indicted for fraud in aiding and abetting mother-in-law to obtain welfare benefits); In re Seraphim, 294 N.W.2d 485 (Wis. 1980) (multiple incidents of sexual harassment and improper courtroom remarks).
45. In re Becker, 834 P.2d 290 (Idaho 1992).
46. 42 U.S.C. §11101 (2000) *et seq.*; 45 C.F.R. Part 60 (2003).
47. 42 U.S.C. §11131.
48. Furrow, *supra* note 36, at 80-81.
49. ABA Model R. for Law. Disc. Enforcement, R. 16 (2001).

nominating commission[50] as well as state licensing boards, subject to Title II of the ADA.[51] Health care professionals also have raised ADA claims (though often unsuccessfully on the merits) against public professional schools,[52] residency programs,[53] and public hospitals in disputes over staff privileges.[54]

Conclusion

Overall, lawyers and other professionals are subject to similar conditions for licensure: age, education, examination and moral character. Lawyers have led the way in successfully challenging both citizenship and residency requirements.

Once licensed, lawyers and other professionals become subject to the continuing standards of professional licensure embodied in relevant positive law. Both the number and complexity of these regulations have grown exponentially in the past quarter century. Perhaps because lawyer codes lead the way in these trends, professional discipline appears to be more rigorously enforced against lawyers than against any other group of professionals.

B. Professional Discipline

Problems

2-2. Martyn & Fox represent Lawyer during a tax audit. When the IRS backs off, Lawyer tells Martyn: "You are the best. Thank God they didn't discover the income I earned on my beach house. Thanks to you, I can sleep again. And I'll bet I can get away with this for another five years." What should Martyn do?

2-3. Martyn & Fox are successor counsel for Client, and discover that Client's former lawyer stole client's money from his trust account. What should Martyn & Fox recommend?

2-4. Martyn discovers that an associate in the firm has stolen money from a client's trust account. Martyn tells Fox that she has investigated the matter and that Associate has repaid the money and will not repeat the conduct because he is now on medication for his bipolar disorder. Should Fox concur?

Consider: Model Rules 5.1, 5.2, 8.3, 8.4, 8.5
Model Code DR 1-102, 1-103
RLGL §5

---

50. Doe v. Jud. Nominating Commn., 906 F. Supp. 1534 (S.D. Fla. 1995).

51. *E.g.*, Hason v. Med. Bd., 279 F.3d 1167 (9th Cir. 2002) (denial of license to practice medicine); Firman v. Dept. of St., 697 A.2d 291 (Pa. Commonwealth 1997) (revocation of nursing and midwifery licenses).

52. *E.g.*, Darian v. Univ. of Mass., 980 F. Supp. 77 (D. Mass. 1997) (nursing student); Wong v. Regents of the Univ. of Cal., 192 F.3d 807 (9th Cir. 1999) (medical student).

53. Swanson v. Univ. of Cincinnati, 268 F.3d 307 (6th Cir. 2001).

54. Menkowitz v. Pottstown Meml. Med. Ctr., 154 F.3d 113 (3d Cir. 1998).

Attorney U v. The Mississippi Bar

678 So. 2d 963 (Miss. 1996)

En Banc.

ON PETITION FOR REHEARING

James L. ROBERTS, JR., J., for the Court:[1]

INTRODUCTION

The petitions for rehearing are granted. Original opinions are withdrawn and these opinions are substituted therefor. . . .

In this matter we are presented with the opportunity to define the point at which a member of the bar has sufficient knowledge concerning an unprofessional act of another member of the bar to be compelled to report that knowledge to the disciplinary authority. The range to be considered stretches from "any information" to "personal knowledge" sufficient to qualify one as a witness under our rules of evidence. M.R.E. 602. We opt for a line short of the latter but considerably beyond the former. . . .

I.

Pulmonary Function Laboratory (PFL) began performing pulmonary function testing and other similar services for clients of Attorney S in 1988. The details of their agreement are unclear. At the time this action was commenced there still existed a dispute between William T. McNeese, part owner of PFL, and S as to the exact financial agreement between the two of them.

In the summer of 1989, a dispute arose between S and McNeese over the amount of money S was to pay PFL. To aid them in settling this dispute, both parties obtained legal counsel with S hiring Frank Trapp and McNeese hiring attorney U. According to U, soon after he began representing McNeese, McNeese brought him a writing which he said was a proposed contract which provided for a splitting of legal fees between PFL and, at that time, an unidentified attorney. . . . U advised McNeese that the proposed agreement, as written, was unenforceable because it violated the Rules of Professional Conduct. U then prepared for his client McNeese a "substitute contingent fee agreement to be used between PFL and individuals it tested and for whom it performed other services who could not afford to pay for them, not with the attorney."

In September, 1989, McNeese told U that PFL had been operating under an oral fee-splitting agreement with S for several months and that S was now denying the existence of the agreement and disputing the amounts owed PFL under it. McNeese also told U "that Trapp was representing S in this dispute; and that Trapp, on behalf of S, had suggested a flat fee arrangement, though the parties were not able to agree on the amount." . . .

There followed a series of letters between U and Frank Trapp. . . .

1. Several portions of Justice Bank's original majority opinion have been used verbatim, as those portions accurately explain the procedural history and facts involved.

On November 8, 1989, Frank Trapp wrote U:

> This letter is written in response to your October 10, 1989 and October 27, 1989 letters. It also is to confirm my conversation with you and [your associate] on October 31, 1989.
>
> First I would reiterate, on behalf of my client, [S], that, without admitting or conceding any arrangement ever existed, he does renounce, declare void and disclaim any arrangement with Pulmonary Functions Laboratory (the "Lab") or Bill McNeese to (1) share legal fees or (2) pay compensation or give anything in connection with the referral of clients who had tests performed at the Lab. . . .

U responded on November 17, 1989:

> PFL has advised me that they have no intention of renouncing the fact that there was a fee-sharing arrangement between them and Mr. S. Further, PFL will do no further retesting on any of Mr. S's clients until a flat fee agreement has been negotiated and signed.
>
> As you know, I have advised PFL of its options, including the availability of the complaint proceedings available through the Mississippi State Bar Association. Again, unless something can be worked out along the lines of a negotiated flat fee arrangement, it is the intention of PFL to seek relief through whatever legal avenues are available to it.
>
> Please discuss this with Mr. S and inform us of his decision. If we have not received a response from Mr. S by November 27, 1989, our clients will perform no further retesting on Mr. S's clients and will pursue whatever legal remedies it considers appropriate. . . .

The final letter was sent by Trapp to U on December 6, 1989.

> I am in receipt of your letter of December 1, 1989. In that letter, you unilaterally announce that Bill McNeese's retesting would only be done at a significant sum above the competitive quote of $423.00 given by a pulmonologist. You did not specify what that "significant" figure is. Also, your letter again couples the demand with a reference to filing a bar complaint.
>
> Mr. McNeese charges the clients of Paul Minor and other lawyers less than the $400.00 fee paid for the initial testing. . . .
>
> Everyone recognizes the arrangement alleged by Mr. McNeese would be an unenforceable contract. Moreover, that alleged arrangement runs afoul with the spirit of the runner and champerty statutes. Thus it is clear Mr. McNeese's demand for $4,000.00 per client is either (1) to pay blackmail to keep Mr. McNeese from filing a complaint with the bar association or (2) to pay Mr. McNeese for allegedly referring clients to Mr.[S]. In either case, the *payment would be illegal*. . . .

U did not reply to this letter. In January, 1990, McNeese filed a bar complaint against S. One year later, in January of 1991, S filed a bar complaint against U. U never filed a bar complaint against S. . . .

II.

This Court conducts a:

> *de novo* review in a bar disciplinary matter which necessarily includes a review of the sanctions imposed. Deference is accorded the findings of the Complaint Tribunal but this Court "has the non-delegable duty of ultimately satisfying itself as to the facts, and reaching such conclusions and making such judgments as it considers appropriate and just."

Furthermore, although "Bar disciplinary proceedings are quasi-criminal in nature," "the beyond-a-reasonable doubt standard does not apply; rather, we require an intermediate level of certainty regarding the facts at issue, to-wit; a clear and convincing evidence standard."

Rule 8.3(a) of the Mississippi Rules of Professional Conduct reads:

> A lawyer having knowledge that another lawyer has committed a violation of the Rules of Professional Conduct that raises a substantial question as to that lawyer's honesty, trustworthiness or fitness as a lawyer in other respects, shall inform the appropriate professional authority.

The central issue here is whether the attorney in question had sufficient knowledge of another attorney's misconduct to require his reporting it to the proper authority.... The Terminology section of the Rules does not define "knowledge" but it does define similar terms. "'Knowingly,' 'Known,' or 'Knows' denotes actual knowledge of the fact in question. A person's knowledge may be inferred from circumstances."...

This question has rarely been addressed by the courts, and this is the first instance for this Court. We have found but three cases discussing the duty to report, Matter of Lefkowitz, 483 N.Y.S. 2d 281 (A.D. 1984); In re Himmel, 533 N.E.2d 790 (Ill. 1988); and In re Ethics Advisory Panel Opinion No. 92-1, 627 A.2d 317 (R.I. 1993). Unfortunately, all fail to discuss "knowledge."

Various state bar associations through their Ethics Opinions treated the subject. The Maine Professional Ethics Commission of the Board of Overseers of the Bar wrote in 1989, "The lawyer has no duty to report the other lawyer's misconduct to disciplinary authorities unless the lawyer himself has knowledge, based on a substantial degree of certainty, that the lawyer has committed an offense that raises a substantial question regarding his honesty, trustworthiness, or fitness to practice law." Maine Ethics Op. 100 (1989). The Advisory Committee of the Nebraska State Bar Association has also addressed this issue, writing, "Because 'knowledge' in the reporting rule means more than a suspicion, a lawyer need not report mere suspicions of code violations." Nebraska Ethics Op. 89-4. That opinion does not, however, reach the issue as to what must be reported.

According to the Advisory Opinions Committee of the State Bar of New Mexico:

> The duty to report misconduct is mandatory and arises when a lawyer has a substantial basis for believing a serious ethical violation has occurred, regardless of the source of that information. This "substantial basis" test for knowledge of misconduct is intended to be greater than a "mere suspicion" or "probable cause" test. While no duty to report arises without a substantial basis for knowledge of misconduct, a lawyer may choose to report information of misconduct to the appropriate professional authority. New Mexico Ethics, Op. 1988-8.

The Committee on Professional Ethics of the Association of the Bar of the City of New York gives one of the stricter definitions of knowledge stating, "The degree of certainty required to constitute knowledge under the rule must be greater than a mere suspicion; the reporting lawyer must be in possession of facts that clearly establish a violation of the disciplinary rules." New York City Ethics, Op. 1990-3 (1990). In contrast, the guidelines given by the Committee on Legal Ethics and Professional Responsibility of the Pennsylvania Bar Association appear more subjective—"If the lawyer believes that opposing counsel's conduct raises a substantial question about his honesty, trustworthiness, or fitness to practice, then the lawyer should report the other lawyer's misconduct to the disciplinary counsel." Pennsylvania Ethics, Op. 89-247 (undated). It is unclear from the materials available, however, whether

the word "believed" refers to the legal conclusion whether the conduct is a violation or to the factual conclusion whether the conduct occurred.

Just recently the District of Columbia Bar adopted the position that a lawyer is compelled to report "only if she has a clear belief that misconduct has occurred, and possesses actual knowledge of the pertinent facts." D.C. Bar, Op. 246 (revised 1994).

An excellent discussion of "knowledge" in the context of the Rules of Professional Conduct can be found in The Law of Lawyering by Geoffrey C. Hazard, Jr., and W. William Hodes (1993). Section 402 states:

> In the final analysis, all conclusions about someone else's state of mind must be derived from circumstantial evidence. . . . It is impossible to look into a lawyer's head, and it is unacceptable simply to take his word for his state of mind when the probity of his own conduct is at issue. As the Terminology section points out, a person's belief or knowledge "may be inferred from circumstances."
>
> This practical method of proof has enormous significance. Even where a violation requires "knowledge," the circumstances may be such that a disciplinary authority will infer that a lawyer must have known. In such a case the lawyer will be legally chargeable as if actual knowledge had been proved. In terms of what can be proved, the "knows" standard thus begins to merge with the "should have known" standard, for often it will be impossible to believe that a lawyer lacked knowledge unless he deliberately tried to evade it. But one who knows enough to evade legally significant knowledge already knows too much.

Hazard and Hodes write of a lawyer's unbelief as opposed to his knowledge:

> Although his professional role may require a lawyer to take a detached attitude of unbelief, the law of lawyering does not permit a lawyer to escape all accountability by suspending as well his intelligence and common sense. . . .

Here is the Hazard and Hodes pragmatic approach to knowledge:

> [A] lawyer's conduct will be assessed according to a legal standard that assumes a lawyer can "know" the truth of a situation, even if he cannot be absolutely sure. Even the criminal law, after all, does not require absolute certainty; it requires only a conclusion that is beyond a reasonable doubt. . . . More than this, the law takes account of a lawyer's legal training and experience in assessing his or her state of mind. A lawyer is an adult, a man or a woman of the world, not a child. He or she is also better educated than most people, more sophisticated and more sharply sensitized to the legal implications of a situation. The law will make inferences as to a lawyer's knowledge with those considerations in mind.
>
> Looking forward into his professional conduct as it proceeds, a lawyer must imagine how his conduct will appear to others, later looking back at it. And he must imagine the inferences that will be drawn as to what he must have known at the time. In pragmatic terms, this is what a lawyer knows.

U would have this court define "actual knowledge" as "personal knowledge." Only if a lawyer had such knowledge as would enable him to testify as a witness that another lawyer had violated the Rules of Professional Conduct would he have to inform the proper authorities. We believe that a higher standard may be fairly inferred to be required. That standard must be an objective one, however, not tied to the subjective beliefs of the lawyer in question. The supporting evidence must be such that a reasonable lawyer under the circumstances would have formed a firm opinion that the conduct in question had more likely than not occurred and that the conduct, if it did occur, raises a substantial question as to the purported offender's honesty, trustworthiness or fitness to practice law in other respects. . . .

The circumstances under consideration here reflect that U's client told him of an arrangement which appeared to be fee splitting. The record tells us nothing concerning corroboration of the client's story or of the client's trustworthiness. The other party to the purported arrangement denies that it existed. These circumstances do not dictate a firm opinion on the part of a reasonable lawyer that the conduct in fact occurred. . . .

It is not for the lawyer to believe or disbelieve the client. Ultimately, it is for the fact-finder, either judge or jury. A lawyer must be free to assert his client's claims, at least until there is evidence apparent that the client is lying. The state of mind necessary to assert the claim, however, falls well short of that required for a "firm opinion" as to whether specific conduct occurred. We must allow lawyers at least this degree of detachment if we are to assure the competent and vigorous representation essential to our adversary system of justice. . . .

As measured by the standard we announce here, the proof falls short of that necessary to demonstrate by clear and convincing evidence that lawyer U had sufficient evidence before him such that any reasonable lawyer would have formed a firm opinion that the conduct alleged by his client had in fact occurred.

Because we conclude that the evidence was insufficient to support a finding of "knowledge" we need not reach the issue whether the alleged entry into a fee-splitting arrangement, which was apparently renounced before any fees were actually split, was conduct bearing on S's honesty, trustworthiness or fitness to practice law. We pause only to note that a lawyer is not obliged to report every transgression of our disciplinary rules, only the most serious of them.

Whether a particular violation of the disciplinary rules meets the "substantial question" test must be determined on a case-by-case basis, using "a measure of judgment" rather than a clear litmus test. Advisory opinions from other juris-dic-tions are somewhat helpful in this regard but suggest no bright line test. Compare Arizona Op. 87-26 (failure to file tax returns should have been reported), Alabama Op. 90-97 (same for misappropriation of escrow funds), and New Mexico Op. 1988-8 (same for attempt to bribe witnesses); with Illinois Op. 90-36 (threats to bring criminal charges to gain advantage in a civil suit need not be reported), Virginia Op. 962 (1987) (same for attempt to persuade clients to change wills to detriment of Society for the Prevention of Cruelty to Animals), and Pennsylvania Op. 88-225 (same for failure to comply with statute of limitations). D.C. Bar, Op. 246.

There are cases and opinions from other jurisdictions dealing with the question of fee-splitting. Where substantial sanctions are imposed, the fee-splitting transgression is usually attended by other misconduct. It should suffice to say, however, that the sanction to be imposed in a particular case will depend upon all of the attendant circumstances.

III.

Having found that U never had a Formal Complaint filed with the Clerk of this Court to pursue charges against him for violation of M.R.P.C. 1.16(a), or 1.2(d), the issue regarding the "threats of a bar complaint to exact a settlement" was not previously and is not now properly before the Court. Additionally, to institute disciplinary proceedings at the appellate level raises glaring due process concerns....

...We do not in any manner condone the alleged acts of U, but are required to construe the disciplinary rules strictly. Therefore, U will not have any more disciplinary proceedings instigated against him with regard to the issues already addressed by this Court or originally found to be lacking probable cause by the Complaints Committee absent a reinstitution of proceedings by the Bar Complaints Committee. It is hoped that similar cases shall not arise. Those so tempted would be better served by persistent and continual study of the Mississippi Rules of Professional Conduct. The conclusion of this case is based upon its peculiar history, as are all cases, and its very close decision affords little comfort to those who may be similarly situated....

BANKS, J., concurring in part and dissenting in part:

I agree that the reprimand imposed by the complaint tribunal should be rejected.... In my view, however, the fact that a complaints committee has failed to authorize a formal complaint on the charge of wrongfully threatening to file a bar complaint in order to gain an advantage is no bar to subsequent proceeding on such a charge. Accordingly, I dissent from today's resolution of this matter and adhere to the views expressed in the original majority opinion[1]....

MCRAE, J., dissenting:

The Complaint Tribunal properly found that Attorney U violated Rule 8.3 of the Rules of Professional Conduct. At the very least, the Tribunal's modest sanction of a public reprimand should be affirmed, and the matter referred to the Bar for further action on Attorney U's threatened blackmail of Attorney S. To let Attorney U emerge unscathed and unsanctioned for his misdeeds reflects the majority's unabashed bias in favor of partners in major Jackson law firms.

The majority's finding that Attorney U had no knowledge that Attorney S was engaged in a fee-splitting arrangement with McNeese and PFL is incredible. Rather than insulting our intelligence, the majority should simply repeal a rule it so obviously dislikes....

We are faced with a most egregious set of facts wherein one attorney attempted to use the threat of a bar complaint to induce another to extract from more than 1,000 asbestosis claimants fees of $4,000.00 apiece for a test that cost other people only about $400.00. Moreover, he used the threat of a bar complaint to sidestep any possible expose to liability for a breach of contract action. Despite this attempt to extort more than four million dollars from our hardworking citizens, the majority pays lip service to our Rules of Professional Conduct and allows the offending attorney, a partner in a distinguished Jackson law firm whose members include a former president of the Bar Association, to walk away without so much as a slap

1. The following is an excerpt from the original majority opinion ...

> The more troublesome conduct apparent from the exhibits in this case is the rather obvious use of the threat of a bar complaint in an effort to secure a favorable settlement. U denies an intent to do so but his letters appear to be amenable to that conclusion.
>
> This is conduct not charged here, however. We, therefore, remand this matter to the Complaint Tribunal for further proceedings with regard to this issue.

on the hand.[1] Would we be so quick to merely wink at even a minor indiscretion and spare the heavy hand were the offending party a small-town sole practitioner? I fear not.

I.

Admission to the Mississippi Bar carries with it privileges as well as solemn responsibilities. Only Bar members may sign pleadings, represent clients in court, or hold themselves out as attorneys. One of membership's greatest privileges is being a part of a self-regulating profession. Members of the Bar decide who is to be admitted and, when an attorney's conduct warrants it, who is to be sanctioned....

Rule 8.3(a) provides the linchpin for self-regulation... [and] makes each attorney a policeman of the profession. The rationale behind this rule is simple—no one is better suited to recognize a breach of the Rules or better situated to observe one. The gravamen of Rule 8.3(a) is such that if its precepts are not enforced, the Bar's hallowed concept of self-regulation will become a pathetic mockery. It applies to all who call themselves lawyers—sole practitioners and large firm partners alike. The majority, however, would have us not only reduce the rule to a shadow, but vanish the shadow as well.

Actual knowledge is required to satisfy Rule 8.3(a), but actual knowledge can be, and indeed often must be, inferred. If it is possible to infer by circumstances and prove by clear and convincing evidence that Attorney A, as a reasonable attorney, knew that Attorney B had violated the Rules of Professional Conduct, then Attorney A should be held to have sufficient knowledge of Attorney B's wrongdoing to warrant the imposition of sanctions under Rule 8.3(a). Thus, Attorney A must have more than a mere suspicion of Attorney B's unprofessional conduct; he cannot ignore his own common sense and legal training. The majority, however, states:

> The standard must be an objective one, not tied to the subjective beliefs of the lawyer in question. The supporting evidence must be such that a reasonable lawyer under the circumstances would have formed a firm opinion that the conduct in question had more likely than not occurred and that the conduct, if it did occur, raises a substantial question as to the purported offender's honesty, trustworthiness or fitness to practice law in other respects.

This standard replaces the vague term "actual knowledge" with the equally vague term "firm opinion." Thus, the majority provides an attorney with no further insight as to what is required of him under Rule 8.3(a). Moreover, semantics aside, the record indicates that Attorney U actually knew of Attorney S's misconduct.

II.

How can the majority assert that a lawyer placed sufficient reliance on information furnished to him by his client to blackmail another attorney, but did not have sufficient knowledge to relay that information to the Bar? Ordinary people are found guilty beyond a reasonable doubt and sentenced to decades in prison on less proof than this. One wonders what it would take to prove to the majority that Attorney U knew of the fee-splitting arrangement.

Take your pick or select them all. Under every authority quoted in the majority opinion, Attorney U hit the bull's eye. There can be no question but

1. We can only speculate as to what sort of fee agreement Attorney U might have had with McNeese. Because the majority has elected to sweep his transgressions under the carpet, we will never know.

that his client, McNeese, told him of the fee-splitting contract between Attorney S and PFL, and that he believed it. How else could he have accused Attorney S and so doggedly threatened him with a lawsuit?

The majority tells us that "the other party to the purported arrangement denies that it existed." To find such a denial in this case, one must go outside the record. Trapp certainly did not deny that such an agreement had ever been made by his client. He was too good a lawyer for that: he pled nolo contendere....

The majority also contends that the fact that Attorney U wrote letters to Trapp, accusing Attorney S of conduct which could cost him his license to practice law, does not mean anything. It says, "Lawyers do that all the time." Does the majority really believe this? Has the majority not read Rule 11 of the Mississippi Rules of Civil Procedure? Moreover, practically speaking, I have never met an attorney, and doubt very seriously that I will ever meet one, who makes idle threats based upon information he does not believe. Only a very naive lawyer would write a letter threatening to file suit based on facts he, himself, did not believe. Even more fatuous is the majority's conclusion that Attorney U did not necessarily believe McNeese's detailed description of the fee splitting arrangement with Attorney S. He just "believed" it enough to attempt blackmail. Strange routes are taken by the majority in its apologia for Attorney U's conduct and its protection of old, established Jackson law firms.

III.

Finally, the majority finds that it is required to render the issue of charges that Attorney U also violated Rule 1.16(a) or 1.2(d) on grounds that the issue of using "threats of a bar complaint to exact a settlement" was not properly before us since no formal complaint had been filed with the Clerk of this Court on that charge. I thought that we reviewed attorney discipline cases de novo. Attorney U was treated with utmost leniency by the Complaint Tribunal, which levied only the sanction of a public reprimand against him. He would not have lost a single day or a single dollar in his law practice. Totally oblivious to any wrongdoing on his part, however, and with not a kernel of contrition for all he did, Attorney U appeals to this Court, expressing outrage at the injustice done him. And the majority concurs, forbidding even a slap on the wrist.

In recent years we have seen the public's trust in the legal profession erode to almost nothing. With this case, however, we might have been able to show that the legal profession is so committed to policing itself that it will punish those who do not assist in this goal, regardless of the stature or prestige of the offending attorney's practice and reputation. Opportunities to prove oneself worthy of another's trust are extremely rare. The facts in this case are clear—Attorney U did know of the illicit fee-spitting arrangement between an attorney and his client, a non-attorney, and did not report it. The law is clear as well—not only are attorneys required to act in professional manner, they also are required by Rule 8.3(a) to report conduct of other attorneys which they know has violated the rules. Today's result should therefore be no less straightforward—Attorney U should be sanctioned. If attorneys are to be self-regulating and have their own Rules of Professional Conduct, these rules must be enforced, especially those designed to aid in self-regulation. A true profession can do no less.

Obviously, membership has its privileges. I would affirm the sanction, and remand for a hearing on what clearly was blackmail as we originally ordered. Accordingly, I dissent.

State ex rel. Oklahoma Bar Association v. Busch

919 P.2d 1114 (Okla. 1996)

SUMMERS, J.:

The Oklahoma Bar Association filed a six-count formal complaint against Respondent Michael Busch alleging neglect of client matters, failure to adequately keep the client informed, failure to appeal twice, and intentional misrepresentation as to the status of a case, both to the court and the client. After a hearing the Professional Responsibility Tribunal recommended discipline in the form of an eighteen-month suspension, and that after the period of suspension Respondent be subject to monitoring for his mental condition, Attention Deficit Disorder. Both parties have filed briefs, the Bar seeking a two year suspension, and the Respondent urging he be allowed to continue his practice subject to medication and supervision.

All incidents giving rise to this complaint involved Respondent's handling of Connie Bateman's medical malpractice claim.[1] Respondent filed on behalf of Bateman and her daughter a lawsuit against the doctor who delivered Bateman's daughter. The daughter, now an adult, suffers permanent physical and mental handicaps, allegedly caused by the doctor's negligence. On November 9, 1989, Bateman's motion for default judgment was granted, giving her a judgment against the doctor for ten million dollars. The doctor made no attempt to set aside the judgment.

A few months later Respondent sent the doctor a letter, stating that Respondent would not execute on any personal assets, but would instead collect from any insurance proceeds available. Respondent testified that a brief investigation led him to believe that the doctor had insurance and did not have substantial personal assets. Bateman testified that she did not agree to having such a letter sent. In response to this letter the doctor wrote to his insurance carrier, admitting negligence and making demand that it pay the policy limits. The carrier refused to pay. After further contact the insurer stated that no coverage was in effect at the time of the incident.

When it was later discovered by Respondent that the doctor had substantial amounts of money in several different bank accounts, as well as a ranch which was not his homestead and a collection of valuable antique cars, Respondent attempted to execute against his personal assets. But the letter from Respondent was upheld in a state court as being a valid covenant not to execute. Bateman was thus barred from executing against the personal assets of the doctor and has, to this date, received nothing on her ten million dollar judgment.

Bateman told Respondent to appeal the state court ruling and he agreed. He filed a Notice of Intent to Appeal. However, he failed to file a Petition in Error. He did not notify Bateman of this, and later testified that he decided not to file the appeal because he felt the chances of winning were slim.

In 1990 Respondent filed a second lawsuit for Bateman against Drumright

1. Count I of the complaint alleges violation of Rule 1.1 and 1.3 by signing a letter agreeing not to pursue the personal assets of the doctor. Count II alleges that he failed to appeal the district court's ruling. Count III alleges violations of Rules 1.4(a) and (b) in failing to inform Bateman of his decision not to appeal. Count IV alleges violations of Rule 1.1 and 1.3 in failing to timely appeal from the ruling in favor of the hospital. Count V alleges that he failed to inform his client that the appeal had been dismissed. Count VI alleged intentional misrepresentation to a court regarding the status of the case.

Memorial Hospital, alleging negligence on the part of the hospital for permitting the doctor to have hospital privileges. The hospital filed a motion for summary judgment, which was sustained. Bateman asked Respondent to appeal. He agreed and filed a Petition in Error. However, due to his preoccupation with another case he filed the Petition in Error a day late. In 1991 this Court dismissed the appeal as being out of time. He did not notify Bateman of these events.

In February, 1993, Respondent appeared in front of District Judge Woodson, in a hearing to determine the enforceability of the covenant not to execute. Judge Woodson specifically questioned Respondent as to the status of the lawsuit against the hospital, and Respondent stated that the appeal was pending and he "expected a decision shortly."

During this ongoing attorney-client relationship with Bateman, she testified that he repeatedly refused to return her calls as to the status of her case. Respondent's secretary confirmed this, and stated that she repeatedly urged Respondent to tell Bateman of its status. Bateman was in the courtroom when he told Judge Woodson that the appeal was pending. She did not know it had been dismissed until she inquired with the Supreme Court Clerk's office.

Respondent testified that in June and July 1993 he was diagnosed as having Attention Deficit Disorder. Since that time he has been on medication, and the problem has, for the most part, resolved itself. He continues to seek counseling for other problems in his personal life which have resulted from his disorder. He believes that his handling of the Bateman case was a direct result of Attention Deficit Disorder.

His psychiatrist testified on his behalf, stating that Respondent has done well since the implementation of a regime of medication. He stated that the general symptom of ADD is impulsive and inattentive behavior. When asked specific questions by the trial panel, he testified that ADD does not create an inability to tell the truth. However, ADD does cause impulsive and stupid behavior without thought to the consequences. He specifically stated that "Lying is not a symptom of ADD."

At the request of the trial panel the psychiatrist also submitted, in written form, a proposed program to help attorneys in Respondent's situation. The first step, and most critical, is to maintain a steady course of medication. The second step includes surveillance and monitoring of the professional practice of Respondent. The doctor suggests that someone who does not have ADD must oversee his workload. The third step includes monitoring for periods of "flooding."[2] During these periods, Respondent would need another attorney to take over his case load. This last step requires that Respondent continue his involvement with Lawyers Helping Lawyers. The doctor did not believe it necessary to inform Respondent's clients of his problem.

As for Respondent's prior history of discipline, he received a private reprimand in 1990 for his failure to respond to a grievance, a public censure in 1992 for his neglect of a client matter, and a 90 day suspension in 1993 with one years probation for neglect of a client matter. State ex rel. Oklahoma Bar Assn. v. Busch, 853 P.2d 194 (Okla. 1993).

The trial panel determined that Respondent's conduct violated the Rules of Professional Conduct. Specifically, the panel found: As to Counts I, II and IV Respondent violated Rules 1.1 and 1.3 with regard to his actions (sending the letter agreeing not to execute on

2. Flooding is described as a neurologic phenomenon in which a person with ADD cannot focus, despite medication and extra effort.

personal assets from the judgment in the first case, and failing to appeal the district court's rulings as to both cases) which bar Bateman from executing on the doctor's personal assets. As to Count III Respondent violated Rule 1.4(a) and (b) by failing to keep Bateman informed about her case and in failing to explain the legalities. As to Count V Respondent violated Rule 1.4 and 8.4(c) by failing to inform Bateman that the appeal against the hospital had been dismissed and misleading her to believe it was still pending. As to Count VI, Respondent violated Rules 3.3(a)(1) and 8.4(c) by making a false statement to Judge Woodson. The trial panel continued by finding that Respondent's conduct in Counts I, III, V and VI were not a result of his disorder, and "do not relate to his diagnosis [of attention deficit disorder]." It found, however, that Counts II and IV do relate to the symptoms of his disorder. The trial panel concluded that Respondent should be disciplined for his conduct in Counts I, III, V, and VI, and that after his period of suspension, Respondent should be subject to the guidelines set forth by his doctor.

This Court's review of a disciplinary proceeding is de novo. As the licensing court exercising exclusive jurisdiction, it is the duty of this Court to review the evidence presented, along with the trial panel report, to determine whether the allegations have been proven by clear and convincing evidence. "The nondelegable, constitutional responsibility to regulate both the practice and the ethics, licensure, and discipline of the practitioners of the law is solely vested in this Court." State ex rel. Okla. Bar Assn. v. Downing, 804 P.2d 1120, 1122-3 (Okla. 1990).

Respondent asserts that the trial panel erred in its imposition of discipline by failing to follow the mandates of the American with Disabilities Act (ADA). *See* 42 U.S.C. 12101 et seq. He asserts that as an individual with a disability recognized under the ADA,[3] he is entitled to a "reasonable accommodation" for his disability, and that the trial panel's imposition of punishment is not a "reasonable accommodation." . . .

Prior to the enactment of the Americans with Disabilities Act, courts traditionally held that mental illness did not prevent attorney discipline. Because of the importance of maintaining the integrity of the bar, courts held that discipline was necessary regardless of the reason for unfitness. However, mental infirmity might be a basis for mitigation. *See* Matter of Hoover, 745 P.2d 939 (Ariz. 1987) (manic depression was not a complete bar to discipline but was a factor to consider when deciding the punishment); Carter v. Gonnella, 526 A.2d 1279 (R.I. 1987) (bipolar disorder did not prevent bar discipline); Matter of Hein, 516 A.2d 1105 (N.J. 1986) (alcoholism was not a defense to bar discipline). To hold otherwise would erode the public's confidence in the bar. The sympathy felt for those with mental illnesses does not extend "to the point of lowering the barriers to the protection we have attempted to give to that portion of the public who are clients, especially clients who entrust their money to lawyers."

The Americans with Disabilities Act, enacted 1990, states as its goal "equality of opportunity, full participation, independent living and economic self-sufficiency" for disabled individuals.

3. We note that the Bar Association does not dispute that Respondent's disorder is recognized under the ADA. After conducting our independent research, the ADA defines "disability" as "a physical or metal impairment that substantially limits one or more of the major life activities of such individual. . . ." 28 C.F.R. §35.104 interprets this definition to include "any mental or psychological disorder such as mental retardation, organic brain syndrome, emotional or mental illness, and specific learning disabilities." Respondent's psychiatrist testified that ADD is a neurological disorder, and is recognized in the Diagnostic and Statistical Manual. He also stated that it does fall within the Americans with Disabilities Act and is mentioned in the Individuals with Disabilities Education Act of 1979.

42 U.S.C. §12101(8). It has been described as a "nationwide mandate to provide reasonable accommodations for disabled persons." Petition of Rubenstein, 637 A.2d 1131, 1136 (Del. 1994) quoting Morrissey, The Americans With Disabilities Act: The Disabling of the Bar Examination Process, The Bar Examiner, May 1993.

Relevant to this case is Subchapter II of the ADA which deals with "public entities." 42 U.S.C. 12131 et seq. "Public entity" is defined to include "any State or local government" and "any department, agency, special purpose district or other instrumentality of a State or States or local government." *Id.* This definition has been interpreted to include many instrumentalities of the courts, such as Boards of Bar Examiners, judicial nominating commissions, and disciplinary committees. In Section 12132, public entities are prohibited from discrimination on the basis of a disability.

The Bar Association urges that the ADA is inapplicable to the association in general and more specifically, the Professional Responsibility Tribunal. The basis for this argument is that the Bar Association is not an "employer" of attorneys. However, the ADA has three subchapters. The first deals with employers, the second with public entities and the third with public accommodation. It is the second subchapter—public entities—which is involved here.... Clearly, the ADA applies to the Oklahoma Bar Association, an arm of this Court.

Because the parties do not dispute that the Respondent's disability falls within the purview of the ADA, and because the Oklahoma Bar Association is subject to the ADA, we next must decide what impact this Act has on Respondent's disciplinary proceeding. Thus far, the issues raised by the ADA have primarily centered in two areas: bar admissions and disciplinary proceedings. While we are obviously concerned with its effect in disciplinary proceedings, we should not disregard the reasoning used in the bar application cases.

Two states have been called upon to reconcile the duty of the bar association in monitoring and disciplining its members with the mandate of the ADA. The Florida Supreme Court, in Florida Bar v. Clement, 662 So. 2d 690 (Fla. 1995), addressed the issue when an attorney who was suffering from bipolar disorder (manic depresssion) was accused of ethical violations. The disciplinary referee recommended disbarment, but the attorney disputed the recommendation, urging that it violated the ADA. The Florida Supreme Court disbarred the attorney although his sickness was one recognized by the ADA.

The Court held that "the ADA does not prevent this Court from sanctioning [an attorney]." This holding was based on two grounds. First, the conduct complained of (misuse and misappropriation of client funds) was not causally connected to his mental illness. Second, even if the conduct has been causally related:

> [T]*he ADA would not necessarily bar this Court from imposing sanctions*.... Clement is not "qualified" to be a member of the Bar because he committed serious misconduct, and no "reasonable modifications" are possible....
>
> *Thus, while the ADA applies to the Bar, it does not prevent this Court from taking disciplinary action against Clement*....

A slightly different result has occurred when the issue is bar admission rather than attorney discipline. These attacks have focused on either the questions asked on the bar application or on the examination process itself. In Petition of Rubenstein, 637 A.2d 1131 (Del. 1994), the applicant suffered from a learning disability which kept her from passing the bar. She filed a petition requesting extra time to take both portions of the exam. The Board of Bar Examiners granted her request as to one portion but denied it as to the other. She sought relief from the Delaware Supreme Court. The Court held that once a disability is established which meets the criteria of the ADA, the public entity must make reasonable accommodations to facilitate the disabled person. As an instrumentality of the court, the Board of Bar Examiners was subject to the "reasonable accommodation" standard of the ADA. Extra time for the taking of the examination was considered a reasonable accommodation.

In McCready v. Illinois Board of Admissions to the Bar, 1995 WL 29609 (N.D. Ill. 1995), an applicant alleged violations of the ADA when he was denied admission to the bar after passing the examination. The denial was based on his mental health history which included prolonged problems with drug addiction and other mental disorders. The court held that the denial of admission was proper and did not violate the ADA.

> Under Title II, the protected class is limited to "qualified individuals with a disability." By protecting "qualified individuals with a disability" (and not all individuals with disabilities), the ADA expressly recognizes that, in some cases, an individual may be unqualified by reason of the disability. . . . It is not enough to be qualified "but for" a disability; "the right inquiry is whether the person can satisfy the program's requirements despite his handicap." . . .

The ADA clearly applies to the Oklahoma Bar Association, as an arm of this Court. However, unlike *Rubenstein*, we see no "reasonable accommodation" which can be made with regard to Respondent's neglect of client matters and deceit in court which would accomplish the purpose of maintaining the integrity of the Bar and promoting the public's confidence in the state's many attorneys. This Court has a constitutional duty in overseeing the Bar to insure that its members are fit to practice.

Our case is closer to *Clement*. As the Florida Supreme Court stated, the ADA does not prevent the discipline of attorneys with disabilities. . . . It is undisputed that Respondent failed to pursue an appeal in the first case and failed to timely file the petition in error in the second. We find the evidence to be clear and convincing that Respondent agreed—without his client's knowledge or permission—to pursue the ten million dollar judgment only against the doctor's insurance rather than against the doctor's personal assets. We similarly find that he told Judge Woodson that an opinion in the appeal was expected soon, when, in fact, Respondent knew that the appeal had been dismissed as untimely.

As mitigation we find that Respondent was suffering from Attention Deficit Disorder, that he is now being treated for this illness, and take that into account in the imposition of our discipline. We also note that Respondent has worked with Lawyers Helping Lawyers because of his illness.

We would be shirking our duty as the guardians of the state's bar were we to permit Respondent to avoid discipline. Such would surely erode public confidence in the bar. Respondent's client testified that due to Respondent's gratuitous letter she has received no compensation for her daughter's injuries in spite of the fact that she obtained a ten million dollar judgment. We find no excuse for Respondent's deceitful behavior in a court of this state. While his neglectful behavior may have been influenced by his ADD, his physician testified that lying is not a direct result of the illness. Because we find that the

Bar Association has proven by clear and convincing evidence all counts as alleged in the complaint, we agree that discipline is necessary.

Taking his neurological deficit, now under control, into account as mitigation, Respondent is hereby suspended from the practice of law for two years and one day. After completion of the suspension, if Respondent resumes his practice, he shall be subject to the guidelines set forth by Dr. Dodson in his letter of August 1, 1995. This plan shall include Respondent's involvement with Lawyers Helping Lawyers. If disagreement as to the plan arises, Lawyers Helping Lawyers shall immediately contact the office of the General Counsel for the Oklahoma Bar Association. We also find that Respondent should be, and is hereby, assessed costs in this matter totalling $2,272.54 to be paid within thirty days of the date this opinion becomes final....

OPALA, J., with whom SIMMS and WATT, JJ., join, concurring in part and dissenting in part.

I concur in the court's view that respondent breached professional discipline and that the A.D.A. does not pose a legal impediment to imposition of sanctions; I dissent from today's suspension. I would order respondent's disbarment.

The Law Governing Lawyers: *Professional Discipline*

Attorney U and *Busch* illustrate aspects of a system of professional discipline that forms the backbone of lawyer professional regulation. We will see additional examples of lawyer discipline for violations of applicable lawyer code provisions throughout these materials. In this note, we consider the mechanics of the disciplinary process and the effect of these standards and procedures on lawyer behavior.

Over the past 30 years, state and federal courts have extensively reformed the substance of lawyer codes, updated the procedures for disciplinary enforcement, and implemented guidelines to standardize disciplinary sanctions. The result has been more extensive discipline for a wider variety of professional misconduct. At the same time, because professional discipline continues to reach only a small fraction of client and third-party complaints, other remedies, such as malpractice, fee forfeiture, disqualification, and procedural sanctions also have expanded to fill the regulatory void.

The Emergence of Modern Disciplinary Systems

Courts rely on their inherent power to regulate the practice of law in establishing disciplinary proceedings, which are *sui generis*, neither civil nor criminal in nature.[1] The potential for loss of professional license is less serious than loss of liberty, but a more severe penalty than civil damages. Lawyer codes that serve as the legal standards in the process vindicate public norms of professional responsibility, yet private clients can initiate a complaint. These realities explain why the Supreme Court has required procedural due process guarantees such as notice of the charge[2] and the right to invoke a Fifth Amendment privilege against self-incrimination in disciplinary

1. ABA Model R. for Law. Disc. Enforcement, R. 18 (2001).

2. In re Ruffalo, 390 U.S. 544 (1968) (lawyer entitled to notice of charge in disbarment proceeding). The adequacy of due process in a state disciplinary proceeding also determines whether a federal court can impose reciprocal discipline for the same conduct without plenary review. *See* Selling v. Radford, 243 U.S. 46 (1917); In re Ruffalo, 390 U.S. at 550; In re Edelstein, 214 F.3d 127 (2d Cir. 2000).

proceedings.[3] At the same time, the Fifth Amendment protection against double jeopardy does not apply, because the purpose of a disciplinary proceeding is not to punish the lawyer but to protect the public.[4] The unique nature of the process further justifies the use of a jurisdiction's rules of civil procedure and evidence, a requirement of clear and convincing evidence, no right to a jury trial, and a right to appeal a hearing committee decision.[5] The Supreme Court also has applied the *Younger* abstention doctrine to state disciplinary proceedings, which requires federal courts to refrain from considering constitutional challenges to pending state proceedings that afford the lawyer an opportunity to present the constitutional issues.[6]

In 1970, a special ABA committee chaired by former United States Supreme Court Justice Thomas Clark evaluated the efficacy and efficiency of disciplinary enforcement nationwide. The Clark Commission reported the existence of a "scandalous situation" that required the "immediate attention of the profession."[7] Grievance processes suffered from insufficient funding and staffing, inadequate procedures, decentralized organization, and delay.[8] Lawyers disciplined in one jurisdiction often were admitted elsewhere, and those convicted of serious crimes sometimes continued to practice for years before any disciplinary action resulted.[9]

In 1992, a similar study by the ABA Commission on Evaluation of Disciplinary Enforcement (The McKay Commission) determined that "revolutionary changes" had occurred because most states had implemented many of the changes prescribed by the Clark report.[10] Professional staff, largely in statewide offices, now conducted lawyer discipline. Many had public disciplinary hearings. The ABA had opened a new Center for Professional Responsibility, which administered a National Lawyer Regulatory Data Bank, enabling jurisdictions to share information about public lawyer regulatory sanctions and thus enhancing reciprocal disciplinary enforcement.[11] ABA Model Rules for Lawyer Disciplinary Enforcement and Standards for Imposing Lawyer Sanctions also encouraged uniform procedures and expanded the range of sanctions.[12]

Despite this progress, the McKay Commission identified some persistent inadequacies. Funding and staffing levels, while improved, had not kept pace with the growth in the profession.[13] Although most agencies handled serious matters well, some continued to offer little protection against unethical lawyers. Many state courts

3. Spevack v. Klein, 385 U.S. 511 (1967) (lawyer may not be disbarred for properly invoking the Fifth Amendment privilege against self-incrimination in disciplinary proceeding). A federal court has added the constitutional right to clear and convincing evidence, In re Medrano, 956 F.2d 101 (5th Cir. 1992).
4. *See, e.g.,* People v. Cardwell, 50 P.3d 897 (Colo. 2002); In re Caranchini, 160 F.3d 420 (8th Cir. 1998); In re Brown, 906 P.2d 1184 (Cal. 1995); Disc. Counsel v. Campbell, 345 A.2d 616 (Pa. 1975).
5. ABA Model R. for Lawyer Disc. Enforcement, *supra* note 1, R. 11 and R. 18.
6. Middlesex County Ethics Comm. v. Garden St. Bar Assn., 457 U.S. 423 (1982). The federal courts also are barred from asserting appellate jurisdiction over a state disciplinary matter by the *Rooker-Feldman* doctrine, which deprives lower federal courts of subject matter jurisdiction to review issues presented to and decided by state proceedings or inextricably intertwined with questions state decisions. *See, e.g.,* Allstate Ins. Co. v. W. Va. St. Bar, 233 F.3d 813 (4th Cir. 2000) (*Rooker-Feldman* doctrine prevents federal court review of state bar committee's ruling regarding unauthorized practice of law).
7. ABA, Special Comm. on Evaluation of Disc. Enforcement, *Problems and Recommendations in Disciplinary Enforcement* 1 (Final Draft 1970).
8. *Id.* at 5-7.
9. *Id.* at 116-135.
10. ABA, *Lawyer Regulation for a New Century: Report on the Commission on Evaluation of Disciplinary Enforcement* xiv (1992).
11. *Id.* at 123.
12. *Id.* at xix, 93, 108.
13. *Id.* at xviii. *See also* In re Atty. Disc. System, 967 P.2d 49 (Cal. 1998) (state supreme court has inherent authority to assess a fee from each licensed lawyer to fund disciplinary functions).

continued to delegate control over lawyer discipline to bar associations, which created the appearance of conflicts of interest and impropriety. Secret disciplinary procedures and lack of immunity for complainants continued to shield errant lawyers in too many jurisdictions. Equally important, huge numbers of disciplinary complaints filed by clients that alleged neglect, incompetence, or failure to communicate were being dismissed by disciplinary authorities as minor infractions, which meant that nothing was done to correct the lawyer's behavior or compensate the client.[14]

Most of these problems have been addressed by continual improvements in state and federal disciplinary proceedings over the past ten years. For example, reciprocal discipline, which imposes a disciplinary sanction on a lawyer for conduct that has been the basis for prior discipline in another jurisdiction, has become increasingly common, in part because of the ABA's National Lawyer Regulatory Data Bank that provides information to disciplinary and bar admission officials.[15] Similarly, interim suspension has become a reality for conviction of a serious crime or where serious harm to the public is threatened, such as by a lawyer who abandons a law practice.[16]

The scope of public protection has been further expanded by the addition of component agencies, such as client protection funds, fee arbitration, mediation of malpractice complaints, law practice assistance and substance abuse counseling.[17] These component agencies address issues that may be dismissed as less serious than those that warrant formal discipline, and by doing so they can respond to a greater number of legitimate client complaints that cannot be addressed by the disciplinary system. More states could benefit the public by mandating financial record keeping, trust account maintenance, and overdraft notification, establishing a system of random audits of trust accounts, requiring lawyers to carry malpractice insurance and studying the possibility of recertification.[18] A few jurisdictions have expanded the scope of professional regulation even further by making law firms as well as individual lawyers subject to disciplinary sanctions.[19]

Who Is Disciplined?

Complaints to disciplinary authorities can come from clients, judges, other lawyers, or third parties. In 2000, the ABA reported that disciplinary authorities in 49 jurisdictions received 114,281 complaints and investigated 90,359 of them, resulting in 9,478 public and private sanctions.[20] The differences in disciplinary systems in these jurisdictions create vast differences in the rate of discipline as well. For example,

---

14. *Id.* at xvii.
15. *E.g.*, In re Kersey, 40 Fed. Appx. 613 (1st Cir. 2002) (federal court correctly imposed reciprocal discipline following earlier discipline imposed by two state jurisdictions for the same conduct); Atty. Grievance Commn. v. McCoy, 798 A.2d 1132 (Md. 2002) (lawyer disbarred in Delaware disbarred in Maryland for the same conduct); In re Monaghan, 743 N.Y.S.2d 519 (A.D. 2002) (state court imposed reciprocal discipline following federal court's earlier determination that lawyer committed misconduct).
16. ABA Model R. for Law. Disc. Enforcement, *supra* note 1, Rules 19 and 20.
17. ABA, *A National Action Plan on Lawyer Conduct and Professionalism,* 80 (1999). ABA Model R. for Law. Disc. Enforcement, *supra* note 1, at Rule 1(A). For a discussion of the impact of practice assistance programs as an alternative to discipline, *see* Diane M. Ellis, *A Decade of Diversion: Empirical Evidence that Alternative Discipline is Working for Arizona Lawyers,* 52 Emory L.J. 1221 (2003).
18. *National Action Plan, supra* note 17, at 37.
19. *See, e.g.,* N.Y. Code of Prof. Resp. DR 1-102(a) (2003). *See also* Ted Schneyer, *Professional Discipline for Law Firms?*, 77 Cornell L. Rev. 1 (1991); *Cf.* Julie Rose O'Sullivan, *Professional Discipline for Law Firms? A Response to Professor Schneyer's Proposal,* 16 Geo. J. Legal Ethics 1 (2002).
20. Idaho and Montana did not provide data for the report. ABA, Standing Comm. on Lawyer Disc., *Survey on Lawyer Discipline Systems 2000.*

Arkansas led the states, disciplining nearly 2 percent of its lawyer population in 2000.[21] Ohio was last, disciplining only 0.13 percent.[22] Although the states with the largest lawyer populations (California, New York, Texas, Illinois, New Jersey, Florida, Pennsylvania, District of Columbia, Massachusetts, and Ohio) also discipline the largest number of lawyers, most are not at the top of the list of percentage of lawyers disciplined.[23]

The dissent in *Attorney U* complains that U emerged unsanctioned for his misdeeds because he was a partner in a major law firm in the state. This allegation mirrors long-standing commentary and empirical evidence that solo practitioners and small firm lawyers are much more often subject to discipline than their large firm or inside counsel counterparts.[24]

More recently, a California State Bar study found that only one in twenty disciplinary investigation files were opened against lawyers in firms of more than ten attorneys.[25] Solo practitioners and small firm lawyers accounted for 95 percent of the investigations opened, and nearly 98 percent of the completed disciplinary cases, but only 56 percent of the lawyer population. The report nevertheless concluded that qualitative factors, such as the protection of the public and the courts, drove the disciplinary system. The percentages of disciplinary prosecutions were a function of the disproportionate number of complaints filed against small firm and solo practitioners, rather than any institutional bias against these lawyers.[26] For example, two thirds of client's complaints were made against solo practitioners, resulting in 68 percent of investigations opened and 78 percent of completed disciplinary prosecutions.[27]

The report noted that solo and small firm practitioners were more at risk for both professional discipline and malpractice suits and identified several "factors unique to the practice environment" that explain this result. First, lawyers in large firms tend to represent clients with more money and power, very often, large institutions. If these clients become unsatisfied, they have the ability to change lawyers, negotiate reduced fees, or litigate. On the other hand, clients of small firm lawyers tend to be individuals who often lack the money or power to leverage such alternatives. They therefore are more likely to seek the assistance of bar authorities when something goes wrong.

Beyond clients, lawyers in large firms also have a great deal more peer assistance available to them. Colleagues can cover for lawyers who become ill or overwhelmed.

---

21. Arkansas imposed 126 sanctions on a lawyer population of 12,942, or 1.95 percent of its licensed lawyers. *Id.*, Charts I and II.

22. Ohio imposed only 50 sanctions on a lawyer population of 38,549. *Id.*

23. The ABA does not rank jurisdictions, so we calculated these rankings using ABA data by dividing the total number of private and public sanctions in a jurisdiction by the number of lawyers licensed to practice. California disciplined 0.45 percent of its licensed lawyers, ranking 30 among all jurisdictions; New York, 0.82 percent, ranked 15; Texas, 0.67 percent, ranked 23; Illinois, 0.17 percent, ranked 47; New Jersey, 0.36 percent, ranked 37; Florida, 0.65 percent, ranked 25; Pennsylvania, 0.26 percent, ranked 43; Washington, D.C., 0.19 percent, ranked 45; Massachusetts, 0.34 percent, ranked 38; Ohio, 0.13 percent, ranked 48.

24. *E.g.*, Sharon Tisher, Lynne Bernabei & Mark J. Greene, *Bringing the Bar to Justice: A Comparative Study of Six Bar Associations* 102-106 (Public Citizen 1977). *Cf.* Philip Shuchman, *Ethics and Legal Ethics: The Propriety of the Canons as a Group Moral Code*, 37 Geo. Wash. L. Rev. 244, 254-269 (1968) (the power and influence of large law firms allows them to shape the substance of professional code provisions to protect their own practices).

25. St. Bar of Cal., *Investigation and Prosecution of Disciplinary Complaints Against Attorneys in Solo Practice, Small Size Law Firms and Large Size Law Firms* (June 2001). Available at *http://www.calbar.ca.gov/calbar/pdfs/sb143report01.pdf*, visited July 29, 2002.

26. *Id.* at 14-16.

27. *Id.* at 14.

Larger firms are more likely to institutionalize procedures and policies that can prevent many rule violations, such as those dealing with client trust funds and conflicts of interest. Small firm lawyers may lack such support systems or office procedures. Financial pressures further may induce some small firm or solo practitioners to "borrow" from client trust accounts. Time pressures may cause missed deadlines, failure to communicate with clients, or lack of documentation that could assist in defending against unfounded allegations.

The California study candidly admits that budget difficulties characteristic of most disciplinary systems have forced administrators to prioritize complaints. The first step ferrets out "non-serious, minor, and technical allegations," which would likely not result in discipline. These include many fee disputes and failures to communicate. Once an investigation is undertaken in a more serious matter, "the main determinants of the outcome of the investigation are whether there is harm to a client or the public, whether the burden of proof can be sustained, and the appropriate level of disposition in accordance with case law and [other] standards."[28]

Of course, sustaining the burden of proof can be a function of the perceived size and power of the defense mounted against an allegation. Here the report notes that lawyers in large firms cooperate with the disciplinary authorities, and usually hire counsel to assist them. This means both that large firm lawyers probably will not be the subject of disciplinary complaints unless the evidence appears strong, and when it is, that counsel will advise them to make personal or professional changes to prevent further malfeasance. It also may be the case that some practices of some large firms, like billing fraud, have not yet come to the attention of disciplinary authorities.[29] On the other hand, the report finds that the "vast majority of non-cooperating and defaulting attorneys in the discipline system are solo practitioners,"[30] who may lack retained counsel and therefore not be able to present a substantial defense or benefit from advice that may salvage a career.

What Behavior Triggers Discipline?

Attorney U makes clear that lawyers are not required by Model Rule 8.3 to report every violation of the Rules of Professional Conduct. First, *U* illustrates that a lawyer must "know" that another lawyer has committed a violation of the professional rules. Second the violation should raise a "substantial question as to that lawyer's honesty, trustworthiness or fitness as a lawyer in other respects," that is, the misconduct should not be minor. Both cases and bar regulations offer some guidance to lawyers faced with determining the magnitude of a violation. For example, Florida defines "minor misconduct" in the context of a rule that guides sanctions in disciplinary cases.[31] The rule provides five categories of serious conduct that are not minor and therefore do not qualify for the sanction of admonishment. Presumably, these categories of conduct also would raise a substantial question regarding a lawyer's fitness to practice law. These include misappropriation of a

28. *Id.* at 13.
29. *See, e.g.,* Lisa G. Lerman, *Blue-Chip Bilking: Regulation of Billing and Expense Fraud by Lawyers,* 12 Geo. J. Leg. Ethics 204 (1999); Lisa G. Lerman, *Lying to Clients,* 138 U. Penn. L. Rev. 659 (1990), discussed in Practice Pointers: Fee Agreements, *infra* p.385.
30. Cal. Bar Report, *supra* note 25, at 18.
31. Fla. Bar Reg. Rule 3-5.1 (2003).

client's funds or property, misconduct that resulted in actual loss of money or legal right to a client or third person, prior discipline, misconduct that includes dishonesty and, last, the commission of a felony.[32] Cases and ethics opinions in other jurisdictions generally follow these definitions.[33] Less serious matters, such as a single act of incompetence or conflicts of interest that do not cause harm have been found not to trigger the reporting requirement.[34]

Third, in those cases where a lawyer knows of a violation that does raise a substantial question, Rule 8.3(c) further conditions disclosures on the requirements of client confidentiality in Rule 1.6. This generally has been interpreted to mean that where a lawyer gains information about another lawyer's misconduct while representing a client, the duty of confidentiality only allows disclosure with the client's consent.[35] If another exception to confidentiality allows the disclosure, then Rule 8.3 requires it as well.[36] One jurisdiction, Illinois, has read this confidentiality exception narrowly to include only information protected by the attorney-client privilege.[37]

Of course, Model Rule 8.4(a) makes every rule violation, as well as every attempted rule violation, grounds for professional discipline. Lawyers may not be required to report every violation, but clients and judges can, and do. Most jurisdictions also authorize disciplinary authorities to investigate matters without a request for investigation. The remaining chapters in this book will provide a number of examples of lawyers who violated a myriad of professional code provisions, including lawyers who were incompetent or failed to communicate with clients (such as occurred in *Busch*), violated confidentiality,[38] committed a crime[39] or a fraud,[40] violated conflicts of interest rules,[41] charged unreasonable fees,[42] and improperly communicated ex parte with a judge.[43] Rule 8.4(a) also prohibits inducing others to violate the rules of professional conduct. For example, lawyers who use an agent to solicit cases or make contact with a represented person have been disciplined under

outline

32. *Id.*

33. *See, e.g.,* Prue v. Statewide Grievance Commn., 680 A.2d 898 (Conn. 1995) (failure to safeguard client's funds); Iowa S. Ct. Bd. v. Miller, 568 N.W.2d 665 (Iowa 1997) (former lawyer's demand to repurchase her shares of stock bordered on extortion); St. Bar of Ariz. Op. 94-09 (1994) (excessive fee charged by another lawyer); Assn. of the Bar of the City of N.Y. Formal Op. 1995-5 (pattern of neglect of matters); Atty. Grievance Commn. v. Brennan, 714 A.2d 157 (Md. 1998) (suspended lawyer misrepresented his status to clients); St. Bar of Wis. Op. E-85-11 (1985) (billing client for fictitious expenses); Matter of Dowd, 559 N.Y.S.2d 365 (A.D. 1990) (kickbacks to city officials); Conn. Bar Assn. Informal Op. 94-11 (1994) (cocaine use, spousal abuse); Pa. Bar Assn. Op. 92-8 (1992) (threats of physical violence).

34. *E.g.,* Ill. St. Bar. Assn. Op. 01-02 (2002) (failure to pay a referral fee); Conn. Bar Assn. Informal Op. 97-8 (1997) (malpractice); Pa. Bar Assn. Informal Op. 97-40 (1997) (dual representation that does not adversely affect a lawyer's relationship with either client).

35. *E.g.,* In re Ethics Advisory Panel Op. No. 92-1, 627 A.2d 317 (R.I. 1993).

36. Conn. Bar Assn. Informal Op. 95-17 (1995) (Conn. exception to rule 1.6 that permits disclosure to rectify the consequences of a client's criminal or fraudulent act requires disclosure under Rule 8.3).

37. Ill. R. of Prof. Conduct, Rule 8.3(c) (2003); Ill. St. Bar Assn. Advisory Op. 96-09 (1997); In re Himmel, 533 N.E.2d 790 (Ill. 1988).

38. Matter of Anonymous, *infra* p.123; In re Pressly, *infra* p.153.

39. People v. Casey, *infra* p.218.

40. In re Forrest, *infra* p.224.

41. In re Halverson, *infra* p.271; In re Wildermuth, *infra* p.314.

42. Matter of Fordham, *infra* p.371; In re Sather, *infra* p.393.

43. In re Ragatz, *infra* p.123.

this provision,[44] as have those who direct others, such as legal assistants or secretaries to do acts that violate the professional rules.[45]

In notes to come, we will examine the provisions of Model Rule 8.4(b), which prohibits lawyers from committing criminal acts that reflect adversely on their ability to practice law,[46] and Rule 8.4(c), which prohibits dishonestly, fraud, deceit and misrepresentation.[47] Note that these provisions apply to lawyer conduct whether inside or outside of law practice.[48] Rule 8.4(d), which prohibits conduct prejudicial to the administration of justice, also has been applied in a wide variety of contexts. Former President Bill Clinton was suspended from law practice in Arkansas for violating this rule. After he was found in contempt of court by the trial judge,[49] Clinton admitted "he knowingly gave evasive and misleading answers," but would not admit to lying. He did, however, agree to a five-year suspension from practice for violating Rule 8.4(d), rather than the more specific dishonesty standard in Rule 8.4(c).[50]

Rule 8.4(d) also has been applied to lawyers who abandon law practice without notifying clients,[51] and prosecutors who seriously misuse their discretion.[52] The rule has provided the basis for discipline for misconduct during litigation, such as shoving another lawyer in the courtroom,[53] making court appearances while intoxicated,[54] or making insulting remarks during a deposition.[55] Lawyers have been uniformly unsuccessful in challenging Model Rule 8.4(d) as void for vagueness.[56]

---

44. *E.g.*, In re Brass, 696 So. 2d 967 (La. 1997) (lawyer who paid investigator to refer personal injury and criminal cases suspended for two and one half years); Emil v. Miss. Bar, 690 So. 2d 301 (Miss. 1997) (lawyer who asked highway patrol officer to refer automobile injury cases in exchange for 15 percent of eventual settlements indefinitely suspended).
45. *E.g.*, In re Ositis, 40 P.3d 500 (Or. 2002) (lawyer who directed a private investigator to pose as a journalist to interview a potential opposing party to a legal dispute suspended for 30 days); In re Morris, 953 P.2d 387 (Or. 1998) (lawyer who directed legal assistant to alter and file final account in a probate matter after it had been signed and notarized suspended for 120 days); Disc. Counsel v. Bandy, 690 N.E.2d 1280 (Ohio 1998) (lawyer who tried to validate a will naming himself as beneficiary six years after its execution by requesting that his former secretary, who was not present when the will was signed nevertheless sign it as an additional witness suspended for two years).
46. The Limits of the Law: Criminal Conduct, *infra* p.220.
47. The Limits of the Law: Lawyer Dishonesty, Fraud, Deceit, and Misrepresentation, *infra* p.101.
48. *E.g.*, In re Morrissey, 305 F.3d 211 (4th Cir. 2002) (lawyer who, while suspended from practice, tried to bribe a Habitat for Humanity official in order to evade his community service obligations required by his criminal sentence, disbarred for engaging in criminal and dishonest conduct).
49. Jones v. Clinton, 36 F. Supp. 2d 1118 (E.D. Ark. 1999).
50. Tom Brune, *No Clinton Indictment; President Makes a Deal*, Newsday, at A05 (Jan. 20, 2001).
51. *E.g.*, In re Kendrick, 710 So. 2d 236 (La. 1998) (lawyer who moved without notifying bankruptcy client, which resulted in repossession of client's vehicles suspended from practice for one year and a day and ordered to pay restitution); People v. Crist, 948 P.2d 1020 (Colo. 1997) (lawyer who left state, abandoning law practice of sixty pending cases disbarred).
52. In re Christoff, 690 N.E.2d 1135 (Ind. 1997) (prosecutor and chief deputy prosecutor who renewed a long dormant criminal investigation against another lawyer who sought the prosecutor's job suspended for 30 days and publicly admonished).
53. In re Jaques, 972 F. Supp. 1070 (E.D. Tex. 1997) (lawyer who, inter alia, assaulted a person and verbally abused another lawyer during a deposition suspended).
54. In re Wyllie, 952 P.2d 550 (Or. 1998).
55. In re Golden, 496 S.E.2d 619 (S.C. 1998) (lawyer who made threatening and degrading comments during two depositions publicly reprimanded).
56. *See, e.g.*, Fla. Bar v. Zamft, 814 So. 2d 385 (Fla. 2002) (ex parte communication with a judge by a lawyer who did not represent either party in the matter); In re Stanbury, 561 N.W.2d 507 (Minn. 1997) (refusing to pay a law-related judgment and make payment on a court filing fee); In re Stuhff, 837 P.2d 853 (Nev. 1992) (intentionally interfering with sentencing of a criminal defendant by filing a disciplinary complaint against a judge just before the sentencing hearing); In re Haws, 801 P.2d 818 (Or. 1990) (failure to respond to bankruptcy trustee's inquiry and disciplinary complaint); St. ex rel Neb. Bar Assn. v. Kirshen, 441 N.W.2d 161 (Neb. 1989) (failing to respond to bar complaint and properly supervise office staff); In re Jones, 534 A.2d 336 (D.C. App. 1987) (failure to respond to inquiries of bar counsel).

Rules 8.4(e) and (f) further prohibit specific kinds of conduct that is prejudicial to the administration of justice. Rule 8.4(e) proscribes conduct that suggests a lawyer can obtain results by improperly influencing a governmental agency or official. Lawyers have violated this provision by suggesting that they could improperly influence a judge or other public official.[57] The rule also has been applied to judges who misuse their positions.[58] Rule 8.4(f) further prohibits lawyers from assisting judges in violating the rules of judicial conduct, for example, by making loans to judges before whom they appear.[59]

Some jurisdictions have added additional grounds for discipline to Rule 8.4. For example, Massachusetts and New York prohibit lawyers from engaging in "any other conduct that adversely reflects on the lawyer's fitness to practice law."[60] Louisiana prohibits lawyers from failing to cooperate with an investigation into alleged misconduct, "except upon the expressed assertion of a constitutional privilege.[61] Colorado, California, and Florida provisions make nonpayment of child support obligations grounds for license suspension.[62] Several jurisdictions also have enacted express prohibitions against discrimination. California prohibits "Discriminatory Conduct in a Law Practice,"[63] the District of Columbia prohibits "Discrimination in Employment,"[64] Illinois, New York, and Ohio forbid unlawful discrimination,[65] Michigan requires lawyers to treat persons involved in the legal process "with courtesy and respect,"[66] Minnesota prohibits harassment "on the basis of sex, race, age, creed, religion, color, national origin, disability, sexual preference, or marital status,"[67] and Texas prohibits lawyers from manifesting "by words or conduct bias based on race, color, national origin, religion, disability, age, sex, or sexual orientation."[68] The ABA opted to address these issues in Comment 3 to Rule 8.4 rather than black letter. Courts have not had trouble disciplining lawyers for truly outrageous conduct either under these provisions or the more general language of Rule 8.4(d), conduct prejudicial to the administration of justice.[69]

---

57. Disc. Counsel v. Cicero, 678 N.E.2d 517 (Ohio 1997) (lawyer who led prosecutor and client-defendant to believe he was having a sexual relationship with a judge after she recused herself from the case suspended from practice for one year); Disc. Proceeding Against Bennett, 376 N.W.2d 861 (Wis. 1985) (lawyer who, inter alia, told his client a bankruptcy matter could be handled in some "extra-legal" way suspended for six months).

58. *E.g.*, In re Yaccarino, 564 A.2d 1184 (N.J. 1989) (judge who contacted police and prosecutor about the arrest of his daughter and who conspired to obtain property that was the subject of a lawsuit over which he presided properly removed from office and subject to disbarment).

59. Lisi v. Several Attorneys, 596 A.2d 313 (R.I. 1991) (lawyers who made loans to judges before whom they appeared subject to suspension and reprimand).

60. Mass. R. of Prof. Conduct, Rule 8.4(h) (2003); N.Y. DR 1-102(a)(7) (2003).

61. La. R. of Prof. Conduct, Rule 8.4(g) (2003).

62. Cal. Bus. & Prof. Code §490.5 (2003); Colo. R. C. P. §251.8.5(b) (2002); Fla. R. of Prof. Conduct 8.4(h) (2003).

63. Cal. R. of Prof. Conduct 2-400 (2003).

64. D.C. R. of Prof. Conduct 9.1 (2003).

65. Ill. R. of Prof. Conduct 8.4(a)(9)(A) (2003) (discrimination in violation of federal, state or local law); N.Y. DR 1-102(a)(6); Ohio DR 1-102(B) (2003).

66. Mich. R. of Prof. Conduct 6.5 (2003).

67. Minn. R. of Prof. Conduct 8.4(g) (2003). Rule 8.4(h) also forbids discriminatory acts prohibited by federal, state, or local law.

68. Tex. Rule 5.08 (2003).

69. *E.g.*, In re Monaghan, 743 N.Y.S.2d 519 (A.D. 2002) (race-based abuse of opposing counsel at a deposition was conduct prejudicial to the administration of justice and unlawful discrimination); Fla. Bar v. Martocci, 791 So. 2d 1074 (Fla. 2001) (sexist, racial, and ethnic insults constituted conduct prejudicial to the administration of justice); In re Panel File 98-26, 597 N.W.2d 563 (Minn. 1999) (prosecutor who sought to disqualify defense counsel solely on the basis of race engaged in conduct prejudicial to the administration of justice). *See also* In re Charges of Unprofessional Conduct, *infra* p.443.

Defenses and Sanctions

Attorney U illustrates that the best defense to a disciplinary complaint is the failure of disciplinary counsel to meet the burden of proof.[70] *Busch* illustrates the importance of mitigating factors, which can be raised in initial discussions with counsel before formal charges, during a disciplinary hearing, and after a finding of misconduct in determining a sanction.

Disciplinary sanctions differ from jurisdiction to jurisdiction, although an increased range of sanctions and their uniformity has been encouraged by the ABA Standards for Imposing Lawyer Sanctions, relied on by several courts in these materials.[71] These Standards call for a wide range of sanctions, including disbarment, suspension, reprimand, admonition, probation, restitution, assessment of costs, limitation upon practice, appointment of a receiver, requiring that a lawyer take continuing legal education or retake all or part of a bar examination, and any other requirement deemed "consistent with the purposes of lawyer sanctions."[72] In determining the appropriate sanction, the Standards list four factors to be considered by a court: the duty violated, the lawyer's mental state, the actual or potential injury caused by the misconduct and the existence of aggravating and mitigating factors.[73]

Aggravating factors include past discipline, dishonest or selfish motive, a pattern of misconduct or multiple offenses, obstruction of a disciplinary proceeding, refusal to acknowledge responsibility, a vulnerable victim, substantial experience in law practice, and illegal conduct.[74] Mitigating factors encompass personal and emotional problems, physical or mental disability, the absence of prior disciplinary violations or selfish motive, timely efforts to rectify harm, a cooperative attitude toward the disciplinary board, delay in the disciplinary proceedings, inexperience in law practice, good character and reputation, other penalties or sanctions, remorse, and remoteness of prior offenses.[75] One disability that plagues lawyers—substance abuse—has been the cause of a large number of disciplinary complaints. Here, most courts regard successful treatment for substance abuse as a mitigating factor, and failure to seek treatment as an aggravating circumstance.[76]

Busch also illustrates how a disability may mitigate a disciplinary sanction, but only if the disability caused the problem and can be accommodated to prevent it in the future. Recall that the court distinguished Busch's dishonesty, which was not caused by his disability, from his incompetence and failure to communicate, which

70. *See, e.g.*, In re Karr, 722 A.2d 16 (D.C. App. 1998) (state bar counsel did not prove by clear and convincing evidence that lawyer was guilty of neglect rather than by consideration of an ethical dilemma caused by his client's perjury). Of course, Constitutional challenges also have met with some success. *See* The Limits of the Law: The Constitution, *infra* p.477. Laches and entrapment also have been raised on rare occasions in disciplinary proceedings. *See, e.g.*, In re Carson, 845 P.2d 47 (Kan. 1993) (ten-year delay in disciplinary proceedings not available as a defense where no prejudice to lawyer occurred); In re Porcelli, 397 N.E.2d 830 (Ill. 1979) (entrapment not available as a defense to a lawyer who paid a police officer to alter a client's blood alcohol report).

71. In re Halverson, *infra* p.271; In re Sather, *infra* p.393. *See also* Sarah A. Hirsch, *The Illusive Consistency: A Case for Adopting the ABA Standards for Imposing Lawyer Sanctions in In re Martin*, 40 S.D. L. Rev. 300 (1995).

72. ABA Standards for Imposing Law. Sanctions, 2.1-2.8 (1986).

73. *Id.* at Standard 3.0.

74. *Id.* at Standard 9.2.

75. *Id.* at Standard 9.3.

76. *Id.* at 9.32 (mental disability or chemical dependency are mitigating factors only when they caused the misconduct, have been confirmed by medical evidence, and recovery is demonstrated by a meaningful and sustained period of successful rehabilitation, which arrested the misconduct and makes recurrence unlikely).

arguably was. Unfortunately, three years later the same court faced similar misconduct by the same lawyer. This time, Busch was disbarred.[77]

Finally, recall that the lawyer codes have been influenced by and continue to influence the broader law governing lawyers.[78] For example, courts often rely on professional code provisions that embody other legal obligations of lawyers (such as fiduciary duty) to create the standard of conduct outside of discipline (such as in a malpractice case or disqualification motion.) This reliance on lawyer code provisions outside of the disciplinary context means that your study of the professional code provisions that create the basis for professional discipline also will inform your more extensive study of professional obligation found in the law governing lawyers.

---

77. St. ex rel. Okla. Bar Assn. v. Busch, 976 P.2d 38 (Okla. 1998).
78. *See* The Law Governing Lawyers: Sources of Law, *supra* p.16.

Part II

Lawyers and Clients: Fiduciary Duty

A lawyer who agrees to represent a client also agrees to assume four basic fiduciary duties: competence, communication, confidentiality and loyalty (avoiding conflicts of interest.) This part of the book explores these obligations and the various remedies available to clients if they are breached. Since none of these obligations exists until a client-lawyer relationship has been created, each chapter in Part II begins by addressing the basic question of what factors determine when lawyers have created client-lawyer relationships and their concomitant fiduciary duties. In this chapter, we explore court appointments and lawyer choice as two ways that lawyers assume professional duties to clients, including service *pro bono publico,* for the public good.

Chapter 3

Deciding Whom to Represent

Problems

3-1. Should Martyn & Fox represent Credit Suisse in a case brought by descendants of Holocaust victims who deposited money in the bank before the war? Would you be willing to have us limit our representation to a statute of limitations motion?

3-2. Should Martyn & Fox represent the Ku Klux Klan, which has been denied a permit to parade downtown?

3-3. Should Martyn & Fox represent a defendant on death row who brutally abused and then stabbed two young girls?

3-4. Should Martyn & Fox represent a disagreeable, nasty, racist old woman who wants to force her Hispanic landlord to repair the building she lives in? What if she has no money to pay a lawyer?

3-5. Should Martyn & Fox represent a client who wants to disinherit an adult child because he is gay? What if the prospective client is near death in a hospice and Martyn & Fox are the only lawyers available?

Consider: Model Rules 1.2, 6.1, 6.2

A. Court Appointments

Bothwell v. Republic Tobacco Co.

912 F. Supp. 1221 (D. Neb. 1995)

PIESTER, Magistrate Judge.

Before me for consideration is a motion, submitted by plaintiff's appointed counsel, Paula Metcalf, seeking reconsideration and vacation of my order appointing her to represent plaintiff in this case....

BACKGROUND

In March 1994 plaintiff Earl Bothwell, who at the time was incarcerated at the Hastings Correctional Center, submitted to this court a request to proceed in forma pauperis, a civil complaint, and a motion for appointment of counsel....

In his complaint plaintiff alleged that he "immediately ceased" purchasing and smoking factory-manufactured cigarettes after Congress enacted the Federal Cigarette Labeling and Advertisement Act of 1969 ("FCLAA"), 15 U.S.C. §1333 et seq, which mandated that a warning label be conspicuously placed on packages of such cigarettes. Plaintiff alleged that he thereafter switched to "roll your own" cigarettes, which were not covered by the FCLAA.... Plaintiff alleged that he switched to the defendants' products on the belief that, because the government had not mandated warning labels on loose tobacco and because the defendants had not voluntarily issued such warnings, those products were not harmful or hazardous. Plaintiff alleged that in 1986 he became aware that he suffered from emphysema, asthma, heart disease, and "bronchial and other respiratory diseases." He later learned that the loose tobacco products he had been using "were stronger that [sic] [factory-produced] cigarettes and were twice as harmful and deadly."...

DISCUSSION

In her brief in support of her motion to reconsider and vacate, Metcalf contends that my order appointing her as counsel is "contrary to law and clearly erroneous" because "a federal court has no statutory or inherent authority to force an attorney to take an ordinary civil case for no compensation."

Statutory Authority

Insofar as concerns statutory authority, Metcalf is correct. Plaintiff in this case is proceeding in forma pauperis pursuant to 28 U.S.C. §1915(d). In Mallard v. U.S. Dist. Ct., 490 U.S. 296 (1989), the United States Supreme Court held, in a 5-4 decision, that section 1915(d) does not authorize a federal court to require an unwilling attorney to represent an indigent litigant in a civil case. In so holding, the Court focused on the language of section 1915(d), which provides that a court may "request" an attorney to accept a court appointment.... However, the Court in *Mallard* left open the question of whether federal courts possess the inherent power to require an unwilling attorney to accept an appointment....

Inherent Authority...

Since its inception the federal judiciary has maintained that federal courts possess inherent powers which are not derived from statutes or rules. These inherent powers vest in the courts upon their creation. Anderson v. Dunn, 19 U.S. 204, 227 (1821) ("courts of justice are universally acknowledged to be vested, by their very creation, with power to impose silence, respect, and decorum, in their presence, and submission to their lawful mandates")....

... [T]he power to conscript lawyers to represent the indigent... exists for two primary purposes: (1) to ensure a "fair and just" adjudicative process in individual cases; and (2) to maintain the integrity and viability of the judiciary and of the entire civil justice system. These two purposes mirror the dual functions that lawyers serve in the civil justice system. First, they act as advocates in individual cases working to peacefully resolve civil disputes between citizens. Second, by their ready availability to act in that capacity, they preserve the credibility of the courts as a legitimate arm of the civil justice system....

(1) "Fair and Just" Process in Individual Cases

... While it is established that a plaintiff has no constitutional right to counsel in a civil case, counsel nevertheless may be necessary in a particular civil proceeding to ensure fairness and justice in the proceeding and to bring about a fair and just outcome.

The American legal system is adversarial in nature. Gideon v. Wainwright, 372 U.S. 335, 344 (1963). The adversarial system has been embraced because it is believed that truth is best divined in the crucible of cross examination and adversarial argument. Attorneys, because they are trained in the advocacy skills of cross-examination and argument, are a necessary component in a properly functioning adversarial system. Thus, the notion that the adversarial system is an effective method for ferreting out the truth presumes that both sides have relatively equal access to adequate legal assistance from those trained in the art of advocacy....

If the lack of legal representation is the free choice of the unrepresented party or if it results from factors unrelated to the indigency of the plaintiff, our system is not offended. Where, however, one party is unable to obtain legal representation because of indigency, the resulting disparity of advocacy skills clearly offends the principle of "equality before the law" underlying our system. Further, a substantial disparity in access to legal representation caused by the indigency of one of the parties threatens the adversarial system's ability to produce a just and fair result.

Access to legal representation in this country is gained primarily through the private market. For the most part, the market is an effective mechanism for providing legal services to those who need them. However, the market sometimes fails to provide counsel regardless of the merits of the claims at issue. Where the person whose claims have been rejected by the private market is indigent, he or she may seek representation through a legal aid organization. However, the ability of such organizations to meet the needs of the indigent has taken a serious hit over the past fifteen years in the form of reduced funding to the Legal Services Corporation ("LSC"), the federal entity responsible for funding state and local legal aid offices.... Rather than increasing that budget, however, the current Congress is considering further cuts in legal services funding. Also being considered are greater restrictions on the types of practice which legal aid organizations can provide to the indigent. Compounding the problem of legal access for the poor is the growing apathy of the private bar to the plight of many indigent litigants. The inevitable net result of these factors is that the poor, indeed most of the so-called "middle class," have less realistic access to advocacy services from lawyers....

... I conclude that, when indigency is the principal reason for disparate access to the civil justice system in an individual case, a federal court does possess the inherent authority to bring about a fair and just adjudicative process by conscripting an unwilling lawyer to represent the indigent party....

(2) *Preserving the Integrity of the Civil Justice System*

The very purposes for the establishment of the judicial branch of government included the peaceful resolution of private disputes between citizens and the protection of the minority from loss of their rights to the majority, either at the ballot box or through force.

In order to be viable in delivering on these goals, a justice system must be both trustworthy and trusted. The judicial branch of our government was created powerless to enforce its own decisions; it relies on the respect of litigants for adherence to the law it declares, or, if necessary, actions of the executive branch. It is, to be sure, a living example of "the consent of the governed." To be accorded respect among the people it serves, it must be perceived as fair. If it is not trusted, it will not be seen as a legitimate means to serve its purposes of peacefully resolving disputes and protecting minority rights. . . .

While the purposes of peacefully resolving disputes and protection of the minority from the overbearing will of the majority remain as essential today as they were at our country's founding, the ability of the courts to fulfill them is currently being eroded by a number of forces. First, the use of violence as a means to settle differences is increasing at an alarming rate. . . . Second, the reduction of governmental resources to provide legal services to the poor is, for them, a removal of the civil justice system's accessibility (and thus, its legitimacy). Third, the other two forces are accommodated by the failure of attorneys to recognize that the legitimacy of the system in which they operate depends upon its equal accessibility to all population groups and by the concomitant attitude that the license to practice law is an entitlement to practice law *solely* for private gain. . . .

Lawyers as Officers of the Court. . .

. . . Because the ready availability of lawyers is necessary to ensuring the perception, and indeed the reality, of fairness, their accessibility as officers of the court is necessary not only to the preservation of the justice system itself but to the ordered liberty of our society. . . .

Monopoly of Lawyers

A further justification which has been advanced for the view that attorneys are obligated to comply with court-ordered appointments is the monopoly theory. Under that theory, attorneys must provide legal services to indigents without compensation by virtue of the exclusive privilege they have been granted to practice law. Regulation of attorney licensing limits the number of individuals who may practice law. As a result, those relatively few individuals who are licensed benefit financially, thereby compensating them for any financial losses incurred by representing indigents. Also, because meaningful access to the courts can be had only through these licensed attorneys, they are required to represent those who are unable to afford representation. . . .

Finally, critics claim that other groups enjoying monopolies as a result of state licensing, such as doctors, nurses, teachers, insurance agents, brokers, and pharmacists, do not bear an obligation to provide free services to the poor. While that is true, it misses the point. The practice of law — that is, the representation of others before the civil courts — is not simply a private enterprise. It is, in addition, a contribution to society's ability to manage its domestic affairs, a necessary condition of any civilized culture. Attorneys have a unique relationship to government not shared by other licensed groups. This relationship, which has been described as "symbiotic," places attorneys in "an intermediary position between the court and the public" where they are "inextricably linked to the public sector despite [their] dual position as a private businessperson."

By virtue of this special relationship between the bench and the bar, courts are dependent upon attorneys to aid in carrying out the administration of justice. While other professions also contribute to private gain and to the betterment of society's standards of living, no other group holds the exclusive key to meaningful participation in a branch of government and the protection of rights. This monumental difference between attorneys and other licensed groups justifies imposition of different conditions on the practice of the profession.

Ethical Obligation of Lawyers

An additional justification for the court's exercise of inherent power to compel representation is the ethical obligation of attorneys to provide representation to indigent litigants. . . . [The court cites Model Rule 6.1.]

While these obligations are not expressed in mandatory terms, they clearly indicate that service to the indigent is an essential characteristic of any ethical attorney. Two aspects deserve further attention.

First, these moral and ethical obligations to provide legal services to the poor do not exist merely to prompt the practicing lawyer to be a "good" person, respected in the profession. Rather, they are a recognition of the critical role of the lawyer in ensuring the fair and just adjudication of disputes, and the need for such advocacy in ensuring the existence of the system.

Second, these obligations are not self-executing. . . . It makes little sense to give only lip service to these ideals while the legitimacy of the court system is being challenged by other means of resolving private disputes. If our society is to have a legitimate civil justice system, the courts must be empowered to take necessary measures to create and maintain it. In a more genteel and public-spirited time, the mere suggestion by a court that a private attorney should provide free representation might be met with acceptance of the duty as a necessary means to ensure fairness and the justice system itself; perhaps that history contributes to the lack of mandatory requirements today. . . .

Necessity of Exercising Authority

In deciding whether to exercise the authority to compel representation I first note that a court must exercise its inherent powers "with restraint and discretion." The common thread running through inherent powers jurisprudence is the concept of necessity. Thus, while this court possesses the inherent power to compel representation of an indigent plaintiff, the power should be exercised only where reasonably necessary for the administration of justice. In other words, the appointment of counsel must be necessary to bring about a fair and just adjudicative process.

. . . [W]hen determining whether counsel should be appointed for an indigent plaintiff, the court should consider such factors as (1) the factual complexity of the case, (2) the ability of the plaintiff to investigate the facts, (3) the existence of conflicting testimony, (4) the plaintiff's ability to present his claims and (5) the complexity of the legal issues. In re Lane, 801 F.2d 1040, 1043-44 (8th Cir. 1986). An additional factor . . . is the plaintiff's ability to obtain counsel on his own. . . .

. . . I conclude that the plaintiff's failure to obtain private counsel was not the result of his indigency but rather a result of the "marketability," or lack thereof, of his claims. This "marketability" analysis, which I believe to be a proper additional consideration in determining whether to appoint counsel, involves . . . several steps.

The first step in the "marketability" analysis is to ask whether, realistically, there is a "market" of lawyers who practice in the legal area of the plaintiff's claims. Many indigent litigants, particularly prisoners, raise civil rights claims pursuant to 42 U.S.C. §1983. There are relatively few private attorneys who practice in the area of civil rights. Also, there are few, if any, lawyers willing to assume cases on a contingent-fee basis where the indigent plaintiff primarily seeks forms of relief other than monetary damages, such as injunctive or declaratory relief. As a result, in many cases, there simply is no true "market" to look to when determining whether an indigent plaintiff should be appointed counsel. In such cases, there should be no further inquiry into the "marketability" of a plaintiff's claims. Rather, the appointment of counsel should rest on those other factors commonly used in determining whether to appoint counsel. *See* In re Lane, *supra*.

In cases where such a "market" of lawyers is found to exist, a second question must be addressed: Does the plaintiff have adequate access to that market? This inquiry is necessary for two major reasons. First, many indigent litigants are physically unable to access private counsel regardless of the merits of their claims. This is especially true where the litigant is incarcerated. . . . Second, there may be communication barriers of language or language skills; barriers of physical, emotional, or mental disabilities; or educational or cultural barriers that block understanding between attorney and client. . . . Where a "market" of attorneys exists but a party does not have adequate, realistic access to it, no further "marketability" inquiry is necessary because such inquiry could not yield a reliable conclusion regarding the involvement of indigence as a factor in the litigant's failure to obtain counsel. In such situations, the appointment of counsel should be analyzed using factors from In re Lane, *supra*.

If there is a market and the litigant had realistic access to it, the third step in the "marketability" analysis must be performed. That step requires an examination of the typical fee arrangements used in the particular area of the law implicated by the indigent plaintiff's complaint. Specifically, if contingent-fee or other low-cost financing arrangements are generally available in the area of law and would be feasible for the plaintiff, further examination is proper. The absence of contingent fee arrangements or other low cost arrangements, however, may undercut the reliability of the market's failure to provide counsel to the litigant.

Once it is determined that an accessible market exists, that the plaintiff has the ability to access that market, and that feasible fee arrangements are available, the final and most important step in the analysis must be performed. The court must determine whether the market's rejection of the party's claims was the result of indigency, for, as noted above, indigency is the touchstone which authorizes the court to exercise the inherent power to correct unequal access to advocacy services. There are many factors to consider when a lawyer is approached about taking a person's claims into litigation. These factors might include, but would not be limited to, the merits of the claims; the existence of precedent to support the claims; the costs of investigating the claims, handling the discovery needed to prepare the case for trial, and trying the case; the relationship of those costs to the amount of a likely recovery, discounted by the probability of recovery; the lawyer's time available to pursue the claims and the impact upon his/her other practice obligations, as well as upon those of partners or associates; the likeability of the litigant;[18] the popularity of the claims; and the potential settlement value of the claims. So long as the market's rejection of the claims was based on the interplay of these and other such factors, and not on the indigency of the plaintiff, the notions of equal justice discussed above are not offended and compelling an attorney to represent that plaintiff is not necessary to the achievement of a fair and just adjudicative process.

Applying the foregoing "marketability" analysis to this case, I first conclude that there was an adequate "market" of lawyers practicing in the general area of plaintiff's claims. Plaintiff raises product liability claims, as opposed to civil rights claims under

18. While even the most despicable character is, by rights, entitled to the same access to the courts to voice his grievances as is the most attractive, wealthy, and urbane individual, the private market may exclude the former from access because of this intangible factor. It is not inappropriate for a court to consider this factor in determining whether the plaintiff's personal characteristics might have been a force behind the market's rejection of his claims.

42 U.S.C. §1983. As such, a greater number of private attorneys were available to represent him than would be for a typical indigent litigant. The potential for joining a class action lawsuit against the tobacco companies further enhanced the "market" that was available to plaintiff. In sum, there was a realistic "market" of lawyers who could litigate the claims raised by plaintiff.

I further conclude that plaintiff had ready access to that "market" of lawyers. Plaintiff is not incarcerated nor has he alleged any other substantial barriers[20] which might have prevented him from communicating with private attorneys. He thus had the unfettered ability to communicate with private attorneys in his immediate locale and elsewhere. Additionally, many of the attorneys who work in products liability and personal injury claims do so on a contingent fee basis.... Under a contingent fee arrangement, there typically is no requirement that the plaintiff advance costs, although the plaintiff would remain liable for them ultimately. Thus, despite plaintiff's indigency, there were feasible fee arrangements available to plaintiff.

The foregoing factors indicate that, unlike most cases initiated by indigent litigants, there was a "market" of private attorneys for plaintiff's claims and that, unlike most indigent litigants, plaintiff had open access to that market and has, in fact, accessed that market, albeit unsuccessfully. It thus is proper to determine whether that market's rejection of plaintiff's claims was the result of his indigency.

I conclude that it was not. The mere existence of indigency as a condition of the plaintiff did not prevent him from suggesting to lawyers that they consider his claims. Rather, he has had the same opportunity as middle- or upper-class plaintiffs to subject his claims to the scrutiny of tort attorneys. That this "market" of attorneys has thus far rejected his claims is the result of factors unrelated to his indigency. Primary among these factors is undoubtedly the enormous cost of litigating claims against tobacco companies....

Plaintiff asserts that most of the attorneys he contacted requested payment of a retainer which he was unable to afford. However, due to the enormous costs involved in this type of litigation and the unlikelihood of settlement, the amount of money required for an adequate retainer would likely be so great that even a middle-class or upper-middle-class citizen would be unable to afford it. As such, the rejection of plaintiff's claims was not based on his indigency, but rather on marketability factors such as the expenses involved and the unlikelihood of settlement.

Because it is the lack of marketability of his claims, as opposed to his indigency, which has prevented plaintiff from obtaining counsel, the notions of equal justice discussed above have not been offended. As such, it is not reasonably necessary to the administration of justice for this court to compel Metcalf to represent plaintiff. Accordingly, I shall not exercise this court's inherent authority to do so.[22]

20. While plaintiff has alleged health problems, he presents no evidence indicating that these problems would inhibit him from seeking out counsel either in person or via telephone or mail.

22. Because I decline to exercise the court's inherent authority, I need not address Metcalf's contention that the exercise of that authority in this case would contravene the Fifth and Thirteenth Amendments of the Constitution. However, the majority of courts which have addressed those issues have found no constitutional violations. *See* Williamson v. Vardeman, 674 F.2d 1211 (8th Cir. 1982) (collecting federal and state cases); In re Amendment to R. Reg. the Fla. Bar, 573 So. 2d 800, 805 & n.11 (citing federal appellate cases); Bradshaw v. U.S. Dist. Court, 742 F.2d 515, 517 n.2 (9th Cir. 1984); Family Div. Trial Lawyers v. Moultrie, 725 F.2d 695, 712 (D.C. Cir. 1984); United States v. Dillon, 346 F.2d 633 (9th Cir. 1964), *cert. denied*, 382 U.S. 978 (1965); ... To the extent these constitutional claims attack the very existence of the inherent power itself, I also reject them.

B. *Pro Bono* Service

The Law Governing Lawyers: *Service Pro Bono Publico*

The *Bothwell* opinion cites disturbing statistics, which indicate that the goal of access to justice remain elusive for most of the poor and much of the middle class in America. This concern is not new, nor is it restricted to our country. In 1919, Reginald Heber Smith wrote: "Without equal access to the law, the system not only robs the poor of their only protection, but it places in the hands of their oppressors the most powerful and ruthless weapon ever invented."[1] Judge Piester echoes this concern, finding that the court's inherent power to conscript lawyers is necessary both to achieve justice in an individual case and to preserve the credibility of the courts as a legitimate arm of the civil justice system. In other words, lawyers are essential to ensure the principle of equality before the law.

These comments reflect one set of values in American society: the value of equality and the value of community, of volunteerism and helping those in need. At the same time, Americans in general and lawyers in particular believe that working hard and accumulating wealth are also worthy social and personal goals.[2] How should we resolve this tension? Should the market dictate the distribution of legal services? Or should lawyers be required to provide some legal services free of charge? Is access to justice a public obligation, dependent on public, but not professional, funding? Or should lawyers lose their monopoly on law practice, permitting others, perhaps with less training to fill the need? Commentators have suggested all of these strategies to address the problem of access to justice, and some combination of strategies will be required to remedy the unmet need for legal services.

The first and most prominent strategy involves reliance on the market to create access to legal services. The second acknowledges public responsibility for access to justice by creating legal rights to representation by lawyers, and by publicly funding legal services programs to provide them. In the third strategy, individual lawyers or groups such as bar associations assume responsibility to promote the common good by serving *pro bono publico*, that is, providing free or reduced-rate services to clients. Finally, some commentators advocate deregulation, or breaking the lawyers' monopoly on delivering legal services, which would permit unlicensed persons or institutions to provide some kinds of legal assistance.

Market Reliance

Bothwell makes clear that the first strategy, reliance on the market, has predominated in this country. This reliance parallels our economic dependence on market transactions, which increasingly require lawyers to facilitate financial matters. At the same time, lawyers administer the complex legal rules designed to restrain the excesses of private enterprise and protect it from government intrusions that threaten individual rights. It follows that those with the most money get the most

1. Reginald Heber Smith, *Justice and the Poor, A Study of the Present Denial of Justice to the Poor and of the Agencies Making More Equal their Position Before the Law, with Particular Reference to Legal Aid Work in the United States* 9 (Carnegie Foundation 1919).
2. Cynthia Fuchs Epstein, *Stricture and Structure: The Social and Cultural Context of Pro Bono Work in Wall Street Firms*, 70 Fordham L. Rev. 1689, 1690 (2002).

legal services and usually the best lawyers, leaving those with little money or power to fend on their own. Since much of the market for legal services is driven by corporate demand, "the legal system prices itself out of the reach of all individuals except those with a claim on corporate wealth."[3]

Reliance on market transactions explains why America has no shortage of lawyers, but the gap between rich and poor continues to expand. Overall, the national lawyer to nonlawyer population ratio currently stands at about 1:275, up from 1:418 in 1980 and only 1:627 in 1960.[4] During the same period, the ratio of lawyers to poor clients (those at or below the poverty level) also has grown, but the poor continue to be grossly underserved. In 1960, voluntary legal aid projects provided one lawyer for every 120,000 poor persons and legal services were provided to less than 1 percent of those in need.[5] By 1980, when legal services funding reached its height, the service level of one lawyer for every 5,000 poor people was met. Even then, legal services were provided to barely 20 percent of those with serious legal problems. Today the ratio of lawyers to poor persons has doubled, back to about 1:10,000.[6]

The disparity between lawyers available for paying clients and those available to serve the poor explains why Judge Piester identified market failure as a salient and inevitable feature of our civil justice system.[7] For at least the past century, judges have exercised their inherent power to offset this market failure, first in criminal and then in civil cases. In civil cases, *Bothwell* represents the modern trend, which recognizes inherent judicial power to appoint lawyers in cases where the market fails to provide access to representation. Model Rule 6.2 reflects these developments by requiring lawyers to present very weighty reasons to avoid court appointments.

Several well-executed empirical studies conducted over approximately the past decade also document market failure in the civil legal services market, not only for the poor but also for the middle class. These surveys conclude that the existing legal services network is simply not meeting the need for civil legal services for low and moderate-income persons. The most extensive analysis, published by the American Bar Association in 1994, found that 71 percent of those in low-income households and 61 percent of those in moderate-income households never brought a serious legal claim to the civil justice system.[8] These neglected legal

---

3. Gillian K. Hadfield, *The Price of Law: How the Market for Lawyers Distorts the Justice System*, 98 Mich. L. Rev. 953, 998 (2000).

4. Barbara A. Curran & Clara N. Carson, *The Lawyer Statistical Report, A Statistical Profile of the U.S. Legal Profession in the 1990's* 1 (Am. Bar Found. 1995). Year 2000 figures based on 275 million Americans and 1 million lawyers. *See* Judith L. Maute, *Changing Conceptions of Lawyers' Pro Bono Responsibilities: From Chance Noblesse Oblige to Stated Expectations,* 77 Tulane L. Rev. 91 (2002).

5. National Legal Aid & Defender Association, History of Civil Legal Aid, available at *http://www.nlada.org*.

6. This figure is based on a U.S. population of 275 million people, 17 percent of whom fall below 125 percent of the poverty line (the Legal Services eligibility standard), and approximately 4,500 legal aid lawyers, about 3,500 of whom work for the Legal Services Corporation and 1,000 who are employed by other nonprofit legal aid offices. Telephone interview with Martha Burgmark, National Legal Aid and Defender Association V.P. for Program Development, January 27, 2000.

7. In addition to asking for a lawyer, Bothwell sought and was granted leave to commence his suit *in forma pauperis,* that is, without payment of court fees, pursuant to 28 U.S.C. §1915 (2000). *See* Bothwell v. Republic Tobacco Co., 912 F. Supp. 1221, 1223 (1995).

8. ABA Consortium on Legal Services and the Public's Legal Needs: *Comprehensive Legal Needs Study* 19 (1994). Low Income Households were defined as those at 125 percent of the official U.S. poverty line or less, Moderate Income Households as those just above this mark but earning less that $60,000 per year in 1992. *Id.* at A-1. This report was later summarized in ABA, Consortium on Legal Services and the Public, *Agenda for Access: The American People and Civil Justice, Final Report on the Implication of the Comprehensive Legal Need Study* (1996).

matters most frequently involved personal finances and consumer issues, housing and real property matters, domestic, and employment related problems. Over half of those persons, especially those who tried to handle the matter themselves or did nothing, were dissatisfied with the result. On the other hand, those few who did take a serious legal matter to the civil justice system reported the highest satisfaction with the result, 48 percent for low-income individuals and 64 percent for those of moderate means.[9] There also is little doubt that those able to obtain a lawyer get significantly better results.[10]

Similar studies in individual states document even more need. For example, a 1991 study in Ohio found that lawyers were addressing only 17 percent of the legal needs of the poor.[11] Consumer, housing, medical and family problems were the most frequently mentioned needs. A more recent Oregon study reports that lawyers there are meeting only 18 percent of the need for legal assistance for low- and moderate-income citizens. Housing, public services, family and consumer cases create the highest unmet need.[12] Studies in Europe document similar need.[13]

Several conclusions can be drawn from these studies. First, the unmet need for civil legal services has remained relatively constant even though the number of lawyers per capita has increased. Second, publicly funded legal services programs are able to meet only a small percentage of the documented need for low-income persons and none of the need for those of moderate means. Third, *pro bono* efforts by individual lawyers and bar associations have helped, but still fall far short of meeting the need. Over the past 20 years, renewed attention has been given to finding a better solution to the problem. Two of the four strategies have predominated: increasing public funding for legal services and expanding *pro bono* service by individual lawyers. Neither has become a reality.

Public Responsibility

Public funding for legal services exists in some form in most western democratic countries.[14] In this country, as in most others, it has never been enough to meet even one fifth of the needs of those who have serious legal problems, and has declined in the past quarter century. The Legal Services Corporation, created by federal statute in 1974, reached a high point in funding ($321million) during the Carter administration in 1980. This figure declined by about one-fourth during the

---

9. *Id.* at 4-5.

10. *E.g.*, Carroll Seron, Gregg Van Ryzin & Martin Frankel, *The Impact of Legal Counsel on Outcomes for Poor Tenants in New York City's Housing Court: Results of a Randomized Experiment*, 35 Law & Society Rev. 419 (2001) (legal counsel provided to poor tenants produced large differences in outcome independent of the merits of the case).

11. Ohio Legal Needs Advisory Committee, *"Thou Shalt Not Ration Justice": An Assessment of the Unmet Civil Legal Needs of Ohio's Poor* 4 (1992).

12. D. Michael Dale, *The State of Access to Justice in Oregon,* Part I: Assessment of Legal Needs, at i-ii (2000). The Oregon study indicated that, of the small percent of cases that do reach a lawyer, legal aid lawyers handle slightly more than half of the matters. The other half are split nearly equally between lawyers who take the cases on a *pro bono* basis, and those who charge a full fee. *Id.* at ii. A decade earlier, the ABA reported that the private bar handled over three-fourths of the cases that received legal attention, with over half charging a reduced or no fee. ABA Final Report, *supra* note 8, at 26.

13. Geoffrey C. Hazard & Angelo Dondi, *Legal Ethics: A Comparative Study,* Section 2.12 (Mullino Press 2002). Chinese lawyers also have established nearly 200 legal aid offices to serve the poor. Benjamin L. Liebman, *Legal Aid and Public Interest in China,* 34 Texas Intl. L.J. 211, 212 (1999).

14. Hazard & Dondi, *supra* note 13, at 2.37-2.40. In Eastern Europe, free legal counsel is available in criminal cases. Council of Europe, *The Role and Responsibilities of the Lawyer in a Society in Transition* 199 (1997). Some countries, including Azerbaijan, Croatia, and Hungary, also provide free counsel in civil cases. *Id.* at 174, 178-179, 183.

Reagan administration. It is now estimated that current funding, at about $300 million, would have to double to meet the services levels of 1980, and would have to increase tenfold to meet the real need.[15]

In the past decade, private funding from foundations, charitable gifts and state Interest on Lawyer Trust Accounts (IOLTA) programs have accounted for a growing percentage of legal services budgets, up to 45 percent by the year 2000. IOLTA funds, discussed in more detail in Chapter 7, also help fund criminal defense representation by public defender offices in many jurisdictions.[16]

Pro Bono Service

The simple truth is that we lack the political will to provide equal access to justice, just as we lack the political will to provide equal access to housing, health care, child care, and education. Yet the lack of access to justice differs from the lack of access to these other essential services. The provision of legal services nearly always depends on advocating a particular point of view that will affect at least one other person's interest. This means that lack of legal representation not only deprives the poor and middle class of access to redress for a legal wrong, but also creates the opportunity for dishonest or exploitive conduct by those aware of this disparity. Further, when individuals or groups lack access to legal advocacy, their views rarely will be reflected in the resulting law. Put another way, the health of the legal system requires that all sides of an issue be heard.

Although about one in five lawyers currently respond to this need in some significant manner, most lawyers focus on their paying clients, often not giving much thought to the cumulative impact of their own practice on the lives of others. Lawyers and judges aware of this situation have created a number of innovative voluntary *pro bono* programs. Four examples will provide some sense of the rich opportunities that are available for the conscientious lawyer.

The Support Center for Child Advocates This innovative Philadelphia-based program provides lawyers for children who find themselves parties to family court proceedings and whose interests otherwise might go unrepresented. Volunteer lawyers are matched with a minor and the Support Center provides resources in terms of training, staff lawyers and social workers to assist *pro bono* counsel in this sensitive and rewarding work.

American Bar Association Death Penalty Representation Project Hundreds of prisoners on death row have no counsel to represent them in *habeas corpus* proceedings. This national project seeks to match law firms with unrepresented death

15. Deborah L. Rhode, *Access to Justice*, 69 Fordham L. Rev. 1785, 1788 (2001). Similar estimates have been made in statewide studies. A recent study in Pennsylvania, for example, concluded that the impact of inflation on the growth in total funding for legal services over the past twenty years resulted in a net decline to 57 percent of the amount available two decades ago. Report of the Statewide Planning Task Force on Small Programs and Configuration, *Configuration of the Pennsylvania Integrated Legal Services System: Maximizing the Effective and Economical Delivery of High-Quality Legal Services Throughout the State* 5 (1998).

16. In Brown v. Legal Found. of Wash., 123 S. Ct. 1406 (2003), the Supreme Court held that state use of IOLTA funds to pay for legal services for those in need qualified as a taking for a "public use" justifying the state's authority to confiscate private property under the Just Compensation Clause of the Fifth Amendment. The Court nevertheless upheld the continuing viability of state IOLTA requirements by finding that no Fifth Amendment violation occurred because the value of the client's "just compensation" was zero in a properly administered fund.

row inmates and funds full-time lawyers in the field to provide the essential guidance these law firms need to negotiate the labyrinthine procedures and difficult jurisprudence associated with *habeas* proceedings.

Legal Assistance Partnership Project The ABA Legal Assistance Partnership project matches public interest law firms and legal services offices with private firms so that the latter can help the former handle litigation, particularly complex cases that strain the resources of the public service community. Examples include test cases, class actions, and matters that require massive discovery. Several states have initiated similar programs modeled after the ABA project.

Community Economic Development Law Program *Pro bono* is hardly limited to litigation matters. This Chicago project provides a full scope of transactional representation and strategic legal advice to community organizations to build affordable housing, to set up job-training programs, and to work with individuals starting their own small businesses.

Although these projects help some, they have never been enough. This is why another alternative, mandatory *pro bono* service, has been proposed. The first recognition of *pro bono* service as an integral part of professional responsibility appeared in 1980, when the Kutak Commission circulated a discussion draft that proposed a mandatory *pro bono* service requirement. Vehement opposition soon followed, and the ABA eventually adopted a rule that lawyers "should," but were not required to, render such service. The immediate past version of Model Rule 6.1 was adopted by a narrow margin in 1993. The basic duty remained aspirational, but the text quantified the necessary service at 50 hours per year.[17]

Mandatory *pro bono* service has been adopted by a few local bar associations and considered by several jurisdictions. Proposals that mandate *pro bono* service recognize that lawyers enjoy a monopoly on the provision of legal services and that the moral justification for lawyer advice and advocacy depends on adequate access to justice. Most of these recommendations include a buyout provision, which would enable an individual lawyer to make a payment to a legal services agency in lieu of personally providing legal services. To date, none of these proposals has been adopted, despite growing evidence of the acute need for better provision of legal services to persons of low and moderate incomes.

Florida has adopted yet another option, a mandatory-reporting requirement.[18] The Florida Rule has increased voluntary *pro bono* service for two reasons.[19] First, reporting requirements remind lawyers that the need for *pro bono* legal assistance is great, something they may forget in the course of a busy, demanding practice. Second, a reporting requirement may carry a bit of coercion: Lawyers who report little or no *pro bono* service may fear peer or official disapproval. They also may worry that the reporting requirement could become the precursor to a mandatory service requirement.

---

17. For a chart that details each state *pro bono* rule, *see* Judith L. Maute, *Pro Bono Publico in Oklahoma: Time for a Change,* 53 Okla. L. Rev. 527, 597-609 (2000).
18. Schwartz v. Kogan, 132 F.3d 1387 (11th Cir. 1998) (upholding the constitutionality of Florida's rule that requires a report of compliance with its aspirational goal of 20 hours or a contribution of $350 to a legal aid organization on each annual bar dues statement).
19. Thomas C. Mielenhausen & Charles A. Krekelberg, *A Better Idea: Reporting Pro Bono Services,* Bench and Bar 21, 24 (March 1999).

Other Alternatives

Because all these efforts still fall far short of meeting the need for legal services, some commentators have suggested a network of other alternatives.[20] Most proposals see lawyer *pro bono* as an indispensable element of an overall plan.[21] Many focus on increased public funding, through federal and state grants, IOLTA, filing fee surcharges or service taxes on for-profit legal services, allocating punitive damage or unpaid class actions funds to a civil justice fund and improved fee awards for successful poor claimants who establish entitlement to public benefits.[22] Some proposals include simplifying legal procedures and rules that govern recurring situations, such as more use of small claims courts, providing readily accessible mediation procedures, or creating plain English regulations that simplify current complex legal provisions or remedies.[23]

Some lawyers are experimenting with unbundling legal services, or delivering legal services a la carte, as a useful means of providing more clients with discrete lawyer services rather than a full-service representation.[24] Proponents encourage lawyers to break down current legal services into discrete tasks, such as advice, legal research, fact gathering, negotiation, document drafting or court representation, as well as issues, such as custody, visitation, property valuation (real, personal, business, investments, pensions, etc.), and insurance benefits.[25] Clients then are offered a menu of these separate tasks and issues, and are given the opportunity to select those that fit the client's budget, or defer to the client's own abilities. Lawyers who offer unbundled services often refer to themselves as client coaches who perform some but not all aspects of a legal representation. Some lawyers provide such services free of charge as part of a nonprofit or court-annexed limited legal services program.[26]

The success of unbundling depends on lawyers to identify all aspects of the matter and to assist the client in understanding the ramifications of self-representation on each aspect. Lawyers must provide competent representation with respect to those items the client cedes to the lawyer and adequate advice to the client about how to accomplish the rest.[27] As you review the materials in the next chapter, consider what kinds of lawyer-client agreements are necessary to validate such limited-scope arrangements.[28]

A number of other proposals also involve some degree of deregulation of the legal monopoly, thereby allowing more persons to become lawyers or nonlawyers to provide some legal services.[29] Through deregulation, nonlawyers could offer all kinds of legal assistance outside of court proceedings, such as drafting wills and tax forms, handling corporate and real estate transactions, collecting debts, and providing

---

20. Roger C. Cramton, *Delivery of Legal Services to Ordinary Americans*, 44 Case Western L. Rev. 531 (1994).
21. *Id.*; Deborah L. Rhode, *Access to Justice*, 69 Fordham L. Rev. 1785 (2001); *Recommendations of the Conference on the Delivery of Legal Services to Low-Income Persons*, 67 Fordham L. Rev. 1751 (1999).
22. Talbot D'Alemberte, *Tributaries of Full Justice: The Search for Full Access*, 25 Fla. St. L. Rev. 631 (1998).
23. *See, e.g.*, Derrick C. Bok, *A Flawed System of Practice and Training*, 33 J. Legal Educ. 570 (1983).
24. *See* Forrest S. Mosten, *Unbundling Legal Services: A Guide to Delivering Legal Services a la Carte* (ABA Law Practice Management 2000).
25. *Id.* at 50, 51.
26. Model Rule 6.5 encourages lawyers to participate in such activities by suspending ordinary conflicts of interest rules except where the lawyer knows that representing a client involves a conflict.
27. Mosten, *supra* note 24, at 92-97.
28. For a sample of such an agreement, *see* Mosten, *supra* note 24, at 29.
29. *See, e.g.*, Richard L. Abel, *American Lawyers* 245-248 (Oxford 1989).

divorce or adoption services. Most of these measures would require reversal of current unauthorized practice restrictions, discussed in Chapter 10. Although deregulation is theoretically possible, it will likely prove unpopular to many lawyers in practice.[30] As long as lawyers and judges are making the decision, these changes seem extremely unlikely to happen.

Licensure of lawyers excludes nonlawyers from providing legal services. This leaves licensed lawyers to shoulder the responsibility of access to justice. Yet current voluntary *pro bono* efforts in the minds of some amount to "little more than a rallying cry for the status quo."[31] This explains why Model Rule 6.1 was amended in 2002 to add: "Every lawyer has the professional responsibility to provide legal services to those unable to pay."

Ultimately, the fairness of the legal representation that is provided by a market-driven system will be measured by the capacity of the justice enterprise to make itself available to those whose interests are affected. Economic differences in the ability of persons to access justice lead to disparity in the legal rights of these groups. As you work through the materials that follow, consider how a lawyer's role depends on a reasonably just legal system, and how lack of access to that system undermines confidence in the justice the legal system produces.

30. *See, e.g.*, ABA, *Nonlawyer Activity in Law-Related Situations: A Report with Recommendations* (ABA 1995).

31. This is the view of the Marrero Commission, which unsuccessfully recommended a mandatory *pro bono* program to the New York Court of Appeals. *See* Vincent Marrero, *Commission to Improve the Availability of Legal Services, Final Report to the Chief Judge of the State of New York* 106 (1990).

Chapter 4

Competence and Communication

This chapter explores the most basic fiduciary duties that lawyers owe clients: competence and communication. Two common themes run throughout these materials. First, the authority to represent a client always remains subject to the client's control over the goals of the representation. Lawyers assume fiduciary duties of communication to ensure that clients stay in charge. Second, the law governing lawyers provides for multiple remedies when professional duties of communication and competence are breached.

The problems in the first sections of this chapter explore two of the possible multiple remedies that may be available to redress incompetence and lack of communication: professional discipline and civil liability. Recall that *Busch* in Chapter 2 involved the remedy of professional discipline for one major instance of incompetence and failure to communicate with a client. Civil actions include both legal malpractice and breach of fiduciary duty. The third section of this chapter addresses another tort, the tort of misrepresentation, which provides an additional basis for relief by both clients and aggrieved third parties. The final section examines lack of communication and incompetence in the context of criminal defense representation and introduces yet another remedy: reversal of a conviction for ineffective assistance of counsel.

A. Who Is Your Client?

Problem

4-1. Martyn interviewed a prospective client about a potential personal injury case and told him that Martyn & Fox did not want to handle the matter. Two months later the same person called, leaving a message that he wanted to check on the "status of his case." Before returning the call, Martyn discovered that the applicable statute of limitations on the claim had run last week. What should Martyn do?

Consider: Model Rule 1.18
RLGL §§14, 15

Togstad v. Vesely, Otto, Miller & Keefe

291 N.W.2d 686 (Minn. 1980)

PER CURIAM.

This is an appeal by the defendants from a judgment of the Hennepin County District Court involving an action for legal malpractice. The jury found that the defendant attorney Jerre Miller was negligent and that, as a direct result of such negligence, plaintiff John Togstad sustained damages in the amount of $610,500 and his wife, plaintiff Joan Togstad, in the amount of $39,000. . . .

In August, 1971, John Togstad began to experience severe headaches and on August 16, 1971, was admitted to Methodist Hospital where tests disclosed that the headaches were caused by a large aneurism of the left internal carotid artery. The attending physician, Dr. Paul Blake, a neurological surgeon, treated the problem by applying a Selverstone clamp to the left common carotid artery. The clamp was surgically implanted on August 27, 1971, in Togstad's neck to allow the gradual closure of the artery over a period of days. . . .

In the early morning hours of August 29, 1971, a nurse observed that Togstad was unable to speak or move. . . . Togstad is now severely paralyzed in his right arm and leg, and is unable to speak.

Plaintiff's expert, Dr. Ward Woods, testified that Togstad's paralysis and loss of speech was due to a lack of blood supply to his brain . . . [which] resulted from the clamp being 50% closed and that the negligence of Dr. Blake and the hospital precluded the clamp's being opened in time to avoid permanent brain damage. . . .

Dr. Blake and defendants' expert witness . . . both alleged that the blood clots were not a result of the Selverstone clamp procedure. . . .

About 14 months after her husband's hospitalization began, plaintiff Joan Togstad met with attorney Jerre Miller regarding her husband's condition. Neither she nor her husband was personally acquainted with Miller or his law firm prior to that time. John Togstad's former work supervisor, Ted Bucholz, made the appointment and accompanied Mrs. Togstad to Miller's office. Bucholz was present when Mrs. Togstad and Miller discussed the case.

Mrs. Togstad had become suspicious of the circumstances surrounding her husband's tragic condition due to the conduct and statements of the hospital nurses shortly after the paralysis occurred. One nurse told Mrs. Togstad that she had checked Mr. Togstad at 2 a.m. and he was fine; that when she returned at 3 a.m., by mistake, to give him someone else's medication, he was unable to move or speak; and that if she hadn't accidentally entered the room no one would have discovered his condition until morning. Mrs. Togstad also noticed that the other nurses were upset and crying, and that Mr. Togstad's condition was a topic of conversation.

Mrs. Togstad testified that she told Miller "everything that happened at the hospital," including the nurses' statements and conduct which had raised a question in her mind. She stated that she "believed" she had told Miller "about the procedure and what was undertaken, what was done, and what happened." She brought no records with her. Miller took notes and asked questions during the meeting, which lasted 45 minutes to an hour. At its conclusion, according to Mrs. Togstad, Miller said that "he did not think we had a legal case, however, he was going to discuss this with his partner." She understood that if Miller changed his mind after talking to his partner, he would call her. Mrs. Togstad "gave it" a few days and, since she did not hear from Miller, decided "that they had come to the conclusion that there wasn't a case." No fee arrangements were discussed, no medical authorizations were requested, nor was Mrs. Togstad billed for the interview.

Mrs. Togstad denied that Miller had told her his firm did not have expertise in the medical malpractice field, urged her to see another attorney, or related to her that the statute of limitations for medical malpractice actions was two years. She did not consult another attorney until one year after she talked to Miller. Mrs. Togstad indicated that she did not confer with another attorney earlier because of her reliance on Miller's "legal advice" that they "did not have a case."

On cross-examination, Mrs. Togstad was asked whether she went to Miller's office "to see if he would take the case of [her] husband. . . ." She replied, "Well, I guess it was to go for legal advice, what to do, where shall we go from here? That is what we went for." Again in response to defense counsel's questions, Mrs. Togstad testified as follows:

Q And it was clear to you, was it not, that what was taking place was a preliminary discussion between a prospective client and lawyer as to whether or not they wanted to enter into an attorney-client relationship?

A I am not sure how to answer that. It was for legal advice as to what to do.

Q And Mr. Miller was discussing with you your problem and indicating whether he, as a lawyer, wished to take the case, isn't that true?

A Yes.

On re-direct examination, Mrs. Togstad acknowledged that when she left Miller's office she understood that she had been given a "qualified, quality legal opinion that [she and her husband] did not have a malpractice case."

Miller's testimony was different in some respects from that of Mrs. Togstad. Like Mrs. Togstad, Miller testified that Mr. Bucholz arranged and was present at the meeting, which lasted about 45 minutes. According to Miller, Mrs. Togstad described the hospital incident, including the conduct of the nurses. He asked her questions, to which she responded. Miller testified that "the only thing I told her [Mrs. Togstad] after we had pretty much finished the conversation was that there was nothing related in her factual circumstances that told me that she had a case that our firm would be interested in undertaking."

Miller also claimed he related to Mrs. Togstad "that because of the grievous nature of the injuries sustained by her husband, that this was only my opinion and she was encouraged to ask another attorney if she wished for another opinion" and "she ought to do so promptly." He testified that he informed Mrs. Togstad that his firm "was not engaged as experts" in the area of medical malpractice, and that they associated with the Charles Hvass firm in cases of that nature. Miller stated that at the end of the conference he told Mrs. Togstad that he would consult with Charles Hvass and if Hvass's opinion differed from his, Miller would so inform her. Miller recollected that he called Hvass a "couple days" later and discussed the case with him. It was Miller's impression that Hvass thought there was no liability for malpractice in the case. Consequently, Miller did not communicate with Mrs. Togstad further.

On cross-examination, Miller testified as follows:

Q Now, so there is no misunderstanding, and I am reading from your deposition, you understood that she was consulting with you as a lawyer, isn't that correct?

A That's correct.

Q That she was seeking legal advice from a professional attorney licensed to practice in this state and in this community?

A I think you and I did have another interpretation or use of the term "Advice." She was there to see whether or not she had a case and whether the firm would accept it.

Q We have two aspects; number one, your legal opinion concerning liability of a case for malpractice; number two, whether there was or wasn't liability, whether you would accept it, your firm, two separate elements, right?

A I would say so....

Kenneth Green, a Minneapolis attorney, was called as an expert by plaintiffs. He stated that in rendering legal advice regarding a claim of medical malpractice, the "minimum" an attorney should do would be to request medical authorizations from the client, review the hospital records, and consult with an expert in the field. John McNulty, a Minneapolis attorney, and Charles Hvass testified as experts on behalf of the defendants. McNulty stated that when an attorney is consulted as to whether he will take a case, the lawyer's only responsibility in refusing it is to so inform the party. He testified, however, that when a lawyer is asked his legal opinion on the merits of a medical malpractice claim, community standards require that the attorney check hospital records and consult with an expert before rendering his opinion.

Hvass stated that he had no recollection of Miller's calling him in October 1972 relative to the Togstad matter. He testified that:

A ... [W]hen a person comes in to me about a medical malpractice action, based upon what the individual has told me, I have to make a decision as to whether or not there probably is or probably is not, based upon that information, medical malpractice. And if, in my judgment, based upon what the client has told me, there is not medical malpractice, I will so inform the client.

Hvass stated, however, that he would never render a "categorical" opinion. In addition, Hvass acknowledged that if he were consulted for a "legal opinion" regarding medical malpractice and 14 months had expired since the incident in question, "ordinary care and diligence" would require him to inform the party of the two-year statute of limitations applicable to that type of action.

This case was submitted to the jury by way of a special verdict form. The jury found that Dr. Blake and the hospital were negligent and that Dr. Blake's negligence (but not the hospital's) was a direct cause of the injuries sustained by John Togstad; that there was an attorney-client contractual relationship between Mrs. Togstad and Miller; that Miller was negligent in rendering advice regarding the possible claims of Mr. and Mrs. Togstad; that, but for Miller's negligence, plaintiffs would have been successful in the prosecution of a legal action against Dr. Blake; and that neither Mr. nor Mrs. Togstad was negligent in pursuing their claims against Dr. Blake. The jury awarded damages to Mr. Togstad of $610,500 and to Mrs. Togstad of $39,000....

1. In a legal malpractice action of the type involved here, four elements must be shown: (1) that an attorney-client relationship existed; (2) that defendant acted negligently or in breach of contract; (3) that such acts were the proximate cause of the plaintiffs' damages; (4) that but for defendant's conduct the plaintiffs would have been successful in the prosecution of their medical malpractice claim....

We believe it is unnecessary to decide whether a tort or contract theory is preferable for resolving the attorney-client relationship question raised by this appeal. The tort and contract analyses are very similar in a case such as the instant one,[4] and we conclude that under either theory the evidence shows that a lawyer-client relationship is present here. The thrust of Mrs. Togstad's testimony is that she went to Miller for legal advice, was told there wasn't a case, and relied upon this advice in failing to pursue the claim for medical malpractice. In addition, according to Mrs. Togstad, Miller did not qualify his legal opinion by urging her to seek advice from another attorney, nor did Miller inform her that he lacked expertise in the medical malpractice area. . . . [W]e believe a jury could properly find that Mrs. Togstad sought and received legal advice from Miller under circumstances which made it reasonably foreseeable to Miller that Mrs. Togstad would be injured if the advice were negligently given. Thus, under either a tort or contract analysis, there is sufficient evidence in the record to support the existence of an attorney-client relationship.

Defendants argue that even if an attorney-client relationship was established the evidence fails to show that Miller acted negligently in assessing the merits of the Togstads' case. They appear to contend that, at most, Miller was guilty of an error in judgment which does not give rise to legal malpractice. . . . However, this case does not involve a mere error of judgment. The gist of plaintiffs' claim is that Miller failed to perform the minimal research that an ordinarily prudent attorney would do before rendering legal advice in a case of this nature. The record, through the testimony of Kenneth Green and John McNulty, contains sufficient evidence to support plaintiffs' position. . . .

There is also sufficient evidence in the record establishing that, but for Miller's negligence, plaintiffs would have been successful in prosecuting their medical malpractice claim. Dr. Woods, in no uncertain terms, concluded that Mr. Togstad's injuries were caused by the medical malpractice of Dr. Blake. Defendants' expert testimony to the contrary was obviously not believed by the jury. Thus, the jury reasonably found that had plaintiff's medical malpractice action been properly brought, plaintiffs would have recovered. . . .

Practice Pointers: *Engagement, Nonengagement, and Disengagement Letters*

Togstad illustrates that misunderstandings between lawyers and clients can create real problems for both. Commentators recommend various types of engagement letters to remedy these potential differences. In their treatise entitled Legal Malpractice, Ronald Mallen and Jeffrey Smith identify four basic situations where such a misunderstanding can occur:

- The lawyer wants to decline a specific request for representation (as in *Togstad*);

4. Under a negligence approach it must essentially be shown that defendant rendered legal advice (not necessarily at someone's request) under circumstances which made it reasonably foreseeable to the attorney that if such advice was rendered negligently, the individual receiving the advice might be injured thereby. *See, e.g.*, Palsgraf v. Long Island R.R. Co., 162 N.E. 99 (N.Y. 1928). . . . A contract analysis requires the rendering of legal advice pursuant to another's request and the reliance factor, in this case, where the advice was not paid for, need be shown in the form of promissory estoppel. See . . . *Restatement (Second) of Contracts*, §90.

- The lawyer provides legal services to some, but not all, of the parties to a transaction;
- The lawyer wants to prevent reliance by unrepresented third parties who are beneficiaries of the lawyer's service to another client; and
- The lawyer wants to prevent a claim for negligent misrepresentation (as occurred in *Greycas*, p.96).[1]

Nonengagement Letters

The first situation involves facts like those in *Togstad*: the lawyer thinks he has declined representation, but the prospective client believes she has received legal advice. In that circumstance, a simple nonengagement letter such as the one below, recommended by Professors Munneke and Davis, can clarify any misunderstandings.[2] Consider how you would modify this form to address the facts in *Togstad*.

[Date]
[Prospective Client] Certified Mail No.
Return Receipt Requested
Re: Potential Engagement Regarding [Matter]
Dear [Name]

Thank you for your visit [phone call] today. As we discussed, although I have not investigated the merits of your matter, I do not feel it would be appropriate for [me/Law Firm Name] to represent you in your possible [matter]. In declining to undertake this matter, [I am/law firm is] not expressing an opinion on [the likely outcome of the matter].

Please be aware that whatever claim, if any, that you have may be barred by the passage of time. Because deadlines may be critical to your case, I recommend that you immediately contact another lawyer/law firm for assistance regarding your matter. [*Optional:* For your information, the telephone number of the legal referral service of the (State) Bar Association is:__________.]

Thank you again for your interest in [me/Law Firm Name]. [*Optional:* We appreciate your having approached us regarding your matter. If you ever have need of legal assistance in the field of (practice or concentration), we hope that you will think of us again in that context. We enclose a copy of our brochure describing our practice in that area.]

Sincerely,

Engagement Letters

Just as nonengagement letters can help clarify the absence of a duty to a prospective client, engagement letters are intended to prevent misunderstandings by clarifying the scope and basis for undertaking a client representation. But an engagement

1. Ronald E. Mallen & Jeffrey M. Smith, *Legal Malpractice* §2.12 (5th ed., West Group 2000).
2. Gary A. Munneke & Anthony E. Davis, *The Essential Formbook: Comprehensive Management Tools for Lawyers* 280 (ABA, Law Practice Management Section 2000).

letter also can be used to address other issues that might arise during the course of the representation. A complete list is probably impossible to compile, but commentators offer the following topics as candidates for inclusion in an engagement letter:[3]

- Identification of the client and related parties;
- Identification of third party neutrals, such a judges, arbitrators, or mediators;
- Identification and consents to conflicts of interest;
- Resolution of confidentiality issues, especially in multiple representations;
- Description of the respective responsibilities of the client and the lawyer;
- Identification of goals of the representation;
- Proposed staffing, including agents of the client and lawyer;
- Methods of communication;
- Definition of the scope of the engagement;
- Fee agreement and billing schedule;
- Grounds for withdrawal or termination;
- Policy on file retention; and
- Methods of dispute resolution between client and lawyer.

New York recently enacted a new professional rule that requires engagement letters in all cases except those where the lawyer charges a fee of less than $3000 or the "attorney's services are of the same general kind as previously rendered to and paid for by the client."[4] The letter must address the following matters: (1) explanation of the scope of the legal services to be provided; (2) explanation of attorney's fees to be charged, expenses and billing practices; and (3) information about the client's right to arbitrate fee disputes.[5]

Fox has drafted the following letter to comply with this New York Rule. What advice do you give him about his work product?

> Dear Client,
>
> We really enjoyed meeting you today and the chance we had to describe to you our firm's capabilities and special expertise in so many different areas of the law. We plan to become your outside general counsel and look forward to fulfilling all your legal needs. We want you to know how much we value your retention of our firm.
>
> It is our plan to provide our services to you at our normal hourly rates. In addition, we will handle expenses and disbursements, for which you are responsible, in our usual way.
>
> We know your faith in hiring our firm will be rewarded with excellent results.
>
> Sincerely,
> Martyn & Fox

---

3. Mallen & Smith, §2.10; Munneke & Davis, 141-144.
4. N.Y. Ct. Rules §§1215.1, 1215.2 (2003). In domestic relations matters, New York requires lawyers to provide clients with both a Statement of Client's Rights and Responsibilities and a written retainer agreement, regardless of the fee charged. *Id.* at §§1400.2, 1400.3.
5. *Id.* at §1215.1(b).

Disengagement Letters

To prevent misunderstandings at the close of a matter, commentators recommend a disengagement letter. Disengagement letters can be helpful when a lawyer completes a matter, decides to withdraw or is fired by the client, or when lawyers leave law firms and do not intend to continue work on a matter. The letter should make clear the reason the relationship has ended, and include appropriate warnings about unfinished work and time deadlines.[6] The letter also can address whether the client wishes the lawyer to communicate with successor counsel, and can provide for the orderly transmission of client files and documents.[7]

Disengagement letters essentially transform a current client into a former client and thereby limit (but, as we will see in the next two chapters, do not extinguish) the duties the lawyer continues to owe that person or entity. Although the use of a disengagement letter can clarify the lawyer's lack of continuing obligation to the client, it is not an unmixed blessing. The lawyer also may hope that the client will call on the lawyer or the law firm for other services in the future. For this reason, the termination letter should be clear, but also can convey a willingness to serve in additional matters.

B. Competence

Problems

4-2. What if Martyn agreed to take the case in Problem 4-1 when she first met with the prospective client?

(a) Must she tell the client that the statute has run?

(b) Can Martyn be disciplined?

(c) Can Martyn & Fox be disciplined?

(d) Will Martyn & Fox be liable for malpractice?

4-3. Martyn & Fox recommended a settlement of $1 million to a client in a Ford Explorer rollover case. Later, the client learns a similar case ended in a jury verdict of $3 million. Can the client recover the difference from Martyn & Fox? What if Martyn & Fox was retained only to advise regarding the tax consequences of the settlement?

Consider: Model Rules 1.1-1.4, 2.1, 5.1
Model Code DR 6-101
N.Y. DR 1-102(a)
RLGL §52

C. Communication

Problem

4-4. Is Martyn & Fox liable if, in preparing the final employment contract, it forgot to insert a covenant not to compete that its client had requested?

6. *See, e.g.,* Gilles v. Wiley, Malehorn & Sirota, *infra* p.402 (client stated cause of action against former lawyers who withdrew at the last minute without adequately warning her that the statute of limitations was about to run on her medical malpractice case).
7. Mallen & Smith, §2.13.

What if Martyn & Fox forgot to advise its client that a covenant not to compete could be included?

Consider: Model Rule 1.4
RLGL §§20, 21, 49

dePape v. Trinity Health Systems, Inc.

242 F. Supp. 2d 585 (N.D. Iowa 2003)

BENNETT, Chief Judge . . .

The plaintiff in this breach-of-contract and legal malpractice case, Dr. Gregory dePape, is a Canadian citizen who completed his medical studies and training in Canada. Thousands of miles away in the small city of Fort Dodge, Iowa, Trimark Physicians Group, Ltd. ("Trimark") [a wholly owned subsidiary of Trinity Health Systems, Inc.] sought a family physician to fill a vacancy and to meet the burgeoning needs of the Fort Dodge medical community. Through a consulting firm, Trimark successfully recruited Dr. dePape to fill this vacancy, and in March of 1999, Trimark and Dr. dePape, while still living and working in Canada, entered into a five-year employment contract.

As part of the contract negotiations process, the parties discussed immigration matters and the fact that Dr. dePape needed to obtain a visa for lawful entry and permission to work in the United States prior to beginning employment. In order to obtain such permission, Trimark engaged the services of a St. Louis, Missouri law firm, Blumenfeld, Kaplan & Sandweiss, P.C. . . .

On April 23, 1999, one month after Trimark and Dr. dePape entered into their employment contract, Blumenfeld held an initial conference regarding its representation of Trimark and Dr. dePape. Partners A and B of the Blumenfeld firm, [and representatives of Trimark] participated in this initial conference. Notably, Blumenfeld did not advise Dr. dePape to participate, nor did it even inform him of the conference. At this conference, Blumenfeld outlined Dr. dePape's immigration options. At the time of this conference, Blumenfeld learned (1) that Dr. dePape had a five-year employment contract with Trimark; (2) that both Dr. dePape and Trimark expected an employment relationship that would endure longer than five years and, ideally, the entirety of Dr. dePape's medical career; and (3) that Dr. dePape had not taken a three-stage set of examinations, known as the USMLE's, [United States Medical Licensing Examination] which precluded him from receiving one of the two visas available to foreign physicians—namely, the H-1B visa. . . .

After holding the initial conference, Partner A sent [Trimark] an engagement letter on April 26, 1999, confirming the parties' agreement and Blumenfeld's commitment to represent Trimark *and* Dr. dePape throughout the immigration process. . . . The engagement letter specifically states that both Trimark and Dr. dePape are Blumenfeld's clients, but Partner A sent a copy of the letter only to Trimark. . . . The engagement letter outlines Dr. dePape's immigration options; yet Blumenfeld did not send a copy to him, nor did Blumenfeld advise Trimark to forward the engagement letter to Dr. dePape, who. . . did not see the letter until preparing for this trial. . . .

It is undisputed that an H-1B visa is the preferred method of bringing a foreign physician into the United States....

In order to perform direct patient care on an H-1B visa, the foreign physician must have successfully completed the USMLE's.

...Blumenfeld never attempted to ascertain whether Dr. dePape would complete the USMLE's, nor did it advise Dr. dePape that completion of the USMLE's was a necessary prerequisite to obtaining an H-1B visa and would be in his best interest....Dr. dePape declined that option because he held misconceptions about the length of time that it took to complete the exams. Dr. dePape believed that the USMLE's could not be completed in fewer than two years, while Partner A and Partner B testified that the process could be completed in six to eight months, [which Dr. dePape could have completed while waiting for his Iowa medical license]....

When Blumenfeld [8 months later] belatedly ascertained that Dr. dePape could not enter the country on an H-1B visa, it switched gears and began working on a TN visa....

When Blumenfeld began work on a TN visa for Dr. dePape, it knew that the position described in his Employment Agreement would not pass muster as an acceptable TN classification job description....Because Dr. dePape had a contract that outlasted the duration of the TN visa and was for a job that was not permitted by the visa, Blumenfeld, without consulting its clients, concocted a fictitious job title and description. Blumenfeld labeled this position "Physician Consultant" and described the duties of this position as a "community health care needs assessment." Blumenfeld did not discuss with Dr. dePape or Trimark the newly created position or the fact that Dr. dePape could not enter the United States and practice family medicine on the TN visa....

...[W]hile Blumenfeld was billing for an H1B visa for which Dr. dePape was not qualified and preparing its sham TN application, Dr. dePape... worked in Canada doing locum tenens, which is temporary substitution work for vacationing physicians.

When Dr. dePape learned that he would be granted his Iowa medical license, he and Trimark...then worked with Blumenfeld to arrange a June 8, 2000 entry at the Peace Bridge in Buffalo, New York, which Blumenfeld chose because of its arrangement with a particular INS officer. Dr. dePape ended his lease, shipped all of his belongings and his vehicle to Fort Dodge, and terminated his locum tenens. He and his fiancée...flew from Vancouver to Toronto, and then rented a car to drive to Buffalo, New York. They planned to drive across the border, drop the car off at the rental station in Buffalo, and then fly to Fort Dodge, Iowa, where Dr. dePape intended to begin his new life....

Because the costs of accompanying Dr. dePape to his INS interview at the Peace Bridge were prohibitively high, Blumenfeld, consistent with its usual practice, retained its local immigration lawyer, Mr. Eiss, to assist Dr. dePape. Mr. Eiss met Dr. dePape at a coffee shop near the INS office in Fort Erie, Canada on the morning of June 8, 2000. There, for the first time, Dr. dePape was shown the letter describing his position as a Physician Consultant and told that he could not work in the United States as a family physician....

...During this short meeting, Mr. Eiss played the role of an immigration officer and asked Dr. dePape what he was planning on doing in the United States. Dr. dePape responded that he was going to be a family physician. Mr. Eiss shook his head and handed Dr. dePape the TN application letter. Dr. dePape was shocked, surprised, and outraged by the letter's description of his position and its temporary nature because, as far as he knew, he was permanently moving to Fort Dodge to be a doctor, not a temporary Physician Consultant doing a community health care needs assessment—something he had never heard about or even knew what it was. Dr. dePape was skeptical and concerned about the lawfulness of representing to INS that he intended to perform a community health care needs assessment and then return to Canada. However, Mr. Eiss convinced Dr. dePape that the community health care needs assessment was legal and only a mere technicality that would not impede him from practicing medicine. Hesitant but confident in the legal advice of his attorney, Dr. dePape proceeded with Mr. Eiss to the INS office to attempt Dr. dePape's entry under TN status.

There, the INS official interviewing Dr. dePape did not believe that Dr. dePape sought entry to perform a community health care needs assessment. When the INS official asked Dr. dePape directly why he was going to the United States, Dr. dePape truthfully answered that he intended to practice family medicine. Because the TN visa does not permit this, the INS official turned Dr. dePape away and sent him back to Canada. Mr. Eiss did not return with Dr. dePape to counsel him further.

Devastated and shocked by his failed entry and with no direction from Mr. Eiss or the Blumenfeld firm, Dr. dePape found a pay phone and called [a Trimark representative, who] advised him to wait thirty minutes and to try to enter the United States as a visitor. If he accomplished that, she instructed him to drop the rental car off at the Buffalo airport and to fly to Fort Dodge in order to work out a "plan B." Dr. dePape and his fiancée followed [this] advice, but the INS officials immediately recognized Dr. dePape. The officials not only interrogated him and accused him of being a liar, they searched his car and belongings and Dr. dePape and his fiancée felt as if they were being treated like criminals. INS again denied Dr. dePape entry to the United States, told him not to come back, and escorted him back to Canada. Dr. dePape felt helpless, humiliated, and angry.

When that entry attempt failed, Dr. dePape was literally stranded. He had no job, no home, and no possessions—not even his medical bag. Fortunately, he had a credit card with him and, at his own expense, he and his fiancée drove back to Toronto, where they paid over two thousand U.S. dollars for last-minute plane tickets back to Vancouver. Throughout this entire ordeal, there was no backup contingency plan and no advice from Blumenfeld.

Ultimately, Dr. dePape returned to British Columbia and, in his words, "re-started his life." He made several attempts to contact Trimark, [whose representative eventually] implored Dr. dePape to attempt another entry in Buffalo, New York, but he refused. She then asked if he was willing to take the USMLE's, but because he labored under the impression that the exams would have taken years to complete, he refused that option as well. Instead, Dr. dePape explored his employment options in Canada and ultimately began his own private practice in October of 2001.

Shockingly, no one at Blumenfeld ever attempted to contact Dr. dePape after his failed entry attempt on June 8, 2000.... [The court dismissed all of Dr. dePape's claims against Trinity and Trimark.]

D. COUNT IV: LEGAL MALPRACTICE...

It is well established that an attorney-client relationship may give rise to a duty, the breach of which may be legal malpractice. In a legal malpractice case, the plaintiff must demonstrate:

(1) the existence of an attorney client relationship giving rise to a duty, (2) the attorney, either by an act or failure to

act, violated or breached that duty, (3) the attorney's breach of duty proximately caused injury to the client, and (4) the client sustained actual injury, loss, or damage.

In this case, there is no dispute that an attorney-client relationship (the first element) existed between Dr. dePape and Blumenfeld....

1. Failure to pursue H-1B visa

...There is no question that Dr. dePape was not eligible for an H-1B visa because he had not taken the requisite examinations—the USMLE's. There is also no question that Blumenfeld was negligent when it failed to advise Dr. dePape of the consequences of not taking the USMLE's and failed to correct his misconception about the length of time the exams took to complete.

However, the record is devoid of any evidence establishing that Dr. dePape would have taken the USMLE's and become eligible for an H-1B visa if Blumenfeld had advised him to do so. Thus, this claim fails for lack of causation....

2. Failure to communicate and advise

a. Breach of duty

..."An attorney breaches the duty of care owed to the client when the attorney fails to use 'such skill, prudence and diligence as lawyers of ordinary skill and capacity commonly possess and exercise in the performance of the task which [is undertaken].'" Expert testimony is generally required to establish that an attorney's conduct is negligent, but, when the negligence is so obvious that a layperson can recognize or infer it, such testimony is unnecessary.

In this case, the plaintiff offered the deposition testimony of Bart Chavez to establish Blumenfeld's negligence. The court has reviewed Mr. Chavez's deposition, and his testimony strongly supports a finding of negligence in this case. Moreover, the court finds that Blumenfeld's breach is of the ilk that does not necessitate expert testimony because it is so obvious and outrageous that a lay person could easily recognize it without the assistance of an expert. Even in the absence of Mr. Chavez's expert testimony, which clearly identifies and articulates a standard of care that Blumenfeld failed to meet, the court is not without guidance in assessing the level of care Blumenfeld is charged with maintaining. "Although the Iowa Code of Professional Responsibility for Lawyers does not undertake to define standards of civil liability, it constitutes some evidence of negligence."...

Because Partners A and B are subject to the Missouri Rules of Professional Conduct, the court will utilize them as a guidepost.[10] Accordingly, the minimum communication Blumenfeld should have maintained with Dr. dePape is as follows: [The court cites Model rule 1.4]

In fact, Blumenfeld itself understands the importance of communication with its clients, and it prides itself on maintaining regular client contact. Indeed, the "letterhead" on each link of Blumenfeld's webpage advertises that Blumenfeld "recognize[s] the importance of personal contact with clients as an integral part of being a responsive firm." www.bks-law.com....

That Blumenfeld breached its duty of communicating with and advising

10. While Iowa law applies to the substantive issues presented in this case, Partners A and B are subject to Missouri's ethical code.... Iowa's code has no direct counterpart to Missouri's rule on communication. However, read together, three provisions in the Iowa Code of Professional Responsibility for Lawyers encompass the same aspirations envisioned by the drafters of the rule on communication. [The court cites DR 6-101(A)(3), EC 7-8, and EC 9-2.]

Dr. dePape does not present the court with a close call. Because Dr. dePape had no information, he indisputably lacked sufficient information upon which to make an informed decision about his immigration. A 20 minute meeting with Mr. Eiss at the border on the morning of Dr. dePape's entry attempt, which was preceded by months of silence, did not cure Blumenfeld's failure to communicate with Dr. dePape because, by that time, it was too late for Dr. dePape to make an informed decision regarding his immigration to the United States. Moreover, the only decision Dr. dePape was ever allowed to make was the one he was faced with at the border—lie and proceed with the immigration charade or tell the truth and be rejected....

While there are a myriad of ways Blumenfeld could have fulfilled its obligation to Dr. dePape, there is no question that Blumenfeld's failure to communicate at all with Dr. dePape is inadequate to meet its obligation under any conceivable option. For example, Blumenfeld could have (1) sent a copy of the retention letter to Dr. dePape, (2) written Dr. dePape a follow-up letter to the initial conference explaining the requirements of the TN and the H-1B visas, (3) followed-up the written explanation with a telephone call to ensure that Dr. dePape understood the visa requirements and to answer any questions that Dr. dePape may have had, and (4) if it was not intended to be a sham, explained the community health care needs assessment to the hospital to determine if they needed or wanted it and to Dr. dePape to determine if he was ready, willing, and able to perform it. Because Blumenfeld failed to do anything to explain Dr. dePape's immigration options and their requirements and, in addition, sprung the community health care needs assessment on Dr. dePape at the border, the court finds that Blumenfeld breached its duty to communicate with and advise Dr. dePape....

b. Causation

..."The burden of proving proximate cause in a legal malpractice action is the same as any other negligence action. To recover, the injured must show that, but for the attorney's negligence, the loss would not have occurred." As applied to this situation, the plaintiff must demonstrate that, but for Blumenfeld's failure to communicate with and ad-vise Dr. dePape, Dr. dePape would have (1) gained entry to the United States or (2) would have chosen to pursue other employment options in Canada instead of attempting to immigrate to the United States. ...

...[B]ecause of Blumenfeld's implausible interpretation of "temporary entry" and because of its exceedingly broad interpretation of the level of patient care permissible under the TN classification, the court finds that Blumenfeld attempted to perpetrate a fraud on the INS by representing that Dr. dePape sought entry to the United States as a Physician Consultant....

However, this conclusion does not relieve Blumenfeld of liability because the court also finds that, had Dr. dePape been informed of his immigration options at the outset, he would have pursued other employment in Canada. Therefore, he would have been able to start his own practice or to begin work in an established practice as soon as he was licensed in Canada.

c. Damages...

i. Lost income....The court previously found that, had Blumenfeld explained the implications of this to him, Dr. dePape would have chosen to remain in Canada and would have started his practice as soon as possible....

The difference between the net income Dr. dePape could have earned during the damages period and what he actually earned is . . . $203,736.20 United States dollars in lost income.

ii. Emotional distress. . . . "Under the tort theory of negligence, there is no general duty of care to avoid causing emotional harm to another. However, where the parties assume a relationship that is contractual in nature and deals with services or acts that involve deep emotional responses in the event of a breach, [Iowa courts] recognize a duty of care to protect against emotional distress."

In this case, Dr. dePape shares a special relationship with Blumenfeld that gives rise to a duty to avoid causing Dr. dePape emotional harm. This is not the sort of legal malpractice case in which mental distress damages are not recoverable. In Lawrence v. Grinde, 534 N.W.2d 414, 422 (Iowa 1995), the Iowa Supreme Court held that a legal malpractice plaintiff could not recover mental distress damages in his legal malpractice action because his distress was too remote to be reasonably foreseeable. There, the plaintiff's attorney failed to disclose a recent settlement on a bankruptcy petition, and the United States government subsequently indicted the plaintiff for bankruptcy fraud. The plaintiff was acquitted, but his indictment and trial gave rise to considerable media coverage.

In that case, the mental distress damages sought were indistinguishable from the damages sought for the plaintiff's alleged damages to his reputation. But because the damage to the plaintiff's reputation as a result of the indictment was one-step removed from the defendant's negligent act in preparing the bankruptcy petition, the Iowa court held that the plaintiff's claim for mental distress damages failed on causation.

Here, Blumenfeld was retained to assist Dr. dePape with his immigration, but instead of assisting Dr. dePape, Blumenfeld's negligence placed Dr. dePape directly in harm's way. It should be noted that Blumenfeld would not be liable for the mental distress that might have accompanied a failed legitimate entry attempt because it would be unfair under those circumstances to hold a lawyer responsible for the independent decision of an independent governmental entity. But in this case, Blumenfeld not only failed to provide Dr. dePape with sufficient information for him to make an informed decision about his immigration, moments before the entry attempt, Blumenfeld (through Mr. Eiss) counseled Dr. dePape to lie to INS officials in order to gain entry to the United States under false pretenses.

Aside from being unethical, this conduct directly led to the INS official's decision to deny Dr. dePape's visa request and formed the basis of the INS official's accusation that Dr. dePape was a liar. . . . Thus, the emotional distress damages resulting from Blumenfeld's negligence in this case are not one-step removed, and Dr. dePape may recover for them.

The court finds that, while short-lived, Dr. dePape suffered severe and intense emotional distress. He was ambushed at the United States border, asked to perpetrate a fraud on the United States government in order to gain entry, and then sent on his way without even the courtesy of a phone call from his lawyers. At the border, INS officials degraded Dr. dePape, and he felt extraordinarily humiliated. Moreover, he had spent the past fifteen months planning to begin his professional career with Trimark and had made the arrangements to do so. . . .

Fortunately, Dr. dePape is a person of strong character and incredible integrity. While he was setback by the emotional turmoil surrounding the ambush at the border, he was able to move on and begin anew. Accordingly, the court finds that Dr. dePape is entitled to $75,000 USD for emotional distress to compensate him for the severe level of mental anguish directly caused by Blumenfeld's negligence. . . .

THEREFORE, upon consideration of the evidence and the parties' arguments, the court finds (1) that there is no basis in fact or in law to hold Trinity or Trimark liable for Dr. dePape's damages; and (2) that Blumenfeld was extraordinarily negligent in failing to inform and communicate with Dr. dePape concerning his immigration and in counseling him to perpetrate a fraud on the INS in order to gain entry to the United States; and (3) that, as a result of the damages caused by this negligence, Dr. dePape is entitled to recover from defendant Blumenfeld a total of $278,736.20 USD for his lost income and emotional distress. . . .[13]

Lawyers and Other Professionals: *Malpractice Liability*

In formulating legal malpractice standards, courts often analogize to malpractice suits against other professionals.[1] Since World War II, both the number and complexity of malpractice cases against professionals has grown.[2] The exact numbers are difficult to determine, because insurers report claims, and many professionals do not carry malpractice insurance.[3] In Oregon, the only state that mandates malpractice insurance for lawyers, statistics for the past 20 years

13. The evidence in this case strongly supports an award of punitive damages against Blumenfeld. Dr. dePape was bushwhacked at the border by Blumenfeld's egregious breach of duty and its willful and wanton disregard for Dr. dePape's rights. The plaintiff did not request punitive damages in his prayer for relief, and the court recognizes its authority to award them when supported by the evidence, even in the absence of a specific prayer for punitive damages. *See* Boeckmann v. Joseph, 889 F.2d 1094 (9th Cir. 1989) (table op.) (affirming district court's award of punitive damages in absence of request because plaintiff plead fraud and, therefore, the defendant was on notice because a finding of fraud supports an award of punitive damages).

In Iowa, the standard for punitive damages is "Whether, by a preponderance of clear, convincing, and satisfactory evidence, the conduct of the defendant from which the claim arose constituted willful and wanton disregard for the rights or safety of another." Iowa Code §668A.1(1)(a). The court has carefully reviewed the plaintiff's initial and amended complaints but finds that Dr. dePape did not plead sufficient facts to put Blumenfeld on notice that punitive damages were at issue. Therefore, despite the overwhelming evidence to support an award of punitive damages in this case, the court will not impose them.

1. Cases against lawyers can be traced to 1767. John W. Wade, *The Attorney's Liability for Negligence*, 12 Vand. L. Rev. 755 (1959) and those against physicians to 1374. *See* Allan H. McCoid, *The Care Required of Medical Practitioners*, 12 Vand. L. Rev. 549, 550 (1959).

2. For lawyers, *see* ABA Standing Committee on Lawyers' Professional Liability, *Legal Malpractice Claims in the 1990s*, 20 (ABA 1996). The vast array of treatises concerning other professionals also attests to this growth. *See, e.g.*, Dan L. Goldwasser & Thomas Arnold, *Accountants' Liability* (Practicing Law Institute 2001); James Acret, *Architects and Engineers* (3d ed., Shepard's McGraw-Hill 1993); Norman L. Schafler, *Dental Malpractice, Legal and Medical Handbook* (John Wiley & Sons, Inc. 1996); Ronald E. Mallen & Jeffrey M. Smith, *Legal Malpractice* (5th ed., West 2000); Warren Freedman, *Malpractice Liability in the Helping and Healing Professions* (Quorum 1995); David W. Louisell & Harold Williams, *Medical Malpractice* (2001); Lawrence E. Lifson & Robert I. Simon, eds., *The Mental Health Practitioner and the Law: A Comprehensive Handbook* (Harvard U. Press 1998); Nancy J. Brent, *Nurses and the Law: A Guide to Principles and Applications* (2d ed., W. B. Saunders Company 2000); David B. Brushwood, *Pharmacy Malpractice: Law and Regulations* (2d ed., Aspen Press 1998). The lack of licensure combined with First Amendment concerns has led most courts to refuse to recognize a cause of action for clergy malpractice. John F. Wagner, Jr., *Cause of Action for Clergy Malpractice*, 75 A.L.R.4th 750 (1990).

3. For example, one commentator estimates that 11 to 50 percent of lawyers do not carry malpractice insurance. Manuel R. Ramos, *Legal Malpractice: The Profession's Dirty Little Secret*, 47 Vand. L. Rev. 1657, 1672 (1994). *See also* Ronald E. Mallen & Robert J. Romero, eds., *Legal Malpractice: The Law Office Guide to Purchasing Legal Malpractice Insurance* (West 1999). A few jurisdictions require lawyers to inform clients if they lack insurance. *E.g.*, Cal. Bus. & Prof. Code §6148(a)(4) (2001); N.H. R. of Prof. Conduct 1.17 (2003), R. of the S. Ct. of Va., Part 6, §IV, ¶18 (2001). Several jurisdictions also require malpractice insurance for lawyers who form professional corporations. *Restatement (Third) The Law Governing Lawyers* §58, Comment c (2000).

indicate that 8.7 to 13.2 percent of lawyers there have claims filed against them each year. Nationally, between 1979 and 1986, the number of legal malpractice cases doubled, and the average settlement rose from $3,000 to $45,000.[4] For physicians, a New York study shows a 13 percent annual claims rate and a fivefold increase in the number of claims between 1976 and 1988. In this same time span, the average settlement rose from $28,000 to $158,000.[5] Although these statistics for physicians and lawyers seem quite close, some think that the true incidence of legal malpractice incidents is "probably closer to 20% or more."[6]

A malpractice action is a specialized negligence case with evidentiary rules that generally defer to professional custom. To establish legal malpractice, for example, *Togstad* and *dePape* illustrate that a plaintiff must prove four elements: the existence of a client-lawyer relationship, breach of a professional duty of care, causation (actual and proximate), and damages. The requirement that a plaintiff establish a relationship with the professional is an application of the *Palsgraf* rule, that the plaintiff must be foreseeable, or in other words, the one to whom a duty is owed.[7] Expert testimony is not only admissible but is required to establish breach of the standard of care. Causation rules may be modified due to the special expertise of professionals or the kind of harm professionals can cause. Finally, proof of damages often requires more precision than that demanded by ordinary negligence cases. The remainder of this note examines each of these elements of a cause of action alleging professional malpractice.

Client-Professional Relationship

In *dePape,* there was no dispute that the law firm deliberately agreed to represent Dr. dePape and therefore owed him a duty of care. *Togstad,* however, illustrates how professionals who do not agree or even intend to create a client-professional relationship can be surprised by a claim from such a person. Courts find duties to prospective clients such as Mr. and Mrs. Togstad when they reasonably rely on a lawyer's advice during a conversation to determine whether they have a matter worth pursuing or whether they wish to engage that particular lawyer to handle the matter.[8] Although some courts continue to insist on privity of contract between client and lawyer before allowing a professional malpractice suit, most courts today impose duties of care not only to clients, but also to some prospective clients, to nonclients who are intended third-party beneficiaries of clients, and also to nonclients who are invited to rely on or benefit from the lawyer's work.[9]

The next case in this chapter, Greycas v. Proud, illustrates how most courts extend the client-professional relationship to third-party beneficiaries; those the

4. Ramos, *supra* note 3, at 1663-1671.

5. The same study estimates that only about one in eight persons injured by medical malpractice ever filed a malpractice claim, and that about half of those who file do not recover. *See* Paul C. Weiler, et al., *A Measure of Malpractice* 68-69 (Harvard U. Press 1995).

6. Ramos, *supra* note 3, at 1664. This estimate explains Ramos' conclusion that legal malpractice may be a "tip of the iceberg problem, while medical malpractice more likely involves "a few bad apples." *See also* Manuel E. Ramos, *Legal Malpractice: No Lawyer or Client Is Safe*, 47 Fla. L. Rev. 1, 17 (1995).

7. *See* Palsgraf v. Long Island R.R. Co., 162 N.E. 99 (N.Y. 1928).

8. *See, e.g.,* DeVaux v. Am. Home Assurance Co., 444 N.E.2d 355 (Mass. 1983) (secretary who spoke to prospective client and told her to write a letter asking for representation and have a physician document injuries had actual or apparent authority to create client-lawyer relationship).

9. For lawyers, *see Restatement (Third) The Law Governing Lawyers* §51 (2000). For other professionals, *see* Lawyers and Other Professionals: Duties to Third Persons, *infra* p.165. We also will address this issue in the context of insurance defense representation in Paradigm Ins. Co. v. The Langerman Law Offices, P.A., *infra* p.330.

client intends to benefit in documents created by a lawyer for a client. For lawyers, the earliest cases involved situations where a client seeks the lawyer's help to make a third party the beneficiary of a will or trust. Here, courts found that the client's intent to benefit a third person created a duty of care by the client's lawyer to that third person as well. This meant that breach of a duty of care to the client, such as negligent drafting of the document, which later caused frustration of the testator's intent, created a cause of action by the intended beneficiary against the testator's or settlor's lawyer.[10] In the same manner, unrepresented parties to transactions may request assistance from another party's lawyer. A client-lawyer relationship has been found to exist in situations where a lawyer for one party to a transaction voluntarily provides services to other parties who reasonably rely on the lawyer's assistance.[11]

On the other hand, where the parties are potential adversaries or incidental rather than intended beneficiaries, courts have refused to apply the third-party beneficiary doctrine.[12] For example, many courts refuse to impose duties on lawyers for personal representatives of an estate to the estate beneficiaries, reasoning that the latter are not intended beneficiaries and their interests may well collide with those of the client's personal representative.[13]

Duty

Plaintiffs must prove not only that a client-professional relationship existed, but also that it existed with respect to the acts or omissions that form the basis of a malpractice suit.[14] This rule recognizes that client and lawyer can limit the scope of representation to certain specific matters.[15] Once both the client-professional relationship and the scope of representation are established, courts impose a duty to follow a professional standard of care, that is, the reasonable knowledge, skill, and diligence of a similarly

---

10. *E.g.*, In re Guardianship of Karan, 38 P.3d 396 (Wash. App. 2002) (minor child has cause of action against mother's lawyer who set up child's trust to allow pilfering of the estate); Lucas v. Hamm, 364 P.2d 685 (Cal. 1961) (intended beneficiaries of a will could recover from lawyer whose negligence in drafting document caused them to lose their testamentary rights). We discuss a similar trend toward recognition of nonclients as foreseeable plaintiffs in tort actions against other professions in Lawyers and Other Professionals: Duties to Third Persons, *infra* p.165.

11. *E.g.*, Kremser v. Quarles & Brady, L.L.P. 36 P.3d 761 (Ariz. App. 2001) (corporation's lawyers undertook responsibility to perfect nonclient creditor's security interest); Nelson v. Nationwide Mortgage Corp., 659 F. Supp. 611 (D.D.C. 1987) (lawyer volunteered to answer questions and explain document). Persons claiming such an implied client-lawyer relationship must reasonably believe that the lawyer represented their interests.

12. *See, e.g.*, Capitol Indem. Corp. v. Fleming, 58 P.3d 965 (Ariz. App. 2002) (surety who posted bond for an estate's conservator incidental, not intended beneficiary of services provided by conservator's lawyer); Bovee v. Gravel, 811 A.2d 137 (Vt. 2002) (bank shareholders were not beneficiaries of law firm's representation of bank); MacMillian v. Scheffy, 787 A.2d 867 (N.H. 2001) (buyers in real estate transaction unable to prove that seller's lawyer, who drafted the deed, had the purpose to benefit them; mere fact they were grantees under the deed was not enough); Kilpatrick v. Wiley, Rein & Fielding, 37 P.3d 1130 (Utah 2001) (law firm's representation of a limited partnership does not create implied client-lawyer relationship with individual limited partners unless the latter reasonably believe the firm represents their discrete interests).

13. *See, e.g.*, Jensen v. Crandall, 1997 Me. Super. LEXIS 72; Trask v. Butler, 872 P.2d 1080 (Wash. 1994); Neal v. Baker, 551 N.E.2d 704 (Ill. App. 1990).

14. *See, e.g.*, Kates v. Robinson, 786 So. 2d 61 (Fla. App. 2001) (lawyer hired only to execute a judgment not responsible for recognizing other potential defendants); *cf.* Nichols v. Keller, 19 Cal. Rptr. 2d 601 (Cal. App. 1993) (initial lawyer consulted by injured worker had duty to advise about availability of third-party action as well as worker's compensation claim, but second lawyer who undertook only worker's compensation case, had no duty to advise).

15. *See* Model Rule 1.2(c), *Restatement (Third) The Law Governing Lawyers* §19 (2000).

situated professional.[16] Because jurors usually lack familiarity with what a particular professional should do, the duty requirement in professional malpractice cases requires expert testimony to establish the professional standard of care.[17] This legal requirement also reflects a social judgment that courts should rely on professionals because they can be trusted to establish their own standards of care.[18]

The defendant in *Togstad* attempted to rely on a doctrine related to judicial reliance on professional judgment when he argued that lawyers should not be liable for "honest errors in judgment."[19] The court's response, that errors in judgment should be subject to the rigors of expert testimony, comports with a similar outcome in medical malpractice cases. There, courts also reject the honest error in judgment (sometimes called the "respectable minority") defense in favor of the general malpractice standard: whether a reasonable and prudent member of the profession would have undertaken such an action.[20]

Until the middle of the twentieth century, medical malpractice actions were further governed by the locality rule, which held that the only admissible source of expert testimony was a physician who practiced in the substantially the same community as the defendant. As medical specialties and training became national in scope, the law of medical malpractice followed the professional custom of physicians, replacing the locality rule with a national standard of care. Today, courts require physicians to use "reasonable diligence, skill, competence, and prudence as are practiced by minimally competent physicians in the same specialty or general field of practice throughout the United States, who have available to them the same general facilities, services equipment and options."[21]

In legal malpractice suits, admissibility of expert testimony similarly reflects the professional practice. State licensure of lawyers translates into the admissibility of the testimony of any lawyer licensed to practice in that state.[22] As lawyers specialize, their recognition of specialty areas also has become a component of the standard of care.[23] So, for example, lawyers as well as physicians have been held responsible for understanding the intricacies of specialized tasks or for failing to refer to a specialist who can competently provide the service.[24] Specialty designations can be established by state regulations, by expert testimony, or by a specific holding out by the defendant lawyer.[25]

---

16. *E.g.*, Ziegelheim v. Apollo, 607 A.2d 1298 (N.J. 1992) (lawyers who negotiate settlements are subject to the general rule that requires them to exercise reasonable knowledge, skill, and diligence possessed by members of that profession in good standing in similar communities). A few courts have isolated some areas of practice, such as negotiation of settlements, from malpractice scrutiny. *See, e.g.*, Muhammad v. Strassburger, McKenna, Messer, Shilobod & Gutnick, 587 A.2d 1346 (Pa. 1991) (absent proof of fraud, dissatisfied litigants may not recover from their lawyers for malpractice in negotiating settlements accepted by the clients). The modern trend, however, subjects all of a lawyer's practice to the expert judgment of similarly situated professionals.

17. *See, e.g.*, Robert M. Schoenhaus, *Necessity of Expert Testimony to Show Malpractice of Architect,* 3 A.L.R.4th 1023 (1981).

18. Expert witnesses are subject to the appropriate professional standard of care as well. *See, e.g.*, Marrogi v. Howard, 805 So. 2d 1118 (La. 2002) (accountant who held himself out as an expert witness in medical billing cases not protected by witness immunity).

19. *See, e.g.*, Hodges v. Carter, 80 So. E.2d 144 (N.C. 1954).

20. *See, e.g.*, Ouellette v. Subak, 391 N.W.2d 810 (Minn. 1986); Henderson v. Heyer-Schulte Corp., 600 S.W.2d 844 (Tex. Civ. App. 1980).

21. *See, e.g.*, Hall v. Hillbun, 466 So. 2d 856, 873 (Miss. 1985).

22. *See, e.g.*, Russo v. Griffin, 510 A.2d 436 (Vt. 1986).

23. Mallen & Smith, *supra* note 2, at §19.4.

24. Horne v. Peckham, 158 Cal. Rptr. 714 (Cal. App. 1979) (lawyer who acknowledged the need for expertise in tax had duty to refer client to an expert practitioner or to comply with the specialty standard of care).

25. *See, e.g.*, Battle v. Thornton, 646 A.2d 315 (D.C. 1994) (absent proof that the defendants held themselves out as specialists in Medicaid fraud defense, or that jurisdiction or profession recognizes such a specialty, lawyer is required to exercise skill and care of lawyers acting under similar circumstances).

The power of professional custom also plays a role in mitigating the doctrine of negligence per se in malpractice cases. In ordinary negligence cases, courts treat relevant safety statutes as conclusive proof of the standard of care.[26] Professional malpractice cases give statutory and regulatory standards different weight, holding that violation of a rule or statute may be evidence but usually is not determinative of the standard of care.[27] Courts often allow or require expert testimony to explain the legislative standard or its application.[28] This rule has special application in legal malpractice cases when a plaintiff claims that a lawyer violated a rule of professional conduct. *dePape* illustrates the view of the majority of courts, which hold that such a violation is relevant and admissible to prove breach of the professional standard of care, but not negligence per se.[29]

Breach

Once qualified as an appropriate expert, an expert witness's testimony must clearly articulate the standard of care or customary practice of the profession.[30] The jury then determines whether the defendant breached this standard of practice. *dePape* illustrates another similarity between medical and legal malpractice cases: the common knowledge exception to the requirement of expert testimony.[31] This exception was created to address situations where expert opinion was not necessary to help the jury understand the alleged duty and breach, because the professional's error was not related to advanced skill, knowledge, or judgment. For example, in medical malpractice cases, plaintiffs need not present expert testimony against physicians who operate on or injure a remote body part or leave surgical implements inside a patient's body.[32]

Three categories of cases create similar common knowledge exceptions in legal malpractice cases. In the first, lawyers ignore basic fiduciary duty, by failing to obey client instructions,[33] or failing to keep a client informed, or failing to obtain informed consent (as in *dePape* and *Roe*); or breaching confidentiality (as in Perez

26. *See, e.g.*, Martin v. Herzog, 126 N.E. 814 (N.Y. 1920). *Restatement (Second) of Torts* §286.
27. *See, e.g.*, Smith v. Haynsworth, Marion, McKay & Geurard, 472 S.E.2d 612 (S.C. 1996) (bar rules intended to protect a person in the client's position or addressing the particular harm are admissible to assess the legal duty of a lawyer); Thayer v. Hicks, 793 P.2d 784, 792 (Mont. 1990) (accountant's deviation from national rules and codes is admissible, but does not automatically constitute negligence). On the other hand, failure to adhere to a building code standard may constitute negligence per se by an architect or an engineer, *See, e.g.*, Burran v. Dambold, 422 F.2d 133 (10th Cir. 1970). Further, recent federal legislation that specifically redefines the role of pharmacists may make negligence per se easier to prove against that group of professionals. *See* Steven W. Huang, *The Omnibus Reconciliation Act of 1990: Redefining Pharmacists' Legal Responsibilities*, 24 Am. J.L. & Med. 417 (1998).
28. *See, e.g.*, Edwards v. Brandywine Hosp., 652 A.2d 1382 (Pa. Super. 1995).
29. Model R. of Prof. Conduct, Scope ¶20; *Restatement (Third) The Law Governing Lawyers* §52(2) (2000).
30. *See, e.g.*, Clark v. D.C., 708 A.2d 632 (D.C. 1997) (expert witness' personal opinion not sufficient to establish the standard of care for medical malpractice); Childers v. Spindor, 754 P.2d 599 (Or. App. 1988) (expert witness' general discussion of deposition practice not sufficient to establish standard of care for legal malpractice).
31. *See, e.g.*, Jones v. Chicago HMO Ltd. of Ill., 739 N.E.2d 1119 (Ill. 2000) (expert testimony not always required to prove the standard of care of a "reasonably careful HMO.").
32. *See, e.g.*, Toy v. Mackintosh, 110 N.E. 1034 (Mass. 1916) (dentist allowed unconscious plaintiff to inhale an extracted tooth); Jefferson v. United States, 77 F. Supp. 706 (D. Md. 1948) (surgeon left towel in patient's abdominal cavity following gallbladder surgery). Some of the cases involving unexplained injuries to a healthy body part rely on the res ipsa loquitur doctrine to infer negligence. *See, e.g.*, Meadows v. Patterson, 109 S.W.2d 417 (Tenn. App. 1937) (eye injury during appendectomy); Ybarra v. Spangard, 154 P.2d 687 (Cal. 1944) (shoulder injury following appendectomy).
33. *See, e.g.*, Olfe v. Gordon, 286 N.W.2d 573 (Wis. 1980) (no expert testimony required to show that lawyer breached fiduciary duty to client by failing to draft a first mortgage the client specifically instructed the lawyer to include in a property transaction).

v. Kirk & Carrigan[34]). The second group of cases involves lawyers who miss time deadlines, such as statutes of limitations.[35] Finally, some courts have concluded that plaintiffs do not need expert testimony to prove that lawyers should perform two basic functions: research applicable law[36] and investigate relevant facts.[37] In all of these situations, juries do not need an expert to assess whether the lawyer failed to perform a basic duty owed to the client.

Causation

Once duty is established, courts require plaintiffs who allege professional malpractice to prove both actual and proximate causation. In legal malpractice actions, the "but-for" standard of actual causation and the foreseeable risk rule in proximate causation can present formidable obstacles. Dr. dePape, for example, was unable to prove malpractice based on a duty of the law firm to pursue an H-1B visa, because he did not establish that he would have taken the medical exams that were required to qualify for it. He was, however, able to establish that he would have started his medical practice in Canada 15 months sooner had the law firm properly informed him of his legal options.

When a time period has expired on a claim, plaintiffs who allege legal malpractice are required to prove a "case within a case," as was done in *Togstad*.[38] The law has not been quite so solicitous in protecting physicians. Recent cases have modified traditional "but-for" causation standards to allow plaintiffs to recover where the physician's negligence "increased the risk" of harm to the plaintiff or caused only a small lost chance of survival.[39] Some commentators argue that this doctrine should be applied to lawyers as well.[40] A later case in this volume, Wolpaw v. General Accident Insurance Company,[41] recognizes an alternative option; using expert testimony to prove what might have happened at trial. This would mean that plaintiffs could recover if a negligent lawyer caused them to lose a chance of recovery, with the value of the loss measured by the settlement value of the underlying matter.[42]

---

34. *See* p.125, *infra*.
35. *See, e.g.*, George v. Caton, 600 P.2d 822 (N.M. 1979).
36. *See, e.g.*, Smith v. Lewis, 107 Cal. Rptr. 95 (Cal. App. 1973) (lawyer who failed to research law, which would have indicated a potential, though unclear client claim in a divorce).
37. *See, e.g.*, Schmidt v. Crotty, 528 N.W.2d 112 (Iowa 1995) (lawyer who failed to investigate property descriptions in valuing estate taxes after he was put on notice they were inaccurate).
38. *E.g.*, Viner v. Sweet, 70 P.3d 1046 (Cal. 2003) (case-within-a-case proof required for errors in transactional work as well as litigation); Bevan v. Fix, 42 P.3d 1013 (Wyo. 2002) (summary judgment granted against client who proved that former lawyer breached fiduciary duty but did not allege facts indicating that the underlying divorce action would have been more favorable to him); Winskunas v. Birnbaum, 23 F.3d 1264 (7th Cir. 1994) (former client must prove that lawyer who failed to file appeal of state court action could have gotten his loss reversed on appeal). *Cf.* Whitley v. Chamouris, 574 S.E.2d 251 (Va. 2003) (jury question whether client proved merits of underlying case, no expert testimony required). The rule also burdens persons convicted of crimes, who must have their convictions reversed or prove their innocence to establish causation. *See* The Law Governing Lawyers: Criminal Defense Representation, *infra* p.113.
39. *See, e.g.*, Herkovits v. Group Health Coop., 664 P.2d 474 (1983) (cancer patient can recover against a physician who failed to timely diagnose her disease, even though she had less than a 39 percent chance of survival if timely diagnosed); Roberts v. Ohio Permanente Med. Group, Inc., 668 N.E.2d 480 (1996) (patient can recover percentage of damages in direct proportion to the chance of survival or recovery that the plaintiff lost).
40. *See, e.g.*, John Leubsdorf, *Legal Malpractice and Professional Responsibility,* 48 Rutgers L. Rev. 101, 149-150 (1995).
41. *See* p.312, *infra*.
42. *Cf.* Jones Motor Co. Inc. v. Holtkamp, Liese, Beckemeier & Childress, P.C., 197 F.3d 1190 (7th Cir. 1999) (malpractice plaintiff who alleged former lawyer's failure to make a timely jury trial request failed to prove causation using a lawyer-expert witness whose opinion of probable jury verdicts was unsubstantiated by actual verdicts in comparable cases).

Damages

Since malpractice is a species of negligence, damages must be shown. For example, even if the jury determines that the plaintiff would have prevailed in a previous case, a defendant who can show that any judgment won would have been uncollectible will be relieved from being accountable for that portion of the verdict.[43] Traditionally, proving damages meant proving monetary or physical injury. Increasingly, clients and patients who allege foreseeable emotional harm also may be able to recover from the professional who caused it.[44] For example, the court in *dePape* recognized the availability of damages for emotional harm against some lawyers, at least where their breach of fiduciary duty is egregious and directly causes severe emotional distress.[45] *dePape* also illustrates the willingness of modern cases to extend punitive damages to professionals where their conduct is grossly negligent or outrageous in character.[46] Query whether Dr. dePape's malpractice lawyers themselves committed malpractice by failing to plead punitive damages.

Defenses

Professionals often allege several defenses to malpractice suits. Increasingly, they seek to implead or be granted contribution from other professionals who provided services to the client.[47] Statutes of limitations also are commonly alleged.[48] Most courts agree that, because clients depend on professionals, the statute is tolled during the time the client-professional relationship continues.[49] Most courts also apply the "discovery rule" to professionals: the statutory time period does not begin until the plaintiff reasonably should have discovered the elements of the cause of action.[50] Courts follow similar reasoning when deciding whether comparative negligence should apply. A lawyer cannot claim comparative fault as a defense in a case

43. *See, e.g., Restatement (Third) The Law Governing Lawyers* §53, Comment b; *cf.* Garretson v. Miller, 121 Cal. Rptr. 2d 317 (Cal. App. 2002) (plaintiff must prove that judgment would be collectible).
44. *See, e.g., Restatement (Third) The Law Governing Lawyers* §53, Comment g. For a similar result in medical practice, *see, e.g.*, Oswald v. Legrand, 453 N.W.2d 634 (Iowa 1990).
45. *See also* Perez v. Kirk & Carrigan, *infra* p.125, which upheld emotional distress damages against lawyers whose breach of confidentiality caused a multiple-count criminal indictment against their client. *Cf.* Long-Russell v. Hampe, 39 P.3d 1015 (Wyo. 2002) (damages for emotional distress not recoverable in malpractice case alleging negligent legal advice about child custody). *See also* Lawrence v. Grinde, 534 N.W.2d 414 (Iowa 1995), cited in *dePape*.
46. *Restatement (Third) The Law Governing Lawyers* §53, Comment h; Jacobson v. Oliver, 201 F. Supp. 2d 93 (D.D.C. 2000) (terrorism victim in legal malpractice case could recover punitive damages if his lawyer negligently failed to raise the issue in the underlying action). The same is true for physicians. *See, e.g.*, Henry v. Deen, 310 S.E.2d 326 (N.C. 1984) (wrongful death and civil conspiracy to destroy documentation).
47. *E.g.*, Sheetz, Inc. v. Bowles, Rice, McDavid, Graff & Love, PLLC, 547 S.E.2d 256 (W. Va. 2001) (predecessor and successor law firms may be joint tortfeasors); Parler & Wobber v. Miles & Stockbridge, P.C., 756 A.2d 526 (Md. 2000) (lawyer being sued by former client may implead or obtain contribution or indemnification from successor lawyer).
48. A few states also have statutes of repose for malpractice suits, which start to run on the date of the act or omission. *See, e.g.*, Sorenson v. Law Offices of Theodore Poehlmann, 764 N.E.2d 1227 (Ill. App. 2001) (six-year statute of repose time stricture applies even where underlying acts only produce injury after that period of time).
49. *See, e.g.*, Shumsky v. Eisenstein, 750 N.E.2d 67 (N.Y. 2001) (analogizing to the continuous treatment rule in medical malpractice cases); Lima v. Schmidt, 595 So. 2d 624 (La. 1992).
50. United States v. Kubrick, 444 U.S. 111 (1979) (in medical malpractice actions against the federal government, the statute of limitations starts to run when the plaintiff learns of the injury and its probable cause); Mastro v. Brodie, 682 P.2d 1162 (Colo. 1984) (statute of limitations against a physician begins to run when the plaintiff learns of the injury, its cause and that it was tortiously inflicted).

such as *dePape* where the client's failure to understand has been caused by the lawyer's negligent explanation or the client's reasonable reliance.[51]

Overall, courts continue to insist on special rules to govern professional malpractice suits. They also acknowledge the similarity in malpractice suits against a myriad of professionals and seek to make these rules consistent. The development of this law has made malpractice suits a primary means of addressing professional incompetence. Understanding the remedy can help you avoid liability in practice.

D. Misrepresentation

Problem

4-5. Is Martyn & Fox liable because it forgot to check the exact language of an applicable case or statute in drafting an opinion letter for a municipal bond issue that stated "all applicable law" had been complied with?

Consider: Model Rules 1.1, 2.3, 4.1, 8.4(c)
Model Code DR 1-102(A)(4), 6-101, 7-102(A)(5)
RLGL §51

Greycas, Inc. v. Proud

826 F.2d 1560 (7th Cir. 1987), cert. denied, 484 U.S. 1043 (1988)

POSNER, Circuit Judge.

Theodore S. Proud, Jr., a member of the Illinois bar who practices law in a suburb of Chicago, appeals from a judgment against him for $833,760, entered after a bench trial. The tale of malpractice and misrepresentation that led to the judgment begins with Proud's brother-in-law, Wayne Crawford, like Proud a lawyer but one who devoted most of his attention to a large farm that he owned in downstate Illinois. The farm fell on hard times and by 1981 Crawford was in dire financial straits. He had pledged most of his farm machinery to lenders, yet now desperately needed more money. He approached Greycas, Inc., the plaintiff in this case, a large financial company headquartered in Arizona, seeking a large loan that he offered to secure with the farm machinery. He did not tell Greycas about his financial difficulties or that he had pledged the machinery to other lenders, but he did make clear that he needed the loan in a hurry. Greycas obtained several appraisals of Crawford's farm machinery but did not investigate Crawford's financial position or discover that he had pledged the collateral to other lenders, who had perfected their liens in the collateral. Greycas agreed to lend Crawford

---

51. *See, e.g., Restatement (Third) The Law Governing Lawyers* §54, Comment d. On the other hand, a client who defrauded a third party was not entitled to indemnification from his lawyers, because "fraudfeasors" cannot hold others liable for harm caused by their own fraudulent conduct. Trustees of the AFTRA Health Fund v. Biondi, 303 F.3d 765 (7th Cir. 2002); Clark v. Rowe, 701 N.E.2d 624 (Mass. 1988) (upholding jury verdict that client was 70 percent negligent in refinancing a loan). For an example of a similar application of comparative fault to medical malpractice, *see, e.g.*, Ostrowski v. Azzara, 545 A.2d 148 (N.J. 1988).

$1,367,966.50, which was less than the appraised value of the machinery.

The loan was subject, however, to an important condition, which is at the heart of this case: Crawford was required to submit a letter to Greycas, from counsel whom he would retain, assuring Greycas that there were no prior liens on the machinery that was to secure the loan. Crawford asked Proud to prepare the letter, and he did so, and mailed it to Greycas, and within 20 days of the first contact between Crawford and Greycas the loan closed and the money was disbursed. A year later Crawford defaulted on the loan; shortly afterward he committed suicide. Greycas then learned that most of the farm machinery that Crawford had pledged to it had previously been pledged to other lenders.

The machinery was sold at auction. The Illinois state court that determined the creditors' priorities in the proceeds of the sale held that Greycas did not have a first priority on most of the machinery that secured its loan; as a result Greycas has been able to recover only a small part of the loan. The judgment it obtained in the present suit is the district judge's estimate of the value that it would have realized on its collateral had there been no prior liens, as Proud represented in his letter.

That letter is the centerpiece of the litigation. Typed on the stationery of Proud's firm and addressed to Greycas, it identifies Proud as Crawford's lawyer and states that, "in such capacity, I have been asked to render my opinion in connection with" the proposed loan to Crawford. It also states that "this opinion is being delivered in accordance with the requirements of the Loan Agreement" and that

> I have conducted a U.C.C., tax, and judgment search with respect to the Company [i.e., Crawford's farm] as of March 19, 1981, and except as hereinafter noted all units listed on the attached Exhibit A ("Equipment") are free and clear of all liens or encumbrances other than Lender's perfected security interest therein which was recorded March 19, 1981 at the Office of the Recorder of Deeds of Fayette County, Illinois.

The reference to the lender's security interest is to Greycas's interest; Crawford, pursuant to the loan agreement, had filed a notice of that interest with the recorder. The excepted units to which the letter refers are four vehicles. Exhibit A is a long list of farm machinery—the collateral that Greycas thought it was getting to secure the loan, free of any other liens. . . .

Proud never conducted a search for prior liens on the machinery listed in Exhibit A. His brother-in-law gave him the list and told him there were no liens other than the one that Crawford had just filed for Greycas. Proud made no effort to verify Crawford's statement. The theory of the complaint is that Proud was negligent in representing that there were no prior liens, merely on his brother-in-law's say-so. No doubt Proud was negligent in failing to conduct a search, but we are not clear why the misrepresentation is alleged to be negligent rather than deliberate and hence fraudulent, in which event Greycas's alleged contributory negligence would not be an issue (as it is, we shall see), since there is no defense of contributory or comparative negligence to a deliberate tort, such as fraud. . . . Proud did not merely say, "There are no liens"; he said, "I have conducted a U.C.C., tax, and judgment search"; and not only is this statement, too, a false one, but its falsehood cannot have been inadvertent, for Proud knew he had not conducted such a search. The concealment of his relationship with Crawford might also support a charge of fraud. But Greycas decided, for whatever reason, to argue negligent misrepresentation rather than fraud. It may have feared that Proud's insurance policy for professional malpractice excluded deliberate wrong-doing from its coverage, or may not have wanted to bear the higher burden of proving fraud, or may have feared that an accusation of fraud would make it harder to settle the case. . . . In any event, Proud does not argue that either he is liable for fraud or he is liable for nothing.

He also does not, and could not, deny or justify the misrepresentation; but he argues that it is not actionable under the tort law of Illinois, because he had no duty of care to Greycas. . . . He argues that Greycas had an adversarial relationship with Proud's client, Crawford, and that a lawyer has no duty of straight dealing to an adversary, at least none enforceable by a tort suit. In so arguing, Proud is characterizing Greycas's suit as one for professional malpractice rather than negligent misrepresentation, yet elsewhere in his briefs he insists that the suit was solely for negligent misrepresentation—while Greycas insists that its suit charges both torts. . . . So we shall discuss both.

Proud is undoubtedly correct in arguing that a lawyer has no general duty of care toward his adversary's client; it would be a considerable and, as it seems to us, an undesirable novelty to hold that every bit of sharp dealing by a lawyer gives rise to prima facie tort liability to the opposing party in the lawsuit or negotiation. The tort of malpractice normally refers to a lawyer's careless or otherwise wrongful conduct toward his own client. Proud argues that Crawford rather than Greycas was his client and . . . we shall assume for purposes of discussion that Greycas was not Proud's client.

Therefore if malpractice just meant carelessness or other misconduct toward one's own client, Proud would not be liable for malpractice to Greycas. But in Pelham v. Griesheimer, 440 N.E.2d 96 (1982), the Supreme Court of Illinois discarded the old common law requirement of privity of contract for professional malpractice; so now it is possible for someone who is not the lawyer's (or other professional's) client to sue him for malpractice. The court in *Pelham* was worried, though, about the possibility of a lawyer's being held liable "to an unlimited and unknown number of potential plaintiffs," so it added that "for a nonclient to succeed in a negligence action against an attorney, he must prove that the primary purpose and intent of the attorney-client relationship itself was to benefit or influence the third party." That, however, describes this case exactly. Crawford hired Proud not only for the primary purpose, but for the sole purpose, of influencing Greycas to make Crawford a loan. The case is much like Brumley v. Touche, Ross & Co., 487 N.E.2d 641, 644-45 (Ill. App. 1985), where a complaint that an accounting firm had negligently prepared an audit report that the firm knew would be shown to an investor in the audited corporation and relied on by that investor was held to state a claim for professional malpractice. In Conroy v. Andeck Resources '81 Year-End Ltd., 484 N.E.2d 525, 536-37 (1985), in contrast, a law firm that represented an offeror of securities was held not to have any duty of care to investors. The representation was not intended for the benefit of investors. Their reliance on the law firm's using due care in the services it provided in connection with the offer was not invited.

All this assumes that *Pelham* governs this case, but arguably it does not, for Greycas, as we noted, may have decided to bring this as a suit for negligent misrepresentation rather than professional malpractice. We know of no obstacle to such an election; nothing is more common in American jurisprudence than overlapping torts.

The claim of negligent misrepresentation might seem utterly straightforward. It might seem that by addressing a letter to Greycas intended (as Proud's counsel admitted at argument) to induce reliance on the statements in it, Proud made himself prima facie liable for any material misrepresentations, careless or deliberate, in the letter, whether or not Proud was Crawford's lawyer or for that matter anyone's lawyer. Knowing that Greycas was relying on him to determine whether the collateral for the loan was encumbered and to advise Greycas of the results of his determination, Proud negligently misrepresented the situation, to Greycas's detriment. But merely labeling a suit as one for negligent misrepresentation rather than professional malpractice will not make the problem of indefinite and perhaps excessive liability, which induced the court in *Pelham* to place limitations on the duty of care, go away. So one is not surprised to find that courts have placed similar limitations on suits for negligent misrepresentation—so similar that we are led to question whether, . . . these really are different torts, at least when both grow out of negligent misrepresentations by lawyers. For example, the *Brumley* case, which we cited earlier, is a professional-malpractice case, yet it has essentially the same facts as Ultramares Corp. v. Touche, Niven & Co., 174 N.E. 441 (N.Y. 1931), where the New York Court of Appeals, in a famous opinion by Judge Cardozo, held that an accountant's negligent misrepresentation was not actionable at the suit of a lender who had relied on the accountant's certified audit of the borrower.

The absence of a contract between the lender and the accountant defeated the suit in *Ultramares*—yet why should privity of contract have been required for liability just because the negligence lay in disseminating information rather than in designing or manufacturing a product? The privity limitation in products cases had been rejected, in another famous Cardozo opinion, years earlier. *See* MacPherson v. Buick Motor Co., 111 N.E. 1050 (N.Y. 1916). Professor Bishop suggests that courts were worried that imposing heavy liabilities on producers of information might cause socially valuable information to be underproduced. *See* Negligent Misrepresentation Through Economists' Eyes, 96 L. Q. Rev. 360 (1980). . . . For example, information produced by securities analysts, the news media, academicians, and so forth is socially valuable, but as its producers can't capture the full value of the information in their fees and other remuneration the information may be underproduced. Maybe it is right, therefore—or at least efficient—that none of these producers should have to bear the full costs. . . . At least that was once the view; and while *Ultramares* has now been rejected, in Illinois as elsewhere . . . a residuum of concern remains. So when in Rozny v. Marnul, 250 N.E. 2d 656 (Ill. 1969), the Supreme Court of Illinois, joining the march away from *Ultramares*, . . . was careful to emphasize facts in the particular case before it that limited the scope of its holding—facts such as that the defendant, a surveyor, had placed his "absolute guarantee for accuracy" on the plat and that only a few person would receive and rely on it, thus limiting the potential scope of liability.

Later Illinois cases, however, influenced by section 552 of the Second Restatement of Torts (1977), . . . hold that "one who in the course of his business or profession supplies information for the guidance of others in their business transactions" is liable for negligent misrepresentations that induce detrimental reliance. Whether there is a practical as distinct from a merely semantic difference between this formulation of the duty limitation and that of *Pelham* may be doubted but cannot change the outcome of this case. Proud, in the practice of his profession, supplied information (or rather misinformation) to Greycas that was intended to guide Greycas in commercial dealings with Crawford. Proud therefore had a duty to use due care to see that the information was correct. He used no care....

There is no serious doubt about the existence of a causal relationship between the misrepresentation and the loan. Greycas would not have made the loan without Proud's letter. Nor would it have made the loan had Proud advised it that the collateral was so heavily encumbered that the loan was as if unsecured, for then Greycas would have known that the probability of repayment was slight....

Proud argues, however, that his damages should be reduced in recognition of Greycas's own contributory negligence, which, though no longer a complete defense in Illinois, is a partial defense, renamed "comparative negligence." It is as much a defense to negligent misrepresentation as to any other tort of negligence....

But we think it too clear to require a remand for further proceedings that Proud failed to prove a want of due care by Greycas. Due care is the care that is optimal given that the other party is exercising due care. It is not the higher level of care that would be optimal if potential tort victims were required to assume that the rest of the world was negligent. A pedestrian is not required to exercise a level of care (e.g., wearing a helmet or a shin guard) that would be optimal if there were no sanctions against reckless driving. Otherwise drivers would be encouraged to drive recklessly, and knowing this pedestrians would be encouraged to wear helmets and shin guards. The result would be a shift from a superior method of accident avoidance (not driving recklessly) to an inferior one (pedestrian armor).

So we must ask whether Greycas would have been careless not to conduct its own UCC search had Proud done what he had said he did—conduct his own UCC search. The answer is no. The law normally does not require duplicative precautions unless one is likely to fail or the consequences of failure (slight though the likelihood may be) would be catastrophic. One UCC search is enough to disclose prior liens, and Greycas acted reasonably in relying on Proud to conduct it. Although Greycas had much warning that Crawford was in financial trouble ..., that was a reason for charging a hefty interest rate and insisting that the loan be secured; it was not a reason for duplicating Proud's work. It is not hard to conduct a UCC lien search; it just requires checking the records in the recorder's office for the county where the debtor lives. *See* Ill. Rev. Stat. ch. 26, para. 9-401. So the only reason to backstop Proud was if Greycas should have assumed he was careless or dishonest; and we have just said that the duty of care does not require such an assumption. Had Proud disclosed that he was Crawford's brother-in-law this might have been a warning signal that Greycas could ignore only at its peril. To go forward in the face of a known danger is to assume the risk. But Proud did not disclose his relationship to Crawford....

A final point. The record of this case reveals serious misconduct by an Illinois attorney. We are therefore sending a copy of this opinion to the Attorney Registration and Disciplinary Commission of the Supreme Court of Illinois for such disciplinary action as may be deemed appropriate in the circumstances. AFFIRMED.

The Limits of the Law: *Lawyer Dishonesty, Fraud, Deceit, and Misrepresentation*

Lawyers are trained to give legal advice, that is, to inform clients just how close to the limits of the law their proposed conduct will take them. Yet, some lawyers, like those in *dePape* and *Greycas,* seem unaware that generally applicable law also applies to their own personal conduct. This series of notes, entitled "The Limits of the Law," will examine several kinds of generally applicable law that limit a lawyer's representation of a client. We focus here on when a lawyer must say "no" to a client to avoid violating a legal limitation on the lawyer's own conduct. In this note, we pause to consider the legal limits on a lawyer's behavior created by various bodies of law concerning deceitful conduct.

In *Greycas,* Judge Posner makes clear that the law of fraud limits the legally acceptable conduct of lawyers, just as it constrains the behavior of any other citizen. He further indicates that facts which support relief in tort also reveal "serious misconduct by an Illinois attorney," and refers the matter to the appropriate state disciplinary commission. In *dePape,* the court characterized the lawyer's "implausible interpretation" of the law as an attempt to perpetrate a fraud on the INS. Both cases illustrate how crucial it is for lawyers to understand the law of fraud, because lawyers who flirt with fraud face not only criminal and civil consequences, but unlike other persons, also risk a third peril: professional discipline.

The Model Rules

The Model Rules of Professional Conduct include four provisions that incorporate nearly all of the general civil and criminal law of fraud and misrepresentation into professional obligations. The first two provisions provide that lawyers can be disciplined for knowingly making false statements of "material fact or law" to a tribunal,[1] or to a third person[2] when representing clients. The third forbids lawyers from engaging in any "conduct involving dishonesty, fraud, deceit or misrepresentation,"[3] both in representing clients and apart from law practice. The fourth provision requires that lawyers assess their client's conduct as well as their own, by prohibiting lawyers from counseling or assisting a client to engage in conduct the lawyer knows to be criminal or fraudulent, a topic we consider in Chapter 5.[4]

With respect to lawyer frauds on tribunals,[5] Model Rule 3.3 prohibits lawyers from making false statements in court,[6] depositions,[7] as well as in written submissions,[8] and applies whether the lawyer acts as a party or a representative of a party.[9]

put in outline

---

1. Model Rule 3.3(a)(1).
2. Model Rule 4.1(a).
3. Model Rule 8.4(c).
4. Model Rule 1.2(d), discussed in The Limits of the Law: Client Fraud, *infra* p.196.
5. The term "tribunal" has been applied to adjudicative or trial-type proceedings, including courts, as well as arbitration and mediation proceedings. Disc. Action Against Zotaley, 546 N.W.2d 16 (Minn. 1996). *But see* Model Rule 1.0(m), which excludes mediation from the definition of tribunals. Model Rule 3.9 extends the antifraud provision of Rule 3.3 to nonadjudicative proceedings such as legislative or administrative hearings.
6. In re Neitlich, 597 N.E.2d 425 (Mass. 1992).
7. In re Porter, 449 N.W.2d 713 (Minn. 1990) (false deposition testimony by a lawyer).
8. In re Meade-Murphy, 410 S.E.2d 99 (Ga. 1991) (false garnishment affidavits); In re Celsor, 499 S.E.2d 809 (S.C. 1998) (false notarization of client's signature).
9. People v. Kolbjornsen, 917 P.2d 277 (Colo. 1996) (lawyer testified falsely); In re Barratt, 663 N.E.2d 536 (Ind. 1996) (lawyer who was party to civil action testified falsely).

Lawyers have been disciplined under this rule for a wide variety of false statements, including the location of a client,[10] reasons the lawyer was unprepared,[11] and false offers of proof.[12]

Model Rule 4.1 applies to statements lawyers make to third parties in the course of representing clients outside of court. It prohibits intentional misstatements made by lawyers in documents, as in *Greycas*,[13] as well as oral statements made in the course of negotiating or closing a transaction or settlement.[14] Lawyers have been found to violate this rule by lying in the course of debt collection efforts, and acting as escrow agents.[15] Courts also have relied on Rule 4.1(a) to grant other relief, such as tort or contract damages.[16]

Model Rule 8.4(c) both overlaps with and expands upon the scope of Rules 3.3 and 4.1. It prohibits all fraud, deceit, dishonesty, and misrepresentation, whether before a tribunal or in other statements. For example, it applies to dishonesty with clients, such as billing or expense fraud[17] and lies about the status of a case.[18] It also applies to lying to other lawyers, including bar officials.[19] Beyond professional obligations not to lie to clients, other lawyers and bar officials, the private dishonest behavior of lawyers also can subject them to professional discipline. Examples include a lawyer who represented that he was a notary public when he knew he was not,[20] a lawyer who knowingly provided a false answer on a handgun permit application,[21] and another who postdated and then stopped payment on a check to a travel agent.[22] Lawyers also have been disciplined under this provision for deceit committed as a trustee[23] and as a corporate board member.[24] Because of its

10. In re Fletcher, 694 N.E.2d 1143 (Ind. 1998).
11. In re Chovanec, 640 N.E.2d 1052 (Ind. 1994) (lawyer who was not prepared falsely told court he was too sick to proceed); Disc. Proceedings Against Urban, 574 N.W.2d 651 (Wis. 1998) (lawyer who failed to prepare documents falsely told several probate judges that he was waiting for resolution of tax disputes).
12. *E.g.*, Disc. Proceedings of Phelps, 637 F.2d 171 (10th Cir. 1981); Edward L. Raymond, Jr., *Attorney's Misrepresentation to Court of His State of Health or Other Personal Matter in Seeking Trial Delay as Ground for Disciplinary Action*, 61 A.L.R.4th 1216 (1988).
13. *E.g.*, In re Apt, 946 P.2d 1002 (Kan. 1997) (real estate deed); In re Holland, 713 A.2d 227 (R.I. 1998) (foreclosure deed).
14. *E.g.*, Ky. Bar Assn. v. Geisler, 938 S.W.2d 578 (Ky. 1997) (lawyer settled personal injury case without disclosing client's death); In re Bennett, 501 S.E.2d 217 (Ga. 1998) (lawyer lied about representing a client in order to receive insurance settlement); Slotkin v. Citizens Casualty Co. of New York, 614 F.2d 301 (2d Cir. 1979) (defense lawyer who lied about excess insurance coverage liable for fraud); Disc. of Granham, 395 N.W.2d 80 (Minn. 1986) (lawyer in a real estate transaction lied to parties about sending their deed to the county recorder's office).
15. *E.g.*, In re Eliasen, 913 P.2d 1163 (Idaho 1996) (debt collection lawyer lied to debtor about consequences of debt); Disc. Action Against Pyles, 421 N.W.2d 321 (Minn. 1988) (lawyer serving as escrow agent promised to pay money when account had been closed).
16. *E.g.*, Copp v. Breskin, 782 P.2d 1104 (Wash. App. 1989) (law firm that assured expert witness he would be paid could not later claim it was client's responsibility); Malewich v. Zacharias, 482 A.2d 951 (N.J. App. 1984) (lawyer who promised but did not inform opposing counsel if case was not adjourned violated Model Rule 4.1, subjecting lawyer to damages).
17. Lisa G. Lerman, *Blue-Chip Bilking: Regulation of Billing and Expense Fraud by Lawyers*, 12 Geo. J. Legal Ethics, 205 (1999).
18. Atty. Grievance Commn. v. Lane, 790 A.2d 621 (Md. 2002); Welts' Case, 620 A.2d 1017 (1993).
19. Conduct of Wyllie, 957 P.2d 1222 (Or. 1998) (imposing two-year suspension for submitting fraudulent MCLE forms and failing to cooperate with investigation); In re Porter, 890 P.2d 1377 (Or. 1995) (imposing 63-day suspension for misrepresenting intentions to opposing counsel); In re Siegel, 627 A.2d 156 (N.J. 1993) (lawyer who defrauded his own law firm disbarred).
20. Conduct of Kluge, 27 P.3d 102 (Or. 2001).
21. In re Kotok, 528 A.2d 1307 (N.J. 1987).
22. Fla. Bar v. Schultz, 712 So. 2d 386 (Fla. 1998).
23. Disc. Counsel v. Kurtz, 693 N.E.2d 1080 (Ohio 1998).
24. Disc. Action Against Shinnick, 552 N.W.2d 212 (Minn. 1996).

breadth, courts often cite Rule 8.4(c) in combination with other rules in discipline cases.[25] In addition to expanding the scope of the disciplinary rules to all lawyer fraudulent conduct, the broad language of Model Rule 8.4(c) also "can be envisioned as designed to catch violations of *civil* law norms."[26] Together, these include all intentional, reckless, and negligent misrepresentations.[27] Judge Posner no doubt had this provision in mind when he referred Proud to the Illinois Disciplinary Commission.

The Law of Fraud

This brief review indicates that the lawyer code provisions incorporate the external law of fraud, which is vast, both in its depth and in its breadth. Morally, this law reflects the fact that most of us feel betrayed when deceived because liars seek a benefit by hiding the truth.[28] Sissela Bok calls liars "free riders": persons who hope to gain from everyone else's honesty while excusing their own deviation from social norms.[29] The law reflects this common sense morality and addresses deceit in a wide variety of contexts. This law includes criminal provisions and is also a significant source of tort liability.[30] Dishonest conduct also creates defenses to claims based upon contract and arising from other transactions. Fraud invalidates an otherwise lawful consent in tort, property, and contract law. As one early treatise writer put it: "Fraud vitiates everything, even judgments and orders of the Court."[31]

Historically, the law of fraud can be traced to biblical times.[32] The tort of misrepresentation developed in the thirteenth century with the writ of deceit, which was used to provide relief from deceptive practices before courts. The writ was extended to include out-of-court transactions and gradually developed into a civil remedy for fraudulent acts that caused actual harm.[33] The criminal law responded to frauds in court by prohibiting perjury, and responded to frauds on the public outside of court by creating the offense of common law cheat, committed by using a

---

25. *E.g.*, In re Mozingo, 497 S.E.2d 729 (S.C. 1998); In re Hyde, 950 P.2d 806 (N.M. 1997). The recent disbarment of F. Lee Bailey provides us with an example. Bailey's client entrusted millions of dollars of stock to him, which the client intended to forfeit to the United States. Bailey claimed most of the money as his fee, spent the money in defiance of several court orders, and then falsely denied that he was aware of the orders. When the client fired him, Bailey wrote *ex parte* letters to the judge disparaging the client in an effort to protect his interest in the money. The Florida Supreme Court disciplined him for violating Rule 8.3(c) and several other rules, finding that he "committed multiple counts of egregious misconduct, including offering false testimony, engaging in *ex parte* communications, violating a client's confidences, violating two federal court orders, and trust account violations, including commingling and misappropriation." Fla. Bar v. Bailey, 803 So. 2d 683 (Fla. 2001).

26. Geoffrey C. Hazard, Jr. & W. William Hodes, *The Law of Lawyering* §65.5 (3d ed., Aspen Publishers, Inc. 2002).

27. Some courts view "dishonesty" as connoting a lack of trustworthiness and integrity and therefore view it as being broader than "fraud" and "deceit." *E.g.*, In re Leonard, 784 P.2d 95, 100 (Or. 1989); In re Servance, 508 A.2d 178 (N.J. 1986) (lawyer represented investments were sound although "he knew little or nothing about them"). Other courts require that reckless or knowing misrepresentations be established to violate Rule 8.4(c). *E.g.*, Disc. Counsel v. Anonymous Atty. A, 714 A.2d 402 (Pa. 1998); Disc. Matter Involving West, 805 P.2d 351 (Alaska 1991).

28. Anthony Arlidge, Jacques Parry & Ian Gatt, *Arlidge & Parry on Fraud* 34 (2d ed., Sweet & Maxwell 1996).

29. Sissela Bok, *Lying: Moral Choice in Public and Private Life* 23 (2d ed., Vintage Books 1999).

30. *E.g.*, Melville M. Bigelow, *The Law of Fraud* (Little Brown 1877).

31. Sydney Edward Williams, *Kerr on Fraud and Mistake* 4 (Sweet & Maxwell Ltd. 1928). For an example of fraud vitiating a court judgment, *see* Spaulding v. Zimmerman, *infra* p.161.

32. Ellen S. Podgor, *Criminal Fraud*, 48 Am. U. L. Rev. 729, 736 (1999).

33. Thomas Atkins Street, *Foundations of Legal Liability* 375-376 (1906). Early cases included a lawyer who colluded with his adversary and a lawyer who failed to come to court, losing his client's case.

false weight or measure.[34] In the past century, frauds on courts, on the government, and between private parties all have become the subject of state and federal criminal law.[35] Many of these statutes also recognize civil actions by private parties.[36] State law, such as the Uniform Commercial Code, incorporates the common law of fraud in a number of provisions.[37] The common law also has expanded to provide tort damages for misrepresentations that cause harm, regardless of whether they were committed intentionally, recklessly, or negligently.[38]

The modern law of criminal fraud includes both generic and specific statutes.[39] The general provisions prohibit general conduct such as "conspiracy to defraud,"[40] mail fraud[41] and wire fraud.[42] The mail and wire fraud statutes prohibit "schemes to defraud" committed by using the mail, or wires, including radio and television. They have been used to address a wide variety of frauds, including insurance, securities, franchise, and even divorce mill fraud.[43] Specific fraud statutes have grown in the past century to address dishonest conduct that occurs in a specific context. Examples include access device fraud,[44] bankruptcy fraud,[45] bank fraud,[46] computer fraud,[47] food stamp fraud,[48] health care fraud,[49] marriage fraud,[50] securities fraud,[51] and tax fraud.[52] Most states also prohibit a wide variety of frauds, including insurance[53] and consumer fraud.[54]

misrepresentation

Modern law also provides for tort recovery for fraud. The tort of misrepresentation, as *Greycas* makes clear, includes intentional, reckless, and negligent misstatements of material fact that cause harm to foreseeable third parties who reasonably relied on the statements. In tort, "fraud" includes both intentional and reckless misrepresentation. To be liable for fraud, a defendant such as Proud does not have to intend harm to the plaintiff. It is enough if he knows he is lying, the misrepresentation

34. Stuart P. Green, *Lying, Misleading and Falsely Denying: How Moral Concepts Inform the Law of Perjury, Fraud, and False Statements*, 53 Hast. L.J. 159, 176, 185 (2001).
35. Podgor, *supra* note 32, at 736.
36. Dan B. Dobbs, *The Law of Torts* 1343 (West 2000).
37. Peter A. Alces, *The Law of Fraudulent Transactions* 1-7 (Warren Gorham & Lamont 1989).
38. *Restatement (Second) of Torts* §§525-552 (1977).
39. For a compilation of some of the major federal antifraud provisions, *see Lawyers' Desk Book on White-Collar Crime* 325-494 (Nat'l Legal Center for the Public Interest, Milton Eisenberg, ed., 1991).
40. 18 U.S.C. §371 (2000) ("Conspiracy to Commit Offense or to Defraud United States").
41. 18 U.S.C. §1341 (2000) ("Frauds and Swindles").
42. 18 U.S.C. §1342 (2000) ("Fraud by Wire, Radio or Television").
43. Podgor, *supra* note 32, at 753-754.
44. 18 U.S.C. §1029 (2000). Access devices include credit cards and personal identification numbers used to access accounts in order to obtain money or services. 18 U.S.C. §1029(e)(1). *See generally* Jerry Iannacci & Ron Morris, *Access Device Fraud and Related Financial Crimes* (CRC Press 2000).
45. 18 U.S.C. §157 (2000).
46. 18 U.S.C. §1344 (2000).
47. 18 U.S.C. §1030 (2000).
48. 7 U.S.C. §2015(b) (2000).
49. 18 U.S.C. §1347 (2000). *See generally* Carrie Valiant & David E. Matyas, *Legal Issues in Healthcare Fraud and Abuse: Navigating the Uncertainties* (2d ed., American Health Lawyers Association 1997).
50. 8 U.S.C. §1325(c) (2000). This statute prohibits "sham marriages" intended to evade immigration laws.
51. 15 U.S.C. §§78j(b), 78ff(a); 17 C.F.R. §240.10b-5. *See generally* Alan R. Bromberg & Lewis D. Lowenfels, *Bromberg & Lowenfels on Securities Fraud and Commodities Fraud* (2d ed. 2001).
52. 26 U.S.C. §7206 (2000). *See generally* Ian M. Comisky, Lawrence S. Feld & Steven M. Harris, *Tax Fraud and Evasion* (6th ed., Warren, Gorham & Lamont 1995).
53. H. Brent Brennenstuhl, *Negligent Misrepresentation as "Accident" or "Occurrence" Warranting Insurance Coverage*, 58 A.L.R.5th 483 (1998).
54. Debra T. Landis, *What Constitutes "Fraudulent" or "Unconscionable" Agreement or Conduct Within Meaning of State Consumer Credit Protection Act*, 42 A.L.R.4th 293 (1985).

concerns a material fact, and reasonable reliance causes harm. This explains why Proud was liable even though he did not intend to harm Greycas, and did not know about the liens on his brother-in-law's property. His knowing lie that he had conducted a UCC search, combined with reasonable reliance, was enough to subject him to liability. When a misrepresentation is fraudulent, the lawyer's liability extends beyond a client to all foreseeable third persons who reasonably relied on the false information.[55]

Proud's legal task in *Greycas*, drafting an opinion letter, also illustrates the vulnerability of lawyers to tort damages for negligent misrepresentation. Proud also could have been held liable for negligent (but not intentional) misrepresentation if he completed the search, but negligently examined the wrong files or database. In that case, he would not have lied about a material fact, but his legal opinion (that no liens existed on the property) would have been based on a failure to exercise reasonable care in obtaining the information.[56] In most jurisdictions, his liability would not extend to any person who reasonably relied on the information, but only to those in a limited class of persons "for whose benefit and guidance he intends to supply the information or knows the recipient intends to supply it."[57]

Although the law of misrepresentation usually requires an affirmative misrepresentation, there are a few occasions when failure to speak can create liability as well. Fiduciary duties create obligations to disclose, which means that lawyers, who owe fiduciary duties to clients, have affirmative duties to disclose material information to clients.[58] A duty to disclose also arises when previous statements have become untrue, misleading, or material.[59] For example, a lawyer may have a duty to disclose tax liens to a prospective purchaser at a foreclosure sale if the buyer was induced to bid by the lawyer's prior incomplete representations.[60]

Like everyone else, lawyers are subject to the law of fraud and misrepresentation. Lawyers who misrepresent a material fact can be held criminally or civilly accountable, or lose a benefit they lied to obtain. Beyond these consequences, lawyers, unlike others, can be professionally disciplined for acts of misrepresentation or dishonesty, whether they involve client representation or conduct of the lawyer apart from law practice. Understanding the law of fraud in any of its permutations can help you avoid suffering any or all of these adverse consequences.

55. *Restatement (Second) of Torts* §531 (1977); Ultramares Corp. v. Touche, Niven & Co., 174 N.E. 441 (N.Y. 1931).

56. *Restatement (Second) of Torts* §552 (1977). Most courts refuse to extend the concept of innocent misrepresentation to lawyers who are sued by nonclients, because the misrepresentations have not been made in a transaction between the parties as required by *Restatement (Second) of Torts* §552C. *E.g.*, Garcia v. Rodey, Dickason, Sloan, Akin & Robb, 750 P.2d 118 (1988); Pasternak v. Sagittarius Recording Co., 617 F. Supp. 1514 (E.D. Mich. 1985), *aff'd*, 816 F.2d 681 (6th Cir. 1987).

57. *Restatement (Second) of Torts* §552(2) (1977).

58. *E.g.*, Baker v. Dorfman, 239 F.3d 415 (2d Cir. 2000) (lawyer who lied in his resume about the extent of his legal experience to a client liable for fraud, including compensatory, emotional distress, and punitive damages). Clients have multiple remedies in such a case, including a suit for fraud, malpractice, and breach of fiduciary duty, as occurred in *dePape*.

59. *Restatement (Second) of Torts* §551 (1977). *E.g.*, In re Alcorn, 41 P.3d 600 (Ariz. 2002) (trial lawyers who made a secret agreement with opposing counsel to dismiss action against their client fined and disciplined for failing to disclose agreement to trial judge who indicated he did not want any sweetheart deals or anything "crafted" that "would be misleading" to him); People v. Rolfe, 962 P.2d 981 (Colo. 1998) (lawyer who stated that a social worker had "begun" her investigation of the matter, but failed to inform the court about the existence of social worker's letter that concluded no abuse could be substantiated, censured for violating Model Rule 3.3 (a)(1)).

60. Gerdin v. Princeton St. Bank, 371 N.W.2d 5 (Minn. App. 1985).

E. Ineffective Assistance of Counsel

Problem

4-6. Is Fox in trouble because he failed to inform a criminal defendant about a plea bargain offered by the prosecutor? What if Fox considered the offer "ridiculous"? What if the defendant was eventually convicted and sentenced to five years and the plea bargain would have resulted in a two-year sentence?

Consider: Model Rules 1.1-1.4, 2.1
Model Code DR 6-101

Roe v. Flores-Ortega

528 U.S. 470 (2000)

Justice O'CONNOR delivered the opinion of the Court.

In this case we must decide the proper framework for evaluating an ineffective assistance of counsel claim, based on counsel's failure to file a notice of appeal without respondent's consent.

I

The State of California charged respondent, Lucio Flores-Ortega, with one count of murder, two counts of assault, and a personal use of a deadly weapon enhancement allegation. In October 1993, respondent appeared in Superior Court with his court-appointed public defender, Nancy Kops, and a Spanish language interpreter, and pleaded guilty to second-degree murder. The plea was entered pursuant to a California rule permitting a defendant both to deny committing a crime and to admit that there is sufficient evidence to convict him. . . . In exchange for the guilty plea, the state prosecutor moved to strike the allegation of personal use of a deadly weapon and to dismiss both assault charges. On November 10, 1993, respondent was sentenced to 15 years to life in state prison. After pronouncing sentence, the trial judge informed respondent, "You may file an appeal within 60 days from today's date with this Court. If you do not have money for Counsel, Counsel will be appointed for you to represent you on your appeal."

Although Ms. Kops wrote "bring appeal papers" in her file, no notice of appeal was filed within the 60 days allowed by state law. (A notice of appeal is generally a one-sentence document stating that the defendant wishes to appeal from the judgment.) Filing such a notice is a purely ministerial task that imposes no great burden on counsel. During the first 90 days after sentencing, respondent was apparently in lockup, undergoing evaluation, and unable to communicate with counsel. About four months after sentencing, on March 24, 1994, respondent tried to file a notice of appeal, which the Superior Court Clerk rejected as untimely. Respondent sought habeas relief from California's appellate courts, challenging the validity of both his plea and conviction, and (before the California Supreme Court) alleging that Ms. Kops had not filed a notice of appeal as she had promised. These efforts were uniformly unsuccessful.

Respondent then filed a federal habeas petition pursuant to 28 U.S.C.

§2254, alleging constitutionally ineffective assistance of counsel based on Ms. Kops' failure to file a notice of appeal on his behalf after promising to do so. The United States District Court for the Eastern District of California referred the matter to a Magistrate Judge, who in turn ordered an evidentiary hearing on the limited issue of whether Ms. Kops promised to file a notice of appeal on respondent's behalf. At the conclusion of the hearing, the Magistrate Judge found:

"The evidence in this case is, I think, quite clear that there was no consent to a failure to file [a notice of appeal]....

"It's clear to me that Mr. Ortega had little or no understanding of what the process was, what the appeal process was, or what appeal meant at that stage of the game.

"I think there was a conversation [between Ortega and Kops] in the jail. Mr. Ortega testified, and I'm sure he's testifying as to the best of his belief, that there was a conversation after the pronouncement of judgment at the sentencing hearing where it's his understanding that Ms. Kops was going to file a notice of appeal.

"She has no specific recollection of that. However, she is obviously an extremely experienced defense counsel. She's obviously a very meticulous person. And I think had Mr. Ortega requested that she file a notice of appeal, she would have done so.

"But, I cannot find that he has carried his burden of showing by a preponderance of the evidence that she made that promise."...

The Court of Appeals for the Ninth Circuit reversed.... We granted certiorari... to resolve a conflict in the lower courts regarding counsel's obligations to file a notice of appeal....

II

In Strickland v. Washington, 466 U.S. 668 (1984), we held that criminal defendants have a Sixth Amendment right to "reasonably effective" legal assistance, and announced a now-familiar test: A defendant claiming ineffective assistance of counsel must show (1) that counsel's representation "fell below an objective standard of reasonableness," and (2) that counsel's deficient performance prejudiced the defendant. Today we hold that this test applies to claims, like respondent's, that counsel was constitutionally ineffective for failing to file a notice of appeal.

IAC Test (2)

A

As we have previously noted, "no particular set of detailed rules for counsel's conduct can satisfactorily take account of the variety of circumstances faced by defense counsel." Rather, courts must "judge the reasonableness of counsel's conduct on the facts of the particular case, viewed as of the time of counsel's conduct," and "judicial scrutiny of counsel's performance must be highly deferential."

We have long held that a lawyer who disregards specific instructions from the defendant to file a notice of appeal acts in a manner that is professionally unreasonable. This is so because a defendant who instructs counsel to initiate an appeal reasonably relies upon counsel to file the necessary notice. Counsel's failure to do so cannot be considered a strategic decision; filing a notice of appeal is a purely ministerial task, and the failure to file reflects inattention to the defendant's wishes. At the other end of the spectrum, a defendant who explicitly tells his attorney not to file an appeal plainly cannot later complain that, by following his instructions, his counsel performed deficiently. *See* Jones v. Barnes, 463 U.S. 745, 751, (1983) (accused has ultimate authority to make fundamental decision whether to take an appeal). The question presented in this case lies between those poles:

Is counsel deficient for not filing a notice of appeal when the defendant has not clearly conveyed his wishes one way or the other?...

In those cases where the defendant neither instructs counsel to file an appeal nor asks that an appeal not be taken, we believe the question whether counsel has performed deficiently by not filing a notice of appeal is best answered by first asking a separate, but antecedent, question: whether counsel in fact consulted with the defendant about an appeal. We employ the term "consult" to convey a specific meaning—advising the defendant about the advantages and disadvantages of taking an appeal, and making a reasonable effort to discover the defendant's wishes. If counsel has consulted with the defendant, the question of deficient performance is easily answered: Counsel performs in a professionally unreasonable manner only by failing to follow the defendant's express instructions with respect to an appeal.... If counsel has not consulted with the defendant, the court must in turn ask a second, and subsidiary, question: whether counsel's failure to consult with the defendant itself constitutes deficient performance. That question lies at the heart of this case: Under what circumstances does counsel have an obligation to consult with the defendant about an appeal?

Because the decision to appeal rests with the defendant, we agree with Justice Souter that the better practice is for counsel routinely to consult with the defendant regarding the possibility of an appeal. *See* ABA Standards for Criminal Justice, Defense Function §4-8.2(a) (3d ed. 1993). In fact, California imposes on trial counsel a per se duty to consult with defendants about the possibility of an appeal. *See* Cal. Penal Code Ann. §1240.1(a) (West Supp. 2000). Nonetheless, "prevailing norms of practice as reflected in American Bar Association standards and the like... are only guides," and imposing "specific guidelines" on counsel is "not appropriate." And, while States are free to impose whatever specific rules they see fit to ensure that criminal defendants are well represented, we have held that the Federal Constitution imposes one general requirement: that counsel make objectively reasonable choices.... We cannot say, as a constitutional matter, that in every case counsel's failure to consult with the defendant about an appeal is necessarily unreasonable, and therefore deficient.... For example, suppose that a defendant consults with counsel; counsel advises the defendant that a guilty plea probably will lead to a 2 year sentence; the defendant expresses satisfaction and pleads guilty; the court sentences the defendant to 2 years' imprisonment as expected and informs the defendant of his appeal rights; the defendant does not express any interest in appealing, and counsel concludes that there are no nonfrivolous grounds for appeal. Under these circumstances, it would be difficult to say that counsel is "professionally unreasonable,"... as a constitutional matter, in not consulting with such a defendant regarding an appeal. Or, for example, suppose a sentencing court's instructions to a defendant about his appeal rights in a particular case are so clear and informative as to substitute for counsel's duty to consult. In some cases, counsel might then reasonably decide that he need not repeat that information. We therefore reject a bright-line rule that counsel must always consult with the defendant regarding an appeal.

We instead hold that counsel has a constitutionally imposed duty to consult with the defendant about an appeal when there is reason to think either (1) that a rational defendant would want to appeal (for example, because there are nonfrivolous grounds for appeal), or (2) that this particular defendant reasonably demonstrated to counsel that he was interested in appealing. In making this determination, courts must take into account all the information counsel knew or should have known.... Although not determinative, a highly relevant factor in this inquiry will be whether the conviction follows a trial or a guilty plea, both because a guilty plea reduces the scope of potentially appealable issues and because such a plea may indicate that the defendant seeks an end to judicial proceedings. Even in cases when the defendant pleads guilty, the court must consider such factors as whether the defendant received the sentence bargained for as part of the plea and whether the plea expressly reserved or waived some or all appeal rights. Only by considering all relevant factors in a given case can a court properly determine whether a rational defendant would have desired an appeal or that the particular defendant sufficiently demonstrated to counsel an interest in an appeal.

Rather than the standard we announce today, Justice Souter would have us impose an "almost" bright-line rule and hold that counsel "almost always" has a duty to consult with a defendant about an appeal.... The relevant question is not whether counsel's choices were strategic, but whether they were reasonable. We expect that courts evaluating the reasonableness of counsel's performance using the inquiry we have described will find, in the vast majority of cases, that counsel had a duty to consult with the defendant about an appeal. We differ from Justice Souter only in that we refuse to make this determination as a per se (or "almost" per se) matter.

B

The second part of the *Strickland* test requires the defendant to show prejudice from counsel's deficient performance.

1

In most cases, a defendant's claim of ineffective assistance of counsel involves counsel's performance during the course of a legal proceeding, either at trial or on appeal. *See, e.g.*, 466 U.S. at 699 (claim that counsel made poor strategic choices regarding what to argue at a sentencing hearing); United States v. Cronic, 466 U.S. 648, 649-650 (1984) (claim that young lawyer was incompetent to defend complex criminal case); Penson v. Ohio, 488 U.S. 75, 88-89 (1988) (claim that counsel in effect did not represent defendant on appeal); Smith v. Robbins, 528 U.S. 259 (2000) (claim that counsel neglected to file a merits brief on appeal); Smith v. Murray, 477 U.S. 527, 535-536 (1986) (claim that counsel failed to make a particular argument on appeal). In such circumstances, whether we require the defendant to show actual prejudice—"a reasonable probability that, but for counsel's unprofessional errors, the result of the proceeding would have been different,"—or whether we instead presume prejudice turns on the magnitude of the deprivation of the right to effective assistance of counsel. That is because "the right to the effective assistance of counsel is recognized not for its own sake, but because of the effect it has on the ability of the accused to receive a fair trial, or a fair appeal." . . .

2

In some cases, however, the defendant alleges not that counsel made specific errors in the course of representation, but rather that during the judicial proceeding he was—either actually or constructively—denied the assistance of counsel altogether. "The presumption that counsel's assistance is essential requires us to conclude that a trial is unfair if the accused is denied counsel at a critical stage." The same is true on appeal. Under such circumstances, "no specific showing of prejudice [is] required," because "the adversary process itself [is] presumptively unreliable."

Today's case is unusual in that counsel's alleged deficient performance arguably led not to a judicial proceeding of disputed reliability, but rather to the forfeiture of a proceeding itself. According to respondent, counsel's deficient performance deprived him of a notice of appeal and, hence, an appeal altogether. Assuming those allegations are true, counsel's deficient performance has deprived respondent of more than a fair judicial proceeding; that deficiency deprived respondent of the appellate proceeding altogether. In *Cronic*, *Penson*, and *Robbins*, we held that the complete denial of counsel during a critical stage of a judicial proceeding mandates a presumption of prejudice because "the adversary process itself" has been rendered "presumptively unreliable."... The even more serious denial of the entire judicial proceeding itself, which a defendant wanted at the time and to which he had a right, similarly demands a presumption of prejudice. Put simply, we cannot accord any "'presumption of reliability,'" to judicial proceedings that never took place.

3

The Court of Appeals below applied a per se prejudice rule, and granted habeas relief based solely upon a showing that counsel had performed deficiently under its standard. Unfortunately, this per se prejudice rule ignores the critical requirement that counsel's deficient performance must actually cause the forfeiture of the defendant's appeal. If the defendant cannot demonstrate that, but for counsel's deficient performance, he would have appealed, counsel's deficient performance has not deprived him of anything, and he is not entitled to relief. *Cf.* Peguero v. United States, 526 U.S. 23, (1999) (defendant not prejudiced by court's failure to advise him of his appeal rights, where he had full knowledge of his right to appeal and chose not to do so). Accordingly, we hold that, to show prejudice in these circumstances, a defendant must demonstrate that there is a reasonable probability that, but for counsel's deficient failure to consult with him about an appeal, he would have timely appealed.

In adopting this standard, we follow the pattern established in *Strickland* and *Cronic*, and reaffirmed in *Robbins*, requiring a showing of actual prejudice (i.e., that, but for counsel's errors, the defendant might have prevailed) when the proceeding in question was presumptively reliable, but presuming prejudice with no further showing from the defendant of the merits of his underlying claims when the violation of the right to counsel rendered the proceeding presumptively unreliable or entirely nonexistent.... [W]e hold that when counsel's constitutionally deficient performance deprives a defendant of an appeal that he otherwise would have taken, the defendant has made out a successful ineffective assistance of counsel claim entitling him to an appeal.

We believe this prejudice standard breaks no new ground, for it mirrors the prejudice inquiry applied in Hill v. Lockhart, 474 U.S. 52 (1985), and Rodriquez v. United States, 395 U.S. 327 (1969). In *Hill*, we considered an ineffective assistance of counsel claim based on counsel's allegedly deficient advice regarding the consequences of entering a guilty plea. Like the decision whether to appeal, the decision whether to plead guilty (i.e., waive trial) rested with the defendant and, like this case, counsel's advice in *Hill* might have caused the defendant to forfeit a judicial proceeding to which he was otherwise entitled. We held that "to satisfy the 'prejudice' requirement [of *Strickland*], the defendant must show that there is a reasonable probability that, but for counsel's errors, he would not have pleaded guilty and would have insisted on going to trial." Similarly, in *Rodriquez*, counsel failed to file a notice of appeal, despite being instructed by the defendant to do so. We held that the defendant, by instructing counsel to perfect an appeal, objectively indicated his intent to appeal and was entitled to a new appeal without any further showing....

As with all applications of the *Strickland* test, the question whether a given defendant has made the requisite showing will turn on the facts of a particular case. Nonetheless, evidence that there were nonfrivolous grounds for appeal or that the defendant in question promptly expressed a desire to appeal will often be highly relevant in making this determination. We recognize that the prejudice inquiry we have described is not wholly dissimilar from the inquiry used to determine whether counsel performed deficiently in the first place; specifically, both may be satisfied if the defendant shows nonfrivolous grounds for appeal.... But, while the performance and prejudice prongs may overlap, they are not in all cases coextensive. To prove deficient performance, a defendant can rely on evidence that he sufficiently demonstrated to counsel his interest in an appeal. But such evidence alone is insufficient to establish that, had the defendant received reasonable advice from counsel about the appeal, he would have instructed his counsel to file an appeal.

By the same token, although showing nonfrivolous grounds for appeal may give weight to the contention that the defendant would have appealed, a defendant's inability to "specify the points he would raise were his right to appeal reinstated," will not foreclose the possibility that he can satisfy the prejudice requirement where there are other substantial reasons to believe that he would have appealed.... We similarly conclude here that it is unfair to require an indigent, perhaps pro se, defendant to demonstrate that his hypothetical appeal might have had merit before any advocate has ever reviewed the record in his case in search of potentially meritorious grounds for appeal. Rather, we require the defendant to demonstrate that, but for counsel's deficient conduct, he would have appealed.

III

The court below undertook neither part of the *Strickland* inquiry we have described, but instead presumed both that Ms. Kops was deficient for failing to file a notice of appeal without respondent's consent and that her deficient performance prejudiced respondent. Justice Souter finds Ms. Kops' performance in this case to have been "derelict," presumably because he believes that she did not consult with respondent about an appeal. But the Magistrate Judge's findings do not provide us with sufficient information to determine whether Ms. Kops rendered constitutionally inadequate assistance. Specifically, the findings below suggest that there may have been some conversation between Ms. Kops and respondent about an appeal (Ms. Kops wrote "'bring appeal papers'" in her file), but do not indicate what was actually said. Assuming, arguendo, that there was a duty to consult in this case, it is impossible to determine whether that duty was satisfied without knowing whether Ms. Kops advised respondent about the advantages and disadvantages of taking an appeal and made a reasonable effort to discover his wishes. Based on the record before us, we are unable to determine whether Ms. Kops had a duty to consult with respondent (either because there were potential grounds for appeal or because respondent expressed interest in appealing), whether she satisfied her obligations, and, if she did not, whether respondent was prejudiced thereby. Accordingly, the judgment of the Court of Appeals is vacated, and the case is remanded for further proceedings consistent with this opinion....

Justice SOUTER, with whom Justice STEVENS and Justice GINSBURG join, concurring in part and dissenting in part.

I join Part II-B of the Court's opinion, but I respectfully dissent from Part II-A. As the opinion says, the crucial question in this case is whether, after a criminal conviction, a lawyer has a duty to consult with her client about the choice to appeal. The majority's conclusion is sometimes; mine is, almost always in those cases in which a plea of guilty has not obviously waived any claims of error.[1] It is unreasonable for a lawyer with a client like respondent Flores-Ortega to walk away from her representation after trial or after sentencing without at the very least acting affirmatively to ensure that the client understands the right to appeal....

While *Strickland*'s disclaimer that no particular set of rules should be treated as dispositive respects the need to defer to reasonable "strategic choices" by lawyers, no such strategic concerns arise in this case. Strategic choices are made about the extent of investigation, the risks of a defense requiring defendant's testimony and exposure to cross-examination, the possibility that placing personal background information before a jury will backfire, and so on. It is not, however, an issue of "strategy" to decide whether or not to give a defendant any advice before he loses the chance to appeal a conviction or sentence. The concern about too much judicial second-guessing after the fact is simply not raised by a claim that a lawyer should have counseled her client to make an intelligent decision to invoke or forgo the right of appeal or the opportunity to seek an appeal.

The Court's position is even less explicable when one considers the condition of the particular defendant claiming *Strickland* relief here. Flores-Ortega spoke no English and had no sophistication in the ways of the legal system. The Magistrate Judge found that "it's clear... that Mr. Ortega had little or no understanding of what the process was, what the appeal process was, or what appeal meant." To condition the duty of a lawyer to such a client on whether, inter alia, "a rational defendant would want to appeal (for example, because there are nonfrivolous grounds for appeal)," is not only to substitute a harmless-error rule for a showing of reasonable professional conduct, but to employ a rule that simply ignores the reality that the constitutional norm must address.[2] Most criminal defendants, and certainly this one, will be

1. I say "almost" always, recognizing that there can be cases beyond the margin: if a legally trained defendant were convicted in an error-free trial of an open-and-shut case, his counsel presumably would not be deficient in failing to explain the options. This is not what we have here. Nor is this a case in which the judge during the plea colloquy so fully explains appeal rights and possible issues as to obviate counsel's need to do the same; such a possibility is never very likely and exists only at the furthest reach of theory, given a defendant's right to adversarial representation.... Finally, of course, there is no claim here that Flores-Ortega waived his right to appeal as part of his plea agreement; although he pleaded guilty, the record shows that he and the State argued before the trial court for different sentences, and he had little understanding of the legal system. The fact of the plea is thus irrelevant to the disposition of the case.

2. The Court holds that a duty to consult will also be present if "this particular defendant reasonably demonstrated to counsel that he was interested in appealing." Because for most defendants, and certainly

utterly incapable of making rational judgments about appeal without guidance. They cannot possibly know what a rational decisionmaker must know unless they are given the benefit of a professional assessment of chances of success and risks of trying. And they will often (indeed, usually) be just as bad off if they seek relief on habeas after failing to take a direct appeal, having no right to counsel in state post-conviction proceedings. . . .

The Law Governing Lawyers: *Criminal Defense Representation*

Roe offers us a portal through which to glimpse the reality of criminal defense representation in America. In most criminal cases today, defendants have a constitutional right to counsel, but the dream that every person charged with a serious crime "will be capably defended . . . sure of the support needed to make an adequate defense"[1] remains elusory. This note explores three legal remedies—ineffective assistance of counsel, malpractice, and discipline—theoretically available to defendants saddled with incompetent counsel. A closer look at the legal requirements necessary to qualify for these remedies illuminates why, in practice, they offer rare relief to criminal defendants and little incentive to incompetent defense counsel and the system that funds them.[2] Yet in spite of difficult doctrinal obstacles, the surprising number of cases that have granted relief points to the continuing pervasiveness of deficient representation.[3] This is especially true in death penalty cases where the costs of error are high, both to the accused and the government.[4]

The Right to Counsel

The constitutional right to effective assistance of counsel grew out of judicial recognition of a constitutional right to counsel.[5] This right to defense representation was recognized first in some,[6] and then in all felony cases, on the ground that defense lawyers "are necessities, not luxuries," both to protect against the risk of wrongful conviction and to provide due process of law.[7] Rights to counsel in juvenile and certain

---

for unsophisticated ones like Flores-Ortega who are unaware even of what an appeal means, such a demonstration will be a practical impossibility, I view the Court as virtually requiring the defendant to show the existence of some nonfrivolous appellate issue.

1. Anthony Lewis, *Gideon's Trumpet* 205 (Random House 1964).

2. Although no statistics about direct appeals exist, one study of habeas corpus review found that 99 percent of ineffective assistance claims were unsuccessful. Victor E. Flango & Patricia McKenna, *Federal Habeas Corpus Review of State Court Convictions*, 31 Cal. Western L. Rev. 237, 259-260 (1995).

3. *See* David Cole, *No Equal Justice* (The New Press 1999).

4. James S. Liebman, *The Overproduction of Death*, 100 Colum. L. Rev. 2030, 2052-2054 (2000) (state and federal courts reversed 68 percent of the capital judgments they fully reviewed from 1973-1995); Stephen B. Bright, *Counsel for the Poor: The Death Sentence Not for the Worst Crime but for the Worst Lawyer,* 103 Yale L.J. 1835 (1994). In capital cases, ineffective defense lawyers are part, but not the entire problem. *See* Edward Connors, Thomas Lundregan, Neal Miller & Tom McEwen, *Convicted by Juries, Exonerated by Science: Case Studies in the Use of DNA Evidence After Trial* (U.S. Dept. of Justice 1996).

5. For a history of the American tradition of an independent criminal defense bar, *see* Susan P. Koniak, *The Law Between the Bar and the State*, 70 N.C. L. Rev. 1389, 1448-1460 (1992).

6. Powell v. Ala., 287 U.S. 45, 60 (1932) (Sixth Amendment requires counsel if fundamental unfairness would result). *See also* Johnson v. Zerbst, 304 U.S. 458 (1938) (Sixth Amendment requires counsel in all federal criminal proceedings).

7. Gideon v. Wainwright, 372 U.S. 335, 344 (1963) (Sixth Amendment requires right to counsel in all felony cases).

misdemeanor cases followed.[8] Today, a person accused of a crime has a right to retained or appointed counsel in all "critical stages"[9] of criminal felony prosecutions and in misdemeanor cases where the defendant is sentenced to a term of imprisonment.[10] In addition, a person convicted of a crime has a Fourteenth Amendment right to counsel for capital sentencing hearings and for the first appeal of right.[11]

The recognition of these constitutional rights created the need for increasingly larger numbers of lawyers qualified to handle criminal trials. That need has accelerated over the past twenty years, as the number of those charged and convicted of crimes has increased exponentially.[12] Initially, judges relied on appointed counsel. The need for specialized expertise hastened the development of public defender offices. In the late 1960s, the American Bar Association drafted and promulgated basic standards for providing defense counsel, and for the administration of criminal justice, intended to assist lawyers in criminal practice.[13] Today, about two-thirds of those accused of a felony are poor enough to qualify for appointed counsel.[14] As a result, lawyers in public defender offices usually shoulder huge caseloads. At the same time, private appointed counsel, because of inadequate fee schedules, often face an "inherent conflict between remaining financially solvent and the defendant's need for vigorous advocacy.[15] These workload and financial pressures result in little or no incentive to provide effective legal assistance.

The Right to Effective Assistance of Counsel

Although the Supreme Court has always recognized that the Sixth Amendment requirement of counsel presupposed *effective* assistance of counsel, it did not provide a framework to evaluate the adequacy of counsel until 1984 in Strickland v. Washington[16] and United States v. Cronic.[17] In these opinions, the Court found that the Sixth Amendment right to effective assistance of counsel included the right

---

8. In re Gault, 387 U.S. 1 (1966) (Sixth Amendment requires counsel for juvenile proceedings that may lead to commitment in state institutions); Argersinger v. Hamlin, 407 U.S. 25 (1972) (Sixth Amendment requires counsel in misdemeanor cases where defendant is imprisoned); Ala. v. Shelton, 535 U.S. 654 (2002) (Sixth Amendment requires counsel in misdemeanor cases where defendant receives a suspended sentence).
9. Critical stages include preliminary hearings, some pretrial identification proceedings, and questioning by prosecutor or police designed to elicit inculpatory statements. Wayne R. LaFave, Jerold H. Israel & Nancy J. King, *Criminal Procedure* 569 (3d ed., West 2000).
10. Scott v. Ill., 440 U.S. 367 (1979) (counsel not required in misdemeanor cases where defendant fined but not imprisoned); Nichols v. United States, 511 U.S. 738 (1994) (defendant can receive enhanced term of incarceration under federal sentencing guidelines even if prior misdemeanor conviction resulted in a fine where no counsel was provided).
11. Douglas v. Cal., 372 U.S. 353 (1963); Ross v. Moffit, 417 U.S. 600 (1974) (no right to counsel for discretionary state appeals); Pa. v. Finley, 481 U.S. 551 (1987) (no right to counsel in state *habeas corpus* proceedings).
12. Arrest rates (per 100,000 inhabitants) have increased from 897 in 1971 to 954 in 1998, but were over 1100 from 1987 to 1995. Ann L. Pastore & Kathleen Maguire, eds., *Sourcebook of Criminal Justice Statistics* 339 (U.S. Dept. of Justice 1999). Incarceration rates (the number of prison and jail inmates per 100,000 U.S. residents) have more than doubled, from 313 in 1985 to 682 in 1999. *Id.* at 497.
13. ABA, *Standards for Criminal Justice, Providing Defense Services*, (3d ed. 1993); ABA, *Standards for Criminal Justice, The Defense Function* (3d ed. 1993).
14. Deborah H. Rhode, *In the Interest of Justice: Reforming the Legal Profession* 61 (Oxford 2000).
15. *Report of the Committee to Review the Criminal Justice Act*, reprinted at 52 Crim. L. Rptr. 2265, 2284-2285 (1993); Cole, *supra* note 3, at 81-89. *See also* Olive v. Maas, 811 So. 2d 644 (Fla. 2002) (lawyers in capital cases may petition the court for additional compensation beyond mandatory fee cap to preserve right to counsel).
16. 466 U.S. 668 (1984).
17. 466 U.S. 648 (1984).

to a lawyer who would play "a role that is critical to the ability of the adversarial system to produce just results."[18] As *Roe* indicates, it then established a two-prong test to assess whether a defendant had been deprived of the effective assistance of counsel. The first prong, "that counsel's representation fell below an objective standard of reasonableness," parallels the duty-breach analysis in legal malpractice suits. The second, "that counsel's deficient performance prejudiced the defendant" parallels the "but-for" actual causation requirement and functions like a harmless error analysis in criminal appeals. In subsequent case law, the Supreme Court has interpreted both prongs to create very difficult proof burdens for defendants.

Proving the first prong of the *Strickland* test, that counsel's performance fell below an objective standard, requires defendants first to identify the precise error or errors of defense counsel and then to present some kind of expert testimony that those errors should not have occurred.[19] To meet this requirement, a defendant may offer testimony from an expert criminal defense practitioner or rely on what the Supreme Court in *Roe* referred to as evidence of "prevailing norms of practice as reflected in American Bar Association standards and the like." *Roe* typifies cases that find such standards (including the Model Rules) relevant but not determinative of the appropriate standard of care.

The dissent and the lower court in *Roe* believed that such precision should not have been required because they deemed the errors of Mr. Flores-Ortega's lawyer to fit within a per se category that would allow the court to presume incompetence. The majority of the Supreme Court found such a per se rule too imprecise when reversal of a conviction was at stake, requiring instead a "circumstance-specific reasonableness inquiry." This difference of opinion reflects a decades-long debate about the value of per se categories of reversible error. Those who favor the per se approach agree with the dissent in *Roe* that a per se rule creates clear standards that protect indigent defendants from incompetence. Per se rules also prevent the time and cost of further fact-finding and act to counterbalance institutional incentives that foster incompetence, such as huge caseloads, poor funding, and lack of time. The absence of such a categorical approach gives defense counsel little incentive to honor basic fiduciary duties like consultation, and allows such errors by counsel to be labeled as "strategic choices." *Roe* is typical of a wide variety of cases that have rejected these per se rules because of a preference to uphold convictions unless obvious error can be demonstrated. As *Roe* indicates, unless the accused can show total deprivation of counsel, the Sixth Amendment requires no such per se rule.[20]

Even when expert testimony is presented, the first prong of the *Strickland* test has proved difficult to meet because *Strickland* also instructs courts to "indulge in a strong presumption that counsel's conduct falls within the wide range of reasonable professional assistance." This essentially invites courts to evaluate whether any established error was due to a strategic decision or came about because of an inexcusable lack of attentiveness.[21] If counsel errs following a reasonably complete

---

18. *Strickland*, 466 U.S. 668, 685. The defendant also has the alternative of representing herself, if she knowingly and intelligently waives her Sixth Amendment right. *See* Faretta v. Cal., 422 U.S. 806 (1975). Standby counsel can be appointed to assist the defendant. *Id.*; McKaskle v. Wiggins, 465 U.S. 168 (1984).
19. A claim of ineffective assistance often requires an evidentiary hearing to develop what happened and why. The remand in *Roe* seemed designed to accomplish this objective.
20. Of course, the states can impose per se rules as a matter of state constitutional or statutory law, as California had done in *Roe*. But such a breach will be irrelevant in a federal habeas corpus proceeding that alleges violation of the United States Constitution. *See, e.g.*, Bell v. Cone, 535 U.S. 685 (2002).
21. Joshua Dressler, *Understanding Criminal Procedure* 621-622 (3d ed., Lexis-Nexis 2002).

investigation of the law and facts, deference usually wins the day. For example, in Burger v. Kemp,[22] the defendant alleged ineffective assistance during a capital punishment sentencing hearing, where mitigating evidence is crucial to avoid the death penalty. The Court found that defense counsel could have performed a more complete investigation, but his less than thorough efforts constituted a reasonable strategic decision. Once again, only when the Court has found that a defense lawyer failed to discover or offer any evidence in a capital sentencing hearing will it find ineffective assistance.[23]

Where defendants have met the first prong of *Strickland*, they then face equal difficulty establishing the second prong, prejudice.[24] The *Roe* court equates this prong with the but-for causation test, which requires that the defendant show that the professional mistake of counsel actually caused a wrongful conviction, sentence, or failure to appeal.[25] For example, where an inadequate investigation caused defense counsel to fail to introduce powerful mitigating evidence in the penalty phase of a capital trial, the Court found that "had the jury been confronted with this considerable mitigating evidence, there is a reasonable probability that it would have returned with a different sentence."[26]

In other words, on the facts in *Roe,* even if the defendant can show that his counsel failed to consult with him, such an error will be deemed "harmless" unless he also can show that, if consulted, he would have appealed his conviction. The defendant in *Roe* argued that the magnitude of his counsel's error meant that prejudice (like incompetence) should be presumed. The Court agreed, but only if he could establish that there was "a reasonable probability that, but for counsel's deficient failure to consult with him about an appeal, he would have timely appealed."

On remand, the district court found that the public defender did not consult with Mr. Flores-Ortega, but if she had done so, she would have advised against filing an appeal because there were no nonfrivolous grounds to support it. The Ninth Circuit reversed, largely on the basis of the lawyer's handwritten note on the client's file to "bring appeal papers." The appellate court found that it was unlikely she would have written such a note unless Mr. Flores-Ortega had demonstrated an interest in filing an appeal. Once this was established, the court found as a matter of law that prejudice was presumed, because it led to forfeiture of the proceeding.[27]

Such a presumption of prejudice is not common, as the cases cited by the Supreme Court in *Roe* demonstrate. The Court has presumed prejudice where

---

22. 483 U.S. 776 (1987).
23. Williams v. Taylor, 529 U.S. 362 (2000); Silva v. Woodford, 279 F.3d 825 (9th Cir. 2002).
24. *E.g.,* Lockhart v. Fretwell, 506 U.S. 364 (1993) (counsel's incompetence, failing to raise an objection to inadmissible evidence in a sentencing hearing, did not prejudice the defendant because the claim was based on precedent that was subsequently overruled); St. v. Hongo, 706 So. 2d 419 (La. 1998) (failure to object to an erroneous jury instruction constituted harmless error); Melancon v. St., 66 S.W.3d 375 (Tex. App. 2001) (failure to subpoena alibi witness not prejudicial because witness' testimony not presented to prove it would have helped).
25. *E.g.,* Glover v. United States, 531 U.S. 198 (2001) (defense counsel's failure to group charges under Federal Sentencing Guidelines, which increased defendant's sentence by 6-21 months, constitutes prejudice).
26. Wiggins v. Smith, 123 S. Ct. 2527, 2543 (2003).
27. Flores-Ortega v. Roe, 39 Fed. Appx. 604 (9th Cir. 2002). The court ordered the district court to "issue a conditional writ of habeas corpus releasing Flores from state custody, unless the state permits Flores to initiate and prosecute a direct appeal from his conviction within a reasonable period of time as determined by the district court." *Id.* at 606. The dissent pointed out that "this rule implicates another question apparently unrecognized by the Court: has a petitioner . . . still suffered prejudice if he or she has no non-frivolous issue to raise on appeal?" *Id.* at 608.

counsel has been actually or constructively denied during a critical stage of the proceeding, or counsel's error led to its forfeiture, as in *Roe*. Other situations require proof of actual prejudice, that is, the circumstances must be "so likely to prejudice the accused that the cost of litigating their effect in a particular case is unjustified."[28] The "sleeping lawyer" cases illustrate the significant proof required to reach this threshold. When defense lawyers nap during a trial, courts have held that one episode of inattention or sleep does not alone rise to the level of a breakdown in the adversary process necessary to presume prejudice. However, repeated periods of unconsciousness may become the equivalent of no counsel at all so that prejudice can be presumed.[29]

One group of cases that ease the burden of proving prejudice in some situations involve defense counsel who labor under a conflict of interest. In Holloway v. Arkansas,[30] the Supreme Court held that the failure of a judge to inquire into a conflict raised by the defense counsel was enough to presume prejudice.[31] However, when the potential conflict is not raised on the record, prejudice is not presumed even where the defendant is unaware of a conflict known by the prosecutor, defense lawyer, and the trial judge.[32] Another situation involves "actual" conflicts of interest that compel defense counsel to compromise his or her duty of loyalty.[33] A defendant who can demonstrate that a specific actual conflict existed need prove only that it "adversely affected" the lawyer's performance at trial instead of the usual but-for prejudice requirement.[34]

This brief review of the law of ineffective assistance of counsel leads to the observation that despite frequent allegations of ineffective assistance of counsel in criminal appeals, very few defendants succeed in overturning convictions. Part of this is due to the fact that over 90 percent of criminal convictions (like *Roe*) result from a guilty plea,[35] a situation where far less scrutiny of counsel's performance is usually possible, and where, even when it is, courts have been especially reluctant to reverse convictions.[36] Of course, the difficulty of satisfying both prongs of the *Strickland* test means that very few convictions are reversed for trial error as well.[37]

---

28. United States v. Cronic, 466 U.S. 648, 658 (1984).
29. *See, e.g.*, Burdine v. Johnson, 231 F.3d 950 (5th Cir. 2000), *rev'd en banc*, 262 F.3d 336 (5th Cir. 2001); *cert. denied sub nom.* Cockrell v. Burdine, 535 U.S. 1120 (2002).
30. 435 U.S. 475 (1978).
31. The trial judge can grant a motion to disqualify defense counsel if necessary to guarantee a fair trial. *See, e.g.*, United States v. Edwards, 39 F. Supp. 2d 716 (M.D. La. 1999).
32. Mickens v. Taylor, 535 U.S. 162 (2002).
33. Cuyler v. Sullivan, 446 U.S. 335 (1980).
34. *See, e.g.*, Perillo v. Johnson, 205 F.3d 775 (5th Cir. 2000).
35. *See* Ann L. Pastore & Kathleen Maguire, eds., *Sourcebook of Criminal Justice Statistics* 429, 460 (U.S. Dept. of Justice 1999) (guilty or *nolo contendere* pleas occurred in 95 percent of federal criminal convictions and in 94 percent of state court convictions in 75 largest counties).
36. Bruce A. Green, *Judicial Rationalization for Rationing Justice: How Sixth Amendment Doctrine Undermines Reform*, 70 Fordham L. Rev. 1729 (2002).
37. Several Supreme Court justices have pointed out the "impotence" of the *Strickland* standard. In a dissent to a denial of certiorari, Justice Blackman chronicled the denial of ineffective assistance claims in death penalty cases where the clients were executed. The lawyers in these cases were addicted to drugs and incarcerated on federal drug charges a few weeks following the client's trial, suspended from practice on unrelated grounds, and unaware of a recent Supreme Court decision that would have reduced a client's death sentence. They committed errors such as failing to present any evidence at the penalty phase of the case and failing to appear for oral argument. One lawyer, asked to name a criminal case, could cite only "Miranda and Dred Scott," yet survived two challenges in state court. McFarland v. Scott, 512 U.S. 1256 (1994) (Blackmun, J., dissenting to the denial of *certiorari*). *See also* Mitchell v. Kemp, 483 U.S. 1026 (1987) (Marshall, J., dissenting to the denial of *certiorari*).

Despite these hurdles, state and federal cases do indicate several categories of blunder by defense counsel that constitute constitutional error in some cases. Most obvious is a lawyer who failed to inform his client that he no longer represented him in an appeal, essentially depriving the accused of any lawyer at all.[38] Similarly, when counsel is present, but fails to test the prosecution's case, for example by conceding the defendant's guilt to the jury when the defendant consistently maintained his innocence,[39] or by a total lack of effort and explanation,[40] courts have no trouble finding a violation. Following a fact-specific inquiry, courts also have found counsel ineffective for failing to adequately investigate facts,[41] finding or understanding relevant law,[42] giving defective advice about whether to testify or accept a plea bargain,[43] and for failing to object to improper evidence or procedures.[44]

Malpractice

Convicted defendants also can bring a legal malpractice action against their former lawyers.[45] Theoretically, such a case should not differ much from ordinary malpractice litigation. Yet courts have created some special doctrines that make malpractice recovery against criminal defense lawyers very difficult to obtain. Consider, for example, whether the facts in *Roe* would justify a successful malpractice claim.

In such a suit, Mr. Flores-Ortega would first be confronted with the defense of governmental immunity. Although the courts agree that publicly employed lawyers such as prosecutors should be protected from suit by governmental immunity,[46] they generally do not grant such immunity to appointed counsel[47] and are split

38. Fields v. Bagley, 275 F.3d 478 (6th Cir. 2001).
39. *E.g.*, St. v. Carter, 14 P.3d 1138 (Kan. 2000).
40. *E.g.*, People v. Bass, 636 N.W.2d 781 (Mich. App. 2001) (defense counsel had no memory of trial, lost most of the file, and offered no reason for failing to call witnesses); People v. Spann, 765 N.E.2d 1114 (Ill. App. 2002) (defense counsel failed to challenge defective indictment, move to quash arrest or suppress evidence, give opening statement or cross-examine the only witness against the defendant); Wenzy v. St., 855 S.W.2d 47 (Tex. App. 1993) (when not allowed to withdraw, counsel refused to take an active role in defense).
41. *E.g.*, Wesley v. St., 753 N.E.2d 686 (Ind. App. 2002) (failure to get psychiatric record of victim who had a history of false accusations); In re K.J.O., 27 S.W.3d 340 (Tex. App. 2000) (failure to conduct investigation into juvenile's defense); People v. Truly, 595 N.E.2d 1230 (Ill. App. 1992) (failure to investigate and present alibi).
42. *E.g.*, People v. Hayes, 593 N.E.2d 739 (Ill. App. 1992) (mistake as to the burden of proof of insanity defense); Stanford v. Stewart, 554 S.E.2d 480 (Ga. 2001) (appellate counsel failed to recognize the significance of an error in jury instructions); Pena-Mota v. St., 986 S.W.2d 341 (Tex. App. 1999) (failure to object to jury instruction resulted in a double jeopardy violation).
43. *E.g.*, Ross v. Kemp, 393 S.E.2d 244 (Ga. 1990) ("fractured" defense by two lawyers who failed to effectively help defendant decide whether to testify); St. v. Donald, 10 P.3d 1193 (Ariz. App. 2000) (receipt of a fair trial did not cure rejection of favorable plea bargain due to counsel's ineffective assistance); Crabbe v. St., 546 S.E.2d 65 (Ga. App. 2001) (defense counsel did not advise defendant that guilty pleas would remove the possibility of parole).
44. Kimmelman v. Morrison, 477 U.S. 365 (1986) (failure to move to suppress due to a total failure to conduct pretrial discovery); Dawkins v. St., 551 S.E.2d 260 (S.C. 2001) (failure to object to hearsay statements of victim); St. v. Crislip, 785 P.2d 262 (N.M. App. 1989) (failure to protect defendant against unsworn, out-of-court accusation by co-defendant); St. v. Scott, 602 N.W.2d 296 (Wis. App. 1999) (failure to object to prosecutor's breach of plea bargain); Alaniz v. St., 937 S.W.2d 593 (Tex. App. 1996) (failure to object to seating of a juror excused for cause); Evans v. St., 28 P.3d 498 (Nev. 2001) (failure to challenge prosecutor's remarks during penalty phase of trial); Ross v. St., 726 So. 2d 317 (Fla. App. 1999) (failure to object to improper remarks of prosecutor made during closing argument).
45. *See*, Gregory G. Sarno, *Legal Malpractice in Defense of Criminal Prosecution*, 4 A.L.R.5th 273 (1992).
46. *See, e.g.*, Durham v. McElynn, 772 A.2d 68 (Pa. 2001).
47. *See, e.g.*, Ferri v. Ackerman, 444 U.S. 193 (1979) (federal law does not immunize appointed defense lawyers); Mossow v. United States, 987 F.2d 1365 (8th Cir. 1993) (federal law does not bar malpractice suit against military lawyer).

about whether public defenders share similar immunity.[48] Thus, depending on the jurisdiction, his suit may be completely barred.[49]

Even if not barred by immunity, the statute of limitations also must be confronted. Most courts hold that the statute begins to run at the time of the reversal of the conviction.[50] Others prefer to reason that the cause of action accrues at the time of the conviction, or the last day services were rendered by the defendant lawyer, which may require the defendant to bring the civil suit while his appeal is pending in order to prevent the statute of limitations from running.[51]

If Mr. Flores-Ortega could surmount these defenses, proof of breach of a professional duty of care would not be as problematic. He most likely would be able to present expert testimony regarding the duty of trial counsel to consult and obtain adequately informed consent about whether to appeal a criminal conviction. In fact, his case arguably fits within the common-knowledge exception explained in *dePape,* because his lawyer apparently breached a basic fiduciary duty of consultation, obedience, or both.

On the other hand, proving causation in Mr. Flores-Ortega's case would be impossible in most jurisdictions. The majority of courts require proof of actual causation by showing that but for the error of counsel, the defendant would not have been convicted. These courts further require that the defendant's conviction must be reversed in order to show that his lawyer's error actually caused him harm.[52] This means that defendants like Mr. Flores-Ortega who pled guilty will be unable to recover for legal malpractice unless they can convince a court to vacate their guilty plea.[53] Some jurisdictions require more: an affirmative proof of innocence.[54] A few jurisdictions allow alternative proof, especially where the lawyer failed to inform the defendant of a plea bargain. They hold that defendant need only show that he would have accepted the plea if it had been presented to him.[55] In the few cases where causation can be shown, courts do not hesitate to approve recovery for emotional distress due to incarceration caused by the lawyer's negligence.[56]

---

48. *See, e.g.,* Barner v. Leeds, 13 P.3d 704 (Cal. 2000) (public defenders not protected by statutory immunity for discretionary acts); Johnson v. Halloran, 742 N.E.2d 741 (Ill. 2000) (public defenders not protected by sovereign immunity). *But see* Public and Appellate Defender Immunity Act, 745 ILCS 19/1 (2000); Wooton v. Vogele, 769 N.E.2d 889 (Ohio App. 2001) (Ohio Tort Immunity Statute protects public defenders from suit); Dziubak v. Mott, 503 N.W.2d 771 (Minn. 1993) (public defenders protected from suit by judicial immunity).

49. Public defenders have been held not to act under color of state law under 42 U.S.C. §1983 because they act contrary to the government's interests. Polk County v. Dodson, 454 U.S. 312 (1981); Miranda v. Clark County, Nevada, 319 F.3d 465 (9th Cir. 2003) (en banc) (assistant public defender who represented defendant in a traditional role, was not a state actor, but administrative head of public defender office, who determined how resources were spent was amenable to suit under §1983). *See also* Catherine R. Lazuran, *Court-Appointed Attorney as Subject to Liability Under 42 U.S.C. §1983,* 36 A.L.R. Fed. 594 (1978).

50. *E.g.,* Schreiber v. Rowe, 814 So. 2d 396 (Fla. 2002).

51. *E.g.,* Gebhardt v. O'Rourke, 510 N.W.2d 900 (Mich. 1994).

52. *Restatement (Third) The Law Governing Lawyers* §53, Comment d (2000).

53. *E.g.,* Gibson v. Trant, 58 S.W.3d 103 (Tenn. 2001); *cf.* Falkner v. Foshaug, 29 P.3d 771 (Wash. App. 2001) (*Alford* plea, which allowed client to plead guilty without admitting guilt, did not preclude later proof of client's innocence in malpractice action against defense counsel).

54. *E.g.,* Schreiber v. Rowe, 814 So. 2d 396 (Fla. 2002); Rodriguez v. Nielsen, 650 N.W.2d 237 (Neb. 2002) (allegation that defendant acted in self-defense does not establish actual innocence); Wiley v. County of San Diego, 966 P.2d 983 (Cal. 1998); Glenn v. Aiken, 569 N.E.2d 783 (Mass. 1991); Carmel v. Lunney, 511 N.E.2d 1126 (N.Y. 1987).

55. *See, e.g.,* Krahn v. Kinney, 538 N.E.2d 1058 (Ohio 1989); Levine v. Kling, 123 F.3d 580 (7th Cir. 1997) (innocence need not be shown where defendant alleges error such as failure to press double jeopardy defense).

56. *E.g.,* Holiday v. Jones, 264 Cal. Rptr. 448 (Cal. App. 1989); Gautam v. De Luca, 521 A.2d 1343 (N.J. Super. 1987); Bowman v. Doherty, 686 P.2d 112 (Kan. 1984).

Discipline

Of course, a defendant who complains about incompetent defense counsel also may file a disciplinary complaint against his former lawyer. In most of the cases were discipline has occurred, the lawyer exhibited a pattern practice of incompetence. For example, lawyers have been disciplined for abandoning criminal clients,[57] failing to appear after being retained to do so,[58] and repeated incompetence in handling criminal matters.[59] Very few cases address the issue of whether incompetence in one criminal matter also can constitute a violation of the Model Rules. In one case involving an experienced defense lawyer whose client's felony conviction was reversed for ineffective assistance of counsel, the Arizona Supreme Court suspended the lawyer for violating Model Rules 1.1, 1.3, and 1.4.[60] The court held that the prior finding of ineffective assistance did not necessarily indicate that the lawyer should be subject to discipline, but at the same time, it recommended that when such a determination has been made "trial judges and appellate courts look to the circumstances and determine whether there is arguably some infraction that should be called to the attention of the appropriate bar authorities."[61]

The State Bar of Arizona later clarified a similar obligation for prosecutors, judges, and other lawyers involved in a case where ineffective assistance is alleged or proved. The opinion responded to the practice of criminal defense lawyers who execute an affidavit acknowledging their own ineffective assistance to assist the defendant's appeal. It then applied Model Rule 8.3 to the situation, concluding that a lawyer who became aware of such an affidavit would have a duty to report the conduct to the disciplinary authorities if it raised a "substantial" question regarding the averring lawyer's "honesty, trustworthiness, or fitness as a lawyer in other respects."[62]

Criminal defense lawyers function in a system that is usually underfunded and overworked. They often labor in difficult conditions where the stakes are exceedingly high. The legal standards and the result in *Roe* illustrate that the law of ineffective assistance of counsel produces few counterincentives to these difficult circumstances. State courts have created similar rules in legal malpractice cases, making that remedy nearly as unavailable. Professional discipline, while possible, also rarely occurs. At the same time, the number of cases where allegations of ineffective assistance of counsel is alleged suggests continuing problems of quality in criminal defense representation, even where the high *Strickland* threshold cannot be met. Further, the number of cases that have granted relief (such as *Roe* on remand) despite these considerable proof burdens suggests a continuing wide range of egregious conduct and raises serious questions about whether our constitutional guarantee of right to counsel is an effective one.

57. *E.g.*, In re Mohling, 2001 Ariz. LEXIS 84.
58. In re Lewis, 689 A.2d 561 (D.C. App. 1997).
59. In re Fox, 522 N.E.2d 1229 (Ill. 1988); Atty. Grievance Commn. v. Middleton, 756 A.2d 565 (Md. 2000); Law. Disc. Bd. v. Turgeon, 557 S.E.2d 235 (W. Va. 2000).
60. In re Wolfram, 847 P.2d 94 (1993).
61. *Id.* at n.5.
62. St. Bar of Ariz. Op. 98-02.

Chapter Five

Confidentiality

A. Introduction

This chapter addresses another basic fiduciary duty: confidentiality. We begin by examining the scope of the professional obligation and proceed to consider exceptions to the doctrine. Throughout the chapter, we refer to both the fiduciary duty of confidentiality, which is found in the lawyer codes and the law of agency and the evidentiary client-lawyer or attorney-client privilege, which blocks disclosure of client confidences in litigation. These bodies of law parallel each other, as the chart below demonstrates.

CLIENT CONFIDENTIALITY

	Attorney-Client Privilege	Ethical/Fiduciary Duty
Source of Law:	Statute; Common Law of Evidence	Agency Law; CPR Canon 4 and MR 1.6, 1.8(b), 1.9, 1.18
Definition:	A communication made between privileged persons in confidence for the purpose of obtaining or providing legal assistance. RLGL §68	DR 4-101(A): Confidences and Secrets; MR 1.6(a): Information relating to the representation of a client
	Exceptions:	
Client Consent	Waiver: RLGL §§78-79	Client consent, express, or implied: MR 1.6(a)
Physical Harm	Future and continuing crime or fraud: RLGL §82	Future serious bodily harm (crime): MR 1.6(b)(1)
Lawyer Self-Defense	Lawyer self-protection: RLGL §83	Lawyer self-defense: MR 1.6(b)(5)

(continued)

CLIENT CONFIDENTIALITY *(continued)*

Seeking Advice		MR 1.6(b)(4)
Financial Harm/ Client Crime or Fraud	Future and continuing crime or fraud: RLGL §82	Future crime, prevent, rectify, mitigate substantial financial loss: MR 1.6(b)(2)(3)
Required by Law or Court Order	Invoking the privilege: RLGL §86	Required by law or court order: MR 1.6(b)(6)

In considering the law governing confidentiality, it is instructive to begin by examining the origins of and justifications for the professional obligation.

The recognition of confidentiality as a core professional obligation arose first in cases applying the attorney-client privilege, which Wigmore dates to the seventeenth century.[1] In the twentieth century, the idea that lawyers were forbidden from disclosing client confidences created the basis for the recognition in agency law that confidentiality is an integral part of the fiduciary duty that lawyer-agents owe to client-principals.[2] Both the attorney-client privilege and the agency duty of confidentiality then became incorporated into lawyer codes as the obligation not to divulge confidences and secrets of a client beginning about 100 years ago.[3]

Throughout this legal development, client-lawyer confidentiality has been justified by both a consequential utilitarian rationale as well as a rights or duty-based deontological rationale. The utilitarian view usually concludes that confidentiality promotes the greatest good for the greatest number because it is essential to making the legal system work. The deontological view holds that confidentiality promotes respect for human autonomy by guaranteeing trust and privacy in the client-lawyer relationship.

Utilitarians focus on consequences and argue that to do their job, lawyers need complete and accurate facts, both about what has already occurred and what the client contemplates doing. Lacking these facts, the lawyer will either apply the wrong law or give incorrect legal advice or both, which in turn will reduce public confidence in the legal system and in lawyers.[4] Others disagree, arguing that confidentiality actually harms society and the legal system. Jeremy Bentham, for example, argued that the attorney-client privilege should be abolished, because it obscured the truth from the courts and allowed those with something to hide to get away with unlawful behavior.[5]

---

1. Geoffrey C. Hazard, Jr., *An Historical Perspective on the Attorney-Client Privilege,* 66 Cal. L. Rev. 1061, 1069-1070 (1978).
2. The First Restatement of Agency included the prohibition against using or disclosing confidential information with other duties of loyalty. *Restatement (First) of Agency* §395 (1933).
3. ABA Canons of Professional Ethics, Canon 6 (1908) provided: "The obligation to represent the client with undivided fidelity and not to divulge his secrets or confidences forbids also the subsequent acceptance of retainers or employment from others in matters adversely affecting any interest of the client with respect to which confidence has been reposed."
4. *See* Deborah L. Rhode & Geoffrey C. Hazard, Jr., *Professional Responsibility and Regulation* 64 (Foundation Press 2002).
5. Jeremy Bentham, *Rationale of Judicial Evidence*, Vol. V, Book IX, Chap. 5, at 324 (1827). It is important to note that Bentham wrote at a time when no privilege against self-incrimination existed, so he reasoned that getting the facts from the lawyer was no different from getting them from the mouth of the defendant. *Id.*

Immanual Kant argued that deontological justifications, which rest on categorical imperatives or fundamental rights, should provide the yardstick for moral accountability. According to this notion, confidentiality obligations are essential to the purpose of the legal system, which exists to protect individual rights, such as the right to contract, own property, or due process. These rights, which respect persons by protecting individual liberty and promoting respect for human autonomy, easily can become vulnerable to infringement by powerful majoritarian interests of the government or others. Law and the legal system provide the means to ensure that such infringements are prevented or redressed.

Confidentiality promotes both the individual rights of citizens and the trust that is central to a client-lawyer relationship. It is a fundamental ethical value, just as loyalty and honesty are integral to a trusting relationship. Privacy also promotes the individual rights of citizens by giving them personal space to plan and define their own meaning in life. The government should not be able to infringe on that private space when it is used to promote that individual's autonomous sense of self. A lawyer's obligation not to share the information further protects the client's own defined sphere of privacy, which can become especially important when government compulsion through the legal system seeks to invade it.

The cases and other materials in this chapter illustrate how both of these justifications begin with an understanding of the inequality inherent in a client-lawyer relationship. On the one hand, clients have the power to select, supervise, and fire lawyers, and to decide when a lawyer acts in the client's best interests. On the other, once a client empowers a lawyer to handle a matter, the superior knowledge and skill of lawyers enable them to use or abuse client information for the benefit or themselves or others.

Problems

5-1. May Martyn & Fox tell a reporter for the Wall Street Journal, "If you want additional information about my client, you might want to check Vol. III, p.227 of the accountant's deposition on file in the county courthouse"?

5-2. Martyn & Fox represents Disney as undisclosed principal for the purpose of purchasing property to develop a new theme park. May Fox purchase adjacent property he discovers for sale during our representation of Disney?

Consider: Model Rules 1.6, 1.8(b)
Model Code DR 4-101
RLGL §60

Matter of Anonymous

654 N.E.2d 1128 (Ind. 1995)

PER CURIAM.

The respondent has been charged by the Disciplinary Commission in a verified complaint for disciplinary action with violating Rules 1.6(a), 1.8(b), and 1.16(a)(1) of the Rules of Professional Conduct for Attorneys at Law. . . .

As stipulated by the parties, the respondent was contacted by an individual (the "mother") in April or May of 1994 about representing her in seeking a child support arrearage due to her from the father ("father") of her minor child. She supplied the respondent with records concerning her support action and her income. Also included in these documents was information regarding the father, including the fact that he was going to receive a substantial inheritance, his salary, his place of employment, and his address.

In the course of reviewing the documents supplied by the mother, the respondent discovered that on July 17, 1992, a judgment had been entered against the mother and father, making them jointly liable for almost $4,500 of medical and hospital debt resulting from the birth of their child. The judgment was in favor of the local county welfare department. The respondent was, at all times relevant to this proceeding, the attorney under contract to represent the local county welfare department.

The respondent contacted the mother to determine if the medical debt owed to the welfare department had been paid by either her or the father. It had not. The respondent then informed the mother that he would be unable to represent her in the case because of a conflict of interest, then forwarded her documents, at her request, to another attorney. Thereafter, the respondent received approval from the local county welfare department to file a collection suit against the father, which he did on April 26, 1994. Later, the father's counsel joined the mother as a party defendant in the collection suit. The respondent ultimately obtained a summary judgment against the mother and the father. The respondent did not withdraw from the case after the mother was joined as a party defendant.

We find that, by revealing information relating to the representation of the mother without her consent, the respondent violated Ind. Professional Conduct Rule 1.6(a). By using that information to her disadvantage without her consent, he violated Prof. Cond. R. 1.8(b). By failing to withdraw as counsel for the local welfare department during the collection suit against the mother when such representation violated the Rules of Professional Conduct, the respondent violated Prof. Cond. R. 1.16(a)(1).

The respondent and the Commission agree that several factors mitigate the severity of his misconduct. They agree that the information gained by the respondent about the mother's case was readily available from public sources and not confidential in nature. The respondent declined to represent the mother after he learned of her outstanding debt owed to the county welfare department, and advised her to seek other counsel. He did not at any time request that she sign an employment agreement, seek a retainer fee, or otherwise charge her. We see no evidence of selfish motive on the respondent's part.

The respondent's use of information gained during consultations with the mother represents misuse of information entrusted to him in his capacity as a lawyer. Such conduct not only threatens harm to the individuals involved, but also erodes the integrity of the profession. At the same time, we note that the respondent appears to have had no sinister motives. For these reasons, we accept the agreed sanction of a private reprimand. . . .

B. Who Is Your Client?

Problems

5-3. Small Co. asks Martyn & Fox to bring a huge fraud and RICO claim against Magna Co. A conflicts check reveals that Martyn & Fox currently represents Big Bank in a $600 million loan to Magna that is scheduled to close next Tuesday. What can we tell Big Bank?

5-4. CEO of Megacorp asks Martyn & Fox to draft a deed transferring vacant land owned by Mega to CEO. "It's just a liability for Mega," CEO explains. What should we do?

Consider: Model Rules 1.4, 1.13, 1.18
Model Code DR 4-101
RLGL §§14, 15, and 20

Perez v. Kirk & Carrigan

822 S.W.2d 261 (Tex. App. 1991)

DORSEY, J. . . .

The present suit arises from a school bus accident on September 21, 1989, in Alton, Texas. Ruben Perez was employed by Valley Coca-Cola Bottling Company as a truck driver. On the morning of the accident, Perez attempted to stop his truck at a stop sign along his route, but the truck's brakes failed to stop the truck, which collided with the school bus. The loaded bus was knocked into a pond and 21 children died. Perez suffered injuries from the collision and was taken to a local hospital to be treated.

The day after the accident, Kirk & Carrigan, lawyers who had been hired to represent Valley Coca-Cola Bottling Company, visited Perez in the hospital for the purpose of taking his statement. Perez claims that the lawyers told him that they were his lawyers too and that anything he told them would be kept confidential.[1] With this understanding, Perez gave them a sworn statement concerning the accident.[2] However, after taking Perez' statement, Kirk & Carrigan had no further contact with him. Instead, Kirk & Carrigan made arrangements for criminal defense attorney Joseph Connors to represent Perez. Connors was paid by National Union Fire Insurance Company which covered both Valley Coca-Cola and Perez for liability in connection with the accident.

Some time after Connors began representing Perez, Kirk & Carrigan,

---

1. The summary judgment affidavits offered by Perez show the following with regard to Kirk & Carrigan's representations to him at the time they took Perez' statement:

> Ruben Perez—"Kirk told me that they were lawyers hired by Valley Coca Cola, that they were my lawyers too, and that whatever I told them would be kept confidential. I trusted what these lawyers told me and I answered their questions."
>
> Israel Perez (Ruben's father)—"Before beginning the questions, Kirk told Ruben that they were his lawyers, that they were going to help him, and that what they . . . learned from Ruben would be kept a secret."
>
> Joe Perez (Ruben's uncle)—"Before Ruben gave his statement, to Kirk, Kirk told Ruben that they (the lawyers) represented Valley Coca Cola, that they were Ruben's lawyers too, and that they did not want anyone else to come in the room and to talk to Ruben. Kirk then told Ruben 'I know you are in pain, but we need to ask you these questions. Your mind would be fresh to tell us what happened. This will be kept confidential. We will get you a copy of it tomorrow. We will not give anyone a copy. It is between you and us.' Kirk and Carrigan did not say that they represented only Valley Coca Cola."

2. Among other things, Perez generally stated that he had a previous accident while driving a Coke truck in 1987 for which he was given a citation, that he had a speeding violation in 1988, that he had not filled out a daily checklist to show that he had checked the brakes on the morning of the accident, that he had never before experienced problems with the brakes on his truck and that they were working just before the accident, that he tried to apply the brakes to stop the truck, but that the brakes for the trailer were not working at all to stop the truck (the truck had two sets of brakes: the ones for the cab worked; the ones for the trailer did not and the greater weight of the trailer had the effect of pushing the entire truck, even though the cab brakes were working), that Perez did not have enough time to apply the emergency brakes, and that there was nothing the managers or supervisors at Valley Coca-Cola could have done to prevent the accident.

without telling either Perez or Connors, turned Perez' statement over to the Hidalgo County District Attorney's Office. Kirk & Carrigan contend that Perez' statement was provided in a good faith attempt to fully comply with a request of the district attorney's office and under threat of subpoena if they did not voluntarily comply. Partly on the basis of this statement, the district attorney was able to obtain a grand jury indictment of Perez for involuntary manslaughter for his actions in connection with the accident.[3]...

...Perez asserted numerous causes of action against Kirk & Carrigan for breach of fiduciary duty, negligent and intentional infliction of emotional distress, violation of the Texas Deceptive Trade Practices Act and conspiracy to violate article 21.21 of the Texas Insurance Code....

With regard to Perez' cause of action for breach of the fiduciary duty of good faith and fair dealing, Kirk and Carrigan contend that no attorney-client relationship existed and no fiduciary duty arose, because Perez never sought legal advice from them.

An agreement to form an attorney-client relationship may be implied from the conduct of the parties. Moreover, the relationship does not depend upon the payment of a fee, but may exist as a result of rendering services gratuitously.[4]

In the present case, viewing the summary judgment evidence in the light most favorable to Perez, Kirk & Carrigan told him that, in addition to representing Valley Coca Cola, they were also Perez' lawyers and that they were going to help him. Perez did not challenge this assertion, and he cooperated with the lawyers in giving his statement to them, even though he did not offer, nor was he asked, to pay the lawyers' fees. We hold that this was sufficient to imply the creation of an attorney-client relationship at the time Perez gave his statement to Kirk & Carrigan.

The existence of this relationship encouraged Perez to trust Kirk & Carrigan and gave rise to a corresponding duty on the part of the attorneys not to violate this position of trust. Accordingly, the relation between attorney and client is highly fiduciary in nature, and their dealings with each other are subject to the same scrutiny as a transaction between trustee and beneficiary. Specifically, the relationship between attorney and client has been described as one of *uberrima fides*, which means, "most abundant good faith," requiring absolute and perfect candor, openness and honesty, and the absence of any concealment or deception. In addition, because of the openness and candor within this relationship, certain communications between attorney and client are privileged from disclosure in either civil or criminal proceedings under the provisions of Tex. R. Civ. Evid. 503 and Tex. R. Crim. Evid. 503, respectively.[5]

There is evidence that Kirk & Carrigan represented to Perez that his statement would be kept confidential.

3. By his summary judgment affidavit offered in support of Perez, Joseph Connors stated that, in his professional opinion as a board certified criminal law specialist, if he had known that the statement had been provided and had been able to have Perez explain his lack of training or knowledge about the brake system to the grand jury, Perez would not have been indicted for manslaughter. Ruben Perez also stated in his affidavit that Valley Coca-Cola Bottling Company had not given him any instruction in brake inspection, maintenance, or use in an emergency situation.

4. An attorney's fiduciary responsibilities may arise even during preliminary consultations regarding the attorney's possible retention if the attorney enters into discussion of the client's legal problems with a view toward undertaking representation.

5. Disclosure of confidential communications by an attorney, whether privileged or not under the rules of evidence, is generally prohibited by the disciplinary rules governing attorneys' conduct in Texas.

Later, however, without telling either Perez or his subsequently-retained criminal defense attorney, Kirk & Carrigan voluntarily disclosed Perez' statement to the district attorney. Perez asserts in the present suit that this course of conduct amounted, among other things, to a breach of fiduciary duty.

Kirk & Carrigan seek to avoid this claim of breach, on the ground that the attorney-client privilege did not apply to the present statement, because unnecessary third parties were present at the time it was given. However, whether or not the Rule 503 attorney-client privilege extended to Perez' statement, Kirk & Carrigan initially obtained the statement from Perez on the understanding that it would be kept confidential. Thus, regardless of whether from an evidentiary standpoint the privilege attached, Kirk & Carrigan breached their fiduciary duty to Perez either by wrongfully disclosing a privileged statement or by wrongfully representing that an unprivileged statement would be kept confidential. Either characterization shows a clear lack of honesty toward, and a deception of, Perez by his own attorneys regarding the degree of confidentiality with which they intended to treat the statement....

In addition, however, even assuming a breach of fiduciary duty, Kirk & Carrigan also contend that summary judgment may be sustained on the ground that Perez could show no damages resulting from the breach. Kirk & Carrigan contend that their dissemination of Perez' statement could not have caused him any damages in the way of emotional distress, because the statement merely revealed Perez' own version of what happened. We do not agree. Mental anguish consists of the emotional response of the plaintiff caused by the tortfeasor's conduct. It includes, among other things, the mental sensation of pain resulting from public humiliation.

Regardless of the fact that Perez himself made the present statement, he did not necessarily intend it to be a public response as Kirk & Carrigan contend, but only a private and confidential discussion with his attorneys. Perez alleged that the publicity caused by his indictment, resulting from the revelation of the statement to the district attorney in breach of that confidentiality, caused him to suffer emotional distress and mental anguish. We hold that Perez has made a valid claim for such damages....

[The Court reversed the summary judgment rendered against Perez on all counts and remanded for trial.]

Lawyers' Roles: *The Directive Lawyer and Fiduciary Duty*

Viewed from the client's perspective, the lawyers in *Perez* breached all four basic fiduciary duties that lawyers owe clients. They violated their client's confidentiality by disclosing his confidences to the prosecutor without his consent. They disregarded loyalty by favoring one client's interests over another, and by pursuing their own interests. They acted incompetently by failing to recognize clear legal limits to their conduct. They ignored basic obligations to communicate by failing to obtain Mr. Perez's informed consent about key issues that surfaced during the representation.

See Supreme Court of Texas, Rules Governing the State Bar of Texas art. X, §9 (Disc. R. of Prof. Conduct) Rule 1.05. In addition, the general rule is that confidential information received during the course of any fiduciary relationship may not be used or disclosed to the detriment of the one from whom the information is obtained. Numed, Inc. v. McNutt, 724 S.W.2d 432, 434 (Tex. App.—Fort Worth 1987, no writ) (former employee is obligated not to use or divulge employer's trade secrets).

All of this caused incalculable damage to Mr. Perez, who was 25 years old when the accident occurred, and was just beginning to realize his life-long ambition to be a truck driver like his father. The accident killed 21 of the 81 children on the bus, who drowned in a water-filled pit after the truck driven by Mr. Perez pushed it off the road. Following the accident, Mr. Perez spent three-and-one-half years awaiting trial in a self-imposed bedroom prison as penance, never leaving his house.[1] At trial on the criminal charges, Mr. Perez was acquitted on all 21 counts after only 4 hours of jury deliberation.[2] Today, he continues to suffer from brain injuries he received in the accident that reduced his intellectual capacity to that of a fifth-grader and is permanently unable to work.[3]

The behavior of Mr. Perez's lawyers indicates that they somehow misconstrued their role in representing their client, thinking that they owed him none of the fiduciary duties they assumed even though they had promised all of them. They apparently saw their client as a legal problem, rather than a person with a legal problem. Perhaps they viewed the law as a means to restore some semblance of social order disrupted by the tragic deaths of the truck-bus collision. They appear to have acted as directors, who arrogantly imposed their own private judgment about the matter on a trusting, unsuspecting client. They perceived themselves as professional authorities in charge of directing a relationship, rather than agents with fiduciary duties subject to their client's instructions. Judge John Noonan calls this "underidentification with a client."[4]

Fiduciary Duties

The client-lawyer relationship is one of the oldest examples of an agency relationship. An agent (the lawyer) agrees to act on behalf of a principal (the client). The agreement between principal and agent confers power and imposes several fiduciary duties on the agent, all designed to ensure that the agent acts on the principal's behalf and subject to the principal's control.[5] Agency law long has recognized the problem of generalized expertise: the tendency of experts to transfer their professional expertise to a general control over all decisions and aspects of the relationship. Professionals easily can assume that professional competence equates with the ability to know what is best for clients. To ensure that the client's moral values control the agency relationship, lawyer agents owe client principals four basic fiduciary duties: competence, communication, confidentiality, and loyalty or proper response to conflicts of interest. All these duties steer lawyers away from benefiting someone other than the client. They also protect clients from lawyers who might take advantage of the trust and power reposed in them.

1. Maggie Rivas, *Truck Driver Says He Spent Years After Bus Crash Doing Penance; He Went into Self-Imposed Exile at Home as Punishment*, Dallas Morning News, at 1A (May 7, 1993).
2. Maggie Rivas, *Trucker Absolved of Bus Deaths; '89 Alton Tragedy Killed 21 Students*, Dallas Morning News, at 1A (May 6, 1993).
3. *A Tragedy Remembered*, Dallas Morning News, at 17A (Sept. 21, 1999).
4. John T. Noonan Jr., *The Lawyer Who Overidentifies with his Client*, 76 Notre Dame L. Rev. 827, 833 (2001). Other commentators identify this defect as "paternalism" or "parentalism." *See, e.g.*, Richard A. Wasserstrom, *Lawyers as Professionals: Some Moral Issues*, 5 Human Rights 1, 19 (1975). We would prefer, with Professors Shaffer and Cochran, not to see parenthood as a morally objectionable image. Parents are supposed to limit a child's freedom for the child's benefit. The problem is that lawyers should not act like parents, because they should not assume that they know what is best for the client. Thomas L. Shaffer & Robert F. Cochran, Jr., *Lawyers, Clients, and Moral Responsibility* 6 (1994).
5. *Restatement (Third) of Agency* §1.01 (Tentative Draft No. 2, 2001).

The first, and most obvious breach of fiduciary duty in *Perez* was the blatant violation of the duty of confidentiality.[6] Mr. Perez's lawyers offered to represent him, promised him confidentiality, obtained his statement about the accident, and then turned it over to a hostile third person (the prosecutor) without their client's consent. The court makes the point that the lawyers' promise both to represent Mr. Perez's interests and to keep his confidences encouraged him to confide in the lawyers. This alone is sufficient to establish an agency relationship, complete with fiduciary duties imposed by law. Mr. Perez's lawyers appeared to understand confidentiality (because they promised it), but they failed to understand the extent of their obligation under the professional rules.

Why did these lawyers make such an obvious mistake? One answer might be found in their breach of the fiduciary duty of loyalty.[7] Mr. Perez's lawyers initially were hired by an insurance company, which covered both Valley Coca-Cola and Mr. Perez. Prior to representing Mr. Perez, they no doubt believed that the interests of both clients were consistent, that is, that the accident was not the fault of either client. In his statement, however, Mr. Perez admitted to several possible violations of company policy, such as a prior speeding violation, as well as failure to check the truck's brakes the day of the accident. Mr. Perez's lawyers then appeared to realize that they had a conflict of interest: protecting the interests of their first client (Valley Coca-Cola) might require that they take action contrary to the interest of their second client (Perez). This may explain why they "had no further contact with him" and made arrangements for another lawyer to defend Mr. Perez's interests.

At this point, however, Mr. Perez's lawyers seemed to assume that they had no further duties of any kind to their now former client. Perhaps they misunderstood their initial promise of confidentiality to Mr. Perez, thinking that it legally included only "privileged" communications, rather than an obligation not to use or reveal information relating to the representation without his consent.[8] They apparently ignored the fact that this fiduciary obligation continues without limit after the client-lawyer relationship ends as well.[9] They also seemed to be oblivious to Model Rule 1.9, which prohibits not only use or disclosure of a former client's confidential information, but also any *potential* use or disclosure of former client confidences. It does this by prohibiting any representation of a subsequent client in the same or substantially related matter without the consent of the former client.[10] Together, these provisions meant that after the representation ceased, Mr. Perez's lawyers were prohibited both from using or disclosing his confidences and unless Mr. Perez consented, from continuing their representation of Valley Coca Cola. Yet, apparently no such consent was sought.

There are at least two possible explanations for this behavior. First, their errors may indicate confusion about their duties following the joint representation. The lawyers' continuing loyalty to Valley Coca Cola, combined with their own interest in staying in the matter, simply may have blinded them to their competing continuing

6. *Restatement (Third) The Law Governing Lawyers* §60 (2000); *Restatement (Second) of Agency* §§395-396 (1958); Model Rule 1.6, 1.8(b), 1.9(a).

7. *Restatement (Third) The Law Governing Lawyers* §121 (2000); *Restatement (Second) of Agency* §387 (1958); Model Rule 1.7.

8. Model Rule 1.6(a), 1.8(b).

9. Model Rule 1.9(c); *Restatement (Third) The Law Governing Lawyers* §60(1)(a) (2000) (prohibiting use or disclosure that would "adversely affect a material interest of the client" "during or after the representation of a client").

10. Model Rule 1.9(a) and (b).

confidentiality duty to Mr. Perez. Second, Mr. Perez's lawyers may have ignored their continuing obligation of confidentiality simply because they did not know it existed. If so, they probably breached another fiduciary duty, the duty of competence.[11] If they mistakenly believed that withdrawing from the representation of Mr. Perez meant no further duty to a former client, or that they had the prerogative to disclose client information they deemed not privileged, they had either never heard of, or never understood, the meaning of either their own professional code provisions or case law that imposed a similar obligation as a matter of fiduciary duty.[12] *Perez* illustrates that both agency law and the professional codes impose fiduciary duties on lawyers whether they understand them or not.

Finally, at several key points, Mr. Perez's lawyers appear to have breached their most basic fiduciary duty: communication.[13] Lawyers and other agents must keep clients informed so that clients can make critical decisions and agents can obey them.[14] In *Perez,* there is no indication that the lawyers disclosed in their first meeting with Perez that certain conflicts of interest might develop, which could require them to withdraw from representing either Mr. Perez, or Valley or both. Second, it is not clear whether they told Mr. Perez that they no longer represented him, or why. Third, they did not seek Mr. Perez's consent to disclosing his statement to the prosecutor; something that his subsequent lawyer claimed could have avoided 21 criminal indictments. These breaches of the duty of communication deprived Mr. Perez of the right to make critical decisions, and meant that his lawyers also breached the fiduciary duty of obedience.

The Problem with Directive Behavior

Judge Noonan recalls a strikingly similar incident that became the focus of future Justice Louis Brandeis' Senate confirmation hearings.[15] Brandeis recommended that a client assign his business assets for the benefit of creditors. He did not tell the client that this assignment constituted an act of bankruptcy, or that Brandeis' law firm represented one of the creditors. Five days later, Brandeis, representing the creditor, instituted involuntary bankruptcy proceedings against the client. Brandeis later claimed that he had been "counsel to the situation," not counsel to the clients. Compare Judge Noonan's characterization of Brandeis' conduct with the acts of the lawyers in *Perez.*

> Underidentification is here, no doubt, carried to the point of caricature. The lawyer does not remember that he took the client as a client. The lawyer does not give the client the most elementary advice about the consequences of the act the lawyer is advising him to perform. The lawyer represents another client and, acting for that client, puts his unremembered client into bankruptcy. At the heart of the situation is the lawyer's desire

---

11. *Restatement (Third) The Law Governing Lawyers* §§48-50 (2000); *Restatement (Second) of Agency* §379 (1958); Model Rule 1.1.

12. The Texas equivalent of Model Rule 1.9 was adopted Oct. 17, 1989, about one month after the accident, and became effective Jan. 1, 1990. Tex. Govt. Code Ann. T.2, Subt. G, App. A, Art. 10, §9, R. 1.09 (2001). The comments to the rule indicate it was based on prior case law, including a case decided about six months before the accident where the Texas Supreme Court mandated that this rule be applied to all former client representations. *See* NCNB Tex. Bank v. Coker, 765 S.W.2d 398 (Tex. 1989).

13. *Restatement (Third) The Law Governing Lawyers* §20 (2000); *Restatement (Second) of Agency* §381 (1958).

14. *Restatement (Third) The Law Governing Lawyers* §§21, 22 (2000); *Restatement (Second) of Agency* §§383, 385 (1958).

15. Judge Noonan points out that this episode was far from typical, but was the "most damaging episode" that Brandeis' enemies could cull from a distinguished 30-year career in law practice. Noonan, *supra* note 4, at 829.

> to abstract himself from the needs and pressures of a particular individual in order to go on and straighten out a mess. In some other world, law could be practiced in that fashion. It is not the way law has been generally practiced in ours.[16]

Perhaps Mr. Perez's lawyers believed that they too were hired "to straighten out a mess," or to direct or implement their own view of social retribution. If so, they made all the mistakes that Noonan attributes to Brandeis. Mr. Perez's lawyers recognized the legal significance of his failure to check the brakes, just as Brandeis knew the legal significance of the assignment for the benefit of creditors. They then transformed themselves into agents for their other client, Valley Coca-Cola, just as Brandeis became the advocate for his other creditor-client. Mr. Perez's lawyers gave his confidential statement to the prosecutor's office, just as Brandeis used his client's confidences against him to force a bankruptcy proceeding. Brandeis and Mr. Perez's lawyers became lawyers for the situation, rather than the client. Each apparently assumed that his private judgment about the matter could dominate, even at the direct expense of his fiduciary duties. Conveniently, sacrificing one client's goals to the lawyers' view of the greater good also happened to dovetail neatly with the lawyers' own interests in continuing to represent the first client.

Lawyers who abstract themselves from clients like this ignore fiduciary duty and often assume the role of an authority who knows best and directs the relationship. Like Brandeis, they act as judges when they are called on to advise and advocate. We have already seen examples of this kind of behavior in the last few chapters. The lawyers in those cases who acted incompetently also incorrectly took for granted that they could define the scope, outcome, or process of a client-lawyer representation. For example, Busch in Chapter 2 waived his client's rights to collect a judgment without her consent, failed to file an appeal as she directed, and lied to both his client and a judge about the status of the matter. In Chapter 4, the Togstads' lawyer also incorrectly assumed he could define whether he had taken them on as clients. Similarly, Dr. dePape's lawyer failed to explain his client's options, and Mr. Flores-Ortega's lawyer in *Roe* failed to facilitate his decision about appealing his case.

The law has long recognized fiduciary duty as the cure for this misguided private judgment. Clients bestow power on lawyers to handle a matter for them. This power allows lawyers to manipulate the representation for their own or another's benefit. The lawyer unwilling to offer legally permissible options from among which the client will decide allows her own subjective moral or legal formulation to determine the client's fate. Fiduciary duty curbs this power by guarding against both intentional and unintentional exploitation by agents. For lawyers, developing experience with similar matters over time can lead even the best intentioned to control the service clients receive because they assume that most clients want a similar result. Yet, even when this is generally true, each client is entitled to the right to choose which legal options to pursue and how far to pursue them.

Directive behavior is most endemic and least justified when lawyers represent individual clients unfamiliar with the law. As in *Perez,* these clients often face litigation concerning past actions. Professors Freedman and Smith focus on advocacy in litigation as the primary circumstance justifying zealous advocacy. Here, where clients are most vulnerable, lawyers should be most diligent in guarding against preempting their client's moral judgments. Outside of litigation, Freedman and Smith argue that lawyers should view the advice they give about contracts and wills

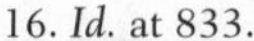

16. *Id.* at 833.

"with an adversary's eye" as well.[17] This advice would have helped avoid the harm foisted on Mr. Perez and Brandeis' client.

In the end, Mr. Perez settled his lawsuit against his former lawyers for an undisclosed amount, and also reached a settlement of $462,619 against Valley Coca-Cola, which paid over $133 million in overall settlements to those injured in the tragedy, largely because of its failure to properly maintain the truck's brakes. The company that manufactured the bus also paid $23 million to accident victims, because of improperly designed hatches that did not allow the children to escape as water filled the bus.[18]

The result in *Perez* is consistent with the result in *Busch, Togstad, dePape,* and *Roe*: lawyers will be liable for tort damages and subject to professional discipline when they breach fiduciary duties, regardless of their intent. On the other hand, lawyers who learn and implement into their practice the four basic fiduciary duties of competence, communication, confidentiality, and loyalty should not fall prey to professional discipline or subject themselves to the civil relief afforded to clients whose lawyers betray them. They also will move toward respecting client interests, and begin to think of themselves as collaborators in representing clients, rather than as authorities or judges who know best.

C. Attorney-Client Privilege

Problems

5-5. At Client's request, Fox returns goods stolen by Client to the police. Can Fox be forced to testify about the identity of Client?

5-6. Martyn interviews 25 maintenance workers to determine how our client is disposing of used oil. Can Martyn be forced to testify about those conversations?

5-7. Can Martyn & Fox turn over notes of 25 interviews with maintenance workers to the Justice Department as part of a settlement on behalf of our corporate client?

5-8. Can Fox testify to privileged communications with old CEO of our client, if new CEO of our corporate client directs him to do so?

5-9. Can Martyn & Fox's client be required to testify where he was on the night in question if he already told us this information in a privileged discussion?

5-10. Can Martyn be forced to testify about a conversation she had alone with an investment banker to understand what was required for our corporate client to pursue a merger?

5-11. Client dies of natural causes one week after he confides to Fox that he committed a crime for which some other person currently is serving a 15-year sentence. Can Fox disclose the confession?

5-12. Martyn & Fox are ready to try the High Energy Case against Arthur Touche and five former High Energy directors. Fox's secretary hands him a thick fax with a cover page that says: "To all Defense Counsel. Privileged and Confidential. Summary of Decision Quest's Jury Profile." What should Fox

17. Freedman & Smith, p.5 *supra.*

18. *Truck Driver Settles Suit from Crash that Killed 21 Schoolchildren in '89*, Dallas Morning News, at 29A (May 26, 1994).

do? What if the fax reveals misconduct by the other side? What if the same document is sent to us in a plain brown envelope with a note "Knew you'd find this interesting"?

Consider: Model Rules 3.4(c) and (e), 4.4
Model Code DR 7-106(A), (C)(1)
RLGL §§68-93

Hughes v. Meade

453 S.W.2d 538 (Ky. 1970)

CLAY, Commissioner.

This is an original proceeding for a writ of prohibition against the Honorable N. Mitchell Meade, Judge of the Fayette Circuit Court. Petitioner, an attorney, seeks to restrain the respondent from enforcing a contempt ruling entered against him because of his refusal to answer a question as a witness in a criminal trial. Petitioner was not a party to, nor did he represent anyone as an attorney in such proceeding.

The proceeding in which he was called as a witness was the trial of one Williams on a criminal charge involving the theft of an IBM typewriter. Petitioner had participated in the return of an IBM typewriter to the Lexington Police Department. His testimony with respect thereto, and so much thereof as is pertinent to the question presented, is as follows:

Q "Would you tell the jury the circumstances and how you happened to deliver that typewriter?

A "Well, a certain party called me and employed me because of, first of all, my relationship with the Lexington Police Department, which is very good, and I do entirely criminal law and know all of the policemen and members of the Police Department, and asked me if I could get some property returned without getting me involved in it.

Q "Without getting who involved—you or him?

A "Without getting me involved....
"So I called Morris Carter, who was then either assistant chief or a major. I know Morris well, and I asked him, I said, 'Morris, are you all interested in getting some stolen property back?' And he said 'Yes we are,' and he said, 'What is it?' I said 'I don't know, I have no idea,' and I said, 'Morris, I don't want to get involved in this thing, I don't want to be called as a witness, all I want to do is get this taken care of.' He said, 'All right, how is it going to be delivered?' And I said, 'Well, I'm watching the cartoons.' It was Saturday morning, and I said, 'Somebody is going to leave it on my front porch,' and the shades were down and I heard a car come up and left, and I called Morris back and I said 'Morris, it's out here,' and he said, 'Okay I'll send somebody out to get it,'....
(Officer Sparks arrived and a taped box was opened disclosing a typewriter.)...

Q "And then did Officer Sparks take possession of the box and the typewriter at that time?

A "He took it and took it down town, I guess.

Q "And do I understand you correctly that during the period of time from when it arrived and up until Officer Sparks got there you had not seen this typewriter?

A "Never seen it.

Q "Was this delivered on your property?

A "Yes, it was.

Q "You didn't want to see who it was?

A "No, that's right.

Q "You say that the certain party called you and employed you to do what you have just described and said you did, is that correct?

A "Yes, sir.

Q "Was this the extent of your employment?

A "Yes, sir.

Q "Have you been paid for that service?

A "Yes, sir.

Q "And I'll ask you now if you will tell us the name of the individual who employed you?

A "I refuse to answer."

Petitioner was found in contempt of court for failure to identify the person who had called him. It is his contention that this information was a privileged communication under KRS 421.210(4), and the trial court improperly sought to compel him to disclose it. That subsection of the statute provides (insofar as pertinent):

> "No attorney shall testify concerning a *communication* made to him, *in his professional character*, by his client, or his advice thereon without the client's consent; . . . ." (Emphasis added.)

This statutory provision generally conforms to the common law policy and principle of attorney-client privilege (developed since 1800) and it is generally recognized in the United States. See 8 Wigmore, Evidence §2291 (McNaughton rev. 1961). This same author thus phrases the principle:

> "(1) Where legal advice of any kind is sought (2) from a professional legal adviser in his capacity as such, (3) the communications relating to that purpose, (4) made in confidence (5) by the client, (6) are at his instance permanently protected (7) from disclosure by himself or by the legal adviser, (8) except the protection be waived." . . .

Wigmore states the object:

> ". . . is to protect the perfect working of a special relation, wherever confidence is a necessary feature of that perfect working. . . ."

. . . On the other hand, if the act in question fairly cannot be said to fall within the scope of professional employment, the privilege cannot be invoked. As said in 97 C.J.S. Witnesses §280, page 793:

> "Neither is there any privilege as to communications with reference to a matter in which the attorney acts, not in his professional capacity, but merely as an agent or attorney in fact, or in which the attorney acts merely as a depositary or as a trustee, particularly where he has instructions to deliver the instrument deposited to a third person, or abstracter of titles."

Returning to the facts of this case, it is the opinion of the majority of the court that whether or not a bona fide attorney-client relationship existed between the petitioner and the undisclosed person, the principal transaction involved, i.e., the delivery of stolen property to the police department, was not an act in the professional capacity of petitioner nor was it the rendition of a legal service. He was acting as an agent or conduit for the delivery of property which was completely unrelated to legal representation. While repose of confidence in an attorney is something much to be desired, to use him as a shield to conceal transactions involving stolen property is beyond the scope of his professional duty and beyond the scope of the privilege.

Dean v. Dean

607 So. 2d 494 (Fla. App. 1992)

FARMER, J.

The issue raised here is whether the attorney-client privilege can be used to prevent the disclosure of the identity of a person who had previously consulted an attorney regarding the return of stolen property belonging to one of the parties in a civil case. As we explain along the way, under the circumstances of this case the privilege bars such disclosure.

The facts are unusual, to say the least. During the pendency of the Deans' dissolution of marriage case, the husband's place of business was allegedly burgled, resulting in the loss of two duffel bags containing various personal items belonging to husband's daughter, and from $35,000 to $40,000 in cash. Sometime after the theft, an unidentified person telephoned Krischer at his office. He related the conversation as follows:

> I received a telephone call from an individual who knew that I was an attorney that was involved in the Baltes[1] matter and the individual asked me for advice with regard to returning property. I advised this person on the telephone that the experience that I have had in the State Attorney's office was that the best avenue was to turn the property over to an attorney and let the attorney bring it to the State Attorney's office or to the law enforcement.

At another point, Krischer added:

> Obviously I have been through this before and I knew all the questions to ask this person and I got all the responses back which indicates to me this person knew I was a lawyer, was asking for legal advice and did not want their identity revealed.

Krischer met twice and had one telephone conversation with this person. Nearly six weeks after the second meeting, the two duffel bags containing only the daughter's personal property were delivered to Krischer's office by someone who told his receptionist that he "would know what they are." No cash was included with the returned items. Krischer then delivered the bags to the police, telling them that they "may have some connection with" husband.

In a twist of irony, these events came to light through Krischer's former secretary, who had also by then become a client of husband's lawyer. Soon after, husband's lawyer served Krischer with a subpoena for a deposition, seeking the identity of Krischer's contact. Krischer asserted the privilege at the deposition. Husband then moved to compel the testimony. After a hearing, the trial court granted the motion....

Krischer's testimony makes plain the intent of his client....

> "The individual called—I can expedite this if I can state a couple of things, judge. I had obviously been through this previously in another case. I was well aware of what was needed to be established in order to protect this client. I inquired of this client if that individual knew I was an attorney. That individual indicated that they did. I inquired if they were seeking legal

1. This refers to a widely publicized case in which a hit-and-run driver consulted Krischer for advice and, afterwards, Krischer asserted the attorney-client privilege when asked to disclose the name of the driver. The fact that the person consulting Krischer in this case referred to the widely publicized case when Krischer kept the identity of his contact confidential might reasonably be taken as evidencing the contact's strong interest in confidentiality.

> advice. They indicated that they did. They discussed a legal problem with me. I gave them legal advice.
>
> A condition precedent to this person discussing the legal problem with me was that I not divulge their identity. . . ."

The trial judge . . . decided that the issue should turn on what the undisclosed person sought to accomplish with the legal advice obtained, or on what Krischer did in conesquence of the contact, citing . . . Hughes v. Meade, 452 S.W.2d 538 (Ky. 1970). . . .

[W]e conclude that the trial court has misinterpreted the privilege and the policies underlying it. . . . It is indisputable that his contact . . . consulted Krischer as an attorney. It is indisputable that the client sought legal advice about a specific matter. It is indisputable that the specific matter concerned a crime that had already been committed, not a planned or future act which might be a crime. And it is indisputable that the client insisted on confidence.

The focus, as we have seen from the common law development of the privilege and our own Florida Evidence Code section 90.502 definition of "client," is on the perspective of the person seeking out the lawyer, not on what the lawyer does after the consultation. As we have also seen, it has long been understood that the representation of a client in a court or legal proceeding is not indispensable for the invocation of the privilege. That Krischer's client sought him out for purely legal advice was enough. Legal advice, after all, is by itself a legal service. It is not necessary to the existence of the privilege that the lawyer render some additional service connected with the legal advice. Nor, as we know, is it even necessary that the lawyer appear in court or contemplate some pending or future legal proceeding.

And even if it were, the engagement of an attorney to effect the return of stolen property should certainly qualify. Surely there is a public purpose served by getting stolen property in the hands of the police authorities, even if the identity of the thief is not thereby revealed. Here the consultation resulted in exactly that. Krischer advised his client to turn over the property to the state attorney or the police. A lawyer's advice can be expected to result in the return of the property if the confidentiality of the consultation is insured.

. . . [T]he mere fact that the consulted attorney acts as a "conduit" for the return of stolen property does not support the conclusion that the attorney has engaged in unprotected consultation with the person seeking the advice.[7] A legal service has been rendered just as surely as when the lawyer represents the accused thief in a criminal trial. . . .

Upjohn Co. v. United States

449 U.S. 383 *(1981)*

Justice Rehnquist delivered the opinion of the Court. . . .

Petitioner Upjohn Co. manufactures and sells pharmaceuticals here and abroad. In January 1976 independent accountants conducting an audit of one of Upjohn's foreign subsidiaries discovered that the subsidiary made payments to or for the benefit of

---

7. In contrast, the attorney in Hughes testified that he had been contacted only to deliver stolen property to the police. His contact reached out for him, not because he was a lawyer, but instead because he was a good friend of many members of the police force. Unlike Krischer here, he gave no legal advice. His services amounted to a phone call informing the police that, if they were interested in the return of stolen property, they could pick it up on the attorney's front porch. Not surprisingly, the court determined that this attorney rendered no legal service, and therefore could not invoke the attorney-client privilege.

foreign government officials in order to secure government business. The accountants so informed petitioner Mr. Gerard Thomas, Upjohn's Vice President, Secretary, and General Counsel. Thomas is a member of the Michigan and New York Bars, and has been Upjohn's General Counsel for 20 years. He consulted with outside counsel and R. T. Parfet, Jr., Upjohn's Chairman of the Board. It was decided that the company would conduct an internal investigation of what were termed "questionable payments." As part of this investigation the attorneys prepared a letter containing a questionnaire which was sent to "All Foreign General and Area Managers" over the Chairman's signature. The letter began by noting recent disclosures that several American companies made "possibly illegal" payments to foreign government officials and emphasized that the management needed full information concerning any such payments made by Upjohn. The letter indicated that the Chairman had asked Thomas, identified as "the company's General Counsel," "to conduct an investigation for the purpose of determining the nature and magnitude of any payments made by the Upjohn Company or any of its subsidiaries to any employee or official of a foreign government." The questionnaire sought detailed information concerning such payments....

On March 26, 1976, the company voluntarily submitted a preliminary report to the Securities and Exchange Commission on Form 8-K disclosing certain questionable payments.... A copy of the report was simultaneously submitted to the Internal Revenue Service, which immediately began an investigation to determine the tax consequences of the payments. Special agents conducting the investigation were given lists by Upjohn of all those interviewed and all who had responded to the questionnaire.... [but an IRS demand for the questionnaires themselves was opposed by Upjohn on the ground of privilege and work product]....

Federal Rule of Evidence 501 provides that "the privilege of a witness . . . shall be governed by the principles of the common law as they may be interpreted by the courts of the United States in light of reason and experience." The attorney-client privilege is the oldest of the privileges for confidential communications known to the common law. 8 J. Wigmore, Evidence §2290 (McNaughton rev. 1961). Its purpose is to encourage full and frank communication between attorneys and their clients and thereby promote broader public interests in the observance of law and administration of justice. The privilege recognizes that sound legal advice or advocacy serves public ends and that such advice or advocacy depends upon the lawyer's being fully informed by the client. As we stated last Term in Trammel v. United States, 445 U.S. 40, 51 (1980): "The lawyer-client privilege rests on the need for the advocate and counselor to know all that relates to the client's reasons for seeking representation if the professional mission is to be carried out." And in Fisher v. United States, 425 U.S. 391, 403 (1976), we recognized the purpose of the privilege to be "to encourage clients to make full disclosure to their attorneys."...

The Court of Appeals, however, considered the application of the privilege in the corporate context to present a "different problem," since the client was an inanimate entity and "only the senior management, guiding and integrating the several operations, . . . can be said to possess an identity analogous to the corporation as a whole." The first case to articulate the so-called "control group test" adopted by the court below, Philadelphia v. Westinghouse Electric Corp., 210 F. Supp. 483, 485 (E.D. Pa.), *petition for mandamus and prohibition denied sub nom.* General Electric Co. v. Kirkpatrick, 312 F.2d 742 (3d Cir. 1962), *cert. denied*, 372 U.S. 943 (1963), reflected a similar conceptual approach.

> Keeping in mind that the question is, Is it the corporation which is seeking the lawyer's advice when the asserted privileged communication is made?, the most satisfactory solution, I think, is that if the employee making the communication, of whatever rank he may be, is in a position to control or even to take a substantial part in a decision about any action which the corporation may take upon the advice of the attorney,... then, in effect, *he is (or personifies) the corporation* when he makes his disclosure to the lawyer and the privilege would apply. (Emphasis supplied.)

Such a view, we think, overlooks the fact that the privilege exists to protect not only the giving of professional advice to those who can act on it but also the giving of information to the lawyer to enable him to give sound and informed advice....

In the case of the individual client the provider of information and the person who acts on the lawyer's advice are one and the same. In the corporate context, however, it will frequently be employees beyond the control group as defined by the court below—"officers and agents... responsible for directing [the company's] actions in response to legal advice"—who will possess the information needed by the corporation's lawyers. Middle-level—and indeed lower-level—employees can, by actions within the scope of their employment, embroil the corporation in serious legal difficulties, and it is only natural that these employees would have the relevant information needed by corporate counsel if he is adequately to advise the client with respect to such actual or potential difficulties....

The control group test adopted by the court below thus frustrates the very purpose of the privilege by discouraging the communication of relevant information by employees of the client to attorneys seeking to render legal advice to the client corporation. The attorney's advice will also frequently be more significant to noncontrol group members than to those who officially sanction the advice, and the control group test makes it more difficult to convey full and frank legal advice to the employees who will put into effect the client corporation's policy.

The narrow scope given the attorney-client privilege by the court below not only makes it difficult for corporate attorneys to formulate sound advice when their client is faced with a specific legal problem but also threatens to limit the valuable efforts of corporate counsel to ensure their client's compliance with the law. In light of the vast and complicated array of regulatory legislation confronting the modern corporation, corporations, unlike most individuals, "constantly go to lawyers to find out how to obey the law".... The test adopted by the court below is difficult to apply in practice, though no abstractly formulated and unvarying "test" will necessarily enable courts to decide questions such as this with mathematical precision. But if the purpose of the attorney-client privilege is to be served, the attorney and client must be able to predict with some degree of certainty whether particular discussions will be protected. An uncertain privilege, or one which purports to be certain but results in widely varying applications by the courts, is little better than no privilege at all. The very terms of the test adopted by the court below suggest the unpredictability of its application. The test restricts the availability of the privilege to those officers who play a "substantial role" in deciding and directing a corporation's legal response....

The communications at issue were made by Upjohn employees to counsel for Upjohn acting as such, at the direction of corporate superiors in order to secure legal advice from counsel. As the

Magistrate found, "Mr. Thomas consulted with the Chairman of the Board and outside counsel and thereafter conducted a factual investigation to determine the nature and extent of the questionable payments *and to be in a position to give legal advice to the company with respect to the payments.*" (Emphasis supplied.) Information, not available from upper-echelon management, was needed to supply a basis for legal advice concerning compliance with securities and tax laws, foreign laws, currency regulations, duties to shareholders, and potential litigation in each of these areas. The communications concerned matters within the scope of the employees' corporate duties, and the employees themselves were sufficiently aware that they were being questioned in order that the corporation could obtain legal advice. The questionnaire identified Thomas as "the company's General Counsel" and referred in its opening sentence to the possible illegality of payments such as the ones on which information was sought. A statement of policy accompanying the questionnaire clearly indicated the legal implications of the investigation. The policy statement was issued "in order that there be no uncertainty in the future as to the policy with respect to the practices which are the subject of this investigation." It began "Upjohn will comply with all laws and regulations," and stated that commissions or payments "will not be used as a subterfuge for bribes or illegal payments" and that all payments must be "proper and legal." Any future agreements with foreign distributors or agents were to be approved "by a company attorney" and any questions concerning the policy were to be referred "to the company's General Counsel." This statement was issued to Upjohn employees worldwide, so that even those interviewees not receiving a questionnaire were aware of the legal implications of the interviews. Pursuant to explicit instructions from the Chairman of the Board, the communications were considered "highly confidential" when made, and have been kept confidential by the company. Consistent with the underlying purposes of the attorney-client privilege, these communications must be protected against compelled disclosure.

The Court of Appeals declined to extend the attorney-client privilege beyond the limits of the control group test for fear that doing so would entail severe burdens on discovery and create a broad "zone of silence" over corporate affairs. Application of the attorney-client privilege to communications such as those involved here, however, puts the adversary in no worse position than if the communications had never taken place. The privilege only protects disclosure of communications; it does not protect disclosure of the underlying facts by those who communicated with the attorney:

> [The] protection of the privilege extends only to communications and not to facts. A fact is one thing and a communication concerning that fact is an entirely different thing. The client cannot be compelled to answer the question, "What did you say or write to the attorney?" but may not refuse to disclose any relevant fact within his knowledge merely because he incorporated a statement of such fact into his communication to his attorney.

Here the Government was free to question the employees who communicated with Thomas and outside counsel. Upjohn has provided the IRS with a list of such employees, and the IRS has already interviewed some 25 of them. While it would probably be more convenient for the Government to secure the results of petitioner's internal investigation by simply subpoenaing the questionnaires and notes taken by petitioner's attorneys, such considerations of convenience do not overcome the policies served by the attorney-client privilege....

...[W]e conclude that the narrow "control group test" sanctioned by the Court of Appeals in this case cannot, consistent with "the principles of the common law as... interpreted... in the light of reason and experience," Fed. Rule Evid. 501, govern the development of the law in this area....

...To the extent that the material subject to the summons is not protected by the attorney-client privilege as disclosing communications between an employee and counsel, we must reach the ruling by the Court of Appeals that the work-product doctrine does not apply to summonses.

...This doctrine was announced by the Court over 30 years ago in Hickman v. Taylor, 329 U.S. 495 (1947). In that case the Court rejected "an attempt, without purported necessity or justification, to secure written statements, private memoranda and personal recollections prepared or formed by an adverse party's counsel in the course of his legal duties." The Court noted that "it is essential that a lawyer work with a certain degree of privacy" and reasoned that if discovery of the material sought were permitted "much of what is now put down in writing would remain unwritten. An attorney's thoughts, heretofore inviolate, would not be his own. Inefficiency, unfairness and sharp practices would inevitably develop in the giving of legal advice and in the preparation of cases for trial. The effect on the legal profession would be demoralizing. And the interests of the clients and the cause of justice would be poorly served."

The "strong public policy" underlying the work-product doctrine... has been substantially incorporated in Federal Rule of Civil Procedure 26 (b)(3).

...While conceding the applicability of the work-product doctrine, the Government asserts that it has made a sufficient showing of necessity to overcome its protections....

The Government stresses that interviewees are scattered across the globe and that Upjohn has forbidden its employees to answer questions it considers irrelevant. The above-quoted language from *Hickman*, however, did not apply to "oral statements made by witnesses... whether presently in the form of [the attorney's] mental impressions or memoranda." As to such material the Court did "not believe that any showing of necessity can be made under the circumstances of this case so as to justify production. If there should be a rare situation justifying production of these matters, petitioner's case is not of that type." Forcing an attorney to disclose notes and memoranda of witnesses' oral statements is particularly disfavored because it tends to reveal the attorney's mental processes.[8]

Based on the foregoing, some courts have concluded that no showing of necessity can overcome protection of work product which is based on oral statements from witnesses.

We do not decide the issue at this time. It is clear that the Magistrate applied the wrong standard when he concluded that the Government had made a sufficient showing of necessity to overcome the protections of the work-product doctrine. The Magistrate applied the "substantial need" and

---

8. Thomas described his notes of the interviews as containing "what I considered to be the important questions, the substance of the responses to them, my beliefs as to the importance of these, my beliefs as to how they related to the inquiry, my thoughts as to how they related to other questions. In some instances they might even suggest other questions that I would have to ask or things that I needed to find elsewhere."...

"without undue hardship" standard articulated in the first part of Rule 26(b)(3). The notes and memoranda sought by the Government here, however, are work product based on oral statements. If they reveal communications, they are, in this case, protected by the attorney-client privilege. To the extent they do not reveal communications, they reveal the attorneys' mental processes in evaluating the communications. As Rule 26 and Hickman make clear, such work product cannot be disclosed simply on a showing of substantial need and inability to obtain the equivalent without undue hardship.

While we are not prepared at this juncture to say that such material is always protected by the work-product rule, we think a far stronger showing of necessity and unavailability by other means than was made by the Government or applied by the Magistrate in this case would be necessary to compel disclosure.

Swidler & Berlin v. United States

524 U.S. 399 (1998)

Chief Justice REHNQUIST delivered the opinion of the Court.

Petitioner, an attorney, made notes of an initial interview with a client shortly before the client's death. The Government, represented by the Office of Independent Counsel, now seeks his notes for use in a criminal investigation. We hold that the notes are protected by the attorney-client privilege.

This dispute arises out of an investigation conducted by the Office of the Independent Counsel into whether various individuals made false statements, obstructed justice, or committed other crimes during investigations of the 1993 dismissal of employees from the White House Travel Office. Vincent W. Foster, Jr., was Deputy White House Counsel when the firings occurred. In July, 1993, Foster met with petitioner James Hamilton, an attorney at petitioner Swidler & Berlin, to seek legal representation concerning possible congressional or other investigations of the firings. During a 2-hour meeting, Hamilton took three pages of handwritten notes. One of the first entries in the notes is the word "Privileged." Nine days later, Foster committed suicide.

In December 1995, a federal grand jury, at the request of the Independent Counsel, issued subpoenas to petitioners Hamilton and Swidler & Berlin for, inter alia, Hamilton's handwritten notes of his meeting with Foster. Petitioners filed a motion to quash, arguing that the notes were protected by the attorney client privilege and by the work product privilege.... The District Court, after examining the notes in camera, concluded they were protected from disclosure by both doctrines and denied enforcement of the subpoenas.

The Court of Appeals for the District of Columbia Circuit reversed....

Petitioners sought review in this Court on both the attorney client privilege and the work product privilege.[1] We granted certiorari, and we now reverse....

The Independent Counsel argues that the attorney-client privilege should not prevent disclosure of confidential communications where the client has died and the information is relevant to

1. Because we sustain the claim of attorney-client privilege, we do not reach the claim of work product privilege.

a criminal proceeding. There is some authority for this position. One state appellate court, Cohen v. Jenkintown Cab Co., 357 A.2d 689 (Pa. Super. 1976), and the Court of Appeals below have held the privilege may be subject to posthumous exceptions in certain circumstances. In *Cohen*, a civil case, the court recognized that the privilege generally survives death, but concluded that it could make an exception where the interest of justice was compelling and the interest of the client in preserving the confidence was insignificant.

But other than these two decisions, cases addressing the existence of the privilege after death—most involving the testamentary exception—uniformly presume the privilege survives, even if they do not so hold. . . .

IC argues.

The Independent Counsel . . . argues that the exception reflects a policy judgment that the interest in settling estates outweighs any posthumous interest in confidentiality. He then reasons by analogy that in criminal proceedings, the interest in determining whether a crime has been committed should trump client confidentiality, particularly since the financial interests of the estate are not at stake.

But the Independent Counsel's interpretation simply does not square with the caselaw's implicit acceptance of the privilege's survival and with the treatment of testamentary disclosure as an "exception" or an implied "waiver." And the premise of his analogy is incorrect, since cases consistently recognize that the rationale for the testamentary exception is that it furthers the client's intent. There is no reason to suppose as a general matter that grand jury testimony about confidential communications furthers the client's intent.

Commentators on the law also recognize that the general rule is that the attorney-client privilege continues after death. Undoubtedly, as the Independent Counsel emphasizes, various commentators have criticized this rule, urging that the privilege should be abrogated after the client's death where extreme injustice would result, as long as disclosure would not seriously undermine the privilege by deterring client communication. See, e.g., C. Mueller & L. Kirkpatrick, 2 *Federal Evidence* §199, at 380-381 (2d ed. 1994); *Restatement (Third) of the Law Governing Lawyers* §127, Comment d (Proposed Final Draft No. 1, Mar. 29, 1996). But even these critics clearly recognize that established law supports the continuation of the privilege and that a contrary rule would be a modification of the common law.

Despite the scholarly criticism, we think there are weighty reasons that counsel in favor of posthumous application. Knowing that communications will remain confidential even after death encourages the client to communicate fully and frankly with counsel. While the fear of disclosure, and the consequent withholding of information from counsel, may be reduced if disclosure is limited to posthumous disclosure in a criminal context, it seems unreasonable to assume that it vanishes altogether. Clients may be concerned about reputation, civil liability, or possible harm to friends or family. Posthumous disclosure of such communications may be as feared as disclosure during the client's lifetime.

The Independent Counsel suggests, however, that his proposed exception would have little to no effect on the client's willingness to confide in his attorney. He reasons that only clients intending to perjure themselves will be chilled by a rule of disclosure after death, as opposed to truthful clients or those asserting their Fifth Amendment privilege. This is because for the latter group, communications disclosed by the attorney after the client's death purportedly will reveal only information that the client himself would have revealed if alive. . . .

The contention that the attorney is being required to disclose only what the client could have been required to disclose is at odds with the basis for the privilege even during the client's lifetime. In related cases, we have said that the loss of evidence admittedly caused by the privilege is justified in part by the fact that without the privilege, the client may not have made such communications in the first place. This is true of disclosure before and after the client's death. Without assurance of the privilege's posthumous application, the client may very well not have made disclosures to his attorney at all, so the loss of evidence is more apparent than real. In the case at hand, it seems quite plausible that Foster, perhaps already contemplating suicide, may not have sought legal advice from Hamilton if he had not been assured the conversation was privileged.

The Independent Counsel additionally suggests that his proposed exception would have minimal impact if confined to criminal cases, or, as the Court of Appeals suggests, if it is limited to information of substantial importance to a particular criminal case.... However, there is no case authority for the proposition that the privilege applies differently in criminal and civil cases.... In any event, a client may not know at the time he discloses information to his attorney whether it will later be relevant to a civil or a criminal matter, let alone whether it will be of substantial importance. Balancing *ex post* the importance of the information against client interests, even limited to criminal cases, introduces substantial uncertainty into the privilege's application. For just that reason, we have rejected use of a balancing test in defining the contours of the privilege. *See* Upjohn, 449 U.S. at 393.

In a similar vein, the Independent Counsel argues that existing exceptions to the privilege, such as the crime-fraud exception and the testamentary exception, make the impact of one more exception marginal. However, these exceptions do not demonstrate that the impact of a posthumous exception would be insignificant, and there is little empirical evidence on this point.[4] The established exceptions are consistent with the purposes of the privilege, while a posthumous exception in criminal cases appears at odds with the goals of encouraging full and frank communication and of protecting the client's interests. A "no harm in one more exception" rationale could contribute to the general erosion of the privilege, without reference to common law principles or "reason and experience."

It has been generally, if not universally, accepted, for well over a century, that the attorney-client privilege survives the death of the client in a case such as this. While the arguments against the survival of the privilege are by no means frivolous, they are based in large part on speculation—thoughtful speculation,

4. Empirical evidence on the privilege is limited. Three studies do not reach firm conclusions on whether limiting the privilege would discourage full and frank communication. Alexander, *The Corporate Attorney Client Privilege: A Study of the Participants*, 63 St. John's L. Rev. 191 (1989); Zacharias, *Rethinking Confidentiality*, 74 Iowa L. Rev. 352 (1989); Comment, *Functional Overlap Between the Lawyer and Other Professionals: Its Implications for the Privileged Communications Doctrine*, 71 Yale L.J. 1226 (1962). These articles note that clients are often uninformed or mistaken about the privilege, but suggest that a substantial number of clients and attorneys think the privilege encourages candor. Two of the articles conclude that a substantial number of clients and attorneys think the privilege enhances open communication, Alexander, *supra*, at 244-246, 261, and that the absence of a privilege would be detrimental to such communication, Comment, 71 Yale L.J., *supra*, at 1236. The third article suggests instead that while the privilege is perceived as important to open communication, limited exceptions to the privilege might not discourage such communication, Zacharias, *supra*, at 382, 386. Similarly, relatively few court decisions discuss the impact of the privilege's application after death. This may reflect the general assumption that the privilege survives—if attorneys were required as a matter of practice to testify or provide notes in criminal proceedings, cases discussing that practice would surely exist.

but speculation nonetheless—as to whether posthumous termination of the privilege would diminish a client's willingness to confide in an attorney. In an area where empirical information would be useful, it is scant and inconclusive.

. . . Interpreted in the light of reason and experience, that body of law requires that the attorney client privilege prevent disclosure of the notes at issue in this case. The judgment of the Court of Appeals is Reversed.

Dissent: Justice O'CONNOR, with whom Justice SCALIA and Justice THOMAS join, dissenting.

Although the attorney-client privilege ordinarily will survive the death of the client, I do not agree with the Court that it inevitably precludes disclosure of a deceased client's communications in criminal proceedings. In my view, a criminal defendant's right to exculpatory evidence or a compelling law enforcement need for information may, where the testimony is not available from other sources, override a client's posthumous interest in confidentiality. . . .

I agree that a deceased client may retain a personal, reputational, and economic interest in confidentiality. But, after death, the potential that disclosure will harm the client's interests has been greatly diminished, and the risk that the client will be held criminally liable has abated altogether. . . . The privilege does not "protect[] disclosure of the underlying facts by those who communicated with the attorney," *Upjohn, supra*, at 395, and were the client living, prosecutors could grant immunity and compel the relevant testimony. After a client's death, however, if the privilege precludes an attorney from testifying in the client's stead, a complete "loss of crucial information" will often result.

. . . Extreme injustice may occur, for example, where a criminal defendant seeks disclosure of a deceased client's confession to the offense. See State v. Macumber, 544 P.2d 1084, 1086 (Ariz. 1976). . . . Indeed, even petitioner acknowledges that an exception may be appropriate where the constitutional rights of a criminal defendant are at stake. An exception may likewise be warranted in the face of a compelling law enforcement need for the information. . . .

. . . The American Law Institute, moreover, has recently recommended withholding the privilege when the communication "bears on a litigated issue of pivotal significance" and has suggested that courts "balance the interest in confidentiality against any exceptional need for the communication." *Restatement (Third) of the Law Governing Lawyers* §127, at 431, Comment d.

Where the exoneration of an innocent criminal defendant or a compelling law enforcement interest is at stake, the harm of precluding critical evidence that is unavailable by any other means outweighs the potential disincentive to forthright communication. In my view, the cost of silence warrants a narrow exception to the rule that the attorney-client privilege survives the death of the client. . . .

Accordingly, I would affirm the judgment of the Court of Appeals. . . .

The Limits of the Law: *Court Orders*

Hughes, Dean, Upjohn, and *Swidler & Berlin* illustrate another legal limit on the conduct of both lawyers and clients: the power of a court order. Each of these cases recognizes a court's inherent power to order disclosures consistent with the confines of the attorney-client privilege. In Chapter 3, *Bothwell* discussed the inherent power of a court to order a lawyer to provide uncompensated representation.[1] In fact, courts order all kinds of conduct in order to carry out their duties.[2] Lawyers must be aware of the importance of these orders to avoid both contempt sanctions and professional discipline.[3]

The Model Rules of Professional Conduct recognize the power of court orders in several key provisions. Most prominent are Model Rule 1.6(b)(6), which allows lawyers to disclose confidential information where required by a court order, and Model Rule 3.4(c), which states the lawyer's basic obligation to obey the rules of tribunals, including court orders.

These provisions recognize and integrate the legal limit of a court order into the requirement of a professional obligation. They also presume that lawyers have a clear fiduciary and procedural obligation to properly raise and protect client interests.[4] Lawyers have an obligation to assert the attorney-client privilege on the client's behalf whenever a nonfrivolous claim against disclosure can be made.[5] Failure to do so could result in legally effective waiver of the privilege by the lawyer, who a court will later characterize as acting with apparent authority as the client's agent.[6] Any harm that results from such a nonconsensual disclosure could then subject the lawyer to claims of malpractice or breach of fiduciary duty.[7]

Once a court has declared that confidential information is not privileged, the lawyer either must comply with the court order to disclose, or appeal the court's decision.[8] The clients and lawyers in *Hughes*, *Upjohn*, and *Swidler & Berlin* elected to raise claims about the privilege on appeal. In two of these cases (*Upjohn* and *Swidler & Berlin*), the lawyers were successful in convincing appellate courts that the information was privileged, which resulted in reversal of the lower court's order to disclose or remand for further factual findings about the matter.

The lawyer in *Hughes* did not succeed on appeal, which meant that any further failure to disclose his client's identity would result in the enforcement of the trial court's contempt order. Judges use contempt sanctions to coerce or punish a lawyer or litigant. Civil contempt occurs when a judge orders fines or imprisonment to accrue until the person in contempt complies with the court order.[9] Criminal

---

1. We will see further illustrations of inherent court power in the notes in The Law Governing Lawyers: Losing a Client by Disqualification or Injunction, *infra* p.261, and in several cases in Chapters 9 and 10.
2. *See Restatement (Third) The Law Governing Lawyers* §105 (2000).
3. *E.g.*, In re Shearin, 765 A.2d 930 (Del. 2000) (lawyer who, inter alia, violated court order enjoining her from interfering with the quiet title, operation, use, enjoyment, and governance of a church property suspended for three years); Herschfeld v. Super. Ct., 908 P.2d 22 (Ariz. 1995) (lawyer who continued to verbally assault a party opponent after being admonished to stop by the judge convicted of criminal contempt); In re Anonymous, No. 34 D.B. 93, 32 Pa. D. & C. 4th 23 (1995) (lawyer who violated a protective order barring him from contact with woman and her child held in contempt and disciplined); In re Belue, 766 P.2d 206 (Mont. 1988) (lawyer who violated federal judge's order to release property from attachment suspended from practice for three months and censured).
4. In an extreme case, a court may dismiss an action for failure to comply with a court order. *See* Washington v. Alaimo, 934 F. Supp. 1395 (S.D. Ga. 1996) (plaintiff's failure to respond to a show-cause order regarding Rule 11 sanctions after plaintiff was warned that failing to respond would cause dismissal resulted in dismissal with prejudice).
5. Model Rule 1.6, comment 11. *See Restatement (Third) The Law Governing Lawyers* §86 for a description of the procedure that should be followed in invoking the privilege.
6. *Restatement (Third) The Law Governing Lawyers* §77 (2000).
7. *Restatement (Third) The Law Governing Lawyers* §63, Comment b (2000). Unauthorized disclosure subjected the lawyers in *Perez*, *supra* p.125, to similar penalties for out of court conduct.
8. *Restatement (Third) The Law Governing Lawyers* §105, Comment d (2000).
9. Courts also can sanction lawyers who use obstructive tactics to assist clients in violating court orders. *See, e.g.*, Guardianship of Melissa W., 18 Cal. Rptr. 2d 42 (Cal. App. 2002) (lawyer who helped clients

contempt punishes refusal to comply and requires elaborate procedural guarantees, similar to those in criminal trials.[10] Occasionally, a lawyer will risk contempt by violating a court order for the express purpose of challenging its validity, scope or meaning.[11] Usually this is done only if no other procedural avenue of appeal is open to the client.[12] In situations where procedural rules provide for appeal, however, lawyers have been both held in contempt and disciplined for failing to obey the court order or properly challenging it.[13]

While these cases illustrate the legal limit created by a court order, the availability of court orders also gives lawyers the opportunity to challenge otherwise unassailable legal rules. For example, Model Rules 3.5(b) and (c) prohibit communication with jurors, unless authorized by law or a court order. Similarly, the prohibition in Rule 4.2 against communication with a represented person recognizes the exception of "law or a court order." Thus, lawyers with nonfrivolous legal reasons to seek communication with jurors or represented persons may seek court approval in order to protect themselves against both contempt and disciplinary action.

The lawyers in the cases discussed in this note understood that court orders, combined with a court's contempt power, could limit their duties to a client. At the same time, they vigorously advocated (often successfully) for legal recognition of their client's interests within and up to this limit of the law.

ABA Formal Opinion 92-368

American Bar Association Standing Committee on Ethics and Professional Responsibility

The Committee has been asked to opine on the obligations under the Model Rules of Professional Conduct of a lawyer who comes into possession of materials that appear on their face to be subject to the attorney-client privilege or otherwise confidential, under circumstances where it is clear that the materials were not intended for the receiving lawyer. The question posed includes situations in which the sending lawyer has notified the receiving lawyer of the erroneous transmission and has requested return of the materials sent as well as those situations in which

---

evade custody order caused dismissal of client's appeal, and also was sanctioned $13,004 for opposing party's attorney's fees, and referred to the bar for further investigation).

10. International Union, UMWA v. Bagwell, 512 U.S. 821 (1994). Criminal contempt proceeding requires proof beyond a reasonable doubt, a special prosecutor, and a jury trial for any imprisonment beyond six months. Fleming James, Jr., Geoffrey C. Hazard, Jr. & John Leubsdorf, *Civil Procedure* §5.14 (5th ed., Foundation 2001). *See, e.g.,* Downey v. Clauder, 30 F.3d 681 (6th Cir. 1994) (criminal contempt citation reversed because lawyer not given adequate notice of the charges against him and did not willfully disobey court order).

11. *Restatement (Third) The Law Governing Lawyers* §94, Comment e (2000). Such a claim may be raised about the scope of the attorney-client privilege, the work product doctrine, or other evidentiary claims, such as irrelevancy or hearsay. *Id.* at §63, Comment b (2000).

12. *E.g.,* Maness v. Meyers, 419 U.S. 449 (1975) (lawyer who advised a client to refuse to obey a court order to testify in order to trigger immediate appellate review of the issue and to protect the client's Fifth Amendment rights could not be punished where procedural rules provided no other means to test the validity of the trial court's ruling and the lawyer believed in good faith that disclosure of the information tended to incriminate the client).

13. *E.g.,* Fla. Bar v. Gersten, 707 So. 2d 711 (Fla. 1998) (lawyer who refused to obey a court order that required him to give a sworn statement suspended); Disc. Action Against Giberson, 581 N.W.2d 351 (Minn. 1998) (lawyer who refused to pay court-ordered child support indefinitely suspended); Davis v. Goodson, 635 S.W.2d 226 (Ark. 1982) (contempt upheld against a lawyer who advised a client in open court to disregard a judge's order).

the inadvertent sending lawyer and his client remain ignorant that the materials were missent. It also extends to situations in which the receiving lawyer has already reviewed the materials as well as those in which the sending lawyer intercedes before the receiving lawyer has had such an opportunity. This opinion is intended to answer a question which has become increasingly important as the burgeoning of multiparty cases, the availability of xerography and the proliferation of facsimile machines and electronic mail make it technologically ever more likely that through inadvertence, privileged or confidential materials will be produced to opposing counsel by no more than the pushing of the wrong speed dial number on a facsimile machine.

A satisfactory answer to the question posed cannot be drawn from a narrow, literalistic reading of the black letter of the Model Rules. But it is useful, and necessary, to bear in mind the thoughts in the Preamble to the Model Rules that "many difficult issues of professional discretion . . . must be resolved through the exercise of sensitive professional and moral judgment guided by the basic principles underlying the Rules," and that "the Rules do not exhaust the moral and ethical considerations that should inform a lawyer, for no worthwhile human activity can be completely defined by legal rules." In that larger, and more fundamental, framework, the Committee's views, expressed in this opinion, have been informed by (i) the importance the Model Rules give to maintaining client confidentiality, (ii) the law governing waiver of the attorney-client privilege, (iii) the law governing missent property, (iv) the similarity between the circumstances here addressed and other conduct the profession universally condemns, and (v) the receiving lawyer's obligations to his client.

Giving due weight to each of the foregoing considerations, it is the view of the Committee that the receiving lawyer, as a matter of ethical conduct contemplated by the precepts underlying the Model Rules, (a) should not examine the materials once the inadvertence is discovered, (b) should notify the sending lawyer of their receipt and (c) should abide by the sending lawyer's instructions as to their disposition.

I. *Confidentiality*

The concept of confidentiality is a fundamental aspect of the right to the effective assistance of counsel. As reflected in each iteration of the rules of professional responsibility, the obligation of the lawyer to maintain and to refuse to divulge client confidences is virtually absolute.

The confidentiality principle rests on the vital importance society places upon the "full, free and frank" exchange between lawyer and client, shielded from the intrusive eyes and ears of adverse parties, the government, the media and the public. The principle's primary basis is that, absent the guarantee of confidentiality, critical discussions will be either proscribed, circumscribed or intruded upon in a way that will impact directly on the ability of the lawyer to serve his or her client. If the lawyer cannot gather all the necessary information and is not free to explore with the client the client's options, free from the threat that these confidential communications will be shared with those whose interests may be adverse to the client, the chilling effect on the lawyer-client relationship becomes plain. The benefits of confidentiality were recognized over 150 years ago when Justice Shaw observed in Hatton v. Robinson, 31 Mass. (14 Pick.) 416, 422 (1833):

> This principle we take to be this; that so numerous and complex are the laws by which the rights and duties of citizens are governed, so important is it that they should be permitted to avail themselves of the superior skill and learning of [attorneys] both in

ascertaining their rights in the country, and maintaining them most safely in court... that the law has considered it the wisest policy to encourage and sanction this confidence, by requiring that on such facts the mouth of the attorney should be forever sealed.

Model Rule 1.6 codifies a lawyer's obligation to keep the confidences of his client....

A. *Competing Principles*

If the Committee were to countenance, or indeed encourage, conduct on the part of the receiving lawyer which was in derogation of this strong policy in favor of confidentiality, the Committee would have to identify a more important principle which supports an alternative result. As the Committee examines the potentially competing principles, we conclude that their importance pales in comparison to the importance of maintaining confidentiality.

First, it might be argued that keeping the confidential materials and not letting the sending lawyer know they were received will punish carelessness on the part of the sending lawyer and those with whom that lawyer works. However, loss of confidentiality is a very high penalty to pay for a mere slip, particularly when the person or entity paying the "price" is not the individual lawyer responsible for the inadvertent conduct, but rather the client who presumably had nothing to do with the mis-sending of the materials.

Second, it could be asserted that letting the receiving lawyer keep the confidential materials in this situation will encourage more careful conduct on the part of other counsel in the future. Once the catastrophic consequences of a misstep are recognized, lawyers and their clients will conform their future conduct to avoid such an unfortunate result. However, this rationale undervalues the lawyer's existing strong motivation. Lawyers already have significant incentives to protect confidential materials, not the least of which is the mandate of Model Rule 1.6 itself. Having an inadvertent disclosure act as a total waiver of confidentiality can add little to this equation. The argument also ignores the persistence of human frailty. The possibility of "punishment," no matter how severe, will never prevent, in this modern age of electronic transmission, unlimited photocopies and cases with hundreds of parties, accidents from occurring. The wrong number on the facsimile machine will still be "mis-speed-dialed;" the contents of two envelopes will get switched; "send copies to all defense counsel" will be misunderstood as "send copies to all counsel."

Third, it may be asserted that once confidential materials are missent there is nothing really to protect. Of course, this argument does not apply if the receiving lawyer becomes aware of the inadvertence before the materials are examined. If the facsimile cover sheet says "to All Defense Counsel" and the receiving lawyer represents the plaintiff, the confidentiality can be completely protected so long as the lawyer refrains from giving in to temptation. But even where the receiving lawyer examines the materials before discovering that they were missent, there is still value in maintaining what confidentiality remains.

First, disclosure to counsel does not have to result in disclosure to counsel's client. Second, there is a significant difference between a lawyer's knowing the contents of documents and that lawyer's being able to use them, for example, at trial either as a basis for questions or by presentation of them to a fact finder. Third, inadvertent disclosure to one counsel or party does not necessarily lead to disclosure to other parties or their counsel if precautions, such as those in confidentiality orders, are taken.

Finally, it might be urged that a receiving lawyer has an obligation to maximize the advantage his client will gain from careful scrutiny of the missent materials. . . .

However, there are many limitations on the extent to which a lawyer may go "all out" for the client. The examples cited in Part IV of this opinion are all "opportunities" the lawyer may not seize. Similarly, the Model Rules carefully circumscribe factual and legal representations a lawyer may make, people counsel may contact and clients counsel can represent. The limitation contemplated by this opinion is entirely consistent with these ethical restraints on uncontrolled advocacy.

B. *The Analogy to Inadvertent Waiver of the Attorney-Client Privilege*

In concluding that inadvertent disclosure of confidential materials should not result in the loss of their confidential character we find persuasive the manner in which courts have treated the inadvertent disclosure of materials subject to the attorney-client privilege. While the privilege is a rule of evidence which addresses when an attorney can be compelled to disclose otherwise protected material, whereas confidentiality is a principle designed to govern the lawyer's voluntary conduct, both concepts are designed to further the attorney-client relationship in a similar manner and for the same reasons.

A review of the relevant cases demonstrates, with few exceptions, an unwillingness to permit mere inadvertence to constitute a waiver. Something more, like a failure of counsel to spend any time reviewing the documents to be produced in discovery, is required before a waiver is found. An example of this approach is the decision by the New Mexico Supreme Court in Hartman v. El Paso Natural Gas Co., 763 P.2d 1144, 1152 (N.M. 1988) in which the Court explained how it would examine counsel's conduct in determining if there is a waiver:

> [There are] five factors which should assist a court in determining whether a document has lost its privilege: (1) The reasonableness of the precautions taken to prevent inadvertent disclosure in view of the extent of the document production; (2) the number of inadvertent disclosures; (3) the extent of the disclosure; (4) any delay and measures taken to rectify the disclosures; (5) whether the overriding interests of justice would be served by relieving a party of its error.

The Committee recognizes that the view that inadvertence should not necessarily give rise to a waiver of the attorney-client (privilege) is not universally accepted. Some cases and commentators endorse Wigmore's view that "the privilege stands in derogation of the public's right to everyman's evidence," that the privilege results in the suppression of evidence, that the cost of the privilege is clear: evidence which would have been used in the search for truth is excluded. . . .

The cases reflecting what appears to be the minority view conclude that any unforced disclosure of attorney-client privileged communications destroys confidentiality and terminates the privilege, not only for the communications disclosed but also for all related communications.

> [I]f a client wishes to preserve the privilege, it must treat the confidentiality of attorney-client communications like jewels—if not crown jewels. Short of court compelled disclosure, [citation omitted] or equally extraordinary circumstances, we will not distinguish between various degrees of "voluntariness" in waivers of the attorney-client privilege. In re Sealed Case, 877 F.2d 976, 980 (D.C. Cir. 1989). . . .

II. *Law Governing Missent Property*

While the Committee does not answer questions of law, this principle does not preclude consideration, for present purposes, of the black letter of the law of bailment as it applies to missent property. . . .

In the question presented to the Standing Committee, the receiving lawyer lawfully possesses the missent materials, but the sending lawyer clearly did not intend to relinquish title to them, either the physical objects or the ideas reflected on each page, such that they would become the "property" of the receiving attorney. The common law of bailments characterizes such mistaken possession as a bailment implied by law, or a constructive bailment. . . .

An essential element of the bailment relationship is the absolute obligation of the bailee to return the subject matter of the bailment upon termination of the bailment. This obligation to return the property is necessarily implied from the mere fact of lawful possession of personal property of another. Where the bailment is not for any particular time, the bailor may terminate it at will. Indeed, the bailment terminates when an unauthorized use is made of the property. If the bailee refuses to return the property, makes an unauthorized disposition of it, or uses it for purposes other than those agreed on, he may be liable for its conversion.

The right of a bailee to use the bailed property and the extent to which it may be used is governed by the intention of the parties to the bailment. In the absence of any express agreement between the parties, as is the case in the question presented the Committee, no rule of universal application can be laid down:

> Each case must be governed by its own circumstances, such as the character and purpose of the bailment and the nature of the property, in connection with other attending incidents. One test or principle applicable to the subject is whether, from the circumstances, *the consent of the owner to the use may be fairly presumed*. 8 Am. Jur. 2d Bailments §207 (1980) (emphasis added).

The sending lawyer here, of course, cannot begin to be presumed to have consented to any use of the missent materials by the receiving lawyer. Indeed, the only "use" to which the sending lawyer could be presumed to have consented is the immediate return of the missent property. Any attempt by the receiving lawyer to use the missent letter for his own purposes would thus constitute an "unauthorized use."

III. *Analogous Cases*

The present issue is not unlike that presented to the Standing Committee in Informal Opinion 86-1518, Notice to Opposing Counsel of Inadvertent Omission of Contract Provision (February 9, 1986). In that case a contract was negotiated including one hotly disputed provision insisted upon by B. When B's lawyer forwarded a draft of the agreement to A's lawyer, the key provision, though agreed to, was missing. The Committee was asked what duty, if any, A's lawyer had in the circumstances.

The opinion concluded that A's lawyer had no duty to notify A of the error under Model Rule 1.4 because the client has no decision to make. Nor was the lawyer barred by the confidentiality provisions of Model Rule 1.6 from informing the other side because this disclosure was "impliedly authorized" by the representation. Because under Model Rule 1.2 the lawyer has the authority to decide the technical means to carry out the representation and because the client's right under the same Model Rule to committed and dedicated representation is not unlimited, the opinion concluded that the "error is appropriate for correction between the lawyers without client consultation." In reaching this result the opinion was concerned that to do otherwise and "capitalize on the clerical error," might violate the proscription of Model Rule 1.2(d) not to counsel the client to engage in conduct the lawyer knows is fraudulent as well as the admonishment of Model Rule 4.1(b) not knowingly to fail to disclose a material fact when disclosure is necessary to avoid a client fraud.

While Informal Opinion 86-1516 is not on all fours with the instant situation, its charitable view toward inadvertence, its unwillingness to permit parties to capitalize on errors, its recognition of a limitation on client decision-making authority and its respect for the role of counsel all support the position advanced in this opinion as to counsel's proper conduct upon the inadvertent receipt of confidential information.

The Committee has also considered other hypothetical situations in which an opposing lawyer may have opportunity to "take advantage" of a chance to review and use confidential information. It is the view of the Committee that its dim view of a lawyer's doing so in each of these examples supports the conclusion reached by this opinion. For example, if during a lunch break in a deposition, lawyer B left notes or other materials in a conference room, either in an unlocked briefcase or on the conference room table, there is no respectable argument that competent and diligent representation requires or even permits lawyer A, arriving back from lunch early, to review the materials to which he now has easy access. Nor if, after a closing at lawyer A's office, lawyer B accidentally leaves a file or a briefcase behind would it be proper to assert that lawyer A could take advantage of this inadvertence and rifle the file or inspect the briefcase before returning it. Indeed, in the view of the Committee that lawyer would have an obligation to notify the lawyer who left her briefcase that it had been found. Finally, if in positioning an overhead projector on a shared counsel table in a courtroom during a recess, court personnel inadvertently move the prosecutor's notes into a position in front of the defense counsel's place at the table, it seems clear to the Committee that defense counsel would have an absolute obligation to return the materials without any examination or copying.

IV. Good Sense and Reciprocity

The analysis of this issue as an ethical matter should not obscure some more practical considerations that suggest the correct course for the receiving lawyer is to inform sending lawyer and return the documents. The immediate reaction of receiving counsel might be that the use of the missent materials can only serve to advantage his client. Nonetheless, it is clear there are advantages to doing just the opposite. First, instances of inadvertent production of documents tend not to occur only on one side. While a lawyer today may be the beneficiary of the opposing lawyer's misstep, tomorrow the shoe could be on the other foot. Second, when it is discovered that the confidential materials were retained and used the result could be similar to that which occurred recently in Baltimore when the court learned after jury selection that defendants' jury selection strategy was misdirected to plaintiffs' counsel by fax. "I find that the plaintiffs' attorneys have an advantage over the defense attorneys. Specifically, the plaintiffs know pretty well which prospective jurors the defense is going to strike.... They knew the inner-most thinking of the defense counsel." The judge struck the jury and ordered the entire process to begin again, at no small cost to plaintiffs, a cost that would have been expanded exponentially if the judge had not learned of this fact until the trial was over or when it was on appeal. Of similar effect is the recent example involving the Washington, D.C. office of a Texas law firm.

Though in that case the confidential materials were intentionally delivered and, because they were from the government, special statutory provisions were involved, the fact that the firm felt compelled to withdraw because the firm was exposed to these materials, suggests the hazardous pathway which one must traverse after receipt of confidential materials. "Taking a bet" on what reaction a court may have when an inadvertent disclosure becomes known can be a risky proposition indeed. Third, the credibility and professionalism inherent in doing the right thing can, in some significant ways, enhance the strength of one's case, one's standing with the other party and opposing counsel, and one's stature before the Court.

Conclusion

The preamble to the Model Rules correctly notes that "virtually all difficult ethical problems arise from the conflict between a lawyer's responsibility to clients, to the legal system and to the lawyer's interest in remaining an upright person while earning a satisfactory living." Similarly, the same introduction observes that "a lawyer is also guided by personal conscience and the approbation of professional peers." In this instance, those principles, as well as the Model Rules, the law of bailment and good sense all come together to support our conclusion that receiving counsel's obligations under those circumstances are to avoid reviewing the materials, notify sending counsel if sending counsel remains ignorant of the problem and abide sending counsel's direction as to how to treat the disposition of the confidential materials. This result not only fosters the important principle of confidentiality, avoids punishing the innocent client and conforms to the law of bailment, but also achieves a level of professionalism which can only redound to the lawyer's benefit.

D. Exceptions to Confidentiality

Exceptions to confidentiality have coexisted with the obligation since its inception. If the rationales that support the obligation of confidentiality in the first place make sense, then the same policies should justify exceptions to lawyer obligations of client confidentiality. In other words, if preserving confidentiality promotes efficient functioning of the legal system, an exception can be justified to restore or promote effective operation of the system of justice. Similarly, if preserving client confidences is deemed important to promote trust or privacy in the client-lawyer relationship, an exception can be justified where preserving client confidences in fact creates a breach of trust or fosters misuse of the relationship to violate legal norms.

1. Express or Implied Authority

The most widely recognized and easiest to justify exception to client confidentiality occurs when clients decide for themselves whether to allow the use or disclosure of such information. On utilitarian grounds, the legal system needs information to function, and therefore clients who wish to take advantage of the system's protections or allowances must agree as a condition of using the system to supply it with some information. Deontologists agree that client consent makes sense as an exception to confidentiality because they view consent as the client's autonomous authorization to disclosure or use of the information. Agency law rests on such a consensual foundation, and protects extensions of autonomy by granting individuals the opportunity to act through others.

Problems

5-13. Martyn recommends that Martyn & Fox add the following clause to all personal injury retainer agreements. Should Fox agree?

"Client agrees to allow Martyn & Fox discretion to disclose any information relating to the representation and to settle the above entitled matter whenever Martyn & Fox determines such action will promote the best interests of Client."

5-14. What may (must) Fox do if Client, in the course of estate planning, tells Fox that she is terminally ill and plans on taking a lethal dose of medication as soon as she signs the documents?

Consider: Model Rules 1.0(e), 1.2(a), 1.6, 1.14
Model Code DR 4-101(C)(1)
RLGL §§19, 22

In re Pressly

628 A.2d 927 (Vt. 1993)

PER CURIAM.

Respondent Thomas Pressly appeals from a decision of the Professional Conduct Board recommending a public reprimand as discipline for his misconduct in violating Disciplinary Rule (DR) 4-101(B)(1) ("a lawyer shall not knowingly . . . reveal a confidence or secret of his client"). DR 1-102(A)(1); ("a lawyer shall not violate a disciplinary rule." . . . We affirm and impose the recommended sanction.

In 1989, respondent, a member of the Vermont bar since 1975, represented complainant in connection with relief from abuse and divorce proceedings. Complainant informed respondent that her husband had a history [of] alcoholism, battering, and abuse. After a hearing at which she was represented by respondent, complainant was granted a temporary order requiring her husband to refrain from abusing her, and, by stipulation of the parties, temporary custody of the couple's two children with supervised visitation by the father. About a month later, respondent filed a divorce complaint on his client's behalf. The parties negotiated an agreement under which complainant would retain temporary custody of the children and her husband would be allowed unsupervised visitation. Complainant, on respondent's advice, reluctantly agreed to the visitation provision.

At that time, complainant told respondent that she was being harassed by her husband, that his alcoholism was a continuing problem, and that she wanted the children's visits with their father to be supervised. Respondent advised her, however, that there were insufficient legal grounds to require supervised visits. Complainant continued to press respondent to help her prevent her husband from continuing unsupervised visitation, but no motion was filed seeking supervised visitation.

Near the end of August 1989, complainant told respondent her suspicions, based on consultation with a counselor, that her nine-year-old daughter had been sexually abused by the father. According to the counselor, a "yellow flag" went up when she observed several symptoms of abuse. Complainant told respondent her suspicions, the basis for them, and her plan to arrange for a doctor's appointment for the daughter, which she thought might provide needed evidence against the father. She asked that respondent not discuss her suspicions or plans with her husband's lawyer.

In response to opposing counsel's question as to why the wife continued to request supervised visitation and whether sexual abuse was an issue in the case, respondent, notwithstanding his client's request, revealed to him the suspicions of sexual abuse. Respondent then asked the husband's lawyer not to communicate this information to the husband.* The next day, opposing counsel wrote respondent stating, "I mentioned to [my client] the representation [your client] had made to you about their daughter making statements to her counselor about sexual abuse.... [They] are totally unfounded and he views them to be a blatant attempt on the part of [your client] to manufacture evidence to keep him away from his children."

Complainant confronted her attorney about the disclosure, and was told by respondent that he provided the information in response to questions from opposing counsel. She discharged respondent and retained new counsel. After the disclosure, complainant perceived that her husband became increasingly uncooperative, which heightened her sense of fear and anxiety and created emotional distress.

The report of the panel appointed to hear the wife's complaint was adopted verbatim by the Board, which agreed that respondent had violated Disciplinary Rule 4-101 of the Code of Professional Responsibility. In approving a public reprimand, the Board agreed that respondent, although he did not intend to harm his client, knew the disclosure he made was confidential....

In recommending public reprimand, the Board looked to the American Bar Association's Standards for Imposing Lawyer Sanctions (ABA Standards). The standards are a model for imposing sanctions on attorneys based on the ethical duty involved, the party to whom the duty is owed, the lawyer's motives and intentions, and the injury caused by the misconduct....

Whatever mental state we ascribe to respondent's conduct, he should have known not to disclose his client's confidence. He testified before the panel that he knew the information was to be held in confidence, but felt that when pressured as to why his client wanted supervised visitation, informing opposing counsel was best. When asked whether he had thought of ending the conversation with counsel by stating that an attorney-client privilege precluded him from revealing anything further, he stated "If I say that, I think I'm letting the cat out of the bag also." He understood that he should not have revealed what his client had requested him to hold in confidence....

The Board gave respondent the benefit of the doubt on whether he knew that his disclosure to opposing counsel would cause his client anguish or jeopardize her case. If respondent did

* Complainant's testimony indicated that she directed her attorney not to disclose anything about sexual abuse to the husband. No mention was made of the opposing counsel. Although respondent points out this distinction as being contrary to the findings, we fail to understand its significance. The only ethical way respondent could communicate about the case was through the husband's lawyer. DR 7-104(A)(1) (lawyer not to communicate directly with adverse party). Respondent could not reasonably expect husband's counsel to keep the wife's confidences unrevealed. Respondent acknowledged that if he had been given similar information by opposing counsel, he would have disclosed it to his client, notwithstanding a request not to do so.

not actually know that his conduct would injure his client—his conduct being negligent because of his good intention (good faith) in making the disclosure—he still knew that his conduct violated a confidence....

The Board found that complainant suffered "emotional distress" as a result of the disclosure, which "heightened her level of fear and anxiety...." As the Board discussed,

Complainant was shocked by this news. She had relied upon respondent to protect the confidentiality of this information. She felt that Respondent had betrayed her trust....

Respondent's conduct was injurious to his client to the extent that his actions caused her emotional distress. We do not find, however, that the disclosure had an adverse impact on the pending litigation although there was a potential for such injury....

We adhere to the Board's recommendation. Respondent's infraction violated a core component of the attorney-client relationship, of which he, as an attorney in practice in this state for approximately sixteen years at the time of the infraction, should have been well aware. Respondent does not contend, nor does the record reflect, that his disclosure was intended or necessary to protect the child. His hope that opposing counsel would not disclose the information to the husband demonstrates naiveté, rather than any intent to simply disregard his client's confidence. Consequently, we agree with the Board that a suspension would be too harsh. On the other hand, a private admonition would unduly depreciate the violation.

The decision of the Professional Conduct Board is affirmed and its recommendation for discipline is approved. Thomas Pressly is publicly reprimanded for violation of DR 4-101(B)(1) of the Code of Professional Responsibility by knowingly revealing a confidence of his client.

2. Physical Harm

Confidentiality seems less important when another human good such as life itself is at stake. Here, a utilitarian would argue that lawyers guarantee confidentiality in part to encourage clients to blow off steam, which affords lawyers an opportunity to counsel clients to abstain from vigilante justice. Occasionally this goal fails, either because the lawyer cannot talk the client out of dangerous behavior, or because the client describes the behavior of someone with whom the lawyer has no relationship. In that situation, the lawyer is justified in disclosing client confidences to promote the greater good of preserving human life and preventing injurious behavior. John Stuart Mill, for example, argued that "[a]s soon as any part of a person's conduct affects prejudicially the interests of others, society has jurisdiction over it."[1] The deontologist would argue that a client who wishes to use the relationship with her lawyer to harm someone else is misusing a trusting relationship and therefore forfeits the client's right to trust or privacy.

Problems

5-15. May (must) Martyn & Fox disclose that a client plans to kill his spouse? What if we learn from the client that his son plans mayhem but the client told us that in confidence?

1. John Stuart Mill, *On Liberty*, Chap. IV (1859).

5-16. May (must) Martyn & Fox disclose that our client just discovered arsenic drums out back of the plant it bought last year? What if our client has owned the plant for 50 years?

5-17. May (must) Martyn & Fox, as lawyers for defendants, disclose that our physician's examination of plaintiff reveals that plaintiff has a life-threatening aneurysm, a condition not uncovered by plaintiff's own physician?

5-18. May (must) Martyn & Fox disclose that our client has committed a crime for which another person is now serving time? What if the innocent person faces the death penalty?

Consider: Model Rule 1.6(b)(1)
Model Code DR 4-101(C)(3)
RLGL §66

Hawkins v. King County

602 P.2d 361 (Wash. App. 1979)

SWANSON, A.C.J.

Michael Hawkins, acting through his guardian ad litem, and his mother Frances M. Hawkins, appeal from a summary judgment dismissing attorney Richard Sanders from an action sounding in tort. Appellants contend Sanders, court appointed defense attorney for Michael Hawkins, was negligent and committed malpractice by failing to divulge information regarding his client's mental state at a bail hearing. We find no error and affirm.

On July 1, 1975, Michael Hawkins was booked for possession of marijuana. Following his court appointment as Hawkins' defense counsel on July 3, 1975, Richard Sanders conferred with Hawkins for about 45 minutes, at which time Hawkins expressed the desire to be released from jail.

Also on July 3, 1975, Sanders talked with Palmer Smith, an attorney employed by Hawkins' mother Frances Hawkins, to assist in having Hawkins either hospitalized or civilly committed. Smith told Sanders then, and reiterated by letter, that Hawkins was mentally ill and dangerous. On July 8, 1975, Dr. Elwood Jones, a psychiatrist, telephoned and wrote Sanders and averred Hawkins was mentally ill and of danger to himself and others and should not be released from custody. Sanders represented that he intended to comply with his client's request for freedom.

On July 9, 1975, a district judge released Hawkins on a personal surety bond. At the bail hearing, Sanders did not volunteer any information regarding Hawkins' alleged illness or dangerousness, nor were any questions in that vein directed to him either by the judge or the prosecutor. Smith, Jones, and Mrs. Hawkins were informed of Hawkins' release, and all parties later met on two occasions in a counseling environment.

On July 17, 1975, about 8 days after his release, Michael Hawkins assaulted his mother and attempted suicide by jumping off a bridge, causing injuries resulting in the amputation of both legs. The Hawkinses commenced an action for damages against King County, the State of Washington, Community Psychiatric Clinic, Inc., and one of its employees on August 16, 1976, and amended the suit on November 30, 1977, to name Sanders a party defendant. Sanders filed a motion to dismiss for failure to state a claim. On June 16, 1978, the trial court granted Sanders' motion. . . .

On appeal, the Hawkinses essentially present two arguments. First, that by his failure at the bail hearing to disclose the information he possessed regarding Michael Hawkins' mental state, defense counsel Sanders subjected himself to liability for malpractice, as court rules and the Code of Professional Responsibility mandate such disclosure on ethical and legal grounds. Second, that by the same omission Sanders negligently violated a common-law duty to warn foreseeable victims of an individual he knew to be potentially dangerous to himself and others. *See* Tarasoff v. Regents of Univ. of Cal., 551 P.2d 334 (Cal. 1976).

Sanders asserts the Hawkinses have failed to demonstrate that he breached any duty owed to them. . . .

[The court examines the court rules that govern bail hearings and finds that they do not require a defense lawyer to disclose "information damaging to his client's expressed desire to be released from custody."]

We believe that the duty of counsel to be loyal to his client and to represent zealously his client's interests overrides the nebulous and unsupported theory that our rules and ethical code mandate disclosure of information which counsel considers detrimental to his client's stated interest. Because disclosure is not "required by law," appellants' theory of liability on the basis of ethical or court rule violations fails for lack of substance.

Turning then to the Hawkinses' theory of a common-law duty to warn or disclose, we note common-law support for the precept that attorneys must, upon learning that a client plans an assault or other violent crime, warn foreseeable victims. *See* Tarasoff v. Regents of Univ. of Cal., *supra*; State ex rel. Sowers v. Olwell, 394 P.2d 681 (Wash. 1964); Dike v. Dike, 448 P.2d 490 (Wash. 1968). *Olwell* and *Dike* make clear our Supreme Court's willingness to limit the attorney's duty of confidentiality when the values protected by that duty are outweighed by other interests necessary to the administration of justice. The difficulty lies in framing a rule that will balance properly "the public interest and safety from violent attack" against the public interest in securing proper resolution of legal disputes without compromising a defendant's right to a loyal and zealous defense. We are persuaded by the position advanced by amicus "that the obligation to warn, when confidentiality would be compromised to the client's detriment, must be permissive at most, unless it appears beyond a reasonable doubt that the client has formed a firm intention to inflict serious personal injuries on an unknowing third person."

Because appellants rely to a great extent upon *Tarasoff* in arguing a common-law duty to disclose, we will demonstrate that the *Tarasoff* decision is inapposite even though the facts are equally atypical and tragic. Tatiana Tarasoff was killed by one Prosenjit Poddar. The victim's parents alleged that 2 months earlier Poddar confided his intention to kill Tatiana to a defendant, Dr. Moore, a psychologist employed by the University of California. After a brief detention of Poddar by the police at Moore's request, Poddar was released pursuant to order of Dr. Moore's superior. No one warned Tatiana of her peril. The plaintiffs claimed the defendant psychologists had a duty to warn foreseeable victims. Defendants denied owing any duty of reasonable care to Tatiana. . . . The Supreme Court of California concluded that the complaint could be amended to state a cause of action against the psychologists by asserting that they had or should have determined Poddar presented a serious danger to Tatiana, pursuant to the standards of their profession, but had failed to exercise reasonable care for her safety.

In *Tarasoff*, the defendant psychologists had first-hand knowledge of Poddar's homicidal intention and knew it to be directed towards Tatiana Tarasoff, who was wholly unaware of her danger. The knowledge of the defendants in *Tarasoff* was gained from statements made to them in the course of treatment and not from statements transmitted by others. Further, the California court in *Tarasoff* did not establish a new duty to warn, but only held that psychologists must exercise such reasonable skill, knowledge, and care possessed and exercised by members of their profession under similar circumstances.

In the instant case, Michael Hawkins' potential victims, his mother and sister, knew he might be dangerous and that he had been released from confinement, contrary to Tatiana Tarasoff's ignorance of any risk of harm. Thus, no duty befell Sanders to warn Frances Hawkins of a risk of which she was already fully cognizant. Further, it must not be overlooked that Sanders received no information that Hawkins planned to assault anyone, only that he was mentally ill and likely to be dangerous to himself and others. That Sanders received no information directly from Michael Hawkins is the final distinction between the two cases.

The common-law duty to volunteer information about a client to a court considering pretrial release must be limited to situations where information gained convinces counsel that his client intends to commit a crime or inflict injury upon unknowing third persons. Such a duty cannot be extended to the facts before us. . . .

Purcell v. District Attorney for the Suffolk District

676 N.E.2d 436 (Mass. 1997)

WILKINS, C.J.

On June 21, 1994, Joseph Tyree, who had received a court order to vacate his apartment in the Allston section of Boston, consulted the plaintiff, Jeffrey W. Purcell, an attorney employed by Greater Boston Legal Services, which provides representation to low income individuals in civil matters. Tyree had recently been discharged as a maintenance man at the apartment building in which his apartment was located. On the day that Tyree consulted Purcell, Purcell decided, after extensive deliberation, that he should advise appropriate authorities that Tyree might engage in conduct harmful to others. He told a Boston police lieutenant that Tyree had made threats to burn the apartment building.

The next day, constables, accompanied by Boston police officers, went to evict Tyree. At the apartment building, they found incendiary materials, containers of gasoline, and several bottles with wicks attached. Smoke detectors had been disconnected, and gasoline had been poured on a hallway floor. Tyree was arrested and later indicted for attempted arson of a building.

In August, 1995, the district attorney for the Suffolk district subpoenaed Purcell to testify concerning the conversation Purcell had had with Tyree on June 21, 1994. A Superior Court judge granted Purcell's motion to quash the subpoena. The trial ended in a mistrial because the jury were unable to reach a verdict.

The Commonwealth decided to try Tyree again and once more sought Purcell's testimony. Another Superior Court judge concluded that Tyree's statements to Purcell were not protected by the attorney-client privilege, denied Purcell's motion to quash an anticipated subpoena, and ordered Purcell to testify. Purcell then commenced this action, . . . in the single justice session of this court. The parties entered into a stipulation of facts, and a single justice reserved and reported the case to the full court.

There is no question before this court, directly or indirectly, concerning the ethical propriety of Purcell's disclosure to the police that Tyree might engage in conduct that would be harmful to others. As bar counsel agreed in a memorandum submitted to the single justice, this court's disciplinary rules regulating the practice of law authorized Purcell to reveal to the police "the intention of his client to commit a crime and the information necessary to prevent the crime." S.J.C. Rule 3:07, Canon 4, DR 4-101(C)(3).[1] The fact that the disciplinary code permitted Purcell to make the disclosure tells us nothing about the admissibility of the information that Purcell disclosed. . . .

The attorney-client privilege is founded on the necessity that a client be free to reveal information to an attorney, without fear of is disclosure, in order to obtain informed legal advice. It is a principle of long standing. The debate here is whether Tyree is entitled to the protection of the attorney-client privilege in the circumstances.

The district attorney announces the issue in his brief to be whether a crime-fraud exception to the testimonial privilege applies in this case. He asserts that, even if Tyree's communication with Purcell was made as part of his consultation concerning the eviction proceeding, Tyree's communication concerning his contemplated criminal conduct is not protected by the privilege. . . .

"It is the purpose of the crime-fraud exception to the attorney-client privilege to assure that the 'seal of secrecy, . . . between lawyer and client does not extend to communications 'made for the purpose of getting advice for the commission of a fraud' or crime." There is no public interest in the preservation of the secrecy of that kind of communication. . . .

We, therefore, accept the general principle of a crime-fraud exception. The Proposed Massachusetts Rules of Evidence adequately define the crime-fraud exception to the lawyer-client privilege set forth in rule 502(d)(1) as follows: "If the services of the lawyer were sought or obtained to enable or aid anyone to commit or plan to commit what the client knew or reasonably should have known to be a crime or fraud." . . . The applicability of the exception, like the existence of the privilege, is a question of fact for the judge.

The district attorney rightly grants that he, as the opponent of the application of the testimonial privilege, has the burden of showing that the exception applies. . . . We conclude that facts supporting the applicability of the crime-fraud exception must be proved by a preponderance of the evidence. However, on a showing of a factual basis

1. The same conclusion would be reached under Rule 1.6(b)(1) of the Proposed Mass. R. of Prof. Conduct, now pending before the Justices. Under rule 1.6(b)(1), as now proposed, a lawyer may reveal confidential information relating to a client "to prevent the commission of a criminal or fraudulent act that the lawyer reasonably believes is likely to result in death or substantial bodily harm, or in substantial injury to the financial interests or property of another." Unlike DR 4-101(C)(3), which allows disclosure of a client's intention to commit any crime, disclosure of a client's intention to commit a crime is permissible under proposed rule 1.6(b)(1) only as to crimes threatening substantial consequences, and disclosure is permitted based on an attorney's reasonable belief of the likely existence of the threat rather than, as is the case under DR 4-101(C)(3), a known intention of the client to commit a crime.

adequate to support a reasonable belief that an in camera review of the evidence may establish that the exception applies, the judge has discretion to conduct such an in camera review. Once the judge sees the confidential information, the burden of proof normally will be unimportant.

In this case, in deciding whether to conduct a discretionary in camera review of the substance of the conversation concerning arson between Tyree and Purcell, the judge would have evidence tending to show that Tyree discussed a future crime with Purcell and that thereafter Tyree actively prepared to commit that crime. Without this evidence, the crime of arson would appear to have no apparent connection with Tyree's eviction proceeding and Purcell's representation of Tyree. With this evidence, however, a request that a judge inquire in camera into the circumstances of Tyree's apparent threat to burn the apartment building would not be a call for a "fishing expedition," and a judge might be justified in conducting such an inquiry. The evidence in this case, however, was not sufficient to warrant the judge's finding that Tyree consulted Purcell for the purpose of obtaining advice in furtherance of a crime. Therefore, the order denying the motion to quash because the crime-fraud exception applied cannot be upheld.

There is a consideration in this case that does not appear in other cases that we have seen concerning the attorney-client privilege. The testimony that the prosecution seeks from Purcell is available only because Purcell reflectively made a disclosure, relying on this court's disciplinary rule which permitted him to do so. Purcell was under no ethical duty to disclose Tyree's intention to commit a crime. He did so to protect the lives and property of others, a purpose that underlies a lawyer's discretionary right stated in the disciplinary rule. The limited facts in the record strongly suggest that Purcell's disclosures to the police served the beneficial public purpose on which the disciplinary rule was based.

We must be cautious in permitting the use of client communications that a lawyer has revealed only because of a threat to others. Lawyers will be reluctant to come forward if they know that the information that they disclose may lead to adverse consequences to their clients. A practice of the use of such disclosures might prompt a lawyer to warn a client in advance that the disclosure of certain information may not be held confidential, thereby chilling free discourse between lawyer and client and reducing the prospect that the lawyer will learn of a serious threat to the well-being of others. To best promote the purposes of the attorney-client privilege, the crime-fraud exception should apply only if the communication seeks assistance in or furtherance of future criminal conduct. When the opponent of the privilege argues that the communication itself may show that the exception applies and seeks its disclosure in camera, the judge, in the exercise of discretion on the question whether to have an in camera proceeding, should consider if the public interest is served by disclosure, even in camera, of a communication whose existence is known only because the lawyer acted against his client's interests under the authority of a disciplinary rule. The facts of each situation must be considered.

It might seem that this opinion is in a posture to conclude by stating that the order denying the motion to quash any subpoena to testify is vacated and the matter is to be remanded for further proceedings concerning the application of the crime-fraud exception. However, the district attorney's brief appears to abandon its earlier concession that all communications between Tyree and Purcell should be treated as protected by the attorney-client privilege unless the crime-fraud exception applies. The question whether the attorney-client privilege is involved at all will be open on remand. We, therefore, discuss the issue.

The attorney-client privilege applies only when the client's communication was for the purpose of facilitating the rendition of legal services. The burden of proving that the attorney-client privilege applies to a communication rests on the party asserting the privilege. The motion judge did not pass on the question whether the attorney-client privilege applied to the communication at all but rather went directly to the issue of the crime-fraud exception, although not using that phrase.

A statement of an intention to commit a crime made in the course of seeking legal advice is protected by the privilege, unless the crime-fraud exception applies. That exception applies only if the client or prospective client seeks advice or assistance in furtherance of criminal conduct. It is agreed that Tyree consulted Purcell concerning his impending eviction. Purcell is a member of the bar, and Tyree either was or sought to become Purcell's client. The serious question concerning the application of the privilege is whether Tyree informed Purcell of the fact of his intention to commit arson for the purpose of receiving legal advice or assistance in furtherance of criminal conduct. Purcell's presentation of the circumstances in which Tyree's statements were made is likely to be the only evidence presented.

This is not a case in which our traditional view that testimonial privileges should be construed strictly should be applied. A strict construction of the privilege that would leave a gap between the circumstances in which the crime-fraud exception applies and the circumstances in which a communication is protected by the attorney-client privilege would make no sense. The attorney-client privilege "is founded upon the necessity, in the interest and administration of justice, of the aid of persons having knowledge of the law and skilled in its practice, which assistance can only be safely and readily availed of when free from the consequences or the apprehension of disclosure." Unless the crime-fraud exception applies, the attorney-client privilege should apply to communications concerning possible future, as well as past, criminal conduct, because an informed lawyer may be able to dissuade the client from improper future conduct and, if not, under the ethical rules may elect in the public interest to make a limited disclosure of the client's threatened conduct.

A judgment should be entered in the county court ordering that the order denying the motion to quash any subpoena issued to Purcell to testify at Tyree's trial is vacated and that the matter is remanded for further proceedings consistent with this opinion....

Spaulding v. Zimmerman

116 N.W.2d 704 (Minn. 1962)

THOMAS GALLAGHER, J.

Appeal from an order of the District Court of Douglas County vacating and setting aside a prior order of such court dated May 8, 1957, approving a settlement made on behalf of David Spaulding on March 5, 1957, at which time he was a minor of the age of 20 years; and in connection therewith, vacating and setting aside releases executed by him and his parents, a stipulation of dismissal, an order for dismissal with prejudice, and a judgment entered pursuant thereto.

The prior action was brought against defendants by Theodore Spaulding, as father and natural guardian of David Spaulding, for injuries sustained by David in an automobile accident, arising out of a collision which occurred August 24, 1956, between an automobile driven by John Zimmerman, in which David was a passenger, and one owned by John Ledermann and driven by Florian Ledermann.

On appeal defendants contend that the court was without jurisdiction to vacate the settlement solely because their counsel then possessed information, unknown to plaintiff herein, that at the time he was suffering from an aorta aneurysm which may have resulted from the accident, because (1) no mutual mistake of fact was involved; (2) no duty rested upon them to disclose information to plaintiff which they could assume had been disclosed to him by his own physicians; (3) insurance limitations as well as physical injuries formed the basis for the settlement; and (4) plaintiff's motion to vacate the order for settlement and to set aside the releases was barred by the limitations provided in Rule 60.02 of Rules of Civil Procedure.[1]

After the accident, David's injuries were diagnosed by his family physician, Dr. James H. Cain, as a severe crushing injury of the chest with multiple rib fractures; a severe cerebral concussion, probably with petechial hemorrhages of the brain; and bilateral fractures of the clavicles. At Dr. Cain's suggestion, on January 3, 1957, David was examined by Dr. John F. Pohl, an orthopedic specialist, who made X-ray studies of his chest. Dr. Pohl's detailed report of this examination included the following:

> "... The lung fields are clear. The heart and aorta are normal."

Nothing in such report indicated the aorta aneurysm with which David was then suffering. On March 1, 1957, at the suggestion of Dr. Pohl, David was examined from a neurological viewpoint by Dr. Paul S. Blake, and in the report of this examination there was no finding of the aorta aneurysm.

In the meantime, on February 22, 1957, at defendants' request, David was examined by Dr. Hewitt Hannah, a neurologist. On February 26, 1957, the latter reported to Messrs. Field, Arvesen & Donoho, attorneys for defendant John Zimmerman, as follows:

> "The one feature of the case which bothers me more than any other part of the case is the fact that this boy of 20 years of age has an aneurysm, which means a dilatation of the aorta and the arch of the aorta. Whether this came out of this accident I cannot say with any degree of certainty and I have discussed it with the Roentgenologist and a couple of Internists.... Of course an aneurysm or dilatation of the aorta in a boy of this age is a serious matter as far as his life. This aneurysm may dilate further and it might rupture with further dilatation and this would cause his death.
>
> "It would be interesting also to know whether the X-ray of his lungs, taken immediately following the accident, shows this dilatation or not. If it was not present immediately following

1. Rule 60.02 of Rules of Civ. Proc. provides in part: "On motion ... the court may relieve a party ... from a final ... order, or proceeding for the following reasons: (1) Mistake, inadvertence, surprise, or excusable neglect; (2) newly discovered evidence which by due diligence could not have been discovered in time to move for a new trial under Rule 59.03; (3) fraud (whether ... intrinsic or extrinsic), misrepresentation, or other misconduct of an adverse party; ... or (6) any other reason justifying relief from the operation of the judgment. The motion shall be made within a reasonable time, and for reasons (1), (2), and (3) not more than one year after the judgment, order, or proceeding was entered or taken.... This rule does not limit the power of a court to entertain an independent action to relieve a party from a judgment, order, or proceeding, ... or to set aside a judgment for fraud upon the court."

> the accident and is now present, then we could be sure that it came out of the accident."

Prior to the negotiations for settlement, the contents of the above report were made known to counsel for defendants Florian and John Ledermann.

The case was called for trial on March 4, 1957, at which time the respective parties and their counsel possessed such information as to David's physical condition as was revealed to them by their respective medical examiners as above described. It is thus apparent that neither David nor his father, the nominal plaintiff in the prior action, was then aware that David was suffering the aorta aneurysm but on the contrary believed that he was recovering from the injuries sustained in the accident.

On the following day an agreement for settlement was reached wherein, in consideration of the payment of $6,500, David and his father agreed to settle in full for all claims arising out of the accident.

Richard S. Roberts, counsel for David, thereafter presented to the court a petition for approval of the settlement, wherein David's injuries were described as:

> ". . . severe crushing of the chest, with multiple rib fractures, severe cerebral concussion, with petechial hemorrhages of the brain, bilateral fractures of the clavicles."

Attached to the petition were affidavits of David's physicians, Drs. James H. Cain and Paul S. Blake, wherein they set forth the same diagnoses they had made upon completion of their respective examinations of David as above described. At no time was there information disclosed to the court that David was then suffering from an aorta aneurysm which may have been the result of the accident. Based upon the petition for settlement and such affidavits of Drs. Cain and Blake, the court on May 8, 1957, made its order approving the settlement.

Early in 1959, David was required by the army reserve, of which he was a member, to have a physical checkup. For this, he again engaged the services of Dr. Cain. In this checkup, the latter discovered the aorta aneurysm. He then reexamined the X rays which had been taken shortly after the accident and at this time discovered that they disclosed the beginning of the process which produced the aneurysm. He promptly sent David to Dr. Jerome Grismer for an examination and opinion. The latter confirmed the finding of the aorta aneurysm and recommended immediate surgery therefor. This was performed by him at Mount Sinai Hospital in Minneapolis on March 10, 1959.

Shortly thereafter, David, having attained his majority, instituted the present action for additional damages due to the more serious injuries including the aorta aneurysm which he alleges proximately resulted from the accident. As indicated above, the prior order for settlement was vacated. In a memorandum made a part of the order vacating the settlement, the court stated:

> "The facts material to a determination of the motion are without substantial dispute. The only disputed facts appear to be whether . . . Mr. Roberts, former counsel for plaintiff, discussed plaintiff's injuries with Mr. Arvesen, counsel for defendant Zimmerman, immediately before the settlement agreement, and, further, whether or not there is a causal relationship between the accident and the aneurysm.
>
> "Contrary to the . . . suggestion in the affidavit of Mr. Roberts that he discussed the minor's injuries with Mr. Arvesen, the Court finds that no such discussion of the specific injuries claimed occurred prior to the settlement agreement on March 5, 1957.

"...the Court finds that although the aneurysm now existing is causally related to the accident, such finding is for the purpose of the motions only and is based solely upon the opinion expressed by Dr. Cain (Exhibit 'F'), which, so far as the Court can find from the numerous affidavits and statements of fact by counsel, stands without dispute.

"The mistake concerning the existence of the aneurysm was not mutual. For reasons which do not appear, plaintiff's doctor failed to ascertain its existence. By reason of the failure of plaintiff's counsel to use available rules of discovery, plaintiff's doctor and all his representatives did not learn that defendants and their agents knew of its existence and possible serious consequences. Except for the character of the concealment in the light of plaintiff's minority, the Court would, I believe, be justified in denying plaintiff's motion to vacate, leaving him to whatever questionable remedy he may have against his doctor and against his lawyer.

"That defendants' counsel concealed the knowledge they had is not disputed. The essence of the application of the above rule is the character of the concealment. Was it done under circumstances that defendants must be charged with knowledge that plaintiff did not know of the injury? If so, an enriching advantage was gained for defendants at plaintiff's expense. There is no doubt of the good faith of both defendants' counsel. There is no doubt that during the course of the negotiations, when the parties were in an adversary relationship, no rule required or duty rested upon defendants or their representatives to disclose this knowledge. However, once the agreement to settle was reached, it is difficult to characterize the parties' relationship as adverse. At this point all parties were interested in securing Court approval....

"When the adversary nature of the negotiations concluded in a settlement, the procedure took on the posture of a joint application to the Court, at least so far as the facts upon which the Court could and must approve settlement is concerned. It is here that the true nature of the concealment appears, and defendants' failure to act affirmatively, after having been given a copy of the application for approval, can only be defendants' decision to take a calculated risk that the settlement would be final....

"To hold that the concealment was not of such character as to result in an unconscionable advantage over plaintiff's ignorance or mistake, would be to penalize innocence and incompetence and reward less than full performance of an officer of the Court's duty to make full disclosure to the Court when applying for approval in minor settlement proceedings."

1. The principles applicable to the court's authority to vacate settlements made on behalf of minors and approved by it appear well established. With reference thereto, we have held that the court in its discretion may vacate such a settlement, even though it is not induced by fraud or bad faith, where it is shown that in the accident the minor sustained separate and distinct injuries which were not known or considered by the court at the time settlement was approved, and even though the releases furnished therein purported to cover both known and unknown injuries resulting from the accident. The court may vacate such a settlement for mistake even though the mistake was not mutual in the sense that both parties were similarly mistaken as to the nature and extent of the minor's injuries, but where it is shown that one of the parties had additional knowledge with respect thereto and was aware that neither the court nor the adversary party possessed such knowledge when the settlement was approved.

2. From the foregoing it is clear that in the instant case the court did not abuse its discretion in setting aside the settlement which it had approved on plaintiff's behalf while he was still a

minor. It is undisputed that neither he nor his counsel nor his medical attendants were aware that at the time settlement was made he was suffering from an aorta aneurysm which may have resulted from the accident. The seriousness of this disability is indicated by Dr. Hannah's report indicating the imminent danger of death therefrom. This was known by counsel for both defendants but was not disclosed to the court at the time it was petitioned to approve the settlement. While no canon of ethics or legal obligation may have required them to inform plaintiff or his counsel with respect thereto, or to advise the court therein, it did become obvious to them at the time that the settlement then made did not contemplate or take into consideration the disability described. This fact opened the way for the court to later exercise its discretion in vacating the settlement and under the circumstances described we cannot say that there was any abuse of discretion on the part of the court in so doing under Rule 60.02(6) of Rules of Civil Procedure. . . . Affirmed.

Lawyers and Other Professionals: *Duties to Third Persons*

Spaulding, Purcell, and *Hawkins* all raise issues about a professional's duty to nonclient third persons. In *Spaulding,* the court found no duty to disclose a serious medical condition in the applicable professional code, but nevertheless imposed it in the context of a Rule 60 motion. In *Purcell* and *Hawkins,* however, the courts imposed no such legal duty on lawyers to third persons. How are we to make sense of these disparate results? *Hawkins* offers some clue. The Washington Court relied heavily on the California Supreme Court's classic decision in Tarasoff v. Regents of the University of California,[1] which defined duties to third persons owed by mental health professionals. In this note we examine *Tarasoff* further, both because it has been followed in most jurisdictions,[2] and because the court's reasoning will help us discover the keys to understanding the law that extends certain professional obligations to persons other than clients.

First, consider the tremendous scope of potential liability to third persons faced by professionals in modern society. Although courts continue to disagree about the extent of a professional's accountability to a third party, in the past century a substantial number of cases have found that such a duty exists for lawyers as well as other professionals. Design professionals such as architects and engineers, whose negligent design causes a later structural collapse, may be held liable to all those injured as a result.[3] Physicians or pharmacists who negligently fail to warn a patient about the dangers of a disorder or a medication's side effects also may be held accountable to injured third persons.[4] Beyond physical injury, accountants and lawyers whose negligence causes economic harm may be liable to persons who rely on their work.[5]

1. 551 P.2d 334 (Cal. 1976).

2. Texas and Virginia appear to be the only dissenters. Thapur v. Zezulka, 994 S.W.2d 635 (Tex. 1999); Nasser v. Parker, 455 S.E.2d 502 (Va. 1995). For a list of cases, *see* Turner v. Jordan, 957 S.W.2d 815 (Tenn. 1997). Some jurisdictions have enacted statutes that impose the duty. Dan B. Dobbs, *The Law of Torts* 897 (West 2000).

3. *See* Constance Frisby Fain, *Architect and Engineer Liability* 35 Washburn L.J. 32, 40-41 (1995).

4. *See* Gregory G. Sarno, *Liability of Physician, for Injury to or Death of Third Party, Due to Failure to Disclose Driving-Related Impediment,* 43 A.L.R.4th 154 (1986).

5. *See* Christine M. Guerci, *Liability of Independent Accountant to Investors or Shareholders*, 48 A.L.R.5th 389 (1997); Joan Teshima, *Attorney's Liability, to One Other Than Immediate Client, for Negligence in Connection with Legal Duties,* 61 A.L.R.4th 615 (1988).

The easiest cases involve intentional torts, where most courts find duties to third persons. Thus, lawyers and other professionals who commit fraud,[6] abuse of process,[7] malicious prosecution,[8] conversion,[9] or the intentional infliction of emotional distress[10] do not escape liability simply because they did so in the act of providing services to a client. The most difficult situations involve allegations like those in *Tarasoff* and *Hawkins*, where creating a duty to a third party appears to conflict directly with a professional obligation to the client, such as confidentiality. Here, courts impose liability only where they find an important public policy in a statute, court rule, or professional code.

Consistent Professional and Public Duties

In cases like *Hawkins,* where negligence is alleged, the courts generally agree that liability to a third party should attach only if the duty imposed is consistent with the professional responsibility owed a client or patient. The *Tarasoff* court relied on sections 315-320 of the Restatement (Second) of Torts, which provide that a duty can arise from either a professional's special relation to the client or patient whose conduct needs to be controlled, or from a special relation between the professional and the foreseeable victim of that conduct. The court noted that in most cases where liability has been imposed both relationships existed.[11]

Recall, for example, the situation where a client seeks the professional's help primarily to benefit a third party, such as a lawyer who negligently drafts a will, which subsequently causes frustration of the testator's intent. In these cases, courts find that the duties owed to the client, competence and obedience, correspond exactly with the duty to the intended third-party beneficiary and uphold a duty to the third person. On the other hand, where the duties do not correspond exactly, courts have refused to apply the third-party beneficiary doctrine. Recall, for example, that many courts refuse to recognize a duty to estate beneficiaries by lawyers for personal representatives of an estate, because the personal representative has other duties (such as the duty to pay debts of the estate) that do not necessarily coincide with those of the estate beneficiaries.[12]

Greycas illustrates another application of the third-party beneficiary theory because the client requested a letter from his lawyer to a third-party lender. The duty

---

6. *E.g.,* Hartford Accident & Indem. Co. v. Sullivan, 846 F.2d 377 (7th Cir. 1988), *cert. denied,* 490 U.S. 1089 (1989) (lawyer liable for fraud in helping client obtain fraudulent bank loan); Bonvire v. Wampler, 779 F.2d 1011(4th Cir. 1985) (lawyer who knowingly misrepresented client's honesty and experience liable for fraud); Fire Ins. Exch. v. Bell, 643 N.E.2d 310 (Ind. 1994) (lawyer who misrepresented policy limits liable for fraud); St. Paul Fire & Marine Ins. Co. v. Touche Ross & Co., 507 N.W.2d 275 (Neb. 1993) (cause of action stated by third parties against accountants for fraud).

7. *E.g.,* Givens v. Mullikin, 75 S.W.3d 383 (Tenn. 2002) (cause of action stated against lawyer for abuse of process (as well as insured client and insurer who directed the lawyer's conduct) for barraging opposing party with subpoenas, interrogatories, and a deposition seeking information that had already been turned over).

8. *E.g.,* Raine v. Drasin, 621 S.W.2d 895 (Ky. 1981) (lawyer liable for malicious prosecution for joining two physicians in malpractice case after reviewing records that clearly showed they had treated patient only after his injury had occurred).

9. *E.g.,* ERA Realty Co. v. RBS Properties, 586 N.Y.S.2d 831 (A.D. 1992) (lawyer who used void process to acquire funds liable for conversion).

10. *E.g.,* Bevan v. Fix, 42 P.3d 1013 (Wyo. 2002) (cause of action stated by child who witnessed lawyer physically abuse his mother/client); Mack v. Soung, 95 Cal. Rptr. 2d 830 (Cal. App. 2000) (cause of action stated by children of elder patient against patient's physician who covered up nursing home abuse and abandoned patient when patient's condition became critical).

11. *Tarasoff,* 551 P.2d at 343-344.

12. *See* Lawyers and Other Professionals: Malpractice Liability, *supra* p.89.

of care owed the client coincided exactly with the duty owed the third party. Note that if Proud had competently completed a UCC search, he would have discovered that his client had lied to him about the absence of liens on the farm property. His duty to his client would have required him to inform the client of that fact, as well as the fact that he would have to disclose those liens if he wrote the letter to the lender. His client then could decide whether it would be better to send the letter or drop the matter. Either way, the lawyer would have succeeded in satisfying his ethical obligation to the client and would not have committed any tort toward the third party.[13]

Beyond a specific intent to benefit a third party, most courts impose a duty on professionals to avoid physical (as opposed to economic) injury to third persons where that duty coincides with the duty undertaken to the client. For example, courts have long applied the rule of MacPherson v. Buick,[14] which abrogated the privity requirement in cases of personal injury, to design professionals whose negligence causes injury to third persons.[15] Similarly, most courts have imposed a duty on physicians when a patient whom the professional has negligently failed to warn about the side effects of medication causes harm to a third person, reasoning that the duty to warn the patient is entirely consistent with the duty to the third party.[16] Presumably, the adequately warned patient would have refrained from the injury causing conduct (such as driving), thereby avoiding the injury. On the other hand, if the patient had been warned but ignored the danger, then the physician would have breached no duty to patient or third party.[17]

With respect to economic harm, *Greycas* also relied on the tort law of misrepresentation, which follows a similar trend in duty to warn cases. Today, some jurisdictions continue to require privity for malpractice or "general" liability, but are willing to extend liability to third persons in negligent misrepresentation cases.[18] They reason that professionals have no duty to warn third persons, but when they undertake a duty to speak, they must do so with care.[19] Initially, this duty extended beyond those in privity of contract with the professional only if the misrepresentation was made intentionally or recklessly.[20] The availability of professional liability insurance

13. These obligations are restated in Model Rule 2.3 and *Restatement (Third) The Law Governing Lawyers* §95.

14 111 N.E. 1050 (N.Y. 1916).

15. *See, e.g.*, Donald M. Zupanec, *Architect's Liability for Personal Injury or Death Allegedly Caused by Improper or Defective Plans or Design*, 97 A.L.R.3d 455 (1980); Francis M. Dougherty, *Personal Injury Liability of Civil Engineer for Negligence in Highway or Bridge Construction or Maintenance*, 43 A.L.R.4th 911 (1986).

16. *See, e.g.*, Shepard v. Redford Community Hosp., 390 N.W.2d 239 (Mich. App. 1986) (physician liable for negligence in diagnosing son's spinal meningitis, which caused his mother's contagion and death); Myers v. Quesenberry, 193 Cal. Rptr. 733 (Cal. App. 1983) (physician liable to third party injured by his patient who was not warned about the dangers of driving).

17. A few courts have limited the scope of the duty to situations where the patient causes harm immediately following a medical treatment, *e.g.*, Lester v. Hall, 970 P.2d 590 (N.M. 1998) (physician who failed to warn patient of side effects of medication not liable to third party injured five days later).

18. *See, e.g.*, Bily v. Arthur Young & Co., 834 P.2d 745 (Cal. 1992) (accountants not liable to third parties for negligence in preparing an audit report, but may be liable for negligent misrepresentation to nonclients who are specifically intended beneficiaries of the audit report); Orshoski v. Krieger, 2001 Ohio App. LEXIS 5018 (prospective buyers who relied on negligent misrepresentations of lawyer for developer concerning subdivision's restrictive covenants could sue for negligent misrepresentation, but not for legal malpractice).

19. *E.g.*, Rubin v. Schottenstein, Zox & Dunn, 143 F.3d 263 (6th Cir. 1998) (*en banc*) (lawyer who represented seller in a securities transaction assumes a duty to provide complete and nonmisleading information with respect to subjects on which he undertakes to speak under Rule 10b-5).

20. Ultramares Corp. v. Touche, 174 N.E. 441 (N.Y. 1931); Conroy v. Andeck Resources '81 Year-End Ltd., 484 N.E.2d 525 (Ill. 1985).

and the evolution of more clear standards of professional practice gradually eroded this rule, so that lawyers and other professionals now are liable to a larger circle of those who reasonably rely on their opinions. Some jurisdictions have completely replaced the privity rule with one that depends solely on foreseeability,[21] while others have adopted the limited foreseeability rule of the *Restatement (Second) of Torts* §552, which restricts liability to "a limited group of persons for whose benefit and guidance" the professional "intends to supply the information."[22]

Inconsistent Professional and Public Duties

When a professional duty directly conflicts with a client obligation, courts impose liability in negligence only when a clear public policy requires it. The most obvious example is the often-repeated statement that lawyers owe no duties to adverse parties.[23] The *Tarasoff* court identified several potential sources of competing public policy.

First, the court cited several cases that upheld a physician's duty to warn a patient's caregivers about the contagious nature of the patient's disease.[24] All of these cases relied on state statutes that required physicians to report diagnosis of contagious diseases to public health officials. The courts reasoned that the public duty to report created by state statute was entirely consistent with and created a duty to warn a third-party caregiver about the nature of the illness.[25] A more recent example can be found in cases that allege a physician should have warned a third person about a patient's diagnosis of AIDS. Once again, courts hinge their finding of such a responsibility on the presence of a clear statutory signal.[26] Similar cases involve the duty to warn state agencies about child abuse. State statutes vary considerably about who has that duty,[27] but most courts agree that a clear statutory duty is required to create liability in tort.[28] The presence of statutes designed to protect the

21. *E.g.*, Molecular Tech. Corp. v. Valentine, 925 F.2d 910 (6th Cir. 1991).
22. *See, e.g.*, Walpert, Smullian & Blumenthal, P.C. v. Katz, 762 A.2d 582 (Md. 2000) (accountant malpractice); *Restatement (Third) The Law Governing Lawyers* §51.
23. *E.g.*, James v. The Chase Manhattan Bank, 173 F. Supp. 2d 544, 550 (N.D. Miss. 2001).
24. Hofmann v. Blackmon, 241 So. 2d 752 (Fla. App. 1970); Wojcik v. Aluminum Co. of America, 183 N.Y.S.2d 351 (A.D. 1959); Jones v. Stanko, 160 N.E. 456 (Ohio 1928); Davis v. Rodman, 227 S.W. 612 (Ark. 1921); Skillings v. Allen, 173 N.W. 663 (Minn. 1919); *See* Tracy A. Bateman, *Liability of Doctor or Other Health Practitioner to Third Party Contracting Contagious Disease from Doctor's Patient*, 3 A.L.R.5th 370 (1992).
25. A similar example occurred in Krejci v. Akron Pediatric Neurology, Inc., 511 N.E.2d 129 (Ohio App. 1987), where the court based a physicians' duty to a third party to use reasonable care in certifying the driving ability of a patient with epilepsy on state statute.
26. *E.g.*, Doe v. Roe, 599 N.Y.S.2d 350 (A.D. 1993) (cause of action stated against a physician who disclosed HIV infection in violation of AIDS confidentiality statute); Doe v. Marselle, 675 A.2d 835 (Conn. 1996) (physician's unauthorized disclosure was "willful" with the meaning of the AIDS confidentiality statute); Tex. Dept. of Health v. Doe, 994 S.W.2d 890 (Tex. App. 1999) (Health Dept. not immune from suit for violating AIDS confidentiality statute). *Cf.* Doe v. High-Tech Inst., Inc., 972 P.2d 1060 (Colo. App. 1998) (disclosure of HIV status required by AIDS statute based on blood test not authorized by AIDS statute states a cause of action for public disclosure of private facts). *See, e.g.*, Krejci v. Akron Pediatric Neurology, Inc., 511 N.E.2d 129 (Ohio App. 1987) (physicians' duty to third party to use reasonable care in certifying the driving ability of a patient with epilepsy based on statute).
27. Some states require "any person" to report, *e.g.*, Fla. Stat. §39.201 (2003), others require specific reporters, such as teachers, physicians, and counselors to report, *e.g.*, Cal. Penal Code §11165.7 (2003); Mass. Ann. Laws §51A (2003). A few statutes designate lawyers as mandated reporters and waive the attorney-client privilege in some or all circumstances, *e.g.*, Tex. Fam. Code §261.1010 (2003); Ohio Rev. Code §2151.421 (2003).
28. *See, e.g.*, Landeros v. Flood, 551 P.2d 389 (Cal. 1976) (physician who breached statutory duty to report child abuse may be liable to the child); Wilson v. Darr, 553 N.W.2d 579 (Iowa 1996) (priest who knew and did not report child abuse not liable to abused child because not a "mandatory reporter" under

public from harm also explains the third party liability of lawyers and accountants in securities cases.[29]

Spaulding offers us another example of the identification of a public policy. The court finds neither a statute nor a lawyer professional code provision to justify the disclosure that the court found should have occurred. Instead, the court bases its decision on a procedural rule (identical to current Fed. R. Civ. P. 60(b)) that gives the court power to modify a judgment if it constitutes a fraud upon the court. The requirement of judicial approval, designed to protect minors from harm or exploitation, embodies the strong public policy that allows the court to find grounds to reform the final order. The court reasons that in joining the plaintiff's lawyers to apply for judicial approval of the settlement, the defense lawyers assumed an obligation to disclose facts material to the court in approving the settlement.[30]

It is also interesting to speculate about the physician's duty in *Spaulding*. In a remarkably similar case nearly 30 years later, a Minnesota court followed the uniform view at the time that physicians who examined individuals at the request of another were deemed to have no physician-patient relationship, and hence, no duty to the person they examined.[31] This view of limited duty explains why the insurance company physician in *Spaulding* disclosed his findings only to his immediate employer. More recently, courts have held that physicians who perform physicals for insurers or employers have duties of disclosure or care to the patients they examine.[32] Interestingly, some of the courts that have made this change rely either on the fact the physician voluntarily undertook a duty to speak to the patient,[33] or base their decision on state statutes that mandate ordinary care.[34]

---

state statute); Kimberly S.M., 649 N.Y.S.2d 588 (A.D. 1996) (cause of action stated against a teacher who breached statutory duty to report child abuse). Several states have codified a civil duty to report. *See, e.g.*, Campbell v. Burton, 750 N.E.2d 539 (Ohio 2000) (teacher, superintendent, and board of education liable under state statute creating liability for not reporting child abuse).

29. *See, e.g.*, Jill E. Fisch, *The Scope of Private Securities Litigation: In Search of Liability Standards for Private Defendants*, 99 Colum. L. Rev. 1293 (1999); James D. Cox, *Just Deserts for Accountants and Attorneys After Bank of Denver*, 38 Ariz. L. Rev. 519 (1996); Richard J. Link, *Persons Liable for False Registration Statement Under Sec. 11 of Securities Act of 1933*, 114 A.L.R. Fed. 551 (1993); F.S. Tinio, *Who Is An "Insider" Within the Meaning of §10(b) of the Securities Exchange Act of 1943 and SEC Rule 10b-5 Promulgated Thereunder—Making Unlawful Corporate Insider's Nondisclosure of Information to Seller or Purchaser of Corporation's Stock*, 2 A.L.R. Fed. 274 (1969).

30. Amazingly, the lawyers in *Spaulding* failed to ask their client Zimmerman, in whose car Spaulding was riding and who had a personal relationship with Spaulding's family, whether he would consent to the disclosure. This is undoubtedly because they incorrectly viewed themselves primarily as insurance company lawyers rather than Zimmerman's lawyer, a serious ethical lapse we shall discuss in Chapter 6. *See* Roger C. Cramton & Lori P. Knowles, *Professional Secrecy and Its Exceptions: Spaulding v. Zimmerman Revisited*, 83 Minn. L. Rev. 63 (1998).

31. Henkemayer v. Boxall, 465 N.W.2d 437 (Minn. App. 1991) (no duty to diagnose or disclose presence of aneurysm to person examined by insurance carrier physician to determine worker's compensation benefits).

32. *See, e.g.*, Green v. Walker, 910 F.2d 291 (5th Cir. 1990) (physician hired by employer failed to discover plaintiff's lung cancer); Ranier v. Frieman, 682 A.2d 1220 (N.J. App. 1996) (physician retained to examine applicant for social security disability benefits owed duty of reasonable care in examination and diagnosis); Greenberg v. Perkins, 845 P.2d 530 (Colo. 1993) (physician hired by opposing counsel to perform an independent medical exam of the plaintiff in a personal injury action owed duty to act with reasonable care so as not to cause injury in testing plaintiff).

33. *E.g.*, Hoover v. Williamson, 203 A.2d 861 (Md. 1964).

34. *See, e.g.*, Daly v. United States, 946 F.2d 1467 (9th Cir. 1991) (Washington medical malpractice act does not require physician-patient relationship for failure to follow the accepted standard of care); Webb v. T.D., 951 P.2d 1008 (Mont. 1997) (statutory law of Montana imposes a duty on physicians who perform examinations at the request of a third person to disclose an imminent danger to the examinee's physical or mental well-being); Cleghorn v. Hess, 853 P.2d 1260 (Nev. 1993) (Nevada evidence statutes define "patient" as one who consulted or was examined or interviewed by a doctor for purposes of diagnosis or treatment).

The Relevance of Professional Codes

Of course, no such court rule or statute existed in *Tarasoff*. This explains why the court went on to cite the relevant professional code, the Principles of Medical Ethics of the American Medical Association, which at the time provided: "A physician may not reveal the confidence entrusted to him in the course of medical attendance . . . unless he is required to do so by law or unless it becomes necessary in order to protect the welfare of the individual or of the community." Recall that the defendant psychologist had already determined it was necessary to protect the community welfare by warning the police about his client's behavior. This meant that the court's imposition of liability simply followed the professional code and practice. In other words, the court's rule corresponded exactly with the professional custom. Imposing that duty on mental health professionals was no different from an ordinary malpractice case that depends on expert testimony.

This legal basis for *Tarasoff* helps to explain the Washington Court's application of the case to the facts in *Hawkins*. First, no statute created the duty to warn. Second, the applicable lawyer code provision in *Hawkins* allowed but did not require disclosure to prevent a future client crime.[35] The physician code cited in *Tarasoff*, on the other hand, prohibited disclosure unless it became necessary to protect the welfare of the community, which the psychologist had already determined had occurred. Further, unlike the psychologist in *Tarasoff*, Hawkins' lawyer received no information from his client that Hawkins planned to assault anyone, and had little or no professional training to make a prediction that he might.[36] Even if he had believed his client was dangerous, the court points out that a warning was not necessary to avoid the harm to the client's mother, who was already aware of his threatening behavior. The lack of an unaware, identifiable victim as well as the lack of a professional duty to diagnose dangerous behavior also has led juries and courts to exonerate mental health professionals from liability in cases subsequent to *Tarasoff*.[37]

Contrast the lawyer in *Purcell* who did exercise his discretion to warn. What if he had not? Suppose the client had burned down the building, killing a tenant. Would a court impose liability on Purcell for failing to warn? The Washington court's rule, that a duty would only exist if the lawyer "believed beyond a reasonable doubt" that the client would harm an identifiable person, suggests that the answer turns on the certainty of the lawyer's belief. Further support for this proposition can be found in the ABA Standards for the Defense Function, which provide that the lawyer "must" reveal the client's intention and information necessary to prevent the crime "if the contemplated crime is one which would seriously endanger the life or safety of any person or corrupt the processes of the courts and the lawyer believes such action on his part is necessary to prevent it."[38] The only other case that

---

35. The Model Code of Professional Responsibility governed Washington lawyers at the time. DR 4-101(C)(3) provided: "A lawyer may reveal . . . [t]he intention of his client to commit a crime and the information necessary to prevent the crime."

36. Some bar opinions emphasize the requirement of Model Rule 1.6(b), holding that mere suspicion is not enough to trigger the future crime exception to confidentiality because the lawyer must have a "reasonable basis" for such a belief. *See, e.g.*, Assn. of the Bar of the City of N.Y. Op. 2002-1, *Client Confidentiality and the Intention to Commit a Crime*.

37. *See* John C. Williams, *Liability of One Treating Mentally Afflicted Patient for Failure to Warn or Protect Third Persons Threatened by Patient*, 83 A.L.R.3d 1201 (1978).

38. ABA, *Standards for Criminal Justice, The Defense Function* §4-3.7(d) (3d ed. 1993). Only two cases cite this standard, and both involve crimes corrupting court process. United States v. Del Carpio-Cotrina, 733 F. Supp. 95 (S.D. Fla. 1990) (jumping bond); In the Matter of Doe, 551 F.2d 899 (2d Cir. 1976) (bribery of a juror).

specifically addresses this issue for lawyers is a subsequent Washington case, where a prospective client told a lawyer that he was "going to get a gun and blow them all away, the prosecutor, the judge and the public defender."[39] The lawyer warned these identified persons, and the court upheld the client's subsequent conviction for intimidating a judge. This time the court commented that lawyers "have a duty to warn of true threats to harm a judge made by a client or a third party when the attorney has a reasonable belief that such threats are real."[40]

The Restatement of the Law Governing Lawyers disagrees with this basis of potential liability. With respect to professional codes, it agrees that a lawyer may, but is not required, to disclose threats of serious bodily harm or death when the lawyer reasonably believes it necessary, and also instructs lawyers, where feasible, to make efforts to dissuade clients not to act.[41] It then provides that the lawyer "is not, solely by reason of such action or inaction, subject to professional discipline, liable for damages to the lawyer's client or any third person."[42] In other words, some clear public policy beyond the applicable professional rule, like the court rule in *Spaulding*, must require the disclosure. The comments reason that disclosure conflicts with the lawyer's "customary role of protecting client interests" and point out that "critical facts may be unclear, emotions may be high and little time may be available" for lawyers to decide whether to warn.[43] Further, because the reasonableness of the lawyer's belief at the time should be controlling, subsequent reexamination of the circumstances would be "unwarranted."[44]

Of course, these same problems apply to mental health professionals. The only way they differ significantly from lawyers is in their specific training to diagnose dangerous behavior, though the psychological professions argue that they are notoriously unable to achieve much accuracy in their predictions.[45] Interestingly, a California case subsequent to *Tarasoff* does seem to find this professional training important. In Nally v. Grace Community Church of the Valley,[46] the court refused to impose any duty of care to prevent a suicide on a nontherapist clergy counselor who was neither licensed nor professionally trained as a medical expert. While the court based its decision in part on the defendant's lack of training, they also emphasized that the state legislature specifically left the religious counselor's activity unregulated.

---

39. St. v. Hansen, 862 P.2d 117, 118 (Wash. 1993).
40. *Id.* at 122. The issue of a lawyer's warning also has arisen in the context of the exceptions to the attorney-client privilege, as it did in *Purcell. See, e.g.,* In re Gonnella, 570 A.2d 53 (N.J. Super. 1989) (public defender's warning to prosecutor after his client told him to warn co-counsel to resign and threatened co-counsel with harm if he did not comply fell within both the waiver and crime-fraud exceptions); People v. Fentress, 425 N.Y.S.2d 485 (Dutchess County Ct. 1980) (lawyer's call to the police about client's crime not "tainted evidence" because call authorized by his client and lawyer acted to prevent client's suicide).
41. *Restatement (Third) The Law Governing Lawyers* §66(1) and (2) (2000).
42. *Id.* §66(3).
43. *Id.* Comment g.
44. *Id.* The Model Rules are not quite so unequivocal, but arguably produce the same result. The Preamble recognizes that the Rules "are not designed to be the basis for civil liability," but also admits that because they "establish standards of conduct by lawyers, a lawyer's violation of a Rule may be evidence of breach of the applicable standard of conduct." Scope ¶20. Since disclosures of threats of danger are discretionary under Rule 1.6, a lawyer would not breach the rule either by disclosing or choosing not to disclose, though some worry that the permission to disclose can be used to create liability.
45. *See* Alan A. Stone, *The Tarasoff Decisions: Suing Psychotherapists to Safeguard Society*, 90 Harv. L. Rev. 358 (1976).
46. 763 P.2d 948 (Cal. 1988).

Lawyers fall right in the middle between unlicensed clergy and licensed mental health professionals. Although lawyers share with clergy a lack of formal psychological training, unlike clergy, lawyers are licensed and heavily regulated by the state. Licensure means that persons who may be dangerous are funneled to certain professionals (like therapists and lawyers) to receive essential services (such as therapy or criminal defense).

The *Tarasoff* court spoke of our society as "crowded," "computerized," "risk infected," and "interdependent," and stated that "we can hardly tolerate the further exposure to danger that would result from a concealed knowledge of the therapist that his patient was lethal."[47] Like therapists, at least some lawyers encounter some very dangerous persons as clients. Should this mean that a lawyer, like a therapist, has a duty to warn foreseeable victims targeted by a client? Perhaps the most that can be said for the moment is that no case has yet imposed liability on a lawyer for failure to warn. Further, precisely because lawyers are not trained to recognize dangerous characteristics, the potential cases where a court might impose such an obligation on lawyers are considerably fewer than those that might involve mental health workers.[48] On the other hand, in the limited number of cases where a lawyer believes a client creates a significant risk, a lawyer like Purcell can exercise his discretion to disclose. If it turns out that the client's threat is very credible and the lawyer fails to disclose, that lawyer could conceivably be the subject of a suit like *Tarasoff* in the future.

We can conclude that courts find duties to nonclients in any one of four situations. First, professionals are liable to nonclients for intentional torts. Second, the client's intent to benefit a third person generally justifies liability. Third, where a breach of a duty to a client causes the client to harm a third person, liability also may attach. In the last situation, where professional duty conflicts with a duty to a third person, courts look for some clear public policy to justify the imposition of a duty to the third person. Statutes can create such duties, as can duties to a tribunal imposed by procedural rules. *Tarasoff* and *Hawkins* show how a duty can be imposed where a professional code requires or recognizes it as well.

3. Seeking Advice and Self-Defense

When an accusation of misconduct against a lawyer has occurred, utilitarians would argue that the need for information to produce a just outcome allows lawyers the freedom to disclose the information necessary to defend themselves. Lawyers also are justified in seeking advice about their own conduct or in making an affirmative claim for fees, at least as long as the client has violated a legal obligation that should be redressed. The deontologist would defend the lawyer's right to seek advice and to respond to an accusation on the grounds that the lawyer deserves a chance to explain her conduct, especially when unjustly accused. Similarly, the lawyer who has provided legal services to a client deserves to be paid for those services because the client has promised to do so and promises should be kept. In all of these situations, the personal interest of the lawyer often is corralled by protective orders or limitations on the permissible scope of disclosure.

47. *Tarasoff*, 551 P.2d at 347.
48. One recent study finds that lawyers themselves are increasingly the target of such violence, citing examples from domestic, employment, and criminal law. Stephen Kelson, *Violence Against Lawyers: The Increasingly Attacked Profession*, 10 Pub. Interest L.J. 261 (2001).

Problems

5-19. If Martyn & Fox's client threatens to sue us for malpractice, can we threaten to disclose confidential information regarding the client? Can we use confidential information in a lawsuit against our client for payment of our fee? What if anything can we disclose when a lender to our client sues us for our role on the loan?

5-20. Martyn & Fox and its client have unhappily parted company. What, if anything, may Martyn & Fox disclose to lawyer A, our successor counsel?

5-21. Lawyer B, from another law firm, consults Martyn & Fox to determine how she should proceed in the representation of her client. She is worried that her client, Big Bank's CEO, is lying to her and wants to go into a considerable amount of detail explaining why. What do we say?

Consider: Model Rule 1.6(b)(4) and (5)
Model Code DR 4-101(C)(4)

Meyerhofer v. Empire Fire & Marine Insurance Co.

497 F.2d 1190 (2d Cir. 1974), cert. denied, 419 U.S. 998 (1974)

MOORE, Circuit Judge:

This is an appeal by . . . plaintiffs, and their counsel, from an order of the United States District Court for the Southern District of New York . . . (a) dismissing without prejudice plaintiffs' action against defendants, (b) enjoining and disqualifying plaintiffs' counsel, Bernson, Hoeniger, Freitag & Abbey, and Stuart Charles Goldberg from acting as attorneys for plaintiffs in this action or in any future action against defendant Empire Fire and Marine Insurance Company (Empire) involving the same transactions, occurrences, events, allegations, facts or issues, and (c) enjoining Bernson, Hoeniger, Freitag & Abbey and Stuart Charles Goldberg from disclosing confidential information regarding Empire to others. Intervenor Stuart Charles Goldberg also appeals from said order.

The full import of the problems and issues presented on this appeal cannot be appreciated and analyzed without an initial statement of the facts out of which they arise.

Empire Fire and Marine Insurance Company on May 31, 1972, made a public offering of 500,000 shares of its stock, pursuant to a registration statement filed with the Securities and Exchange Commission (SEC) on March 28, 1972. The stock was offered at $16 a share. Empire's attorney on the issue was the firm of Sitomer, Sitomer & Porges. Stuart Charles Goldberg was an attorney in the firm and had done some work on the issue.

Plaintiff Meyerhofer, on or about January 11, 1973, purchased 100 shares of Empire stock at $17 a share. He alleges that as of June 5, 1973, the market price of his stock was only $7 a share—hence, he has sustained an unrealized loss of $1,000. . . . Plaintiff Federman, on or about May 31, 1972, purchased 200 shares at $16 a share, 100 of which he sold for $1,363, sustaining a loss of some $237 on the stock sold and an unrealized loss of $900 on the stock retained.

On May 2, 1973, plaintiffs, represented by the firm of Bernson,

Hoeniger, Freitag & Abbey (the Bernson firm), on behalf of themselves and all other purchasers of Empire common stock, brought this action alleging that the registration statement and the prospectus under which the Empire stock had been issued were materially false and misleading. Thereafter, an amended complaint, dated June 5, 1973, was served. The legal theories in both were identical, namely, violations of various sections of the Securities Act of 1933, the Securities Exchange Act of 1934, Rule 10b-5, and common law negligence, fraud and deceit. Damages for all members of the class or rescission were alternatively sought.

The lawsuit was apparently inspired by a Form 10-K which Empire filed with the SEC on or about April 12, 1973. This Form revealed that "The Registration Statement under the Securities Act of 1933 with respect to the public offering of the 500,000 shares of Common Stock did not disclose the proposed $200,000 payment to the law firm as well as certain other features of the compensation arrangements between the Company [Empire] and such law firm [defendant Sitomer, Sitomer and Porges]." Later that month Empire disseminated to its shareholders a proxy statement and annual report making similar disclosures.

The defendants named were Empire, officers and directors of Empire, the Sitomer firm and its three partners, A. L. Sitomer, S. J. Sitomer and R. E. Porges, Faulkner, Dawkins & Sullivan Securities Corp., the managing underwriter, Stuart Charles Goldberg, originally alleged to have been a partner of the Sitomer firm, and certain selling stockholders of Empire shares.

On May 2, 1973, the complaint was served on the Sitomer defendants and Faulkner. No service was made on Goldberg who was then no longer associated with the Sitomer firm. However, he was advised by telephone that he had been made a defendant. Goldberg inquired of the Bernson firm as to the nature of the charges against him and was informed generally as to the substance of the complaint and in particular the lack of disclosure of the finder's fee arrangement. Thus informed, Goldberg requested an opportunity to prove his non-involvement in any such arrangement and his lack of knowledge thereof. At this stage there was unfolded the series of events which ultimately resulted in the motion and order thereon now before us on appeal.

Goldberg, after his graduation from Law School in 1966, had rather specialized experience in the securities field and had published various books and treatises on related subjects. He became associated with the Sitomer firm in November 1971. While there Goldberg worked on phases of various registration statements including Empire, although another associate was responsible for the Empire registration statement and prospectus. However, Goldberg expressed concern over what he regarded as excessive fees, the nondisclosure or inadequate disclosure thereof, and the extent to which they might include a "finder's fee," both as to Empire and other issues.

The Empire registration became effective on May 31, 1972. The excessive fee question had not been put to rest in Goldberg's mind because in middle January 1973 it arose in connection with another registration (referred to as "Glacier"). Goldberg had worked on Glacier. Little purpose will be served by detailing the events during the critical period January 18 to 22, 1973, in which Goldberg and the Sitomer partners were debating the fee disclosure problem. In summary, Goldberg insisted on a full and complete disclosure of fees in the Empire and Glacier offerings. The Sitomer partners apparently disagreed and Goldberg resigned from the firm on January 22, 1973.

On January 22, 1973, Goldberg appeared before the SEC and placed before it information subsequently embodied in his affidavit dated January 26, 1973, which becomes crucial to the issues now to be considered.

Some three months later, upon being informed that he was to be included as a defendant in the impending action, Goldberg asked the Bernson firm for an opportunity to demonstrate that he had been unaware of the finder's fee arrangement which, he said, Empire and the Sitomer firm had concealed from him all along. Goldberg met with members of the Bernson firm on at least two occasions. After consulting his own attorney, as well as William P. Sullivan, Special Counsel with the Securities and Exchange Commission, Division of Enforcement, Goldberg gave plaintiffs' counsel a copy of the January 26th affidavit which he had authored more than three months earlier. He hoped that it would verify his nonparticipation in the finder's fee omission and convince the Bernson firm that he should not be a defendant. The Bernson firm was satisfied with Goldberg's explanations and, upon their motion, granted by the court, he was dropped as a defendant. After receiving Goldberg's affidavit, the Bernson firm amended plaintiffs' complaint. The amendments added more specific facts but did not change the theory or substance of the original complaint.

By motion dated June 7, 1973, the remaining defendants moved "pursuant to Canons 4 and 9 of the Code of Professional Responsibility, the Disciplinary Rules and Ethical Considerations applicable thereto, and the supervisory power of this Court" for the order of disqualification now on appeal.

By memorandum decision and order, the District Court ordered that the Bernson firm and Goldberg be barred from acting as counsel or participating with counsel for plaintiffs in this or any future action against Empire involving the transactions placed in issue in this lawsuit and from disclosing confidential information to others.

...The basis for the Court's decision is the premise that Goldberg had obtained confidential information from his client Empire which, in breach of relevant ethical canons, he revealed to plaintiffs' attorneys in their suit against Empire....

There is no proof—not even a suggestion—that Goldberg had revealed any information, confidential or otherwise, that might have caused the instigation of the suit. To the contrary, it was not until after the suit was commenced that Goldberg learned that he was in jeopardy. The District Court recognized that the complaint had been based on Empire's—not Goldberg's—disclosures, but concluded because of this that Goldberg was under no further obligation "to reveal the information or to discuss the matter with plaintiffs' counsel."

Despite the breadth of paragraphs EC4-4 and DR4-101 (B), DR4-101(C) recognizes that a lawyer may reveal confidences or secrets necessary to defend himself against "an accusation of wrongful conduct." This is exactly what Goldberg had to face when, in their original complaint, plaintiffs named him as a defendant who wilfully violated the securities laws.

The charge, of knowing participation in the filing of a false and misleading registration statement, was a serious one. The complaint alleged violation of criminal statutes and civil liability computable at over four million dollars. The cost in money of simply defending such an action might be very substantial. The damage to his professional reputation which might be occasioned by the mere pendency of such a charge was an even greater cause for concern.

Under these circumstances Goldberg had the right to make an appropriate disclosure with respect to his role in the public offering. Concomitantly, he had the right to support his version of the facts with suitable evidence.

The problem arises from the fact that the method Goldberg used to accomplish this was to deliver to Mr. Abbey, a member of the Bernson firm, the thirty page affidavit, accompanied by sixteen exhibits, which he had submitted to the SEC. This document not only went into extensive detail concerning Goldberg's efforts to cause the Sitomer firm to rectify the nondisclosure with respect to Empire but even more extensive detail concerning how these efforts had been precipitated by counsel for the underwriters having come upon evidence showing that a similar nondisclosure was contemplated with respect to Glacier and their insistence that full corrective measures should be taken. Although Goldberg's description reflected seriously on his employer, the Sitomer firm and, also, in at least some degree, on Glacier, he was clearly in a situation of some urgency. Moreover, before he turned over the affidavit, he consulted both his own attorney and a distinguished practitioner of securities law, and he and Abbey made a joint telephone call to Mr. Sullivan of the SEC. Moreover, it is not clear that, in the context of this case, Canon 4 applies to anything except information gained from Empire. Finally, because of Goldberg's apparent intimacy with the offering, the most effective way for him to substantiate his story was for him to disclose the SEC affidavit. It was the fact that he had written such an affidavit at an earlier date which demonstrated that his story was not simply fabricated in response to plaintiffs' complaint....

The burden of the District Court's order did not fall most harshly on Goldberg; rather its greatest impact has been felt by Bernson, Hoeniger, Freitag & Abbey, plaintiffs' counsel, which was disqualified from participation in the case. The District Court based its holding, not on the fact that the Bernson firm showed bad faith when it received Goldberg's affidavit, but rather on the fact that it was involved in a tainted association with Goldberg because his disclosures to them inadvertently violated Canons 4 and 9 of the Code of Professional Responsibility. Because there are no violations of either of these Canons in this case, we can find no basis to hold that the relationship between Goldberg and the Bernson firm was tainted. The District Court was apparently unpersuaded by appellees' salvo of innuendo to the effect that Goldberg "struck a deal" with the Bernson firm or tried to do more than prove his innocence to them. Since its relationship with Goldberg was not tainted by violations of the Code of Professional Responsibility, there appears to be no warrant for its disqualification from participation in either this or similar actions. A fortiori there was no sound basis for disqualifying plaintiffs or dismissing the complaint.

Order dismissing action without prejudice and enjoining Bernson, Hoeniger, Freitag & Abbey from acting as counsel for plaintiffs herein reversed.... To the extent that the orders appealed from prohibit Goldberg from acting as a party or as an attorney for a party in any action arising out of the facts herein alleged, or from disclosing material information except on discovery or at trial, they are affirmed.

4. Financial Harm

No one disputes that lawyers cannot counsel or assist a client crime or fraud. Specific exceptions to client confidentiality that allow disclosure to prevent, rectify or mitigate financial harm caused by a client, however, continue to generate substantial disagreement among lawyers and the public, including the authors of this book. Yet, perhaps because the human willingness to lie can cause serious harm, confidentiality exceptions have long been recognized when clients seek to use lawyers to promote fraudulent activity.

Utilitarians recognize that efficient operation of both a market economy and a democratic government requires honesty. If everyone could use lawyers to promote their own illegal deception, the market system, many aspects of government and the legal system itself would lose the confidence of its citizens. To prevent this erosion in confidence, some lawyers argue that they should be able to disclose activities of clients that seek to use the lawyer's services to perpetrate a fraud when the greater good would be promoted by disclosure. Others maintain that confidentiality remains an essential incentive for clients to disclose their plans to lawyers, who then are in the best position to dissuade clients from engaging in fraudulent activity. Focusing on trust and privacy, the deontologist would agree that clients should be encouraged to facilitate their plans through the client-lawyer relationship. They would add, however, that when the client seeks to use the relationship to create a legal mess by violating another categorical imperative such as honesty, then the client's right to confidentiality has been lost. If the lawyer's services unwittingly have been used to further that fraud, the lawyer's duty of reparation for her own acts also comes into play.

Problems

5-22. Martyn admonished Client about the importance of fully disclosing all assets on a bankruptcy filing. Client failed to do so and was indicted for bankruptcy fraud. Can Martyn be forced to testify about the original warning?

5-23. May Martyn tell the other side that our client "won't possibly pay more than $500,000" when she has recommended that our client settle the case quickly or face far more extensive liability? How about if Martyn tells the other side that she "isn't authorized to settle for more than $500,000," when she has settlement authority of $5,000,000?

5-24. Martyn & Fox, acting under a misunderstanding while representing seller, told buyer's lawyer that the property is zoned commercial. What happens if we later discovered the mistake but did not correct it, the deal closed, and then the buyer found out that in fact the property is zoned industrial?

5-25. What may (must) Martyn & Fox disclose if at a celebration dinner the night before the initial public offering the CEO tells us, "I sure am glad we didn't have to disclose that threatened patent infringement suit"? What if it's the CFO and he tells us, "I sure am glad the auditors didn't put that footnote in about the $65 million in off-balance sheet financing"? What if we learn these things a week after the IPO? What happens if we tell the CEO or CFO to disclose and either refuses? If we withdraw, can our client sue us?

Consider: Model Rules 1.0(d), 1.2(d), 1.6(b)(2) and (3), 1.13, 1.16, 2.1, 4.1, 8.4(c)
Model Code DR 4-101(C)(2) and (3), DR 7-102(A) and (B)
RLGL §§67, 82

United States v. Chen

99 F.3d 1495 (9th Cir. 1996), cert. denied, 520 U.S. 1167 (1997)

KLEINFELD, Circuit Judge:

This case deals with the scope of the crime-fraud exception to the attorney-client privilege, where the attorney is innocent of any wrongdoing or guilty knowledge.

FACTS

Mr. Chen and his wife own Sunrider Corporation and operate TF Chen Products, Inc., a subsidiary of Sunrider. The companies manufacture health food and skin care products and import from Taiwan, Hong Kong, Japan, and other countries. The importation tariffs the companies pay depend on the price they declare they paid for the goods. Undervaluation may result in administrative, civil, and criminal penalties. A statutory procedure allows an importer to mitigate or avoid penalties by filing a disclosure statement before the Customs Service learns of the undervaluation independently. *See* U.S.C. §1592(c)(4).

Of course an importer also pays taxes on profits. The higher the cost of goods sold, then, other things being equal, the lower the level of income taxes. Thus, an importer saves money on tariffs to the extent the goods are cheap, but pays more in income tax. Conversely, the company saves money on taxes, but pays higher tariffs, to the extent its cost of goods is higher.

The Customs duties on the higher values are much less than the additional taxes which would be due based on the true values. Thus an importer can come out ahead by overpaying tariffs and underpaying income taxes, by overstating the cost of the goods imported.

Mr. and Mrs. Chen and Sunrider were indicted for conspiracy, tax evasion, and other crimes. The indictment alleged that Mr. and Mrs. Chen imported their inventory and paid tariffs based on the true invoiced price. Then Mr. Chen's sister, Jau Hwa, the comptroller of Sunrider, would prepare entirely fictional invoices on blank forms from Sunrider's Hong Kong affiliate, owned largely by the Chens and operated by Mrs. Chen's brother. The fake invoices purported to charge much higher prices for the goods. The fake invoices were then given to Sunrider's accountants to prepare trial balances, which were themselves given to Sunrider's tax preparers. Thus, tariffs would be paid on the true lower price of the goods, but taxes would be paid as though the goods had cost much more than they really did. Mr. Chen periodically instructed Jau Hwa to wire excess money to the Hong Kong affiliate's bank accounts, to maintain the fiction that Sunrider's payments were based on the fake invoices, not the real ones. Mr. and Mrs. Chen would subsequently recover the excess with the connivance of Mrs. Chen's brother. The government alleges that the Chens skimmed almost $90 million this way.

According to the indictment, the Chens eventually became concerned that IRS and Customs enforcement agents might communicate on their case and discover the difference in the claimed cost of their inventory. To protect themselves, they caused a disclosure to be made to Customs, purporting to acknowledge that they had understated their cost of goods imported. In the disclosure, they stated that the true cost of the goods was what they had reflected in their tax returns. Thus, the original Customs declarations were true, but the correcting disclosure was actually not a disclosure at all, but a fraud, intended to shield their tax evasion scheme. This scheme is entirely theoretical at this point, because nothing has yet been proven.

Mr. Chen's attorneys, Stein, Shostak, Shostak & O'Hara, filed a prior disclosure pursuant to 19 U.S.C. §1592(c)(4) and section 162.74 of the Customs regulations stating that a review gave rise to the discovery that "certain charges relating to the imported products may not have been properly included in the entered value." A check for over $381,000 was enclosed with the disclosure. The law firm said that more money would be paid as more data were assembled revealing underpayments.

Jau Hwa eventually left Sunrider. She then gave the government materials she had taken from Sunrider's files, and gave a customs agent her account of events on which the indictment is based. The Customs agent filed an affidavit saying that according to Jau Hwa, "Marjorie Shostak [Sunrider's lawyer] proposed that Sunrider should file a disclosure with Customs." Though this affidavit does not say in so many words that Ms. Shostak knew that the disclosure would be false, and intended to hide a tax evasion scheme, the Assistant United States Attorney argued that the differences between the initial and supplemental invoices was "substantial enough to put any reasonable professional on notice that this was, in all likelihood, a fraudulent scheme."

Joseph P. Cox had worked on the Sunrider matter for the Stein, Shostak firm; James D. Wilets was in-house Sunrider counsel. Both were subpoenaed before the Grand Jury. The Chens and Sunrider moved to quash these two subpoenas based on their attorney-client privilege. . . .

Ms. Shostak filed a declaration that her firm was employed to avoid litigation by bringing Sunrider into compliance with the Customs laws, by voluntarily disclosing supplemental payments already reported to the IRS. Ms. Shostak countered the attack on her professional integrity by the Assistant United States Attorney and stated that the accountants "consistently said that the payments to Paget were legitimately a part of the costs of the goods sold for tax purposes." She explained in detail the nature of the transactions and why her firm "saw nothing to suggest that a prior disclosure would further some alleged tax evasion scheme." She stated plainly that neither she nor any attorney to her knowledge had engaged in the conduct alleged by Jau Hwa, done anything to mislead Customs, or had any knowledge of or participation in any fraud on the government. Mr. Wilets and Mr. Cox also filed affidavits explaining what services they had performed on behalf of the Chens and Sunrider, stating that to the best of their knowledge neither they, the accountants, the Ernst & Young Customs group assisting with the prior disclosure, nor anyone else involved, including the Chens, had ever intended to further any tax evasion scheme or known about such a scheme. General counsel for Sunrider, Cynthia Muldrow, filed an affidavit establishing that no one had authorized Jau Hwa to take any documents with her when she left the corporation, or to disclose any attorney-client information to anyone outside Sunrider.

After considering all the evidence, the district judge made a finding of fact in favor of the attorneys regarding the government's imputation of wrongdoing on their part. He found "the attorneys are not involved in the involved crime," because there was not even a "prima facie case that these attorneys in any way participated in or joined the alleged criminal conspiracy." . . . The judge nevertheless denied the Chens' motions to quash the Grand Jury subpoenas, "provided the questioning is confined to matters concerning the disclosures which TFCP/Sunrider made to United

States Customs in 1989-1990." The district judge expressly found a prima facie case establishing reasonable cause to believe that the Chens and Sunrider had used their lawyers to make false statements, albeit not known to the lawyers to be false, to the Customs Service. . . .

ANALYSIS. . .

The attorney-client privilege is essential to preservation of liberty against a powerful government. People need lawyers to guide them through thickets of complex government requirements, and, to get useful advice, they have to be able to talk to their lawyers candidly without fear that what they say to their own lawyers will be transmitted to the government. *See* United States v. Zolin, 491 U.S. 554, 562 (1989).

. . . This valuable social service of counseling clients and bringing them into compliance with the law cannot be performed effectively if clients are scared to tell their lawyers what they are doing, for fear that their lawyers will be turned into government informants. *See* Fisher v. United States, 425 U.S. 391, 403 (1976). . . .

Lawyers are constantly called upon to tell people, in advance of action or developed controversy, what their duties are to other people and to the government, and what the duties of others are to them. In the case of tightly defined requirements, such as the return and payment of taxes, this may call for close, meticulous guidance. For the most part, however, what are involved are prohibitions. Safe-side counselling is commonly the lawyer's task. When a continuing course of conduct is in question, this may require not only an informed appraisal of risk but the preparation of a plan of action to minimize it. . . .

It is a truism that while the attorney-client privilege stands firm for client's revelations of past conduct, it cannot be used to shield ongoing or intended future criminal conduct. *Zolin*, 491 U.S. at 563. That principle is easily applied when a lawyer is retained to defend a client in a criminal prosecution or civil litigation relating to an entirely completed course of conduct. But it is difficult to apply when the lawyer's role is more in the nature of business planning or counseling or bringing the client into compliance for past wrongs, as opposed to simply defending the client against a charge relating to past wrongs. The act of bringing a client into compliance with the law ordinarily and properly engages the lawyer in an effort to assure the client is sanctioned no more harshly than the law requires. Because of the delicacy and importance of the attorney-client privilege in the counseling relationship, both the district court's task and ours are especially difficult when the United States Attorney insists upon using a person's own lawyer against him.

The government argues without citation that "where attorneys are involved in business decision-making, or, as Cox and Wilets acted here, as spokespersons for a company, they are clearly not acting as 'professional legal advisors.'" The government argues that this proposition takes the lawyers' planning for correcting understated customs declarations out of the privilege.

The lawyers in this case were "spokespersons" only in the sense that, as lawyers, they communicated their clients' positions to the government agencies dealing with their clients. They were not engaged in a public relations business separate from their law firm, as the government's term "spokespersons" may imply. For a lawyer to tell a judge, jury, or administrative agency, his client's position and the basis for it, that is, to be his client's spokesman, is a traditional and central attorney's function as an advocate. The communications between lawyer and client which enable a lawyer to perform this function are privileged. The government's argument implies that when a lawyer speaks on a client's behalf to a jury, the client forfeits his privilege for the attorney-client communications relating to the lawyer's statements on the client's behalf, obviously an untenable proposition.

The government's phrase, "involved in business decision-making," obscures the issue. A client is entitled to hire a lawyer, and have his secrets kept, for legal advice regarding the client's business affairs. This principle has long been the law....

That a person is a lawyer does not, ipso facto, make all communications with that person privileged. The privilege applies only when legal advice is sought "from a professional legal advisor in his capacity as such."... For example, where a counterfeiter hired a man who was a lawyer to buy printing equipment for him, no privilege could be asserted because the lawyer was merely a "business agent" and not a "legal advisor." United States v. Huberts, 637 F.2d 630, 640 (9th Cir. 1980). Likewise, lawyer-client communications were not privileged where the "clients did not approach him for legal advice and assistance, but rather with the aim of finding [investment opportunities]." Liew v. Breen, 640 F.2d 1046, 1050 (9th Cir. 1981). A lawyer's account ledgers revealing a client's financial transactions with third parties, which did not reveal the client's communications with the lawyer, or the lawyer's advice, were not privileged. In re Fischel, 557 F.2d 209, 212 (9th Cir. 1977).

If a person hires a lawyer for advice, there is a rebuttable presumption that the lawyer is hired "as such" to give "legal advice," whether the subject of the advice is criminal or civil, business, tort, domestic relations, or anything else. But the presumption is rebutted when the facts show that the lawyer was "employed without reference to his knowledge and discretion in the law."... That the lawyers were "involved in business decision-making," as the government puts it, is irrelevant. What matters is whether the lawyer was employed with or without "reference to his knowledge and discretion in the law," *id.*, to give the advice. In this case, the attorneys were employed for their legal knowledge, to bring their clients into compliance with the law in the least burdensome way possible (so far as the lawyers knew). Their communications with their client were therefore within the scope of the attorney-client privilege.

Appellants correctly argue that Jau Hwa, a past employee of Sunrider Corporation, lacked authority to waive the corporation's attorney-client privilege. The attorney-client privilege applies to communications between corporate employees and counsel, made at the direction of corporate superiors in order to secure legal advice. This "same rationale applies to the ex-employees." "The power to waive the corporate attorney-client privilege rests with the corporation's management and is normally exercised by its officers and directors." Commodity Futures Trading Commn. v. Weintraub, 471 U.S. 343, 348 (1985). "When control of a corporation passes to new management, the authority to assert and waive the corporation's attorney-client privilege passes as well." *Id.* at 349. It follows a fortiori that since a corporate employee cannot waive the corporation's privilege, that same individual as an ex-employee cannot do so. An employee must generally keep an employer's confidences. *See Restatement (Second) of Agency* §395 (1958). The uncontradicted evidence in the record established that Jau Hwa never was given any authority to waive the attorney-client privilege. Thus, Jau Hwa's disclosures of attorney-client communications could not and did not waive the privilege.

Appellants next argue that the government improperly submitted Jau Hwa's affidavit and Agent Diciurcio's affidavit, thereby disclosing to the judge material protected by the attorney-client privilege, before the court decided that such a disclosure should be made. They are correct. The Supreme Court established in *Zolin* that the parties seeking to strip attorney-client communications of their privilege under the crime-fraud exception must satisfy the court with some showing prior to judicial in camera review of the privileged material. . . .

. . . Thus there are two steps. First the government must satisfy the judge that there is "a factual basis adequate to support a good faith belief by a reasonable person that in camera review of the materials may reveal evidence to establish the claim that the crime-fraud exception applies," and then if the judge decides this question in favor of the government, the otherwise privileged material may be submitted for in camera examination. *Id.* The government cannot show the otherwise privileged material to the judge unless and until the judge has made this preliminary judgment. In *Zolin*, the prosecutor thought that it was unduly cumbersome to approach the district court twice, first to make a showing that the judge should read the putatively privileged material in order to decide whether the crime-fraud exception applied, and second to decide whether the exception applied. The Supreme Court decided that, cumbersome or not, that is what the prosecutor had to do.

In the case at bar, the United States Attorney submitted Jau Hwa's disclosures of attorney-client communications, and Diciurcio's affidavit telling more about her disclosures, without first making a prima facie showing and obtaining the court's permission. This was incorrect under *Zolin*. . . .

But the district judge recognized that there was an incorrect submission. He disregarded what Jau Hwa said in making his decision that the crime-fraud exception applied, and expressly said he was disregarding it. Violation of the *Zolin* two-step procedure was therefore harmless.

What is left of the case is whether the government's showing, without Jau Hwa's disclosures, was adequate to invoke the crime-fraud exception. It was. "To invoke the crime-fraud exception successfully, the government has the burden of making a prima facie showing that the communications were in furtherance of an intended or present illegality and that there is some relationship between the communications and the illegality." Mere allegations or suspicion by the government are insufficient. But proof beyond a reasonable doubt is not necessary to justify application of the crime-fraud exception. The test for invoking the crime-fraud exception to the attorney-client privilege is whether there is "reasonable cause to believe that the attorney's services were utilized in furtherance of the ongoing unlawful scheme." *Id.* (internal quotations and alterations omitted). Reasonable cause is more than suspicion but less than a preponderance of evidence. The government must submit "evidence that if believed by the jury would establish the elements of an ongoing violation."

In this case, there was reasonable cause to believe that the Chens and Sunrider were using attorneys' services to conceal income tax fraud. The government submitted copies of blank presigned invoices from Sunrider's supplier, which would facilitate the kind of fraud claimed by the government. The portions of Jau Hwa's affidavit other than her disclosures of attorney-client communications, tended to show, if true, that the company was claiming a low value of goods purchased for Customs' purposes, a high value for income tax purposes, and was proposing to make a fraudulent corrective disclosure to Customs in order to evade income taxes. The evidence, excluding the improperly submitted disclosures of attorney-client communications, further gave reasonable cause to believe that the Chens were using their lawyers to help prepare the paperwork for this fraudulent scheme, and using their prestige in the customs bar to hide it.

The district judge found that the lawyers in this case were innocent of any wrongful intent, and had no knowledge that their services were being used to trick the Customs' Service or the IRS. But the lawyers' innocence does not preserve the attorney-client privilege against the crime-fraud exception. The privilege is the client's, so "it is the client's knowledge and intentions that are of paramount concern to the application of the crime-fraud exception; the attorney need know nothing about the client's ongoing or planned illicit activity for the exception to apply. It is therefore irrelevant . . . that [the lawyers] may have been in the dark." . . .

CONCLUSION

The prosecution should have followed the two-step submission procedure in *Zolin*, and did not. But that error was harmless, because the judge disregarded the incorrectly submitted attorney-client communications. The attorneys' lack of any guilty knowledge did not matter, because the privilege was the client's, and the client's misconduct sufficed to lose it, despite the lawyers' innocence of wrongdoing. The properly submitted materials established reasonable cause to believe that the Chens and Sunrider were using their lawyers as part of an ongoing scheme to evade taxes, so the district judge was within his discretion in allowing the government to compel disclosures under the crime-fraud exception.

AFFIRMED.

Lawrence J. Fox

Legal Tender: A Lawyer's Guide to Handling Professional Dilemmas

157-166 (ABA 1995)

The Opinion Letter

Forty years ago they were in the third grade at Highlands School. George was the new kid on the block, Lonnie the veteran from kindergarten. They met in the playground before school, quickly learned they both loved baseball (even the hapless Philadelphia A's), and soon found themselves as rival pick-up team captains. How many times they had used that elaborate ritual of alternately grabbing the baseball bat to determine who would choose first.

George's family's move to the suburbs five years later did not separate the boys for long, as Lonnie's folks followed them to Claymont one year later. There they found themselves teammates on the Claymont High School baseball team (Class B Delaware High School champions in 1959), sharing both the visits to colleges and the springtime anxiety as they awaited the results of the torturous college admissions process. When both lads were accepted at Syracuse, the fact that Lonnie had also been admitted to his original first choice, Trinity College, was quickly ignored as the friends deliciously contemplated spending four more years together—two hundred miles from home. Visions of intercollegiate athletics, fraternity memberships, new friendships, and football weekends soon became reality; Lonnie and George thrived despite the harsh winters of upstate New York.

College was a total success, launching the new graduates into their first period of separation in nearly ten years; George went off to Villanova Law School and Lonnie to the business school at Northwestern. They had often discussed their differing interests into the night over coffee and even, it had to be admitted, over more than a few Genessee beers, jokingly suggesting that Lonnie might some day become George's biggest client. But this was no more than a joke designed to ease the pain of their going down different paths since, at the time, George envisioned himself as Assistant District Attorney in New Castle County, prosecuting the clients of Perry Mason.

Nonetheless, twenty years later, with George firmly established at the Wilmington office of the prestigious, old-line Philadelphia firm, Caldwell & Moore—practicing corporate law no less—Lonnie, who had risen to president and chief operating officer of the Mercury Maintenance Company, was presented with his first opportunity to send business George's way. Mercury, whose growth had been spectacular, found itself in need of major new financing. Its old law firm had recently forced the retirement of Mercury's original lawyer and board member, Lewis Stern. Thus Lonnie felt free to steer this important matter to George.

During the interim they had remained friends. Both moved to Greenville as they each rose up their respective ladders. Their children were friends, baseball had given way to golf (now played regularly at Wilmington Country Club), and the two couples socialized at every opportunity. But this was the first time they had actually worked together.

At Lonnie's initial visit, he explained the plan to George. Mercury had a series of long-term contracts to replace streetlights and traffic controls for municipalities throughout the Delaware Valley. Because of its reputation for high-quality, prompt, and low-cost service, Mercury had signed multi-year contracts with over two hundred boroughs, townships, three of the five major counties surrounding Philadelphia, and, of course, the City of Wilmington. In discussions with Integrity Bank it had become clear that these contracts were Mercury's biggest asset. Based on the cash flow stability they represented, the bank was prepared to lend significant sums to Mercury. Lonnie had negotiated the broad outline of a deal in which Mercury would receive a $5 million loan to be drawn down in equal installments quarterly across four years, permitting Mercury, as it expanded its operations into New Jersey, to purchase the additional trucks and cherry pickers that were critical to its delivery of service. He called on George to document the transaction, represent Mercury, and provide Integrity with any routine legal opinions it required.

"Protect us as best you can," Lonnie implored George, "but none of your aggressive stuff—we need this money and you know how cussedly independent these banks can be."

"You can count on me, Lonnie. I want your board to be proud of your selection of lawyers, even though I know the real reason you hired me is to make up for your stealing my Mickey Mantle rookie card. That's something that you should feel guilty about. Do you know what that would be worth today?"

"Your mom would've thrown it out with your old Lionel trains anyway," Lonnie replied.

George returned to the office, called up his friend Vince Almond at Integrity to inquire who would be "lawyering" this transaction for the bank, learned that Vince himself would be working on it, and made a date with Vince to meet within a week to discuss the matter.

The loan processing could not have been easier. The bank officials were so impressed with Mercury's success that many of the issues typically raised did not need to be addressed. Similarly, the documentation went smoothly, and George's firm was only asked to provide opinion letters on the corporate authority of Mercury to enter into the loan transaction and the enforceability of the long-term contracts, including the effect of the penalty clauses, if any of Mercury's customers attempted to terminate them early. Neither legal question was difficult, and George confidently and, if truth be told, proudly delivered each opinion—printed on crisp ivory Caldwell & Moore letterhead—to Vince at closing. This was the final step prior to the delivery of the first $300,000-plus installment to Mercury. New equipment would soon be on its way, and George could only think that his good friend Lonnie might be well on his way to being CEO of a major public corporation, now that Mercury had this assured flow of capital.

A celebratory dinner at the Hotel duPont brought the old friends, their spouses, and a few key colleagues together for one of those events where the fact that the wine bill actually exceeded the cost of the food only seemed embarrassing the next morning. The repeated toasts to all involved only confirmed what high hopes everyone present shared as they dined among the Winterthur reproductions.

It was just one year later that George got the call from Lonnie. George immediately could tell something was wrong. There was a tension in Lonnie's voice, a hesitancy in his approach, and no desire for small talk. Rather, Lonnie asked George if they could meet right away at the club. George knew this was important, but his idle speculation as to why they had to meet immediately did not include anything close to the story that unfolded.

Lonnie's face was drawn, his normally neatly combed auburn hair, now just flecked with grey, appeared a little disheveled, and he sat poised at the edge of his highback club chair, as he began his tale.

"George, it's just terrible. I don't even know what to say. We just had a meeting with the folks from Arthur Andersen, our auditors. They have uncovered a massive fraud. We don't even know how big it is. Seems our best sales representative, Arnold Plinger, has been systematically bribing township officials to get these contracts—not just to get them, but to have the contracts include a five-year term when the governing body has only authorized two or three. He even did it with New Castle County! All those contracts we thought were for five years paid Arnold a commission based on five years. Now it turns out some expire as soon as December of this year."

"How many are there?" George interrupted more to ease his anxiety than to learn any information.

"We don't know. At least twenty. Maybe more, many more. Arnold isn't cooperating. His psychiatrist has put him on sedatives and ordered him not to talk to anyone. But he has hired a lawyer, on our advice. We only know from contacting a few officials who, of course, had not admitted the bribes but have stated that their versions of the contract are only for two years or, at most, three years. Arnold had over one hundred customers, so who knows?"

"Well," George observed, silently thanking his lucky stars he had not opined on the genuineness of the contracts, "we must act in a forthright manner. Tell the bank. After all, they are about to give you guys another $300,000 in a few weeks, if I'm not mistaken. Based on our firm's opinion that those five-year contracts are enforceable according to their terms. We can't let that happen."

"We can't do that," replied Lonnie. "That's why I wanted to meet with you today. I remember way back when, how you told me that everything a client told you you had to keep confidential. I even remember you and I having a major fight over that case of the lawyer who knew his client had killed those kids in upstate New York. I said he had to tell the victims' families. You said it was unethical to do so."

"That was different," said George, realizing he was shouting. "That client wasn't the lawyer's best friend. The lawyer hadn't given an opinion to anyone."

"That's what Lewis Stern said you would say."

"When did you talk to him?" George inquired, not hiding his annoyance.

"We had a special board meeting yesterday to discuss all of this. One of the board members invited Lewis to join us—said we needed someone who knew the company better than you, someone who wouldn't panic. The board decided that Mercury had no choice but to keep this under wraps. If we tell the bank, they'll never lend us another dime and they'll demand repayment of what they've already paid. Without that $300,000 per quarter, we'd probably have to file a chapter proceeding. We've already spent that money, y'know. Anyway, Lewis told us that we should tell you what had happened so that you would understand why we were consulting him."

"Caldwell & Moore will have to resign if you go forward like this."

"He told us you would say that, too, and he agreed you would have to resign. In fact, he thought that was best. But he also told us you would not be able to tell anyone about our little problems with Arnold."

"But the bank is relying on my opinion. Certainly I can call them up and tell them they shouldn't continue to do so."

"Not according to Lewis. He says you lawyers call these 'noisy withdrawals.' The rules don't permit them when the fraud's complete."

"But you're taking down more money from the bank."

"That may be so. Otherwise, our company will die and your best friend Lonnie will be sleeping in your garage. But we aren't requiring any further services from you. In fact, you've withdrawn. But I must warn you, as Lewis instructed me, we better not hear another peep out of Caldwell & Moore . . . especially if you ever want to see any of the $100,000 we still owe you."

"You're being impossible. I better talk to Lewis myself. I'll be back to you shortly. Maybe all of this will seem less explosive with the passage of a few days. But those kind of threats will get you nowhere, Lonnie. If our friendship means anything, you'll not repeat such outrageous statements," George intoned, now almost unable to control his mixture of anger and shock.

George returned to his office and, after consulting with his most trusted colleague, Henry Gill, the conscience of Caldwell & Moore, it was agreed that he would make a personal call on Lewis the very next day. It was a meeting George did not look forward to at all. Lewis Stern was a giant at the bar. A member of the American College of Trial Lawyers, he had served for years as chairman of the Ethics Committee of the Delaware Bar Association, of which he had also been president. Jousting with Lewis on the issue of confidentiality was, at best, a formidable task.

The meeting began pleasantly enough. Lewis's office was spacious and encrusted with the memorabilia from a career of service to clients, charities, and the bar. Lewis greeted him warmly, an approach George found both welcoming and intimidating: he knew Lewis was planning to charm him into acquiescence.

"This is all very sad stuff, George. It's terrible that your friend, Lonnie, and the others at Mercury have been so injured by Arnold's unfortunate conduct. Now all we can do is make sure this doesn't snowball into a total disaster. I am sure you agree with Lonnie and the others that, despite the fact that these contracts are for a shorter time than we thought, Mercury is likely to obtain renewals of contracts because of its reputation for speedy, low-cost service."

"But not once they find out about the bribes," George rejoined. "At that point, Mercury may not be eligible even to bid on the renewals."

"That's true if you go blabbing about. But the way this is structured," Lewis continued, "no one has to find out—as long as you recognize your professional responsibility not to violate Model Rule 1.6."

"That's easy enough for you to say. It's not your opinion on the line. Your firm didn't tell the bank these contracts were enforceable in accordance with their terms when, in fact, we didn't even have the versions of the contracts with the correct number of years in front of us. If we don't take some step to tell the bank it can't rely on our opinion anymore, we will certainly violate Rule 1.2(d)," said George, proud that he remembered the rule number. "You know, the rule that bars an attorney from assisting a client fraud—to say nothing of becoming civilly liable to the bank as an accessory to our client's fraud."

"Now, now George," Lewis said patronizingly. "Surely you can see how in your panic you are not analyzing this correctly. Caldwell & Moore will now be asked to do *nothing* having anything to do with the financial transactions—the loan, its extension, or its repayment. All of *that* will be undertaken by others. Your firm will be completely shielded from all contact with any transaction. The only hint of Caldwell & Moore's existence in those ongoing transactions (whatever they may be) is your once-issued opinion. Under that fact situation, I fail to see how Caldwell & Moore's conduct will result in violation of Rule 1.2(d); Caldwell & Moore will *not* be *assisting* a client in conduct it knows is criminal or fraudulent. Clearly, Rule 1.2(d) contemplates ongoing assistance by the lawyer. It could have spoken, but it does not, about the client's possible use of a lawyer's prior *work product*; but that's not what it says. It *says* that a lawyer 'shall not . . . *assist* a client, in conduct that the lawyer knows is criminal or fraudulent': and based on what the Mercury folks have told you, Caldwell & Moore will not be assisting your former client in such conduct because Caldwell & Moore will have nothing to do with that aspect, or any other aspect, of the client's affairs.

"As for your claim of possible civil liability, when a lawyer owes a duty of confidentiality to a client, that duty cannot be sacrificed to some attenuated argument that the lawyer might, just might, be liable to a third party. Otherwise, lawyers would always be conjuring up unwarranted fears as a way of protecting themselves and, at the same time, rendering the duty of keeping confidences a meaningless one.

"Clearly, Caldwell & Moore was entitled, as it did, to withdraw voluntarily—and if I were you, I would have done the same thing—under Rule 1.16(b)(2). You understood that Mercury had used your services 'to perpetrate a crime or fraud' (in the initial obtaining of the loan using your opinion letter). I do not, however, see how anything your firm does from this day forward 'will *result* in violation of' Rule 1.2(d), by assisting the client to commit a fraud."

George listened carefully. The argument seemed too pat. Where was the place where the rabbit went into the hat? Then it struck him: "Lewis, I admire you greatly and your advocacy skills have never been greater. But frankly, you are wrong. This is a mandatory withdrawal situation under Model Rule 1.16(a). That's why I must let the bank know they can't rely on my opinion."

"You're wrong again," Lewis replied. "The mandatory withdrawal provisions of Rule 1.16(a)(1) come into play 'if the lawyer's *services will be used* by the client in materially furthering a course of criminal or fraudulent conduct.' The operative words here are 'services' and 'will be used.' Here the 'services' of Caldwell & Moore will not be used to further criminal or fraudulent conduct. Only Caldwell & Moore's past, completed 'work product'—the opinion letter—will remain at the bank. Thus, even under that unauthorized ridiculous comment to Rule 1.6—the one that purports to permit a 'noisy withdrawal' under Rule 1.16(a)(1), withdrawal is only permitted if the lawyer's services are involved (which they are not) and only if those services 'will be used' by the client for fraudulent purposes."

"I can't believe you are telling me this. It's pure sophistry, Lewis. Your reading of 'assisting' is far too narrow. Surely, one can assist a person in the future through work that is completed. The fact that the work is completed renders the assistance no more or less helpful, or actionable, I might add, than if it were taking place at the same time as the client's conduct. Indeed, in order to reach your unfortunate result, Lewis, you have to graft onto Rule 1.2(d) the word 'ongoing.' I dare say no court of law would let a lawyer off the hook because the assistance by the lawyer for the client took the form of services that were provided before the client's conduct. If the lawyer knew, before the client conduct, that the lawyer's earlier work product was going to be used to further the client's improper or illegal purpose, the lawyer is in trouble. Your reliance on the words 'services will be used' is entirely misplaced. The phrase does not contain any modifier as to when the services were performed, only when they will be used." George concluded, increasingly confident that he was matching Lewis verbal blow for verbal blow.

But Lewis remained indomitable. "What you are saying is that by hiding behind an overly broad interpretation of 1.2(d), you can call up the bank and withdraw your opinion. You know the effect, if not the purpose, of that call is to make certain that the bank understands that Caldwell & Moore is not responsible for the content of the opinion that was prepared in reliance on client representations that you have discovered are untrustworthy." Counting off by fingers to emphasize each point, Lewis further observed, "The Model Rules only contain three explicit exceptions to the obligation to maintain client confidences. The first is the case of client conduct likely to result in imminent death or substantial bodily harm. The second is to establish a claim or defense on behalf of the lawyer. The third is in the case of a violation of Model Rule 3.3: candor to the tribunal. None of those apply here. We're only talking about money, no one's made a claim against you and don't start telling me about Hazard's theory of a preemptive strike, and we are not in court. Nor does this represent a situation where the disclosure of a confidence is impliedly authorized.

"Indeed, Rule 1.6 itself recognizes only one kind of 'implied' authority to breach confidentiality, and that is in the case of 'disclosures that are impliedly authorized in order to carry out the representation . . . ' Rule 1.6(a). Clearly, a 'noisy withdrawal,' which contemplates both the mandatory withdrawal under 1.16(a)(1) and the withdrawal or disaffirmance of something the lawyer wrote or said while he was representing the client, is not something the lawyer is doing 'to carry out the representation.' Rather, it is something the lawyer is doing to *rectify* what he did during the representation, to the supposed unfair detriment of nonclients. Thus, a 'noisy withdrawal' does not fall within the sorts of disclosures that are 'impliedly authorized' in the *only* rule that recognizes impliedly authorized disclosures contrary to the mandate of confidentiality—Rule 1.6(a)."

Remembering one last argument that Gill had shared with him yesterday, George offered his surrebuttal. "It is true that there is no explicit exception to Rule 1.6 that covers this situation. However, when the drafters of the Model Rules wanted to make it clear that a duty in a rule was 'trumped' by the confidentiality provisions of 1.6, they explicitly stated that fact. Just look at Model Rule 4.1(b). But there is no reference to 1.6 in the text of 1.2. So all we have is a conflict between two rules that appear to give contradictory advice. And when you realize that the purpose of Caldwell & Moore's withdrawing its opinion is not to disclose a client confidence, not to rectify a fraud, but merely to avoid a violation of 1.2 using the most limited means at our disposal, you can understand why Rule 1.2 duty should overcome any impediment implicit in 1.6.

"If you would only persuade *your* client to do the right thing, we wouldn't be in this pickle. And if I thought just withdrawing would accomplish the purpose, I would do that. But here I know that our silent withdrawal won't do anything. It's not like the bank is calling us up each week to find out if we are still representing Mercury. Under these special circumstances, we simply have no choice."

Now Lewis stood, pressing his palms on his mammoth desk as he leaned forward for emphasis. "You're right about no choice. But you're wrong about the result. You have no basis for disclosing Arnold's indiscretions to the bank. And if you do so, I can assure you that Caldwell & Moore will find itself not only the subject of a malpractice suit for the damages flowing from the bank's cutting off the credit and calling the loan, but also before the disciplinary board defending its unethical conduct. If you do anything other than withdraw, it will be a very sad day for all of us. Think about it, son. Think of Lonnie; think of your firm; think of your fine reputation. I know you'll do the right thing."

Stunned, George slowly rose from the chair and, without a word or a gesture, shuffled out of Lewis's office, his legs heavy and wooden, his hands clammy, his forehead beaded with sweat, and his psyche a battlefield of conflicting emotions—remorse, anger, regret, dismay. How difficult it was to be a lawyer, an ethical lawyer, the conscientious lawyer he always wanted to be.

In re American Continental Corporation/ Lincoln Savings & Loan Securities Litigation

794 F. Supp. 1424 (D. Ariz. 1992)

BILBY, District Judge....

Five separate actions are consolidated before this court....

[1.] ... a class action on behalf of "all persons who purchased securities, stock or debentures, of American Continental Corporation ("ACC") between January 1, 1986 and April 14, 1989," [that] alleges the following violations: Section 10(b) of the Securities Exchange Act of 1934 ("Exchange Act") and Rule 10b-5, 15 U.S.C. §78j(b), 17 C.F.R. 240.10b-5; Section 18 of the Exchange Act, 15 U.S.C. §78r; the Racketeer Influenced and Corrupt Organizations Act ("RICO"), 18 U.S.C. §1961 et seq.; the Arizona Racketeering Act ("AZRAC"), 13 A.R.S. §13-2301 et seq.; and Sections 11 and 12 of the Securities Act of 1933 ("Securities Act"), 15 U.S.C. §77k.

[2.] ... a state action on behalf of the same class of securities purchasers, states claims for fraud, negligent misrepresentation, breach of fiduciary duty, and violations of California Corporations Code Sections 1507 and 25401.

[3.] ... federal and state actions on behalf of approximately 100 individual ACC securities purchasers.... [These] plaintiffs allege violations of Section 10(b), RICO, negligent misrepresentation, breach of fiduciary duty, conspiracy to breach fiduciary duty, California

Corporations Code Section 25401, Sections 11 and 12(2) of the Securities Act, professional negligence, and negligent infliction of emotional distress.

[4.] . . . the Resolution Trust Corporation ("RTC"), as receiver for Lincoln, brings claims under RICO, AZRAC, and various state and common law theories of liability.

[5.] Finally, this opinion addresses claims made [by] investors in an ACC-related limited partnership [who] brought claims for securities fraud, RICO, unjust enrichment, and negligent misrepresentation.

These actions originate from the business dealings of Charles H. Keating, Jr. ("Keating"), former chairman of ACC. The claims at issue here were brought principally against professionals who provided services to ACC and/or Lincoln Savings. . . .

II. LAW OF GENERAL APPLICATION

Section 10(b) of the Exchange Act. . . .

[A] primary violation of Section 10(b) and Rule 10b-5 entails: (1) a scheme or artifice to defraud; (2) an affirmative misrepresentation or omission of a fact necessary to make other statements not misleading; or (3) a course of business which operates as a fraud or deceit. In addition, the act or omission must be made or conducted "in connection with" the purchase or sale of securities, with resultant damage to plaintiffs.

Proof of scienter is a requisite to any 10b-5 action. The United States Supreme Court has defined scienter as "a mental state embracing intent to deceive, manipulate, or defraud." Ernst & Ernst v. Hochfelder, 425 U.S. 185 (1976). In Hollinger v. Titan Capital Corp., 914 F.2d 1564 (9th Cir. 1990), *cert. denied*, 499 U.S. 975 (1991), the Ninth Circuit adopted a standard for the minimal culpable mindset, referred to hereinafter by this court as "reckless scienter." . . . The *Hollinger* court observed that "the danger of misleading buyers must be actually known or so obvious that any reasonable [person] would be legally bound as knowing, and the omission must derive from something more egregious than even 'white heart/empty head' good faith." Thus, the court concluded, "recklessness is a lesser form of intent rather than a greater degree of negligence." . . .

Section 11 of the Securities Act

Section 11 of the Securities Act provides that every person who acquires a security burdened by an untrue statement or omission of material fact may sue: (1) every person who signed the registration statement; (2) every director and officer of the offeror; (3) "every accountant, engineer, or appraiser, or any person whose profession gives authority to a statement made by him, who has with his consent been named as having prepared or certified" any part of the registration statement or any report or valuation used in connection with it; and/or (4) every underwriter with respect to such security. 15 U.S.C. §77k.

A purchaser's reliance on the registration statement need not be proven unless the plaintiff "acquired the security after the issuer made generally available to its security holders an earning statement covering a period of twelve months beginning after the effective date of the registration statement." Section 77k further provides that reliance may be shown without proof that the plaintiff read the registration statement. . . .

Racketeering Influenced and Corrupt Organizations Act

Section 1962(c) of RICO provides:

> It shall be unlawful for any person employed by or associated with any

> enterprise engaged in, or the activities of which affect, interstate or foreign commerce, to conduct or participate, directly or indirectly, in the conduct of such enterprise's affairs through a pattern of racketeering activity or collection of unlawful debt.

18 U.S.C. §1962(c). RICO also provides that it is unlawful for any person to conspire to violate subsection (c). The Code defines "racketeering activity" as any act indictable under various provisions of Title 18, including . . . mail fraud, . . . wire fraud, and "any offense involving fraud connected with a case under Title 11, fraud in the sale of securities. . . ."

To establish a RICO claim, plaintiffs must prove defendants intended to devise and did devise a scheme to defraud. . . . "The fraudulent scheme need not be one which includes an affirmative misrepresentation of fact, since it is only necessary [to prove] that the scheme was calculated to deceive persons of ordinary prudence." "Deceitful concealment of material facts is not constructive fraud but actual fraud."

The standard for aiding and abetting a RICO violation parallels that under Section 10(b). A defendant must have knowledge or act with reckless scienter. . . .

Arizona RICO ("AZRAC")

To establish a primary violation of AZRAC, plaintiffs must prove defendants were associated with an enterprise and conducted or participated in the conduct of such enterprise's affairs through racketeering. A.R.S. §13-2312. "Racketeering" is defined, in pertinent part, to include any act, "committed for financial gain which is chargeable or indictable under the laws of this state and punishable by imprisonment for more than one year," including:

> (r) Fraud in the sale of securities.
> (t) A scheme or artifice to defraud.

The definition of "fraud in the sale of securities" parallels Rule 10b-5. . . . A "scheme or artifice to defraud" involves a plan to knowingly obtain benefit by means of false or fraudulent pretenses, representations, promises or material omissions.

California Corporations Code

Section 1507 of the California Corporations Code imposes liability on any corporate director, officer, employee, or agent who publishes a prospectus, report, financial statement or other public document which is false in any material respect, or who falsifies or erases in any material aspect the books, minutes, records, or accounts of a corporation. . . .

It is a violation of Section 25401 of the Code to sell securities through written or oral communications which are materially untrue or omit to state material facts. Under Section 25401, proof of reliance is unnecessary. . . .

Common Law Fraud and Negligent Misrepresentation

Under California common law, an action for fraud and deceit requires proof of: (1) a false representation; (2) knowledge of the falsity; (3) an intent to induce reliance; (4) actual and reasonable reliance; and (5) resulting damage to the plaintiff. Secondary liability, or aiding and abetting, is defined in Restatement (Second) of Torts, §876b. It requires proof of knowledge of the primary violation, which may be inferred from the circumstances, and substantial assistance, which may be in the form of encouragement or advice. . . . The aider and abetter's conduct must be a substantial factor in causing the plaintiff's harm.

A negligent misrepresentation claim involves the following elements: (1) a misrepresentation of past or existing material facts; (2) a lack of reasonable grounds for believing in the truth of the representation; (3) an intent to induce reliance; (4) actual and justifiable reliance; and (5) resulting damage. . . .

Conspiracy

A conspiracy involves a knowing agreement by two or more persons to take concerted action to commit an illegal act. The existence of a conspiracy may be inferred from the nature of the acts, the relation of the parties, the interests of the conspirators, or other circumstances. *Id.* Express agreement or tacit consent will, if proven, suffice to create liability. *Rest. 2d of Torts* §876(a).

Where the objective of a conspiracy has not yet been achieved when a co-conspirator manifests his or her agreement to further the objective, the co-conspirator becomes liable for all acts done in furtherance of the common objective, including acts previously done. This is so "irrespective of whether or not [the conspirator] was a direct actor and regardless of the degree of his activity. . . ." A conspirator may not be held liable for an offense committed before his or her agreement to join the conspiracy, if that prior offense completed the ultimate objective of the conspiracy. . . .

V. RULINGS PERTINENT TO INDIVIDUAL DEFENDANTS

D. Jones, Day, Reavis & Pogue

Jones Day, a defendant in [actions 1-4], focuses its summary judgment motion on an individual opinion letter given in connection with a 1986 registration statement. Jones Day claims this opinion letter was neither false, nor was it written in an expert capacity. Jones Day generally claims that it has not engaged in conduct for which it could be held liable because lawyers are obligated to keep their clients' confidence and to act in a ways that do not discourage their clients from undergoing regulator compliance reviews.

1. The Record

The record reveals the following facts concerning Jones Day's involvement with ACC and Keating.

Prior to joining Jones Day, defendant William Schilling was director of the FHLBB Office of Examinations and Supervision. In that capacity, he was directly involved in the supervision of Lincoln Savings. During the summer of 1985, he wrote at least one memorandum and concurred in another, expressing serious regulatory concerns about numerous aspects of Lincoln's operations. For example, he wrote:

> [U]nder new management, Lincoln has engaged in several serious regulatory violations. Some of these violations, such as the overvaluation of real estate and failure to comply with Memorandum R-4l(b), are the same type of violations that have lead to some of the worst failures in FSLIC's history.

Later in 1985, Schilling was hired by Jones Day to augment its expertise in thrift representation. On January 31, 1986, Schilling and Jones Day's Ron Kneipper flew to Phoenix to solicit ACC's business. ACC retained Jones Day to perform "a major internal audit of Lincoln's FHLBB compliance and a major project to help Lincoln deal with the FHLBB's direct investment regulations."

During the regulatory compliance audit, which Jones Day understood to be a pre-FHLBB examination compliance review, the law firm found multiple regulatory violations. There is evidence that Jones Day knew that Lincoln had backdated files, destroyed appraisals, removed appraisals from files, told appraisers not to issue written reports when their oral valuations were too low, and violated affiliated transaction regulations. Jones Day found that Lincoln did no loan underwriting and no post-closure loan followup to ensure that Lincoln's interests were being protected. Jones Day learned Lincoln had multiple "loans" which were, in fact, joint ventures which violated FHLBB regulations, made real estate loans in violation of regulations, and backdated corporate resolutions which were not signed by corporate officers and did not reflect actual meetings. There is evidence that Jones Day may have tacitly consented to removal of harmful documents from Lincoln files. For example, one handwritten notation on a memorandum memorializing Jones Day's advice not to remove documents from files reads, "If something *is* devastating, consider it individually." (Emphasis in original.)

There is evidence that Jones Day instructed ACC in how to rectify deficiencies so that they would not be apparent to FHLBE examiners. Jones Day attorneys, including Schilling, testified that they told ACC/Lincoln personnel to provide the Jones Day-generated "to do" lists only to the attorneys responsible for rectifying the deficiencies, and to destroy the lists so that FHLB-SF would not find them in the files. For the same reason, Jones Day's regulatory compliance reports to ACC/Lincoln were oral. Jones Day paralegals testified that responsibilities for carrying out the "to do" lists were divided among Jones Day and ACC staff. Jones Day continued this work into the summer of 1986.

The evidence indicates that Jones Day may have been aware that ACC/Lincoln did not follow its compliance advice with respect to ongoing activities. There are material questions of fact concerning the procedures Jones Day used—if any—to ascertain whether their compliance advice was being heeded. The testimony suggests that Jones Day partners knew ACC/Lincoln personnel were preparing loan underwriting summaries contemporaneously with Jones Day's regulatory compliance review, even though the loan transactions had already been closed. Moreover, the evidence reveals that Jones Day attorneys participated in creating corporate resolutions to ratify forged and backdated corporate records.

On April 23, 1986, Jones Day partner Fohrman wrote:

> I received Neal Millard's memo on ACC. In looking at the long list of people involved, it occurred to me that there will be times when individuals may be called upon to render legal services that might require the issuance of opinion letters from Jones, Day. As we all know, we now possess information that could affect the way we write our opinion letters and our actual ability to give a particular opinion may be severely restricted. However, this large list of individuals may not be aware of knowledge that is held by Messrs. Fein and Schilling. I would suggest that a follow up memo be issued by Ron Fein indicating that any work involving ACC which requires the issuance of opinions, must be cleared by Ron....

Also in April 1986, ACC's Jim Grogan wrote to Jones Day's Kneipper, soliciting a strategy to "sunset" the FHLBB direct investment regulation. Jones Day subsequently made multiple Freedom of Information Act requests to FHLBB in furtherance of a direct investment rule strategy, for which Lincoln was billed. In a September 12, 1986 telephone conversation, Grogan allegedly told Kneipper: "Comment letters were great success FHLBB picked it up 'hook, line and sinker'... Charlie wants to do again...."

The record indicates that the concept of selling ACC debentures in Lincoln savings branches may have originated at an April 9, 1986 real estate syndicate seminar given by Jones Day Defendant Ron Fein. There is evidence that Fein may have contributed to the detailed bond sales program outline, attending to details such as explaining how the sales would work, and insuring that the marketing table was far enough from the teller windows to distinguish between ACC and Lincoln Savings employees. The evidence indicates that Jones Day reviewed the debenture registration statement and prospectus, which is corroborated by Jones Day's billing records. As a result, in January 1987, ACC was able to assure the California Department of Savings & Loan that:

> The process of structuring the bond sales program was reviewed by Kaye, Scholer and Jones Day to assure compliance not only with securities laws and regulations, but also with banking and FSLIC laws and regulations.

Moreover, there is evidence which suggests that political contributions were made on behalf of ACC, in exchange for ACC's consent that Jones Day could "bill liberally." On June 23, 1986, Kneipper memorialized a phone conversation:

> (1) 1:15 p.m. Ron Kessler—in past, firm has given $amt. to PAC, has premium billed, & PAC contri. to candidate; concern that we're an out of state law firm and that a $# in excess of $5,000.00 would look like an unusual move; Barnett and Kessler have done before; question re whether and how we can get some busi. from GOV. for this.
>
> (2) 3:40 p.m. Jim Grogan
>
> Ten tickets at $1,000.00 equals $10,000.00
>
> Barr wants limits of $5,000.00/contribution.
>
> Agreed that we could bill liberally in future in recognition of this.

At deposition, Kneipper testified that his note—"agreed could bill liberally in recognition for this,"—"is what it appears to be." Jones Day set up an Arizona Political Action Committee ("PAC") specifically for the purpose of making a contribution to an Arizona gubernatorial candidate. The PAC was opened on September 4, 1986 and closed in December, 1986, after the contribution was made.

In June 1986, Jones Day solicited additional work from ACC. Jones Day attorney Caulkins wrote, in part:

> Rick Kneipper reports that ACC is very explicit that it does not care how much its legal services cost, as long as it gets the best. He states that Keating gave him an unsolicited $250,000 retainer to start the thrift work, and sent another similar check also unsolicited in two weeks. On the down side, he reports that he has never encountered a more demanding and difficult client, . . .
>
> It appears to Rick and to me that American Continental is made for us and we for them.

On October 28, 1986, Jones Day provided an opinion letter, required by Item 601(b) of SEC regulation S-K, for inclusion in an ACC bond registration statement. Jones Day's opinion letter stated that the indenture was a valid and binding obligation under California law.

2. *Section 10(b), RICO, and Common Law Fraud*

Jones Day seeks summary judgment on Plaintiffs' claims under Section 10(b), RICO and common law fraud. Jones Day contends that it may not be held liable for counseling its client. The line between maintaining a client's confidence and violating the securities law is brighter than Jones Day suggests, however. Attorneys must inform a client in a clear and direct manner when its conduct violates the law. If the client continues the objectionable activity, the lawyer must withdraw "if the representation will result in violation of the rules of professional conduct or other law." Ethical Rule 1.16 ("ER"). Under such circumstances, an attorney's

ethical responsibilities do not conflict with the securities laws. An attorney may not continue to provide services to corporate clients when the attorney knows the client is engaged in a course of conduct designed to deceive others, and where it is obvious that the attorney's compliant legal services may be a substantial factor in permitting the deceit to continue.

The record raises material questions about whether Jones Day knew of ACC/Lincoln's fraud, but nevertheless provided hands-on assistance in hiding loan file deficiencies from the regulators, offered detailed advice about setting up the bond sales program, carried out a lobbying strategy with respect to the direct investment rule, made political contributions on ACC's behalf, reviewed SEC registration statements and prospectuses, and lent its name to a misleading legal opinion. This evidence raises material questions concerning . . . RICO, AZRAC, common law fraud and deceit, and violations of Cal. Corp. Code §§25401 and 25504.1.

3. *Section 11 Liability . . .*

b. Expert Status

Jones Day further contends that it cannot be held liable under Section 11 because it did not issue an "expert" opinion. Section 11 applies to misleading statements made by one "whose profession gives authority to statements made by him." 15 U.S.C. §77l. Jones Day concedes that its October 28, 1986 opinion letter was required by SEC Regulation S-K, which provides in part:

> (5) Opinion Re Legality—(i) An opinion of counsel as to the legality of the securities being registered, indicating whether they will, when sold, be legally issued, fully paid and non-assessable, and, if debt securities, whether they will be binding obligations of the registrant.

The court holds that an attorney who provides a legal opinion used in connection with an SEC registration statement is an expert within the meaning of Section 11.

4. *Breach of Fiduciary Duty to Lincoln . . .*

An attorney who represents a corporation has a duty to act in the corporation's best interest when confronted by adverse interests of directors, officers, or corporate affiliates. It is not a defense that corporate representation often involves the distinct interests of affiliated entities. Attorneys are bound to act when those interests conflict. There are genuine questions as to whether Jones Day should have sought independent representation for Lincoln.

Moreover, where a law firm believes the management of a corporate client is committing serious regulatory violations, the firm has an obligation to actively discuss the violative conduct, urge cessation of the activity, and withdraw from representation where the firm's legal services may contribute to the continuation of such conduct. Jones Day contends that it would have been futile to act on these fiduciary obligations because those controlling ACC/Lincoln would not have responded. Client wrongdoing, however, cannot negate an attorney's fiduciary duty. Moreover, the evidence reveals that attorney advice influenced ACC/Lincoln's conduct in a variety of ways. Accordingly, summary judgment as to this claim is denied.

5. *Professional Negligence Claims*

Jones Day issued an opinion letter that was included with ACC's 1986 shelf registration statement. California authority provides that independent public accountants have a duty to those who are foreseeably injured from representations made in connection with publicly held corporations. While this duty does not extend to confidential advice which an attorney gives to its clients, it would apply where an attorney issues an SEC opinion letter to the public. Roberts v. Ball, Hunt, Hart, Brown & Baerwitz, 128 Cal. Rptr. 901 (Cal. App. 1976).

Accordingly, a question of fact remains as to whether the . . . Plaintiffs who purchased bonds issued pursuant to the November, 1986 shelf registration and amendments, were injured by the Jones Day opinion letter.

The Limits of the Law: *Client Fraud*

In a previous note about lawyer dishonesty, we saw that lawyers, like everyone else, are subject to the law of fraud and misrepresentation and need to understand this law in all its permutations to avoid suffering a number of adverse consequences.[1] *American Continental Corporation (ACC)* indicates that the law of fraud also plays a significant role in the advice lawyers give to clients. Some of the most notorious corporate frauds of the past 50 years have raised similar questions about the lawyer's role in advising clients. This note examines the way the criminal and civil law of fraud and the lawyer codes create legal limits on what lawyers are able to do for clients as well as what lawyers may do for themselves.

The vast scope of the modern law of fraud reflects its equally frequent and widespread occurrence.[2] The lawyer's advice can play a central role in avoiding the massive personal and social costs of criminal and fraudulent activity both to a client,[3] and to the others such as shareholders and employees of corporations and family members of individuals. Proper legal advice also may prevent injury to the economic system itself. Fraudulent practices can undercut competition, raise the price of goods, and cause loss of confidence in the market system. Potential economic actors may refrain from market transactions if they do not trust its mechanisms. This chilling effect further impedes the market and can damage social ties, many of which also depend upon trust.[4]

The Model Rules

The Model Rules of Professional Conduct recognize the central role of legal advice in representing clients. The four basic fiduciary duties (competence, communication, confidentiality, and loyalty) all contribute to trust between lawyer and client, enabling lawyers to get the information necessary to advise clients accurately about the legal ramifications of their proposed conduct. At the same time, all of these essential fiduciary duties are limited by several rules that prohibit lawyers from knowingly furthering a course of criminal or fraudulent conduct by their clients.

---

1. *See* The Limits of the Law: Lawyer Dishonesty, Fraud, Deceit, and Misrepresentation, *supra* p.101.
2. Overall statistics concerning fraud are not available in the United States, but a comparison of several studies indicates that fraud crimes account for ten times the loss that more conventional crimes (such as burglary, robbery, and auto theft) cause. Brenda L. Nightingale, *The Law of Fraud and Related Offences* 1-24.1 (Carswell 2000). One example is the failure of Lincoln Savings & Loan, which cost taxpayers at least $2.5 billion. *Bad Day at Jones Day; A Record Payment gets the Law Firm off the Hook in the S&L Debacle,* Time 23 (May 3, 1993). Canadian statistics for the year 1999 indicate that over one quarter of all criminal prosecutions were for fraud related crimes. Nightingale, *supra* at 1-21.
3. Charles Keating was convicted of 90 federal and state counts of fraud, racketeering, and conspiracy. He served less that five years of a twelve and one-half year sentence and was released after two appellate courts found legal error in his convictions. Adam Zagorin, *Charlie's an Angel? Charles Keating, Demon of the $500 Billion S&L Fiasco, Is Now Innocent, Sort Of,* Time 36 (Feb. 3, 1997).
4. Nightingale, *supra* note 2, at 1-24.2 to 1-25.

Model Rule 1.2(d) prohibits lawyers from counseling or assisting clients in conduct the lawyer knows to be criminal or fraudulent. Model Rules 3.3 and 4.1(b) further require lawyers to disclose information where necessary to avoid knowingly assisting a criminal or fraudulent act by a client on a tribunal or third person.[5] Lawyers who represent organizations also are given discretion to disclose violations of law beyond the entity by Model Rule 1.13 but "only if and to the extent the lawyer reasonably believes necessary to prevent substantial injury to the organization."[6] Ethics opinions over the past 20 years illustrate that lawyers more than occasionally need guidance understanding these provisions. For example, lawyers have sought guidance from ethics committees concerning a client's fraud on a bank,[7] an insurance company,[8] and on the INS.[9] Lawyers also have needed advice when a client was threatening or has committed bankruptcy fraud,[10] tax fraud,[11] welfare fraud,[12] and worker's compensation fraud.[13]

The Lawyer's Knowledge

Note that Model Rules 1.2(d), 1.13, 3.3, and 4.1 all hinge on the lawyer's knowledge of the client's activity (knowledge that it constitutes a fraud or crime is not required).[14] A lawyer has no duty to withdraw to avoid assisting client fraud under Rule 1.2(d) unless the lawyer "knows" about it.[15] If the client refrains from or stops the wrongful activity after the lawyer learns of it, the lawyer will not have assisted or counseled it. However, if a prospective client expresses an intent to undertake the conduct, the lawyer will have to decline the representation to avoid violating Rule 1.2(d). When the lawyer learns of the client's intent to begin or continue the wrongful conduct after the representation has commenced, withdrawal from the representation is mandated by Rule 1.16(a), because continuing to represent the client in the matter will result in a violation of rule 1.2(d). If the lawyer does not "know, " but only "reasonably believes" that that client's course of action is criminal or fraudulent, then the lawyer may, but is not required to withdraw under Rule 1.16(b).

The knowledge requirement raises the question whether a lawyer who suspects but does not know of client wrongdoing should investigate further. On the one hand, not investigating seems an easy way to avoid triggering these rules. On the other, not investigating risks incompetent representation, or even worse, later allegations of complicity. Failure to investigate facts or law could result in incompetent legal advice

5. The duty to disclose to third persons in Rule 4.1(b) (client frauds on third persons) is subject to Rule 1.6 with respect to confidentiality, but the duty in Rule 3.3(b) (frauds on tribunals) is not. As we have seen in a previous note about lawyer dishonesty, Model Rule 8.4(c) also prohibits lawyers themselves from engaging "in conduct involving dishonesty, fraud, deceit or misrepresentation."
6. Model Rule 1.13(c)(2).
7. ABA Formal Op. 93-375, 92-366; Conn. Informal Op. 93-8.
8. Pa. Bar Assn. Op. 98-27; Pa. Bar Assn. Op. 98-5; Pa. Bar Assn. Op. 91-22; R.I. Op. 93-1.
9. D.C. Op. 296 (2000); Maryland Op. 99-17; Va. LEO 1687 (1996).
10. *E.g.*, Conn. Informal Op. 96-5; Texas Op. 480 (1993); Va. LEO 1643 (1995).
11. ABA Informal Op. 1490 (1982); ABA Informal Op. 1470 (1981).
12. Pa. Bar. Assn. Op. 91-39 (1992).
13. Ala. Op. RO-94-08; Pa. Bar Assn. Op. 97-21.
14. *See* In re Bloom, 745 P.2d 61 (Cal. 1987) (lawyer unsuccessfully argued that he thought helping a client transport plastic explosives to Libya was not unlawful).
15. The Model Rules define knowledge as "actual knowledge of the fact in question, which may be inferred from the circumstances," a definition that seems to include willful blindness as well as actual subjective knowledge. *E.g.*, In re Wahlder, 728 So. 2d 837 (La. 1999) (lawyer who permitted his client to place the client's wife's signature on a settlement document and witnessed the signature when he knew wife did not personally sign the document violated Model Rules 4.1(a) and 8.4(a) and (d)); In re Disbarment Proceedings, 184 A. 59 (Pa. 1936) (lawyer disbarred for knowingly participating in a numbers racket by agreeing in advance to regularly represent the organized criminals and their henchmen).

and a lost opportunity for the lawyer to assist the client in some manner that would avoid a crime or a fraud.[16] For example, the lawyer may be able to structure a transaction in an alternate way, or additional facts may create the basis for a new claim or defense in litigation. Further, the law that governs some tasks lawyers undertake for clients requires "due diligence"; that is, a competent investigation into the facts surrounding the transaction. Failure to meet these obligations or to explore alternatives for clients could result in discipline, civil and criminal liability.[17]

Beyond competence, anyone who contemplates future behavior, including lawyers and clients, faces the problem of "hindsight bias," a cognitive distortion that causes humans to believe that the fact a past event (like fraud) has occurred must have meant the event could have been anticipated in advance.[18] Lawyers should anticipate that hindsight bias is especially likely to occur in situations where they have some warning of wrongdoing and then encourage a client to push the law to its limits.[19] Finally, discovery of a client's ongoing or contemplated crime or fraud may mean that a lawyer loses a client's business, but it also affords the lawyer an opportunity to extricate herself from the client misconduct before it results in massive liability.[20]

The Duty to Withdraw: *ACC* Revisited

Consider the way these rules that limit lawyer services and shape legal advice to clients apply to the behavior of the Jones Day lawyers in *ACC*. There is no question that the firm's first legal service for ACC, a major internal audit of Lincoln's compliance with federal regulations, found multiple regulatory violations. Judge Bilby found that there were triable issues of fact concerning what Jones Day did with this information. It was not clear whether they told their client "in a clear and direct manner" that "its conduct violated the law." The court found some evidence, however, that despite their knowledge of these violations, Jones Day continued to represent ACC while the violations continued.

Judge Bilby also found that material issues of fact existed concerning whether Jones Day, knowing about these violations, actually helped cover them up rather than stop them. He correctly summarized the professional codes on this subject, which state that lawyers may not continue to represent clients who are engaged in a course of deceptive conduct. This means that a lawyer either must convince the client to stop the conduct or withdraw from the representation. If ACC's violations were continuing rather than past, and Jones Day knew about them, it was required to withdraw to avoid violating Model Rule 1.2(d).[21]

---

16. *E.g.*, Janet Fairchild, *Legal Malpractice for Advising Client to Commit a Crime or Unlawful Act*, 51 A.L.R.4th 1227 (1987).

17. *E.g.*, United States v. Benjamin, 328 F.2d 854 (2d Cir. 1964) (criminal prosecution of lawyers and accountants for aiding clients in mail and securities fraud).

18. *See* Jeffrey J. Rachlinski, *A Positive Psychological Theory of Judging in Hindsight*, 65 U. Chi. L. Rev. 571 (1998).

19. *See, e.g.*, FDIC v. O'Melveny & Myers, 969 F.2d 744 (9th Cir. 1992), *rev'd and remanded on other grounds*, 512 U.S. 79 (1994), *reaffirmed on remand*, 61 F.3d 17 (9th Cir. 1995) (receiver of a failed financial institution stated a cause of action against the institution's lawyer assigned to the receiver by investors for not questioning auditors and a law firm that resigned just before the firm assisted the client in a private real estate syndication); FDIC v. Clark, 978 F.2d 1541 (10th Cir. 1992) (jury verdict against failed financial institution's outside counsel upheld for negligence in failing to investigate or inform the bank directors of claims of fraud made against the bank's president in a civil suit).

20. *See* Lawyer's Roles: The Instrumental Lawyer and the Limits of the Law, *infra* p.202, for details of the financial consequences of Jones Day's representation of ACC.

21. Today, Model Rule 1.13(d) and Comment [4] clarify this distinction as well.

One Jones Day lawyer, Ronald Fein, testified that he warned ACC's inside counsel that ACC's conduct would have to stop and was assured that it would not recur. He also told ACC that if the regulatory violations continued, Jones Day would have to withdraw.[22] At that point, its initial work on regulatory compliance "wound down." But, just two days later, Fein himself solicited ACC's securities business, and Jones Day then was hired for that purpose.[23] *ACC* indicates that material questions of fact existed regarding whether Jones Day, knowing about ACC's fraud, turned to actively assisting it, by reviewing securities registration statements and lending "its name to misleading legal opinions."[24] One of the statements made in these documents was: "Lincoln Savings complies with the rules and regulations promulgated by the FHLBB (Federal Home Loan Bank Board) and the California Department of Savings and Loan regarding appraisals. . . ."[25] If the firm knew this language was incorrect, Jones Day not only violated Rule 1.2(d), but also engaged in deceit itself in violation of Rule 8.4(c). If this occurred, Jones Day crossed the line from counseling a client about the limits of the law to assisting a client in violating it.

Disclosure?

Withdrawing from a representation that involves the lawyer in a client's crime or fraud may not exhaust the lawyer's obligations. Model Rules 1.13, 3.3, and 4.1 raise the question of whether the lawyer also must disclose some or all of the facts to avoid or remedy the client's fraud. With respect to frauds on tribunals, Rule 3.3(b) makes clear that even if the lawyer withdraws, the lawyer also must disclose if that step is necessary to avoid assisting the client's criminal or fraudulent act. Outside of tribunals, Rule 4.1(b) conditions the duty to disclose on the exceptions in Rule 1.6 regarding disclosing confidential information. Model Rule 1.13, however, specifically grants an entity lawyer discretion to disclose violations of law regardless of Rule 1.6 exceptions where "the lawyer reasonably believes [this is] necessary to prevent substantial injury to the organization."[26]

The question of whether a lawyer should be able to disclose a client's fraud has been the subject of unrelenting debate for over a quarter century. Original drafts of the Model Rules in 1980 included a provision that would have permitted a lawyer to disclose information to prevent or to rectify criminal or fraudulent acts of clients on both tribunals and third persons. These proposals prevailed where the fraud was perpetrated on a tribunal (Model Rule 3.3), but failed where the fraud occurred outside of tribunals (Model Rules 1.6 and 4.1). As a compromise, the so-called noisy withdrawal provision was added to the comments in Model Rule 1.6:

> After withdrawal the lawyer is required to refrain from making disclosure of the client's confidences, except as otherwise permitted in Rule 1.6. Neither this Rule nor Rule 1.8(b) nor Rule 1.16(a) prevents the lawyer from giving notice of the fact of withdrawal, and the lawyer may also withdraw or disaffirm any opinion, document, affirmation or the like.[27]

Disagreement about these provisions resurfaced when the American Law Institute adopted the Restatement of the Law Governing Lawyers, and again when the ABA debated the Revised Model Rules in the summers of 2001 and 2003. The Restatement

---

22. Rita Henley Jensen, *Lawyers Share the Blame for the Savings and Loan Scandal*, 95 Bus. & Socy. Rev. 54 (Sept. 22, 1995).
23. *Id.*
24. *ACC*, *supra* p.195.
25. *Id.*
26. Model Rule 1.13(c)(2). This language reflects ABA amendments adopted in August 2003.
27. Model Rule 1.6, Comment [15] (1983).

debate resulted in the adoption of §67 which allows lawyers to use or disclose client information to prevent, rectify or mitigate substantial financial loss. The Ethics 2000 Commission recommended similar exceptions to confidentiality, which initially were rejected by the ABA. In 2003, following Enron and other corporate disasters, the ABA reversed course, abandoning "noisy withdrawal" for the current explicit exceptions in Model Rule 1.6(b)(2) and (3), which allow disclosure to prevent, mitigate, or rectify client acts that constitute a crime or fraud and are "reasonably certain to result in substantial injury to the financial interest or property of another and in furtherance of which the client has used or is using the lawyer's services."

As jurisdictions consider their own version of the Model Rules, debate over these provisions continues. Today, jurisdictions agree on two rules and disagree about a third. They agree that lawyers cannot counsel or assist criminal or fraudulent client activity (Rule 1.2(d)), and that lawyers have duties to tribunals, which may require disclosure of client confidences when fraud has occurred (Rule 3.3).

Jurisdictions disagree strongly, however, on the lawyer's obligations outside of tribunals when the client contemplates or commits fraud (Rules 1.6, 1.13, and 4.1). The following table summarizes the wide variation in these state provisions.

CLIENT FRAUD

	Withdrawal	Noisy Withdrawal	Disclosure
Past Fraud	Not required unless future or continuing, but *permitted* by MR 1.16(b)(3) if "the client has used the lawyer's services to perpetrate a crime or fraud."	*Required* = 1: TN	*Required* = 3: OH, HI, TN *Prohibited* = 30:[28] E.g., CA, IA[29] NY *Permitted* = 18:[30] E.g., MR 1.6(b)(3)
Continuing or Future Fraud	*Required* if the lawyer knows the client is engaging in criminal or fraudulent conduct. MR 1.2(d), 1.16(a)(1).	*Required* = 1: TN *Permitted* = 31[31] E.g., MR 1.6	***Criminal Fraud:*** *Required* = 5[32] *Prohibited* = 9[33] *Permitted* = 38[34]
	Permitted if the lawyer reasonably believes the client's course of action is criminal or fraudulent. MR 1.16(b)(2).	Former Comment 15	***Non-Criminal Fraud:*** *Required* = 3[35] *Prohibited* = 37[36] *Permitted* = 11[37]

28. AL, AK, AR, CA, CO, DC, FL, GA, IA, ID, IL, IN, KS, KY, LA, ME, MS, MO, MT, NE, NH, NM, NY, OR, RI, SC, VT, WA, WV, WY.
29. Prohibited if privileged information, if not, disclosure required.
30. AZ, CT, DE, MD, MA, MI, MN, NJ, NV, NC, ND, OK, PA, SD, TX, UT, VA, WI.
31. AL, AK, AZ, AR, CO, CT, DE, DC, FL, GA, HI, IN, KS, KY, LA, MD, MA, ME, MS, MO, NH, NM, ND, RI, SC, TX, VT, VA, WV, WI, WY.
32. FL, MA, NJ, VA, WI.
33. AL, CA, DC, KY, LA, MO, MT, RI, SD.
34. AK, AZ, AR, CO, CT, DE, GA, HI, ID, IL, IN, IA, KS, ME, MD, MA, MI, MN, MS, NE, NV, NH, NM, NY, NC, ND, OH, OK, OR, PA, SC, TN, TX, UT, VT, WA, WV, WY.
35. MA, NJ, WI.
36. AL, AR, CA, CO, CT, DC, FL, GA, ID, IL, IN, IA, KS, KY, LA, ME, MI, MN, MS, MO, MT, NE, NH, NM, NY, OH, OK, OR, RI, SC, SD, TN, VT, VA, WA, WV, WY.
37. AK, AZ, DE, HI, MD, NC, NV, ND, PA, TX, UT.

Lawyers and jurisdictions that oppose exceptions to confidentiality designed to allow lawyers to warn about or rectify client fraud make several arguments. First, they maintain that narrower exceptions to confidentiality in general create more opportunity for lawyers to encourage full and frank communication with clients and therefore enhance the ability of lawyers to give legal advice to avoid or mitigate wrongful conduct. Second, they point to the nature of "fraud" and worry that adding such an exception might be construed as a duty to warn in a later civil case. They argue that "fraud" is always difficult to identify at the time it occurs, and easier to recognize after the fact. Any exception to confidentiality tied to client fraud therefore increases the likelihood that liability will be extended to lawyers who did not warn or rectify. This in turn will force lawyers to practice law defensively, erring on the side of disclosure and undermining client trust. Third, they maintain that exceptions to save human life recognize a competing value of "unique importance," where no remedy will suffice to prevent the harm.[38] Client fraud, on the other hand, usually results in monetary loss, which can be restored by other legal remedies. Finally, lawyers who oppose client fraud exceptions argue that when client fraud does occur, the lawyer's withdrawal from the matter is sufficient to extricate the lawyer from the client's wrongdoing.[39]

Lawyers and jurisdictions that support exceptions to confidentiality where client fraud occurs or is threatened address the same issues, but disagree on the result. They concede the possibility that clients might be less willing to confide in lawyers, but maintain that clients who misuse the client-lawyer relationship are not entitled to absolute confidentiality.[40] Further, they argue that the ability of the lawyer to encourage the client to act lawfully will be enhanced by a discretionary disclosure provision. With respect to the threat of civil liability, they note that civil liability already exists in many cases (as it did in *ACC*), and to clarify this point, added §67(4) to the Restatement. This section provides that any exercise of discretion under this exception does not create grounds for discipline or liability. Finally, lawyers caught in the web of client wrongdoing argue that an exception to confidentiality where the client perpetrates a fraud by using the lawyer's services actually allows lawyers to extricate themselves from the client's acts before they otherwise might be able to respond under the self-defense exception in Model Rule 1.6. Disclosing client misconduct when they withdraw from the representation also avoids the fiction of limited disclosure by notification and disavowal allowed by "noisy withdrawal."

Whatever their view of the appropriate answers to these issues, lawyers do agree on several key points: First, you must be competent. This means that you must know the relevant facts and law that govern your representation of a client, including whether the activity constitutes a crime or fraud. Second, if you have been retained to defend a client's wrongful activity that is completely ended and not continuing, you are not assisting or counseling it. Third, if a client seeks to use your services to assist in future or ongoing criminal or fraudulent activity, failure to withdraw will subject you to professional discipline as well potential civil and criminal liability. Fourth, if you represent an entity, you have special obligations to take serious legal

38. Freedman & Smith, *Understanding Lawyers' Ethics* 145 (LexisNexis 2002).

39. *Legislative History of the Model Rules of Professional Conduct: Their Development in the ABA House of Delegates* 48-49 (ABA 1987).

40. *Restatement (Third) Law Governing Lawyers* §67, Comment b. Professor Burt argues that the mistrust which pervades the client-lawyer relationship might actually be addressed and alleviated by more discretionary disclosure exceptions because they would force honest exploration of the basis for the mistrust. *See* Robert A. Burt, *Conflict and Trust Between Attorney and Client*, 69 Geo. L.J. 1015 (1981).

violations beyond your immediate supervisor to higher authorities such as corporate boards for reconsideration.[41] Finally, you need to know your own jurisdiction's exceptions to confidentiality to determine whether you also have discretion or an obligation to warn third persons.

Lawyers' Roles: *The Instrumental Lawyer and the Limits of the Law*

Viewed from a public perspective after the massive costs of the fraud were known, the Jones Day lawyers in *ACC*, like Mr. Perez's lawyers, appear to have misconstrued their role in the representation. The court in *ACC* found that that material issues of fact existed about whether Jones Day's representation of its client violated federal and state securities and fraud laws. Indeed, two years before Judge Bilby's decision, Judge Stanley Sporkin upheld the federal receivership of Lincoln Savings, concluding his opinion with these observations:

> There are other unanswered questions presented by this case. Keating testified that he was so bent on doing the "right thing" that he surrounded himself with literally scores of accountants and lawyers to make sure all the transactions were legal. The questions that must be asked are:
>
> Where were these professionals, a number of whom are now asserting their rights under the Fifth Amendment, when these clearly improper transactions were being consummated?
>
> Why didn't any of them speak up or disassociate themselves from the transactions?
>
> Where also were the outside accountants and attorneys when these transactions were effectuated?[1]

ACC involves serious allegations against lawyers who appear to have overidentified with a client and illustrates what can happen when a lawyer fails to maintain the distance critical to evaluating a client's conduct. The lawyer who continues to advocate for such a client unwittingly, negligently, or knowingly can become an instrument of wrongdoing or an accessory to corrupt and dishonorable conduct. The behavior of these lawyers suggests that they saw law as a malleable means to pursue a client's objectives, rather than a set of rules with some clear boundaries that should have shaped both their client's and their own behavior. They apparently also lacked a healthy skepticism that may have helped them avoid entanglement in their client's wrongdoing, and suffered from too little, rather than too much, distance in their professional relationship with their client. From the viewpoint of summary judgment, they allowed themselves, wittingly or unwittingly, to be used as instruments and technicians of inappropriate conduct by a client. How and why might this have happened?

The Limits of the Law

We have seen that the agency relationship between client and lawyer requires fiduciary duties to ensure that a lawyer acts subject to the client's control. At the same time, every agency relationship is subject to one limitation: neither the principal's power nor the agent's duty to obey allows either to violate the limits of the law.[2]

---

41. Model Rule 1.13. For public corporations, this obligation also stems from the Sarbanes-Oxley Act, 15 U.S.C. §7201 *et seq.* (2003); 17 C.F.R. Part 205, 68 Fed. Reg. 6296 (2-6-03).

1. Lincoln Savings & Loan Assn. v. Wall, 743 F. Supp. 901, 919-920 (D.D.C. 1990).

2. *Restatement (Third) The Law Governing Lawyers* §23 (2000); *Restatement (Third) of Agency* §1.01, Comment f(1) (Tentative Draft No. 2, 2001).

When an agent agrees to act subject to the control of a principal, the law does not assume that the principal merges her legal personality into the agent's. Both principal and agent remain responsible for the consequences of their own conduct. Agency law recognizes principal and agent as distinct, autonomous legal persons, and anticipates that they will behave accordingly.[3]

Lawyers can be put in a position of real conflict when it comes to abiding by client instructions. On the one hand, lawyers are admonished to do everything they can to help fulfill the client's goals of the representation, goals that are to be determined by the client. On the other, clients can make decisions that the lawyer believes reflect bad judgment or, worse, that suggest to the lawyer that the client might be engaging in conduct that could run afoul of the law and subject the client to liability. When lawyers place too much weight on the former proposition—simply being instruments unquestioningly abiding their client's instructions—they disserve the client by failing to share their independent view of the merits of the course of action and open their clients to potential liability. *ACC* indicates that they disserve themselves as well, by exposing their own law firm to liability.

It is important to realize that a lawyer can be subjected to allegations of assisting client misconduct in at least three different circumstances. In the first, lawyers like those in *Chen*, unwittingly or innocently participate in the client's fraud by providing legal advice to a client who, unbeknownst to the lawyer, is using it to break the law. In the second, lawyers act negligently by failing to identify or act upon red flags, which with the benefit of 20-20 hindsight, will be characterized as clear warnings that the client was engaged in wrongful conduct. Third, and most serious, involves lawyers who act recklessly or intentionally by blindly ignoring clear warning signs or, worse, purposefully assisting a client to violate the law. Everyone recognizes the last as a clear example of lawyer misconduct. But the middle example can get lawyers in almost as much trouble, and the first, unwitting involvement, requires immediate response at the point the lawyer discovers the client's unlawful activity. In all of these circumstances, the lawyer who fails to keep the proper distance and overidentifies with the client is the lawyer who is most likely to ignore the warning signs that will seem much clearer after the fact.

What Happened in *ACC*?

We turn now to consider whether, or how, this occurred in *ACC*. First, when Charles Keating, Jr., hired Jones Day, Keating and his general counsel met with William Schilling and Rick Kneipper.[4] Note that Schilling, a Jones Day partner, had recently stepped down from his job as director of the Federal Home Loan Bank Board, where he had supervised and participated in an investigation that found serious regulatory concerns about Keating's Lincoln Savings and Loan. Schilling's "personal and substantial involvement" meant that he could not personally represent ACC after he left the government. It also meant that Jones Day could represent ACC only if Schilling was "screened from any participation in the matter and apportioned no part of the fee therefrom," and his former agency was given written notice about these

3. *Id.* at Comment c.
4. Rita Henley Jensen, *Lawyers Share the Blame for the Savings and Loan Scandal*, 95 Bus. & Socy. Rev. 54, 56 (1995). Keating controlled both Lincoln Savings & Loan and American Continental Corporation (ACC), which was a wholly-owned subsidiary of Lincoln.

arrangements.[5] Yet, Schilling testified that he not only solicited ACC's business, but also that he personally performed legal services for ACC (the "to do" lists).[6]

Second, even if Schilling had been properly screened from representing ACC, note that the court found that there was evidence that despite their knowledge of these violations, Jones Day continued to represent ACC while the violations continued. Judge Bilby also found that material issues of fact existed concerning whether Jones Day, knowing about these violations, actually helped cover them up rather than stop them. If that occurred, Jones Day intentionally assisted its client's unlawful conduct.

Third, beyond counseling, if in fact Jones Day knew that the statements they made on behalf of ACC in the legal opinions they prepared to facilitate the bond transactions were false, they crossed the line from counseling a client about the limits of the law to assisting a client in violating it. Jones Day's Neal Millard's memo appears to have anticipated this problem: "... we now possess information that could affect the way we write our opinion letters...." Millard's memo apparently sought to remedy the problem by assigning opinion letter responsibilities to those within the firm who lacked this knowledge of ACC's regulatory violations. Of course, this advice ignores the basic agency rule that attributes the knowledge of one agent to those in the rest of the firm. In other words, there was no way any lawyer at Jones Day could write opinion letters certifying ACC's compliance with banking regulations if some in the firm knew that such compliance was not a reality.

Finally, note that the fourth cause of action for breach of fiduciary duty also withstands summary judgment. This action was instituted by constituents of the client itself; the shareholders who now claim that Jones Day should not have obeyed Keating when he was in fact acting contrary to the best interests of both Lincoln and ACC. Here, the court's response anticipates recent specific amendments to Model Rule 1.13 and the Sarbanes-Oxley Act of 2002.[7] Lawyers who believe that constituents of entity clients are acting against its best interests should seek outside opinions and refer the matter to a higher authority within the organization. If that does not stop the wrongdoing, the lawyer should resign.[8] Model Rule 1.13 today also instructs lawyers who reasonably believe it necessary to prevent substantial injury to the organization to disclose information to prevent, stop, or rectify the wrongdoing.[9]

ACC illustrates that this reality about the many faces of corporate identity often has grave consequences for lawyers when an entity fails. At that point, a successor in interest, such as a trustee in bankruptcy (or the receiver in *ACC*) reassesses the entity's best interests, with a view toward maximizing the funds available to creditors or other stakeholders. In such cases, corporate officials like Keating, who may have

---

5. *See* Model Rule 1.11(b). The "personal and substantial participation" requirement of this rule was borrowed from 18 U.S.C. §207 (2000). This conflict of interest statute prohibits former governmental employees from communicating or appearing before their former agencies within certain time periods in any matters in which they participated personally and substantially while in government service. If Schilling confined his representation of ACC to advising them, and avoided contact on their behalf with the FHLBB, he complied with this statute.

6. The government refused to settle the case unless the settlement included Schilling's agreement not to work on any additional banking matters. John H. Cushman, Jr., *Despite Big Settlement, Firm Feels Little Pinch*, N.Y. Times, at B10 (Apr. 23, 1993).

7. 15 U.S.C. §7201 *et seq.* (2003); 17 C.F.R. Part 205, 68 Fed. Reg. 6296 (2-6-03).

8. Model Rule 1.13, Comment [4]. Comment [6] provides that a lawyer in such a situation also "may" resign and mirrors the *ACC* court's conclusion that withdrawal is mandatory where the ongoing conduct is criminal or fraudulent and the lawyer knows about it. *See* Model Rule 1.2(d).

9. Model Rule 1.13(c)(2).

violated legal regulations, often blame the professionals they say they relied on and waive the attorney-client privilege so that all documents and conversations the lawyer thought would never see the light of day may appear on page one of the Wall Street Journal. The lawyer who acted instrumentally may in fact have agreed to the course of action, knowing it was risky, but believing all along that the corporate official would prevail on behalf of the entity. When that fails, the legal advice will be very carefully scrutinized by a successor in interest to the now failed enterprise.

The Problem with Instrumental Behavior

Professor Rhode warns that this kind of instrumental behavior is especially dangerous and misplaced in representing entities rather than individuals, and in counseling clients rather than litigating on their behalf. When a powerful enterprise rather than an autonomous individual's interests are at stake, the rights-based justification for role-differentiated behavior has much less justification. When lawyers counsel clients, Rhode points out that lawyers deal with future behavior and have an opportunity and obligation to prevent, rather than justify, massive social and person harm.[10] *ACC* illustrates how an initial litigation-minded advocacy (appropriate for defending the entity against bank regulators) may have infected subsequent transactional service as well. Thinking about how to protect the client against legal sanctions may have erased practical wisdom about legal limits on future activity.

ACC also demonstrates that no lawyer or law firm is invulnerable to serious allegations of complicity in client misconduct. In retrospect, what is so amazing about this case is that very well educated and talented lawyers could appear to be so duped by a clever and self-serving client. *ACC* offers one clue to how they might have lost their way when it quotes an ambiguous, but troubling, Jones Day memo from its lawyer Caulkins, written after Jones Day solicited additional business from Keating.

> ACC is very explicit that it does not care how much its legal services cost, as long as it gets the best.... On the down side, he reports that he has never encountered a more demanding and difficult client.... It appears to Rick and to me that American Continental is made for us and we for them.

In fact, Jones Day solicited Keating's business at a time when its managing partner, Richard W. Pogue, was "pushing the Los Angeles branch to break into the lucrative business of advising banks and other financial institutions."[11] In the year before this, Pogue had overseen a firm merger that transformed Jones Day from a five-office 330-lawyer firm to the country's second-largest firm with nearly 600 lawyers. Perhaps a powerful client saw an economic opportunity in this situation to make the law firm a tool of his will.

It is also possible that overidentification with a client may have been caused by nonmonetary considerations. It is conceivable that Jones Day lawyers, like several public figures,[12] found themselves drawn to a charismatic man who no doubt believed himself unfairly targeted and harassed by federal regulators.[13] At the same time, their

---

10. *See supra* pp.9-10.
11. Jensen, *supra* note 4, at 55.
12. The "Keating Five," was the derogatory moniker placed on five United States Senators (Alan Cranston, Dennis DeConcini, John Glenn, Donald Riegle, and John McCain) whose careers were nearly ruined by their close association to Keating. *See* Richard L. Berke, *Cranston Rebuked by Ethics Panel*, N.Y. Times, at A1 (Nov. 20, 1991).
13. For an account of Keating's view of the matter, *see* Michael Binstein & Charles Bowden, *Trust Me: Charles Keating and the Missing Billions* (Random House 1993).

legal audit discovered numerous offenses of federal banking regulations, including key provisions designed to prevent bank failure. Perhaps the power of this man and his organization seduced them to combine their technical skills with their entrepreneurial interests, merging their own desires with those of their client in the process.[14]

Whatever their motivations, the role assumed by these lawyers apparently enabled Keating to turn them into instruments of his wrongful conduct. Although Jones Day correctly identified ACC's regulatory violations and threatened to withdraw if they were not stopped, it also solicited ACC's securities business just two days after it completed the regulatory audit. The second task required the firm to opine that ACC was in compliance with applicable thrift regulations, something it apparently had already discovered not to be the case.[15] The firm appears not only to have allowed but also to have invited Keating and ACC to treat them instrumentally. In the process, the firm apparently lost some of its ability to evaluate objectively its client's conduct, and as a result, was implicated in ACC's wrongdoing.

In the end, it is interesting to note that Jones Day was able to bill ACC about $1.2 million for its services,[16] an amount that pales in relation to the $24 million for which it eventually settled the private claims of the stockholders against the firm. The government claims went to trial, but just after jury selection, the law firm settled these claims for an additional $51 million. At a press conference on the day of the settlement, Pogue denied wrongdoing by the firm but concluded after watching jury selection that the jury would never understand the firm's complex defense.[17] All told, Jones Day settled the public and private claims against the firm for $75 million.

Jones Day's new managing partner said that the settlement would not have a "significant financial impact" on the firm even though $19.5 million of the settlement was uninsured.[18] The firm also claimed it was "infected" by its association with Keating and released a statement that characterized its services to Lincoln as "limited" and "performed competently and in accord with applicable standards of professional conduct."[19] Do you agree?

5. Law or Court Order: Physical Evidence

Legal obligations such as court orders, statutes or procedural rules often require the disclosure of confidential client information. Creating an exception to client confidentiality when other law requires or allows such disclosure promotes the policy of that other law. At the same time, allowing other legal obligations to trump client-lawyer confidentiality may compromise a central justification for confidentiality, especially if the purpose of the other law does not mirror another preexisting exception already justified by the underlying rationales for the protection.

---

14. This is the way Judge Noonan describes the transformation of another influential lawyer, Hoyt Moore, whose representation of Bethlehem Steel led him to bribe a federal judge to secure his client's goals. John T. Noonan, Jr., *The Lawyer Who Overidentifies with His Client*, 76 Notre Dame L. Rev. 827, 840-841 (2001).
15. The Limits of the Law: Client Fraud, *supra* p.196.
16. Jensen, *supra* note 4, at 57.
17. *Id.* at 59.
18. Henry J. Reske, *Firm Agrees to Record S & L Settlement: Shifting Standards Require Lawyers to Disclose More to Regulatory Agencies*, 79 ABA J. 16 (July 1993). The law firm that represented Lincoln on regulatory matters after Jones Day, Kaye, Scholer, Fierman Nays & Handler, also settled with both private investors ($21 million) and the government ($41 million). Stephen Labaton, *Law Firm Will Pay a $41 Million Fine in Savings Lawsuit*, N.Y. Times, at A1 (Mar. 9, 1992).
19. Reske, *supra* note 18.

Utilitarians may argue about the precise line to draw in creating an efficient and fair legal system, but probably would agree that court orders and procedural rules should be obeyed in order to promote the proper functioning of the courts. Some statutes, such as child and elder abuse disclosure provisions, also could be justified if their purpose is to protect child welfare and prevent harm. Similar arguments could be made about the law of fraud. Insofar as it prevents unfair use of the market or the legal system, a lawyer could be justified in disclosing client confidences in order to comply with the criminal or civil law of fraud. A deontologist would agree that court rules or laws designed to protect basic human freedoms are important. When a client seeks to infringe such an obligation, the client's conduct is blameworthy, which creates a valid reason for the lawyer to prevent such a misuse of others.

Problems

5-26. What, if any, obligation to disclose does Martyn have if her client tells her where he hid the stolen money? What if he hands her the key to the safe deposit box where the money is? Can Martyn give it back? If she keeps the key, can she be forced to testify that her client gave it to her?

5-27. May (must) Fox disclose that his client killed two children and Fox knows where the bodies are buried? Does it matter if the parents still hope the children are alive, and the town has been conducting a massive search for two weeks?

Consider: Model Rules 1.6(b)(6), 3.4(a), 8.4(b)
Model Code DR 1-102(A)(3), 4-101(C)(2), 7-109(A)
RLGL §119

In re Original Grand Jury Investigation

733 N.E.2d 1135 (Ohio 2000)

Appellant Jeffrey Helmick was lead defense counsel representing defendant Douglas Coley in a capital trial. During the trial, an investigator retained by Helmick discovered the existence of a threatening letter. The letter, which was written by Coley to his brother, was in the possession of Coley's mother, Victoria Coley. Victoria Coley reluctantly gave the letter to the investigator, who in turn gave it to Helmick.

Since the letter contained threats against others, Helmick contacted Jonathan Marshall, Secretary of the Board of Commissioners on Grievances and Discipline of the Supreme Court, for advice on whether he had an obligation to report the matter. Marshall opined that Helmick should report the matter. Helmick telephoned the presiding trial judge and read the letter to her. The judge then contacted the police. Helmick told a detective the salient facts in the letter so that the detective could understand the nature, severity, and breadth of the threats contained in the letter. Helmick states that he also filed a motion to withdraw as defense counsel, which the trial court granted.

Thereafter, a subpoena was issued to Helmick asking him to appear before the grand jury and to bring with him "any letter(s), correspondence, or writing(s) of any types, including envelopes, originals and/or copies thereof, written by or purportedly authored by Douglas Coley, aka MiMi, which led to or served as a basis for Douglas Coley's trial counsel requesting leave to withdraw as his legal counsel." Helmick refused to comply with the subpoena. Instead, through counsel, Helmick filed two motions to quash the subpoena. Helmick argued that the subpoena should be quashed because otherwise his attorney-client relationship, work-product privilege, and Fifth Amendment rights would be violated. Helmick also argued that compliance with the subpoena would violate his obligations under the Code of Professional Responsibility.

The trial court overruled Helmick's motions to quash and ordered him to comply with the subpoena. Helmick refused to do so. The trial court conducted a show cause hearing and held Helmick in civil contempt under R.C. 2705.02. The court also imposed an ongoing daily fine of $25 until he complied with the order. The sanction was stayed pending appeal. . . .

Francis E. SWEENEY, Sr., J.

The issue presented in this case is whether an attorney can be compelled to disclose to the grand jury a letter written by a client and discovered by an investigator that contains evidence of a possible crime or whether the Ohio Code of Professional Responsibility prohibits such disclosure.

At the outset, we understand that appellant was faced with an ethical dilemma and had the difficult decision of determining how to respond to the competing challenges of maintaining client confidentiality and preserving the safety concerns of the public. We appreciate that appellant confronted the problem head-on by first asking the Secretary of the Board of Commissioners on Grievances and Discipline of the Supreme Court for advice on whether he had an obligation to report a possible crime and then by heeding that advice by reporting the matter to the court and cooperating with the police. Nevertheless, for the reasons that follow, we find that appellant must comply with the grand jury subpoena and relinquish the letter in question.

The concept of client confidentiality, including the attorney's ethical obligations concerning confidentiality, is embodied in DR 4-101. . . .

We must first determine whether the letter sought falls within the definition of a client "secret." Unlike "confidence," which is limited to information an attorney obtains directly from his or her client, the term "secret" is defined in broad terms. . . .

The court of appeals found that the letter was not a secret because it was not information gained in the professional relationship. Instead, the court said that the letter was simply physical evidence, which needed to be disclosed to the authorities. Even though the letter does constitute physical evidence of a possible crime, it also contains information detrimental to appellant. Thus, we find that the letter falls within the definition of a client "secret," since it was obtained in the professional attorney-client relationship, by appellant's agent (the investigator), and since it contains detrimental information detailing a possible crime committed by appellant's former client.

Although the letter is a client secret, this does not necessarily mean that disclosure of the letter is absolutely prohibited. An attorney may disclose a client secret if one of the four listed exceptions in DR 4-101(C) applies.

Appellant concedes that DR 4-101(C)(3) permits him to "reveal . . . the intention of his client to commit a crime and the information necessary to prevent the crime." . . .

We agree with appellant that he was authorized by DR 4-101(C)(3) when he chose to reveal the intent of his client to commit a crime, and, actually, went beyond what DR 4-101(C) (3) allows by reading the entire letter to the trial court and police. However, the fact that he revealed this information does not answer the question whether he is obligated to produce the letter itself. Thus, the question that remains is whether appellant is required to relinquish the letter itself and present it to the grand jury. We find that the exception found in DR 4-102(C)(2) governs disposition of this issue.

DR 4-101(C)(2) provides that an attorney may reveal "confidences or secrets when permitted under Disciplinary Rules or required by law or court order." Although the language contained in DR 4-101(C)(2), like that of DR 4-101 (C)(3), is written in permissive terms, courts have interpreted provisions similar to DR 4-101(C)(2) in such a manner as to require disclosure. The exception of DR 4-101(C)(2) for disclosures required by law has been construed so that "the effect of other rules . . . compels disclosures." Consequently, if a lawyer is "required by law" to disclose information to the authorities, "these legal obligations create 'forced' exceptions to confidentiality." 1 Hazard & Hodes, The Law of Lawyering: A Handbook on the Model Rules of Professional Conduct (2d ed. 1990) 183, Section 1.6:310. Under these circumstances, a lawyer's duty "not to use or disclose confidential client information . . . is superseded when the law specifically requires such use or disclosure." Restatement of the Law 3d, Law Governing Lawyers (Proposed Final Draft No. 1, 1996), Section 115, Comment a.

The exception of DR 4-101(C)(2) for disclosures required by law has been applied in the context of mandating that attorneys relinquish evidence and instrumentalities of crime to law-enforcement agencies. Thus, the rule has emerged that, despite any confidentiality concerns, a criminal defense attorney must produce real evidence obtained from his or her client or from a third-party source, regardless of whether the evidence is mere evidence of a client's crime, *see, e.g.*, Morrell v. Alaska, 575 P.2d 1200 (Alaska 1978), or is a fruit or instrumentality of a crime.[2] In either event, the physical evidence must be turned over to the proper authorities. *See* In re Ryder, 381 F.2d 713 (4th Cir. 1967) (holding that an attorney abuses his professional responsibility by knowingly taking possession of and secreting the fruits and instrumentalities of a crime); State v. Green, 493 So. 2d 1178 (La. 1986) (holding that the attorney had an obligation to relinquish client's gun, an instrumentality of a crime, to authorities). In essence, the confidentiality rules do not give an attorney the right to withhold evidence. *See* People v. Lee, 83 Cal. Rptr. 715, 722 (Cal. App. 1970).

Appellant contends, however, that there are strong policy reasons against mandating disclosure. Appellant believes that mandatory disclosure will discourage attorneys from reporting possible threats made by their clients and will therefore run contrary to the intent of the code, which is to prevent crimes from occurring. Appellant cites the Massachusetts decision of Purcell v. Dist. Atty. for Suffolk Dist., 676 N.E.2d 436 (Mass. 1997), which highlights these concerns.

In *Purcell*, . . . the court noted:

> We must be cautious in permitting the use of client communications that a

2. In *Morrell*, the Supreme Court of Alaska held that a criminal defense attorney was obligated to turn over to authorities a legal pad containing a kidnapping plan written by his client that was given to him by his client's friend. Although the main issue before the court in *Morrell* was whether the defendant was denied effective assistance of counsel, the decision is applicable to this case, since the court also addressed the interplay between the relevant disciplinary rules, including the rules regarding clients' secrets.

> lawyer has revealed only because of a threat to others. Lawyers will be reluctant to come forward if they know that the information that they disclose may lead to adverse consequences to their clients. A practice of the use of such disclosures might prompt a lawyer to warn a client in advance that the disclosure of certain information may not be held in confidence, thereby chilling free discourse between lawyer and client and reducing the prospect that the lawyer will learn of a serious threat to the well-being of others.

Although these may be valid concerns, we find that the *Purcell* decision is distinguishable from the instant case, and that the policy reasons cited in *Purcell* have less validity here. *Purcell* involved direct communications between an attorney and client. The issue in that case was whether the attorney was required to testify against his client. In this case, the attorney-client privilege is not at issue. Nor is appellant being asked to testify against his former client. Instead, the instant case revolves around whether a physical piece of evidence must be relinquished to the grand jury. While we recognize the importance of maintaining a client's confidences and secrets and understand that an attorney may have concerns in turning over incriminating evidence against his or her client, we do not believe that these concerns should override the public interest in maintaining public safety and promoting the administration of justice by prosecuting individuals for their alleged criminal activity.

Since the letter sought in this case contains evidence of a possible crime, we find that the letter must be turned over to the grand jury. Accordingly, we hold that where an attorney receives physical evidence from a third party relating to a possible crime committed by his or her client, the attorney is obligated to relinquish that evidence to law-enforcement authorities and must comply with a subpoena issued to that effect.

Other provisions of the code support our holding that appellant must relinquish the letter to the grand jury. DR 7-109(A) provides, "A lawyer shall not suppress any evidence that he or his client has a legal obligation to reveal or produce." Furthermore, DR 7-102(A)(3) provides, "In his representation of a client, a lawyer shall not . . . conceal or knowingly fail to disclose that which he is required by law to reveal." Reading these rules together, we believe that under the facts presented in this case, appellant has a legal obligation to turn the letter over to the grand jury.[3]

We agree with the court of appeals that the sanction imposed against appellant stemming from the contempt proceedings should be vacated, given that appellant challenged the subpoena on confidentiality grounds in good faith. Under these circumstances, we do not believe appellant should be punished and held in contempt. The finding of contempt is vacated on condition that appellant comply with the subpoena.

Accordingly, we affirm the judgment of the court of appeals and order appellant to relinquish the letter in question to the grand jury.

Judgment affirmed.

PFEIFER, J., concurring in part and dissenting in part.

I agree with the majority that the letter is a client secret and that Helmick was authorized to reveal the intent of his client to commit a crime. DR 4-101(C)(3). Revealing "the information necessary to prevent the crime," DR 4-101(C)(3), should have concluded the matter. Unfortunately, the trial court

---

3. Although appellant has not concealed any evidence, we also note that a person may be charged with obstruction of justice under R.C. 2921.32, for concealment of physical evidence of a crime.

and now a majority of this court chose to read DR 4-101(C)(2) liberally. That reading of the exception swallows the rule of DR 4-101(B)(1), which states that a lawyer "shall not knowingly . . . reveal a confidence or secret of his client," and declares open season on defense attorney files.

The majority relies on cases from other jurisdictions in which attorneys were required to turn over to the proper authorities the fruits and instrumentalities, including a gun, of crime. E.g., In re Ryder, 381 F.2d 713 (4th Cir. 1967); State v. Green, 493 So. 2d 1178 (La. 1986). Those cases are not similar factually to this case. Purcell v. Dist. Atty. for Suffolk Dist., 676 N.E.2d 436 (Mass. 1997), is, and we should have taken a similarly cautious approach. Otherwise, "lawyers will be reluctant to come forward if they know that the information that they disclose may lead to adverse consequences to their clients . . . , thereby chilling free discourse between lawyer and client and reducing the prospect that the lawyer will learn of a serious threat to the well-being of others." *Id.* at 114, 676 N.E.2d at 440.

Helmick acted the way all attorneys with an ethical dilemma should: he sought out competent counsel and followed the advice given. He acted in a manner designed to prevent the commission of a crime, which is what the (C)(3) exception to DR 4-101 is all about.

Today's opinion will likely have two unfortunate results. First, overzealous prosecutors will be more likely to engage in fishing expeditions. Second, attorneys and their clients will be less likely to discuss potential crimes, which will decrease the likelihood that the crimes can be prevented. I concur in part and dissent in part.

DOUGLAS and KENNEDY, JJ., concur in the foregoing opinion.

People v. Belge

372 N.Y.S.2d 798 (S. Ct. 1975), affirmed, 359 N.E.2d 377 (N.Y. 1976)

ORMAND N. GALE, J.

In the summer of 1973 Robert F. Garrow, Jr., stood charged in Hamilton County with the crime of murder. The defendant was assigned two attorneys, Frank H. Armani and Francis R. Belge. A defense of insanity had been interposed by counsel for Mr. Garrow. During the course of the discussions between Garrow and his two counsel, three other murders were admitted by Garrow, one being in Onondaga County. On or about September of 1973 Mr. Belge conducted his own investigation based upon what his client had told him and with the assistance of a friend the location of the body of Alicia Hauck was found in Oakwood Cemetery in Syracuse. Mr. Belge personally inspected the body and was satisfied, presumably, that this was the Alicia Hauck that his client had told him that he murdered.

This discovery was not disclosed to the authorities, but became public during the trial of Mr. Garrow in June of 1974, when to affirmatively establish the defense of insanity, these three other murders were brought before the jury by the defense in the Hamilton County trial. Public indignation reached the fever pitch, . . . [and] the District Attorney of Onondaga County caused the Grand Jury of Onondaga County, then sitting, to conduct a thorough investigation. As a result of this investigation Frank Armani was no-billed by the Grand Jury but Indictment No. 75-55 was returned as against Francis R. Belge, Esq., accusing him of having violated subdivision 1 of section 4200 of the Public Health Law, which, in essence, requires that a decent burial be accorded the dead, and section 4143 of the Public Health Law, which, in essence, requires anyone knowing of the death of a person without medical attendance, to report the same to the proper authorities. Defense counsel moves for a dismissal of the indictment on the grounds that a confidential, privileged communication existed between him and Mr. Garrow, which should excuse the attorney from making full disclosure to the authorities.

The National Association of Criminal Defense Lawyers, as amicus curiae succinctly state the issue in the following language: If this indictment stands, "The attorney-client privilege will be effectively destroyed. No defendant will be able to freely discuss the facts of his case with his attorney. No attorney will be able to listen to those facts without being faced with the Hobson's choice of violating the law or violating his professional code of Ethics."...

The effectiveness of counsel is only as great as the confidentiality of its client-attorney relationship. If the lawyer cannot get all the facts about the case, he can only give his client half of a defense. This, of necessity, involves the client telling his attorney everything remotely connected with the crime.

Apparently, in the instant case, after analyzing all the evidence, and after hearing of the bizarre episodes in the life of their client, they decided that the only possibility of salvation was in a defense of insanity. For the client to disclose not only everything about this particular crime but also everything about other crimes which might have a bearing upon his defense, requires the strictest confidence in, and on the part of, the attorney.

When the facts of the other homicides became public, as a result of the defendant's testimony to substantiate his claim of insanity, "Members of the public were shocked at the apparent callousness of these lawyers, whose conduct was seen as typifying the unhealthy lack of concern of most lawyers with the public interest and with simple decency." A hue and cry went up from the press and other news media suggesting that the attorneys should be found guilty of such crimes as obstruction of justice or becoming an accomplice after the fact. From a layman's standpoint, this certainly was a logical conclusion. However, the Constitution of the United States of America attempts to preserve the dignity of the individual and to do that guarantees him the services of an attorney who will bring to the Bar and to the Bench every conceivable protection from the inroads of the State against such rights as are vested in the Constitution for one accused of crime. Among those substantial constitutional rights is that a defendant does not have to incriminate himself. His attorneys were bound to uphold that concept and maintain what has been called a sacred trust of confidentiality.

The following language from the brief of the amicus curiae further points up the statements just made: "The client's Fifth Amendment rights cannot be violated by his attorney. There is no viable distinction between the personal papers and criminal evidence in the hands or mind of the client. Because the discovery of the body of Alicia Hauck would have presented 'a significant link in a chain of evidence tending to establish his guilt,' Garrow was constitutionally exempt from any statutory requirement to disclose the location of the body. And Attorney Belge, as Garrow's attorney, was not only equally exempt, but under a positive stricture precluding such disclosure. Garrow, although constitutionally privileged against a requirement of compulsory disclosure, was free to make such a revelation if he chose to do so. Attorney Belge was affirmatively required to withhold disclosure. The criminal defendant's self-incrimination rights become completely must weigh

nugatory if compulsory disclosure can be exacted through his attorney."

In the recent and landmark case of United States v. Nixon, 418 U.S. 683, 713 (1974), the court stated: "the constitutional need for production of relevant evidence in a criminal proceeding is specific and neutral to the fair adjudication of a particular criminal case in the administration of justice. Without access to specific facts a criminal prosecution may be totally frustrated." In the case at bar we must weigh the importance of the general privilege of confidentiality in the performance of the defendant's duties as an attorney, against the inroads of such a privilege on the fair administration of criminal justice as well as the heart tearing that went on in the victim's family by reason of their uncertainty as to the whereabouts of Alicia Hauck. In this type situation the court must balance the rights of the individual against the rights of society as a whole. There is no question but Attorney Belge's failure to bring to the attention of the authorities the whereabouts of Alicia Hauck when he first verified it, prevented bringing Garrow to the immediate bar of justice for this particular murder. This was in a sense, obstruction of justice. This duty, I am sure, loomed large in the mind of Attorney Belge. However, against this was the Fifth Amendment right of his client, Garrow, not to incriminate himself. If the Grand Jury had returned an indictment charging Mr. Belge with obstruction of justice under a proper statute, the work of this court would have been much more difficult than it is.

There must always be a conflict between the obstruction of the administration of criminal justice and the preservation of the right against self-incrimination which permeates the mind of the attorney as the alter ego of his client. But that is not the situation before this court. We have the Fifth Amendment right, derived from the Constitution, on the one hand, as against the trivia of a pseudo-criminal statute on the other, which has seldom been brought into play. Clearly the latter is completely out of focus when placed alongside the client-attorney privilege. An examination of the Grand Jury testimony sheds little light on their reasoning. The testimony of Mr. Armani added nothing new to the facts as already presented to the Grand Jury. He and Mr. Belge were co-counsel. Both were answerable to the Canons of professional ethics. The Grand Jury chose to indict one and not the other. It appears as if that body were grasping at straws.

It is the decision of this court that Francis R. Belge conducted himself as an officer of the court with all the zeal at his command to protect the constitutional rights of his client. Both on the grounds of a privileged communication and in the interests of justice the indictment is dismissed.

New York Penal Law (2003)

§205.50. Hindering prosecution; definition of term

... [A] person "renders criminal assistance" when, with intent to prevent, hinder or delay the discovery or apprehension of, or the lodging of a criminal charge against, a person who he knows or believes has committed a crime or is being sought by law enforcement officials for the commission of a crime, or with intent to assist a person in profiting or benefiting from the commission of a crime, he:

1. Harbors or conceals such person; or
2. Warns such person of impending discovery or apprehension; or

3. Provides such person with money, transportation, weapon, disguise or other means of avoiding discovery or apprehension; or
4. Prevents or obstructs, by means of force, intimidation or deception, anyone from performing an act which might aid in the discovery or apprehension of such person or in the lodging of a criminal charge against him; or
5. Suppresses, by any act of concealment, alteration or destruction, any physical evidence which might aid in the discovery or apprehension of such person or in the lodging of a criminal charge against him; or
6. Aids such person to protect or expeditiously profit from an advantage derived from such crime.

(L 1965, c 1030)

6. Law or Court Order: Practice Before a Tribunal

Problems

5-28. If Martyn & Fox's client lies to an IRS agent during an audit, do we have any obligation to correct the record? Does it matter whether we were present? Whether the lie came as a surprise?

5-29. What should Martyn tell a judge who asks Martyn to reveal her client's bottom line?

5-30. If Martyn & Fox's client lies about her name in a criminal case, what should we do?

5-31. If Martyn & Fox's client dies of natural causes while the client's personal injury action is pending, can we settle the case before the other side finds out? What if our client dies as a result of the injury inflicted by the alleged tortfeasor?

5-32. May (must) Martyn & Fox disclose the presence just outside the courtroom of a witness we know the other side has been trying to subpoena for weeks?

5-33. May (must) Martyn & Fox disclose an error by the court (e.g., our client has no prior convictions) that we played no role in causing to occur?

5-34. Martyn is preparing an appellate brief, which argues that the trial court properly dismissed an indictment against her client because the court correctly construed a criminal statute narrowly so as to exclude her client's conduct. Martyn finds only one reported decision citing the statute, a ten-year-old state supreme court case that upheld the statute's constitutionality. The prosecutor's brief does not mention this case, and Martyn doesn't like the case's dicta, which might suggest a broader statutory meaning. Should Martyn cite the case?

5-35. Prior to trial, Fox discusses with Client whether he has ever smoked marijuana. Client asks what that has to do with the matter, and Fox tells him: "Nothing, but I am worried the other side just might ask that question." Client admits he smokes marijuana from time to time. At trial, opposing counsel asks Client whether he has ever smoked marijuana, and he immediately responds "no." Does Fox have any obligation to correct the record? Can we settle the case before the lie is disclosed? What if the same thing happened during Client's deposition?

5-36. How does Martyn & Fox deal with our criminal defendant client who insists on testifying and insists on lying? What if we know in advance? What if it happens as a surprise? Does it matter that we are convinced our client is innocent?

Consider: Model Rules 1.0(m), 1.6(b)(6), 3.3, 3.4, 3.9, 4.1, 8.4(c) and (d)
Model Code DR 4-101(C)(2), DR 7-102(A) and (B), DR 7-106(B)
Code of Judicial Conduct, Canon 3B(7)(d) and (8)
RLGL §§63 and 120

Lawrence J. Fox

Legal Tender: A Lawyer's Guide to Handling Professional Dilemmas

184-188 (ABA 1995)

Don't Ask, Don't Tell

The beads of sweat were totally understandable. What made it worse was that he knew he had contributed to this impossible situation. But the alternative course of conduct seemed as bizarre as this one was turning out to be. Why hadn't the ethical dilemma he faced been resolved by some ethics committee? Or maybe he should blame these new activist judges—unnecessarily meddling in settlement. Well, it was too late to worry about all of that now. He was left with nowhere else to turn. Like a batter a moment after he has committed, checking his swing was no longer an option.

He had been representing the Gilhool Company for a number of years on this matter. Gilhool had been sued by Chase Enterprises for lost profits in September 1989. Chase charged that Gilhool's new assembly line design had not met the level of hourly production that had been specified in the request for proposals that had resulted in Gilhool being awarded the contract. Gilhool had responded that the problem was not in their design, but in the quality of raw materials Chase was buying from outside vendors. Each side had engaged in endless depositions and each had retained a prominent manufacturing expert to fully support its theory of the case. Now the case stood ready for a three-week trial and the parties had been called for a conference before Judge Frankfort for one last-ditch settlement attempt.

Peter had spent a full day in discussion with officers of his client before they went to the conference. They had explored all of the legal and factual issues one more time. Peter had shared his opinion as to the strengths and weaknesses of their position; Peter had discussed, with an embarrassing candor, how much pressure Judge Frankfort was likely to impose, and he shared his estimate of the legal fees and other expenses of taking the case through trial. The Gilhool folks had emphasized the disruption the litigation had already caused and was likely to cause in the future, and they revisited together the parties' last settlement positions.

Then Peter had embarked on the discussion that was now giving him such fits. He wanted the Gilhool executives to come up with a bottom line figure at which they would be happy to settle. After what seemed an endless colloquy, in which the internal division among the Gilhool reps was apparent, they agreed that paying $3.4 million, the number Peter had recommended, was the place where Gilhool would draw a line in the sand. They then decided that the best strategy was for Peter to go into the negotiations by pulling their last offer ($2.1 million) off the table on the ground that Gilhool's deposition of Chase's expert had gone so well. Besides, this tactic showed the company's toughness and an appropriate level of disinterest in settling the case. All of which led the CEO of Gilhool, Robert Marks, to suggest that there was a bonus for Peter's firm of 25 percent of any amount under $3.4 million Peter saved Gilhool at this stage of the proceedings. "Wrap it up for $3 million and we'll pay you an extra $100,000, Peter," Marks said in front of the assembled group.

The meeting with Judge Frankfort opened not quite as the Gilhool team had anticipated. Peter's counterpart, Spud Griffiths, his law school classmate, gave an impassioned speech on behalf of Chase in which he observed that his client was no longer willing to settle for $5.6 million, the offer made a year ago. While his rhetoric (better saved for the jury, thought Peter), went on for some time, Griffiths's two basic points were that a year had passed since his clients offered to accept that number and the interest alone on that sum exceeded $400,000; moreover, a newly produced document demonstrated that a Gilhool employee recognized potential problems with the installation well before its completion.

Peter, of course, in the highest tradition of litigation bluster, felt obliged to match Griffiths's excess, after which he pulled his client's last offer off the table, asserting the ground that had been planned the day before. When he was done, Peter could tell Judge Frankfort was exasperated by these two experienced litigators posturing in this way. Thus, he was not surprised when the judge suggested that he meet with each lawyer individually, if no one had any objection to such an approach. Far be it from Peter to have the temerity to suggest otherwise, given the fact that the judge would preside at the upcoming jury trial. Griffiths, no doubt similarly motivated, also agreed.

The judge's meeting with Griffiths lasted perhaps a half an hour. Then it was Peter's turn to be summoned to meet the great man. After cordial pleasantries, including a review of where their respective children were currently enrolled in college (a surrogate competition all fathers Peter's age seemed to carry on now that they had reached that point in their family's lives), the judge turned to Peter and asked him to cut the palaver. The judge thought this case could be settled, thought it could be settled today; he wanted to clear this potential three-week jury trial from his too full platter (what better did judges have to do, Peter thought), and he wanted Peter to tell him the full amount of his authority to settle the case. Judge Frankfort opined that he knew how these things worked all too well, that the withdrawing of the last best offer was mere posturing with which he was unimpressed, and he knew Peter's client had shared with him a number that the judge now wished Peter, as an officer of the court, to tell him. The judge noted that Griffiths had given him a number, a "nice round figure," and that now the judge needed Peter's response. Repeating the "officer of the court" line, the judge emphasized that this was no time for Peter to start negotiating with the judge; the number he wanted was Peter's authority.

The silence seemed interminable. Peter did not know what to do. His client's $3.4 million was a confidential number reached after a privileged discussion of the merits of the case. Indeed, it reflected his client's acceptance of his best judgment of the case; the Model Rules required Peter to keep his client's confidences; he had no authority to share that number with the court or anyone else. It was true the Model Rules provided for implied authority "to make disclosures . . . in carrying out the representation, except to the extent that the client's instructions or special circumstances limit the authority." But this was not such a situation. Revealing the number was not critical to carrying out the representation and, indeed, he and the client had not discussed the pros and cons of whether to reveal the bottom line. Clearly the injunction of Model Rule 1.4 requiring informing the client of all relevant facts and issues necessary to make intelligent decisions regarding the objectives of the representation would require such a discussion before Peter could feel he had the authority to disclose the number.

Then Peter had a frightening thought. What if Griffiths's round number was $3 million? Would he be costing his client an unnecessary $400,000 by revealing the bottom line number? Perhaps the best thing to do was to answer the judge's question, but just give him a number higher than the $1.8 million (the posturing offer) but significantly less than the $3.4 million. This not only would keep his client's confidence intact, but it had the added benefit of preserving Peter's chance of securing at least some of that delicious bonus money.

Peter started worrying again. He knew Rule 4.1 states that a lawyer, in the course of representing a client, "shall not knowingly make a false statement of a material fact. . . to a third person." Wasn't the judge such a person? How could he lie about the $3.4 million? Then he remembered that the comment to that rule left an out for negotiations: "Whether a particular statement should be regarded as one of fact can depend on the circumstances. . . . Under generally accepted conventions in negotiation, certain types of statements ordinarily are not taken as statements of material fact. Estimates of price or value placed on the subject of a transaction and a party's intentions as to an acceptable settlement of a claim are in this category."

But then Peter thought this provision really couldn't apply to a judge. This comment must contemplate direct negotiations between the parties and their lawyers. Candor toward a judge was really addressed in Rule 3.3, which provided: "A lawyer shall not knowingly make a false statement of material fact or law to a tribunal." But Peter rationalized that provision away with little hesitation. The judge wasn't acting as a tribunal when he got involved in settlement negotiations like this. And settlement authority was no more a "material fact" here that it was in 4.1. Peter would never lie about a fact in the case; settlement positions just were not such facts.

Finally, Peter broke the silence, explaining to the judge that he appreciated the judge's good offices in trying to settle the case, that he had reviewed the merits at length and felt confident his client would win, and that the judge was correct, his client had agreed to a higher number. Gilhool Company was prepared to pay $2.4 million to settle the case.

Peter had no sooner figured out that this confidently offered number would yield him a $250,000 bonus than the judge surprised him with his response. "Peter," the judge intoned, "I've known you too long. You're too good a lawyer to have advised your client to go no higher than $2.4 million. The recent documents your client allegedly just found," said the judge, turning sarcastic, "alone add a million to the settlement value of this case. I'm going to get to the bottom of this." Then, turning toward his intercom, he asked his secretary to send in Peter's client representative.

Before Peter could even get up the courage to ask for time to chat before his client entered the vast chambers, there was a knock on the door and in walked John Bingham, Gilhool's executive V.P. Bingham hadn't taken two steps when Judge Frankfort, rising from behind his vast desk, literally commanded Bingham to share with him Gilhool's bottom-line number. The hurried glances between Peter and Bingham provided no opportunity for meaningful communication and Peter was sure he must have looked nothing but pathetic as the judge repeated his demand to know Gilhool's number. Peter could tell Bingham was overwhelmed by the majesty of the surroundings (did anyone but federal judges have offices the size of ballrooms?) and that Bingham was no match for Judge Frankfort, but as soon as the "$3.4 million" came limply from Bingham's lips, Peter knew this was a day he wold never forget. Not only did all hope of his "bonus" go down the drain, but he knew the judge was dead serious when he said referral to the disciplinary committee of the bar association for violations of the Model Rules was the only way Peter's conduct could be adequately dealt with. Other attorneys coming into Judge Frankfort's courtroom would learn not to trifle with the settlement process. Yes, Peter would be used as an example, a very persuasive example.

People v. Casey

948 P.2d 1014 (Colo. 1997)

PER CURIAM.

A hearing panel of the supreme court grievance committee approved the findings and the recommendation of a hearing board that the respondent in this lawyer discipline case be suspended for forty-five days from the practice of law and be ordered to take and pass the Multi-State Professional Responsibility Examination (MPRE). The respondent has excepted to the recommendation as too severe. We disagree, and we accept the recommendation of the hearing panel and hearing board.

I.

The respondent was licensed to practice law in Colorado in 1989. . . .

In December 1994, S.R., a teenager, and her mother, met with the senior partner at the law firm where the respondent was an associate. In August 1994, S.R. attended a party held in the home of third parties. The police were called and they cited several persons at the party with trespassing and underage drinking. S.R. gave the police a driver's license in her possession that had been issued to her friend, S.J. A criminal summons charging trespass was issued to S.R. in the name of her friend, S.J. Since she was not aware of the summons in her name, S.J. failed to attend the first court hearing and a bench warrant was issued in her name. S.R., posing as S.J., later appeared to reset the matter. S.R. was arrested, jailed, and later released under the name of S.J.

After being assigned the case by the senior partner, the respondent wrote to the Colorado Springs City Attorney's Office, and advised the City Attorney, falsely, that he represented S.J., when he actually represented S.R. He requested and obtained discovery using S.J.'s name. He also notified the court clerk of his entry of appearance in the S.J. case. The senior partner "consulted and advised" the respondent, but the hearing board did not make findings as to when this occurred or as to the details of the conversation.

On February 14, 1995, the respondent appeared at a pretrial conference scheduled for S.J. His client, S.R., waited outside during the hearing. Although he spoke with an assistant city attorney about the case, the respondent did not reveal his client's true identity. The assistant city attorney agreed to dismiss the S.J. matter. The respondent presented the city's motion to dismiss the case and the court entered an order of dismissal on February 14, 1995.

Prior to the pretrial conference, S.J. called the respondent about the case. The respondent told her that he intended to get the trespassing charge dismissed, but that S.J. would then have to petition on her own to get the criminal record sealed. He also told S.J. the date and time of the pretrial hearing.

After the case was dismissed, the respondent met with his client and her mother, and S.J. and her stepfather. S.J. was upset that the respondent had spoken with the assistant city attorney outside of S.J.'s presence and she wanted to know if her name had been cleared. The respondent took S.J. and her stepfather outside, and explained that the trespassing charge had been dismissed and that his client would pay the court costs. The respondent admitted that S.J. would nevertheless have a criminal record and that she would have to petition the court to have her criminal record sealed. S.J.'s stepfather subsequently called his lawyer who reported the events to the district attorney.

The respondent stipulated that the foregoing conduct violated Colo. RPC 1.2(d) (counseling a client to engage, or assisting a client, in conduct that the lawyer knows is criminal or fraudulent)[1]; Colo. RPC 3.3(a)(1) (knowingly making a false statement of material fact or law to a tribunal); Colo. RPC 3.3(a)(2) (failing to disclose a material fact to a tribunal when disclosure is necessary to avoid assisting a criminal or fraudulent act by the client); Colo. RPC 8.4(c) (engaging in conduct involving dishonesty, fraud, deceit or misrepresentation); Colo. RPC 8.4(d) (engaging in conduct prejudicial to the administration of justice)....

II....

The respondent portrays his situation as involving a close question between the loyalty he owed his client, and his duty to the court. He apparently seeks to invoke the status of a "subordinate lawyer," as addressed in Colo. RPC 5.2....

However, ... the respondent admits to having violated [Colo. RPC 3.3].... Colo. RPC 3.3(a)(2) applies because of his initial appearance before the court in which he represented, falsely, that he was appearing on behalf of the named defendant, S.J. At the pretrial conference he presented the motion to dismiss to the court resulting in the case being dismissed. The respondent had the duty to disclose to the court that his client was impersonating S.J. in the criminal proceedings.

Further, Colo. RPC 3.3(b) clearly resolves the respondent's claimed dilemma in that it provides that the duty to be truthful to the court applies even if to do so requires disclosure of otherwise confidential information. It is not "arguable" that the respondent's duty to his client prevented him from fulfilling his duty to be truthful to the court. The protection afforded by Colo. RPC 5.2(b) for a subordinate who acts in accordance with a supervisory lawyer's direction is not available to the respondent. However, ... a good-faith, but unsuccessful, attempt to bring an ethical problem to a superior's attention to receive guidance may be a mitigating factor....

While we have determined that Colo. RPC 5.2(b) does not entitle the respondent to immunity, an attempt to obtain guidance from a senior partner and a failure of a senior partner to suggest a reasonable and ethical course of

1. Section 18-5-113, 6 C.R.S. (1997), provides in part:

18-5-113. Criminal impersonation. (1) A person commits criminal impersonation if he knowingly assumes a false or fictitious identity or capacity, and in such identity or capacity he:

(d) Does an act which if done by the person falsely impersonated, might subject such person to an action or special proceeding, civil or criminal, or to liability, charge, forfeiture, or penalty; or

(e) Does any other act with intent to unlawfully gain a benefit for himself or another or to injure or defraud another.

(2) Criminal impersonation is a class 6 felony.

conduct for the respondent could be a factor to be considered in mitigation. . . . Here, the board's finding that the senior partner "consulted and advised" the respondent, without detail about the advice, if any, given is inadequate to allow us to conclude that the consultation is a mitigation factor.

We conclude that the respondent's misconduct is serious enough to warrant a short suspension. The respondent's professed confusion regarding his professional responsibilities confirms that he should be required to take and pass the MPRE. Accordingly, we accept the board's and panel's recommendations.

The Limits of the Law: *Criminal Conduct*

In two previous notes,[1] we addressed the law of fraud and saw that lawyers have no special immunity from civil or criminal fraud laws, either in representing clients or in their own personal conduct outside of law practice. In this chapter, two cases, *Belge* and *Casey*, illustrate several ways that the equally vast scope of the criminal law imposes significant limitations on a lawyer's behavior.[2] Appellate decisions regarding lawyer discipline reveal that courts impose severe sanctions on lawyers who commit crimes. Lawyers must be aware of the contours of the criminal law both to avoid committing crimes themselves (as happened in *Belge*) and to avoid counseling or assisting client crimes (as did not occur in *Casey*). When either of these dangers occur, Model Rules 8.4(b) and 1.2(d) become relevant. Model Rule 8.4(b) regulates lawyers who commit crimes. When a client commits or plans conduct that constitutes a crime, Model Rule 1.2(d) comes into play.

Belge's conduct implies recognition of a significant legal limit on his own action created by New York's obstruction of justice statute. Belge observed, but did not alter, conceal or destroy the physical evidence of his client's crime. Note that the court says its work would be much more difficult if the grand jury had returned an indictment for that crime, presumably because in that case the lawyer's conduct would have moved beyond merely protecting confidentiality to an active criminal cover-up of a client crime.[3] To understand this point, imagine what would have occurred if, when Belge discovered the bodies, he dug a deep hole and buried them in order to protect his client. His conduct then would have violated the New York obstruction of justice statute, because he would have intended to prevent discovery of the physical evidence and would have done so by an act of concealment.

Lawyer Crimes

If Belge had violated the obstruction of justice statute, he also would have been subject to professional discipline for violation of Model Rule 8.4(b), which prohibits lawyers from committing crimes "that reflect adversely on the lawyer's honesty, trustworthiness or fitness as a lawyer in other respects." Several aspects of this rule have been extensively litigated. First, it has been argued that lawyers who commit

---

1. The Limits of the Law: Lawyer Dishonesty, Fraud, Deceit, and Misrepresentation, *supra* p.101; The Limits of the Law: Client Fraud, *supra* p.196.
2. Although an exact count of criminal prohibitions probably is impossible, one author estimates about 3,600 federal and 985 state crimes in her jurisdiction (Arizona). Susan A. Ehrlich, *The Increasing Federalization of Crime*, 32 Ariz. St. L.J. 825, 826 (2000). *See also* ABA Task Force on the Federalization of Criminal Law, *The Federalization of Criminal Law* (ABA 1998), App. C, which lists over 3,000 federal crimes.
3. *See* Bruce A. Green, *The Criminal Regulation of Lawyers*, 67 Fordham L. Rev. 327 (1998).

crimes do not respect the law and therefore should not be lawyers. However, not all crimes fall within the prohibition of this rule.[4] Consider, for example, whether Belge should have been disciplined if he had been convicted of failing to provide decent burial of the dead. If every misdemeanor (including traffic offenses) qualified, most of us would be in trouble. On the other hand, professional code provisions and courts hold that most serious crimes (defined to include most felonies in some jurisdictions) do reflect on the lawyer's ability to practice law.

Some criminal conduct is so serious and so related to character traits necessary to practice law that courts discipline lawyers involved whether the conduct constitutes a misdemeanor or felony.[5] Crimes involving dishonesty or lack of trustworthiness, such as fraud and theft, clearly fit this category.[6] The same is true of offenses that involve violence, or serious interference with the administration of justice, such as obstruction of justice or bribery.[7] Courts also agree that domestic violence constitutes a ground for professional discipline, not only because of the violent acts involved, but also because the lawyer cannot be trusted with vulnerable or defenseless persons.[8] For similar reasons, courts find sexual misconduct that exploits another indicative of a lack of trustworthiness.[9] On the other hand, Comment 2 to Model Rule 8.4 excludes "some matters of personal morality, such as adultery and

---

4. The Model Code of Professional Responsibility DR 1-102(A)(3) attempted to convey this idea by referring to "illegal conduct involving moral turpitude." That term proved too vague, but the cases under that provision gradually came to convey the idea that the crime must be related to a fitness to practice law. *See* Charles W. Wolfram, *Modern Legal Ethics* §3.3 (West 1986).

5. Rule 19 of the ABA Model R. for Lawyer Disc. Enforcement (1999) defines "serious crime" to include, generally, any felonies or lesser crimes that reflect adversely on the lawyer's fitness to practice and specifically, those that involve "interference with the administration of justice, false swearing, misrepresentation, fraud, deceit, bribery, extortion, misappropriation, theft, or an attempt, conspiracy or solicitation of another to commit a 'serious crime.'"

6. *E.g.*, Atty. Grievance Commn. v. Bereano, 744 A.2d 35 (Md. 2000) (lawyer convicted of mail fraud based on violations of state election fundraising laws disbarred regardless of lack of potential for direct personal gain); In re Mmahat, 736 So. 2d 1285 (La. 1999) (lawyer convicted of felony misapplication of bank funds in a scheme to avoid detection of the bank's insolvency disbarred); In re Moore, 691 A.2d 1151 (D.C. 1997) (lawyer who was convicted of a misdemeanor for willful failure to file tax returns suspended for three years); Wilson v. Neal, 964 S.W.2d 199 (Ark. 1998), *aff'd*, 16 S.W.3d 228 (Ark. 2000) (lawyer who pleaded guilty to misdemeanors of knowingly disposing of soybeans and rice that were mortgaged and pledged to the Farmers Home Administration and knowingly taking money from a Department of Agriculture bank account and using it for unapproved purposes suspended for five years). *See also* The Limits of the Law: Lawyer Dishonesty, Fraud, Deceit, and Misrepresentation, *supra* p.101.

7. In re Convery, 765 A.2d 724 (N.J. 2001) (lawyer who pled guilty to a federal misdemeanor of promising employment in return for political activity, due to his attempts to get zoning variances for a client, suspended for six months); In re Floyd, 527 S.E.2d 357 (S.C. 2000) (lawyer who stole an automobile, robbed bank, and shot a teller disbarred); Fla. Bar v. Simmons, 581 So. 2d 154 (Fla. 1991) (lawyer involved in potential jury tampering suspended for one year); Disc. Proceedings Against Curran, 801 P.2d 962 (Wash. 1990) (lawyer convicted of vehicular homicide of two clients, whom he attempted to drive home after several drinks at lunch, suspended for six months); In re Ettinger, 538 N.E.2d 1152 (Ill. 1989) (lawyer who bribed a police officer disbarred).

8. *E.g.*, Atty. Grievance Commn. v. Painter, 739 A.2d 24 (Md. 1999) (lawyer guilty of repeated domestic violence of wife and child disbarred); Iowa S. Ct. Bd. of Prof. Ethics & Conduct v. Polson, 569 N.W.2d 612 (Iowa 1997) (lawyer guilty of domestic abuse suspended from practice two years); In re Magid, 655 A.2d 916 (N.J. 1995) (lawyer convicted of simple assault, based on isolated incident of domestic violence with girlfriend, publicly reprimanded); In re Walker, 597 N.E.2d 1271, *modified*, 601 N.E.2d 327 (Ind. 1992) (lawyer who assaulted female companion he had previously represented in a divorce and her nine-year-old daughter suspended from practice for 60 days).

9. *E.g.*, In re Boudreau, 815 So. 2d 76 (La. 2002) (lawyer pleaded guilty to possession of child pornography disbarred); Atty. Grievance Commn. v. Thompson, 786 A.2d 763 (Md. 2001) (lawyer who pled guilty to stalking a teenage boy suspended indefinitely); In re Parrott, 480 S.E.2d 722 (S.C. 1997) (lawyer convicted of simple assault for pulling down a woman's bathing suit at a beach suspended). Sexual behavior with clients also may fall into this category. *See* Lawyers and Other Professionals: Sexual Relationships with Clients, *infra* p.278.

comparable offenses" that also may be criminal but do not necessarily indicate that the lawyer is incompetent, dishonest, or untrustworthy.[10]

Second, as long as the evidence in a disciplinary proceeding shows that the lawyer committed the requisite criminal act, professional discipline can occur whether or not that lawyer was convicted or even charged with a crime. Professional discipline has even occurred in cases where a jury has acquitted the lawyer,[11] or where the lawyer was later pardoned for the crime.[12] At the same time, the fact of a conviction becomes conclusive evidence that the lawyer committed the crime.[13]

Third, the cases make clear that the criminal conduct need not involve client representation. Criminal acts such as fraud, negligent homicide, and failing to render assistance to children injured in a hit and run accident all have resulted in successful disciplinary action.[14] Finally, serious criminal conduct may indicate an immediate risk to clients or the public. For this reason, many states allow for immediate interim suspension of a lawyer following the conviction of a serious crime or a felony.[15] The lawyer remains entitled to a disciplinary hearing at a later date that might provide evidence of mitigation of the sanction.

Client Crimes

Unlike Belge, Casey seemed oblivious to the fact that criminal law placed legal limits on his representation of a client. He was either unaware of the Colorado's criminal impersonation statute, or unaware of its application in his client's case. *Casey* illustrates that lawyers must not only avoid criminal acts themselves, but also must understand the criminal law to give competent legal advice to clients. Rule 1.2(d) prohibits lawyers from knowingly assisting or counseling client crimes or frauds.[16] This rule first requires that a lawyer properly identify the legal characterization of his client's conduct. For example, when Casey learned that his client had given the police an assumed name, he also learned that she had committed a crime. Imagine if, at that point, Casey had advised his client of the legal significance of her conduct. Failing to do so meant that he represented her incompetently by failing to provide her with crucial legal advice. This incompetence eventually led him to

10. *See, e.g.,* In re Nuss, 67 P.3d 386 (Or. 2003) (lawyer convicted of misdemeanor crime of harassment for intentionally reaching into another's car and offensively touching the victim's shoulder not subject to discipline). Some of the most difficult cases concern lawyers who commit alcohol or drug crimes. *See, e.g.,* In re Lock, 54 S.W.3d 305 (Tex. 2001) (lawyer's guilty plea to possession of a controlled substance (cocaine), a third degree felony, should not subject lawyer to compulsory discipline, but rather to standard disciplinary procedure where mitigating factors can be considered).

11. *E.g.,* In re Segal, 719 N.E.2d 480 (Mass. 1999) (lawyer acquitted of making false statements to a federally insured bank later suspended for two years for the same conduct); People v. Odom, 941 P.2d 919 (Colo. 1997) (lawyer who committed the felony of concealing property to avoid seizure, but who was never charged with the crime, disbarred).

12. In re Abrams, 689 A.2d 6 (D.C. 1997) (en banc) (lawyer who received presidential pardon after pleading guilty to testifying falsely to Congress publicly censured for dishonesty, deceit, and misrepresentation).

13. *Restatement (Third) The Law Governing Lawyers* §5, Comment g (2000).

14. *E.g.,* In re Capone, 689 A.2d 128 (N.J. 1997) (lawyer who committed mail fraud by making a false statement on loan application suspended for two years); In re Brown, 674 So. 2d 243 (La. 1996) (lawyer convicted of negligent homicide disbarred); Tate v. St. Bar, 920 S.W.2d 727 (Tex. Crim. App. 1996) (lawyer who fled the scene and failed to stop and render assistance to three injured children disbarred).

15. *E.g.,* N.Y. Jud. Law §90(4) (McKinney 2003) (interim suspension for "serious crimes" and for failure to file income tax returns); Ohio Gov. Bar R. V §5 (2003) (interim suspension for felonies and default of child support orders).

16. We discussed the application of this rule to fraud in The Limits of the Law: Client Fraud, *supra* p.196.

facilitate a client felony (criminal impersonation) that was much more serious than the original misdemeanor charge (trespass).

A lawyer who fails to identify his client's crime, also can fail failure to properly categorize the criminal activity as past, continuing, or future. Casey's client's crime did not end when she gave someone else's driver's license to the police. She continued her criminal conduct by using the assumed identity in court records and in negotiations with the prosecutor. Casey's failure to understand that she was engaged in a continuing crime prevented him from recognizing that Rule 1.2(d) had been triggered. Failing to appreciate his client's continuing crime further meant that his appearance on her behalf under an assumed name assisted her crime. It also meant that he lied to the court.

One issue the court did not discuss was whether Casey's conduct went far enough to constitute a violation of Model Rule 8.4(b) as well. Although Casey did not violate the criminal impersonation statute directly, he may have been guilty of accessorial liability—that is, he may have been an accomplice to his client's crime.

Typical accomplice statutes prohibit intentional "aiding," "abetting," "advising," "assisting," "counseling," or "encouraging " the criminal act of another.[17] Model Rule 1.2(d) loosely incorporates these principles of accessorial liability.[18] The knowledge requirement in 1.2(d) roughly parallels the *mens rea* of the crime of accomplice liability[19] and the "counsels or assists" language in the rule tracks the *actus reus* commonly required by most accomplice statutes. This means that a lawyer like Casey who facilitates a client crime may be disciplined not only for violating 1.2(d), but also for violating Model Rule 8.4(b) if that lawyer has committed a criminal act as an accomplice.

Lawyers who intend to commit a serious crime (*mens rea*) and agree to aid the client in committing it (*actus reus*)[20] also can become entangled in client crimes as co-conspirators. In many situations, an accomplice is also a co-conspirator.[21] Unlike accomplice liability, however, conspiracy to commit a crime constitutes a separate crime, even if the underlying crime itself is never completed.[22] The lawyer need not actually aid, abet, or assist, as long as she purposely promotes the criminal act and agrees with the others that one of them will commit it.[23] Like accomplices, lawyer co-conspirators have been subject to professional discipline for violating Model Rule 8.4(b).[24]

Together, *Belge* and *Casey* illustrate the operation of the professional rules involving lawyer and client criminal conduct. Lawyers who commit crimes themselves, or

---

17. Wayne R. LaFave, *Criminal Law* §6.7 (3d ed., West 2000); Model Penal Code §2.06.

18. Other specific examples include Model Rules 3.3(a)(3) (knowing presentation of false testimony), 3.4(a) (unlawfully obstructing access to evidence), and 3.4(b) (falsifying evidence, assisting others in falsifying evidence). Geoffrey C. Hazard, Jr. & W. William Hodes, *The Law of Lawyering* §5.12 (3d ed., Aspen Law & Business 2002).

19. The Model Penal Code requires that an accomplice have the "purpose" or conscious desire to facilitate the commission of the offense. Model Penal Code §2.06(3)(a). *See, e.g.,* In re DeRose, 55 P.3d 126 (Colo. 2002) (lawyer who pled guilty to aiding and abetting a client's illegal structure of financial transactions to evade reporting requirements disbarred).

20. Arnold H. Loewy, *Criminal Law in a Nutshell* 260 (3d ed., West 2000).

21. *See, e.g.,* Joshua Dressler, *Understanding Criminal Law* 487 (3d ed., Lexis 2001).

22. Ellen S. Podgor & Jerold H. Israel, *White Collar Crime in a Nutshell* 40 (2d ed., West 1997).

23. Model Penal Code §5.03. The federal conspiracy statute, 18 U.S.C. §371 (2000), prohibits agreements conspiracies to commit any offense against the United States or to defraud the United States. A number of federal criminal statutes also include conspiracy provisions. For a list of representative provisions, *see* Podgor & Israel, *supra* note 22, at 37.

24. *E.g.,* In re Lee, 755 A.2d 1034 (D.C. App. 2000) (lawyer convicted of conspiracy with client to launder money disbarred); In re Petition of Anderson, 851 S.W.2d 408 (Ark. 1993) (lawyer convicted of conspiracy with client to possess cocaine with intent to distribute failed to gain readmission to the bar).

who assist or counsel clients in committing crimes, may not only be indicted and convicted, but they may also lose their license to practice law. As federal and state criminal codes grow to address ever-widening areas of conduct, lawyers in all kinds of practice need to be alert to this limitation of the law.

In re Forrest

730 A.2d 340 (N.J. 1999)

PER CURIAM. . . .

I

In 1984, respondent was admitted to the New Jersey bar. At the time the ethics complaint was filed, respondent practiced with the law firm of Lieberman & Ryan in Somerville. In March 1993, Robert and Mary Ann Fennimore, husband and wife, retained Lieberman & Ryan to represent them in a personal injury action resulting from a car accident in which the Fennimores' car had been hit by another vehicle. The Fennimores, both of whom were in the car at the time of the accident, sought to recover from the driver of the other car. Mr. Fennimore claimed that as a result of the accident he suffered a rotator cuff tear, limitation of movement in his right ring finger, limitation of strength in his left shoulder, chronic cervical strain, and headaches. He further claimed that all of his injuries were "permanent. . . ."

On April 5, 1993, Lieberman & Ryan filed a complaint against the driver of the other car on behalf of the Fennimores. Respondent was assigned to work on the Fennimores' file.

Mr. Fennimore died sometime between April 1993 and December 1993, for reasons unrelated to the car accident. . . . Mrs. Fennimore notified respondent of her husband's death.

In December 1993, respondent, knowing of Mr. Fennimore's death, served unsigned answers to interrogatories, entitled "Plaintiff Robert A. Fennimore's Answers to Defendant's . . . Interrogatories," on his adversary, Christopher Walls, Esq. Neither the answers nor the cover letter indicated that Mr. Fennimore had died.

On June 8, 1994, respondent and Mrs. Fennimore appeared at an arbitration proceeding apparently conducted pursuant to Rule 4:21A (mandating arbitration in automobile negligence actions with amount in controversy less than $15,000 and other personal injury actions with amount in controversy less than $20,000). Before the proceeding, respondent advised Mrs. Fennimore that when she testified she should not voluntarily reveal her husband's death. When the arbitrator inquired about Mr. Fennimore's absence, respondent replied that Mr. Fennimore was "unavailable." The arbitrator awarded $17,500 to Mrs. Fennimore and $6000 to Mr. Fennimore. At no time before, during, or after the arbitration proceeding did respondent or Mrs. Fennimore inform the arbitrator that Mr. Fennimore had died.

After the arbitration, respondent contacted Walls to discuss a possible settlement. Again, respondent did not inform Walls of Mr. Fennimore's death.

From January to August 1994, Walls propounded several requests on respondent to produce Mr. Fennimore for a medical examination, but respondent did not reply to those requests. Consequently, Walls filed a motion with the trial court to compel Mr. Fennimore to appear for a medical examination.

Respondent did not oppose or otherwise reply to the motion, and the court entered an order on September 9, 1994, that directed Mr. Fennimore to submit to a medical examination on October 4, 1994. After the order was entered, respondent did not disclose Mr. Fennimore's death but nevertheless contacted Walls to further discuss settlement. Only when Mr. Fennimore failed to appear for the court-ordered medical examination did respondent inform Walls of Mr. Fennimore's death.

The DEC [District Ethics Committee] found respondent's conduct in handling the Fennimore matter to be unethical and concluded that respondent violated. . . . RPC 3.3(a)(5) (failure to disclose material fact to tribunal), RPC 3.4(a) (obstructing party's access to evidence of potential evidentiary value), and RPC 8.4(c) (engaging in conduct involving dishonesty, fraud, deceit or misrepresentation). The DEC recommended that respondent be publicly reprimanded.

. . .[T]he DRB [Disciplinary Review Board] issued its decision in June 1998, and concluded that respondent's conduct warranted a three-month suspension. . . .

. . . Respondent admits that he acted imprudently when he failed to disclose Mr. Fennimore's death to the court, the arbitrator, and opposing counsel. Respondent argues, however, that certain circumstances mitigate his conduct. Specifically, respondent contends that he acted out of a desire to enhance the recovery for his clients and always had his clients' best interests in mind; that he made no misrepresentations throughout the Fennimore matter but merely withheld certain information, a negotiation technique he describes as "bluffing" and "puffing"; and that he did not knowingly or intentionally violate the Rules of Professional Conduct. Respondent has expressed regret for his misguided conduct in failing to disclose Mr. Fennimore's death.

II

A

The failure to disclose a material fact to a tribunal is an ethical violation under RPC 3.3(a)(5). Respondent violated that rule when he failed to inform the trial court that opposing counsel's motion to compel Mr. Fennimore to appear for a doctor's examination was moot.

We find guidance in Virzi v. Grand Trunk Warehouse & Cold Storage Co., 571 F. Supp. 507, 512 (E.D. Mich. 1983), in which the court held that, under the relevant rule of professional conduct, plaintiff's attorney had an affirmative duty to disclose the fact of his client's death to the court and his adversary. The attorney in *Virzi*, after learning of his client's death, appeared before the court at a pretrial conference and entered into a settlement agreement without notifying the court or opposing counsel of plaintiff's death. In setting aside the settlement, the court held that "by not informing the court of plaintiff's death, . . . plaintiff's attorney led this court to enter an order of a settlement for a non-existent party." Acknowledging that an attorney has an affirmative duty to zealously represent a client's interests, the court noted that an attorney "also owes an affirmative duty of candor and frankness to the court and opposing counsel when such a major event as the death of the plaintiff has taken place." *See also* Toledo Bar Assn. v. Fell, 364 N.E.2d 872, 873 (Ohio 1977) (imposing indefinite suspension from practice of law on Workmen's Compensation attorney who "understood that it had been the long established practice . . . to deny any claim for permanent-total disability benefits upon notice of the death of the claimant, [and] deliberately withheld information concerning his client's death prior to the hearing on the motion concerning the claim"); American Bar Association, Formal Opinion No. 95-397

(1995) (advising that, when client dies in midst of settlement negotiations, lawyer has duty to inform court and opposing counsel of death in first communication to either); In re Jeffers, 1994 WL 715918 (Cal. Review Dept. of State Bar Court Dec. 16, 1994) (imposing two-year probation on attorney who failed to inform court of client's death and represented to court during settlement discussions that he could not communicate with client because "client's brain was not functioning").

We note that the relevant rule of professional conduct at issue in *Virzi*—Rule 3.3 of the American Bar Association's Model Rules of Professional Conduct—provides, in relevant part, that a "lawyer shall not knowingly make a false statement of material fact or law to a tribunal . . . [nor] fail to disclose a material fact to a tribunal when disclosure is necessary to avoid assisting a criminal or fraudulent act by the client." In contrast, our corresponding rule, RPC 3.3, provides, in relevant part, that an attorney "shall not knowingly fail to disclose to the tribunal a material fact with knowledge that the tribunal may tend to be misled by such failure." RPC 3.3(a)(5). In view of New Jersey's even more stringent requirement of disclosure than the standard set forth by the Model Rules cited in *Virzi*, we hold that respondent's withholding of the material fact of Mr. Fennimore's death was misleading and violative of RPC 3.3(a)(5).

In addition, respondent violated RPC 3.3(a)(5) when he withheld the fact of Mr. Fennimore's death from the arbitrator. The fact that the violation occurred before an arbitrator as opposed to a court does not render the rule inapplicable. Arbitration is "a substitution . . . of another tribunal for the tribunal provided by the ordinary processes of law." . . .

. . . The effectiveness of arbitration as an alternative to formal litigation clearly would be undermined if counsel did not deal candidly with arbitrators.

We view respondent's proffer to the arbitrator that Mr. Fennimore was "unavailable" for the arbitration hearing as nothing less than a concealment of the material fact that Mr. Fennimore was deceased. Unquestionably, the arbitrator would have been compelled to consider Mr. Fennimore's death in determining the amount of any monetary award. Additionally, we note that the cause of action originally filed on behalf of Mr. Fennimore—an automobile negligence/personal injury action—would have been transformed into a survivor's action upon Mr. Fennimore's death. *See* N.J.S.A. 2A:15-3. To withhold information about Mr. Fennimore's death from the arbitrator effectively prevented the arbitrator from properly discharging his responsibilities under the court rules.

B

As did the DEC and the DRB, we find that respondent obstructed opposing counsel's access to potentially valuable evidence, in violation of RPC 3.4(a), by failing to inform opposing counsel that Mr. Fennimore was deceased. Respondent deliberately misled his adversary by serving answers to interrogatories propounded on Mr. Fennimore without disclosing that his client was deceased. Respondent exacerbated that deception by attempting to negotiate a settlement of the claim although his adversary remained uninformed of Mr. Fennimore's death. As the court observed in *Virzi*, *supra*, the attorney

> did not make a false statement regarding the death of plaintiff. He was never placed in a position to do so because during the . . . settlement negotiations defendants' attorney never thought to ask if plaintiff was still alive. Instead, in hopes of inducing settlement, [he] chose not to disclose plaintiff's death. . . . But the fact of plaintiff's death . . .

> would have had a significant bearing on defendants' willingness to settle.

We also find that respondent engaged in conduct involving dishonesty, deceit, and misrepresentation, in violation of RPC 8.4(c). Respondent misrepresented to the arbitrator the reasons for Mr. Fennimore's absence at the arbitration proceeding, encouraged Mrs. Fennimore to withhold from the arbitrator the fact of her husband's death, and misled opposing counsel throughout the discovery and negotiation process.

III

The principal goal of disciplinary proceedings is to foster and preserve public confidence in the bar, and to protect the public from an attorney who does not meet the high standards of professional responsibility....

Attorneys must "possess a certain set of traits—honesty and truthfulness, trustworthiness and reliability, and a professional commitment to the judicial process and the administration of justice."...

A misrepresentation to a tribunal "is a most serious breach of ethics because it affects directly the administration of justice."... Accordingly, we have recognized that "the destructive potential of such conduct to the justice system warrants stern sanctions."...

In the instant matter, respondent concealed a material fact from the court and arbitrator. That concealment was compounded by respondent's misrepresenting to the arbitrator the reasons for Mr. Fennimore's absence at the hearing, encouraging Mrs. Fennimore to evade questions about her husband's death, and obstructing Walls's access to the fact of Mr. Fennimore's death. Respondent's misconduct extended far beyond adversarial tactics that might constitute acceptable "puffing" or "bluffing." Respondent's nondisclosure of Mr. Fennimore's death deceived both his adversary and the arbitrator about a fact that was crucial to the fair and proper resolution of the litigation.

... Respondent's conduct was not an isolated incident but occurred over a period of at least nine months. Respondent engaged in a continuing course of dishonesty, deceit, and misrepresentation. Respondent's deception of his adversary and the arbitrator is inexcusable, and the contention that it occurred because of a sincere but misguided attempt to obtain a permissible tactical advantage in a lawsuit strains our credibility. Misrepresentation of a material fact to an adversary or a tribunal in the name of "zealous representation" never has been nor ever will be a permissible litigation tactic.

We believe that respondent now understands the gravity of his misdeeds. Nonetheless, respondent's ethical transgressions are serious, and he must be sanctioned accordingly. We conclude that respondent should be suspended from the practice of law for six months. Respondent is also ordered to reimburse the Disciplinary Oversight Committee for appropriate administrative costs.

Matter of Hendrix

986 F.2d 195 (7th Cir. 1993)

POSNER, Circuit Judge.

This appeal concerns the effect of a discharge in bankruptcy on litigation against the debtor's liability insurer outside of bankruptcy. In re Shondel, 950 F.2d 1301 (7th Cir. 1991), decided well before the appeal briefs were filed yet cited by neither party, dooms the appeal, but we shall not stop with that observation, as there are a few new wrinkles in this case.

On April 6, 1990, an automobile driven by Daniel Hendrix injured Sara Page. Hendrix had liability insurance, but, . . . he and his wife . . . declared bankruptcy under Chapter 7 of the Bankruptcy Code on June 5, 1990. On July 13, Hendrix added to the list of creditors that he had filed in the bankruptcy court the Pages, who at some time . . . between April 6 and July 13 had filed a personal injury suit against Hendrix in an Indiana state court. The Pages, despite being listed and receiving notice, did not file a claim in the bankruptcy proceeding. On September 12, 1990, the bankruptcy court granted Hendrix a discharge from his debts to the listed creditors. . . .

. . . [T]he Pages filed a motion to reopen the bankruptcy proceeding. The motion asked the bankruptcy judge to modify Hendrix's discharge so that they could ask the Indiana state court to reopen their suit for the purpose of proceeding against Hendrix's insurer. The bankruptcy judge granted the relief sought on September 23, 1991, the district judge affirmed, and Hendrix-which is to say Atlanta Casualty Company, for Hendrix has no interest in the matter, his discharge being secure, unmodified, and unchallenged, as far as any effort by the Pages to collect a judgment against him arising from the accident is concerned—appeals. . . .

The discharge had by virtue of 11 U.S.C. §524(a)(2) the force of an injunction against a suit by any holders of listed debts (such as the Pages) to collect those debts from Hendrix. But as to whether such an injunction extends to a suit only nominally against the debtor because the only relief sought is against his insurer, the cases are pretty nearly unanimous that it does not. In re Shondel, *supra*, 950 F.2d at 1306-09; Green v. Welsh, 956 F.2d 30 (2d Cir. 1992); In re Jet Florida Systems, Inc., 883 F.2d 970 (11th Cir. 1989) (per curiam); In re Western Real Estate Fund, Inc., 922 F.2d 592, 601 n.7 (10th Cir. 1990) (per curiam); 3 Collier on Bankruptcy ¶524.01 at pp. 524-16 to 524-17 (Lawrence P. King ed., 15th ed. 1991); *see also* In re Fernstrom Storage & Van Co., 938 F.2d 731, 733-34 (7th Cir. 1991); *contra*, In re White Motor Credit, 761 F.2d 270, 274-75 (6th Cir. 1985). . . . If this is right, the discharge did not in fact prevent the Pages from proceeding in state court against Hendrix, provided they were seeking only the proceeds of his insurance policy. . . .

We recur in closing to the parties' failure to cite *Shondel*. Although the cases are not identical, this appeal could not succeed unless we overruled *Shondel*. Needless to say, the appellant failed to make any argument for overruling *Shondel*, for it failed even to cite the case. This omission by the Atlanta Casualty Company (the real appellant) disturbs us because insurance companies are sophisticated enterprises in legal matters, *Shondel* was an insurance case, and the law firm that handled this appeal for Atlanta is located in this circuit. The Pages' lawyer, a solo practitioner in a nonmetropolitan area, is less seriously at fault for having failed to discover *Shondel*—and anyway his failure could not have been a case of concealing adverse authority, because *Shondel* supported his position. At all events, by appealing in the face of dispositive contrary authority without making arguments for overruling it, Atlanta Casualty filed a frivolous appeal.

This conclusion may seem questionable because, given the intrinsic difficulty of the issues presented by the appeal, and the fact that *Shondel* is the only case on point, the appellant, although it would still have lost, would not have risked sanctions had it urged us to overrule *Shondel*. But that is true in a great many cases in which sanctions are imposed under Fed. R. App. P. 38 for filing a frivolous appeal. The court does not ask whether the appeal might have been nonfrivolous if presented differently, with arguments and authorities to which the appellant in fact never alluded. If the appeal is blocked by authorities that the appellant ignored, the appellant is sanctioned without inquiry into whether the authorities if acknowledged might have been contested.

There is a further point. Although as we noted in Thompson v. Duke, 940 F.2d 192, 196 n.2 (7th Cir. 1991), the circuits are divided (and we have not taken sides) on whether a failure to acknowledge binding adverse precedent violates Fed. R. Civ. P. 11, if Atlanta Casualty's counsel knowingly concealed dispositive adverse authority it engaged in professional misconduct. ABA Model Rules of Professional Conduct Rule 3.3(a)(3) (1983). The inference would arise that it had filed the appeal for purposes of delay, which would be an abuse of process and thus provide an additional basis for imposition of sanctions under Fed. R. App. P. 38 ("damages for delay"). A frivolous suit or appeal corresponds, at least approximately, to the tort of malicious prosecution, that is, groundless litigation; a suit or appeal that is not necessarily groundless but was filed for an improper purpose, such as delay, corresponds to—indeed is an instance of—abuse of process. Both, we hold, are sanctionable under Rule 38. We direct Atlanta Casualty's counsel to submit within 14 days a statement as to why it or its client, or both, should not be sanctioned under Rule 38 for failing to cite the *Shondel* case to us.

We are not quite done. Rule 46(c) of the appellate rules authorizes us to discipline lawyers who practice before us. In deciding whether a lawyer has engaged in conduct sanctionable under that rule, we have looked not only to the rules of professional conduct but also to Rule 11 of the civil rules, which makes it sanctionable misconduct for a lawyer to sign a pleading or other paper, including a brief, if he has failed to make a reasonable inquiry into whether his position "is well grounded in fact and is warranted by existing law or a good faith argument for the extension, modification, or reversal of existing law." Reasonable inquiry would have turned up *Shondel*. The lawyer who signed Atlanta Casualty's briefs in this court is therefore directed to submit a statement within 14 days as to why he should not be sanctioned under Rule 46(c). . . .

United States v. Shaffer Equipment Co.

11 F.3d 450 (4th Cir. 1993)

NIEMEYER, Circuit Judge:

In an action brought by the United States Environmental Protection Agency ("EPA") under the Comprehensive Environmental Response, Compensation, and Liability Act ("CERCLA"), 42 U.S.C. §9601 et seq., to recover over $5 million in costs incurred in cleaning up a hazardous waste site in Minden, West Virginia, the district court found that the government's attorneys deliberately and in bad faith breached their duty of candor owed to the court during the course of proceedings. The court found that Robert E. Caron, the EPA's on-scene coordinator for the cleanup, had misrepresented his academic achievements and credentials in this and in other cases and that the government's attorneys wrongfully obstructed the defendants' efforts to root out the discrepancies and failed to reveal them once they learned of them.[1] ...

On appeal, the government contends that the district court adopted an overly broad interpretation of the applicable rules of lawyer conduct and abused its discretion in imposing the most severe sanction by dismissing the action....

I...

When the defendants first scheduled the deposition of Caron for September 12, 1991, an EPA assistant regional counsel, Charles Hayden, reviewed Caron's academic credentials. Caron was unable to produce his college diploma (allegedly because his mother failed to mail it to him), but he stated that he had received an undergraduate degree from Rutgers University in 1978 and had taken courses at Drexel University, Trenton State College, and Brookdale Community College....

On the morning of September 12, prior to the deposition, Hayden learned that Caron had not formally received a degree from Rutgers and so advised J. Jared Snyder, a Department of Justice attorney representing the government at the deposition. At the deposition, however, Caron testified, in the presence of Snyder, that he had completed all of the requirements for a degree at Rutgers and that the only reason he had not received his diploma was a question of paperwork. Caron also testified that he had continued taking courses at Drexel for a masters degree. He stated that his bachelors degree work was in environmental science and that his masters degree work was in organic chemistry.

When the deposition was resumed about two months later, on November 27, 1991, Caron was shown a copy of a professional resume on which he had claimed to have received a B.S. degree in environmental science from Rutgers and an M.S. degree in organic chemistry from Drexel. At that point, Snyder directed the witness not to answer any questions about the resume, claiming that the inquiry was not relevant, despite defense counsel's assertion that Caron's credibility was at issue. When counsel for the defendants suggested that the parties obtain a court ruling, Snyder took a recess from the deposition... called his superior at the Department of Justice, William A. Hutchins, who called his superior, Bruce Gelber, who called the Deputy Regional Counsel of the EPA, Michael Vaccaro. Following the various calls, Hutchins eventually called Snyder back and instructed him to advise Caron of the option to refuse giving further testimony until Caron obtained his own attorney. In addition, Hutchins advised Snyder to permit Caron to answer if Caron so elected and to place any objections on the record. When the deposition resumed, Snyder followed Hutchins' instructions, but he continued to maintain that the questioning was irrelevant.... Defense counsel agreed not to proceed on the issue of Caron's credentials further because, as the court found, counsel concluded that to do so would create the appearance of taking advantage of Caron by questioning him without his having first consulted an attorney.

Two days after the deposition, Snyder researched the question of whether Caron's credibility was relevant to the litigation and concluded that it was relevant as a matter of law. Snyder nonetheless did not supplement the government's response to an earlier interrogatory directed to Caron's

1. Caron later resigned from the EPA and pled guilty to the criminal charge of making material false declarations in violation of 18 U.S.C. §1623.

credentials (to which the government had objected on the basis of irrelevance) and did not withdraw the relevancy objection to the discovery, despite his conclusion that the inquiry was relevant under current law.

In early December 1991, Vaccaro began an EPA civil investigation into Caron's credentials, advising Hutchins of the investigation and directing him not to advise anyone about it. Vaccaro also told Hutchins that a discrepancy had appeared in Caron's employment application with the EPA and that Caron had testified under oath in another case that he had earned a masters degree. On December 19, 1991, after Vaccaro told the EPA Office of the Inspector General about "the Caron problem," the Inspector General began a criminal investigation. . . .

Hutchins learned in December, during the course of his own investigation, that of the Superfund sites on which Caron had worked six were in litigation. Hutchins then instructed the government attorneys on each of those six cases that the government was not to rely on Caron's testimony. Hutchins also directed the attorneys not to disclose the existence of any investigation because to do so might prejudice the investigation and might also violate Caron's privacy rights.

As the attorney on this case, Snyder received Hutchins' instructions and followed them. Thus, in December 1991, when Snyder prepared the government's motion for summary judgment, he did not cite any testimony from Caron, nor did he include any affidavits executed by Caron. But Snyder did base the summary judgment motion on the administrative record compiled under Caron's direction as the On-Scene Coordinator during the cleanup. The district court found that "Caron [had] played a significant role in the preparation of documents contained in the administrative record."

On January 7, 1992, the defendants, in an effort to learn more facts about Caron's qualifications and credentials, subpoenaed records from the various colleges identified by Caron during his deposition. When Snyder learned of this, he telephoned counsel for the defendants to object because the subpoena was served after December 31, 1991, the discovery cutoff date. Snyder followed up with a letter requesting that the subpoena be withdrawn and that the documents be returned to the various institutions. Drexel University later reported that it had no record of Caron's attendance there, and Snyder was so advised by defense counsel. In response, Snyder wrote a letter of thanks dated January 17, 1992, stating that "we are looking into the matter and will let you know if Mr. Caron's testimony requires correction." While Snyder had also intended, in that letter, to disclose the existence of the criminal investigation and had so drafted the letter, Hutchins and Gelber directed him to delete the reference, and Snyder followed the instruction.

On January 17, 1992, Snyder filed the government's motion for summary judgment which he had started preparing in December. He made no mention of the EPA investigation, the criminal investigation, or the misstatements or misrepresentations of Caron's credentials.

Still attempting to discover the extent of the Caron problem after the government filed its summary judgment motion, defense counsel discovered in late January 1992, through independent means, that Caron had testified falsely in another case. Defense counsel decided to bring this evidence to the attention of the Assistant United States Attorney on the case who, following consultation with Snyder and Hutchins, then advised the court for the first time in a letter dated January 31, 1992, of the Caron problem and requested a stay.

D.C. - Snyder & Hutchins violated 3.3

Based on these facts, the district court concluded that Snyder and Hutchins violated their general duty of candor to the court as well as the particular duties imposed by West Virginia Rule of Professional Conduct 3.3 (describing the lawyer's duty of candor toward the tribunal) and Federal Rule of Civil Procedure 26(e)(2) (obliging counsel to supplement discovery requests). With respect to Snyder's conduct, the court found that even though Snyder knew, as of September 12, 1991, that Caron had no college degree, he obstructed efforts by defense counsel to discover this at the November 27 deposition by instructing Caron not to answer questions about his resume which claimed that Caron had two college degrees. The court also found that Snyder failed to withdraw his objections to interrogatories submitted earlier and to modify the positions taken in the deposition, or to advise the court or opposing counsel when he concluded two days later, through his own independent legal research, that Caron's credibility in this case was relevant. The court found that despite discovering the discrepancies in Caron's employment application with the EPA, the commencement of an investigation by the EPA, and the commencement of a criminal investigation, Snyder "continued to litigate the matter unabated without disclosing the investigations to the Court."

With respect to Hutchins, Snyder's superior, the district court found that his actions were "egregious" and constituted more severe violations. Hutchins had learned on November 27, 1991, that Caron had no college degree even though Caron's resume stated otherwise. In early December, Hutchins had learned of (1) the EPA civil investigation, (2) the false testimony given by Caron in another litigation claiming that he had a masters degree, and (3) Vaccaro's referral of the matter to the EPA's Office of Inspector General. Shortly thereafter, in January, Hutchins had learned that an actual criminal investigation had been commenced. The district court found that Hutchins improperly continued the litigation without disclosing to the court the existence of the ongoing investigations, and that Hutchins had prevented Snyder from disclosing the facts when Snyder had proposed to do so in a letter to opposing counsel. Finally, the court also found that Hutchins improperly concealed his knowledge that Caron had testified falsely in other cases and in affidavits sent to the EPA Office of Inspector General.

. . . Stating that the only sanction appropriate to address the violation was dismissal, the [district] court dismissed the action under its inherent powers and awarded the defendants their attorney's fees incurred in responding to the government's misconduct, under the Equal Access to Justice Act, 28 U.S.C. §2412.

This appeal followed.

II . . .

Our adversary system for the resolution of disputes rests on the unshakable foundation that truth is the object of the system's process which is designed for the purpose of dispensing justice. However, because no one has an exclusive insight into truth, the process depends on the adversarial presentation of evidence, precedent and custom, and argument to reasoned conclusion—all directed with unwavering effort to what, in good faith, is believed to be true on matters material to the disposition. Even the slightest accommodation of deceit or lack of candor in any material respect quickly erodes the validity of the process. As soon as the process falters in that respect, the people are then justified in abandoning support for the system in favor of one where honestly is preeminent.

. . . [I]t is important to reaffirm . . . the principle that lawyers, who serve as officers of the court, have the first line task of assuring the integrity of the process. Each lawyer undoubtedly has an important duty of confidentiality to his client and must surely advocate his client's position vigorously, but only if it is truth which the client seeks to advance. . . . [W]e recognize that the lawyer's duties to maintain the confidences of client and advocate vigorously are trumped ultimately by a duty to guard against the corruption that justice will be dispensed on an act of deceit.

While Rule 3.3 articulates the duty of candor to the tribunal as a necessary protection of the decision-making process, and Rule 3.4 articulates an analogous duty to opposing lawyers, neither of these rules . . . displaces the broader general duty of candor and good faith required to protect the integrity of the entire judicial process. . . .

. . . For example, in Tiverton Board of License Commissioners v. Pastore, 469 U.S. 238 (1985), counsel failed to apprise the Supreme Court that during the appeal process, one of the respondents, a liquor store challenging the admission of evidence at a Rhode Island liquor license revocation proceeding, had gone out of business, rendering the case moot. Rebuking counsel for failing to comply with a duty of candor broader than Rule 3.3, the Supreme Court stated, "It is appropriate to remind counsel that they have a '*continuing duty to inform the Court* of any development *which may conceivably affect the outcome' of the litigation*." . . .

In this case, the district court found that both Snyder and Hutchins repeatedly failed to advise the court of the Caron problem and the civil and criminal investigations relating to it, continuing "to litigate the matter unabated." . . . [W]e are satisfied that these are matters involving deceit that, when not disclosed, undermine the integrity of the process. Moreover, their disclosure could conceivably have affected the outcome of the litigation, as we discuss more fully, below. Accordingly, the conduct violates the general duty of candor that attorneys owe as officers of the court.

Even limiting our consideration to the provisions of Rule 3.3 which, the government argues, define a lawyer's duty of candor more restrictively, we are nevertheless satisfied that the district court was justified in finding that the government's attorneys breached their duty of candor under that rule. . . .

Addressing first the "actual knowledge" requirement of Rule 3.3, the government contends that, while it may have had suspicions about Caron's misstatements, it did not fully appreciate their falsity until the investigation was completed. While it is true that a mere suspicion of perjury by a client does not carry with it the obligation to reveal that suspicion to the court under Rule 3.3, the government's attorneys in this case cannot find shelter behind any such doubt. Caron admitted to Snyder as early as September 1991 that he did not have a college degree. By December 1991, when an EPA investigation was under way and EPA regional counsel had referred the matter to the Office of Inspector General, the lawyers for the United States had actual knowledge of the discrepancy in Caron's sworn testimony in which he said, on the one hand, that he had no college degree and, on the other, that he had both a bachelor of science degree and a masters degree. At that time, the government's lawyers also had had conversations with Rutgers University which confirmed that no degree had been issued, were aware of misrepresentations on Caron's employment application, and actually possessed a copy of Caron's fraudulent resume. Against this evidence, the government's claim to have held only a suspicion rings hollow.

Δ - info was not material

We move to the government's principal argument under Rule 3.3, that the information which Caron falsified in his credentials was not material to the proceeding. First of all, we find the sincerity of the position undermined because Snyder, the Justice Department attorney in this case, reached the exact opposite conclusion during the course of his independent research in November 1991....

The issue before the district court in this case was whether the defendants are liable to the EPA for costs incurred in cleaning up a hazardous waste site. To establish its case, the government must demonstrate that the release or the threatened release of hazardous wastes caused the EPA to incur "response costs." One method for challenging the appropriateness of the response costs is for the defendant to demonstrate that the methods of cleaning up are not consistent with the National Contingency Plan established by CERCLA. Procedurally, the government relies on the administrative record developed during the cleanup, and the defendant bears the burden of demonstrating that this reliance is arbitrary and capricious. Because this method for establishing its case relies on the administrative record and not testimony, the government argues that Caron's credibility and credentials are not material....

The administrative record in this case is large, consisting of volumes of bills, communications, and authorizations developed primarily from on-site activity. The person placed in overall charge of the site was Robert Caron. While Caron's decisions were subject to approval by superiors, as On-Scene Coordinator he made most of the decisions and, when he sought the approval of superiors, his recommendations were adopted in virtually all of the cases. It was Caron who recommended and obtained approval for the solvent extraction method, side-stepping the traditional method of physically removing the contaminated soil. As it turned out, the pilot process proved unsatisfactory and the traditional method of removing the soil was ultimately utilized. However, the experimental process was abandoned only after over $1 million in costs were incurred, which the EPA now seeks to impose on the defendants. While Caron's role in this litigation relates primarily to supporting response selection, he also had a major role in approving project-related expenditures. Thus, Caron's credentials, capability and credibility are relevant to the examination of the administrative record in this case.

Even where review of a case is confined to the evidence contained in the administrative record, the Supreme Court has concluded that evidence of bad faith or improper behavior by an administrative agency's official in compiling that record justifies inquiry beyond the record compiled. The fact that the government's agent in charge of monitoring expenses and selecting responses filed fraudulent documents with the federal government and perjured himself repeatedly in connection with his federal employment is, we think, of primary relevance to an examination of the integrity and reliability of the administrative record.

It is obviously difficult to assess the impact that Caron's fraud may have had on the development of the record, particularly on the selection of the solvent extraction method, an issue hotly debated by the parties. Would Caron have been given the responsibility for initiating a pilot program if his credentials had not been misrepresented to the EPA in his employment application? Would his recommendations have carried the same weight on review by superiors? To what extent are the defendants saddled in this case with decisions in the administrative record tainted by questions of competence and integrity? . . . Given the great possibility that Caron's deception affected administrative decisions in this case and disguised a weakness in his capabilities, we cannot agree with the government that the sole relevance of the "Caron problem" is with regard to impeachment of Caron's testimony. That approach is too narrow. Moreover, the significance of impeaching the principal EPA witness, who was largely responsible for developing the record, renders impeachment information material. . . .

Once we find the government's attorneys had actual knowledge of Caron's deception and that the deception was material under Rule 3.3, we move to a review of whether Caron's conduct amounted to a fraudulent act of the EPA. . . . Caron's perjury in an attempt to cover up his earlier deception was certainly a fraudulent act. Since Caron was involved in the case as an important agent of the EPA and his misrepresentation was made in the course of his employment with the EPA with the effect of disguising a weakness in the EPA's case, his action is fairly characterized as an act of the EPA.

Distilling the district court's findings, this case reduces to an effort by an important EPA witness to cover up or minimize his long history of fraud. The government's attorneys compounded the problem by obstructing the defendants' efforts to uncover this perjury and in failing themselves to reveal it. When the government's attorneys filed a motion for summary judgment dependent on the administrative record made by Caron and requested a favorable resolution of the case prior to a full documentation of the perjury, these attorneys overstepped the bounds of zealous advocacy, exposing themselves and their employer to sanctions. While this violation was effectively brought to light by opposing counsel, this was not done until after the expenditure of significant time and money.

III

Due to the very nature of the court as an institution, it must and does have an inherent power to impose order, respect, decorum, silence, and compliance with lawful mandates. This power is organic, without need of a statute or rule for its definition, and it is necessary to the exercise of all other powers. Because the inherent power is not regulated by Congress or the people and is particularly subject to abuse, it must be exercised with the greatest restraint and caution, and then only to the extent necessary. Roadway Express, Inc. v. Piper, 447 U.S. 752, 764 (1980). . . .

In this case, the government proposed to the district court a lesser sanction to be imposed if a breach of the duty of candor were to be found. It suggested (1) opening for de novo review the administrative record with respect to the selection of the solvent extraction method; (2) allowing discovery by defendants on the EPA's selection of the solvent extraction method; and (3) allowing discovery on any and all matters involving Caron. The district court rejected this offer as a "rather slight sanction." . . .

In doing so, we believe that the district court did not adequately address the broad policies of deciding the case on the merits where the orderly administration of justice and the integrity of the process have not been permanently frustrated, and of exercising the necessary restraint when dismissal is based on the inherent power. Thus, we reverse its dismissal order. We are confident that the district court's objective of punishing the wrongdoers, deterring similar future conduct, and compensating the defendant can be achieved by a sanction, short of dismissal, tailored more directly to those goals.

The occasion to consider the disciplining of members of the bar is not a happy one, and the district court's response was understandably stern. We are in full agreement with the district court's expressed concern, and we repeat that our adversary system depends on a most jealous safeguarding of truth and candor. But we also observe that through an outright dismissal, the defendants receive the benefit of a total release from their obligations under the environmental protection laws. This would provide the defendants relief far beyond the harm caused by the government attorneys' improper conduct and would frustrate the resolution on the merits of a case which itself has strong policy implications. . . .

Without suggesting a sanction which is appropriate, we point out that in considering the proper role of the administrative record in this case and the respective burdens of proof, the district court may deny the government the benefit of any portion of the record or the right to claim any expense, which may have been tainted by Caron's misconduct, even if it becomes impossible to assess accurately the extent of that taint. Because of the government's misconduct, the benefit of any doubt must be resolved in the defendants' favor. . . .

Accordingly, we affirm the district court's finding that a breach of ethical conduct occurred, but we vacate the judgment of the district court dismissing the case and remand for the imposition of a sanction short of outright dismissal. Since an award of attorney's fees may be part of the district court's overall calculus in selecting a sanction after further proceedings, we leave for later review, if necessary, any question on whether attorney's fees were appropriately awarded.* . . .

Nix v. Whiteside

475 U.S. 157 (1986)

Chief Justice BURGER delivered the opinion of the Court.

We granted certiorari to decide whether the Sixth Amendment right of a criminal defendant to assistance of counsel is violated when an attorney refuses to cooperate with the defendant in presenting perjured testimony at his trial.

I

A

Whiteside was convicted of second-degree murder by a jury verdict which was affirmed by the Iowa courts. The killing took place on February 8, 1977, in Cedar Rapids, Iowa. Whiteside and two others went to one Calvin Love's apartment late that night, seeking marihuana. Love was in bed when Whiteside and his companions arrived; an argument between Whiteside and Love over the marihuana ensued. At one point, Love directed his girlfriend to get his "piece," and at another point got up, then returned to his bed. According to Whiteside's testimony, Love then started to reach under his pillow and moved toward Whiteside. Whiteside

* On remand, the district court ordered lawyers Hutchins and Snyder to pay personal sanctions of $2,000 each and prohibited them from seeking reimbursement from the government. It also accepted a consent decree, which it deemed necessary because of Mr. Caron's misconduct in the case and the government's inability to rely on his testimony. Finally, it vacated its initial award of attorney's fees to the defendants to enhance the value of the consent decree to the government. U.S. v. Shaffer Equipment Co., 158 F.R.D. 80 (S.D. W. Va. 1994).

stabbed Love in the chest, inflicting a fatal wound.

Whiteside was charged with murder, and when counsel was appointed he objected to the lawyer initially appointed, claiming that he felt uncomfortable with a lawyer who had formerly been a prosecutor. Gary L. Robinson was then appointed and immediately began an investigation. Whiteside gave him a statement that he had stabbed Love as the latter "was pulling a pistol from underneath the pillow on the bed." Upon questioning by Robinson, however, Whiteside indicated that he had not actually seen a gun, but that he was convinced that Love had a gun. No pistol was found on the premises; shortly after the police search following the stabbing, which had revealed no weapon, the victim's family had removed all of the victim's possessions from the apartment. Robinson interviewed Whiteside's companions who were present during the stabbing, and none had seen a gun during the incident. Robinson advised Whiteside that the existence of a gun was not necessary to establish the claim of self-defense, and that only a reasonable belief that the victim had a gun nearby was necessary even though no gun was actually present.

Until shortly before trial, Whiteside consistently stated to Robinson that he had not actually seen a gun, but that he was convinced that Love had a gun in his hand. About a week before trial, during preparation for direct examination, Whiteside for the first time told Robinson and his associate Donna Paulsen that he had seen something "metallic" in Love's hand. When asked about this, Whiteside responded:

"[In] Howard Cook's case there was a gun. If I don't say I saw a gun, I'm dead."

Robinson told Whiteside that such testimony would be perjury and repeated that it was not necessary to prove that a gun was available but only that Whiteside reasonably believed that he was in danger. On Whiteside's insisting that he would testify that he saw "something metallic" Robinson told him, according to Robinson's testimony:

> "[We] could not allow him to [testify falsely] because that would be perjury, and as officers of the court we would be suborning perjury if we allowed him to do it; . . . I advised him that if he did do that it would be my duty to advise the Court of what he was doing and that I felt he was committing perjury; also, that I probably would be allowed to attempt to impeach that particular testimony."

Robinson also indicated he would seek to withdraw from the representation if Whiteside insisted on committing perjury.

Whiteside testified in his own defense at trial and stated that he "knew" that Love had a gun and that he believed Love was reaching for a gun and he had acted swiftly in self-defense. On cross-examination, he admitted that he had not actually seen a gun in Love's hand. Robinson presented evidence that Love had been seen with a sawed-off shotgun on other occasions, that the police search of the apartment may have been careless, and that the victim's family had removed everything from the apartment shortly after the crime. Robinson presented this evidence to show a basis for Whiteside's asserted fear that Love had a gun.

The jury returned a verdict of second-degree murder, and Whiteside moved for a new trial, claiming that he had been deprived of a fair trial by Robinson's admonitions not to state that he saw a gun or "something metallic." The trial court held a hearing, heard testimony by Whiteside and Robinson, and denied the motion. The trial court made specific findings that the facts were as related by Robinson.

The Supreme Court of Iowa affirmed respondent's conviction. That court held that the right to have counsel present all appropriate defenses does not extend to using perjury, and that an attorney's duty to a client does not extend to assisting a client in committing perjury. Relying on DR 7-102(A)(4) of the Iowa Code of Professional Responsibility for Lawyers, which expressly prohibits an attorney from using perjured testimony, and Iowa Code §721.2 (now Iowa Code §720.3 (1985)), which criminalizes subornation of perjury, the Iowa court concluded that not only were Robinson's actions permissible, but were required. The court commended "both Mr. Robinson and Ms. Paulsen for the high ethical manner in which this matter was handled." . . .

II

B

In Strickland v. Washington, we held that to obtain relief by way of federal habeas corpus on a claim of a deprivation of effective assistance of counsel under the Sixth Amendment, the movant must establish both serious attorney error and prejudice. . . .

C

We next turn to the question presented: the definition of the range of "reasonable professional" responses to a criminal defendant client who informs counsel that he will perjure himself on the stand. . . .

In *Strickland,* we recognized counsel's duty of loyalty and his "overarching duty to advocate the defendant's cause." Plainly, that duty is limited to legitimate, lawful conduct compatible with the very nature of a trial as a search for truth. Although counsel must take all reasonable lawful means to attain the objectives of the client, counsel is precluded from taking steps or in any way assisting the client in presenting false evidence or otherwise violating the law. . . .

These principles have been carried through to contemporary codifications . . . of an attorney's professional responsibility. [The Court cites DR 7-102 (A) (4) and (7) and Model Rule 1.2(d)]. . . . [B]oth the Model Code and the Model Rules do not merely *authorize* disclosure by counsel of client perjury; they *require* such disclosure. *See* Rule 3.3(a)(4); DR 7-102(B)(1).

These standards confirm that the legal profession has accepted that an attorney's ethical duty to advance the interests of his client is limited by an equally solemn duty to comply with the law and standards of professional conduct; it specifically ensures that the client may not use false evidence. This special duty of an attorney to prevent and disclose frauds upon the court derives from the recognition that perjury is as much a crime as tampering with witnesses or jurors by way of promises and threats, and undermines the administration of justice.

The offense of perjury was a crime recognized at common law, and has been made a felony in most states by statute, including Iowa. An attorney who aids false testimony by questioning a witness when perjurious responses can be anticipated risks prosecution for subornation of perjury under Iowa Code §720.3 (1985). . . .

D

Considering Robinson's representation of respondent in light of these accepted norms of professional conduct, we discern no failure to adhere to reasonable professional standards that would in any sense make out a deprivation of the Sixth Amendment right to counsel. Whether Robinson's conduct is seen as a successful attempt to dissuade his client from committing the crime of perjury, or whether seen as a "threat" to withdraw from representation and disclose the illegal scheme, Robinson's representation of Whiteside falls well within accepted standards of professional conduct and the range of reasonable professional conduct acceptable under *Strickland*. . . .

The Court of Appeals' holding that Robinson's "action deprived [Whiteside] of due process and effective assistance of counsel" is not supported by the record since Robinson's action, at most, deprived Whiteside of his contemplated perjury. Nothing counsel did in any way undermined Whiteside's claim that he believed the victim was reaching for a gun. Similarly, the record gives no support for holding that Robinson's action "also impermissibly compromised [Whiteside's] right to testify in his own defense by conditioning continued representation . . . and confidentiality upon [Whiteside's] restricted testimony." The record in fact shows the contrary: (a) that Whiteside did testify, and (b) he was "restricted" or restrained only from testifying falsely and was aided by Robinson in developing the basis for the fear that Love was reaching for a gun. Robinson divulged no client communications until he was compelled to do so in response to Whiteside's post-trial challenge to the quality of his performance. We see this as a case in which the attorney successfully dissuaded the client from committing the crime of perjury. . . .

Whatever the scope of a constitutional right to testify, it is elementary that such a right does not extend to testifying *falsely*. . . .

The paucity of authority on the subject of any such "right" may be explained by the fact that such a notion has never been responsibly advanced; the right to counsel includes no right to have a lawyer who will cooperate with planned perjury. A lawyer who would so cooperate would be at risk of prosecution for suborning perjury, and disciplinary proceedings, including suspension or disbarment. . . .

E

We hold that, as a matter of law, counsel's conduct complained of here cannot establish the prejudice required for relief under the second strand of the *Strickland* inquiry. . . .

Whether he was persuaded or compelled to desist from perjury, Whiteside has no valid claim that confidence in the result of his trial has been diminished by his desisting from the contemplated perjury. Even if we were to assume that the jury might have believed his perjury, it does not follow that Whiteside was prejudiced. . . .

Whiteside's attorney treated Whiteside's proposed perjury in accord with professional standards, and since Whiteside's truthful testimony could not have prejudiced the result of his trial, the Court of Appeals was in error to direct the issuance of a writ of habeas corpus and must be reversed. . . .

Commonwealth v. Mitchell

781 N.E.2d 1237 (Mass. 2003)

GREANEY, J.

A jury convicted the defendant of two indictments charging murder in the first degree by reason of deliberate premeditation and extreme atrocity or cruelty. The defendant's motion for a new trial was denied by the trial judge, on the basis of affidavits, without an evidentiary hearing. . . . The defendant argues that he was denied constitutionally effective assistance of counsel (and incurred violations of other constitutional rights) when his trial counsel, relying on Mass. R. Prof. C. 3.3(e)[1] . . . advised the judge at trial that the defendant would testify and present false testimony to the jury, that counsel had attempted to persuade the defendant from testifying falsely, that counsel had decided that he would not seek to withdraw from representing the defendant in the ongoing trial, and that counsel needed instruction from the judge on how to proceed before the jury. After receiving instruction, counsel presented the defendant's testimony in narrative form and made a closing argument that reflected his understanding of his ethical obligations. . . .

The evidence and proceedings at the trial may be summarized as follows. The victims, Sonya Shurtliff and David Allen, were murdered in the late evening of June 13, 1996, in their Fall River apartment, within hours of a drug raid at Julius Adams's nearby apartment that resulted in the seizure of drugs and the arrest of Adams. After posting bail, Adams returned to his apartment and told his wife, Barbara, and the defendant (the defendant resided in the same building as Adams), a friend to whom Adams supplied drugs, that he believed that the victims had furnished the police with the information used to obtain the search warrant. Adams had sold drugs to the victims until April, 1996, when he had an altercation with them. After the dispute, the defendant sold drugs to the victims.

After their conversation, the defendant asked Adams if he wanted to do anything about the fact that the victims had talked to the police. Adams responded that he did not. Later, that night, Adams was on his porch talking with his brother-in-law, Willie Smith, when he saw the defendant. The defendant told Adams, "I did it." Adams said, "Did what?" The defendant responded, "Sonya and David." The defendant was dressed in black nylon sweat pants, a black sweatshirt and white "glove liners" that were "kind of reddish." The defendant left, and, approximately fifteen minutes later, Adams saw the defendant leave the apartment building carrying a brown backpack.

[The court summarizes the testimony of several other trial witnesses, including one who sold the defendant a revolver on the night of the murder, one who saw the defendant knocking on the door of the victims' apartment the night of the murder, and two who testified that after the murders, the defendant told them he had killed two people.]

The defendant contended at trial that someone else, probably Adams, had killed the victims. The defendant called an analyst employed by Cellmark Diagnostics, who testified that DNA testing excluded the defendant as a source of DNA obtained from hairs found in Shurtliff's hand. The defendant also called Willie Smith. Smith

1. "In a criminal case, defense counsel who knows that the defendant, the client, intends to testify falsely may not aid the client in constructing false testimony, and has a duty strongly to discourage the client from testifying falsely, advising that such a course is unlawful, will have substantial adverse consequences, and should not be followed. . . . If a criminal trial has commenced and the lawyer discovers that the client intends to testify falsely at trial, the lawyer need not file a motion to withdraw from the case if the lawyer reasonably believes that seeking to withdraw will prejudice the client. If, during the client's testimony or after the client has testified, the lawyer knows that the client has testified falsely, the lawyer shall call upon the client to rectify the false testimony and, if the client refuses or is unable to do so, the lawyer shall not reveal the false testimony to the tribunal. In no event may the lawyer examine the client in such a manner as to elicit any testimony from the client the lawyer knows to be false, and the lawyer shall not argue the probative value of the false testimony in closing argument or in any other proceedings, including appeals."

The rule has separate requirements when the issue arises prior to trial.

testified that, during the early morning of June 14, 1996, he saw the defendant while talking to Adams on the porch to Adams's apartment. Smith stated that the porch lights were on, that he had not noticed any blood on the defendant's clothing, and that the defendant was not wearing any gloves. He denied paying attention to the conversation between Adams and the defendant.

The defendant testified. After his trial counsel had him state his name, counsel asked, "Mr. Mitchell, what do you wish to tell these jurors?" The defendant then proceeded to testify at length in a narrative fashion. The defendant recounted his dealings with Adams and recounted events that tended to implicate Adams as the killer. The defendant denied that he had killed the victims, [and denied the testimony of other prosecution witnesses].

The defendant's trial counsel did not argue the defendant's testimony in his closing argument. He emphasized the Commonwealth's high burden of proof and stressed that Adams had a motive to harm the victims. The defendant's trial counsel stated that the defendant was a small time dealer with no motive to kill the victims. He pointed out inconsistencies in [the testimony or credibility of prosecution witnesses.] The defendant's trial counsel further called to the jury's attention the lack of physical evidence tying the defendant to the crimes, and what he considered failures in the police investigation. . . .

In his motion for a new trial, the defendant argued that his trial counsel did not have an adequate basis to invoke rule 3.3(e), that the judge unconstitutionally applied the rule by failing to conduct a colloquy with him, and that his constitutional rights were violated because he was not present at the sidebar when his trial counsel invoked rule 3.3(e). The defendant also claimed that he should have been afforded the opportunity to be represented by independent counsel, and that he should have been allowed to give an unsworn statement to the jury or to argue his own testimony in closing. In support of his contentions, the defendant offered his affidavit and the affidavit of his trial counsel. In the defendant's affidavit, he stated that "the testimony that I gave at trial was true. I never told [my trial counsel] that I was going to testify falsely and commit perjury." The defendant's trial counsel, in his affidavit, made the following statements:

> "When I first interviewed [the defendant], he told me he did not kill the victims in this case.
>
> "Later on in the course of my representation, he told me that he did. My subjective belief was that this inculpatory story was true. I had no additional inculpatory information other than that provided by the Commonwealth in discovery and by the witnesses at trial. . . .
>
> "Prior to the defendant's testimony, I advised him that he was not permitted to give perjured testimony, and that I could not present perjured testimony or argue it.
>
> "I believed it was perjurious because it contradicted his earlier version of events and was contrary to the evidence provided to me in discovery and presented in the Commonwealth's case.
>
> "The defendant asked me if he could argue his case in addition to my argument. I told him that the judge would not allow it and I thought it would hurt rather than help him. . . ." . . .

a. We first address the defendant's contention that the judge applied the wrong standard to inform the word "knows" in rule 3.3(e). The question what a criminal defense attorney should do when confronted with client perjury at trial has been a subject of considerable debate. The problem raises both ethical and constitutional concerns. Defense counsel must furnish zealous advocacy and preserve client confidences, but, at the same time, defense counsel has a duty under rule 3.3(e) to the court. In addition, the problem has constitutional implications by reason of its potential to deprive a defendant of his right to effective assistance of counsel, and his rights to due process and a fair trial, which include his right to testify in his own defense.

Not unexpectedly, courts have adopted differing standards to determine what an attorney must "know" before concluding that his client's testimony will be perjurious. The standards include the following: "good cause to believe the defendant's proposed testimony would be deliberately untruthful," State v. Hischke, 639 N.W.2d 6, 10 (Iowa 2002); "compelling support," Sanborn v. State, 474 So. 2d 309, 313 n.2 (Fla. App. 1985); "knowledge beyond a reasonable doubt," Shockley v. State, 565 A.2d 1373, 1379 (Del. 1989); a "firm factual basis," United States ex rel. Wilcox v. Johnson, 555 F.2d 115, 122 (3d Cir. 1977); a "good-faith determination," People v. Bartee, 566 N.E.2d 855 (Ill. App.), *cert. denied*, 502 U.S. 1014 (1991); and "actual knowledge," United States v. Del Carpio-Cotrina, 733 F. Supp. 95, 99 (S.D. Fla. 1990) (applying "actual knowledge" standard to require firm factual basis). The judge properly rejected standards that were too lenient (good cause to believe) or too rigid, particularly, the standard sought by the defendant, knowledge beyond a reasonable doubt. The knowledge beyond a reasonable doubt standard essentially would eviscerate rule 3.3(e). That standard, as described by one court, is "virtually impossible to satisfy unless the lawyer had a direct confession from his client or personally witnessed the event in question." The standard would also tend to compel defense attorneys to remain silent in the face of likely perjury that a sharp private warning could nip in the bud. *See* Nix v. Whiteside, 475 U.S. 157, 169 (1986).

The judge correctly settled on the firm basis in fact standard. This standard satisfies constitutional concerns because it requires more than mere suspicion or conjecture on the part of counsel, more than a belief and more information than inconsistencies in statements by the defendant or in the evidence. Instead, the standard mandates that a lawyer act in good faith based on objective circumstances firmly rooted in fact. The lawyer may act on the information he or she possesses, and we decline to impose an independent duty on the part of counsel to investigate because such a duty would be "incompatible with the fiduciary nature of the attorney-client relationship," and is unnecessary when an attorney relies, in significant part, on incriminating admissions made by the client.

b. Under the standard articulated, we are satisfied that the defendant's trial counsel, a lawyer with thirty-five years' experience, acted properly under rule 3.3(e). Contrary to the defendant's contentions, his trial counsel was not faced with mere inconsistent statements. Rather, the defendant initially told his trial counsel that he did not kill the victims, but later stated that he had murdered them.... The defendant's trial counsel was not faced with mere discrepancies in details told to him by the defendant at various times; he was faced with a direct admission from the defendant's own lips combined with substantial evidence produced by the Commonwealth that corroborated the defendant's admission, including the defendant's incriminating conduct and his inculpatory statements to others. The record amply supports the judge's finding that counsel had a firm basis in objective fact for his good faith determination that the defendant intended to commit perjury....

e. It is of no consequence that the defendant's trial counsel informed the judge, in the prosecutor's presence, of his intention to invoke rule 3.3(e). The defendant's trial counsel did not disclose what expected testimony he believed would be perjurious. Had the defendant's trial counsel left the prosecutor out of his discussions with the judge, the defendant's subsequent testimony in narrative form likely would have been met with strong objection from the prosecutor, thereby drawing the jury's attention to the procedure.

f. The narrative form of testimony was properly directed. This approach was adopted by the ABA in 1971. *See* ABA Standards for Criminal Justice 4-7.7 (Approved Draft 1971). Although the ABA later rejected this approach and currently suggests that the lawyer may examine as to truthful testimony, and although the approach has been criticized, *see* United States v. Long, 857 F.2d 436, 446 n.7 (8th Cir. 1988), "the narrative [approach] continues to be a commonly accepted method of dealing with client perjury," Shockley v. State, 565 A.2d 1373, 1380 (Del. 1989). *See* Butler v. United States, 414 A.2d 844, 850 (D.C. 1980); Sanborn v. State, 474 So. 2d 309, 313 & n.3 (Fla. App. 1985); People v. Bartee, 566 N.E.2d 855 (Ill. App. 1991). The defendant suggests that his trial counsel should have conducted a direct examination with respect to the "non-suspect" portions of his testimony and should also have argued the truthful portions of the defendant's testimony in his closing argument. . . . The latter suggestion is impractical, as it may call attention to testimony of the defendant that is not argued by trial counsel, and would likely lead to counsel's making an incoherent final argument. We shall not impose these requirements on counsel. Further, to permit the defendant to make an unsworn statement or his own closing argument, would allow him to do what rule 3.3(e) prohibits his counsel from doing, arguing perjured testimony to the jury. The defendant's testimony was placed before the jury, and his trial counsel made a persuasive, well-reasoned closing argument to the jury. The judge correctly concluded that the defendant was not "denuded" of a defense.

g. The judge reasonably concluded that it was not necessary to conduct a colloquy with the defendant: that the defendant had made a voluntary and knowing waiver of the assistance of counsel with respect to his own testimony; and that the lack of a colloquy did not deprive the defendant of any right. Although the rule does not require a colloquy, the record will not always be as clear as it is in this case. Thus, a judge, if the situation warrants, has discretion to conduct a colloquy at which a defendant is informed of his right to testify and his right to counsel, his attorney's ethical obligation not to place false testimony before the court, and the consequences of his attorney's invocation of rule 3.3(e), namely, that the defendant will testify in narrative form and his counsel will not argue his testimony to the jury in summation.[7] Any colloquy should be carefully controlled and conducted to elicit simple "yes" or "no" answers from the defendant, and, if the defendant expresses doubt or misunderstands, he should be directed to consult with counsel until he fully comprehends what rule 3.3(e) requires.

7. We reject the suggestions in the defendant's brief that the judge should have conducted an evidentiary hearing on whether the defendant's trial counsel had an adequate basis to invoke rule 3.3(e). An evidentiary hearing, at least in these circumstances, poses a strong likelihood that a defense attorney could improperly reveal, directly or indirectly, client confidences in contravention of the rule's requirement that "the lawyer shall not reveal the false testimony to the tribunal." Mass. R. Prof. C. 3.3(e) (1998). Further, an evidentiary hearing would have been premature, as the perjured testimony had not yet occurred. Examination of a defense counsel's "firm factual basis" for invoking the rule usually will be better left, as it was here, for disposition in connection with a motion for a new trial, in which trial counsel, freed from the constraints of preserving confidences, may express the basis for his invocation of rule 3.3(e), and describe his efforts to persuade the defendant to testify truthfully.

A summary of our disposition of this issue is now in order. The duties imposed on a criminal defense lawyer (zealous advocacy, preservation of client confidences, avoidance of a conflict of interest) and the constitutional rights granted a defendant (effective legal representation, opportunity to testify in his own defense, right to a fair trial) are circumscribed by what we demand of honorable lawyers and the core principle of our judicial system that seeks to make a trial a search for truth. The rights of a defendant are not so exclusive that justice can be subrogated to the defendant's perceived interests thereby dismissing or ignoring the interests of victims and the Commonwealth. Perjury, a most serious common-law felony, is antithetical to these values. In Massachusetts it is punishable in a noncapital case by up to twenty years' imprisonment, and in a capital case by possible life imprisonment. . . .

To implement the obligations imposed by rule 3.3(e), when the question of perjured testimony by a defendant arises, we require, as the rule's knowledge element, that the lawyer, before invoking the rule, act in good faith and have a firm basis in objective fact. Conjecture or speculation that the defendant intends to testify falsely are not enough. Inconsistencies in the evidence or in the defendant's version of events are also not enough to trigger the rule, even though the inconsistencies, considered in light of the Commonwealth's proof, raise concerns in counsel's mind that the defendant is equivocating and is not an honest person. Similarly, the existence of strong physical and forensic evidence implicating the defendant would not be sufficient. Counsel can rely on facts made known to him, and is under no duty to conduct an independent investigation.

Once the matter is called to the court's attention, the judge should instruct the lawyer on how to proceed. (In evaluating the situation, the judge will have to rely on the representations of counsel, which of necessity will be cryptic, because counsel is the one who must make the disclosure while maintaining client confidences and allowing for continued zealous advocacy at trial.) Before giving instruction, the judge is not required to hold an evidentiary hearing, to appoint an independent lawyer for the defendant, or conduct a colloquy, although the latter may be appropriate if it appears that the defendant does not clearly understand the situation he has created. It is acceptable for the defendant to testify by means of an open narrative. If the defendant, now informed, moves for appointment of new counsel (and concomitantly, a mistrial), the judge should deny the motions unless the defendant can demonstrate that such motion must be allowed to prevent a miscarriage of justice. No comprehensive canon can be written on all aspects of practical implementation because each case will have its own idiosyncrasies, and the judge cannot then be informed of the details underlying counsel's invocation of rule 3.3(e). The judge possesses considerable discretion to vary any of the procedures discussed, if the interests of justice, or effective management of the trial so requires. As here, full exploration of the ramifications of counsel's invocation of rule 3.3(e) must be postponed until a motion for a new trial, at which time full details may permissibly be revealed.

The judge here anticipated, and followed, these principles (except for the defendant's presence at the sidebar conference), and he properly concluded that the conduct of the defendant's trial counsel fell within the range of reasonable professional response to anticipated client perjury and thus satisfied both rule 3.3(e), and constitutional concerns. . . .

Lawyers' Roles: *Zealous Representation Within the Bounds of the Law*

Several of the cases in this chapter provide dramatic examples of lawyers who underidentified or overidentified with clients. Those who apparently underidentified with clients, like the lawyers in *Perez*, breached fiduciary duties. The lawyers in *Anonymous* and *Pressly* also exhibited this pathology by failing to obey client instructions. The other extreme involves lawyers who apparently overidentified, like the lawyers in *ACC*, and, as a result, were implicated in their client's violations of law. The lawyers in *Casey*, *Forrest*, and *Shaffer Equipment* also fell into this trap and, as a result, facilitated a client crime (*Casey*) and a fraud on the court (*Forrest* and *Shaffer Equipment*).

We pause here to consider the vast majority of lawyers who avoid these extremes. Most of the cases in this chapter reflect most client-lawyer relationships, where lawyers serve their clients well by representing them zealously within the bounds of the law.[1] These lawyers refrained from directive behavior (assuming that they knew what was best) by fulfilling their fiduciary duties and providing zealous representation. At the same time, these lawyers avoided instrumentalism by maintaining a professional objectivity necessary to provide their clients with good legal advice. They were able to recognize definitive legal norms but remained willing to challenge them openly when significant rights of a client were at stake. This is what Judge Noonan calls the "right relation. . . struck most of the time."[2] It is a relation of collaborator, "wise counselor,"[3] or translator, rather than parent or puppet.

Lawyers as Collaborators

Consider first, the lawyers in *Upjohn* and *Swidler & Berlin*. In both cases, they promised confidentiality, used it to generate trust and gain the facts necessary to advise their clients, and then claimed the attorney-client privilege when these facts were sought. In both cases, the Supreme Court thought that the availability of the privilege facilitated the work of the lawyer and protected the client.

Consider second, the lawyers in *Hawkins* and *Purcell*. Each learned facts about a client that indicated a risk of harm to third persons. Hawkins' lawyer did not disclose, either to the court or to others; Purcell's did. Yet both acted appropriately.

In *Hawkins*, the Washington court points out that the lawyer's failure to warn others was not required, since those persons already knew about the potential for dangerous behavior by the client. Further, Hawkins' lawyer did not misrepresent any facts in the bail hearing, and he had no duty to disclose additional facts unless asked. In short, Hawkins' lawyer pursued his client's interests zealously (by seeking his release on bail) within the bounds of the law (by steering clear of fraud on the court and maintaining confidentiality). You may have less sympathy for the lawyer's failure to prevent his client's suicide attempt, but even here, the lawyer acted within the bounds of the law, imperfect though they may have been. As the court indicates, the lawyer's ability to disclose client confidences reached only to future criminal

1. This phrase closely parallels the title of Canon 7 of the Code of Professional Responsibility: "A Lawyer Should Represent a Client Zealously Within the Bounds of the Law."
2. John T. Noonan, Jr., *The Lawyer Who Overidentifies with His Client*, 76 Notre Dame L. Rev. 827, 840 (2001).
3. Lon L. Fuller & John D. Randall, *Professional Responsibility: Report of the Joint Conference*, 44 ABA J. 1159, 1161 (1958).

conduct.[4] Since suicide was not a crime, the only justification for the discretionary disclosure would have been the client's threat to a third party.[5] In any case, it is understandable why Hawkins' lawyer did not disclose. The client was charged with a nonviolent crime and had expressed a desire to be released on bail. All of the information about the client's potential danger came from third parties who did not want him released from custody. Hawkins' lawyer sided with his client, and even accompanied him to two counseling sessions with all of these parties.

Purcell, on the other hand, listened to very credible threats of harm from his own client and realized that the third parties who were likely to be harmed by his client's behavior could not protect themselves. He then exercised his discretion to warn authorities to prevent the harm. But when a court later sought his testimony in order to convict his former client, he protected his client's confidentiality by appropriately asserting the privilege on his client's behalf. The Massachusetts court points out that he too acted within the bounds of the law and zealously protected his client's interests. Note that the result in *Purcell* gives lawyers an incentive to prevent serious harm when efforts to dissuade their clients from harmful conduct prove unsuccessful. Lawyers can act to save lives and at the same time avoid betraying the client's confidence in a subsequent proceeding.

The result in *Chen* also reflects the lawyers' appropriate representation of their clients. These lawyers properly prepared customs disclosures to comply with customs law and avoid litigation, relying on confidential information from their client. The court held that they did not know their client was lying to them and therefore were not involved in furthering their client's criminal conspiracy.[6] Nevertheless, the client's purpose, to use the lawyer's services to further an unlawful scheme, acted to deprive the client of the evidentiary privilege. Whereas in *Purcell*, the client sought legal advice for a lawful purpose (avoiding eviction and discharge from employment), in *Chen*, the clients used the lawyer's services solely to defraud the government.

The disclosures made by the lawyer in *Meyerhofer* also were justified. The securities action against his former client was precipitated by the client's own subsequent SEC filing. Goldberg disclosed the details of his participation in the preparation of the registration statement only after he learned he was about to be joined as a defendant in the case. Further, his disclosure reflected most negatively on his old law firm, which he believed offered defective legal advice to the client, because the contingent liability it advised against disclosing was the law firm's own legal fee. Goldberg, however, remained objective, arguing with the firm about the matter and subsequently leaving the firm when it would not remedy the situation. At that point, he sent his affidavit to the SEC Criminal Fraud Division (to avoid a future crime) and only disclosed it again when another exception to confidentiality (self-defense) justified his disclosure. Goldberg knew these rules well, tried to represent his client competently by providing independent advice that would have avoided the subsequent lawsuit, and acted within the limits of the law when he did disclose some of the facts behind the transaction.

---

4. DR 4-101(C)(3), which allowed lawyers to reveal "the intention of his client to commit a crime and the information necessary to prevent the crime" governed the case.
5. This gap in the rule has been closed by Model Rule 1.6(b)(1), which allows lawyers to disclose information relating to the representation "to prevent reasonably certain death or substantial bodily harm." Model Rule 1.14(c) also classifies these disclosures as impliedly authorized under 1.6(a) if made for the purpose of taking protective action when a client suffers from diminished capacity and is at risk of substantial physical harm.
6. Their lack of knowledge also means that no duty to withdraw was triggered by Model Rule 1.2(d).

Two other examples in this chapter concern lawyers in litigation. The lawyers in *Belge* steered clear of obstructing justice by observing and not actively concealing the buried bodies they discovered. The information was disclosed only after their client blurted it out on the stand. The court holds that their apparent violation of a misdemeanor statute had to give way to the client's Fifth Amendment right. These lawyers not only observed the limits of the law, they also zealously advocated their client's interests throughout the proceeding, by preparing a legally recognized defense (insanity) justified by the facts.

Whiteside's lawyer in *Nix* also investigated the facts, spoke to his client at some length, and prepared a legally recognized defense. When his client switched stories just before trial, he warned Whiteside that he had reached a legal limit, because lawyers cannot present perjured testimony. He did not, however, lose his zeal in defending his client. The trial proceeded with Whiteside's lawyer competently presenting his defense, cross-examining witnesses, and attacking the prosecution's case. Mitchell's lawyer also refused to present perjured testimony, but in every other way offered him zealous representation. Contrast this behavior with that of the EPA lawyers in *Shaffer Equipment*, who, rather than immediately correcting the perjury that had occurred, let the deposition testimony simmer long enough to taint the outcome in the case.

The Collaborative Model

All of these lawyers acted as collaborators with their clients. They did not control or manipulate their clients and observed all of the fiduciary duties the law demands. They acted competently and loyally, communicated with their clients, enabled them to make decisions about the matter, and kept their confidences. At the same time, they did not shirk from clear explanations to clients when the latter's conduct approached legally unacceptable boundaries. When necessary, these lawyers refused to act instrumentally, and told their clients why. They were empathetic, but offered objective advice. They identified enough with their clients to do a good job, but did not become tools of their client's wrongdoing. When they disagreed with a client's proposed conduct, they respected the client enough to remonstrate with the client about the propriety of the client's conduct. When legal competence demanded that they draw a line between their clients' and their own behavior, they did so.

These lawyers realized that, in taking on a client in a collaborative relationship, they had first agreed to share some common interest. It may have been as little as a common interest in making the legal system work appropriately for the client or as much as total belief in the client's point of view. Within this spectrum, these lawyers recognized a duty not to counsel or assist their clients in violating legal norms, civil or criminal. At the same time, these lawyers recognized a duty to defer to the client's determination of goals and course of the representation, as long as the client acted within legal boundaries.[7]

Beyond a common interest, these cases illustrate the mutuality of collaboration. Lawyers assist clients by helping them pursue goals they could not achieve themselves. Clients assist lawyers as well, not only by providing them with a livelihood, but also by giving them the opportunity to exercise their expertise, to be appreciated for making a difference in some small or large way. In order to achieve this, the

---

7. *See* Thomas D. Morgan & Robert W. Tuttle, *Legal Representation in a Pluralist Society*, 63 Geo. Wash. L. Rev. 984, 985 (1995).

lawyers in these cases realized that their clients had a story to tell, one that the lawyer would have to translate into legally recognized language. They needed to be educated by their clients about the client's predicament, and the client's need for legal services.[8] At the same time, these lawyers understood that the law and legal institutions, experienced with similar situations, might force their clients to focus on other issues or competing moral values that needed to be addressed. Therefore, they were prepared to see occasions where they disagreed with clients as opportunities to educate clients about the limits of the law, and if clients did not listen, to extricate themselves from facilitating the client's unlawful behavior.

To consider another way that this collaborative model works beyond the cases in this chapter, Professor James Boyd White invokes the metaphor of lawyers as translators, and invites us to think about it in the context of lawyers for clients who seek a divorce or dissolution of marriage.[9] He reminds us about an empirical study of client-lawyer interactions in divorce cases, which concluded that the clients consistently complained that their lawyers disregarded what the clients told them, especially when they related "who did what to whom."[10] While it is true that good divorce lawyers need to learn about both personal as well as legal dimensions of the client's situation, Professor White offers an alternative explanation for the client's critical assessment of their lawyers: good divorce lawyers understand they have a social role that cannot be reduced simply to meeting all of their client's wishes. The law of marriage dissolution teaches these lawyers that their clients will have to plan realistically for the future, both in economic and relational terms. They know that they will in turn have to educate their clients and divert them from their felt need to express anger and frustration to resolving the future problems they inevitably must face. One of the objectives of good divorce lawyers is to get their clients to "give up the fight, and the claims of right and wrong by which they carry it on" and to move in that direction earlier than they otherwise might.[11]

Similar accounts can be given for almost every kind of law practice. Each client-lawyer relationship brings with it the opportunity to translate the client's desires and moral values into legal categories. It also affords a lawyer the opportunity to gain new insight into the impact of the legal system on a client.[12] The client brings a desire to accomplish some objective, which the lawyer must listen to with care. Lawyers advocate for the client, but also advocate to the client, teaching the client about competing moral values or public policy choices the law has embodied to protect the interests of others.[13] For example, the lawyer who assists a client in a

8. A rich clinical literature explores the art of interviewing and counseling clients. *See, e.g.*, Robert F. Cochran, Jr., John M. A. DiPippa & Martha M. Peteres, *The Counselor-at-Law: A Collaborative Approach to Client Interviewing and Counseling* (Lexis 1999); David A. Binder & Susan C. Price, *Lawyers as Counselors: A Client-Centered Approach* (West 1990); Robert M. Bastress & Joseph D. Harbaugh, *Interviewing, Counseling and Negotiation: Skills for Effective Representation* (Little Brown 1990). *See also* Marcus T. Boccaccini, Jennifer L. Boothby & Stanley L. Brodsky, *Client-Relations Skills in Effective Lawyering: Attitudes of Criminal Defense Attorneys and Experienced Clients,* 26 L. & Psychol. Rev. 97 (2002).

9. James Boyd White, *Translation as a Mode of Thought,* 77 Cornell L. Rev. 1388 (1992).

10. Austin Sarat & William L. F. Felstiner, *Law and Social Relations: Vocabularies of Motive in Lawyer/Client Interaction,* 22 L. & Socy. Rev. 737, 742 (1988).

11. White, *supra* note 9, at 1395.

12. Clark D. Cunningham, *The Lawyer as Translator, Representation as Text: Towards an Ethnography of Legal Discourse,* 77 Cornell L. Rev. 1298 (1992).

13. William F. May, Beleaguered Rulers: The Public Obligation of the Professional 80 (Westminster John Knox 2001).

securities transaction understands that securities law requires certain disclosures to achieve some fairness in market transactions. The same lawyer understands her client's desire to raise money. Both can be met with some effort and collaboration through compromise, though not perhaps in the way the client or the lawyer originally envisioned.

Ultimately, lawyers, like other professionals, listen to clients' stories, translate these client narratives into legal language, and translate law and legal policy back to the client in order to offer guidance. In most cases, lawyers can help a client achieve a legal goal. In some instances, they must inform a client that certain actions cannot be taken or even that certain goals cannot be realized. In each case, they are not only translating the client's desires to the legal system and back again, but they are also acting as private lawmakers, who both influence and are influenced by the law and legal system they function in. To do this well, lawyers must respect each client's moral autonomy, but also help each client understand the moral values and public policy choices embedded in the law itself. The best lawyers also respect their own moral integrity and are willing to deliberate and, if necessary, argue with clients about their goals and interests.

Chapter 6

Loyalty

A. Introduction

This chapter explores another core fiduciary duty, loyalty, which can be traced back several centuries in the law of agency. Loyalty imposes an obligation on lawyers to avoid harm to clients by recognizing and responding to any influences (conflicts of interest) that may interfere with the lawyer's obligation to act in the client's best interests. In the last chapter, we saw that the obligation to maintain client confidences constitutes one facet of the loyalty obligation. This chapter focuses on the principal feature of loyalty: the need to recognize and respond to conflicts of interest created by the lawyer's own interest, the interest of another current or former client or of a third person.

We begin this chapter as we have the other chapters in this section of the book by identifying the client to whom a lawyer owes fiduciary duties. We next turn to consider an additional remedy commonly sought to ameliorate conflicts of interest: judicial disqualification. The bulk of the chapter then addresses the various categories of conflicts of interest that lawyers face. Throughout this material, we find it helpful to address conflicts of interest by following the four-step analysis outlined below.

Conflicts of Interest

1. **Identify the client(s)**
2. **Determine whether a conflict of interest exists. Six categories:**

   A. **Personal Interests of a Lawyer**

General Rule:	1.7(b)	
Specific Rules:	1.8(a)	Business transactions w/clients
	1.8(b)	Use of client information
	1.8(c)	Client gifts to lawyer
	1.8(d)	Literary rights
	1.8(e)	Financial assistance to client
	1.8(h)	Limitation of liability to client
	1.8(i)	Proprietary interest in litigation
	1.8(j)	Lawyer/client sexual relationship
	3.7	Lawyer as witness

B. **Interests of Another Current Client:**

General Rule: 1.7(a)(b)
Specific Rules: 1.8(g), 1.13(g)

C. **Interests of a Third Person**

General Rule: 1.7(b)
Specific Rules: 1.8(f), 5.4(c), 1.13(a)

D. **Interests of a Former Client:**

General Rule: 1.9

E. **Government Lawyers:**

General Rule: 1.11
Specific Rule: 1.12

F. **Imputed Conflicts:**

General Rule: 1.10
Specific Rules: 1.8(k), 1.11, 1.12

3. **Decide whether the conflict is consentable.**
4. **If it is, consult with affected clients and obtain informed consent. (Writing preferred or required.)**

B. Who Is Your Client?

Problem

6-1. Martyn & Fox has been retained by Magnum Industries to defend a products liability action. In-house counsel for Magnum tells Fox that the case is "routine," but she wants to know what to do about the fact that plaintiff's counsel works for a law firm that regularly represents Forest Products, Inc., a wholly owned Magnum subsidiary. Does it make any difference whether Forest Products is a partially owned subsidiary?

Consider: Model Rules 1.7, Comment [34]; 1.13
RLGL §121, Comment d

Lawrence J. Fox

Legal Tender: A Lawyer's Guide to Handling Professional Dilemmas

133-140 (ABA 1995)

Shooting Yourself in the Foot

Roberta Lynn was so pleased with herself. She had just completed a series of depositions in a major case for her most important client, Tranco manufacturing, the largest subsidiary of America's fourth-largest industrial enterprise, United

Amalgamated. The depositions had gone extremely well and for once she looked forward to an upcoming trial, knowing that Abbott Corporation's spurious claim for damages would literally collapse once Roberta has a chance to cross-examine Abbott's CFO, an arrogant, officious fellow whose temper would inevitably come to the surface under Roberta's gentle prodding.

The relationship with Tranco was very important to Roberta, who had been a partner at Butcher & Miller for only three years. She hoped it would impress the management committee of her firm, a difficult task in a firm with 150 partners, particularly if you were in one of the firm's smaller outposts like Austin. Roberta regularly had lunch with the general counsel of Tranco, Jerry Sweet, to see if Butcher & Miller couldn't expand the services it provided this manufacturer of conveyer belts and other nuts-and-bolts industrial equipment. They became good friends and Roberta became a patient listener and confidante as Jerry would share his own professional challenges, which, in some respects, were not unlike Roberta's.

"Can you imagine," Jerry would whine, "here I am, general counsel of a hundred-million-dollar business and I still have to call headquarters to get permission to attend a seminar! I get no appreciation for anything. Last year we saved the parent millions by settling a number of cases and, instead of a thank you, they cut my budget an additional ten percent."

"But they do leave you alone to run your own shop," Roberta consoled Jerry. "You yourself said that on the big issues—selection of counsel, strategy, when to settle—they give you full responsibility."

"That's true, but it's so galling. Everyone around here feels the same way. The parent couldn't be more hands-off in some respects and then they nitpick the minutiae," Jerry continued.

"Sounds familiar to me, Jerry. All the home office in Dallas wants to know is how many billable hours I've logged . . . and that I am not running up any unreimburseable secretarial overtime. Since you guys won't pay for the overtime, I'm in a perfect trap. If I don't get your work done by 5 P.M., I get Dallas or you angry at me."

"Isn't the practice of law glamorous," Jerry responded. "Did any of this occur to you when you were in law school? I'll bet not. Then you were going to be a zealous advocate on behalf of the downtrodden. Now your big issue is the bureaucracy."

"Thank goodness for these professional relationships that permit us to commiserate with one another," Roberta sighed.

It never occurred to Roberta that even that consolation prize would be in jeopardy when she was called by the firm's ethics partner, David Elliot, a week later.

"I have really good news," David began, after the usual pleasantries everyone at Butcher & Miller had come to expect from the patient, gracious, and elegantly handsome Mr. Ethics of the firm. "We've just been retained by Modern Manufacturing to sue United Amalgamated. This is really big. Antitrust implications. Could involve a dozen associates. Budget's $150,000 a month, and that's just for openers."

Roberta was surprised by David's uncharacteristic emphasis on money issues. Elliot usually eschewed such mundane considerations and Roberta was particularly struck by the juxtaposition of the budget numbers with the announcement of a case against the parent of her best client. But before she could give voice to her random initial thoughts, David continued, "I'm calling you because the folks at Modern told us they had no problem with our Austin office doing work for Tranco. Actually, they thought it was helpful that we were willing to bring these serious charges even though we represent the wholly owned subsidiary of the defendant. Lent some credibility, they said."

"But what about Tranco?" Roberta sputtered, now sensing what was coming next.

"What about them," David stated, as if he were not answering Roberta's question with a question.

"Can we sue our client's parent? It makes me uncomfortable. I know you're Mr. Ethics, but it doesn't seem right," Roberta gulped.

"Now, now, my dear," David sounded ever so slightly patronizing," of course there's no problem. I wouldn't have asked Modern if they had a problem if I thought *we* had a problem with Tranco. But you can trust me on this one. Let me explain."

Then followed a ten-minute lecture from David who assured Roberta that "as a courtesy" she ought to call general counsel for Tranco, but that he was sure Tranco would recognize the freedom the Model Rules provided counsel to bring an action adverse to the parent of a client. In one way Roberta was convinced that David was right. But that was more because of the respect she had for him and his articulate and logical approach to the problem than because of the weight of his arguments, for when he was done she still felt sufficiently uneasy that she urged David to join her in calling Jerry Sweet.

"You sound so much more authoritative than I ever will on this issue. If we're both on the line I think Jerry will understand and, that way, I'll have the best chance of keeping Tranco happy," Roberta explained.

"Well, I hardly think that's necessary given your talent as an advocate, but I'll be glad to do so," David replied.

They agreed to call that afternoon, then Roberta got a call from Jerry regarding the Abbott matter, ended up reworking the pretrial memorandum until midnight and it was not until the next day that she was able to find a few minutes to make the call. Roberta went to David's office and she placed the call on his speakerphone.

"Hi, Jerry. It's Roberta," she started.

"You think I don't recognize your cheery voice, Bobbi? Though I can tell you've been sleep-deprived by that pre-trial memo. I can't believe judges require so much detail. Anything to force a settlement, I suppose. Anyway, what's up?"

"I've got you on the speakerphone because I'm calling with my partner David Elliot. You remember David, I think, from the Christmas party. David's a former chairman of the ABA Standing Committee on Ethics and is our ethics maven at Butcher & Miller. I asked David to join me so we could share with you some information and then, if you have any concerns, David can respond wearing his professional responsibility hat," Roberta answered.

"So what is it? Spit it out, Bobbi."

"Butcher & Miller has been asked ...," Roberta stammered, "I mean, Modern Manufacturing has retained our firm...," Roberta still couldn't get a grip. "The defendant is going to be United Amalgamated, well, actually the suit's already been filed, Jerry. We knew there was no problem because of the rules but we thought you should know anyway. It's a courtesy call. We're still going to represent you vigorously, even harder." Roberta's hands went cold and she realized she was running off at the mouth.

"Am I hearing you right, Roberta?" Jerry sounded shocked. "Butcher & Miller has brought a lawsuit against our parent? Without asking consent? You're telling me this after the fact?" Jerry was clearly exercised.

"David'll explain. But there was no need to tell you in advance. David confirmed that for our firm. You can't get more authoritative that that." Roberta was beginning to recover her composure, feeling confident.

"Sure! You guys do something unethical, then get your own partner to confirm it. Sounds fair to me. As fair as suing your own client."

"Now, now, Jerry. Just calm down," Roberta thought David was sounding patronizing as he joined the conversation. "You're surely not arguing that United Amalgamated is our client. We've never dealt with anyone from that company. Our bills go to Tranco. They're paid with Tranco checks. And you're general counsel of Tranco, not United Amalgamated," David intoned.

"Well, you've certainly done your homework on those details, David, but none of that has anything to do with the fact that United Amalgamated is one integrated conglomerate. We're just a profit center for our parent. We all get United Amalgamated stock options and U.A. pensions."

"You're just wrong about this, Jerry," David continued, sounding impatient. "United Amalgamated has Tranco set up as a separate subsidiary. If it chooses to limit its liability in this way, it has to be prepared to suffer the consequences," David summed up.

"I can't believe what I'm hearing. You are prepared to punish your client for using a perfectly legitimate corporate form. You know very well the reason we are a separate unit is purely historical. Besides, since U.A. has an insurance subsidiary, it must be a separate corporation for regulatory purposes. But none of that makes us any less of an integrated enterprise."

"How can you say that, Jerry? Really!" It was Roberta's turn to interject. "You, who spend all your time complaining about how the home office treats you. Sometimes you sound like you'd like to sue United Amalgamated yourself."

"Look, Bobbi," Jerry answered. "I have my gripes with them. Just like your gripes with your executive committee; your firm administrator. But that doesn't mean we're not all one family. I may hate my old man, but I'd never sue him. Y'know what I mean. Let me ask you a question, David. If I represent Chevrolet, can I sue Oldsmobile?"

"Of course not. They're both divisions of the same corporation. Suing Oldsmobile is suing your client," David replied crisply.

"Then the ethics rule you espoused clearly exalts form over substance. We are just as much a part of U.A. as Chevrolet is a part of General Motors. Your just don't get it, David."

David ignored Jerry's General Motors argument and took back the lead. "Perhaps if I explain Model Rule 1.13 to you, Jerry, you will understand. That rule makes it quite clear that when a lawyer represents a corporate client, he or she doesn't represent the officers, the stockholders, or the directors. Indeed, in some cases you may be forced to sue those constituents in fulfilling your duty to your client. It's the same here. We represent Tranco, not its stockholder, United Amalgamated."

"I'm no ethics expert, I admit," Jerry snapped back, "but that's too much. Sure, Rule 1.12 or whatever says that in representing a corporation a lawyer shouldn't make the mistake of confusing the client with these other groups. I worry about that rule all the time as in-house counsel. Everyone thinks I'm his lawyer when, in fact, my client is the corporation, not the plant manager. But that rule is designed to address the situation in which the interest of the constituents and the corporate entity might diverge. In those circumstances, the rule quite correctly states that the lawyer's duty and loyalty is to the entity, not the constituents. However, here we and our parent have the same interest: not to have U.A. get sued. You can't take a position directly adverse to the corporate parent of your own client."

"Well, I hate to rely on our committee's opinions to prove my point, but I am afraid you leave me no choice." David sounded like an exasperated professor with a slow student. "Opinion 91-361 held that when one represents a partnership one does not necessarily represent the partners and Opinion 92-365 held the same with respect to a trade association. If you represent the association you do not thereby represent the members of the association."

Roberta thought David now sounded pompous, but it was only a second until Jerry used that to his advantage. "Held! Your committee *held* something. Come on. You are not the Supreme Court, you know. Just a bunch of superannuated bar association junkies who knew how to wangle an appointment to the committee.

"And as for your opinions, not having ever heard of them, I still have no trouble distinguishing them. After all, I agree if you represent General Motors you can sue a shareholder of GM. But if there is only one general partner in the partnership, I can't imagine that the result would not be different. Here you're suing our *only* shareholder." Jerry was obviously pleased with his response and Roberta was beginning to lose confidence in her senior partner.

David continued undaunted: "Well, I hear you. But I'm not buying. There is nothing you can say, Jerry, that will convince me that if A is my client, A's parent, B, is also my client." David sought to conclude the discussion.

Jerry was silent for a few moments. David and Roberta stared at each other wondering if the exercise was over. "Pardon me," Jerry interrupted the too-long silence. "I was just getting out my Model Rules. Gotta admit it's not my habit to consult them. But I thought I was right. Rule 1.7 says a lawyer cannot undertake a representation that is 'directly adverse to the interest of another client.' Even if United Amalgamated is not your client, suing them sure feels like a representation directly adverse to Tranco."

"Now that's farfetched," said Roberta, sounding too snide and knowing it. "What I mean, Jerry, is whatever impact we have on United Amalgamated is, at best, indirect as to Tranco. After all, you're separate entities." Roberta felt she had recovered.

"Am I hearing my own lawyer say this? Is this a bad dream? Indirect? It's about as indirect as if one of your partners were sued for malpractice. We are one enterprise. We have one consolidated set of financial statements that are filed as part of one Report on Form 10-K with the SEC."

"Now, now, now," it was David's turn. "It's one thing if a lawyer represents a parent and sues the subsidiary. I can see why the parent would object. But the reverse can't be true. Why does the sub care if I sue the parent?"

"You may understand ethics, though I have my doubts now," Jerry responded, "but you sure don't understand business enterprises. When United Amalgamated sneezes, we get chills. Subs are totally dependent on the financial and regulatory health of the parent. If the parent's stock falls, all our options are worthless and it's harder to recruit new employees. If the parent's credit rating is downgraded, it's harder for us to borrow. Our ability to invest in new plant and equipment is totally dependent on the whim of our parent—if it lets us keep earnings or borrow or lends us money we can proceed. If not, we don't." Jerry was not letting go. If anything, he was rising to the challenge.

Roberta thought she had an idea. "Look, all those points just suggest that if the lawyer takes a position adverse to the parent that is really serious, like it might affect the price of the stock, them it's a conflict. But just a regular lawsuit shouldn't count."

"Sounds like a dangerous path to me," Jerry was growing impatient. "If you introduce that concept on suits against a parent, it will only be a few years before you'll say that it's ok to sue your own client if it doesn't hurt too much. I don't know what the world is coming to, but when I was at Caldwell & Moore we were taught you don't take any position adverse to your client. It didn't matter if it was minor. It was a question of loyalty and it still is here at Tranco. That's for sure."

Jerry was now sounding indignant and a bit self-righteous. Roberta was in a panic. This had not gone well at all. David's arguments had fallen flat when presented to a worthy adversary. As she looked across at her revered colleague he appeared more old than distinguished, more troubled than confident. Roberta was ready to throw in the towel, apologize to Jerry for imposing on him, and graciously agree to abandon the case against U.A. As the thought occurred to her, she was already feeling better, knowing that they would be doing the right thing.

"Well then, fire us, Jerry, if you don't agree," said David, shattering Roberta's ruminations. "You're certainly free to dismiss us if you don't agree with our ethics."

Roberta glared at David. What was he doing? Had he gone mad? This client was Roberta's future.

"Fire you? I should say not," Jerry interjected. "Roberta's done a bang-up job on this case. She's an outstanding litigator and we are but weeks from trial. If she weren't such a star, I still wouldn't switch now. No one could get up to speed in such a short period of time. No way! I'm not going to solve *your* problem by replacing Butcher & Miller as counsel. So just go back to your salivating partners, Mr. Ethics, and tell them if you persist in this suit against United Amalgamated, the motion to disqualify will be in the return post and, after it's granted, we'll make sure every reader of the *American Lawyer* knows how you treat your clients!"

With the harsh click of Jerry hanging up rasping over the speakerphone, Roberta looked at David with a mixture of anger and dismay. Whichever way this proceeded, a satisfactory solution would elude Butcher & Miller and Roberta Lynn. Perhaps writing the unfortunate tale for the local bar association magazine would at least alert others in the profession to the dangers that lurked when one attempted to sue the parent of one's client.

C. Remedies

Maritrans GP Inc. v. Pepper, Hamilton & Scheetz

602 A.2d 1277 (Pa. 1992)

PAPADAKOS, J. . . .

Maritrans is a Philadelphia-based public company in the business of transporting petroleum products along the East and Gulf coasts of the United States by tug and barge. Maritrans competes in the marine transportation business with other tug and/or barge companies, including a number of companies based in New York. Pepper is an old and established Philadelphia law firm. Pepper and Messina represented Maritrans or its predecessor companies in the broadest range of labor relations matters for well over a decade. In addition, Pepper represented Maritrans in a complex public offering of securities, a private offering of $115 million in debt, a conveyance of all assets, and a negotiation and implementation of a working capital line of credit. Over the course of the representation, Pepper was paid approximately $1 million for its labor representation of Maritrans and, in the last year of the representation, approximately $1 million for its corporate and securities representation of Maritrans.

During the course of their labor representation of Maritrans, Pepper and Messina became "intimately familiar with Maritrans' operations" and "gained detailed financial and business information, including Maritrans' financial goals and projections, labor cost/savings, crew costs and operating costs." This information was discussed with Pepper's labor attorneys, and particularly with Messina, for the purpose of developing Maritrans' labor goals and strategies. In addition, during the course of preparing Maritrans' public offering, Pepper was furnished with substantial confidential commercial information in Maritrans' possession—financial and otherwise—including projected labor costs, projected debt coverage and projected revenues through the year 1994, and projected rates through the year 1990. Pepper and Messina, during the course of their decade-long representation of Maritrans, came to know the complete inner-workings of the company along with Maritrans' long-term objectives, and competitive strategies in a number of areas including the area of labor costs, a particularly sensitive area in terms of effective competition. In furtherance of its ultimate goal of obtaining more business than does its competition, including the New York-based companies, Maritrans analyzed each of its competitors with Pepper and Messina. These analyses included an evaluation of each competitor's strengths and weaknesses, and of how Maritrans deals with its competitors.

Armed with this information, Pepper and Messina subsequently undertook to represent several of Maritrans' New York-based competitors. Indeed, Pepper and Messina undertook to represent the New York companies in their labor negotiations, albeit with a different union, during which the New York companies sought wage and benefit reductions in order to compete more effectively with, i.e., to win business away from, Maritrans.

In September, 1987, Maritrans learned from sources outside of Pepper that Pepper and Messina were representing four of its New York-based competitors in their labor relations matters. Maritrans objected to these representations, and voiced those objections to many Pepper attorneys, including Mr. Messina. Pepper and Messina took the position that this was a "business conflict," not a "legal conflict," and that they had no fiduciary or ethical duty to Maritrans that would prohibit these representations.

To prevent Pepper and Messina from taking on the representation of any other competitors, especially its largest competitor, Bouchard Transportation Company, Maritrans agreed to an arrangement proposed by Pepper whereby Pepper would continue as Maritrans' counsel but would not represent any more than the four New York companies it was then already representing. In addition, Messina—the Pepper attorney with the most knowledge about Maritrans—was to act not as counsel for Maritrans but, rather, as counsel for the New York companies, while two other Pepper labor attorneys would act as counsel for Maritrans; the attorneys on one side of this "Chinese Wall" would not discuss their respective representation with the attorneys on the other side. Maritrans represented that it agreed to this arrangement because it believed that this was the only way to keep Pepper and Messina from representing yet more of its competitors, especially Bouchard.

Unbeknownst to Maritrans, however, Messina then "parked" Bouchard and another of the competitors, Eklof, with Mr. Vincent Pentima, a labor attorney then at another law firm, at the same time that Messina was negotiating with Pentima for Pentima's admission into the partnership at Pepper. Moreover, notwithstanding Pepper's specific agreement not to represent these other companies, Messina for all intents and purposes was representing Bouchard and Eklof, as he was conducting joint negotiating sessions for those companies and his other four New York clients. On November 5, 1987, Maritrans executives discussed with Pepper attorneys, inter alia, Maritrans' plans and strategies of an aggressive nature in the event of a strike against the New York companies. Less than one month later, on December 2, 1987, Pepper terminated its representation of Maritrans in all matters. Later that month, on December 23, 1987, Pepper undertook the representation of the New York companies. Then, on January 4, 1988, Mr. Pentima joined Pepper as a partner and brought with him, as clients, Bouchard and Eklof. In February, 1988, Maritrans filed a complaint in the trial court against Pepper and Messina.

Discovery procedures produced evidence as follows: (i) testimony by principals of the New York companies to the effect that the type of information that Pepper and Messina possess about Maritrans is of the type considered to be confidential commercial information in the industry and that they would not reveal that information about their companies to their competitors; (ii) testimony by principals of the New York companies that they were desirous of obtaining Maritrans' confidential commercial information; (iii) testimony by principals of the New York companies that labor costs are the one item that make or break a company's competitive posture; (iv) an affidavit from the United States Department of Labor attesting that, contrary to defendant Messina's sworn testimony at the first preliminary hearing in February, 1988, Maritrans' labor contracts are not on file with the Department of Labor and thus not available under the Freedom of Information Act; and other information as well....

[T]he trial court determined that preliminary injunctive relief was both justified and appropriate....

... Concluding that Maritrans was entitled to be able to proceed in its business with confidence that its plans and strategies would not be disclosed or used by Appellees, even inadvertently, the trial court ruled that preliminary injunctive relief was warranted given the existence of material adversity between Maritrans and the New York competitors, of a substantial relationship between the representations, and the fact that Maritrans had carried its burden in proving the necessity for a preliminary injunction.

The Superior Court reversed stating that the trial court erred by issuing a preliminary injunction based upon Pepper's alleged violation of the [Pennsylvania] Rules of Professional Conduct....

The public's trust in the legal profession undoubtedly would be undermined if this Court does not correct the Superior Court's failure to recognize the common law foundation for the principle that an attorney's representation of a subsequent client whose interests are materially adverse to a former client in a matter substantially related to matters in which he represented the former client constitutes an impermissible conflict of interest actionable at law. The Superior

Court's decision is diametrically opposed to law established by the courts of this Commonwealth and throughout the United States which have imposed civil liability on attorneys for breaches of their fiduciary duties by engaging in conflicts of interest, notwithstanding the existence of professional rules under which the attorneys also could be disciplined.

I. ACTIONABILITY AND INDEPENDENT FIDUCIARY DUTY AT COMMON LAW OF AVOIDING CONFLICTS OF INTEREST—INJUNCTIVE RELIEF . . .

Activity is actionable if it constitutes breach of a duty imposed by statute or by common law. Our common law imposes on attorneys the status of fiduciaries vis à vis their clients; that is, attorneys are bound, at law, to perform their fiduciary duties properly. Failure to so perform gives rise to a cause of action. It is "actionable." Threatened failure to so perform gives rise to a request for injunctive relief to prevent the breach of duty.

At common law an attorney owes a fiduciary duty to his client; such duty demands undivided loyalty and prohibits the attorney from engaging in conflicts of interest, and breach of such duty is actionable. As stated by the United States Supreme Court in 1850:

> There are few of the business relations of life involving a higher trust and confidence than those of attorney and client or, generally speaking, one more honorably and faithfully discharged; few more anxiously guarded by the law, or governed by sterner principles of morality and justice; and it is the duty of the court to administer them in a corresponding spirit, and to be watchful and Industrious, to see that confidence thus reposed shall not be used to the detriment or prejudice of the rights of the party bestowing it. Stockton v. Ford, 52 U.S. at 247. . . .

Adherence to those fiduciary duties ensures that clients will feel secure that everything they discuss with counsel will be kept in confidence. . . .

II. AN ATTORNEY'S COMMON LAW DUTY IS INDEPENDENT OF THE ETHICS RULES . . .

Long before the [professional codes] were adopted, the common law recognized that a lawyer could not undertake a representation adverse to a former client in an matter "substantially related" to that in which the lawyer previously had served the client. . . .

As regards misuse of a former client's confidences, the disciplinary rules derive from the lawyer's common law duties, not the other way around.

III. SCOPE OF DUTIES AT COMMON LAW

. . . Attorneys have always been held civilly liable for engaging in conduct violative of their fiduciary duties to clients, despite the existence of professional rules under which the attorneys could also have been disciplined.

Courts throughout the country have ordered the disgorgement of fees paid or the forfeiture of fees owed to attorneys who have breached their fiduciary duties to their clients by engaging in impermissible conflicts of interests. . . .

Courts have also allowed civil actions for damages for an attorney's breach of his fiduciary duties by engaging in conflicts of interest.

Courts throughout the United States have not hesitated to impose civil sanctions upon attorneys who breach their fiduciary duties to their clients, which sanctions have been imposed separately and apart from professional discipline. . . .

IV. EQUITY

Injunctive relief will lie where there is no adequate remedy at law. The purpose of a preliminary injunction is to preserve the status quo as it exists or previously existed before the acts complained of, thereby preventing irreparable injury or gross injustice. A preliminary injunction should issue only where there is urgent necessity to avoid injury which cannot be compensated for by damages. . . .

Pepper and Messina argue that a preliminary injunction was an abuse of discretion where it restrains them from representing a former client's competitors, in order to supply the former client with a "sense of security" that they will not reveal confidences to those competitors where there has been no revelation or threat of revelations up to that point. We disagree. Whether a fiduciary can later represent competitors or whether a law firm can later represent competitors of its former client is a matter that must be decided from case to case and depends on a number of factors. One factor is the extent to which the fiduciary was involved in its former client's affairs. The greater the involvement, the greater the danger that confidences (where such exist) will be revealed. Here, Pepper and Messina's involvement was extensive as was their knowledge of sensitive information provided to them by Maritrans. We do not wish to establish a blanket rule that a law firm may not later represent the economic competitor of a former client in matters in which the former client is not also a party to a law suit. But situations may well exist where the danger of revelation of the confidences of a former client is so great that injunctive relief is warranted. This is one of those situations. There is a substantial relationship here between Pepper and Messina's former representation of Maritrans and their current representation of Maritrans' competitors such that the injunctive relief granted here was justified. It might be theoretically possible to argue that Pepper and Messina should merely be enjoined from revealing the confidential material they have acquired from Maritrans but such an injunction would be difficult, if not impossible, to administer. . . . As fiduciaries, Pepper and Messina can be fully enjoined from representing Maritrans' competitors as that would create too great a danger that Maritrans' confidential relationship with Pepper and Messina would be breached.

Here, the trial court did not commit an abuse of discretion. On these facts, it was perfectly reasonable to conclude that Maritrans' competitive position could be irreparably injured if Pepper and Messina continued to represent their competitors and that Maritrans' remedy at law, that is their right to later seek damages, would be difficult if not impossible to sustain because of difficult problems of proof, particularly problems related to piercing what would later become a confidential relationship between their competitors and those competitors' attorneys (Pepper and Messina). . . . In short, equitable principles establish that injunctive relief here was just and proper. Damages might later be obtained for breach of fiduciary duties and a confidential relationship, but that remedy would be inadequate to correct the harm that could be prevented by injunctive relief, at least until the court could examine the case in greater detail. . . .

The Law Governing Lawyers: *Losing a Client by Disqualification or Injunction*

Maritrans identifies multiple remedies that the law of agency has made available to clients whose lawyers breach fiduciary duties of loyalty or confidentiality. In a famous agency case that has become a classic description of fiduciary duty, then Chief Judge Cardozo explained:

> Many forms of conduct permissible in a workaday world for those acting at arm's length are forbidden to those bound by fiduciary ties. . . . Not honesty alone, but the punctilio of an honor the most sensitive, is then the standard of behavior. As to this there has developed a tradition that is unbending and inveterate. Uncompromising rigidity has been the attitude of courts of equity when petitioned to undermine the rule of undivided loyalty. . . . Only thus has the level of conduct for fiduciaries been kept at a level higher than that trodden by the crowd.[1]

Multiple remedies make clear that the standards of conduct for fiduciaries are kept at this appropriate higher level, consistent with pursuing the best interests of the client. When conflicts of interest have caused harm, clients can bring a malpractice or breach of fiduciary duty claim.[2] They also can seek professional discipline when a violation of the relevant professional code occurs[3] and fee forfeiture.[4] In egregious cases, lawyers have been held criminally accountable as well.[5]

In the past half century, however, courts have examined most conflicts of interest in the context of motions to disqualify lawyers.[6] Often these cases present circumstances like those in *Maritrans*, where harm is threatened but has not yet occurred. *Maritrans* teaches us that clients or former clients can seek injunctive relief to prevent the representation of other clients in transactional representations outside of court. It also makes clear that the breach of a fiduciary duty by one lawyer vicariously disqualifies the entire law firm. Clients, former clients, and other judicial participants can seek similar relief using a disqualification motion in a matter pending before a court.

Injunctive Relief

With respect to the equitable remedy of injunctive relief, the *Maritrans* court first makes clear that ordinary rules concerning injunctions apply. This means that breaches of statute or common law qualify as actionable activity. Since lawyers are fiduciaries, and fiduciaries owe duties of loyalty and confidentially, it follows that agency remedies for breach of fiduciary duty should be available. Injunctive relief is such a remedy, but should only be granted when "there is a urgent necessity to avoid injury" and no adequate legal remedy exists. The facts in *Maritrans* presented just such a case, because Maritrans should not have been forced to wait until damage occurred to stop its former law firm from using its secrets for the benefit of its competitors. To rule otherwise might require them to lose all or part of the company's business before claiming a remedy.[7]

---

1. Meinhard v. Salmon, 164 N.E. 545, 546 (N.Y. 1928).
2. Recall dePape v. Trinity Health Systems, Inc., *supra* p.83, and Perez v. Kirk & Carrigan, *supra* p.125.
3. *See, e.g.,* St. ex rel. Neb. St. Bar Assn. v. Frank, 631 N.W.2d 485 (Neb. 2001) (lawyer who simultaneously represented an insurance company in litigation and another client in a claim against the insurance company publicly reprimanded).
4. *See* The Law Governing Lawyers: Loss of Fee or Other Benefits, *infra* p.291.
5. *See, e.g.,* United States v. Bronson, 658 F.2d 920 (2d Cir. 1981) (mail fraud conviction based on lawyer's conflict of interest).
6. *See, e.g.,* Franklin v. Callum, 782 A.2d 884 (N.H. 2001) (both parties granted disqualification of the other side's lawyer on different legal theories).
7. Of course, if damages had already been caused by the firm's conflict of interest, then Maritrans could seek a remedy at law for the past harm in addition to an equitable remedy to prevent future damage.

Disqualification

Injunctive relief is related to the most common remedy for conflicts of interest: disqualification of lawyers from further participation in a matter pending before a court. Like injunctive relief, disqualification is sought to prevent a lawyer or former lawyer (and that lawyer's current law firm) from representing another client. The party seeking disqualification essentially asks for prophylactic relief from a tribunal, just as Maritrans sought prophylactic relief through injunction in a nonlitigated matter. When granted, disqualification can ensure that the case will be presented without conflicting loyalties or that confidential information of a former client will not be used against that client in the current matter.[8] For example, if Pepper Hamilton had attempted to represent one of Maritrans' competitors against Maritrans in litigation, Maritrans could have asked the court to disqualify its former law firm as a means to prevent the firm's use of its secrets against it in subsequent litigation. We first encountered this remedy in *Meyerhofer* in Chapter 5, and we will see repeated consideration of disqualification as a remedy in the cases in this chapter.

Disqualification motions originated over a century ago as requests for court orders.[9] They are addressed to the inherent power of judges designed to regulate the course of proceedings, through court orders and other relief.[10] Such motions usually are addressed to trial courts, but may be raised in any court where a conflict occurs.[11] The motion to disqualify may be made by the lawyer's client, former client, or any other party to the litigation.[12] Trial judges also are empowered to raise such an issue *sua sponte.*[13] Although a few courts initially thought they had no such power, litigation over the past 50 years has left no doubt that courts can, and should, disqualify lawyers when their conduct threatens the fairness of a judicial proceeding.[14]

While disqualification provides relief from real or serious threats of breaches of loyalty or confidentiality, unlike other remedies, it imposes costs on other parties to a proceeding. When a lawyer is disqualified, the time schedule of a proceeding often must be adjusted to allow the client who has lost a lawyer time to retain new counsel. When the motion to disqualify comes from opposing counsel or the court, clients can be deprived of their chosen lawyers without their consent. For these

8. *Restatement (Third) The Law Governing Lawyers* §6, Comment i.

9. The first case was Gauden v. Ga., 11 Ga. 47 (1852). *See* Kenneth L. Penegar, *The Loss of Innocence: A Brief History of Law Firm Disqualification in the* Courts, 8 Geo. J. Legal Ethics 831, 832 (1995).

10. *Restatement (Third) The Law Governing Lawyers* §6, Comment i. *See also* The Limits of the Law: Court Orders, *supra* p.144.

11. *See, e.g.,* Williams v. St., 805 A.2d 880 (Del. 2002) (appellate counsel disqualified for positional conflict of interest). Appellate courts review disqualification decisions of trial courts using an abuse of discretion standard. *See, e.g.,* People ex rel. Dept. of Corporations v. Speedee Oil Change Sys., Inc. 980 P.2d 371, 378 (Cal. 1999).

12. Ronald E. Mallen & Jeffrey Smith, *Legal Malpractice* §16.15 (5th ed. 2000).

13. This may be especially likely to occur in criminal cases, where judges assume special responsibility for the fairness of the proceeding. *E.g.,* Fed. R. Crim. P. 44(c) (federal district courts required to inquire into any proposed joint representation); Cuyler v. Sullivan, 446 U.S. 335 (1980) (trial judge has important role in assuring fairness of trial of joint defendants).

14. *E.g.,* Ennis v. Ennis, 276 N.W.2d 341, 348 (Wis. App. 1979). Administrative law judges also exercise this power in appropriate circumstances. *See, e.g.,* Prof. Reactor Operator Socy. v. United States NRC, 939 F.2d 1047 (D.C. Cir. 1991) (Administrative Procedure Act's right to counsel guarantee requires concrete evidence that counsel's presence would impede its investigation in order to exclude a lawyer from representing a subpoenaed witness); SEC v. Csapo, 533 F.2d 7 (D.C. Cir. 1976) (same standard required for similar SEC rule granting agency authority to disqualify lawyers); In re Scioto Broadcaster, 5 FCC Rcd. 5158 (1990) (FCC review board and Commission will intervene only in cases of clear conflicts of interest).

reasons, courts recognize that motions to disqualify can be used to tactical advantage by opposing parties in litigation. Courts have responded in three ways to this potential for misuse of the court's power.

First, as we will see in this chapter, courts are careful to scrutinize the facts and law offered in support of disqualification motions. Second, courts increasingly use the doctrine of laches, estoppel, or waiver to deny motions to disqualify when they have not been made timely.[15] Third, orders granting or denying disqualification usually are not appealable until a final judgment on the merits.[16] This means that where disqualification is denied, the targeted lawyer may continue the representation, but the other side can raise the issue on appeal. On the other hand, if the motion is granted, the client represented by the now disqualified lawyer is forced to find new counsel.[17] If that client settles or wins the case, the disqualified lawyer has no independent right to appeal. Only if the client loses the case can the issue be raised on appeal.

The Relevance of Lawyer Codes

In assessing whether a lawyer should be disqualified, courts begin with the relevant conflict of interest rules in the relevant professional code or case law.[18] If lawyer code rules have been violated, disqualification commonly follows, because, as *Maritrans* teaches, the relevant professional rules derive from the lawyer's common law duties. A few courts impose an additional requirement, explicitly limiting disqualification to breaches of the relevant lawyer code conflict of interest provisions that would "taint" the trial.[19] Perhaps because it has faced the greatest number of disqualification motions, the Second Circuit adopts this "restrained approach" to disqualification motions, both to promote judicial economy and because it prefers "disciplinary machinery" for "less serious allegations of ethical impropriety."[20] More typical is the Fifth Circuit, which explicitly rejects this "hands-off approach," finding that "a motion to disqualify counsel is the proper method for a party-litigant to bring the issues of conflict of interest or breach of ethical duties to the attention of the court."[21]

Where the lawyer code rules have been violated, the Fifth Circuit approach makes sense because the lawyer should have recognized the conflict and responded by withdrawing from the representation that created it. Granting a disqualification motion simply requires the lawyer to do what she already should have done—move to withdraw under Rule 1.16(a)—in order to avoid a violation of the professional code.[22] A more difficult situation is presented when a potential or threatened

15. *See, e.g.*, Universal City Studios, Inc. v. Reimerdes, *infra* p.296.
16. In the federal courts, an order granting or denying disqualification cannot be appealed until a final judgment on the merits has been reached. Richardson-Merrell Inc. v. Koller, 472 U.S. 424 (1985); Flanagan v. United States, 465 U.S. 259 (1984); Firestone Tire & Rubber v. Risjord, 449 U.S. 368 (1981). State courts are split on this issue. *See* David B. Harrison, *Appealability of State Court's Order Granting or Denying Motion to Disqualify Attorney*, 5 A.L.R.4th 1251 (1981).
17. Successor counsel will usually be allowed to use the disqualified lawyer's work product if it does not contain impermissible client confidential information. *Restatement (Third) The Law Governing Lawyers* §6, Comment i.
18. In some situations such as bankruptcy, statutory provisions impose additional conflict of interest standards. *See, e.g.*, In re Leslie Fay Companies, 175 B.R. 525 (Bankr. S.D.N.Y. 1994).
19. Armstrong v. McAlpin, 625 F.2d 433 (2d Cir. 1980), *vacated on other grounds*, 449 U.S. 1106 (1981).
20. *See* The European Community v. RJR Nabisco, Inc., 134 F. Supp. 2d 297, 303 (E.D.N.Y. 2001) (reviewing Second Circuit decisions).
21. *See* In re American Airlines, Inc., 972 F.2d 605, 611 (5th Cir. 1992).
22. *See, e.g.*, Williams v. St., 805 A.2d 880 (Del. 2002) (trial counsel's motion to withdraw as appellate counsel granted due to a conflict created by previous Supreme Court argument).

violation of the rules appears in a case. Then, courts look to seriousness of the potential violation and the likelihood that it will affect the fairness of the matter before the court. Relief will be denied unless the possibility of an injury to a party or the fairness of the proceeding can be shown.[23]

It is important to remember that injunctive relief and disqualification are just two of the many remedies that may be pursued by clients who allege that a conflict of interest taints their lawyer's responsibilities. Although disqualification motions are the most common remedy sought by clients and former clients to redress conflicts of interest, *Maritrans* illustrates that other remedies, including civil damages, fee forfeiture, dismissal of a claim or defense, and professional discipline also exist.[24] The potential for each of these remedies will occur throughout the materials in this chapter. Each remedy carries its own legal requirements, but multiple remedies may exist for the same breach of fiduciary duty. One thing is certain: lawyers today have to worry about more than malpractice suits and professional discipline. They also realize that injunctive relief or disqualification may be granted to an opposing party, involuntarily depriving them of the opportunity to represent a client, as well as exposing them to potential liability and loss of compensation.

D. Personal Interests of the Lawyer

Problems

6-2. Should Martyn & Fox agree to accept one third of the shares of stock issued in a new business start-up in lieu of an hourly fee?

6-3. Should Martyn & Fox insert a clause in all of its estate planning documents that appoints a Martyn & Fox lawyer as the fiduciary (executor, administrator or personal representative) of an estate or trustee of a trust? When our lawyers act as fiduciary or trustee, may they hire Martyn & Fox as counsel for the trust or estate?

6-4. Should Martyn & Fox provide free legal services to a criminal defendant who agrees to grant us the movie rights to his story?

6-5. Our client is worried she'll have to settle her case early and for too little in order to survive financially. Should Martyn & Fox pay her living expenses through trial?

6-6. Martyn & Fox failed to file a client's case within the appropriate statute of limitations. Should Martyn sit down with the client, confess her error, and offer to pay the entire amount of the underlying claims?

6-7. Martyn & Fox represents Acme Corp. in contested litigation against Zenon Inc. Can a senior associate assume a major role in the case when he is married to the lead lawyer for Zenon?

---

23. *See, e.g.,* United States v. Kitchin, 592 F.2d 900, 903 (5th Cir.), *cert. denied*, 444 U.S. 843 (1979) (lawyer may be disqualified "only where there is a reasonable possibility that some specifically identifiable ethical impropriety actually occurred, and, in light of the interests underlying the standards of ethics, the social need for ethical practice outweighs the party's right to counsel of his choice"); Bd. of Education v. Nyquist, 590 F.2d 1241, 1246 (2d Cir. 1979) (conflict must "taint the trial"); In re Infotechnology, Inc., 582 A.2d 215, 216 (Del. 1990) (conflict must "adversely affect . . . the fair and effective administration of justice").

24. *See Restatement (Third) The Law Governing Lawyers* §6.

6-8. Client tells Martyn & Fox that he is strapped for cash and cannot afford our requested retainer in a divorce case. Can Martyn & Fox have Client sign a promissory note secured by a mortgage on the family home in lieu of the retainer?

6-9. Martyn & Fox represents Big Bank in a wide variety of matters. A colleague tells Fox at lunch: "Did you hear the latest? Sarah Snyder [an associate at Martyn & Fox] is dating the General Counsel of Big Bank."

Consider: Model Rules 1.7, 1.8, 1.10
Model Code DR 4-101(B), 5-101, 5-104, and 6-102
Cal. Rules 3-120, 3-320, 4-210; D.C. Rule 1.8(d); N.Y. Rule DR 5-111
RLGL §6

Monco v. Janus

583 N.E.2d 575 (Ill. App. 1991)

Justice BUCKLEY delivered the opinion of the court:

In February 1987, plaintiff Dean Monco (Monco) petitioned to dissolve on the grounds of deadlock JI-SCO-NI Enterprises, Inc. (Jisconi), an Illinois corporation, owned 50% each by Monco and defendant Ronald Janus (Janus). Jisconi's sole asset is its ownership of patent rights to an invention which Monco and Janus had assigned to Jisconi. Janus counter-claimed against Monco seeking to vacate the assignment and to compel Monco to turn over the Jisconi shares he owned on the grounds that the invention was Janus' idea, that Monco was Janus' personal attorney, and that the assignment and Monco's stock ownership in Jisconi were the result of Monco's undue influence and breach of fiduciary duty to Janus....

On October 4, 1989, the circuit court of Cook County dismissed Janus' counterclaim holding that, while an attorney-client relationship existed and a breach of fiduciary duty had occurred, Janus knowingly ratified his dealings with Monco....

... The record shows that Janus is a college graduate, a certified teacher, and the sole proprietor of his own landscaping business for over 17 years. Monco is an attorney admitted to practice in Illinois and before the United States Patent and Trademark Office. Monco is also a shareholder in a Chicago law firm.

Prior to the transaction in question, Janus and Monco had been social acquaintances since 1970. In 1981 and 1984, Janus contacted Monco to discuss possible patentable ideas. These ideas were not pursued. In the spring of 1985, Monco engaged Janus to perform landscaping services for his home. On Memorial Day weekend, while performing such services, Janus sat down with Monco at Monco's kitchen table and drew a sketch of an idea for a beverage container to be worn around the neck of the user. The contents of the conversation which next transpired is disputed by the parties and nothing in writing exists to verify either party's version of the agreement.

Janus testified that after Monco told him that his idea was fantastic, Janus asked Monco if he was interested in pursuing the idea together. Janus told Monco that Monco could help him with the idea and share in any profits. Janus testified that he and Monco agreed to share expenses equally and that Monco would provide business contacts and free legal services to the venture. Janus denied that Monco told him to obtain independent legal advice and denied that he and Monco were "50/50" partners.

Monco testified that Janus specifically asked him to go into business and offered Monco a 50% interest in the venture. Monco accepted Janus' offer and the two shook hands. Monco testified they discussed various matters, including licensing the patent to a manufacturing concern, from which they would receive royalties, versus assigning the patent to a separate corporation owned by them equally, which would avoid personal liability but would require business capital and marketing. Monco testified that he specifically advised Janus to obtain outside counsel to make sure that Janus' interests were represented. Janus agreed. Monco's wife, who was present for much of the conversation, corroborated Monco's testimony.

Significantly, at the kitchen table meeting, or any time thereafter, Monco admitted that he never advised Janus that if Janus were to assign the patent to a jointly-owned corporation, Janus would lose exclusive control over the patent in the event of corporate dissolution. In such situation, Janus and Monco as co-owners of the patent would have equal rights to market the patent without accounting to the other for profits. Monco also testified that he did not inform Janus of the option of licensing the patent to Jisconi as opposed to a full assignment. Monco explained that Janus was not his client and that anything less than a full assignment to a jointly-owned company would be inconsistent with their agreement to be "50/50" partners.

In the summer months following the "kitchen table" meeting, Janus and Monco communicated by telephone and letter and exchanged ideas on numerous matters involving the beverage container, including what entity would be best for liability and tax purposes. Ultimately, the parties agreed to incorporate and name the entity using the first names of their children. Monco also suggested and conducted a "prior art" search to determine if Janus' idea was patentable. Based on the results of this search, Monco concluded and Janus agreed that a patent application was appropriate.

On September 19, 1985, Janus and Monco met with Mark Fine, an attorney and friend of Monco, about incorporating Jisconi. Fine prepared draft articles of incorporation and testified that Monco and Janus told him that they were equal partners in the new business; Fine heard nothing during this conversation to indicate to him that Monco and Janus were anything other than business partners. Fine also testified that he advised Janus to obtain independent counsel to prepare a buy/sell and shareholders' agreement in order to protect Janus' interests. Janus' recollection about this meeting conflicted with Fine's. Janus denied ever discussing anything regarding specific ownership interests, and he could not remember Fine's advice to obtain independent counsel.

After the meeting with Fine, Janus asked Monco to prepare the incorporation papers. Monco was reluctant to prepare these papers because he did not practice corporate law. However, using Fine's draft, Monco prepared the papers and forwarded them to Janus for his review and signature. Janus admitted that Monco told him to have his own counsel review the papers but Janus never did. Janus testified that he considered Monco his attorney and thought that Monco would assure that Janus' interests were protected. Jisconi was incorporated on October 2, 1985.

Following the incorporation of Jisconi, Monco prepared the initial patent application for the beverage container. The application, related documents, and the assignment of the patent to Jisconi were forwarded to Janus for his review. Monco testified that he again told Janus to have his own counsel review the documents, but Janus denied ever receiving this advice. On October 28, 1985, without the aid of independent counsel, Janus executed the parent patent application and an initial assignment. Monco filed the parent patent application and related documents on November 12, 1985....

On July 30, 1986, Monco wrote Janus and addressed several subjects, including a proposed shareholders' agreement which Monco had previously drafted and ... also stated that, as he had told Janus on several occasions since forming Jisconi, Janus should obtain independent counsel to review the agreement as well as other matters connected with Jisconi. This was the first time in writing that Monco advised Janus to obtain independent counsel. Neither Janus nor Anthony Vaccarello, an attorney retained shortly thereafter by Janus, raised any concerns about the statements in the letter....

On August 5, 1986, Vaccarello wrote Monco and identified himself as Janus' counsel regarding the proposed shareholders' agreement. In this letter, Vaccarello requested certain corporate documents, including any pre-incorporation agreements, shareholders' meeting minutes and certificates, and directors' resolutions and minutes.

On August 9, 1986, without Vaccarello's presence, Monco and Janus met at Monco's office to sign numerous corporate documents including the documents that Vaccarello requested. In particular, Janus and Monco executed a shareholders' resolution setting forth their original agreement that they each would assign all patent rights to Jisconi; that Monco would prepare the patent applications; and that Monco and Janus would equally share the expenses of the business. Monco and Janus also executed share certificates showing each to own 500 shares of Jisconi stock and meeting minutes of the first shareholders' meeting formally designating themselves as Jisconi's sole directors. Monco and Janus dated these documents as of November 1, 1985, to conform the written record to their agreement as of the time of incorporation. Janus gave the executed documents to Vaccarello; neither Janus or Vaccarello objected to the documents at any time thereafter.

Beginning in late summer, Janus began to voice objections to Monco. ... These differences soon led to a total breakdown in the parties' relationship. In early September, a meeting was held between Monco. and Janus and their respective counsel in an attempt to resolve the deadlock. The meeting was only partially successful. However, despite the parties' differences, on September 29, 1986, Janus executed an application for a design patent and another assignment of all patent rights to Jisconi. Neither Janus, ... or Vaccarello objected.

In December 1986, Janus arranged a meeting with Monco in an attempt to resolve the deadlock.... The parties remained deadlocked.

Monco initiated this lawsuit by filing his petition to dissolve Jisconi in February 1987. Janus counterclaimed in June 1987 alleging undue influence, overreaching and Monco's failure to inform Janus that, upon Jisconi's dissolution, each party could get 100% of the non-exclusive rights to market the patent and keep profits without accounting to the other. Janus alleged that he did not know this legal consequence, as it was a peculiarity of the patent laws, and requested as relief that the assignment to Jisconi be vacated, that Monco's 50% interest in Jisconi be forfeited as an excessive fee, and that damages be awarded.

In July 1988, Monco filed a motion for summary judgment on Janus' counterclaim ... [where he] claimed that he was acting as Janus' business partner and not as his attorney....

The first issue we address is whether a client's subsequent conduct can cure an attorney-client transaction which is the product of the attorney's undue influence. This is an issue of first impresssion in Illinois.

Transactions between attorneys and clients are closely scrutinized. When an attorney engages in a transaction with a client and is benefited thereby, a presumption arises that the transaction proceeded from undue influence. Once a presumption is raised, the burden shifts to the attorney to come forward with evidence that the transaction was fair, equitable and just and that the benefit did not proceed from undue influence. Because a strong presumption of undue influence arises when an attorney engages in a transaction with a client and is benefited thereby, courts require clear and convincing evidence to rebut this presumption. . . . Some of the factors the courts deem persuasive in determining whether the presumption of undue influence has been overcome include a showing by the attorney (1) that he or she made a full and frank disclosure of all relevant information; (2) that adequate consideration was given; and (3) that the client had independent advice before completing the transaction. (McFail v. Braden, 166 N.E.2d 46, 52 (Ill. 1960)). Once the presumption has been rebutted, the burden of production and persuasion is again on the client to show undue influence.

Initially, we agree with the circuit court that an attorney-client relationship existed between Monco and Janus. The evidence supports that Monco was acting as the attorney for Jisconi as well as for both himself and Janus. While the evidence also shows that Monco and Janus were business partners, Monco's role as Janus' partner does not foreclose the conclusion that Monco was also Janus' personal attorney.

We also agree with the circuit court that Monco entered into a beneficial business transaction with Janus. Accordingly, under relevant supreme court precedent, Monco was required to prove by clear and convincing evidence the three *McFail* factors. We agree that Monco failed to meet his burden.

Under the first factor, it cannot be readily disputed that Monco failed to give Janus a "full and frank disclosure of all relevant information" prior to Janus making the first assignment of all his rights in the patent to Jisconi. Monco admitted at trial that he did not learn of the effect of Jisconi's dissolution under the patent laws until shortly before he filed his petition for dissolution in February 1987. Thus, there is no way Monco could have timely given Janus the required information.

Under the second factor, Monco did not present clear and convincing evidence to show that he gave adequate consideration to support the 50% ownership interest in Jisconi he received. Admittedly, Monco was the "brains" behind taking the appropriate measures to assure that Janus' idea became patented and that the idea was marketed profitably. In this regard, Monco spent, as he testified, hundreds of hours of his own time working on Jisconi matters. While Monco worked on Jisconi at a time when he was fully compensated by his firm, Monco testified that his work on Jisconi prevented him from billing firm clients which in turn contributed to a lower yearly salary. Aside from the legal and nonlegal time Monco contributed towards Jisconi, the record shows that Monco contributed over $13,000 in capital contributions. These expenses were never reimbursed by Jisconi. Moreover, Monco fronted Janus' one-half of the expenses from time to time when Janus became unable to pay his share.

Notwithstanding the above consideration contributed by Monco, we agree that it was not clear and convincing evidence of adequate consideration. Monco's 50% interest gave him an equal voice in Jisconi affairs. If Janus and Monco disagreed, Monco's interest gave him the ability to deadlock Jisconi's affairs and potentially hold Janus hostage. It must be remembered that this extreme leverage was given to Monco at a time when an attorney-client relationship existed. More importantly, the beverage container idea originated with Janus. Even in Monco's opinion, the idea had great money-making potential. We agree that Monco's labor and capital contributions were not adequate consideration to support the benefits which Monco could ultimately reap.

As for the third factor, the record shows that Janus did not have independent counsel before executing the first assignment. According to Janus, at this stage of their relationship, Monco was his personal attorney and was looking out for his interests. Although Monco advised Janus to have independent counsel to look over his work, this advice was insufficient. Janus' trust in Monco was great. The two had been personal acquaintances since 1970, and Janus had consulted Monco on two prior occasions regarding other patentable ideas. In light of Janus' extreme trust in Monco, Monco's suggestion that Janus have someone look over his work was insufficient to satisfy Monco's obligation to assure that Janus had independent counsel before executing the assignment.

As the foregoing analysis shows, we agree that Monco failed to rebut the presumption of undue influence. Accordingly, we next focus on Monco's affirmative defense of ratification. . . .

The fact that attorney-client transactions are voidable and not void supports our conclusion that in certain situations, a client's post-transaction conduct can properly amount to an affirmance of that transaction notwithstanding that it is the product of the attorney's undue influence. To hold otherwise would, in our opinion, unsettle attorney-client transactions despite an attorney's reasonable reliance that the transaction was a "done deal." Moreover, to hold otherwise would contradict settled principles of traditional contracts and trusts law relating to ratification. . . .

. . . During its analysis, the circuit court initially concluded that Monco had failed to present clear and convincing evidence as to any of the three *McFail* factors. In its ratification analysis, the circuit court . . . conclude[d] that Janus' ratification occurred with the benefit of independent counsel and full knowledge of the effect the patent laws had on an assignment of a patent to a jointly owned corporation which later dissolved.

Our disagreement with the circuit court's ratification analysis is that the court failed to address for the second time whether the Monco-Janus transaction was fair. . . . As we have stated, the fairness of the transaction is a separate and indispensable inquiry to a ratification analysis of an attorney-client transaction. Because we conclude that the Monco-Janus transaction is unfair, we hold that the affirmative defense of ratification is unavailable to Monco.

As previously discussed, Monco did not present clear and convincing evidence that he gave adequate consideration to support the 50% interest he received in the patent. Monco has not directly appealed this finding and, in any event, it is supported by the manifest weight of the evidence. Even when all of the benefits Monco conferred are taken together, we believe they are out of all proportion to the 50% interest he received and the corresponding rights associated with a shareholder holding such interest. Accordingly, for these reasons, the circuit court erred in dismissing Janus' counterclaim. . . .

The unfairness of the transaction, and this court's duty to set it aside, is made even more clear in light of the Code of Professional Responsibility. This court has found the Canons of Ethics within the Code a relevant consideration in malpractice actions between attorney and client. . . .

Rule 5-104(a) prohibits a lawyer from entering a business transaction with a client if they have conflicting interests therein and if "the client expects the lawyer to exercise his professional judgment therein for the protection of the client, unless the client has consented after full disclosure." Here, the initial assignment of Janus' patent rights to Jisconi and Monco's 50% interest therein allowed Monco to deadlock Jisconi. At the same time as the assignment, Janus expected Monco to exercise professional judgment on his behalf. Monco's representation of Janus and his ownership interest in Jisconi cannot be reconciled, as Monco's position in this case makes apparent. Janus was never informed on these matters, nor for that matter, of his right to expect under the Canons Monco's zealous representation of his interests and Monco's exercise of independent professional judgment on his behalf.

In summary, we conclude that the circuit court erred in dismissing Janus amended counterclaim. . . .

In re Halverson

998 P.2d 833 (Wash. 2000)

En Banc. . . .

IRELAND, J. . . .

Lowell K. Halverson has been a member of the WSBA in private practice since 1968, concentrating on family law for the last 20 years. He has lectured and published extensively in this area. From 1990-91, Halverson served as president of the WSBA.

Although Halverson has been married to his wife, Diane, since 1964, he admits that since the early 1970s he has had consensual sexual relationships with six different female clients. Five of these clients retained Halverson as their attorney before the sexual relationship began. The most recent of these relationships was with Lisa Wickersham, the grievant in this action. Halverson first met Wickersham in 1989 when Wickersham accompanied a friend to Halverson's office. At this point, Wickersham was married to an attorney, Neil Sarles.

During this office visit, Halverson gave Wickersham and her friend a personality questionnaire that he regularly used with clients; he also asked Wickersham if she might like to work in his office on a special project involving artwork. Following this meeting, Wickersham worked at Halverson's office for a few months until early in 1990.

Wickersham retained Halverson as her attorney in May 1991, at which time Halverson administered another personality questionnaire. . . . Halverson filed a dissolution petition on her behalf in June 1991, and Wickersham moved out of her husband's house in early July.

Later in July while at Halverson's office, Wickersham confided to him that she was "attracted to [her] attorney." . . . Shortly thereafter, following a successful court appearance, Halverson took Wickersham on a tour of photographs displayed at the Rainier Club in Seattle. According to Halverson, while on the tour, Wickersham suggested that they get a room, but Wickersham denies this occurred.

Both agree, however, that after the tour they went to a restaurant on the waterfront where they expressed a mutual attraction and discussed Halverson's "ground rules" for a potential relationship: Halverson's wife could not find out about the affair and there could be no bonding between Halverson and Wickersham's young daughter. According to Halverson, he explained to Wickersham that a potential relationship between them would not be of any significance to the pending divorce action if these "ground rules" were followed. Wickersham herself recognized the need for them to be discreet because of Halverson's high profile as president of the WSBA.

Halverson, however, did not advise Wickersham of the possible ramifications if the relationship were to become known. For example he did not tell her that, if Sarles were to discover the relationship, he would most likely become less willing to compromise in the divorce proceeding and that this would increase the complexity and cost of the dissolution and could impact the custody determination. Neither did Halverson advise Wickersham that either his wife's or Sarle's discovery of the affair could lead to his withdrawal as her attorney. . . .

. . . For the next six months, Wickersham and Halverson maintained a sexual relationship seeing each other whenever they could.

On January 1, 1992, Halverson's wife discovered the affair. Within a few days, Halverson withdrew as Wickersham's attorney because he felt that he had lost his objectivity and could no longer keep his roles separate, particularly in view of his wife's position as his office manager.

Halverson temporarily moved out of his home and continued his personal relationship with Wickersham for several weeks. In mid-February, however, Halverson told Wickersham that he was returning to his wife.

Meanwhile, Halverson provided Wickersham with the names of several other attorneys who could take over her case. Although Wickersham wanted Halverson to continue as her attorney, he refused, and Wickersham, thus, hired another attorney, Eric Watness, to complete her dissolution. Halverson transferred the balance of Wickersham's account to Watness and wrote off her outstanding bill to him. There is no evidence that Halverson at any time revealed any client confidences or otherwise used information obtained from Wickersham. . . .

. . . Watness represented Wickersham until September 1992, when her case settled and a decree of dissolution was entered. Overall, Watness felt Wickersham received a "fair outcome" in her case.

A year later in October 1993, Wickersham complained to the WSBA about Halverson's conduct and, in 1994, filed a civil lawsuit. Wickersham's civil suit against Halverson settled in 1995 by sealed agreement for a substantial sum and with no admission of liability. Wickersham's former husband subsequently sued Wickersham and received one-half of the settlement.

The WSBA filed a formal complaint against Halverson in February 1997. Following proceedings in December 1997 and February 1998, the hearing officer issued findings of fact and conclusions of law and recommended a sanction consisting of six months' suspension and two years' probation with the conditions that Halverson disclose to female clients the purpose of his discipline and continue treatment with his mental health physician. . . .

Halverson challenges several of the Board's factual findings. . . .

. . . [T]he record is clear that Wickersham depended upon Halverson regarding temporary living arrangements, custody of her daughter, and a favorable property division in her dissolution action.

As to the power imbalance, an experienced family law practitioner testified to the inherent power imbalance in a dissolution attorney-client relationship. In addition, Dr. Laura Brown, a psychologist who studies sexual relationships between clients and professionals, testified that Halverson's administration of personality tests to Wickersham "added a more psychological aura to what he was doing" and, therefore increased "the risk of harm because the power differential was greater." According to Dr. Brown, Halverson's status as Wickersham's former employer further contributed to a power differential.

... [T]he testimony that Wickersham received a "fair outcome" in her dissolution proceeding does not undermine the substantial testimony from mental health professionals that as a result of Halverson's conduct, Wickersham suffered personal harm in the form of depression and anxiety. In addition, Wickersham's relationship with Halverson had an adverse impact upon her relationship with her former husband. In the years following the divorce, Wickersham described the relationship as "brutally adversarial; abusive and emotionally and financially difficult." Further, after her relationship with Halverson, Wickersham was unable to trust her new attorney....

... Halverson's admission to sexual relationships with five prior clients clearly supports the finding that he knew or should have known the risks of such relationships, particularly because one of these relationships resulted in a fee dispute where the client threatened to disclose the details of the relationship to Halverson's wife unless Halverson wrote off his bill.

Further, Halverson's book, *Divorce in Washington: A Humane Approach*,[5] discouraged those involved in a dissolution from getting involved in a new sexual relationship. A section in the Washington *Family Law Deskbook* of which Halverson was editor and chief,[6] and the written materials for a Continuing Legal Education course at which Halverson spoke, both discussed the potential adverse ramifications of an attorney-client sexual relationship, as did three prominent family law attorneys who testified.

Where the evidence conflicted as to the potential effect of the Wickersham/Halverson affair upon Wickersham's dissolution proceeding, the hearing officer was entitled to credit the testimony of those experts who testified that the affair increased the legal risks to Wickersham....

II. LEGAL CONCLUSIONS....

A. Violation of RPC 1.7(b)...—Duty to Avoid Conflicts of Interest

"RPC 1.7(b) generally prevents a lawyer from representing a client if that representation will be materially limited by the lawyer's own interests unless the lawyer reasonably believes the representation will not be affected and the client consents in writing."... Halverson concedes no written consent was obtained, but argues that this was merely a technical violation of the rule. We disagree.

It was not objectively reasonable for Halverson to believe that the representation would not be adversely affected by the sexual relationship, nor did Halverson disclose to Wickersham the risks involved or the material implications of the sexual relationship upon the dissolution proceeding. Consequently, Halverson's failure to obtain written consent was more than a mere technical violation of the rule.

Halverson should have known that discovery of the affair could worsen the

5. Lowell K. Halverson & John W. Kydd, *Divorce in Washington: A Humane Approach* (1985).
6. Wash. St. Bar Assn., *Family Law Deskbook* §3.9 (1989).

relationship between Wickersham and Sarles and, thus, unnecessarily complicate the dissolution proceeding. Further, Halverson should have known that the affair could impact the custody determination of Wickersham's daughter. Finally, Halverson should have known that discovery of the affair by his wife might lead to his withdrawal as Wickersham's attorney. Thus, Halverson's subjective belief that the relationship would not adversely affect the representation was not objectively reasonable.

In any event, Halverson did not disclose any of these risks to Wickersham before commencing the relationship. Rather, the "ground rules" discussed at the start of the relationship focused primarily on Halverson's own interests: keeping the relationship secret from his wife and avoiding any emotional bonding with Wickersham's daughter. Under these circumstances, the Board properly affirmed the hearing officer's conclusion that Halverson violated RPC 1.7(b).

1.7(b) violation

B. Violation of RPC 1.4(b)—Duty to Communicate

Pursuant to RPC 1.4 (b), "A lawyer shall explain a matter to the extent reasonably necessary to permit the client to make informed decisions regarding the representation." We agree with the Board that the same failures to disclose supporting the conclusion that Halverson violated RPC 1.7(b) also support the conclusion that he violated RPC 1.4(b).

1.4(b) violation

C. Violation of RPC 2.1—Duty to Exercise Independent Professional Judgment

"In representing a client, a lawyer shall exercise independent professional judgment and render candid advice. In rendering advice, a lawyer may refer not only to law but to other considerations such as moral, economic, social and political factors, that may be relevant to the client's situation." RPC 2.1.

As recently noted by the Court of Appeals in a criminal case where the defendant claimed ineffective assistance of counsel, a lawyer who "commences a sexual relationship with the client during the course of the representation . . . creates significant but needless risks that emotions arising from the relationship will impair . . . his or her ability to 'exercise independent professional judgment' . . ." Although we do not adopt a per se rule that a lawyer who commences a sexual relationship with a client always fails to exercise independent professional judgment, we find that under the circumstances here Halverson violated RPC 2.1.

Halverson did not exercise independent professional judgment when he failed to (1) advise Wickersham of the potential ramifications the affair might have on the dissolution or his ability to represent her; (2) advise Wickersham of his published professional opinion that persons involved in a dissolution should be discouraged from getting involved in a new sexual relationship; and (3) take precautions to avoid pregnancy or discuss with Wickersham the consequences of such event. Thus, we affirm the Board's conclusion that Halverson violated RPC 2.1. . . .

F. No Violation of RLD 1.1—Commission of Act of Moral Turpitude

RLD 1.1 provides in pertinent part:

> A lawyer may be subjected to the disciplinary sanctions or actions set forth in these rules for any of the following:
>
> (a) The commission of any act involving moral turpitude, dishonesty, or corruption, or any unjustified act of assault or other act which reflects disregard for the rule of law, whether the

> same be committed in the course of his or her conduct as a lawyer, or otherwise, and whether the same constitutes a felony or misdemeanor or not....

The WSBA argues that Halverson's acts constituted moral turpitude citing, In re Disciplinary Proceeding Against Heard, 963 P.2d 818 (Wash. 1998); Heinmiller v. Department of Health, 903 P.2d 433 (Wash. 1995), *modified*, 909 P.2d 1294 (Wash. 1996); and Haley v. Medical Disciplinary Bd., 818 P.2d 1062 (Wash. 1991). Halverson claims that these cases are distinguishable. We agree.

Heard states that: "Despite the absence of an express rule banning attorney-client sexual relations, an attorney's sexual relations with a client can constitute 'moral turpitude,' justifying the imposition of disciplinary sanctions."... Heard's client was a 23-year-old woman who suffered from a mental disability as a result of injuries from a motorcycle accident, and who also had drug and alcohol problems. All of this was known to Heard. Nonetheless, during the course of settlement negotiations, Heard went to the client's home, took her to two cocktail lounges where they both consumed alcohol, had her drive his vehicle while intoxicated, and then took her to his apartment where they had consensual sexual relations.

This Court concluded that "Heard's use of his professional position to exploit a vulnerable young woman constituted moral turpitude within the meaning of RLD 1.1."...

Heard was based on *Haley*, a case involving a physician-patient sexual relationship. There, Haley, a 66-year-old surgeon, operated on a 16-year-old patient and, thereafter, over the next two years provided the girl with alcohol and engaged in a sexual relationship with her. Haley was given a 10-year stayed suspension on grounds his acts constituted moral turpitude.[9]

This Court also followed the *Haley* holding in *Heinmiller*, where we found a social worker's sexual relationship with a former patient that began one day after the conclusion of counseling constituted moral turpitude. The finding of moral turpitude in *Heinmiller* rested on expert testimony establishing bright line rules in the social work profession prohibiting counselor-patient sexual relations for a period of time even after the discontinuance of therapy.

Here, the aggravating factors present in *Heard* and *Haley* do not exist. Wickersham was not a juvenile. She did not suffer from a mental disability or a drug and alcohol addiction. Halverson did not supply her with intoxicants. Thus, Halverson did not "blatantly misuse[ ] his professional status to exploit [his] client's vulnerability...."

Further, unlike in *Haley* and *Heinmiller*, a bright line rule prohibiting attorney-client sexual relations does not exist. Finally, Halverson's conduct was not an unsolicited advance because Wickersham was arguably the initiator of the relationship. Consequently, the Board properly found that under the circumstances Halverson's affair with Wickersham did not constitute moral turpitude.

III. SANCTION...

A. Sanction Standards

The American Bar Association's Standards for Imposing Lawyer Sanctions govern bar discipline cases in Washington.... After a finding of lawyer misconduct, the Board engages in a two-step process to determine the proper sanction.

9. Halverson notes that *Haley* is distinguishable because it involved a bright line statutory rule prohibiting physician-patient sexual contact. See RCW 18.130.180(24). Although this statute does create a bright line rule, the *Haley* court held it inapplicable because the young woman was a former patient....

First, the Board must determine a presumptive sanction by considering (1) the ethical duty violated; (2) the lawyer's mental state; and (3) the extent of the actual or potential harm caused by the misconduct. As to mental state, the Board must determine whether the lawyer acted intentionally, knowingly, or negligently. In deciding the extent of the actual or potential harm, the Board should consider the "harm to a client, the public, the legal system or the profession that is reasonably foreseeable at the time of the lawyer's misconduct. . . ." The potential for injury caused by the lawyer's misconduct need not be actually realized.

Second, the Board considers whether there are aggravating or mitigating factors that should lead to an alteration of the presumptive sanction or affect the length of a suspension. . . .

As to mental state, the Board also properly determined that Halverson acted knowingly. . . . Although there is no evidence that Halverson intended to harm Wickersham or the legal profession, the evidence clearly establishes that Halverson was aware that his entry into a sexual relationship with Wickersham during her dissolution proceedings exposed her to serious psychological and legal risks. . . .

In light of the above factors, particularly the determination that Halverson acted knowingly, the Board properly concluded that suspension should be the presumed sanction, as opposed to disbarment or a mere reprimand. . . .

Under the circumstances here, we are persuaded that a six-month suspension is inadequate to maintain public confidence in the integrity of the legal profession and deter others from such conduct. As a frequent lecturer and extensive publisher in the family law area, and as the past president of the WSBA, other attorneys as well as the public looked to Halverson for advice. His book demonstrates not only that he knew of the serious psychological and legal risks entering into a new sexual relationship presented to a dissolution client but that he specifically advised others against it. Yet, Halverson knowingly carried on his affair with Wickersham while he was president of the WSBA.

His practice of using personality questionnaires increased his clients' perceptions of him as a personal counselor or quasi-therapist and engendered their trust. Yet, Halverson violated the trust Wickersham placed in him by taking advantage of her status as his dissolution client for his own sexual gratification.

What seems most lacking in the Board's sanction determination is the fact that Halverson engaged in a pattern of misconduct. By his own admission, he has engaged in a sexual relationship with six clients. We find the contradiction between Halverson's published professional advice and status in the legal community, and his personal conduct particularly damaging to the integrity of the legal profession. . . .

CONCLUSION

In conclusion, we uphold all the Board's factual findings, its conclusions of law, and the conditions of the two-year probationary period. We increase the recommended term of suspension from six months to one year to adequately serve the purposes of attorney discipline.

SANDERS, J. (concurring in part, dissenting in part)— . . .

By upholding certain challenged findings of fact, the majority demonstrates its paternalistic perception of female dissolution clients. The majority opines "Wickersham depended upon Halverson," and claims a "power imbalance" Halverson allegedly exercised in his representation of female dissolution clients. . . . However these conclusions are neither supported by the facts of this case nor based on human experience....

Viewing female dissolution clients as "victims" who need the support, assistance and guidance of their powerful male attorneys is degrading because it undermines women's right of independent self-determination. Moreover it does not accurately portray the dynamics of an attorney-client relationship.[1] Rather it is the client who has the power to choose her attorney from the multitude of attorneys competing to gain her business. It is the client who has the power to determine the objectives of the representation and whether to accept or reject an offer of settlement. It is the client who has the power to terminate the services of her lawyer for any reason or no reason at all. It is the client who has the power to sue an attorney if he fails to adequately represent her wishes—a power successfully exercised by Halverson's client here.[2] And it was this client who chose to initiate and enter a consensual sexual relationship with her attorney.

While rules governing attorney-client sex appear to control male sexuality—by disciplining attorneys who engage in the sexual relationships, the vast majority of whom are male—they indirectly control female sexuality by denying self-determination to female clients who desire a dual relationship with an attorney.

Thus, characterizing Halverson's client as a defenseless victim subject to the overwhelming power of her attorney is inaccurate, not supported by the record, and inconsistent with the legal entitlements of all concerned.

The majority also improperly focuses on the emotional harm which purportedly befell Halverson's client as a result of their affair. "As a result of Halverson's conduct, Wickersham suffered personal harm in the form of depression and anxiety."... While this may be true, broken hearts and personal disappointments are not the proper subjects of an attorney discipline proceeding which must focus on state licensure requirements....

...As previously discussed, Halverson advised his client against any sexual relationship, explained that a relationship with him would be improper, and instructed her to tell the truth if asked about their relationship. More fundamentally, there is no showing his advice regarding the substance of the litigation was unsound....

CONCLUSION

No one disputes that Lowell Halverson acted wrongly, foolishly, and hurtfully when he entered into a sexual relationship with Lisa Wickersham. It was a grievous wrong and grievously has Halverson answered for it.... Although Halverson's conduct arguably violated RPC 1.7(b), it did not violate RPC 1.4(b) or RPC 2.1. And as both the hearing officer and the majority acknowledge Halverson "should have known" better, the appropriate sanction under these circumstances is a reprimand.

---

1. Counsel for the WSBA perpetuates this outdated stereotype, arguing: "Mr. Halverson was a very prominent, successful, powerful lawyer, a President of the Bar Association. Ms. Wickersham was a much younger, a woman without a college degree, with a young child, who was intimidated by her attorney husband, and who was terrified of losing custody of her baby daughter..."

2. Not only did Halverson settle his client's civil suit for an undisclosed "substantial sum" of money, Halverson provided his client with over $13,000 of free legal work—described by Wickersham's second attorney as work of "excellent" quality—which greatly aided Halverson's client in obtaining a good outcome....

Lawyers and Other Professionals: *Sexual Relationships with Clients*

Halverson is typical of a growing number of cases that discipline lawyers for engaging in sexual relationships with clients. The fact that Halverson settled a civil suit brought by the same client "for a substantial sum" indicates that lawyers can be subject to civil liability as well as professional discipline. During the past decade, the number of civil, criminal, and professional disciplinary actions brought against a myriad of professionals for sexual misconduct has grown exponentially.[1] *Halverson* refers to some of these cases in determining the appropriate sanction. The rise in the number of claims against clergy, counselors, dentists, lawyers, mental health professionals, nurses, and physicians indicates both that victims are more likely to complain, and that many professionals do not understand or take advantage of the vulnerability of their clients.[2]

Power, Vulnerability, and Transference

Fiduciary duties are imposed on professionals in trusting relationships. Clients repose trust in a professional, empowering that person to act solely on the client's behalf. The professional's power derives not only from the client's retainer, but also from an inherent inequality due to the professional's knowledge and skill. The client's vulnerability stems from both the occasion for seeking a professional's assistance, and the sharing of confidential information. Often, a significant event has caused a loss of control that renders that person vulnerable. A client who seeks a divorce, a bankruptcy, or who has been indicted, injured, or lost a job all face circumstances that have caused them to lose control of some aspect of their life. Further, in order to get professional help, clients must entrust confidential information to professionals, which increases both the professional's power to help and the potential to misuse the information. In many client-professional relationships, these power differentials can be exacerbated by the emotional stress of the legal process itself or the treatment the professional undertakes.

The majority opinion in *Halverson* credits the expert testimony of a lawyer and a psychologist, who agreed that Halverson further exploited his client's trust by administering personality tests, which increased the risk of harm by increasing the power differential in the relationship. This testimony reflects the training of mental health professionals to expect and understand a phenomenon common to all human relationships known as "transference." Literally, transference means that one person unconsciously assigns or transfers onto another feelings or attributes associated with some other person.[3] Persons can transfer negative or positive feelings, and often these feelings involve strong reactions about the underlying legal matter or relationship about which the client or patient seeks advice. Clients and patients also can transfer or project their own needs onto a professional, who is expected to assist the client in working out the underlying issues involved in the matter. The knowledge, experience, power, and social class of most professionals, combined with the client's need for relief and dependence on the professional to get it, may lead the

---

1. *See* Steven B. Bisbing, Linda Mabus Jorgenson & Pamela K. Sutherland, *Sexual Abuse by Professionals: A Legal Guide* (Michie 1995).
2. Detailed statistics are hard to find, but one Illinois study of lawyers documents 50 complaints in 1989 alone, calling the problem a "systematic, unchanging and consistent trend." ABA Formal Op. 92-364.
3. Andrew S. Watson, *Psychiatry for Lawyers* 2-3 (Intl. Universities Press 1978).

client unconsciously to project positive feelings or wishes onto that person that reflect the client's own needs.[4]

Psychotherapists are trained to expect transference in every professional relationship as a normal and therapeutically helpful part of the counseling they provide.[5] They also are trained to recognize countertransference, or the professional's own emotional reactions to the patient or client, that reflect the professional's personal needs.[6] Professionals who are untrained to recognize either phenomenon may assume that a client's expression of personal interest can be taken at face value, and may fail to understand that a client's trust makes undue influence nearly impossible to avoid. About a decade ago, the American Medical Association concluded that both transference and countertransference are common and powerful enough to make any sexual contact with a patient ethically inexcusable.[7]

When Halverson responded to his client's initial expression of sexual attraction by establishing the "ground rules" for the relationship, he reflected either his unawareness of his client's transference or his own willingness to take advantage of it. His response also signals his own countertransference, or projection of his own needs, which were powerful enough to cause him to ignore his own advice to other lawyers and clients to avoid lawyer-client sexual relationships.[8] Both the majority and the dissenting opinions conclude that Halverson's conduct was "a grievous wrong," and that as a result, he was properly subject to professional discipline as well as a civil suit for damages. These same remedies are available to victims of sexual misconduct caused by other professionals. In some cases, professionals also may be held criminally accountable, even when the client or patient "consents" or initiates the contact.

Criminal Accountability

In 1975, Masters and Johnson addressed the American Psychiatric Association and recommended that "sexual seduction of patients . . . regardless of whether the seduction was initiated by the patient or the therapist," should result in an indictment for rape, rather than a civil complaint.[9] In cases of egregious exploitation of professional power, such as rendering patients helpless with medication, some professionals have been convicted of rape.[10] In many cases, however, the consent element of a rape statute creates problems for prosecutors who can establish exploitation, but have difficulty countering a defense raised by facts that show a client who appeared to "consent."

Today, nearly two dozen jurisdictions provide that counseling professionals who intentionally establish sexual contact during a professional relationship are guilty of

---

4. *See, e.g.*, Joel Friedman & Marcia Mobilia Boumil, *Betrayal of Trust: Sex and Power in Professional Relationships* 21 (Praeger 1995).
5. Transference offers insight into the way the client relates to other significant people. *Id.* at 22.
6. The concepts of transference and countertransference were first introduced into the law in a civil case where a patient successfully complained that her psychiatrist committed malpractice by engaging in a sexual relationship with her during the course of her therapy. *See* Zipkin v. Freeman, 436 S.W.2d 753 (Mo. 1969).
7. Am. Med. Assn., Council on Ethical and Judicial Affairs, *Sexual Misconduct in the Practice of Medicine*, 266 JAMA 2741, 2742 (1991).
8. At the very least, his repeated sexual misconduct with clients suggests that he had developed a number of irrational justifications for his conduct. *See* Gene G. Abel & Candice A. Osborn, *Cognitive-Behavioral Treatment of Sexual Misconduct*, in Joseph D. Bloom, Carol C. Nadelson & Malkah T. Notman, eds., *Physician Sexual Misconduct* 188, 230 (Am. Psychiatric Press 1999).
9. Bisbing et al., *supra* note 1, at 833.
10. *Id.* at 835.

criminal conduct.[11] Typical statutes prohibit "sexual exploitation,"[12] or "sexual misconduct,"[13] by mental health and counseling professionals of their clients or patients during the time the professional service was rendered.[14] All of these provisions provide for criminal accountability, regardless of the consent of the victim, on the theory that any consent in such a relationship is coerced or the product of undue influence.[15]

Lawyers are not currently included in sexual exploitation criminal statutes that eliminate consent as a defense. This means that lawyers can be held criminally accountable only under a typical sexual assault law, where proof of the victim's lack of consent will be required as an element of the crime.[16] Some have argued that lawyers should be subject to such provisions, because disciplinary actions do not provide enough relief to injured clients.[17] Others point out that lawyers, unlike psychotherapists, are not trained to recognize transference-like reactions and do not always represent dependent, vulnerable clients.[18]

Civil Remedies

Clients who have been victimized by sexual misconduct during a professional relationship have used several legal theories to seek redress. Some claim battery, arguing that any consent to the contact was fraudulently obtained. Others seek damages for professional malpractice, alleging both harm due to incompetent professional services and emotional distress damages. Most successful have been suits for breach of fiduciary duty, which in essence allege a kind of constructive fraud that coerced or unduly influenced the client or patient to enter into a sexual relationship with the professional.[19]

---

11. *Id.* at §4-7, citing statutes in Ariz., Cal., Colo., Conn., D.C., Fla., Ga., Iowa, Me., Mich., Minn., N.H., N.M., N.D., Ohio, R.I., S.D., Tex., Utah, Wis., and Wyo. In addition to counseling professionals, these provisions also may include teachers, coaches, physicians, nurses, and clergy.
12. *E.g.*, Wis. Stat. §940.22 (2001).
13. *E.g.*, Fla. Stat. §491.0112 (2001).
14. Constitutional challenges to these provisions based on vagueness have not met with success. *See, e.g.*, St. v. McKeeth, 38 P.3d 1275 (Idaho 2001); Ferguson v. St., 824 P.2d 803 (Colo. 1992); St. v. Jenkins, 326 N.W.2d 67 (N.D. 1982).
15. A study of the Wisconsin experience with such a statute concludes that, although two thirds of the confirmed cases of sexual misconduct were prosecuted under the generally applicable sexual assault statute, the specific sexual exploitation statute probably has had a deterrent effect. Andrew W. Kane, *The Effects of Criminalization of Sexual Misconduct by Therapist: Report of a Survey in Wisconsin*, in John C. Gonsiorek, ed., *Breach of Trust: Sexual Exploitation by Health Care Professionals and Clergy* 317, 333 (Sage 1995).
16. Most of these statutes do make consent irrelevant where a mental illness or deficiency causes the victim to be temporarily or permanently incapable of appraising the assaulter's conduct. *E.g.*, Tex. Penal Code §22.011(2)(b)(4) (2002); Wis. Stat. §940.225(2)(b) (2001). Even then, the state has the burden of proof to show that the victim was incapable of appraising the conduct. Further, if such an allegation were made, the defendant probably would be entitled to a psychiatric examination of the client. *See, e.g.*, Jonas v. St., 773 P.2d 960 (Alaska App. 1989).
17. *See, e.g.*, William D. Langford, Jr., Student Author, *Criminalizing Attorney-Client Sexual Relations: Toward Substantive Enforcement*, 73 Tex. L. Rev. 1223, 1239 (1995).
18. *See, e.g.*, Friedman & Boumil, *supra* note 4, at 6, 94-97.
19. *See, e.g.*, Walter v. Stewart, 67 P.3d 1042 (Utah App. 2003). When complaints allege negligence or malpractice, they trigger the duty to defend in professional liability policies. However, the same policies specifically exclude intentional acts, such as battery and fraud. Insurers typically are required to provide a defense when both are pleaded. In such cases, the insurer reserves the right to later claim no duty to indemnify the defendant because sexual misconduct is not a covered occurrence. *See, e.g.*, St. Paul Fire & Marine Ins. Co. v. Engelmann, 639 N.W.2d 192 (S.D. 2002).

Fraud and battery provide relief in situations where the professional has intentionally misrepresented a material fact concerning the sexual relationship.[20] The tort of the intentional infliction of emotional distress has provided relief where a professional refuses or delays professional services as a means of coercing a sexual relationship with a client or patient.[21]

Clients also sue for malpractice, which requires them to prove breach of the standard of care using expert testimony, as well as causation and damage. In sexual misconduct cases, the expert testimony requirement initially created a significant hurdle for plaintiffs until a clear professional custom emerged. Proving the need for further counseling or other professional services shows causation and damages.[22] Malpractice actions also have proven useful when a professional has a sexual relationship with the spouse of the client or patient.[23]

To clarify the common law, several states have enacted statutes that provide a cause of action for civil damages against various named counseling professionals for sexual exploitation.[24] These statutes eliminate the need for expert testimony, providing for damages if sexual contact occurred during the time the patient received counseling, regardless of that person's consent. The same result has been reached when clients allege breach of fiduciary duty against professionals who misuse confidential information to establish sexual contact.[25] In cases against counseling professionals that allege breach of fiduciary duty without any specific showing of misuse of confidences, some courts refuse to find a fiduciary relationship in the absence of a trust relationship concerning property.[26] Others disagree, reasoning that a counselor's position of trust allows him or her to manipulate a patient's emotions.[27]

Lawyers obviously owe fiduciary duties, but in cases that allege sexual misconduct, some courts have narrowly construed them. For example, in Suppressed v. Suppressed, a client alleged breach of fiduciary duty by her former divorce lawyer for psychologically

20. *See, e.g.,* DiLeo v. Nugent, 592 A.2d 1126 (Md. Ct. Spec. App. 1991) (therapist told patient that drugs and sexual intercourse with him were part of his treatment); Barbara A. v. John G., 193 Cal. Rptr. 422 (Cal. App. 1983) (lawyer who told client he "couldn't possibly get anyone pregnant," liable for battery and fraud after client suffered a tubal pregnancy which rendered her sterile).

21. *See, e.g.,* Corbett v. Morgenstern. 934 F. Supp. 680 (E.D. Pa. 1996) (psychologist's 12-year sexual relationship with patient sufficient to allow claim for both intentional and negligent infliction of emotional distress); Figueiredo-Torres v. Nichel, 584 A.2d 69 (Md. 1991) (husband entitled to damages for intentional infliction of emotional distress against marriage counselor who engaged in sexual relationship with his wife and encouraged her to leave husband); McDaniel v. Gile, 230 Cal. Rptr. 242 (Cal. App. 1991) (lawyer whose sexual advances were refused by client stopped working on the client's case and gave her incorrect advice about her legal rights).

22. *See, e.g.,* Zipkin v. Freeman, *supra* note 6 (negligent mishandling of transference reaction). Employers have been found vicariously liable in malpractice cases as well. *See, e.g.,* Simmons v. United States, 805 F.2d 1363 (9th Cir. 1986) (government liable for $150,000 judgment based on negligence of a social worker in Indian Health Service in handling patient's transference); Russell G. Donaldson, *Liability of Hospital or Clinic for Sexual Relationships with Patients by Staff Physicians, Psychologists, and Other Healers,* 45 A.L.R.4th 289 (1986).

23. *See, e.g.,* Rowe v. Bennett, 514 A.2d 802 (Me. 1985) (psychotherapist); Mazza v. Huffaker, 300 S.E.2d 833 (N.C. App. 1983) (psychiatrist). *But see* Kahlig v. Boyd, 980 S.W.2d 685 (Tex. App. 1998) (lawyer).

24. *See* Bisbing et al., *supra* note 1, at §4-7, citing statutes in Cal., Colo., Ill., Minn., N.H., N.C., Tex., and Wis.

25. *See, e.g.,* Tante v. Herring, 453 S.E.2d 686 (Ga. 1994) (lawyer who misused confidential information about the client's mental and emotional condition to convince her to engage in sex with him liable to both client and her husband, no expert testimony required). The lawyer was suspended from practice for 18 months for the same conduct. In re Tante, 453 S.E.2d 688 (Ga. 1994).

26. *See, e.g.,* Gray v. Ward, 929 S.W.2d 774 (Mo. App. 1996).

27. *See, e.g.,* Horak v. Biris, 474 N.E.2d 13 (Ill. App. 1985) (social worker); Norberg v. Wynrib, 92 D.L.R. 449 (Ca. 1992) (dentist); F.G. v. MacDonell, 696 A.2d 697 (N.J. 1997) (clergy counselor).

coercing her into having sexual relations.[28] The court restricted a lawyer's fiduciary duty to the lawyer's "legal representation," and concluded that no cause of action could be stated absent proof that the client's underlying legal action was somehow compromised.[29] Other cases disagree, upholding damages for emotional distress alone if the lawyer has reason to know that a breach of fiduciary duty was likely to cause it.[30]

Professional Discipline

Mental health professionals were the first to address the issue of sexual misconduct with patients or clients in their professional codes. Today, nearly every counseling profession's code includes an absolute prohibition on sexual relationships with current clients or patients.[31] Many professions extend this ban to former clients or patients for a period of time after the professional relationship ends as well.[32] Some courts have interpreted more general professional code provisions that prohibit client exploitation to include such a ban.[33] Some of these prohibitions have been added to state licensing statutes.[34]

Lawyers have taken longer to respond. Today, *Halverson* illustrates the approach found in most jurisdictions, where general professional code provisions are applied to lawyer sexual misconduct. In these cases, lawyers have been disciplined for violating conflict of interest and communication rules, as well as those that prohibit criminal conduct and fraud.[35] The ABA Ethics Committee reached a similar conclusion in 1992, opining that sexual relationships during the course of representation raise

28. 565 N.E.2d 101 (Ill. App. 1990), *rev. denied*, 571 N.E.2d 156 (Ill. 1991).
29. The court admitted that a claim for battery or intentional infliction of emotional distress might be possible, but it was not pleaded, probably because it was barred by the statute of limitations. *Id. See also* Kling v. Landry, 686 N.E.2d 33 (Ill. App. 1997). *But see* Gaspard v. Beadle, 36 S.W.3d 229 (Tex. App. 2001) (lawyer's sexual relationship with a client, while socially inappropriate, was not outrageous as a matter of law).
30. *See, e.g.*, Doe v. Roe, 681 N.E.2d 640 (Ill. App. 1997).
31. *See* Am. College of Phys., *Ethics Manual*, Sexual Contact between Physician and Patient (1998), in Rena A. Gorlin, *Codes of Professional Responsibility: Ethics Standards in Business, Health and Law* 318 (BNA 1999); Am. Counseling Assn., *Code of Ethics and Standards of Practice*, Section A.7. Sexual Intimacies with Clients (1997), *id.* at 422; Am. Psych. Assn., *Principles of Medical Ethics with Annotations Especially Applicable to Psychiatry* §§2-1, 4-14 (1998), *id.* at 455, 457; Am. Psychol. Assn., *Ethical Principles of Psychologists and Code of Conduct*, Standards 4.05 (1992), *id.* at 478; Clinical Social Work Fedn., *Code of Ethics* §II(3)(b) (1997), *id.* at 519; Natl. Assn. of Soc. Workers, *Code of Ethics* §1.09 (1996), *id.* at 537.
32. *See, e.g.*, Am. College of Phys., *supra* note 31 ("Sexual involvement between physicians and former patients raises concern."); Am. Counseling Assn., *supra* note 31 (two-year bar after counseling relationship terminates, after two years, counselors "have the responsibility to thoroughly examine and document that such relations did not have an exploitative nature"); Am. Med. Assn., *supra* note 7 ("Sexual or romantic relationships with former patients are unethical if the physician uses or exploits trust, knowledge, emotions, or influence derived from the previous professional relationship."); Am. Psych. Assn., *supra* note 31 ("Sexual activity with a current or former client is unethical."); Am. Psychol. Assn., *supra* note 31, at §4.07 (two-year bar after treatment terminates, after two years only in the "most unusual circumstances" and psychologist "bears the burden of demonstrating that there has been no exploitation"); Clinical Social Work Fedn., *supra* note 31 (no romantic or sexual contact with either current or former clients).
33. *See* Am. Med. Assn., *supra* note 7; Gorlin, *supra* note 31, at 401; Am. Chiropractic Assn., Ethics Committee, *Sexual Intimacies with a Patient* (1992-3), *id.* at 278; Budde v. Mich. Dept. of Consumer & Indus. Services, 2001 Mich. App. LEXIS 2564 (social worker's license revoked on basis of expert testimony); Heinecke v. Dept. of Com., 810 P.2d 459 (Utah 1991) (nurse's license revoked for having sexual relationship with a mentally ill client that culminated in the client's pregnancy).
34. Bisbing, *supra* note 1, at §4-7.
35. *See, e.g.*, In re Tsoutsouris, 748 N.E.2d 856 (Ind. 2001) (sexual relationship with client violates Rule 1.7(b)); People v. Riddle, 1999 Colo. Discipl. 88 (lawyer who became sexually involved with client who was also a lawyer violated Rules 1.7(b) and 1.16(a)); In re Berg, 955 P.2d 1240 (Kan. 1998) (lawyer who engaged in sexual relations with several divorce clients disbarred for violating MR. 1.7(b), 1.8(b), 2.1,

a significant risk of impairment to the lawyer's representation, which could involve violations of competence (Model Rule 1.1), confidentiality (Model Rules 1.6 and 1.8(b)), loyalty (Model Rule 1.7 and 3.7), or prevent the lawyer from exercising independent judgment (Model Rule 2.1).[36] They also warned about compromise of the attorney-client privilege and concluded that the client's consent will "rarely be sufficient to eliminate" the danger of impairment to the representation, even if a sexual relationship does not result from coercion or exploitation.

Applying general lawyer code provisions to sexual relationships with clients assumes that they are appropriate in some circumstances as long as a lawyer obtains a client's informed consent to legitimate the relationship.[37] California was the first jurisdiction to recognize that such an approach neither clearly warns lawyers about sexual misconduct nor protects clients by deterring it. To "ensure that a lawyer acts in the best interest of his or her client,"[38] the California Supreme Court in 1992 enacted the first specific lawyer code provision, which prohibits coercive or exploitive sexual relationships with clients.[39] Since then, at least 12 other jurisdictions have followed California's lead[40] and several more mention the issue in comments to their professional codes.[41] In the past decade, nine of these jurisdictions have gone further than California's anticoercive approach by enacting total bans on sexual relationships with all clients during the course of the representation.[42] New York has adopted a hybrid rule that prohibits sexual relationships between lawyers and clients in "domestic relations" matters, and creates an anti-exploitive rule for all other client-lawyer relationships.[43]

The revised Model Rules recently endorsed the prohibitive approach, resulting in the enactment of new rule 1.8(j), which flatly bans sexual relations with all clients that did not precede the professional relationship. Enactment of such a provision means that a lawyer must choose between providing legal services and pursuing a personal sexual relationship.[44] The comment points out that the client-lawyer relationship "is almost always unequal" and that a sexual relationship violates "the lawyer's basic ethical obligation not to use the trust of the client to the client's disadvantage."[45] This means that an absolute prohibition applies "regardless of whether

3.7, and 8.4(d)); In re Rinella, 677 N.E.2d 909 (Ill. 1997) (sexual relationships with several clients constitutes conduct prejudicial to the administration of justice and overreaching); In re Kraemer, 546 N.W.2d 186 (Wis. 1996) (sexual relationship with client violates Rules 1.3, 1.7(b), and 8.4(f), which prohibits violations of "supreme court decisions regulating the conduct of lawyers"). *See also* Gregory G. Sarno, Jr., *Sexual Misconduct as Ground for Disciplining Attorney or Judge,* 43 A.L.R.4th 1062 (1986).

36. ABA Formal Op. 92-364, *supra* note 2.

37. *Halverson* illustrates that some jurisdictions also require a written document. *See* Practice Pointers: Written Consents to Conflicts of Interest, *infra* p.322.

38. Cal. Bus. & Prof. Code §6106.8 (1992).

39. Cal. R. Prof. Conduct 3-120 (1992).

40. Ariz R. Prof. Conduct 1.8(j); Del. R. Prof. Conduct 1.8(j); Fla. R. Prof. Conduct 4-8.4(i); Iowa DR 5-101(b); Minn. R. Prof. Conduct 1.8(1); Rev. R. Prof. Conduct of the N.C. St. Bar 1.18; N.Y. DR 5-111(b); Or. Code Prof. Resp., DR 5-110; S.D. R. Prof. Conduct 1.8(j); Utah R. Prof. Conduct 8.4(g); W. Va. R. Prof. Conduct 8.4(g); Wis. S. Ct. R. 20:1.8(k). *See, e.g.,* Fla. Bar v. Bryant, 813 S.2d 38 (Fla. 2002) (lawyer who exchanged sex with exotic dancer client for legal representation violated Rule 8.4(i), which prohibits "sexual conduct with a client that exploits the lawyer-client relationship").

41. *E.g.,* Md. Law. R. Prof. Conduct 1.7, Comment 7; Mich. R. Prof. Conduct 1.8, Comment *Sexual Relations with Clients*; Vt. R. Prof. Conduct 8.4, Comment.

42. Ariz., Del., Iowa, Minn., N.C., Or., S.D., W. Va., Wis.

43. N.Y. DR 5-111(b)(3).

44. *See, e.g.,* Musick v. Musick, 453 S.E.2d 361 (W. Va. 1994) (lawyer who engaged in sexual relationship with client disqualified from further representation on motion of opposing party).

45. Model R. Prof. Conduct 1.8, Comment [17].

the relationship is consensual and regardless of the absence of prejudice to the client," "because of the significant danger of harm to client interests and because the client's own emotional involvement renders it unlikely that the client could give adequate informed consent."[46] When the client is an organization, the rule applies to representatives of entity clients who regularly consult with the lawyer.[47] Unlike other parts of Rule 1.8, this conflict is personal, and therefore another lawyer in the law firm may carry out the representation, subject, of course, to other general conflict of interest provisions.[48]

The Future

Although *Halverson* illustrates that discipline certainly is possible under current general professional code provisions, the lack of clear notice to lawyers and more certain deterrence to protect clients means that a specific provision may be seen as both necessary and preferable in many jurisdictions. If states decide to address the issue specifically in their professional codes, they will have to decide whether to enact an anti-exploitive provision like California's, an absolute prohibition like Model Rule 1.8(j), or some combination or the two such as New York's hybrid provision.

To date, the majority of states that have enacted a specific rule have chosen an absolute prohibition because of both its clarity and ease of administration. On the other hand, good arguments can and have been made that not all clients of lawyers are vulnerable and dependent.[49] This may lead some jurisdictions to opt for the California anti-exploitive approach, or to enact total prohibitions only in some kinds of legal representations where truly voluntary consent is extremely unlikely, as New York has done.

While an anti-exploitive rule may be fairer to lawyers (and according to the dissent in *Halverson,* also to clients), such a rule requires that the lawyer who is emotionally involved with a client make a determination whether his or her own conduct involves coercion, intimidation, or undue influence. If the client later files a disciplinary complaint, such a rule also shifts the burden of proving coercion or other exploitive factors to disciplinary counsel. Other professions have not been willing to let professionals exercise their own judgment in a circumstance where the risk of transference, countertransference, and undue influence is so high.

The analogy to the complete bans in the counseling professions may not be completely helpful, however, if the reason for those prohibitions stem from the belief that virtually every counseling relationship involves some degree of transference and opportunity for undue influence. Nearly every lawyer can imagine some client-lawyer relationships where transference, even if it occurs, does not subject the client or the lawyer to undue influence.[50] Legal rules about business transactions with clients such as *Monco* recognize this, presuming undue influence in every situation, but shifting the burden of proof to the lawyer to justify the fairness of the transaction. This has led some to urge a similar professional rule governing sexual

---

46. *Id.*
47. *Id.*, Comment [19]. *See also* Cal. Rule, *supra* note 39, and Iowa, Minn., Or., Utah, and Wis. Rules, *supra* note 40, which include certain representatives of organizational clients.
48. Model R. Prof. Conduct 1.8(k), 1.10(a).
49. *See, e.g.*, Linda Fitts Mischler, *Reconciling Rapture, Representation, and Responsibility: An Argument Against Per Se Bans on Attorney-Client Sex*, 10 Geo. J. Legal Ethics 209 (1996).
50. *See, e.g.*, Lawrence J. Fox, *When It Comes to Sex With Clients, Whom Do You Trust: Nanny or the ABA?* 19 GP Solo 36 (Oct./Nov. 2002).

relationships that shifts the burden of proof to the lawyer to prove the lack of undue influence on the client's consent to the relationship.[51] Of course, such a rule would require the lawyer to obtain an extensive informed consent, probably in writing. The difficulty of imagining what such a document would contain has led others to call for the simplicity of an absolute prohibition.

Specific professional rules about lawyer sexual misconduct may have other impacts as well. An absolute professional prohibition could lead some to abandon calls for criminal regulation. Such a prohibition also acknowledges "that the professional relationship is inextricably bound up with the personal feelings of the individuals involved."[52] At the same time, proof that a lawyer violated a professional code provision will be admissible, but not determinative, of whether that lawyer should be liable in a civil action. Even without such a professional code provision, most courts are adopting the view that a sexual relationship with a client constitutes a breach of fiduciary duty. The lesson of this chapter is that such a breach leads to many potential remedies, including damages, fee forfeiture, and disqualification.

E. Multiple Clients

1. Aggregate Settlements

Problem

6-10. Martyn & Fox represents wife, child, and grandmother who were injured in a car accident that killed wife and injured the other two. Defendant's insurer tells us it will pay the full policy limits ($1 million) to settle all three clients' claims. Should we accept the settlement?

Consider: Model Rule 1.8(g)
Model Code DR 5-106
RLGL §§6, 37

Burrow v. Arce

997 S.W.2d 229 (Tex. 1999)

Justice Hecht delivered the opinion of the Court.

The principal question in this case is whether an attorney who breaches his fiduciary duty to his client may be required to forfeit all or part of his fee, irrespective of whether the breach caused the client actual damages. Like the court of appeals, we answer in the affirmative and conclude that the amount of the fee to be forfeited is a question for the court, not a jury. . . .

I

Explosions at a Phillips 66 chemical plant in 1989 killed twenty-three workers

51. Linda Mabus Jorgenson & Pamela K. Sutherland, *Fiduciary Theory Applied to Personal Dealings: Attorney-Client Sexual Contact*, 45 Ark. L. Rev. 459 (1992).
52. Anthony E. Davis & Judith Grimaldi, *Sexual Confusion: Attorney-Client Sex and the Need for a Clear Ethical Rule*, 7 Notre Dame J.L. Ethics & Pub. Policy 57, 98 (1993).

and injured hundreds of others, spawning a number of wrongful death and personal injury lawsuits. One suit on behalf of some 126 plaintiffs was filed by five attorneys, David Burrow, Walter Umphrey, John E. Williams, Jr., F. Kenneth Bailey, Jr., and Wayne Reaud, and their law firm, Umphrey, Burrow, Reaud, Williams & Bailey. The case settled for something close to $190 million, out of which the attorneys received a contingent fee of more than $60 million.

Forty-nine of these plaintiffs then filed this suit against their attorneys in the Phillips accident case alleging professional misconduct and demanding forfeiture of all fees the attorneys received. More specifically, plaintiffs alleged that the attorneys, in violation of rules governing their professional conduct, solicited business through a lay intermediary, failed to fully investigate and assess individual claims, failed to communicate offers received and demands made, entered into an aggregate settlement with Phillips of all plaintiffs' claims without plaintiffs' authority or approval, agreed to limit their law practice by not representing others involved in the same incident, and intimidated and coerced their clients into accepting the settlement. Plaintiffs asserted causes of action for breach of fiduciary duty, fraud, violations of the Deceptive Trade Practices—Consumer Protection Act, ... negligence, and breach of contract. The attorneys have denied any misconduct and plaintiffs' claim for fee forfeiture.

The parties paint strikingly different pictures of the events leading to this suit:

The plaintiffs contend: In the Phillips accident suit, the defendant attorneys signed up plaintiffs en masse to contingent fee contracts, often contacting plaintiffs through a union steward. In many instances the contingent fee percentage in the contract was left blank and 33-1/3% was later inserted despite oral promises that a fee of only 25% would be charged. The attorneys settled all the claims in the aggregate and allocated dollar figures to the plaintiffs without regard to individual conditions and damages. No plaintiff was allowed to meet with an attorney for more than about twenty minutes, and any plaintiff who expressed reservations about the settlement was threatened by the attorney with being afforded no recovery at all.

The defendant attorneys contend: No aggregate settlement or any other alleged wrongdoing occurred, but regardless of whether it did or not, all their clients in the Phillips accident suit received a fair settlement for their injuries, but some were disgruntled by rumors of settlements paid co-workers represented by different attorneys in other suits. After the litigation was concluded, a Kansas lawyer invited the attorneys' former clients to a meeting, where he offered to represent them in a suit against the attorneys for a fee per claim of $2,000 and one-third of any recovery. Enticed by the prospect of further recovery with minimal risk, plaintiffs agreed to join this suit, the purpose of which is merely to extort more money from their former attorneys.

These factual disputes were not resolved in the district court. Instead, the court granted summary judgment for the defendant attorneys on the grounds that the settlement of plaintiffs' claims in the Phillips accident suit was fair and reasonable, plaintiffs had therefore suffered no actual damages as a result of any misconduct by the attorneys, and absent actual damages plaintiffs were not entitled to a forfeiture of any of the attorneys' fees. . . .

The Clients contend that the Attorneys' serious breaches of fiduciary duty require full forfeiture of all their fees, irrespective of whether the breaches caused actual damages, but if not, that a determination of the amount of any lesser forfeiture should be made by a jury rather than the court. The Clients also contend that their lack of actual damages has not been established as a matter of law. The Attorneys argue that no fee forfeiture can be ordered absent proof that the Clients sustained actual damages, but even if it could, no forfeiture should be ordered for the misconduct the Clients allege....

II

At the outset we consider whether the Attorneys have established as a matter of law that the Clients have suffered no actual damages as a result of any misconduct by the Attorneys....

... [W]e conclude that the Attorneys failed to establish as a matter of law that the Clients did not suffer actual damages, and thus the Attorneys were not entitled to summary judgment dismissing the Clients' claims on that basis.

III

The Attorneys nevertheless argue that the Clients have not alleged grounds that would entitle them to forfeiture of any of the Attorneys' fees.... The Clients counter that whether they sustained actual damages or not, the Attorneys, for breach of their fiduciary duty, should be required to forfeit all fees received, or alternatively, a portion of those fees as may be determined by a jury. These arguments thus raise four issues: (a) are actual damages a prerequisite to fee forfeiture? (b) is fee forfeiture automatic and entire for all misconduct? (c) if not, is the amount of fee forfeiture a question of fact for a jury or one of law for the court? and (d) would the Clients' allegations, if true, entitle them to forfeiture of any or all of the Attorneys' fees? We address each issue in turn.

A

To determine whether actual damages are a prerequisite to forfeiture of an attorney's fee, we look to the jurisprudential underpinnings of the equitable remedy of forfeiture. The parties agree that as a rule a person who renders service to another in a relationship of trust may be denied compensation for his service if he breaches that trust. Section 243 of the Restatement (Second) of Trusts states the rule for trustees: "If the trustee commits a breach of trust, the court may in its discretion deny him all compensation or allow him a reduced compensation or allow him full compensation." Similarly, section 469 of the Restatement (Second) of Agency provides:

> An agent is entitled to no compensation for conduct which is disobedient or which is a breach of his duty of loyalty; if such conduct constitutes a willful and deliberate breach of his contract of service, he is not entitled to compensation even for properly performed services for which no compensation is apportioned.

Citing these two sections, section 49 of the proposed Restatement (Third) of The Law Governing Lawyers applies the same rule to lawyers, who stand in a relation of trust and agency toward their clients. Section 49 states in part: "A lawyer engaging in clear and serious violation of duty to a client may be required to forfeit some or all of the lawyer's compensation for the matter."

Though the historical origins of the remedy of forfeiture of an agent's compensation are obscure, the reasons for the remedy are apparent. The rule is founded both on principle and pragmatics. In principle, a person who agrees to perform compensable services in a relationship of trust and violates that relationship breaches the agreement, express or implied, on which the right to compensation is based. The person is not entitled to be paid when he has not provided the loyalty bargained for and promised.... Pragmatically, the possibility of forfeiture of compensation discourages an agent from taking personal advantage of his position of trust in every situation no matter the circumstances, whether the principal may be injured or not. The remedy of forfeiture removes any incentive for an agent to stray from his duty of loyalty based on the possibility that the principal will be unharmed or may have difficulty proving the existence or amount of damages. In other words, as comment b to section 49 of the proposed Restatement (Third) of The Law Governing Lawyers states, "forfeiture is also a deterrent."

To limit forfeiture of compensation to instances in which the principal sustains actual damages would conflict with both justifications for the rule. It is the agent's disloyalty, not any resulting harm, that violates the fiduciary relationship and thus impairs the basis for compensation. An agent's compensation is not only for specific results but also for loyalty. Removing the disincentive of forfeiture except when harm results would prompt an agent to attempt to calculate whether particular conduct, though disloyal to the principal, might nevertheless be harmless to the principal and profitable to the agent. The main purpose of forfeiture is not to compensate an injured principal, even though it may have that effect. Rather, the central purpose of the equitable remedy of forfeiture is to protect relationships of trust by discouraging agents' disloyalty....

The Attorneys nevertheless argue that forfeiture of an attorney's fee without a showing of actual damages encourages breach-of-fiduciary claims by clients to extort a renegotiation of legal fees after representation has been concluded, allowing them to obtain a windfall. The Attorneys warn that such opportunistic claims could impair the finality desired in litigation settlements by leaving open the possibility that the parties, having resolved their differences, can then assert claims against their counsel to obtain more than they could by settlement of the initial litigation. The Attorneys urge that a bright-line rule making actual damages a prerequisite to fee forfeiture is necessary to prevent misuse of the remedy. We disagree. Fee forfeiture for attorney misconduct is not a windfall to the client. An attorney's compensation is for loyalty as well as services, and his failure to provide either impairs his right to compensation. While a client's motives may be opportunistic and his claims meritless, the better protection is not a prerequisite of actual damages but the trial court's discretion to refuse to afford claimants who are seeking to take unfair advantage of their former attorneys the equitable remedy of forfeiture. Nothing in the caselaw in Texas or elsewhere suggests that opportunistically motivated litigation to forfeit an agent's fee has ever been a serious problem....

We therefore conclude that a client need not prove actual damages in order to obtain forfeiture of an attorney's fee for the attorney's breach of fiduciary duty to the client.

B

The Clients argue that an attorney who commits a serious breach of fiduciary duty to a client must automatically forfeit all compensation to the client....

... [T]o require an agent to forfeit all compensation for every breach of fiduciary duty, or even every serious breach, would deprive the remedy of its equitable nature and would disserve its purpose of protecting relationships of trust. A helpful analogy, the parties agree, is a constructive trust, of which we have observed:

> Constructive trusts, being remedial in character, have the very broad function of redressing wrong or unjust

> enrichment in keeping with basic principles of equity and justice.... Moreover, there is no unyielding formula to which a court of equity is bound in decreeing a constructive trust, since the equity of the transaction will shape the measure of relief granted.

Like a constructive trust, the remedy of forfeiture must fit the circumstances presented. It would be inequitable for an agent who had performed extensive services faithfully to be denied all compensation for some slight, inadvertent misconduct that left the principal unharmed, and the threat of so drastic a result would unnecessarily and perhaps detrimentally burden the agent's exercise of judgment in conducting the principal's affairs.

The proposed Restatement (Third) of The Law Governing Lawyers rejects a rigid approach to attorney fee forfeiture. Section 49 states:

> A lawyer engaging in clear and serious violation of duty to a client may be required to forfeit some or all of the lawyer's compensation for the matter. In determining whether and to what extent forfeiture is appropriate, relevant considerations include the gravity and timing of the violation, its wilfulness, its effect on the value of the lawyer's work for the client, any other threatened or actual harm to the client, and the adequacy of other remedies.

The remedy is restricted to "clear and serious" violations of duty. Comment d to section 49 explains: "A violation is clear if a reasonable lawyer, knowing the relevant facts and law reasonably accessible to the lawyer, would have known that the conduct was wrongful." The factors for assessing the seriousness of a violation, and hence "whether and to what extent forfeiture is appropriate," are set out in the rule.... Comment a states: "A lawyer is not entitled to be paid for services rendered in violation of the lawyer's duty to a client, or for services needed to alleviate the consequences of the lawyer's misconduct." And comment e observes: "Ordinarily, forfeiture extends to all fees for the matter for which the lawyer was retained...." But comment e adds: "Sometimes forfeiture for the entire matter is inappropriate, for example when a lawyer performed valuable services before the misconduct began, and the misconduct was not so grave as to require forfeiture of the fee for all services." And comment b expands on the necessity for exercising discretion in applying the remedy:

> Forfeiture of fees, however, is not justified in each instance in which a lawyer violates a legal duty, nor is total forfeiture always appropriate. Some violations are inadvertent or do not significantly harm the client. Some can be adequately dealt with by the remedies described in Comment a or by a partial forfeiture (see Comment e). Denying the lawyer all compensation would sometimes be an excessive sanction, giving a windfall to a client. The remedy of this Section should hence be applied with discretion.

The Restatement's approach, as a whole, is consistent with Texas law concerning constructive trusts, and we agree with the forfeiture rule stated in section 49 as explained in the comments we have quoted. This rule, or something similar, also appears to have been adopted in most other jurisdictions that have considered the issue....

Section 49 sets out considerations similar to those for trustees in applying the remedy of fee forfeiture to attorneys.... The several factors embrace broad considerations which must be weighed together and not mechanically applied. For example, the "wilfulness" factor requires consideration of the attorney's culpability generally; it does not simply limit forfeiture to situations in which the attorney's breach of duty was intentional. The adequacy-of-other-remedies factor does not preclude forfeiture when a client can be fully compensated by damages. Even though the main purpose of the remedy is not to compensate the client, if other remedies do not afford the client full compensation for his damages, forfeiture may be considered for that purpose.

To the factors listed in section 49 we add another that must be given great weight in applying the remedy of fee forfeiture: the public interest in maintaining the integrity of attorney-client relationships. . . . The Attorneys' argument that relief for attorney misconduct should be limited to compensating the client for any injury suffered ignores the main purpose of the remedy. . . .

Accordingly, we conclude that whether an attorney must forfeit any or all of his fee for a breach of fiduciary duty to his client must be determined by applying the rule as stated in section 49 of the proposed Restatement (Third) of The Law Governing Lawyers and the factors we have identified to the individual circumstances of each case.

C

The parties agree that the determination whether to afford the remedy of forfeiture must be made by the court. The Clients argue, however, that they are entitled to have the amount of the forfeiture set by a jury. The Attorneys argue, and the court of appeals held, that the amount of any forfeiture is also an issue to be decided by the court.

Forfeiture of an agent's compensation, we have already explained, is an equitable remedy similar to a constructive trust. As a general rule, a jury "does not determine the expediency, necessity, or propriety of equitable relief." Consistent with the rule, whether a constructive trust should be imposed must be determined by a court based on the equity of the circumstances. However, when contested fact issues must be resolved before equitable relief can be determined, a party is entitled to have that resolution made by a jury.

These same principles apply in deciding whether to forfeit all or part of an agent's compensation. Thus, for example, a dispute concerning an agent's culpability—whether he acted intentionally, with gross negligence, recklessly, or negligently, or was merely inadvertent—may present issues for a jury, as may disputes about the value of the agent's services and the existence and amount of any harm to the principal. But factors like the adequacy of other remedies and the public interest in protecting the integrity of the attorney-client relationship, as well as the weighing of all other relevant considerations, present legal policy issues well beyond the jury's province of judging credibility and resolving factual disputes. The ultimate decision on the amount of any fee forfeiture must be made by the court. . . .

Thus, when forfeiture of an attorney's fee is claimed, a trial court must determine from the parties whether factual disputes exist that must be decided by a jury before the court can determine whether a clear and serious violation of duty has occurred, whether forfeiture is appropriate, and if so, whether all or only part of the attorney's fee should be forfeited. Such factual disputes may include, without limitation, whether or when the misconduct complained of occurred, the attorney's mental state at the time, and the existence or extent of any harm to the client. If the relevant facts are undisputed, these issues may, of course, be determined by the court as a matter of law. Once any necessary factual disputes have been resolved, the court must determine, based on the factors we have set out, whether the attorney's conduct was a clear and serious breach of duty to his client and whether any of the attorney's compensation should be forfeited, and if so, what amount. Most importantly, in making these determinations the court must consider whether forfeiture is necessary to satisfy the public's interest in protecting the attorney-client relationship. The court's decision whether to forfeit any or all of an attorney's fee is subject to review on appeal as any other legal issue....

The Law Governing Lawyers: *Loss of Fee or Other Benefits*

In *Burrow,* the Supreme Court of Texas explains the jurisprudential underpinnings of another equitable remedy for breaches of fiduciary duty: fee forfeiture. In *Monco,* the Illinois Appellate court granted a similar remedy: rescission of a transaction with a client, with concomitant loss of benefits to the lawyer. Both of these remedies overlap with other remedies that the law of agency makes available to principals whose agents breach fiduciary duties. Both courts also cite the lawyer code provisions that restate basic fiduciary duty. In this note, we examine some of the details of these remedies in order to understand their relationship to other legal and equitable remedies provided to clients whose lawyers breach fiduciary duties.

Loss of Contractual Benefits

Lawyer-agents who breach duties of obedience, loyalty, or confidentiality lose their entitlement to fees or other contractual rights because they have violated a basic fiduciary duty essential to the contract. In refusing to enforce such contracts, *Monco* illustrates that agency rules, such as a presumption of undue influence, require close scrutiny of business transactions between lawyers and clients in order to give lawyers incentives to preserve fiduciary duties. Similarly, the *Burrow* court typifies the view that the fee forfeiture remedy should be provided both for breaches of fiduciary duty to a particular client, and also to deter similar conduct in other cases.

Either or both of these remedies can arise as an issue when a lawyer sues a client to obtain a contractual benefit, such as Monco's petition to dissolve the corporation, or an unpaid fee. *Burrow* points out that clients can seek such remedies on their own as well. If the fee has already been paid, or the contractual benefit has already occurred, the client can seek return of the benefit through other equitable remedies, such as a constructive trust or fee forfeiture.[1] One example involves civil actions to order lawyers or other agents to account for, return, or hold in constructive trust specific property acquired because of the improper use of confidential information.[2] Lawyers who breach fiduciary duties also may be ordered to disgorge profits to the client.[3]

Fee Forfeiture

Although *Burrow* represents a contemporary example of the usefulness of fee forfeiture, the remedy itself, like the constructive trust, is quite old. In a bankruptcy case, Judge Learned Hand traced the lawyer's duty not to represent opposing interests back three centuries, and found that the usual consequence of doing so had been that the lawyer was "debarred from receiving any fee from either, no matter how

---

1. When a client seeks a forfeiture of fees already paid, courts sometimes refer to the remedy as "fee disgorgement."
2. *Restatement (Third) The Law Governing Lawyers* §6, Comments d and e.
3. *See, e.g.,* In re Estate of Mark F. Corriea, 719 A.2d 1234 (D.C. App. 1998) (the court found that the disgorgement of profits was insurable as damages, unless the insurer could justify refusal of coverage by proving that the lawyer intended to deceive the client in not disclosing his conflict of interest).

successful his labors."[4] *Burrow* represents the well-settled view that the forfeiture follows from breach of the contract, and unlike legal remedies, does not require proof of other damages.

We have already seen examples of legal relief available to clients who can prove that a lawyer's breach of fiduciary duty caused them harm. For example, Dr. dePape was able to show that his lawyers' failure to inform him about legal options caused him $278,760 in lost income and emotional distress. Similarly, Mr. Perez was able to state a claim for emotional distress damages due to his lawyers' breach of confidentiality. Although both of these clients could have sought fee forfeiture as well, neither did, probably for similar reasons.

First, unlike *Burrow,* both fees were insignificant compared to the other damages sought. Dr. dePape's legal fee was paid by the health care system that hoped to hire him. Similarly, Mr. Perez's lawyers did not represent him for long, and appear to have been provided and paid for by his employer's insurer.[5] Second, both of these clients were able to prove causation and damages in their tort suits. Although the *Burrow* court held that proof of actual damages might be possible, it required that each plaintiff show causation, that but for the breach of fiduciary duty, they would have recovered a certain additional sum of money in the underlying action. Expert testimony of some kind may be needed to establish these facts. In contrast, proof that the lawyers do not deserve some or their entire $60 million fee rests only on proof of their breach of a fiduciary duty. The more serious the breach, however, the greater the fee forfeited to the former clients.

Finally, liability insurance would certainly cover a damage award, but rarely will be available to pay a fee forfeiture award. The Minnesota Supreme Court has analogized fee forfeiture to cases about punitive damages and concluded that insurance covering a lawyer's individual breach of fiduciary duty was contrary to public policy, but coverage for a law firm's vicarious responsibility was not.[6] This means that an insurer will be required to pay the fee forfeiture award on behalf of a law firm, but the firm can seek indemnity against the errant lawyer who breached a fiduciary duty to the client.[7]

Clear and Serious Violations

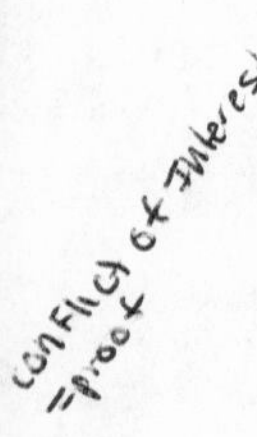

Although clients do not have to prove causation or actual damages to be entitled to fee forfeiture, they do have to prove a clear and serious violation of a duty owed the client. Breaches of the core agency duties of obedience, disclosure, confidentiality, and loyalty usually qualify, although the source of the duty can be civil law (for example, legal malpractice) or criminal law (for example, fraud) as well.[8] Most common are conflicts of interest, such as representing a client's wife in a divorce,[9] failing to disclose that the law firm employed the opposing party's adjuster,[10] or pressuring a client to change a fee contract,[11] all of which evidence clear disloyalty. Settling a client's case without consent also qualifies.[12]

---

4. Silbiger v. Prudence Bonds Corp., 180 F.2d 917, 920 (2d Cir. 1950) (citing cases). *See also* Woods v. City Natl. Bank & Trust Co. of Chicago, 312 U.S. 262 (1941).
5. Mr. Janus also paid no fee to Monco, so he had no fee forfeiture to seek.
6. Perl v. St. Paul Fire & Marine Ins. Co., 345 N.W.2d 209 (Minn. 1984).
7. *Id.* at 216-217.
8. *Restatement (Third) The Law Governing Lawyers* §37, Comment c.
9. Jeffry v. Pounds, 136 Cal. Rptr. 373 (Cal. App. 1977).
10. Rice v. Perl, 320 N.W.2d 407 (Minn. 1982).
11. Searcy, Denney, Scarola, Barnhart & Shipley, P.A. v. Scheller, 629 So. 2d 947 (Fla. App. 1993).
12. Francisco v. Foret, 2002 Tex. App. LEXIS 2610.

The duty breached not only must be owed to the client, but also must be clear and serious enough to justify fee forfeiture. *Burrow* adopts the Restatement factors as a means to determine whether such a breach of a duty constitutes a clear and serious violation. The first factor, whether the violation was "clear" is determined by an objective standard: whether "a reasonable lawyer, knowing the relevant facts and law reasonably accessible to the lawyer, would have known that the conduct was wrongful."[13] For example, the lawyers in *Burrow* will not be able to claim that they had no idea that Model Rule 1.8(g) prohibits aggregate settlements. The court also dismisses their claim that the rule is less than clear. The second factor, whether the violation was "serious," arises in a number of ways. Unlike *Burrow*, some courts hold that no fee forfeiture can occur unless the client was harmed.[14] *Burrow* represents the modern view, that harm is not necessary as long as the breach of a duty is otherwise clear and serious.[15] On the other hand, isolated inadvertent breaches, such as the failure to explain fully the terms of a settlement when the trial judge explained them to the client, do not rise to the level of a clear and serious breach.[16]

Multiple breaches in the same case are much more likely to qualify. For example, in a Texas case following *Burrow*, a law firm succeeded in getting a client a $56 million divorce settlement, even though she had signed a prenuptial agreement that limited her to about $12 million.[17] Along the way, the firm charged an unjustified contingent fee, changed the fee contract after the representation was underway, all while knowing that the client's "alcohol and prescription drug problem impaired her ability to agree to the amount of attorney fees."[18] One of the lawyers pursued a romantic relationship with the client that included his acceptance of expensive gifts and use of her charge card. When the client disputed some of the fee, the lawyers failed to keep the disputed portion in a trust account until the dispute was resolved. The court concluded that the serious breaches of duty to the client "did not affect the value of their legal work but would have if the underlying case had not settled," and ordered forfeiture of the $3 million fee.[19]

Total or Partial Forfeiture

When the client has shown a clear and serious breach, *Burrow* relies on the Restatement of the Law Governing Lawyers for the proposition that, normally, fee forfeiture will be total.[20] The court eschews an absolute rule of total forfeiture in all cases, recognizing that other courts have imposed partial fee forfeiture when the misconduct can be separated in time from other valuable services the lawyer has

---

13. *Restatement (Third) The Law Governing Lawyers* §37, Comment d. *See, e.g.*, Hardison v. Weinshel, 450 F. Supp. 721 (E.D. Wis. 1978) (lawyer who withdrew from case shortly before trial because he mistakenly believed client would not prevail forfeits all fee).
14. *See, e.g.*, Frank v. Bloom, 634 F.2d 1245 (10th Cir. 1980); Crawford v. Logan, 656 S.W.2d 360 (Tenn. 1983); Burk v. Burzynski, 672 P.2d 419 (Wyo. 1983).
15. *See, e.g.*, Hendry v. Pelland, 73 F.3d 397 (D.C. Cir. 1996) (lawyers represented property owners with conflicting interests); In re Eastern Sugar Antitrust Litig., 697 F.2d 524 (3d Cir. 1982) (law firm failed to disclose merger negotiations with opposing party's firm); Jackson v. Griffith, 421 So. 2d 677 (Fla. App. 1982) (lawyer coerced client to sign fee contract).
16. Hoover v. Larkin, 2001 Tex. App. LEXIS 6313.
17. Angela Ward, *Arce Jeopardizes Family Lawyers' Fee; Jury Awards 6.3 Million Verdict for Breach of Fiduciary Duty,* Texas Lawyer 16 (Nov. 15, 1999).
18. Piro v. Sarofim, 80 S.W.3d 717 (Tex. App. 2002).
19. *Id.* The court also upheld the trial judge's finding that the $6 million verdict, half for compensatory damages and half for fee forfeiture, was made in the alternative, but it added that "the trial court could have rendered judgment against the lawyers on both awards without creating a double recovery." *Id.* at 21.
20. *Restatement (Third) The Law Governing Lawyers* §37, Comment e.

performed. The court cites other factors as well, including the willfulness of the violation, its effect on the client, and the adequacy of other remedies. It then adds a final factor to be given great weight: "the public interest in maintaining the integrity of attorney-client relationships." The court avoids, however, the question of burden of proof. The most logical view seems to be that the client must show the clear and serious breach, at which point total forfeiture is presumed. The burden of proof then shifts to the lawyer to justify less than full forfeiture, by establishing the value of the service rendered apart from the breach.[21] Such an approach also parallels the reasoning in *Monco,* where the court presumed undue influence because of the lawyer's self dealing and then shifted the burden of proof to the lawyer to establish that the transaction was indeed reasonable and fair.

How might these factors play out on remand in *Burrow*? First, note that the aggregate settlement rule that the law firm allegedly breached is a long-standing rule that protects each client's right to individualized fiduciary duties. If the rule was violated, it is possible that the court could impose total fee forfeiture regardless of the lack of demonstrable harm to the clients. However, it is also possible that the law firm provided valuable services to each client up until the point of settlement. Suppose, for example, that the firm vigorously developed the liability issues in the case and worked up the damage claims of each client individually. It is conceivable that this work precipitated the settlement negotiations, which would not have otherwise occurred. At that point, the breach of the aggregate settlement rule, while still a serious matter, might be viewed as less of a breach of the total relationship. On the other hand, if the law firm did little of this work and the defendant conceded liability, the breach appears nearly total.

Thus, where the breach of fiduciary duty permeates the entire relationship, the grounds for total fee forfeiture occur. This explains why so many of the full forfeiture cases involve conflicts of interest, which tainted the entire representation. On the other hand, where the conflict occurs during the representation, the lawyer may be reimbursed for services provided before she should have responded to it.[22] Since so much is unknown and disputed in *Burrow,* the court properly remands for additional development of the facts.

Statutory Fee Forfeiture

Fee forfeiture can occur pursuant to statute as well. Most prominent are criminal statutes that provide for forfeiture of the fruits of criminal activity, including lawyer's fees.[23] Of course, lawyers who know that their clients are paying them with the fruits of the crime also risk other criminal penalties, such as aiding and abetting the crime or receiving stolen property.[24] Forfeiture statutes provide for civil forfeiture of the client's funds traceable to criminal activity, on the theory that they passed to the government at the time of the crime.[25] The government can seize all assets of a defendant at the point of indictment on a showing of probable cause to believe that the assets will ultimately be found to be subject to forfeiture.[26] If the criminal case

---

21. *See Restatement (Third) The Law Governing Lawyers* §42(2).
22. *E.g.,* Hill v. Douglas, 271 So. 2d 1 (Fla. 1971) (lawyer did not forfeit fee until he should have known he would be a witness).
23. *E.g.,* 21 U.S.C. §§848, 853 (2000).
24. *See* The Limits of the Law: Criminal Conduct, *supra* p.220.
25. *See* Geoffrey C. Hazard & W. William Hodes, *The Law of Lawyering* §9.32 (2002).
26. United States v. Monsanto, 924 F.2d 1186 (2d Cir. 1991) (en banc).

determines that the assets are the proceeds of the crime, they are permanently forfeited to the government.

The Supreme Court has held that these statutes are intended to reach lawyer's fees, as well as other assets of the defendant, and that using this statutory power to freeze cash paid to a lawyer does not violate a client's rights.[27] The Court was not persuaded by the argument that this meant that some defendants would be deprived of counsel of their choice. The majority pointed out that the Sixth Amendment guaranteed them a lawyer, but gave them no constitutional right "to spend another person's money" for such services. Publicly appointed counsel would suffice if no other untainted sources of money could be found to retain private counsel.[28] The practical reality created by these cases is that a lawyer retained by a defendant where such a statute applies takes a risk of nonpayment. Further, because the statute exempts a "bona fide purchaser for value" of property otherwise subject to forfeiture, lawyers essentially must audit the source of the client's money in order to insure payment.[29]

Overlapping Remedies

Courts have created different equitable remedies to fill gaps in legal relief. Occasionally, these remedies overlap, allowing a client to seek several in the same case. For example, *Burrow* leaves open the possibility that clients who can prove a breach of fiduciary duty that caused harm will be able to recover damages as well as fee forfeiture.[30] Similarly, a former client who succeeded in disqualifying his former lawyer from representing his wife in a divorce also was entitled to reversal of the trial court's order to pay his wife's attorney fees.[31] The client later filed a grievance as well, which resulted in a public reprimand of the lawyer.[32] In an analogous case claiming fee forfeiture under RICO, the court disqualified the law firm because of the defendant's statement that he wanted to plead guilty, but could not, because such a plea would jeopardize the $103,000 fee he had paid his lawyer. Following disqualification, the court also ordered fee forfeiture, including a state common law conversion action to recover the money the firm had already spent.[33]

One issue that commonly arises is whether a law firm that defends a disqualification motion can charge its current client for the defense. If the firm is disqualified, the client may have a partial or complete defense to the payment of legal fees.[34] Such a client also may seek disgorgement of a fee already paid.[35] Some clients in this position agree to defend the action but at the firm's own expense.[36]

27. Caplin & Drysdale v. United States, 491 U.S. 617 (1989); United States v. Monsanto, 491 U.S. 600 (1989).
28. *Caplin & Drysdale, supra* note 27, at 626.
29. A "bona fide purchaser for value" is a person who "was reasonably without cause to believe that the property was subject to forfeiture" when he took the property. 21 U.S.C. §853(c). *See, e.g.,* United States v. McCorkle, 321 F.3d 1292 (11th Cir. 2002) (burden of proof on lawyer F. Lee Bailey to identify the portion of the fee collected while he was a bona fide purchaser for value).
30. *See also Hendry, supra* note 15; *Piro, supra* note 18.
31. Ennis v. Ennis, 276 N.W.2d 341 (Wis. 1979). *See also* Image Tech. Serv. v. Eastman Kodak Co., 136 F.3d 1354 (9th Cir. 1998) (former client not entitled to attorney fees under Clayton Act for work done by lawyer who was later disqualified).
32. In re Conway, 301 N.W.2d 253 (Wis. 1981).
33. United States v. Moffitt, Zwerling & Kemler, P.C., 83 F.3d 660 (4th Cir. 1996), *cert. denied,* 519 U.S. 1101 (1997).
34. *See, e.g.,* In re Bonneville Pacific Corp., 196 B.R. 868 (D. Utah 1996); Goldstein v. Lees, 120 Cal. Rptr. 253 (Cal. App. 1975).
35. *See, e.g.,* In re Fountain, 141 Cal. Rptr. 654 (Cal. App. 1972).
36. *See, e.g.,* Padco v. Kinney & Lange, 444 N.W.2d 889 (Minn. App. 1989).

Together, the common law agency remedies of fee forfeiture and other loss of contractual benefits, as well as statutes that accomplish the same result, create minefields for unwary lawyers. You can avoid the common law remedies by honoring fiduciary duty, including duties of obedience, disclosure, confidentiality, and loyalty. Avoiding statutory fee forfeiture requires careful investigation of facts.

2. Simultaneous Representation of Adversaries

Problems

6-11. Viacom and Disney are both competing for an open TV channel in New York.

- **(*a*)** Can Martyn represent Viacom while Fox represents Disney if each lawyer seeks their client's consent?
- **(*b*)** What if our lawyers feel comfortable taking on the representation of both?
- **(*c*)** If our firm already represents Viacom in another unrelated matter, can we take on representation of Disney?

6-12. Local Municipality filed a motion to disqualify Martyn & Fox, claiming that Martyn & Fox cannot represent a developer in an appeal from a zoning decision because we currently represent local Municipality on some tax collection matters. Martyn, who is handling the zoning appeal, distinctly recalls chatting with the City Solicitor and getting a waiver. Are we safe?

Consider: Model Rules 1.7, 1.10
Model Code DR 5-105
RLGL §128

Universal City Studios, Inc. v. Reimerdes

98 F. Supp. 2d 449 (S.D.N.Y. 2000)

KAPLAN, District Judge.

This is an action by major motion picture studios, including Time Warner Entertainment Company L.P. ("Time Warner"), pursuant to the Digital Millenium Copyright Act[1] to enjoin defendants from posting on Internet web sites a computer program called DeCSS, which allegedly defeats an encryption system used by plaintiffs on digital versatile disks (DVDs) containing their copyrighted motion pictures. The matter now is before the Court on Time Warner's motion to disqualify defendants' new counsel on the ground that these attorneys currently are representing Time Warner in another case.

FACTS

Prior Proceedings in this Action

Shortly after the commencement of this action, plaintiffs moved for a preliminary injunction. . . . The motion was granted. . . . Although the Court

1. 17 U.S.C. §1201 *et seq.*

offered the defendants an immediate trial, that offer was declined and the case became inactive for a time. Indeed, the original defendants other than Eric Corley settled with plaintiffs.

The Court conducted a Rule 16 conference on March 20, 2000 at which Martin Garbus, Esq. of Frankfurt, Garbus, Klein & Selz, P.C. appeared for the first time on behalf of Corley. After conferring with counsel, the Court fixed a schedule and a trial date. Plaintiffs raised no objection to the Frankfurt firm's appearance.

On April 5, 2000, plaintiffs moved to expand the preliminary injunction to restrain defendants not only from making the offending computer program available on their web sites, but from linking to other web sites on which the program remains available. Three weeks later, plaintiff Time Warner moved to disqualify defendants' new counsel on the ground that he simultaneously is representing it in another action.

At present, the parties are engaged in expedited discovery. Trial is scheduled for July 17, 2000.

The Other Action

The source of the Frankfurt firm's alleged conflict is another case pending in this Court, Scholastic, Inc. v. Stouffer, which relates to the popular Harry Potter books. The books were written by J.K. Rowling and published by Scholastic, Inc. ("Scholastic"). Time Warner is the exclusive owner of, inter alia, all copyrights, trademarks, and exploitation rights in the first four Harry Potter books. It has spent millions of dollars registering and protecting various trademarks and indicia of origin from these books, including the term and mark "Muggles." Scholastic is merely a licensee of certain U.S. publishing rights under rights reserved to Rowland.

In or about August 1999, Rowling, Scholastic and Time Warner received a claim from Nancy Stouffer, who purported to own the copyright and trademark in the term "Muggles."... Time Warner and the others retained the Frankfurt firm in connection with the claim in or about September 1999.

In early November, 1999,... Scholastic, Rowling and Time Warner decided to commence a declaratory judgment action against Stouffer.... Time Warner and Scholastic agreed that Scholastic's outside litigation counsel, the Frankfurt firm, would handle the *Stouffer* case and that Scholastic would be responsible for paying its fees....

On or about April 12, 2000, a Time Warner in-house attorney telephoned the Frankfurt partner responsible for the *Stouffer* lawsuit, Edward Rosenthal, to discuss the firm's conflict of interest. Two days later, Mr. Rosenthal advised Time Warner that he had reviewed the two matters and concluded that there was no conflict. Time Warner disagreed and asked that the firm withdraw in this case. Nearly a week later, Mr. Rosenthal wrote Time Warner, stating that the Frankfurt firm did not believe that there was "any disqualifiable conflict created by [its] representation" of defendant Corley in this action and its representation of Time Warner in *Stouffer* because the two cases involve entirely different issues. He suggested that Time Warner retain separate counsel in *Stouffer* if it remained concerned.

Discussion

Attorneys practicing in this Court must adhere to the Code of Professional Responsibility adopted by the Appellate Division of the New York Supreme Court. Canon 5 of the Code states that "[a] lawyer should exercise independent professional judgment on behalf of a client," and Disciplinary Rule DR 5-105 proscribes a lawyer from representing a client if that representation is of interests differing from or adverse to those of another existing client.

In Cinema 5, Ltd. v. Cinerama, Inc.,[16] the Second Circuit held that it is improper per se for an attorney to participate in a lawsuit against his or her own client in a situation in which the lawyer has traditional attorney-client relationships with both clients.[17] More recently, the circuit "has established alternative guidelines for a district court to follow... depending on the particular facts of the case."

Plaintiff's counsel was a partner of two separate firms—one of which represented Cinema 5, Ltd. in the matter before the court, the other which represented Cinerama in an unrelated matter. There was no question that plaintiff's counsel—or his firm—as directly representing both plaintiff and defendant simultaneously.

This more flexible approach stems from Glueck v. Jonathan Logan, Inc.,[19] where the circuit faced the question whether a law firm's suit against a member of an association which it represented implicated the standard of *Cinema* 5. The court framed the inquiry as "whether there exist sufficient aspects of an attorney-client relationship for purposes of triggering inquiry into the potential conflict involved."[20] The court answered this question in the negative, holding that (1) the association member was a client only in a vicarious sense, and (2) the "risks against which Canon 5 guards will not inevitably arise" in such a situation. In those situations, a standard less stringent than *Cinema* 5's per se test applies.

This Court built upon *Cinema* 5 and *Glueck* in Commercial Union Insurance Co. v. Marco International Corp.,[22] a case presenting the question whether an insurance company's longstanding counsel was disqualified from representing the carrier in coverage litigation with its insured because it simultaneously was representing the insured, as a nominal plaintiff, in bringing a subrogation claim to recover for the benefit of the carrier a loss for which the carrier already had indemnified its insured. The Court examined the relationships among the insured, the carrier and the attorneys. It found that the insured was obliged to assign to the carrier its right to prosecute and recover on any claim against third parties for the loss on which the carrier made payment. Thus, the insured had no significant economic or other interest in the subrogation case. Moreover, in light of the provisions of the policy, the insured had no role in selecting, paying or controlling the actions of counsel in pursuing that action. In consequence, the Court held that the lawyers' client in the subrogation case in substance was the carrier, not the insured in whose name the case was brought and refused to disqualify counsel....

Unlike the insured in *Commercial Union*, Time Warner has substantial interests at stake in the *Stouffer* case. It appears, in fact, that its interests there substantially exceed those of either Scholastic or Rowling. If Stouffer were to prevail in her contention that she owns the copyright and trademark in "Muggles," the value of Time Warner's film and ancillary merchandising rights in the Harry Potter books would be impaired. Indeed, the complaint in *Stouffer* alleges that Time

16. 528 F.2d 1384 (2d Cir. 1976).
17. *Id.* at 1387. *Accord, e.g., Restatement of the Law Governing Lawyers* §209(2) (Prop. Final Draft No. 1, 1996) (lawyer may not represent one client against another currently represented client even if matters unrelated).
19. 653 F.2d 746 (2d Cir. 1981).
20. *Glueck*, 653 F.2d at 748-49 (internal citations omitted).
22. 75 F. Supp. 2d 108 (S.D.N.Y. 1999).

Warner currently is developing a theatrical motion picture referring to the imaginary world created by Rowling in the Harry Potter books and that all of the plaintiffs in the *Stouffer* case have plans for merchandising projects intended to build on the books. Moreover, while the extent to which it has participated in the *Stouffer* case thus far appears to have been limited, Time Warner house counsel have been provided drafts of legal papers in advance of filing and have the right to control the actions of the Frankfurt firm as its counsel. This situation is quite distinct from that in *Commercial Union*, where the insured had assigned all of its rights to the carrier and was obliged to cooperate with the carrier's assertion of the subrogation claim. Thus, Time Warner, unlike the insured in *Commercial Union*, is party to a real attorney-client relationship with the Frankfurt firm. The fact that it agreed to use Scholastic's litigation counsel in *Stouffer* and, indeed, that there may be little love lost between Time Warner and Mr. Garbus by virtue of events gone by cannot detract from this fact. When the Frankfurt firm agreed to represent Time Warner along with Scholastic and Ms. Rowling, it surrendered the right to represent another client in litigation against any of them.

The fact that the Frankfurt firm has responded to the motion to disqualify in part by moving in *Stouffer* for leave to withdraw as counsel for Time Warner is of no assistance to it. "It is . . . established law that an attorney cannot avoid disqualification under the *Cinema* 5 rule merely by 'firing' the disfavored client, dropping the client like a hot potato, and transforming a continuing relationship to a former relationship by way of client abandonment." Indeed, the offense inherent in taking on the conflicting representation is compounded by seeking to "fire" the client in pursuit of the attorney's interest in taking on a new, more attractive representation. If, as one judge has written, "the act of suing one's client is a 'dramatic form of disloyalty,'" what might be said of trying to drop the first client in an effort to free the attorney to pursue his or her self-interest in taking on a newer and more attractive professional engagement?

In response to these considerations, the Frankfurt firm has submitted a declaration of Professor Charles W. Wolfram, who contends that Time Warner is a "non-primary" or "accommodation" client, that only "primary" clients may seek disqualification of counsel afflicted with conflicts, and in any case that a lawyer representing a non-primary client "can drop the accommodation client (like a hot potato, or otherwise) and file suit against the former accommodation client." He relies principally on Allegaert v. Perot[27] and the proposed Restatement. With respect, this Court disagrees.

It is worth noting at the outset that Professor Wolfram does not seek to defend the proposition that the Frankfurt firm acted properly in taking on defendants in a case brought against them by Time Warner, among others, while simultaneously representing Time Warner. Rather, his point is limited to whether disqualification at the behest of an accommodation client is an appropriate remedy in such a situation. Indeed, the Restatement upon which he relies makes plain that the firm's action was not appropriate.[28]

Second, Professor Wolfram's conclusion that Time Warner is a non-primary or accommodation client rests on a

27. 565 F.2d 246 (2d Cir. 1977).
28. *Restatement of the Law Governing Lawyers* §209(2) (Proposed Final Draft No. 1, 1996).

series of factual assumptions—that Time Warner must have understood that the Frankfurt firm's ultimate allegiance is to Scholastic in the event of a conflict between Time Warner and Scholastic, that Time Warner "could not reasonably expect that the law firm would keep any information of interest to [Scholastic] confidential from it," that Time Warner has no economic stake in the *Stouffer* case because "(as I assume) its interests [are] fully protected pursuant to its contractual arrangements for indemnification with either or both of Ms. Rowling and Scholastic," that Time Warner was named as a plaintiff in *Stouffer* only at the direction of Scholastic, that Time Warner "plays no part in controlling the activities" of the lawyers, and that Time Warner's minor role in the case "was dictated entirely by considerations of the ultimate success of" Scholastic and Ms. Rowling. These assumptions, however, are demonstrably wrong (e.g., the assumption that Time Warner has no economic stake in the case), unproved, or are unwarranted inferences drawn from assertions made by the Frankfurt firm. The fact, for example, that Time Warner's house counsel have not commented on drafts of legal papers provided to them in advance of filing does not show that Time Warner "plays no part in controlling" the firm's actions. As noted earlier, it may reflect nothing more than satisfaction with the work product. And surely this record, unlike that in *Commercial Union*, does not justify the conclusion that Scholastic is contractually entitled to control the *Stouffer* litigation by virtue of an assignment to it of Time Warner's interests.

Finally, even if the facts warranted the conclusion that Time Warner is an accommodation client in *Stouffer* in the sense that Professor Wolfram uses the term, the Court rejects his contention that the Frankfurt firm is entitled, without Time Warner's consent, to drop it "like a hot potato, or otherwise" simply because it has found a case more to its liking. *Allegaert* involved a different situation entirely. The law firms sought to be disqualified there from suing the bankruptcy estate of duPont Walston Incorporation ("Walston") formerly had represented both their regular clients and Walston, with whom their regular clients then were aligned in something akin to a joint venture, in a derivative suit challenging the alignment. The Circuit affirmed the district court order declining to disqualify the law firms on the ground that Walston, in view of the "joint venture" in which it was engaged with the law firms' regular clients, could not reasonably have believed that any information they gave to the lawyers in the course of the derivative suit would be withheld from the regular clients. The case therefore involved the question whether the lawyers were disabled from suing a former client by virtue of Canon 4's requirement that the lawyer preserve client confidences. The Circuit held only that Canon 4 is not implicated where there could have been no confidences to begin with. But that is a far cry from saying that a lawyer in an existing relationship simply may fire a client for the lawyer's own advantage, a matter that implicates Canon 5's requirement of the lawyer's obligation of utmost fidelity to the client. Thus, the Court concludes that the Frankfurt firm is acting improperly in seeking to represent defendants here despite its representation of Time Warner in *Stouffer*. That, however, does not necessarily mean that it should be disqualified.

Disqualification motions are subject to abuse for tactical purposes. They may require sometimes complex satellite litigation extraneous to the case before the court. Disqualification also deprives a client of counsel of its choice. Moreover, professional disciplinary bodies, including the Grievance Committee of this

Court, are available to police the behavior of counsel. Accordingly, the Second Circuit has made clear that disqualification is appropriate only if a violation of the Code of Professional Responsibility gives rise to a significant risk of trial taint. . . . That is to say, disqualification for an alleged conflict of interest is appropriate only if there is a significant risk that the conflict will affect the attorney's ability to represent his or her client with vigor or if the attorney is in a position to use privileged information acquired in the representation of a client against that client in another matter.

There is substantial reason to believe that the motion to disqualify the Frankfurt firm is motivated at least partly by tactical considerations. Time Warner knew of the conflict as early as March 14 but did not even raise the issue with the firm until April 12, well after a scheduling order was entered and more than a week after plaintiffs had moved to expand the preliminary injunction. Plaintiffs have been pressing for, and recently obtained, an acceleration of the trial in this action and thus stand to gain by forcing defendants to find and educate new counsel. Moreover, Time Warner's belated objection to the Frankfurt firm's appearance here comes against a background of considerable apparent animosity between Martin Garbus, Esq. of the Frankfurt firm and Time Warner.

The view that the motion is tactically motivated, at least in part, draws support from the fact that Time Warner has made no effort to show that its interests either in this case or in *Stouffer* would be affected adversely by the Frankfurt firm's conflict. There is no suggestion that the Frankfurt firm is privy to any Time Warner secrets by virtue of the *Stouffer* representation that could be used to its disadvantage here. There is no suggestion that the firm's representation of Time Warner in *Stouffer* would suffer, which seems unlikely in view of the firm's long standing relationship with Scholastic and the substantial congruence of Time Warner's interests there with those of Scholastic. In short, Time Warner has failed to establish any material risk that it would be prejudiced inappropriately by allowing the Frankfurt firm to continue in this litigation notwithstanding its role in the *Stouffer* case. Moreover, defendants here certainly do not object to Frankfurt's representation of them notwithstanding its obligations to Time Warner in *Stouffer*.

CONCLUSION

The situation before the Court is troublesome. The lawyers' breach of ethics cannot reasonably be minimized. Even acknowledging that the Frankfurt firm, in consequence of sloppy conflict checking procedures, appears to have agreed to take on this case without realizing that doing so would be improper, its insistence on proceeding once it learned of the conflict was improper. In other circumstances, the Court well might disqualify it. But there are substantial factors pointing to a contrary result. There is no real risk of tainting the trial or, putting it another way, of prejudicing Time Warner absent disqualification. Disqualification at this stage would prejudice defendants in that they would be forced either to find and educate new counsel for an important trial that now is less than two months away or seek an adjournment and thus perhaps prolong the duration of the preliminary injunction. Time Warner sat on its hands for too long to have substantial claims on the Court's exercise of its discretion.

Accordingly, the motion to disqualify defendants' counsel is denied. The proper place for this controversy is in the appropriate professional disciplinary body. . . .

3. Joint Clients

Problems

6-13. Husband and Wife ask Martyn & Fox to prepare the papers for their dissolution of marriage. May Martyn & Fox represent both spouses? Does it matter if they have already agreed to property division, child custody, and support obligations? What if Husband and Wife ask Martyn to mediate their disputes regarding these issues? If the mediation is successful, May Martyn represent both in drafting the legal papers necessary to effectuate the dissolution?

6-14. Two defendants are charged with murder arising from a botched bank robbery that resulted in the killing of a customer. Can Martyn & Fox represent both defendants? What if only the "shooter" is eligible for the death penalty? Would it matter is Martyn represents one defendant and Fox represents the other?

6-15. Martyn & Fox is asked to represent driver-son, and passenger-father, in a lawsuit arising from an auto accident where the driver of the other car has been charged with speeding. Can we take on this case? What happens if son tells Fox before his deposition "I had two drinks before I picked up dad"?

6-16. Our long-time corporate brokerage client and two of its stockbrokers have been sued for violating insider-trading regulations. Can Martyn & Fox represent both the corporation and the stockbrokers?

6-17. Buyer and seller of real estate come to Martyn & Fox to handle the deal. They have agreed on the price, date of closing, and identity of the property to be conveyed. Can Martyn & Fox undertake the engagement?

6-18. A long-time client of Martyn & Fox asks us to represent three partners in forming a new business: our long-time client, the money guy, and the new venture's CEO. May we?

6-19. Our corporate client's CEO asks Martyn & Fox to represent his wife and him in drawing up new wills. Can we do so? What if the wife takes Martyn aside and tells her to draft a codicil that diverts a substantial part of her assets to a "friend"? What if later, during divorce proceedings, the wife calls Martyn & Fox to be refreshed as to husband's assets; may (must) Martyn & Fox share that information?

Consider: Model Rules 1.7, 1.8(b), 1.10, 1.12, 1.13, 2.4
Model Code DR 5-105

New York State Bar Opinion 736 (2001)

New York State Bar Association Committee on Professional Ethics

Questions

May an attorney engaged in matrimonial mediation draft and file a separation agreement and divorce papers that incorporate terms agreed upon by the marital parties in the course of the mediation?

Opinion

As we have recognized in the past, a lawyer who serves as a mediator to assist in the resolution of a possible dispute does not "represent" either party as a client for purposes of the conflict-of-interest rules and other rules governing the lawyer-client relationship. Therefore, even in many situations where a lawyer could not properly represent two clients with differing interests, the lawyer may serve them both as a mediator. This is true in matrimonial as well as other legal contexts. In N.Y. State 258 (1972), although we concluded that a lawyer may not jointly represent the spouses in a divorce proceeding, we also observed, "A lawyer approached by husband and wife in a matrimonial matter and asked to represent both, may . . . properly undertake to serve as a mediator or arbitrator." *Accord* N.Y. City 80-23 (1981).

This is not to say that all matrimonial disputes are appropriate candidates for mediation. Matrimonial mediation may be undertaken in many circumstances, but in some circumstances, . . . the complex and conflicting interests involved in a particular matrimonial dispute, the difficult legal issues involved, the subtle legal ramifications of particular resolutions, and the inequality in bargaining power resulting from differences in the personalities or sophistication of the parties make it virtually impossible to achieve a just result free from later recriminations or bias or malpractice, unless both parties are represented by separate counsel. In the latter circumstances, informing the parties that the lawyer "represents" neither party and obtaining their consent, even after a full explanation of the risks, may not be meaningful; the distinction between representing both parties and not representing either, in such circumstances, may be illusory.

Thus, there will be situations where the lawyer-mediator must not initially undertake, or must thereafter end, the mediation because a party's interest cannot fairly be protected without obtaining independent legal advice, or because a party needs a lawyer's assistance to protect against overreaching. However, the fact that the parties may begin with differing interests that would preclude a joint representation does not, in and by itself, foreclose the possibility of mediation.

The question now before us is whether, at the conclusion of any mediation, having assisted the parties in achieving the general terms of a settlement (which the lawyer-mediator would typically outline in a document), the lawyer-mediator may then proceed to represent the parties and draft and file legal documents on their behalf—in particular, the separation agreement and divorce papers. At that point, of course, the lawyer would be representing two clients who expect to become facial adversaries in a matrimonial litigation, and the representation would be subject to DR 5-105(A) and (C), which address the joint representation of clients with differing interests. . . .

. . . Thus, as we recognized in Opinion 258 in the matrimonial context in particular, a lawyer who serves as mediator in a matrimonial dispute may not later represent one party against the other if the dispute is not successfully resolved in mediation. We do not believe, however, that it is categorically improper for a lawyer, after successfully concluding a mediation, to represent both parties to the mediation with the consent of each, if there is no longer a "dispute" between them.

As to whether a lawyer-mediator—or, for that matter, any other lawyer—may represent parties to a divorce for the limited purpose of drafting and filing a settlement agreement and divorce papers, or whether such a joint representation is categorically forbidden by DR 5-105(A) and (C), we turn first to Opinion 258, where we opined:

> It would be improper for a lawyer to represent both husband and wife at any stage of a marital problem, even with full disclosure and informed consent of both parties.

> The likelihood of prejudice is so great in this type of matter as to make impossible adequate representation of both spouses, even where the separation is "friendly" and the divorce uncontested.

We reasoned that dual representation would never satisfy the then "obviousness" test of DR 5-105(C)[1] because of the "substantial likelihood of prejudice or professional conflict of interest in every matrimonial problem."

We now modify our previous view. . . . [B]ecause there will be occasions when a "disinterested lawyer" would believe that the lawyer-mediator can competently represent the interests of each spouse by preparing and filing the settlement agreement and divorce papers, we reject the dictate of Opinion 258 that the joint representation is per se impermissible in any and all circumstances.

We remain convinced, however, that in the generality of cases, even if the spouses agree on the broad outlines of a settlement at the conclusion of the mediation, a disinterested lawyer will not be able to conclude that he or she can competently represent the interests of each spouse. Although there is general agreement on broad settlement terms, many particulars may remain to be worked out in the course of drafting a settlement agreement. Even with respect to the terms on which there appears to be agreement, one or both spouses may benefit from a disinterested lawyer's advice as to whether the agreement meets with the spouse's legitimate objectives and what other procedural alternatives may be available to achieve more favorable terms. One or both spouses may thus benefit from a disinterested lawyer's advice as to (1) his or her legal options, (2) how the settlement terms will or will not meet the client's interests, and (3) alternative ways to fashion a settlement agreement. Likewise, one or both may benefit from the assistance of a disinterested lawyer in negotiating the terms and/or thereafter drafting the terms.

In short, under the disinterested lawyer test of DR 5-105(C), the lawyer may not represent both spouses unless the lawyer objectively concludes that, in the particular case, the parties are firmly committed to the terms arrived at in mediation, the terms are faithful to both spouses' objectives and consistent with their legal rights, there are no remaining points of contention, and the lawyer can competently fashion the settlement agreement and divorce documents. In those circumstances, the per se ban of N.Y. State 258 should be relaxed to permit spouses to avoid the expense incident to separate representation and permit them to consummate a truly consensual parting, provided both spouses consent to the representation after full disclosure of the implications of the simultaneous representation and the advantages and risks involved.[2]

Because the "disinterested lawyer" test cannot easily be met, the lawyer-mediator may not prepare and file a settlement agreement and divorce papers after the conclusion of the mediation as a matter of regular practice on behalf of spouses who are otherwise unrepresented.[3] Nor may the lawyer-mediator, in advertising, a

1. The "obviousness" test has been replaced by the "disinterested lawyer" test, which has been codified in DR 5-101(A) and DR 5-105(C).

2. Full disclosure should include advising both clients of the risk of a legal challenge, since "the absence of independent representation is a significant factor to be taken into consideration when determining whether a separation agreement was freely and fairly entered into" when "the same attorney represented both parties in the preparation of the agreement." Levine v. Levine, 436 N.E.2d 476 (N.Y. 1982).

3. If the spouses are independently represented by lawyers who are prepared, insofar as necessary, to advise about the settlement terms, negotiate unresolved terms, and review the settlement agreement and other papers, then we see no restriction on the lawyer-mediator serving as drafter and reducing to writing an oral agreement that encompasses a mutually agreeable understanding between the parties on all

retainer agreement, or other communications with potential clients, state or imply that, in the ordinary course, the lawyer will routinely prepare and file the divorce papers after the mediation is completed. The likelihood that joint representation will satisfy the standard of DR 5-105(C) is so uncertain prior to the start of the mediation that it would be misleading for the lawyer to indicate that preparing and filing the divorce papers for the spouses is part of the lawyer's standard practice.

In reaching our conclusion, we are not unmindful of the decision in Levine v. Levine, 436 N.E.2d 476 (N.Y. 1982), in which the Court of Appeals held that the mere fact that a separation agreement was prepared by one attorney representing both husband and wife was not sufficient, "in and of itself, to establish overreaching requiring a rescission of the agreement." In *Levine*, after a non-jury trial, the trial court "found no evidence of coercion, undue influence or overreaching practiced by the husband," and made specific factual findings "that the agreement was fair" and "that the attorney had 'managed to preserve neutrality' throughout his joint representation of the couple." Under those circumstances, while acknowledging that "the potential conflict of interest inherent in such joint representation suggests that the husband and wife should retain separate counsel," the Court of Appeals stated that "the parties have an absolute right to be represented by the same attorney provided 'there has been full disclosure between the parties, not only of all relevant facts but also of their contextual significance, and there has been an absence of inequitable conduct or other infirmity which might vitiate the execution of the agreement.'"

Although the Court's reference to the parties' "absolute right to be represented by the same attorney" might be read to supersede DR 5-105(A) and (C), we do not believe that was the Court's intention. We are not aware of any published decisions since 1982, when the Court decided *Levine*, that hold, on the basis of the Court's dicta, that a lawyer may represent spouses jointly in divorce proceedings even when the representation would otherwise be forbidden by DR 5-105(C) because a disinterested lawyer would not believe that the lawyer can competently represent the interests of each. Further, we note that, in *Levine*, the Court did not explicitly address the propriety of the joint representation under the disciplinary rules. Rather, the question before the Court was whether a court would grant the extraordinary remedy of rescission on a particular set of facts. The answer did not turn on whether or not the lawyer properly undertook the representation. Even if, after the representation has come to an end, a court in full possession of all relevant facts concludes that there was "an absence of inequitable conduct or other infirmity which might vitiate the execution of the agreement," it may nevertheless have been improper to undertake the representation at the outset, in light of the facts then known to the lawyer and the risk that one or both spouses would be disadvantaged by the lack of independent counsel.

Finally, we note that, in cases where it is permissible for the lawyer-mediator to draft and file divorce papers, if the lawyer does not make a formal appearance in the divorce proceeding, the lawyer must ensure that his or her role is disclosed to the court. Otherwise, there is a risk that the court will be misled to believe that the papers were prepared by the parties themselves, and, further, the court will not know which lawyer is responsible in the event it has concerns about the preparation and contents of the legal documents.

---

issues. In essence, the lawyer will then be serving as a mere amanuensis, and will not be exercising independent professional judgment on behalf of one spouse or the other with respect to the settlement terms.

CONCLUSION

An attorney-mediator may prepare divorce documents incorporating a mutually acceptable separation agreement and represent both parties only in those cases where mediation has proven entirely successful, the parties are fully informed, no contested issues remain, and the attorney-mediator satisfies the "disinterested lawyer" test of DR 5-105(C).

Lawyers and Other Professionals: *Informed Consent*

All of the cases in this chapter rely heavily on the notion of informed consent as a means to enable clients to maintain control and to prevent lawyers from breaching fiduciary duties. Recent amendments to the Model Rules of Professional Conduct also define and impose the requirement on lawyers as a condition of obedience to a client,[1] limiting the scope of a representation,[2] disclosing or using confidential information,[3] and avoiding conflicts of interest.[4] Although the idea of informed consent can be linked to centuries-old concepts of fiduciary obligation, it is better known in recent legal literature as a doctrine that governs the conduct of physicians and other health care providers. In this note, we trace the similarities and distinctive features of the law of informed consent in both professions in order to discover some of the probable vectors the law might take in the future.

Autonomous Authorization

The recognition of a legal right to decide and the concomitant legal obligation of a professional person to disclose information emphasize the importance of autonomy, or self-governance. The law of informed consent reflects the belief that persons make a real choice only if they have first understood information, second, appreciated the consequences of a choice, and third, have used reason to evaluate this information. The same law imposes dual duties on professionals as a means of promoting the autonomous choices of those they serve: an obligation to provide adequate information and deference to client choice.

Morally, respect for autonomy has deontological roots. Autonomy is essential to both religious and philosophical notions of respect for the dignity of the human person.[5] For example, Kant envisioned persons as inherently valuable because we are self-legislating agents capable of shaping our own destinies.[6] Making decisions requires an application of personal values to determine a future course, which in turn depends upon a view of humans as being free and rational. We respect a human person by relying on that person's own self-determined choices. To withhold or skew relevant information, even for a person's own good, is to treat him or her as an object to be manipulated.[7]

1. Model Rules 1.2(a), 1.4.
2. Model Rule 1.2(c).
3. Model Rules 1.6(a), 1.9, 1.18(d).
4. Model Rules 1.7(b)(4), 1.8-1.12, 2.3(b). These issues often are addressed in engagement letters. *See* Practice Pointers: Engagement, Nonengagement, and Disengagement Letters, *supra* p.79.
5. *See* Marcy Strauss, *Toward a Revised Model of Attorney-Client Relationship: The Argument for Autonomy,* 65 N.C. L. Rev. 315, 336 (1987).
6. *See* Jessica W. Berg et al., *Informed Consent: Legal Theory and Clinical Practice* 22, 31 (2d ed., Oxford 2001).
7. *See* Isaiah Berlin, *Four Essays on Liberty* 136 (1969).

Beyond moral duty, autonomy also has been justified on utilitarian grounds, because it promotes rational decisionmaking. For example, John Stuart Mill argued that individuality was an element of well-being, and that we should assist each other in distinguishing the "better from the worse."[8] Lawyers and physicians often are unable to know what values their clients and patients place on alternative courses of action. The subjectivity of weighing possible consequences and the reality that the client must live with the eventual result of the decision lead many to argue that informed consent maximizes the benefit of decisionmaking to clients, professionals, and the institutions they work in.

There is also considerable empirical evidence for this conclusion. In law, a study of New York City personal injury plaintiffs concluded that clients who actively participate in the conduct of their claims get significantly better results than those who passively delegate decisionmaking responsibility.[9] Similar studies in medicine validate the efficacy of informed consent in clinical decisionmaking.[10]

Lawyers

For lawyers, agency law imposes the obligation of informed consent. The requirement that a lawyer has an affirmative duty to advise a client "promptly whenever he has any information to give which it is important the client receive"[11] originated in nineteenth-century agency cases where lawyers breached client confidentiality, failed to disclose a conflicting personal interest, or neglected to notify their clients about material facts in a transaction. These courts characterized the breach as a constructive fraud, because the client acted without sufficient information.[12] Many of these early cases focused on when such disclosure must be made, creating the foundation for our current understanding that disclosure is required to avoid breaching fiduciary duties of obedience, confidentiality, and loyalty. None of these cases required any expert testimony to establish the breach of fiduciary duty. It was enough if the lawyer failed to disclose sufficient information to allow the client to make an autonomous choice.

In these materials we have already encountered lawyers who did not obey or clarify their client's instructions,[13] lawyers who disclosed confidential information that harmed their clients,[14] and lawyers who used confidential information of their clients for the benefit of others.[15] We also have seen situations where lawyers' disclosures to clients have been insufficient to collect a contingent fee,[16] overcome a presumption of undue influence,[17] justify a sexual relationship with a client,[18] or legitimate a joint representation. In all of these cases, the special knowledge and skill of the lawyers gave them the power, inadvertently or intentionally, to abuse the trust of their clients. The courts' recognition of a fiduciary duty of disclosure, obedience, confidentiality, or loyalty protected these clients' rights to individualized

8. Tom L. Beauchamp & James F. Childress, *Principles of Biomedical Ethics* 125 (Oxford 1994).
9. Douglas E. Rosenthal, *Lawyer and Client: Who's In Charge?* 61 (Russell Sage Found. 1974).
10. Berg et al., *supra* note 6, at 26-30; Susan R. Martyn, *Informed Consent in the Practice of Law*, 48 Geo. Wash. L. Rev. 307, 340-343 (1980).
11. Baker v. Humphrey, 101 U.S. 494, 500 (1879).
12. Martyn, *supra* note 10, at 323.
13. dePape v. Trinity Health Systems, Inc. *supra* p.83; Roe v. Flores-Ortega, *supra* p.106.
14. Perez v. Kirk & Carrigan, *supra* p.125; In re Pressly, *supra* p.153.
15. Matter of Anonymous, *supra* p.123; Maritrans GP Inc. v. Pepper, Hamilton & Scheetz, *supra* p.257.
16. Burrow v. Arce, *supra* p.285.
17. Monco v. Janus, *supra* p.266.
18. In re Halverson, *supra* p.271.

representation of their best interests. At the same time, proper informed consent by the clients would have obviated the breach.

The recently revised Model Rules articulate similar duties to communicate with a client, identifying five different occasions that trigger the requirement that lawyers initiate the information and consultation process. The first duty arises when decisions require client consent, such as the decision to settle or appeal a matter or clarification of the client's wishes regarding contract provisions.[19] The second occasion that requires client consultation concerns the means to be used to accomplish client objectives. This could include, for example, whether to litigate, arbitrate or mediate a matter, whether to stipulate to a set of facts, or whether to consult with another lawyer.[20] Third, a lawyer must update the client periodically on the status of a matter. This duty requires a lawyer to communicate information about both important developments in the matter as well as changes in the lawyer's practice, such as a serious illness of the lawyer or a merger with another law firm.[21] Beyond periodic updates, the lawyer also has a duty to respond to client requests for information.[22] Finally, the lawyer has a responsibility to initiate communication with a client about limitations on the lawyer's conduct, such as the obligation not to counsel or assist client crimes or frauds.[23]

The most difficult part of understanding the duty of informed consent for lawyers and other professionals involves knowing how much and what kind of information to disclose. Most cases require complete disclosure of all information that may be relevant to the lawyer's representation.[24] *Monco* demonstrates that the disclosure must include both material facts as well as an explanation of their legal significance. One issue that repeatedly arises is whether advance waivers of conflicts of interest will later become effective to vitiate a conflict. Comments to the Restatement and Model Rule 1.7 apply the general duty to disclose and explain specific risks and alternatives to answer this question. So, for example, where the consent is open-ended and not specific, such a waiver will probably not be effective against a later conflict. On the other hand, a specific waiver unrelated to the representation entered into after the client received independent legal advice may be upheld.[25]

Lawyer codes gradually have incorporated the agency obligation to disclose and explain all relevant information. The ABA Canons, for example, articulated a full disclosure requirement with respect to conflicts of interest.[26] The Model Code of Professional Responsibility also required full disclosure of relevant facts to clients, both about conflicts and the lawyer's use of confidential information.[27] The original

---

19. *See* Model R. Prof. Conduct 1.2(a), 1.4(a)(1); *Restatement (Third) The Law Governing Lawyers* §22.
20. *See* Model R. Prof. Conduct 1.2(a), 1.4(a)(2); *Restatement (Third) The Law Governing Lawyers* §21. In some matters, such as trials, lawyers have inherent authority to act for clients when the legal system demands an immediate decision without time for consultation. *Id.* at §23, Comment d. This exception roughly correlates to the emergency exception to physician informed consent. *See* note 43, *infra.*
21. *Id.* at §20, Comment c; Model R. Prof. Conduct 1.4(a)(3).
22. *Id.*, Comment d; Model R. Prof. Conduct 1.4(a)(4).
23. *Id.* at §22, Comment c; Model R. Prof. Conduct 1.4(a)(5).
24. Ronald E. Mallen & Jeffrey M. Smith, *Legal Malpractice* §14.19 (5th ed., West 2000).
25. *Restatement (Third) The Law Governing Lawyers* §122, Comment d (2000); Model Rule 1.7, Comment 22. *See also* Lawrence J. Fox, *All's O.K. Between Consenting Adults: Enlightened Rule on Privacy, Obscene Rule on Ethics,* 29 Hofstra L. Rev. 701 (2001).
26. With respect to conflicting interests, lawyers had a duty to disclose "all of the circumstances of his relations to the parties, and any interest in or connection with the controversy, which might influence the client . . . ," and required "express consent of all concerned given after a full disclosure of the facts." ABA Canons of Prof. Ethics, Canon 6 (1908).
27. DR 4-101(C)(1) (reveal or using confidential information); DR 5-101(A) (personal interests of the lawyer); DR 5-104 (business relations with clients); DR 5-107(A) (influence by nonclients). The Code also specified the topics of required disclosure in some conflicts rules. DR 5-105(C) (multiple clients); DR 5-106 (aggregate settlements).

Model Rules modified this full disclosure mandate, replacing it with a new requirement that the client consent "following consultation."[28] "Consultation" was defined to mean the "communication of information reasonably sufficient to permit the client to appreciate the significance of the matter in question."[29] At the same time, specific disclosure requirements for certain conflicts were articulated more clearly.[30] The Model Rules also clarified the lawyer's obligation to keep the client generally informed about the about the status of the matter and to explain the matter "to the extent reasonably necessary to permit the client to make informed decisions regarding the representation."[31] The Restatement generally adopted this "consent following consultation standard."[32] With respect to client waivers of conflicts of interest, however, it articulated the prerequisite of "informed consent," which "requires that the client or former client have reasonably adequate information about the material risks of such representation to that client or former client."[33]

The current Model Rules recognize the importance of both disclosure and explanation of relevant information by substituting a uniform standard of "informed consent" for the original "consents following consultation" obligation.[34] A person's agreement constitutes an informed consent if the lawyer has communicated "adequate information and explanation" about two matters: "the material risks of and reasonably available alternatives to the proposed course of conduct."[35] Disclosure requirements for specific conflicts also have been clarified.[36] Renaming this obligation "informed consent" restates the lawyer's fiduciary obligation recognized in several centuries of cases.[37] Defining the content of required disclosure to include material risks and reasonably available alternatives parallels the same standard that has emerged in the last quarter century in medicine.

Health Care Providers

A patient's consent to a health care provider authorizes what would otherwise be considered a harmful physical invasion of that person's body. While any action or words can convey this authorization, the person's consent is not informed unless she first understands the nature and purpose of the invasion and its probable

28. Model Rules 1.2(c) (scope of the representation), 1.6(a) and 1.8(b) (confidentiality), 1.7 (conflicts of interest), 1.8 (interests of nonclients), 1.8(i) (family conflicts), 1.9 (former client conflicts), 1.10 (imputed disqualification), 1.11 (government lawyers), 1.12 (former judges and arbitrators), 1.13 (organizational employees), 2.3 (evaluations for use by third persons) (1983).
29. *Id.*, Terminology.
30. *Id.* Model Rules 1.8(a) (business transactions with clients), 1.8(g) (aggregate settlements), 2.2 (multiple representation as intermediary).
31. *Id.*, Model Rule 1.4 (communication).
32. *See Restatement (Third) The Law Governing Lawyers* §16 (2000) (lawyer's duty to obey client's lawful instructions "as defined by the client after consultation"), §20 (duty to keep a client "reasonably informed" about a matter), §62 (use or disclosure of confidential information with client consent "after being adequately informed").
33. *Id.* at §122(1).
34. Model Rule 1.0(e) (informed consent).
35. *Id.*
36. *Id.*, Model Rules 1.5(e) (fee division with another lawyer), 1.8(a) (business transactions with clients), 1.8(g) (aggregate settlements), 2.4(b) (third-party neutral).
37. *See, e.g.*, Metrick v. Chatz, 639 N.E.2d 198, 201 (Ill. App. 1994) (allegations that lawyers failed to disclose available options for alternative legal solutions, as well as to explain the foreseeable risks and benefits of each amounts to "nothing more than an application of the long-standing rule pertinent to a cause of action for medical negligence premised upon a lack of informed consent").

results. Courts have recognized this right in civil actions that allege battery, lack of informed consent, and violation of constitutional liberty rights.[38]

Speaking many years ago in a battery case, Judge Cardozo said: "Every human being of adult years and sound mind has a right to determine what shall be done with his own body."[39] The idea that a legally valid consent must include the right to know about foreseeable complications or risks of a medical procedure came later. Shortly after the mid-twentieth century, courts begin to hold that physicians who failed to disclose potential complications of treatment to patients committed a "technical battery," because the consent given did not contemplate the risk that materialized.[40]

In the landmark case of Canterbury v. Spence, the D.C. Circuit Court of Appeals first articulated a negligence theory for an informed consent cause of action.[41] The court held that the "fiducial quality" of the doctor-patient relationship gave rise to a duty to disclose that depended on patient need rather than medical custom. This duty required disclosure of material risks and side effects as well as alternatives to the proposed treatment. Risks are material "when a reasonable person, in what the physician knows or should know to be the patient's position, would be likely to attach significance to the risk."[42] Failure to disclose a material risk constitutes breach of the duty of informed consent.[43] To prove causation in informed consent cases, the plaintiff must show that a reasonably prudent person in the plaintiff's position would have decided otherwise if he or she had been properly informed. Damages are established by showing that the undisclosed risk materialized.[44]

In the past quarter century, this standard of informed consent based on patient need has been adopted in about half of American jurisdictions.[45] The other half recognize custom-based informed consent; that is, the plaintiff must introduce expert testimony that establishes the appropriate standard of care regarding disclosure by similarly situated physicians.[46] Topics of disclosure include information about the nature of the procedure, the material risks and side effects of the proposed intervention, and alternatives to the proposed treatment, including the alternative of no medical intervention.[47] The duty applies not only to situations where a physician proposes treatment, but also where refusing to consent to a diagnostic test or intervention creates a risk.[48] More recent decisions disagree about whether physicians

38. *See, e.g.,* Washington v. Glucksberg, 521 U.S. 702, 724-727 (1997); Cruzan v. Director, 497 U.S. 261, 279 (1990), *id.* at 287 (O'Connor, J., concurring). Recognition of a constitutional right opens the door to a civil rights action against state or federal actors. *See, e.g.,* In re Cincinnati Radiation Litig., 874 F. Supp. 796 (S.D. Ohio 1995).

39. Schloendorff v. Socy. of N.Y. Hosp., 105 N.E. 92, 93 (1914).

40. *See, e.g.,* Gray v. Grunnagle, 223 A.2d 663 (Pa. 1966); Scott v. Wilson, 396 S.W.2d 532 (Tex. Civ. App. 1965), *aff'd,* Wilson v. Scott, 412 S.W.2d 299 (Tex. 1967); Bang v. Charles T. Miller Hosp., 88 N.W.2d 186 (Minn. 1958).

41. 464 F.2d 772 (D.C. Cir. 1972). *See also* Cobbs v. Grant, 502 P.2d 1 (Cal. 1972).

42. *Canterbury*, 464 F.2d at 787.

43. The only exceptions to this rule are true emergencies, when there is no time to ask for consent, and the so-called therapeutic exception, where disclosure would menace the patient's health. In both circumstances, the courts require disclosure to a relative if possible. Dan B. Dobbs, *The Law of Torts* 657 (West 2000). The Model Rules also recognize a limited exception to disclosure that would harm the client. Model Rule 1.7, Comment [7]. *See also* Geoffrey C. Hazard & W. William Hodes, *The Law of Lawyering* §7.4 (3d ed. 2002).

44. *Canterbury*, 464 F.2d at 790-791.

45. Dobbs, *supra* note 43, at 655.

46. *E.g.,* Tashman v. Gibbs, 556 S.E.2d 772 (Va. 2002).

47. Berg et al., *supra* note 6, at 53-61. *E.g.,* Matthies v. Mastromonaco, 733 A.2d 456 (N.J. 1999) (risk of femur displacement and never walking again from bed rest following hip fracture compared to risk of surgical intervention to pin hip).

48. *E.g.,* Truman v. Thomas, 611 P.2d 902 (Cal. 1980) (risk of death from not consenting to a pap smear).

also have a duty to disclose physician-specific information, such as the extent of their experience with a given procedure, and the alternative of other more skilled practitioners.[49]

Increasingly, one group of informed consent cases against physicians parallels those based on breach of fiduciary duty against lawyers. In cases of "economic informed consent," plaintiffs allege that personal and economic interests of the physician conflict with therapeutic motivations. Where this conflict arises in the context of a physician who conducts research on a patient, both federal regulations and common law impose a full disclosure standard.[50] More generally, courts impose a duty on physicians to disclose "personal interests unrelated to the patient's health, whether research or economic, that may affect the physician's professional judgment."[51] Failure to provide this information constitutes both a lack of informed consent and a breach of fiduciary duty.

This theory has been relied on to create duties to disclose economic incentives in managed care plans. The recent trend has been for courts to deny such a separate cause of action, finding it more appropriate to focus on whether any medical malpractice occurred in the treatment.[52] Some suggest that the insurer rather than the physician should have such a duty.[53]

Informed Consent in the Practice of Law and Medicine

Both law and medicine envision informed consent as validating what would otherwise constitute a potentially harmful professional action. This explains why each profession's articulation of informed consent has influenced the other. The notion of informed consent as a means to avoid breaches of fiduciary duty by lawyers has influenced and may continue to inform similar duties for health care professionals.

---

49. *E.g.*, Johnson v. Kokemoor, 545 N.W.2d 495 (1995) (duty to disclose that physician had never done the procedure before and that availability of other more skilled nearby practitioners); Hiding v. Williams, 578 So. 2d 1192 (La. App. 1991) (duty to disclose personal chronic alcohol abuse). *But see* Duttry v. Patterson, 771 A.2d 1255 (Pa. 2001) (no duty to disclose physician-specific information, even when patient asks for it). *See also* Aaron D. Twerski & Neil B. Cohen, *The Second Revolution in Informed Consent: Comparing Physicians to Each Other*, 94 Nw. U. L. Rev. 1 (1999).

50. *See, e.g.*, Blaz v. Michael Reese Hosp. Found., 191 F.R.D. 570 (N.D. Ill. 1999) (duty to warn of results of research discovered at a later time); Kus v. Sherman Hosp., 644 N.E.2d 1214 (Ill. App. 1995) (cause of action for battery and lack of informed consent stated for physician and hospital's failure to monitor informed consent to research); In re Cincinnati Radiation Litig., 874 F. Supp. 796 (S.D. Ohio 1995) (plaintiffs denied procedural and substantive due process by professionals who did not inform them they were the subjects of radiation experiments); Mink v. U. of Chicago, 460 F. Supp. 713 (N.D. Ill. 1978) (plaintiffs state cause of action for battery and lack of informed consent against physicians who failed to inform them they were part of a double-blind experiment with DES). Federal regulations require that the patient be told that he or she is a subject of a research protocol, given a description of the research project, its risks, benefits and alternatives to the research, and participation is voluntary and may be ended at any time. 45 C.F.R. §46.116 (2002).

51. Moore v. Regents of the U. of Cal., 793 P.2d 479 (Cal. 1990). This translated into a duty to inform the patient that the physician has used tissue from the patient's surgically removed spleen to develop a patented cell line, worth millions of dollars. The court left the issue of damages open, but specifically held that the patient had no right to claim all the profits based on a cause of action for conversion.

52. *See, e.g.*, Pegram v. Herdrich, 530 U.S. 211 (2000) (no cause of action for breach of fiduciary duty under ERISA); Neade v. Portes, 739 N.E.2d 496 (Ill. 2000) (breach of fiduciary duty claim duplicates medical malpractice claim).

53. *See, e.g.*, *Neade*, *supra* note 52, at 504, citing an American Medical Association opinion that requires disclosure of "any financial inducements that may tend to limit the diagnostic and therapeutic alternatives that are offered to patients or that may tend to limit patients' overall access to care," but allows physicians to satisfy this duty by assuring that a managed care plan makes adequate disclosure to those enrolled in the plan.

At the same time, the doctrine of informed consent in medicine continues to enlighten duties of disclosure for lawyers.

For lawyers, fiduciary duty makes clear that disclosure must occur whenever the client has a right to decide; specifically, full disclosure must occur to legitimate any potential breach of confidentiality or loyalty. Many of these loyalty cases, like *Monco*, involve personal financial interests of the lawyer that conflict with those of the client. Physicians have not yet seen full implementation of such an economic theory of informed consent. They can benefit from understanding the admonition of lawyer conflict of interest cases that prohibit lawyers from putting their own welfare above that of their clients. When health care providers acquire a particular financial interest that conflicts with the health of a patient, they should be required to disclose that interest.[54]

At the same time, lawyers have learned and benefited from the articulation of the informed consent doctrine in medicine. Although fiduciary notions make clear when a lawyer must disclose, they have not always clearly articulated what must be said. Analogizing to health care cases has assisted such an analysis. For example, informed consent in medicine requires disclosure of risks, benefits, and alternatives to proposed courses of action, topics just recently set out in the Model Rule requirement of informed consent. Further, it is not clear the extent to which lawyer-specific information, such as lack of experience with similar cases, must be disclosed. Cases that allege a parallel duty of lawyers may soon rely on cases against physicians that alleged similar failures to disclose.

Finally, both professions' doctrines of informed consent also agree that consent validates most, but not all proposed conduct by professionals. We have already seen the debate about whether sexual relationships between professionals and their clients or patients can be legitimated by client consent.[55] All counseling professionals, and many lawyer codes, agree that the potential for undue influence makes voluntary consent nearly impossible. Federal regulations governing medical research also classify some interventions as too risky to be the subject of any informed consent.[56] Similarly, several of the cases in the rest of this chapter present additional examples of nonconsentable prohibited conflicts that can be cured only by providing separate independent legal counsel.

Wolpaw v. General Accident Insurance Co.

639 A.2d 338 (N.J. Super. 1994)

BRODY, P.J.A.D.

Defendant issued a homeowners' policy to Saranne Frew. Other members of Frew's household covered by the policy were plaintiff, who is Frew's sister, and plaintiff's son Heath. All three were sued in a personal-injury action for their allegedly negligent conduct during the term of the policy. Defendant assigned the same firm of attorneys, third-party defendants Parker, McCay and

54. *See* Grant H. Morris, *Dissing Disclosure: Just What the Doctor Ordered*, 44 Ariz. L. Rev. 313 (2002); Nancy J. Moore, *What Doctors Can Learn From Lawyers About Conflicts of Interest*, 81 B.U. L. Rev. 445 (2001).

55. *See* Lawyers and Other Professionals: Sexual Relationships with Clients, *supra* p.278.

56. *See* Basic HHS Policy for Protection of Human Research Subjects, 45 C.F.R. Part 46 (2003).

Criscuolo, Esqs., to represent the three insureds even though their interests as defendants in that action were in conflict. Plaintiff brought this action to compel defendant to pay the substantial portion of the negligence-action judgment entered against her that exceeds the policy limit. We agree with the trial judge that defendant breached the policy by assigning a single firm of attorneys to represent insureds having conflicting interests. . . . Defendant's liability is limited to the portion of plaintiff's actual loss attributable to the breach.

On January 9, 1986, plaintiff's eleven-year-old son Heath accidently fired a BB from an air rifle that put out an eye of his playmate and neighbor Michael Heim. Plaintiff was divorced from Heath's father Ivan Wolpaw at the time and lived with Heath in the home of her sister Saranne Frew. Plaintiff, her sister and Heath were covered for the accident under a $50,000 homeowners' policy that defendant General Accident Insurance Company had issued to Frew. Michael and his parents brought an action for the ensuing damages against plaintiff, Heath, Frew, Ivan, the rifle's manufacturer, and the store where Ivan had purchased the rifle as a gift for his son. Defendant immediately deposited in court the $50,000 limit of its policy in offer of settlement. The Heims rejected the offer. A jury awarded the Heims damages totaling $502,000 after finding plaintiff 50% negligent, Ivan 30% negligent and Heath 20% negligent. The jury absolved the manufacturer and the store. The claims against Frew had been dismissed before trial on her motion for a partial summary judgment.

In this action, the trial judge held, on plaintiff's motion for summary judgment, that defendant had breached its policy by providing a single firm of attorneys to represent insureds having conflicting interests. . . .

A liability insurer that insures codefendants whose interests conflict with one another must retain separate and independent counsel for each insured or permit each insured to do so at the insurer's expense. That was the case here. The three insureds had the common interests of minimizing the amount of the Heims's judgment and maximizing the percentage of fault attributable to the other defendants. However, their interests in maximizing the percentage of the other insureds' fault and minimizing their own were clearly in conflict. For instance, it was in plaintiff's interest to argue that she adequately had secured the rifle from Heath's unattended use and had carefully instructed him in its safe use, which he negligently disregarded; on the other hand, it was in Heath's interest to argue that plaintiff negligently failed to secure the rifle, and that he was not negligent in view of his mother's negligence and his youth.

With the general abolition of parental immunity, and in the absence of sufficient liability insurance coverage, separate attorneys representing plaintiff and Heath might well have asserted cross-claims for contribution against the other's client. That was not done here. It was also in plaintiff's interest to assert a cross-claim against her sister and that she remain a codefendant to share the liability burden. Yet the single firm of attorneys, discharging its duty to her sister, not only did not file a cross-claim for contribution on plaintiff's behalf, but successfully moved to have Frew dismissed from the case. A trial is not necessary to determine the obvious. Defendant violated its contractual duty to provide plaintiff with counsel who were free of conflicting interests.

Where conflicting interests impose on a liability insurer the duty to provide multiple insureds with separate counsel, it may be that in a particular case the separate attorneys would manage the case the same way as one attorney representing all insureds. Even so, where there is the risk of a judgment that will exceed the policy limit, separate independent counsel for each insured must be employed to decide whether and how to act in light of the conflict.

A conflict that forms the basis of an insurer's breach, however, does not establish that compensatory damages are to be awarded against the insurer if the breach did not cause the insured an actual loss. . . .

Although it may not be certain that an injured party sustained damages from a breach, where the breach itself destroys the injured party's ability to prove damages with exactitude, the proof may be inexact. This tolerant approach has been applied to the proof of damages where, as here, a liability insurer breached its policy. . . .

. . . In such a case damages in a legal malpractice action can often be approximated by having the successor plaintiff's attorney recreate or create a defective or time-barred tort trial by conducting a "suit within a suit" in which the flawed attorney plays the role of the tort defendant. . . .

. . . Another option, which may be apposite in this case in light of the duality of defendants, the factor of role reversal, and the passage of time, is to proceed through the use of expert testimony as to what as a matter of reasonable probability would have transpired at the original trial. Such experts would testify, in light of their experience and expertise, concerning the outcome of the [malpractice case] if the case had been brought to trial as anticipated by [the attorney] and had been defended in the manner [the attorney] had initially planned. . . .

If the parties use experts to express opinions as to whether or as to how having separate counsel probably would have changed the Heim judgment, their opinions must be confined to changes in the allocation of fault among the three insureds. . . .

Thus, regardless of any reduction in the percentage share of plaintiff's fault, she would remain liable to the Heims for the full amount of their judgment unless but for defendant's breach the jury probably would have found that she was not at fault. Had plaintiff, if properly represented, been absolved of all fault then defendant would be liable to pay the whole judgment on her behalf—including the substantial excess over the policy limits. . . .

Matter of Disciplinary Proceedings Against Wildermuth

416 N.W.2d 607 (Wis. 1987)

Per Curiam . . .

Following a disciplinary hearing, the referee made the following findings of fact. In 1980, Mr. and Mrs. Grabowski, long-standing clients of Attorney Wildermuth, sold their tavern business on land contract to a Mr. King and his minor son. Attorney Wildermuth represented both the sellers and the buyers in that transaction and at the time knew that the Grabowskis were liable on two notes, totaling approximately $7800, secured by mortgages on the property. Shortly after that closing, the Grabowskis left the state, and throughout 1981 and early 1982 Attorney Wildermuth continued to represent them, assisting them in their making mortgage payments, dealing with the mortgagees concerning delinquent payments and collecting payments from the vendees on the land contract.

In the spring of 1981, the Kings agreed to sell their interest in the land contract to Mr. and Mrs. Jones. Mr. King and Mr. Jones asked Attorney Wildermuth to represent both of them in arranging to transfer the land contract interest, the assets of the tavern business and the liquor license. Attorney Wildermuth informed them of the potential conflict of interest inherent in the dual representation and indicated the desirability that they retain separate counsel. He stated that he would have to withdraw from representing either of them in the event any dispute between them arose, and he told them he had represented the Grabowskis and had drafted the land contract itself. He also informed them of the mortgages on the property, as well as the Grabowski's responsibility to make payments on the underlying notes.

Following that disclosure, Mr. King and Mr. Jones, who had been authorized by Mrs. Jones to act on her behalf in arranging the transaction, consented to the dual representation. Subsequently, after talking with Mr. King and Mr. Jones and expressing some uncertainty, Mrs. Jones agreed to Attorney Wildermuth's representation of both sides in the assignment transaction.

At the closing held May 1, 1981, Attorney Wildermuth told the parties of their differing interests in the transaction and suggested they each consider retaining their own attorney. Although this was the first time Mrs. Jones met with Attorney Wildermuth, he did not mention the existence of the mortgages on the property. Attorney Wildermuth was not then aware that the Grabowskis had failed to make the required mortgage payments for the months of March, April and May of 1981, nor had he attempted to ascertain the status of the mortgage loans. He had not caused the abstract to the property to be continued to date of closing and had neither been asked for nor gave an opinion on title to the Joneses. Also, Attorney Wildermuth had not sought the appointment of a guardian ad litem to represent Mr. King's son, who he knew was still a minor. Following the closing, Attorney Wildermuth did not record the assignment of the land contract.

Some time between June 5 and June 15, 1981, Attorney Wildermuth learned of the Grabowskis' delinquency on the mortgage notes. The Grabowskis had sent him a blank check to make the delinquent payments, which totaled $654.25, but that check was subsequently dishonored for insufficient funds. The mortgagee then brought a foreclosure action and Attorney Wildermuth appeared on behalf of the Grabowskis; the Joneses, however, were not named parties in that action. Attorney Wildermuth never told the Joneses of the Grabowskis' delinquency in making mortgage payments, even though he had on a number of occasions called to urge them to make payments on the land contract; neither did he inform them of the foreclosure action. . . .

In December, 1981 the Joneses retained other counsel to represent them in matters concerning the property and the following January Attorney Wildermuth discussed with that attorney the possibility of the Joneses' buying the Grabowskis' interest for $16,000. Prior to that time, Attorney Wildermuth had not told either the Joneses or their attorney that the Grabowskis had wanted to sell their interest. The Joneses did not purchase the interest; subsequently, after the balance due on the land contract had been paid, the business was closed.

On the basis of these facts, the referee found that Attorney Wildermuth's representation of the Joneses terminated the day of closing. . . .

The referee erred in finding that Attorney Wildermuth's representation of the Joneses terminated upon completion of the closing. His professional obligation to the Joneses survived that closing. In order to protect the Joneses' newly acquired interest in the property,

Attorney Wildermuth had a duty to record the assignment of the land contract, which he never did. He also had a duty to inform the Joneses of facts coming to his attention which, had they been known at the time of closing, would likely have affected the outcome of the transaction. Here, that was the fact that at the time of the closing, the Grabowskis were in default on the mortgage notes. Attorney Wildermuth did not learn of that delinquency until six weeks after closing, but he never informed the Joneses of the fact, despite his continued contact with them to have them make payments under the land contract....

We find it unnecessary to determine whether the advice Attorney Wildermuth gave to the Joneses concerning multiple representation problems was sufficient. ... Upon discovery, albeit after the closing, of the Grabowskis' delinquency on the mortgage notes, it became obvious that Attorney Wildermuth could not adequately represent the interest of the Grabowskis and the interest of the Joneses simultaneously. As his professional obligation to the Joneses extended beyond the closing, Attorney Wildermuth's continuing to act in the matter was proscribed by SCR 20.28(2) (1986), which prohibits a lawyer from continuing multiple employment "if the exercise of the lawyer's independent professional judgment on behalf of a client will be or is likely to be adversely affected by the lawyer's representation of another client. ..."

We note that the revised rule in this regard, to become effective January 1, 1988, requires client consent in writing after consultation if the representation of that client will be directly adverse to another client or may be materially limited by the lawyer's responsibilities to another client or to a third person or by the lawyer's own interest, but the rule does not require that the consultation itself be in writing. Because the revised rule requires a writing in any event, it would be good practice for a lawyer to establish compliance with the rule's disclosure requirement by giving the required consultation in writing and having the client give consent to the representation in the same writing....

... [W]e determine that a 60-day suspension of Attorney Wildermuth's license to practice law is appropriate discipline. His clients, the Joneses, had a right to rely on him to represent their interests in the transaction and to inform them in the event the interests of his other clients in the matter adversely affected theirs. Not only did he fail to protect the Joneses after learning of the Grabowskis' default on the mortgage notes, but he also failed to give them the information necessary to act on their own to protect their interests....

A. v. B.

726 A.2d 924 (N.J. 1999)

POLLOCK, J.

This appeal presents the issue whether a law firm may disclose confidential information of one co-client to another co-client. Specifically, in this paternity action, the mother's former law firm, which contemporaneously represented the father and his wife in planning their estates, seeks to disclose the existence of the father's illegitimate child to the wife.

A law firm, Hill Wallack, ... jointly represented the husband and wife in drafting wills in which they devised their respective estates to each other.

The devises created the possibility that the other spouse's issue, whether legitimate or illegitimate, ultimately would acquire the decedent's property.

Unbeknown to Hill Wallack and the wife, the husband recently had fathered an illegitimate child. Before the execution of the wills, the child's mother retained Hill Wallack to institute this paternity action against the husband. Because of a clerical error, the firm's computer check did not reveal the conflict of interest inherent in its representation of the mother against the husband. On learning of the conflict, the firm withdrew from representation of the mother in the paternity action. Now, the firm wishes to disclose to the wife the fact that the husband has an illegitimate child. To prevent Hill Wallack from making that disclosure, the husband joined the firm as a third-party defendant in the paternity action. . . .

I . . .

In October 1997, the husband and wife retained Hill Wallack, a firm of approximately sixty lawyers, to assist them with planning their estates. On the commencement of the joint representation, the husband and wife each signed a letter captioned "Waiver of Conflict of Interest." In explaining the possible conflicts of interest, the letter recited that the effect of a testamentary transfer by one spouse to the other would permit the transferee to dispose of the property as he or she desired. The firm's letter also explained that information provided by one spouse could become available to the other. Although the letter did not contain an express waiver of the confidentiality of any such information, each spouse consented to and waived any conflicts arising from the firm's joint representation.

Unfortunately, the clerk who opened the firm's estate planning file misspelled the clients' surname. The misspelled name was entered in the computer program that the firm uses to discover possible conflicts of interest. The firm then prepared reciprocal wills and related documents with the names of the husband and wife correctly spelled.

In January 1998, before the husband and wife executed the estate planning documents, the mother coincidentally retained Hill Wallack to pursue a paternity claim against the husband. This time, when making its computer search for conflicts of interest, Hill Wallack spelled the husband's name correctly. Accordingly, the computer search did not reveal the existence of the firm's joint representation of the husband and wife. As a result, the estate planning department did not know that the family law department had instituted a paternity action for the mother. Similarly, the family law department did not know that the estate planning department was preparing estate plans for the husband and wife.

A lawyer from the firm's family law department wrote to the husband about the mother's paternity claim. The husband neither objected to the firm's representation of the mother nor alerted the firm to the conflict of interest. Instead, he retained Fox Rothschild to represent him in the paternity action. After initially denying paternity, he agreed to voluntary DNA testing, which revealed that he is the father. Negotiations over child support failed, and the mother instituted the present action.

After the mother filed the paternity action, the husband and wife executed their wills at the Hill Wallack office. The parties agree that in their wills, the husband and wife leave their respective residuary estates to each other. If the other spouse does not survive, the contingent beneficiaries are the testator's issue. The wife's will leaves her residuary estate to her husband, creating the possibility that her property ultimately may pass to his issue. Under N.J.S.A. 3C:1-2, :2-48, the term "issue" includes both legitimate and illegitimate children. When the wife executed her will, therefore, she did not know that the husband's illegitimate child ultimately may inherit her property.

The conflict of interest surfaced when Fox Rothschild, in response to Hill Wallack's request for disclosure of the husband's assets, informed the firm that it already possessed the requested information. Hill Wallack promptly informed the mother that it unknowingly was representing both the husband and the wife in an unrelated matter.

Hill Wallack immediately withdrew from representing the mother in the paternity action. It also instructed the estate planning department not to disclose any information about the husband's assets to the member of the firm who had been representing the mother. The firm then wrote to the husband stating that it believed it had an ethical obligation to disclose to the wife the existence, but not the identity, of his illegitimate child. Additionally, the firm stated that it was obligated to inform the wife "that her current estate plan may devise a portion of her assets through her spouse to that child." The firm suggested that the husband so inform his wife and stated that if he did not do so, it would. . . .

II

This appeal concerns the conflict between two fundamental obligations of lawyers: the duty of confidentiality, Rules of Professional Conduct (RPC) 1.6(a), and the duty to inform clients of material facts, RPC 1.4(b). The conflict arises from a law firm's joint representation of two clients whose interests initially were compatible, but now conflict.

Crucial to the attorney-client relationship is the attorney's obligation not to reveal confidential information learned in the course of representation. [The court cites Model Rule 1.6 (a).]

A lawyer's obligation to communicate to one client all information needed to make an informed decision qualifies the firm's duty to maintain the confidentiality of a co-client's information. [The Court cites Model Rule 1.4 (b).] In limited situations, moreover, an attorney is permitted or required to disclose confidential information. Hill Wallack argues that RPC 1.6 mandates, or at least permits, the firm to disclose to the wife the existence of the husband's illegitimate child. RPC 1.6(b) requires that a lawyer disclose "information relating to representation of a client" to the proper authorities if the lawyer "reasonably believes" that such disclosure is necessary to prevent the client "from committing a criminal, illegal or fraudulent act that the lawyer reasonably believes is likely to result in death or substantial bodily harm or substantial injury to the financial interest or property of another. . . ." Despite Hill Wallack's claim that RPC 1.6(b) applies, the facts do not justify mandatory disclosure. The possible inheritance of the wife's estate by the husband's illegitimate child is too remote to constitute "substantial injury to the financial interest or property of another" within the meaning of RPC 1.6(b).

By comparison, in limited circumstances RPC 1.6(c) permits a lawyer to disclose a confidential communication. RPC 1.6(c) permits, but does not require, a lawyer to reveal confidential information to the extent the lawyer reasonably believes necessary "to rectify the consequences of a client's criminal, illegal or fraudulent act in furtherance of which the lawyer's services had been used." Although RPC 1.6(c) does not define a "fraudulent act," the term takes on meaning from our construction of the word "fraud," found in the analogous "crime or fraud" exception to the attorney-client privilege.

We likewise construe broadly the term "fraudulent act" within the meaning of RPC 1.6(c). So construed, the husband's deliberate omission of the existence of his illegitimate child constitutes a fraud on his wife. When discussing their respective estates with the firm, the husband and wife reasonably could expect that each would disclose information material to the distribution of their estates, including the existence of children who are contingent residuary beneficiaries. The husband breached that duty. Under the reciprocal wills, the existence of the husband's illegitimate child could affect the distribution of the wife's estate, if she predeceased him. Additionally, the husband's child support payments and other financial responsibilities owed to the illegitimate child could deplete that part of his estate that otherwise would pass to his wife.

In effect, the husband has used the law firm's services to defraud his wife in the preparation of her estate....

Under RPC 1.6, the facts support disclosure to the wife....

[T]he husband and wife signed letters captioned "Waiver of Conflict of Interest." These letters acknowledge that information provided by one client could become available to the other. The letters, however, stop short of explicitly authorizing the firm to disclose one spouse's confidential information to the other. Even in the absence of any such explicit authorization, the spirit of the letters supports the firm's decision to disclose to the wife the existence of the husband's illegitimate child.

Neither our research nor that of counsel has revealed a dispositive judicial decision from this or any other jurisdiction on the issue of disclosure of confidential information about one client to a co-client. Persuasive secondary authority, however, supports the conclusion that the firm may disclose to the wife the existence of the husband's child.

The forthcoming Restatement of The Law Governing Lawyers §112 comment l (Proposed Final Draft No. 1, 1996) ("the Restatement") suggests, for example, that if the attorney and the co-clients have reached a prior, explicit agreement concerning the sharing of confidential information, that agreement controls whether the attorney should disclose the confidential information of one co-client to another. ("Co-clients... may explicitly agree to share information" and "can also explicitly agree that the lawyer is not to share certain information... with one or more other co-clients. A lawyer must honor such agreements.")

As the preceding authorities suggest, an attorney, on commencing joint representation of co-clients, should agree explicitly with the clients on the sharing of confidential information. In such a "disclosure agreement," the co-clients can agree that any confidential information concerning one co-client, whether obtained from a co-client himself or herself or from another source, will be shared with the other co-client. Similarly, the co-clients can agree that unilateral confidences or other confidential information will be kept confidential by the attorney. Such a prior agreement will clarify the expectations of the clients and the lawyer and diminish the need for future litigation.

In the absence of an agreement to share confidential information with co-clients, the Restatement reposes the resolution of the lawyer's competing duties within the lawyer's discretion:

> [T]he lawyer, after consideration of all relevant circumstances, has the... discretion to inform the affected co-client of the specific communication if, in the lawyer's reasonable judgment, the immediacy and magnitude of the risk to the affected co-client outweigh the

> interest of the communicating client in continued secrecy. [Restatement (Third) The Law Governing Lawyers §112, comment l.]

Additionally, the Restatement advises that the lawyer, when withdrawing from representation of the co-clients, may inform the affected co-client that the attorney has learned of information adversely affecting that client's interests that the communicating co-client refuses to permit the lawyer to disclose.

In the context of estate planning, the Restatement also suggests that a lawyer's disclosure of confidential information communicated by one spouse is appropriate only if the other spouse's failure to learn of the information would be materially detrimental to that other spouse or frustrate the spouse's intended testamentary arrangement. The Restatement provides two analogous illustrations in which a lawyer has been jointly retained by a husband and wife to prepare reciprocal wills. The first illustration states:

> Lawyer has been retained by Husband and Wife to prepare wills pursuant to an arrangement under which each spouse agrees to leave most of their property to the other. Shortly after the wills are executed, Husband (unknown to Wife) asks Lawyer to prepare an inter vivos trust for an illegitimate child whose existence Husband has kept secret from Wife for many years and about whom Husband had not previously informed Lawyer. Husband states that Wife would be distraught at learning of Husband's infidelity and of Husband's years of silence and that disclosure of the information could destroy their marriage. Husband directs Lawyer not to inform Wife. The inter vivos trust that Husband proposes to create would not materially affect Wife's own estate plan or her expected receipt of property under Husband's will, because Husband proposes to use property designated in Husband's will for a personally favored charity. In view of the lack of material effect on Wife, Lawyer may assist Husband to establish and fund the inter vivos trust and refrain from disclosing Husband's information to Wife. . . .

The other illustration states:

> Same facts as [the prior Illustration], except that Husband's proposed inter vivos trust would significantly deplete Husband's estate, to Wife's material detriment and in frustration of the Spouses' intended testamentary arrangements. If Husband will neither inform Wife nor permit Lawyer to do so, Lawyer must withdraw from representing both Husband and Wife. In the light of all relevant circumstances, Lawyer may exercise discretion whether to inform Wife either that circumstances, which Lawyer has been asked not to reveal, indicate that she should revoke her recent will or to inform Wife of some or all the details of the information that Husband has recently provided so that Wife may protect her interests. Alternatively, Lawyer may inform Wife only that Lawyer is withdrawing because Husband will not permit disclosure of information that Lawyer has learned from Husband. . . .

The Professional Ethics Committees of New York and Florida, however, have concluded that disclosure to a co-client is prohibited. N.Y. St. Bar Assn. Comm. on Prof. Ethics, Op. 555 (1984); Fla. St. Bar Assn. Comm. on Prof. Ethics, Op. 95-4 (1997).

The New York opinion addressed the following situation:

> A and B formed a partnership and employed Lawyer L to represent them in connection with the partnership affairs. Subsequently, B, in a conversation with Lawyer L, advised Lawyer L that he was actively breaching the partnership agreement. B preceded this statement to Lawyer L with the statement that he proposed to tell Lawyer L something "in confidence." Lawyer L did not respond to that statement and

> did not understand that B intended to make a statement that would be of importance to A but that was to be kept confidential from A. Lawyer L had not, prior thereto, advised A or B that he could not receive from one communications regarding the subject of the joint representation that would be confidential from the other. B has subsequently declined to tell A what he has told Lawyer L.

In that situation, the New York Ethics Committee concluded that the lawyer may not disclose to the co-client the communicating client's statement. The Committee based its conclusion on the absence of prior consent by the clients to the sharing of all confidential communications and the fact that the client "specifically in advance designated his communication as confidential, and the lawyer did not demur."

The Florida Ethics Committee addressed a similar situation:

> Lawyer has represented Husband and Wife for many years in a range of personal matters, including estate planning. Husband and Wife have substantial individual assets, and they also own substantial jointly-held property. Recently, Lawyer prepared new updated wills that Husband and Wife signed. Like their previous wills, their new wills primarily benefit the survivor of them for his or her life, with beneficial disposition at the death of the survivor being made equally to their children. . . .
>
> Several months after the execution of the new wills, Husband confers separately with Lawyer. Husband reveals to Lawyer that he has just executed a codicil (prepared by another law firm) that makes substantial beneficial disposition to a woman with whom Husband has been having an extra-marital relationship.

Reasoning that the lawyer's duty of confidentiality takes precedence over the duty to communicate all relevant information to a client, the Florida Ethics Committee concluded that the lawyer did not have discretion to reveal the information. In support of that conclusion, the Florida committee reasoned that joint clients do not necessarily expect that everything relating to the joint representation communicated by one co-client will be shared with the other co-client.

In several material respects, however, the present appeal differs from the hypothetical cases considered by the New York and Florida committees. Most significantly, the New York and Florida disciplinary rules, unlike RPC 1.6, do not except disclosure needed "to rectify the consequences of a client's . . . fraudulent act in the furtherance of which the lawyer's services had been used." RPC 1.6(c). Second, Hill Wallack learned of the husband's paternity from a third party, not from the husband himself. Thus, the husband did not communicate anything to the law firm with the expectation that the communication would be kept confidential. Finally, the husband and wife, unlike the co-clients considered by the New York and Florida Committees, signed an agreement suggesting their intent to share all information with each other.

Because Hill Wallack wishes to make the disclosure, we need not reach the issue whether the lawyer's obligation to disclose is discretionary or mandatory. In conclusion, Hill Wallack may inform the wife of the existence of the husband's illegitimate child. . . .

The law firm learned of the husband's paternity of the child through the mother's disclosure before the institution of the paternity suit. It does not seek to disclose the identity of the mother or the child. Given the wife's need for the information and the law firm's right to disclose it, the disclosure of the child's existence to the wife constitutes an exceptional case "for compelling reason clearly and convincingly shown." . . .

Practice Pointers: *Written Consents to Conflicts of Interest*

The lawyers involved in both *Wildermuth* and *A. v. B.* provided their clients with a written waiver of the conflicts of interest. Until recently, only three jurisdictions (California, Washington, and Wisconsin) required that the client's informed consent be confirmed in writing. The Washington Supreme Court applied this requirement to lawyer Halverson's sexual relationship with his client.

The American Bar Association House of Delegates recently voted to follow the lead of these jurisdictions by amending Model Rules 1.7, 1.8(h), and 1.9 to require a written confirmation of client consent to conflicts governed by these rules.

These amendments to the black letter of Model Rule 1.7 require that "each affected client gives informed consent, confirmed in writing."[1] Comment [20] emphasizes that the writing is just part of the informed consent process:

> Such a writing may consist of a document executed by the client or one that the lawyer promptly records and transmits to the client following an oral consent.... The requirement of a writing does not supplant the need in most cases for the lawyer to talk with the client, to explain the risks and advantages, if any, of representation burdened with a conflict of interest, as well as reasonably available alternatives, and to afford the client a reasonable opportunity to consider the risks and alternatives and to raise questions and concerns. Rather, the writing is required in order to impress upon clients the seriousness of the decision the client is being asked to make and to avoid disputes or ambiguities that might later occur in the absence of a writing.

The move to require written waivers parallels the evolution of other conflicts rules that have come to require written waivers, such as business deals with clients. Earlier versions of this rule, such as DR 5-101(A) that governed the lawyer's conduct in Monco v. Janus, required informed consent of a client, but did not require a writing to memorialize either the lawyer's disclosures or the client's agreement. To prevent similar misunderstandings and to clarify that the burden is on the lawyer to obtain an informed consent, the American Bar Association added a specific writing requirement to Model Rule 1.8(a).

The content of disclosure rules about business transactions with clients also have grown more specific over time because of repeated problems with old rules that did not offer clients enough information to assess the conflict realistically. Other recurring conflicts have generated similar attempts to articulate the information that clients need to control and monitor the representation. For example, Florida recently has mandated that insurance defense lawyers present policyholders with a two and one-half page document entitled "Statement of Insured Client's Rights," intended to explain the conflicts of interest inherent in the three-way relationship between the insurer, the lawyer and the policyholder.[2] The required statement addresses several important issues, including selection and direction of the lawyer, fees and costs, litigation guidelines, confidentiality, conflicts of interest, settlement, risk of judgment beyond policy limits, and how to report violations.

In most cases, however, a lawyer will be called on to draft an individualized consent to a conflict of interest. What should a written waiver look like? The Model

1. Model Rule 1.7(b)(4).
2. *See* Amendments to R. Regulating the Fla. Bar, 820 So. 2d 210 (Fla. 2002) (Rule 1.8(j)).

Rule definition of "confirmed in writing"[3] does not require the client's signature but does require confirmation in a written document of "informed consent," or agreement of a client "after the lawyer has communicated adequate information and explanation about the material risks of and reasonably available alternatives to the proposed course of conduct."[4] We have seen that this definition requires that the writing list the information and explanation of risks and alternatives.[5] The lawyers in *Wildermuth* and *A. v. B.* attempted to do just that. What information or explanation of material risks did they omit? What, if anything did they say about alternatives? Ultimately, each court gives you guidance about both omitted risks (because they materialized) and alternatives (because they were not discussed).

Taken together, the cases in this section illustrate that a written confirmation of informed consent should include at least three categories of information. First, the material risks of the proposed course of conduct (for example, joint representation) must be disclosed. Most of these risks are a function of loyalty conflicts created by the legal rights of the parties involved (such as the legal effect of one spouse's will on the other spouse's children) as well as the individual facts in each representation (such as the fact that one spouse has a child out of wedlock). Both must be disclosed. Any prior or continuing relationship of the lawyer with either party should be explained as well.

Second, *A. v. B.* and *Wildermuth* illustrate that another potential conflict regarding the use of confidential information always lurks in joint representations. Here, the parties can choose either full disclosure, or limited disclosure from the lawyer to each of them. The written confirmation of their informed consent should specifically disclose these alternatives, as well as document which alternative the clients elected.[6] The clients also are entitled to some explanation of the effect of the joint representation on the attorney-client privilege.[7]

Third, each potential client should receive some explanation about the advantages and disadvantages of the available alternatives to joint representation, such as representation by separate lawyers, or representation of one client alone. Here, the joint clients should understand the difference in the lawyer's role in individual and joint representations, that the latter will require each client to assume greater responsibility for making decisions than might be the case if a lawyer were to individually advocate on their behalf.[8] The clients also need to understand their right to discharge the lawyer at any time, as well as changes in their legal rights or their individual situations that might require the lawyer to withdraw. Finally, the clients need an explanation of what will happen if the representation ends before the legal service is completed. Absent explicit consent to the contrary, the lawyer probably will be required to withdraw from both or all of the representations, causing additional expense and effort.[9]

Lawyers in jurisdictions like California indicate that the writing requirement has benefited both clients and lawyers. Clients benefit because a written document provides the client with a continual specific reminder of the nature of the conflict, which allows the client to monitor and control the ongoing course of the lawyer's

---

3. Model Rule 1.0(b).
4. Model Rule 1.0(e).
5. *See* Lawyers and Other Professionals: Informed Consent, *supra* p.306.
6. *See* Model Rule 1.7, Comment 31.
7. *See* Model Rule 1.7, Comment 30.
8. *See* Model Rule 1.7, Comment 32.
9. *See* Model Rule 1.7, Comment 29.

service. Lawyers benefit because articulating the nature of the conflict in writing prods them to be diligent in recognizing and responding to conflicts and gives them protection when a client decides to proceed with the representation. Think, for example, of how such a properly prepared writing would have reminded the clients in *Monco* and *Wildermuth* about the nature of the alternatives and risks if they had agreed to accept them. Or consider how explicit explanation and consent about confidential information would have aided the law firm in *A. v. B.*

That leaves us with *Halverson*. Can you envision the written informed consent the court said could legitimate some sexual relationships with clients? If not, the conflict probably is nonconsentable, as many jurisdictions have concluded. Attempting to draft a written waiver affords lawyers an opportunity to assess whether a conflict can be the subject of adequate informed consent. If the lawyer in *Wolpaw* had attempted such an exercise, perhaps he and the insurer who hired his law firm would have been spared significant additional litigation.

4. Positional Conflicts

Problem

6-20. Client A asks Martyn & Fox to challenge a "poison-pill" provision in a takeover agreement. At the same time, Client B in a different case asks our firm to enforce a similar poison-pill provision against the other side. Can we make both arguments? Does it matter whether Client A wants to challenge the provision's constitutionality in the same district court where Client B's case is filed?

Consider: Model Rule 1.7
Model Code DR 5-105

F. Interests of a Third Person

Problems

6-21. Fox is an estate lawyer. One day he receives a visit from an individual who says: "I need some help for Dad. It is too hard for Dad to travel downtown these days. He needs to change his will to make sure my children's education is paid for." What should Fox do?

6-22. Martyn & Fox is hired by Insurance Company to represent several of its insureds.

(a) Who is our client?

(b) Can Insurance Company tell Martyn & Fox:

- how many depositions to take?
- whether and when to hire an expert witness?
- what motions to file?
- to send bills to an outside auditing company for review?

(c) In the course of investigating our first case, Fox comes across a confidential medical file that shows the insured was fully aware of his acts when he brutally attacked and severely injured the plaintiff. The insured's policy includes standard language that excludes coverage for intentional acts. What should Fox do with this information?

(d) The plaintiff's complaint in our second case demands $300,000 in damages resulting from an auto accident. Plaintiff offers to settle the case for the policy limits of $100,000 but Insurance Company tells Martyn "We'd rather pay you to litigate this case than settle with that malingerer." What should Martyn do?

(e) In our third case, the insured is a physician accused of medical malpractice. Plaintiff offers to settle well within policy limits, and Insurance Company agrees, but the physician refuses saying, "Settling this case will destroy my professional reputation." What should Fox do?

Consider: Model Rules 1.7, 1.8(f), 1.14, 5.4(c)
Model Code DR 5-105, 5-107

In re Rules of Professional Conduct

2 P.3d 806 (Mont. 2000)

Justice W. William LEAPHART delivered the opinion of the Court. . . .

FACTUAL AND PROCEDURAL BACKGROUND

P5 In June, 1985 we adopted the Rules of Professional Conduct "as rules governing the conduct of persons admitted to practice law before this Court and all state courts in the State of Montana." In November, 1998 Petitioners filed an application for original jurisdiction and declaratory relief. Petitioners requested a declaratory ruling on two issues: 1. May an attorney licensed to practice law in Montana, or admitted pro hac vice, agree to abide by an insurer's billing and practice rules which impose conditions limiting or directing the scope and extent of the representation of his or her client, the insured? 2. May an attorney licensed to practice law in Montana, or admitted pro hac vice, be required to submit detailed descriptions of professional services to outside persons or entities without first obtaining the informed consent of his or her client and do so without violating client confidentiality?

P6 We accepted original jurisdiction. We ordered that Petitioners identify insurers doing business in Montana whom they sought to have bound by this Court's determination of the issues, that the insurers (Respondents) file copies of the billing rules that they enforce in Montana, directly or through an auditing agency. . . .

DISCUSSION . . .

P9 We have a constitutional mandate to fashion and interpret the Rules of Professional Conduct. See Article VII, Section 2 of Montana's Constitution, providing that "[the supreme court] may make rules governing appellate procedure, practice and procedure for all other courts, admission to the bar and the conduct of its members." Art. VII, Sec. 2(3), Mont. Const. Further, whether insurers' billing and practice rules conflict with the Rules of Professional Conduct is a question of law that requires no evidentiary hearing. . . .

P11 1. May an attorney licensed to practice law in Montana, or admitted pro hac vice, agree to abide by an insurer's billing and practice rules which impose conditions limiting or directing the scope and extent of the representation of his or her client, the insured?

P12 In addressing this issue, there are several Rules of Professional Conduct that we keep in mind. [The court cites MR 1.1, 1.8 (f), 2.1 and 5.4(c).]

P16 In the present case, the parties do not dispute that insurers' billing and practice rules typically "impose conditions [upon an attorney appointed by an insurer to represent an insured] limiting or directing the scope and extent of the representation of his or her client." The Petitioners have focused on the requirement of prior approval in insurers' billing and practice rules. We therefore address that condition of representation while recognizing that other conditions limiting or directing the scope and extent of representation of a client may also implicate the Rules of Professional Conduct.

P17 As a representative set of litigation guidelines, we briefly consider the guidelines submitted by the St. Paul Companies (hereafter, St. Paul). The declared policy of St. Paul's Litigation Management Plan (hereafter, the Plan) is to "provide a systematic and appropriate defense for St. Paul and its insureds, and to vigorously defend nonmeritorious claims and claims where the demands are excessive."

P18 St. Paul promotes a "team" approach to litigation in which each member has distinct responsibilities. The claim professional is "responsible for disposition of claims, whether in suit or not. We expect the St. Paul claim professional to take the lead in initiating settlement negotiations.... We also expect the claim professional to have significant input into development of the litigation strategy (i.e., settle or try)." The Plan also "recognizes that defense counsel's primary responsibility and obligation are to protect and further the interests of the insured in the conduct of the litigation. Our goal is to cooperate with the insured and defense counsel to achieve the best result possible."

P19 However, the Plan states that "motion practice, discovery and research are items that have historically caused us some concern and which we plan to monitor closely. While we foresee very few differences of opinion, we require that defense counsel secure the consent of the claim professional prior to scheduling depositions, undertaking research, employing experts or preparing motions."

P20 Thus, the Plan expressly requires prior approval before a defense attorney may undertake to schedule depositions, conduct research, employ experts, or prepare motions. The Plan concludes that "we understand that any conflicts between the St. Paul Litigation Management Plan and the exercise of your independent judgment to protect the interests of the insured must be resolved in favor of the insured. We expect, however, to be given an opportunity to resolve any such conflicts with you before you take any action that is in substantial contravention of the Plan."

A. Whether Montana has recognized the dual representation doctrine under the Montana Rules of Professional Conduct.

P21 Petitioners assert that the insured is the sole client of a defense attorney appointed by an insurer to represent an insured pursuant to an insurance policy (hereafter, defense counsel) and that a requirement of prior approval in insurance billing and practice rules impermissibly interferes with a defense counsel's exercise of his independent judgment and his duty of undivided loyalty to his client. Petitioners argue that because the relationship of insurer and insured is permeated with potential conflicts, they cannot be co-clients of defense counsel.

P22 Respondents argue that under Montana law, the rule is that in the absence of a real conflict, the insurer and insured are dual clients of defense counsel. From this fundamental premise, Respondents argue that as a co-client of defense counsel, the insurer may require pre-approval of attorney activities to assure adequate consultation. Respondents argue further that defense counsel must abide by a client's decisions about the objectives of representation and that defense counsel are obliged to consult with a client about the means for the objectives of representation. Respondents also argue that under Montana law, an insurer is vicariously liable for the conduct of defense counsel and that an insurer's control of litigation justifies holding an insurer vicariously liable for the conduct of defense counsel....

B. Whether insurers and insureds are co-clients under Montana's Rules of Professional Conduct....

P37 Respondents argue vigorously that the interests of an insurer and an insured usually coincide and that most litigation is settled within an insured's coverage limits. These arguments gloss over the stark reality that the relationship between an insurer and insured is permeated with potential conflicts.... In cases where an insured's exposure exceeds his insurance coverage, where the insurer provides a defense subject to a reservation of rights, and where an insurer's obligation to indemnify its insured may be excused because of a policy defense, there are potential conflicts of interest.

P38 We reject Respondents' implicit premise that the Rules of Professional Conduct need not apply when the interests of insurers and insureds coincide. The Rules of Professional Conduct have application in all cases involving attorneys and clients. Moreover, whether the interests of insurers and insureds coincide can best be determined with the perfect clarity of hindsight. Before the final resolution of any claim against an insured, there clearly exists the potential for conflicts of interest to arise. Further, we reject the suggestion that the contractual relationship between insurer and insured supersedes or waives defense counsels' obligations under the Rules of Professional Conduct. We decline to recognize a vast exception to the Rules of Professional Conduct that would sanction relationships colored with the appearance of impropriety in order to accommodate the asserted economic exigencies of the insurance market. We hold that under the Rules of Professional Conduct, the insured is the sole client of defense counsel.

P39 We caution, however, that this holding should not be construed to mean that defense counsel have a "blank check" to escalate litigation costs nor that defense counsel need not ever consult with insurers. Under Rule 1.5, M.R. Prof. Conduct, for example, an attorney must charge reasonable fees. Nor, finally, should our holding be taken to signal that defense counsel cannot be held accountable for their work....

C. Whether the requirement of prior approval violates the Rules of Professional Conduct.

P46 Having concluded that the insured is the sole client of defense counsel, we turn to the fundamental issue whether the requirement of prior approval in billing and practice rules conflicts with defense counsels' duties under the Rules of Professional Conduct. The parties appear to agree that defense counsel may not abide by agreements limiting the scope of representation that interfere with their duties under the Rules of Professional Conduct....

P47 We conclude that the requirement of prior approval fundamentally interferes with defense counsels' exercise of their independent judgment, as required by Rule 1.8(f)....

P48 Montana is not alone in rejecting arrangements that fetter lawyers' undivided duty of loyalty to their clients and their independence of professional judgment in representing their clients. In Petition of Youngblood, 895 S.W.2d 322 (Tenn. 1995), the court determined that for inhouse attorney employees of an insurance company to represent insureds was not a per se ethical violation. However, the *Youngblood* court emphasized the loyalty that an attorney owes an insured and concluded that

> Some of the usual characteristics incident to [the employer-employee] relationship cannot exist between the insurer and the attorney representing an insured. The employer cannot control the details of the attorney's performance, dictate the strategy or tactics employed, or limit the attorney's professional discretion with regard to the representation. Any policy, arrangement or device which effectively limits, by design or operation, the attorney's professional judgment on behalf of or loyalty to the client is prohibited by the Code, and, undoubtedly, would not be consistent with public policy.

The court...conclude[d] that "the same loyalty is owed the client whether the attorney is employed and paid by the client, is a salaried employee of the insurer, or is an independent contractor engaged by the insurer."

P49 In addressing whether an insurer is vicariously liable for the malpractice of defense counsel, the Texas Supreme Court was similarly critical of insurer directions to defense counsel that interfere with their independent judgment and undivided loyalty to insureds. See State Farm Mut. Auto. Ins. Co. v. Traver, 980 S.W.2d 625 (Tex. 1998). In *Traver*, the court held that an insurer is not vicariously liable for the malpractice of an independent attorney whom it chooses to defend an insured. The court in *Traver* reasoned that in evaluating whether a principal is vicariously responsible for the actions of its agent, "the key question is whether the principal has the right to control the agent with respect to the details of that conduct." The court determined that "even assuming that the insurer possesses a level of control comparable to that of a client, this does not meet the requisite for vicarious liability."...

P50 Moreover, in Am. Ins. Assn. v. Ky. Bar Assn., 917 S.W.2d 568 (Ky. 1996), the court affirmed an Advisory ethics opinion that proscribed insurers' use of inhouse attorneys to represent insureds. The court in *Ky. Bar Assn.* also affirmed an Advisory ethics opinion concluding that a lawyer may not "enter into a contract with a liability insurer in which the lawyer or his firm agrees to do all of the insurer's defense work for a set fee." The court concluded that the pressures exerted by the insurer through the set fee interferes [*sic*] with the exercise of the attorney's independent professional judgment, in contravention of Rule 1.8(f)(2). The set fee arrangement also clashes with Rule 1.7(b) in that it creates a situation whereby the attorney has an interest in the outcome of the action which conflicts with the duties owed to the client: quite simply, in easy cases, counsel will take a financial windfall; in difficult cases, counsel will take a financial loss....

P51 We hold that defense counsel in Montana who submit to the requirement of prior approval violate their duties under the Rules of Professional Conduct to exercise their independent judgment and to give their undivided loyalty to insureds.

P52 2. May an attorney licensed to practice law in Montana, or admitted pro hac vice, be required to submit detailed descriptions of professional services to outside persons or entities without first obtaining the informed consent of his or her client and do so without violating client confidentiality? [The court cites MR 1.6.]

P54 As a representative set of guidelines concerning the disclosure of detailed descriptions of professional services to third-party auditors, we consider the guidelines submitted by the Zurich-American Insurance Group (hereafter, Zurich). Zurich's litigation guidelines regarding audits provide in pertinent part:

> **Audits**
>
> Zurich-American reserves the right to examine and audit books, records, other documents, and supporting material for the purpose of evaluating compliance with its litigation management guidelines, the billing requirements set forth therein, and the reasonableness of the firm's charges. The books, records, and documents we may examine include, without limitation: original time sheets from attorneys and staff; explanations of billing methods and practices; attorney work product and other contents of open and closed files involving the defense of Zurich-American customers; phone message records; and diaries, etc.
>
> All requested books and records must be made available to us during business hours for examination, audit, or reproduction. We shall employ, at our discretion, internal auditors or independent outside auditors for purposes of accomplishing audits.

P55 Petitioners argue that Respondents' billing and practice rules require the disclosure of confidential detailed descriptions of professional services. These disclosures are not impliedly authorized and do not further representation. Nor does an insured's contractual consent to disclosure of confidential information cure such disclosures, as an insured cannot know in advance of litigation what will be disclosed. Petitioners argue further that third-party auditors are different from insurers and that they do not fall within a protective "magic circle." Petitioners argue that under the Rules of Professional Conduct, disclosures of detailed billing statements to third-party auditors are only permissible if the client gives his informed consent after consultation.

P56 Respondents respond that third-party auditors are agents of insurers. Because they share "common interests" with insureds in reducing costs of litigation, third-party auditors are part of a privileged community. Further, insureds' consent is implied for disclosures that are reasonably necessary for representation. Thus, disclosures to third-party auditors are like disclosures to secretaries and computer technicians. Moreover, insureds have consented to disclosure by contract. Respondents also argue that whether a disclosure to a third-party auditor breaches the attorney-client privilege is a question of fact. Further, Respondents argue that much of the information in billing statements is neither confidential nor privileged. Finally, Respondents contend that the obligation of defense attorneys to charge reasonable fees is meaningless if insurers cannot monitor their services....

P70 We conclude that a third-party auditor is not within the "magic circle" or community of interest.... This asserted common interest in keeping litigation costs and premiums down is not sufficient to bring third-party auditors within the magic circle. The Rules of Professional Conduct do not vary according to commercial exigencies.... We further conclude that disclosure of detailed billing statements to a third-party auditor is "disclosure to a potential adversary." In third-party auditors' review of confidential information, there is always the possibility of disputes between auditors, defense counsel and their clients that could result in litigation....

P74 Having determined that insurers are not clients of defense counsel and that third-party auditors are potential adversaries of defense counsel, we turn to the issue whether the disclosure of billing statements to third-party auditors is "impliedly authorized in order to carry out the representation." Rule 1.6.

P75 Petitioners do not dispute that disclosures of billing information to insurers are impliedly authorized to carry out representation. It does not follow, however, that disclosing billing information to third-party auditors is also impliedly authorized. As previously discussed, third-party auditors lie outside the "magic circle" and do not share a community of interest with insureds. Their mission, as characterized in part by Respondents, is to find fault with legal charges, not to further the representation of insureds. Further, unlike secretaries and computer technicians who are engaged to assist defense counsel, third-party auditors are not employed by defense counsel and as noted they are potential adversaries of defense counsel. As such, third-party auditors stand in potential conflict with the interests of insureds in competent representation by defense counsel who exercise their independent professional judgment.

P76 Further, we reject Respondents' argument that insureds' consent by contract to disclosure of detailed professional billing statements comports with Rule 1.6. An insured executing a liability policy with an insurer cannot know at the time he enters the contract what kind of claim will be brought against him, what the issues will be, or what kinds of services will be undertaken by his defense attorney. Nor can an insured know, at the time he contracts for insurance, the legal consequences that may result from the disclosure of billing information to a third-party auditor. Depending on the facts and circumstances, such disclosure may waive a specific privilege. Thus, under Rule 1.6, for an insured to make a fully informed consent to disclosure of detailed professional billing statements, the consent must be contemporaneous with the facts and circumstances of which the insured should be aware....

P78 We hold that disclosure by defense counsel of detailed descriptions of professional services to third-party auditors without first obtaining the contemporaneous fully informed consent of insureds violates client confidentiality under the Rules of Professional Conduct.

Paradigm Insurance Co. v. The Langerman Law Offices, P.A.

24 P.3d 593 (Ariz. 2001)

En Banc....

FELDMAN, J.

P1 The ultimate question in this case is whether an attorney may be held liable to an insurer, which assigned him to represent an insured, when the attorney's negligence damages only the insurer....

P3 Paradigm issued an insurance policy covering Dr. Benjamin A. Vanderwerf for medical malpractice liability. Vanderwerf, Medical Director of Samaritan Transplant Service, a division of Samaritan Health Service (Samaritan), and another doctor were sued by Renee Taylor, who alleged that Vanderwerf committed malpractice by injuring her during a catheter removal procedure. Taylor included Samaritan as a defendant, alleging that at the time of the negligent act, Vanderwerf was acting as Samaritan's agent or employee....

P4 . . . In due course, Paradigm assigned defense of Taylor's claims to Langerman. Langerman undertook the assignment, with Vanderwerf evidently acquiescing, and appeared in the action as Vanderwerf's counsel. During the course of representation, Langerman advised Paradigm that it believed there was no viable theory of liability against Samaritan. Langerman, however, failed to investigate whether Vanderwerf was covered by Samaritan's liability insurance and, thus, was unable to advise Paradigm whether the defense could be tendered to Samaritan.

P5 After a time, . . . Paradigm terminated Langerman's representation in Taylor and retained new counsel for Vanderwerf.

P6 Vanderwerf's new lawyer discovered that Samaritan had liability coverage through Samaritan Insurance Funding (SIF) that not only covered Vanderwerf for Taylor's claim but probably operated as the primary coverage for the claim. . . . Accordingly, new counsel tendered the claim to SIF, which rejected it on the grounds that the tender was untimely.

P7 Taylor v. Vanderwerf was eventually settled for an amount within Paradigm's policy limits. Thus, Vanderwerf was not injured by Langerman's failure to make a timely tender to SIF. However, Paradigm, compelled to act as Vanderwerf's primary carrier, was forced to settle Taylor's claim with its own funds and without being able to look to SIF for contribution or indemnification.

P8 Langerman then presented Paradigm with its statement for legal services. Paradigm refused to pay, claiming Langerman had been negligent both in failing to advise it of SIF's exposure as the primary carrier and by not promptly tendering the defense. When Langerman sued for fees, Paradigm counterclaimed for damages. . . .

DISCUSSION

A. Whether an express agreement is necessary to form an attorney-client relationship

P10 Langerman argues that, before an attorney-client relationship can form between an insurer and the counsel it retains to represent an insured, express mutual consent must be reached among all of the respective parties. We disagree. The law has never required that the attorney-client relationship must be initiated by some sort of express agreement, oral or written. Quite to the contrary, the current rule is described as follows:

> A relationship of client and lawyer arises when: (1) a person manifests to a lawyer the person's intent that the lawyer provide legal services for the person; and . . . (a) the lawyer manifests to the person consent to do so. *Restatement (Third) of The Law Governing Lawyers* §14.

Indeed, comment c to section 14 indicates that either intent or acquiescence may establish the relationship. . . .

B. Potential and actual conflicts of interest with the insurer as client

P13 Langerman contends that absent the consent of the insured, a lawyer assigned by an insurer to represent the insured forms an attorney-client relationship only with the insured and never with the insurer. Any contrary conclusion, asserts Langerman, inherently creates a strong potential conflict of interest for the attorney, weakens his "undivided allegiance" to the insured, and creates "situations rife with opportunities for mistrust and second guessing." Langerman's concern over conflicts of interest between attorney, insurer, and insured is not unfounded.

This case presents the typical situation found when defense is provided by a liability insurer: as part of the insurer's obligation to provide for the insured's defense, the policy grants the insurer the right to control that defense—which includes the power to select the lawyer that will defend the claim. But the fact that the lawyer is chosen, assigned, and paid by the insurer for the purpose of representing the insured does not automatically create an attorney-client relationship between the insurer and lawyer. . . .

P15 Thus, because the insured has given the insurer control of the defense as part of the agreement for indemnity, the assigned lawyer more or less automatically becomes the attorney for the insured. But does the assigned lawyer automatically also become the attorney for the insurer in every case? . . . Langerman . . . argu[es] that even in the absence of actual conflict between the insured and insurer, there is always a great potential for it. And it is this potential, argues Langerman, that prevents the formation of an attorney-client relationship absent the express consent of the insured—the automatic client. . . .

P16 . . . There can be no doubt that actual conflicts between insured and insurer are quite common and that the potential for conflict is present in every case. Conflicts may arise over the existence of coverage, the manner in which the case is to be defended, the information to be shared, the desirability of settling at a particular figure or the need to settle at all, and an array of other factors applicable to the circumstances of a particular case. This is especially true in cases involving medical malpractice claims.[1] We have recognized such tensions, holding . . . that when a conflict actually arises, and not simply when it potentially exists, the lawyer's duty is exclusively owed to the insured and not the insurer. Because a lawyer is expressly assigned to represent the insured, the lawyer's primary obligation is to the insured, and the lawyer must exercise independent professional judgment on behalf of the insured. Thus, a lawyer cannot allow an insurer to interfere with the lawyer's independent professional judgment, even though, in general, the lawyer's representation of the insured is directed by the insurer.

P17 . . . We have, in fact, previously held that an attorney assigned to represent an insured cannot supply the insurer with information that either may be or actually is detrimental to the insured's interests. . . . Where a substantial danger of harming the client does not exist, there is no actual conflict of interest—only the potential of a future conflict. . . .

P19 We agree with Langerman that the potential for conflict between insurer and insured exists in every case; but we note that the interests of insurer and insured frequently coincide. For instance, both insurer and insured often share a common interest in developing and presenting a strong defense to a claim that they believe to be unfounded as to liability, damages, or both. Usually insured and insurer have a joint interest in finding additional coverage from another carrier. Thus, by serving the insured's interests the lawyer can also serve the insurer's, and if no question arises regarding the existence and adequacy of coverage, the potential for

1. For instance, in the ordinary case in which liability is probable, even if somewhat questionable, it would almost always be in the interest of the insurer to make a reasonable settlement offer within policy limits. However, such a settlement might not be in the insured's interest and he or she may prefer to take a chance at trial because any settlement payment will require reporting that physician to the National Practitioner Data Bank, thus potentially affecting the physician's ability to obtain hospital privileges or malpractice insurance in the future.

conflict may never become substantial. In such cases, we see no reason why the lawyer cannot represent both insurer and insured; but in the unique situation in which the lawyer actually represents two clients, he must give primary allegiance to one (the insured) to whom the other (the insurer) owes a duty of providing not only protection, but of doing so fairly and in good faith.

P20 Perhaps recognizing this, the court of appeals determined that the "majority rule" was "in the absence of a conflict, the attorney has two clients, the insurer and the insured." We believe the court of appeals' characterization of the majority rule is too absolute. A host of potential problems are created by holding that, as a matter of law, a lawyer hired by the insurer to represent an insured always accepts the responsibilities of dual representation until a conflict actually arises—thus always automatically forming an attorney-client relationship with both the insurer and insured. There are many cases in which the potential for conflict is strong enough to implicate ER 1.7 . . . from the very beginning. Think, for example, of a claim with questionable liability against an insured covered by limits much lower than the amount of damages. The potential for conflict is quite substantial unless and until the insurer has committed itself to offering or waiving the policy limits. Thus we do not endorse the view that the lawyer automatically represents both insurer and insured until the conflict actually arises.[3] . . .

C. Duty to a nonclient

P22 The court of appeals gave several reasons for its conclusion that, in the absence of a conflict, an attorney automatically provides dual representation. . . . The primary reason given, and the one most relevant, is that absent an attorney-client relationship, an "insurer cannot maintain a malpractice action against an attorney it hired to represent its insured," thus "immunizing that attorney's malpractice."[5] On this point we must respectfully disagree with the court of appeals.

P23 If a lawyer's liability to the insurer depends entirely on the existence of an attorney-client relationship and for some reason the insurer is not a client,[6] then the lawyer has no duty to the insurer that hired him, assigned the case to him, and pays his fees. There are many problems with that result: if that lawyer's negligence damages the insurer only, the negligent lawyer fortuitously escapes liability. Or if the lawyer's negligence injures both insurer and insured in a case in which the insured is the only client but refuses to proceed against the lawyer, the insurer is helpless and has no remedy. Such

3. To forestall confusion among the bar, we hasten to point out that even when the insurer is not the lawyer's client, it certainly is the insured's agent to prepare and handle the defense. Thus, for instance, communications between the nonclient insurer and the lawyer would generally be entitled to the same degree of confidentiality—as long as the general requirements for privilege are met—as those between the insured client and the lawyer.

5. The court gave two other reasons to support its conclusion of a dual attorney-client relationship. One was the absence of any absolute ethical prohibition against an attorney representing more than one client in a single matter. The final reason given was that having one attorney representing both insurer and insured made "economic and practical sense." We agree with the first reason. As to the other, we believe that in some cases common representation makes economic and practical sense but in others it does not. We have, of course, no way of quantifying those cases in which dual representation makes sense and those in which it does not—much depends on the strength of the potential for conflict and the nature of the issues in the case. Yet neither of these reasons, we believe, are persuasive enough to hold that there is dual representation in every case where an attorney is assigned by an insurer to represent the insured.

6. When, for instance, the insured does not consent to a dual relationship, the potential for conflict is great, or the conflict is real.

unjust results are not just bad policy but unnecessary. The Restatement holds the view that a lawyer may, in certain circumstances, owe a duty to a nonclient. Specifically, Restatement section 51(3) reads, in pertinent part:

> [A] lawyer owes a duty of care . . . to a nonclient when and to the extent that:
>
> (a) the lawyer knows that a client intends as one of the primary objectives of the representation that the lawyer's services benefit the nonclient;
>
> (b) such a duty would not significantly impair the lawyer's performance of obligations to the client; and
>
> (c) the absence of such a duty would make enforcement of those obligations to the client unlikely;

Comment g to this section advises:

> [A] lawyer designated by an insurer to defend an insured owes a duty of care to the insurer with respect to matters as to which the interests of the insurer and insured are not in conflict, whether or not the insurer is held to be a co-client of the lawyer.

In addition, comment f to Restatement section 14 states:

> Because and to the extent that the insurer is directly concerned in the matter financially, the insurer should be accorded standing to assert a claim for appropriate relief from the lawyer for financial loss proximately caused by professional negligence or other wrongful act of the lawyer.

P24 . . . Arizona's courts have long recognized situations in which a professional is under a duty of care to nonclients. In Fickett v. Superior Court, for example, the attorney representing a guardian of an estate was accused of negligence by the ward in failing to discover that the guardian had dissipated the estate by misappropriation, conversion, and improper investing. 558 P.2d 988, 89 (Ariz. 1976). . . . The court of appeals [held] that one could not say, as a matter of law, that the guardian's attorney owed no duty to the ward. . . .

P27 In Napier v. Bertram we recognized that, although the "general rule is that a professional owes no duty to a non-client unless special circumstances require otherwise," there are "special circumstances" where we have "imposed liability on a professional to the extent that a foreseeable and specific third party is injured by the professional's actions." 954 P.2d 1389 (Ariz. 1998). . . . [T]hese circumstances are found in a myriad of contexts. *See, e.g.*, Lombardo v. Albu, 14 P.3d 288 (Ariz. 2000) (purchaser's real estate agent has duty to disclose purchaser's financial difficulties to seller); Hamman v. County of Maricopa, 775 P.2d 1122, 1127-28 (Ariz. 1989) (psychiatrist has duty to exercise reasonable care to protect foreseeable victim of patient); Mur-Ray Mgmt. Corp. v. Founders Title Co., 819 P.2d 1003, 1008-09 (Ariz. App. 1991) (imposing duty of reasonable care for escrow agent's representations to third persons). The "common thread [that] exists between" such cases is that "there was a foreseeable risk of harm to a foreseeable non-client whose protection depended on the actor's conduct."

P28 But Langerman argues that Paradigm need not have depended on it, as every insurer has both the freedom and financial ability to hire separate counsel to protect the insurer's own interests. This, of course, must be done in cases in which a conflict exists or is imminent, but we certainly need not impose such an expense on every insurer in every case just to provide the insurer with protection against malpractice by the lawyer it has chosen to handle the defense. When the interests of insurer and insured coincide, as they often do, it makes neither economic nor practical sense for an insurer to hire another attorney to monitor the actions and decisions of the attorney assigned to an insured. More important, we believe that a special relationship exists between the insurer and the counsel it assigns to represent its insured. The insurer is "in some way dependent upon" the lawyer it hires on behalf of its insureds. For instance, the insurer depends on the lawyer to represent the insured zealously so as to honor its contractual agreement to provide the defense when liability allegations are leveled at the insured. In addition, the insurer depends on the lawyer to thwart claims of liability and, in the event liability is found, to minimize the damages it must pay. Thus, the lawyer's duties to the insured are often discharged for the full or partial benefit of the nonclient. *See Fickett,* 558 P.2d at 990. We reject Langerman's attempt to distinguish the present case from our cases that recognize that a professional has a duty to third parties who are foreseeably injured by the lawyer's negligent actions.

CONCLUSION

P29 ...[B]ased on a long line of precedent, when an insurer assigns an attorney to represent an insured, the lawyer has a duty to the insurer arising from the understanding that the lawyer's services are ordinarily intended to benefit both insurer and insured when their interests coincide. This duty exists even if the insurer is a nonclient. We hold again today that a lawyer has a duty, and therefore may be liable for negligent breach, to a nonclient under the conditions set forth in previous case law and the Restatement....

P30 The record does not allow us, however, to determine whether, as a matter of law, Langerman actually breached its duty to Paradigm in this case. Thus, our holding does not determine whether the applicable standard of conduct would have required Langerman to investigate the existence of a different primary insurer or advise Paradigm to tender the defense to that other insurer. Although we have decided that an attorney-client relationship is not a prerequisite to Paradigm's maintaining a tort action against Langerman for its alleged negligence, whether Langerman actually breached its duty to Paradigm or caused damage is left for the trial court to decide on remand. Under the circumstances of this case, suffice it to say that absent any conflict or significant risk of conflict that compelled Langerman to act as it did, Langerman had a duty to Paradigm—regardless of whether Paradigm was a client....

G. Former Clients

Problems

6-23. Three years ago, Martyn & Fox prepared tax returns for Wife's business. Husband now wants Martyn & Fox to represent him in a divorce. Can we? Does it matter if we prepared the tax returns ten years ago?

6-24. Martyn & Fox represented Client in getting zoning from Abington Township for a new shopping center.

- ***(a)*** Can Martyn & Fox represent potential tenants in lease negotiations for the new center?
- ***(b)*** Can Martyn & Fox represent someone who wants to build a shopping center across the street?

(c) Can Martyn & Fox represent an environmental group that wants to challenge the shopping center because it would lie in a flood plain and would violate applicable federal regulations?

6-25. Martyn & Fox received a call to defend a major accounting firm in a 10b-5 class action involving a dot.com company whose stock has precipitously dropped. The accounting firm sent Fox the pleadings and Fox met with them for three hours yesterday, explaining the firm's approach and the possible lines of defense the accounting firm might use. The firm promised to get back to Martyn & Fox next week. Today Martyn circulated a conflicts memo asking whether the firm could take on the representation of the defendant underwriter in the same matter. What should Fox do?

6-26. Grayson, the senior partner at Martyn & Fox, has been mediating a dispute between Hydrogen Electric and Steel Company over electric rates for the year 2000. He finished facilitating the participants' agreement last Tuesday. Now Martyn has been called by Steel Company to see if the firm will represent Steel Company against Hydrogen Electric for the year 2002 electric charges. May Martyn take the case?

Consider: Model Rules 1.0(k), 1.9, 1.10, 1.12, 1.18, 2.4
Model Code DR 4-101, 5-105(D)

Kanaga v. Gannett Company, Inc.

1993 Del. Super. LEXIS 341

Vincent A. BIFFERATO, J. . . .

In December of 1992, Dr. Kanaga filed a complaint in this Court, alleging that she was defamed by an article printed in The Sunday News Journal on July 5, 1992. The article contained information provided by Pamela Kane, a former patient of Dr. Kanaga. It was authored by Jane Harriman. The Sunday News Journal is published by The News Journal Company, which is owned by Gannett Co., Inc.

Essentially, the article alleged that Dr. Kanaga recommended that Ms. Kane undergo a hysterectomy which later was determined to be unnecessary by another physician. The complaint alleged that the article wrongly criticized Dr. Kanaga's skill and ethics as a practicing obstetrician and gynecologist and caused severe damage to her reputation and medical practice.

In January of 1993, Gannett Co., Inc. and Ms. Harriman (collectively referred to as "Respondents") filed an Answer through counsel of the law firm, Richards, Layton and Finger. Subsequently, Dr. Kanaga filed this motion to disqualify Respondents' counsel on the grounds that Dr. Kanaga was a former client of the firm. Pamela Kane has separate counsel and is not a party to this Motion.

It is undisputed that John A. Parkins, Jr., a member of the law firm Richards, Layton and Finger, represented Dr. Kanaga in a prior action brought against her in 1983. Dr. Kanaga argues that this prior representation by Mr. Parkins has created a conflict of interest and counsel from his firm should be disqualified from representing Respondents in this present action. . . .

[The court cites Del. Rules 1.9(a) and 1.10.]

It is undisputed that Richards, Layton and Finger currently represents new clients, other than Dr. Kanaga; that this action is materially adverse to Dr. Kanaga's interests; that Dr. Kanaga has not consented to this representation; and that this action is not the "same matter." The issue, therefore, is whether the matter presently before this Court is "substantially related" to the former matter.

Essentially, Dr. Kanaga argues that the two matters are "substantially related" because both actions involve allegations of improper medical treatment. Respondents argue that the matters are not "substantially related" because this action is a defamation action which involves different defenses and a different standard of proof than the former medical malpractice action....

In determining whether a "substantial relationship" exists between the two representations, three questions are to be considered. They are:

1) What is the nature and scope of the prior representation at issue?
2) What is the nature of the present lawsuit against the former client?
3) In the course of the prior representation, might the client have disclosed to his attorney confidences which could be relevant to the present action? In particular, could any such confidences be detrimental to the former client in the current litigation.

The first factor is the nature and scope of the prior representation of Dr. Kanaga by Mr. Parkins. He defended her against serious allegations of medical malpractice arising from the performance of a hysterectomy. Dr. Kanaga strongly contested these allegations. The case lasted seven years. It went to trial and the jury returned a verdict in favor of Dr. Kanaga. Ultimately, the Delaware Supreme Court held that a verdict should have been directed in favor of Dr. Kanaga because there was no expert testimony presented against her at trial.

The second factor is the nature of the present lawsuit involving... Dr. Kanaga. Respondents have been sued for their participation in the publication of the article which allegedly defamed Dr. Kanaga by suggesting that she recommended the performance of an unnecessary hysterectomy.

The third factor is the possibility that Dr. Kanaga may have disclosed confidential matter during the first representation by Mr. Parkins which could be relevant and detrimental to Dr. Kanaga's subsequent action for defamation. In order to determine whether counsel may have acquired potentially detrimental confidential information during a former representation, "the court should not allow its imagination to run free with a view to hypothesizing conceivable but unlikely situations in which confidential information 'might' have been disclosed which would be relevant to the present suit...." Rather, "the Court should consider whether a client ought to have discussed the relevant facts or whether it would not have been unusual for the lawyer and client to have discussed the relevant facts."

Dr. Kanaga contends that she shared confidential information during consultations with Mr. Parkins on the Russell case. She asserts that in discussing the specific facts of the Russell case, she disclosed, to Mr. Parkins, her medical practices and procedures as well as her skill as a physician and her reputation and standing in the medical community. She alleges that these facts are critical to the defense in this action and therefore detrimental to her case.

Respondents argue that Dr. Kanaga has failed to demonstrate that potentially detrimental confidential information was gained. Respondents argue that Dr. Kanaga's professional abilities are not confidential because they are held out to the public and that standards of care are not confidential because they are determined by the medical community. In addition, Respondents argue that Dr. Kanaga's professional standing and reputation in the medical community are not confidential because such are based upon other's opinions. By affidavit, Mr. Parkins asserts that he has no recollection of a discussion with Dr. Kanaga on her standing and reputation. Respondents argue that such a conversation is unlikely because it would be irrelevant to medical malpractice cases.

This Court finds Dr. Kanaga's argument to be more persuasive. It is reasonable to assume that a medical malpractice lawsuit would be potentially traumatic for a physician. It would be likely that Dr. Kanaga would engage in open discussion with her attorney on many issues connected with the lawsuit. Her counsel may not have initiated discussion on issues not specifically relevant to a defense in a medical malpractice case. However, it is conceivable that Dr. Kanaga may have volunteered information which fell outside such a scope. Although Dr. Kanaga has not delineated an exact dialogue which could be deemed confidential and explained how it would negatively impact the present action, she is not required to do so.... It is enough to demonstrate that such information could have been acquired, and Dr. Kanaga has proven that this possibility exists.

As the party moving for disqualification, Dr. Kanaga has the burden of proving the "requisite substantial relationship." "A movant for disqualification must have evidence to buttress his claim of conflict because a litigant should, as much as possible, be able to use the counsel of his choice."...

It is the decision of this Court that Dr. Kanaga has proven that a substantial relationship exists between the prior action in which she was represented by the law firm of Richards, Layton and Finger and the present action in which it represents Respondents. Therefore, it is the finding of this Court that a conflict of interests exists.

The Motion to Disqualify Counsel is granted....

Poly Software International, Inc. v. Su

880 F. Supp. 1487 (D. Utah 1995)

WINDER, Chief Judge.

This matter is before the court on cross-motions to disqualify counsel. Plaintiff and Counterdefendant Poly Software International ("Poly Software") has moved for the disqualification of Lynn G. Foster and the firm of Foster & Foster. The current CEO of Poly Software is Xiaowu Wang ("Wang"). Defendants and Counterclaimants Yu Su, et al. ("Su") have moved for the disqualification of Berne S. Broadbent and the firm of Berne S. Broadbent, P.C....

I. BACKGROUND

Treatment of the disqualification motions at issue requires a brief account of the previous dealings of the parties. In 1989, Su was employed as a software engineer by Micromath, Inc., a company specializing in the development and marketing of mathematical software. Wang joined him in the same capacity in 1990.

In the summer of 1992, both Su and Wang left Micromath, formed a partnership ("Polysoft Partnership"), and began producing their own line of mathematical graphing software. Micromath subsequently sued the Polysoft Partnership for copyright infringement. The focus of the Micromath litigation was a Polysoft Partnership product entitled "Techplot," later renamed "PS Plot," and then "PSI-Plot." Micromath claimed that Wang and Su had obtained user's handbooks and computer source code while working for Micromath, and illegally employed that information in their development of Techplot.

Soon after the complaint was filed the parties agreed to submit their dispute to mediation, a non-binding alternative to formal litigation, and chose Berne S. Broadbent ("Broadbent") to serve as mediator. Broadbent conducted a series of intensive meetings, conferring with the parties both individually and together. During Broadbent's private caucuses with the Polysoft Partnership both Wang and Su were present and openly discussed confidential aspects of their case, including detailed analysis of their source codes and handbook comparisons. At the conclusion of the mediation process Micromath and the Polysoft Partnership successfully negotiated a settlement of their dispute.

Subsequent to the settlement of the Micromath litigation, the Polysoft Partnership continued to market PSI-Plot, and began developing new programs. Two of these were "PSI-Stat," and "PSI-Math." However, in December of 1993, Wang and Su dissolved the partnership. Under the terms of the dissolution, Su surrendered his ownership interest in the Polysoft Partnership to Wang, and received the rights to the PSI-Stat software. Wang retained the rights to the PSI-Plot and PSI-Math programs. Subsequently, Wang restructured the business as Poly Software International, Inc., and Su formed Datamost Corporation.

The present litigation was commenced on November 7, 1994, when Poly Software filed an action asserting copyright infringement and other related claims against Su and various other employees of Datamost. In substance, those claims asserted that "Statmost for DOS," Datamost's version of the program PSI-Stat (the rights to which had passed to Su upon dissolution of the Polysoft Partnership) illegally duplicated significant portions of the PSI-Plot User's Handbook, and incorporated source code unique to PSI-Plot.

Prior to commencing suit, Wang interviewed a number of attorneys for the purpose of finding a law firm to pursue his claim against Su and Datamost. One of those attorneys, Lynn G. Foster of the firm Foster & Foster, met with Wang in October of 1994. F for this initial interview. Foster asserts that the meeting began at about 5:30 P.M., and lasted less than 30 minutes.[1] He also claims that Wang was given two options for the interview. One option would primarily focus on the fee schedule of the firm and outline the policies employed in pursuing litigation. Under this option, the potential client would give only a very general description of the litigation proposed. The second option would involve a much more significant interview, focusing on specific details of the potential client's case. Foster asserts that Wang chose the first option, and that Wang disclosed only that "he had a dispute against a former partner, software was

1. Wang testified briefly at the hearing before this court. He speaks and understands English, but his heavy accent nonetheless raises somewhat of a language barrier. In particular, Wang must often repeat what he says in order to make himself effectively understood. Foster claims that communication difficulties in his interview with Wang prevented them from discussing anything beyond the bare essentials of the case during the short time allotted.

involved, and there was some type of prior settlement agreement." Wang, on the other hand, claims that the meeting was over an hour long, that he specifically discussed the evidence relevant to the proposed litigation, disclosed potential strengths and weaknesses of his case, displayed the user's handbooks printed by both companies, and compared a printout of portions of defendants' "materials" with those of Poly Software.

II. DISCUSSION ...

A. The Motion to Disqualify Lynn G. Foster

... [A] party wishing to disqualify opposing counsel under Rule 1.9 must demonstrate three factors: (1) that a previous attorney-client relationship arose with the moving party; (2) that the present litigation is "substantially factually related" to the previous representation; and (3) that the attorney's present client's interests are materially adverse to the movant. In this case, Wang convened with Foster for the purpose of determining whether Foster would represent Poly Software in the very litigation for which Foster eventually was retained by the opposing side. Hence, the second and third factors are clearly demonstrated. The determinative question, then, is whether an attorney-client relationship ever arose between Wang and Foster.

Nevertheless, because ethical rules are generally concerned with the behavior and regulation of the legal profession, and more specifically here with the protection of communications that a reasonable person would assume to be confidential, the various legal criteria employed to determine a client relationship under agency or other contractual employment theories do not necessarily provide the appropriate answer to that question. Nor, frankly, does existing case law. A number of cases, for instance, have formulated a rule for an "implied" attorney-client relationship in situations where formal contracts have not been executed or fees have not been paid....

This rule, however, may not adequately address the situation involving an initial interview (such as that occurring between Wang and Foster) where both parties understand that the relationship is potential, not implied or actual. *See* B.F. Goodrich Co. v. Formosa Plastics Corp., 638 F. Supp. 1050, 1052 (S.D. Texas 1986) (holding all-day interview insufficient to form attorney-client relationship where potential client was in process of conducting several interviews). Even in such an initial interview both the attorney and the potential client may find it quite tempting to discuss the case as frankly as possible, enabling them to more clearly assess the desirability of undertaking a formal, perhaps costly, attorney-client relationship. It also seems quite likely that at the outset nonlawyers will not always appreciate the possibility that, should they choose not to enter a formal relationship, the attorney may be free to work for the other side in the same legal dispute. Justice will be hampered and the stature of the legal profession harmed if, to the surprise and dismay of persons who have assumed that their initial discussion was confidential, attorneys subsequently represent the opposing side in a dispute.

Balanced against these considerations, however, is the public interest of allowing clients (and attorneys) to freely choose their employment arrangements. It may often be necessary for potential clients to interview a number of lawyers before settling on the lawyer or firm that best meets their expectations. In this vein, it is critical to avoid a situation where a person, merely by arranging employment interviews, renders a large number of attorneys unavailable for the opposing party.[3] The present conflict between Wang and Su may well be a case in point. Wang (quite understandably) visited a number of local attorneys who focus on intellectual property litigation before entrusting his proposed lawsuit to one of them. Although the Wasatch Front is a moderately-sized urban area, attorneys specializing in such fields are not overwhelmingly plentiful. If the ethical rules disqualified every attorney granting an initial interview, Wang, in a very short time period, could have (even unintentionally) forced his opponent to seek inexperienced or out-of-state counsel.

Constructing a rule which best strikes the appropriate balance between the competing considerations is not an easy task. The best solution is for attorneys to avoid the dilemma altogether by adequately controlling the initial interview.[5] In this case Foster claims he did precisely that by offering Wang two options for the interview: one to involve a fairly cursory overview of the proposed litigation, and the other to involve a more detailed, in-depth discussion. According to Foster, Wang explicitly chose the first option, their discussion consumed less than a half-hour, and no details of the proposed litigation were revealed. Wang claims he revealed considerably more. After carefully weighing the conflicting affidavits and testimony describing what occurred during the interview and how long it lasted, this court finds Foster's version to be the more credible of the two. As a result, this court also holds that the degree of confidentiality established in the interview was insufficient to preclude Foster's subsequent employment by Su and Datamost.

B. The Motion to Disqualify Berne S. Broadbent

Su and Datamost have brought a similar motion to disqualify Wang's attorney, Berne S. Broadbent. That motion is based on Broadbent's previous role as a mediator in the Micromath litigation. With respect to the appropriate rule governing mediators, this case is one of first impression. In making their arguments on this issue, both parties have cited to the Utah Prof. Conduct Rules, Rule 1.12(a). That provision states that "a lawyer shall not represent anyone in connection with a matter in which the lawyer participated personally and substantially as a judge or other adjudicative officer, arbitrator or law clerk to such a person, unless all parties to the proceeding consent after disclosure." Su also cites to Nancy H. Rogers & Craig A. McEwen, *Mediation: Law, Policy, Practice* (2d ed. 1994), and its proposed code of ethics for mediators, which provides that "without the consent of all parties, a mediator shall not subsequently establish a professional relationship with one of the parties in a related matter." In substance, this proposal is analogous to Model Rule 1.9's proscription of subsequent employment on a "substantially related matter," or in the case of the more specific Utah Prof. Conduct Rules, Rule 1.9, "substantially factually related matter."

Thus, Rules 1.9 and 1.12 promulgate a significant distinction in the scope of prohibited subsequent representation. This distinction becomes important in

3. It is even conceivable that a potential litigant could strategically disqualify those attorneys perceived to be the most valuable or likely choices for the opposition.

5. This may become particularly necessary when dealing with persons who are unfamiliar with legal proceedings. Individuals and organizations that are more accustomed to dealing with lawyers, on the other hand, will more likely understand the importance of avoiding disclosures of sensitive information during the initial interview. Attorneys should also foresee the possibility of being called upon by the opponent of the potential client. If they desire to keep that option open, then they should take greater care to prevent an atmosphere of confidentiality from arising.

this case because the Micromath litigation mediated by Broadbent and the present lawsuit possess a common factual nexus, but are distinct legal disputes. With respect to "matter" as that term is employed by Rule 1.12, there is virtually no case law or other commentary. However, Rule 1.11 contains substantially the same provision as Rule 1.12, and, "as used in [Rule 1.11], the term 'matter' includes . . . any judicial or other proceeding, application, request for ruling or other determination, contract, claim, controversy, investigation, charge, accusation, arrest or other particular matter involving a specific party or parties." Further commentary has observed that

> The same lawsuit or litigation is the same matter. The same issue of fact involving the same parties and the same situation or conduct is the same matter... The same "matter" is not involved [when] . . . there is lacking the discrete, identifiable transaction of conduct involving a particular situation and specific parties. Securities Investor Protection Corp. v. Vigman, 587 F. Supp. 1358, 1365 (C.D. Cal. 1984) [quoting ABA Formal Op. 342 (Nov. 24, 1975)].

A "substantially factually related matter," on the other hand, is not defined by any particular, discrete legal proceeding. By its terms, it includes aspects of past controversies which are similar, but not necessarily identical, to those encompassed within a present dispute. So long as there are substantial factual threads connecting the two matters, the criteria of Rule 1.9 are met.

> For the most part, [this difference] is due to the different purposes served by each rule. The purpose of rule 1.9 is to assure that the confidentiality and loyalty owed to the client is not compromised. . . . The purpose of Rule 1.11 is to prevent a lawyer from exploiting public office for the advantage of a private client.

In this case the lawsuit between Su and Wang is legally distinct from the earlier Micromath litigation because it involves a separate dispute between differing parties, and thereby "lack[s] the discrete, identifiable transaction of conduct involving a particular situation and specific parties." Thus, it is not the same "matter" as that term is understood in Rule 1.12 or 1.11.

The present litigation is, however, "substantially factually related" to the Micromath litigation. Poly Software accuses Su and Datamost of impermissibly copying source code and handbook information from the PSI-Plot program. Micromath accused Wang and Su of pirating source code and handbook information to formulate an earlier version of the very same program. The complaints filed in the two cases are virtually identical in many respects, at times employing precisely the same phrasing. Moreover, as a mediator in the Micromath litigation, Broadbent examined in detail the disputed source code and elicited frank discussions in private caucus with Wang and Su as to which of them might be responsible for alleged illegal copying. Therefore, the determinative question on the issue of the ethical status of Broadbent's current representation of Poly Software is whether mediators should be governed by a same "matter" standard similar to that enunciated in Rule 1.12 and 1.11, or by a "substantially factually related" standard similar to that employed by Rule 1.9.

Preliminary to answering that question a brief discussion of the definition of "mediator," is necessary. For the purposes of this opinion, a mediator is an attorney who agrees to assist parties in settling a legal dispute, and in the course of assisting those parties undertakes a confidential relationship with them. . . . Such mediation may often occur in the context of a court-supervised Alternative Dispute Resolution ("ADR") program. . . . [I]t applies to situations where litigation has already commenced, the parties subsequently agree to suspend their litigation, and also agree to the appointment of an attorney to facilitate settlement. The attorney who thus serves as mediator is a neutral individual who confers with each party in private caucus, learning what results are acceptable to each of them and assessing in confidence the strengths and weaknesses of their cases. The mediator also meets with all parties together to facilitate settlement of the case. In this regard, mediation may well be the most valuable ADR option. . . .

These characteristics of mediation demonstrate that it differs significantly from more formal adversarial proceedings at which an adjudicative officer presides. Most importantly, the mediator is not merely charged with being impartial, but with receiving and preserving confidences in much the same manner as the client's attorney. In fact, the success of mediation depends largely on the willingness of the parties to freely disclose their intentions, desires, and the strengths and weaknesses of their case; and upon the ability of the mediator to maintain a neutral position while carefully preserving the confidences that have been revealed. The Utah District Court ADR Manual, for instance, encourages the parties to disclose to the mediator (in strict confidence) "all critical information, whether favorable or unfavorable to the party's position," and recommends that mediators "advise the parties and their attorneys that it is neither helpful nor productive to withhold information with the intent of gaining some tactical advantage."

Adversarial proceedings, on the other hand, are characterized by vigorous attempts to maintain confidences. Attorneys who have received such confidential information are under a strict duty to avoid, without the consent of the client, any disclosures of that information. And because adjudicators do not occupy a relationship of confidence and trust with the parties akin to that occupied by the attorneys, they do not, for the most part, have access to those confidences. Thus, although mediators function in some ways as neutral coordinators of dispute resolution, they also assume the role of a confidant, and it is that aspect of their role that distinguishes them from adjudicators.

As a result, the appropriate ethical rule for mediators differs somewhat from the text of the Utah Prof. Conduct Rules, Rule 1.12. Where a mediator has received confidential information in the course of mediation, that mediator should not thereafter represent anyone in connection with the same or a substantially factually related matter unless all parties to the mediation proceeding consent after disclosure. This rule also takes into account some important policy considerations. If parties to mediation know that their mediator could someday be an attorney on the opposing side in a substantially related matter, they will be discouraged from freely disclosing their position in the mediation, which may severely diminish the opportunity for settlement. If, on the other hand, the disqualification net is thrown too wide, attorneys will be discouraged from becoming mediators. The "substantially factually related" standard best balances those two interests. It encourages parties to freely disclose their positions during mediation by assuring them that the specific information disclosed will not be used against them at a later time. It also limits disqualification to subsequent situations where there is a substantial factual nexus with the previously mediated dispute. Applying the "substantially factually related" standard to the present motion, it is evident that Broadbent received confidential information in the

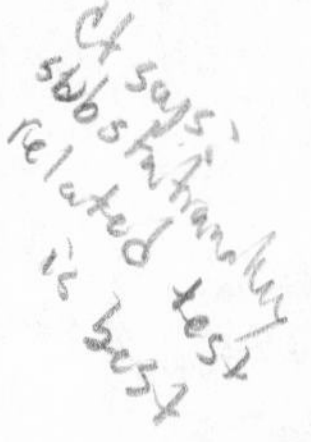

course of the Micromath dispute. It is also undisputed that Su and Datamost did not consent to his subsequent representation of Wang in a substantially factually related lawsuit. Therefore, his current representation constitutes a violation of the rule established by this opinion.

Nevertheless, because this is a case of first impression, the court wishes to make clear that in one respect this violation assumes a dramatically different posture than an infraction of a more clearly established rule. Given the paucity of literature on the issue and the tendency of many commentators to lump all ADR methods under the same ethical rubric, an attorney could have understandably selected the "same matter" standard of the Utah Prof. Conduct Rules, Rule 1.12, and thereby reasonably assumed that no violation would occur. Thus, imposition of sanctions or criticism of Mr. Broadbent's professional reputation is unwarranted in this case.

In this case, Broadbent received a significant amount of confidential information during the mediation of the Micromath litigation. In particular, he was present while Wang and Su conducted heated conversations on the topic of which of them might be responsible for the copying alleged by Micromath. Poly Software argues that, because Wang was present whenever Su revealed anything to Broadbent, Poly Software does not gain access, by employing Broadbent in the present litigation, to any confidential information that it does not already possess. However, this argument ignores the fact that Broadbent's professional expertise afforded him a perspective on the legal significance of the confidences that Wang himself could not possibly obtain or communicate to new counsel. In short his role as a mediator with experience in intellectual property litigation gives him an unfair advantage as an attorney in the present case. Moreover, given the posture of this case, the disqualification of Broadbent must be imputed to the other members of his small firm. *See* Utah Prof. Conduct Rules, Rule 1.10(a).

H. Government Lawyers

Problem

6-27. Martyn & Fox recently hired Julia Davis, a lawyer who worked for the state attorney general's office for the past six years. Ms. Davis' first case in the AG's office was the successful defense of a race discrimination class action against the State Department of Taxation. In her last case, she served as lead counsel in negotiating a settlement in an antitrust suit on behalf of the State Department of Transportation against General Motors.

(*a*) Can Martyn & Fox take on the representation of Local Municipality against General Motors based on facts identical to the State Department of Transportation case?

(*b*) Can Martyn & Fox take on the representation of Paula Pearson who wishes to bring a race discrimination complaint against the State Department of Taxation based on events that occurred four years after Ms. Davis' defense of the Department?

Consider: Model Rules 1.11, 7.6
Model Code DR 9-101

The Limits of the Law: *Federal and State Conflict of Interest Provisions*

The last problems regarding mediators and government lawyers required you to apply special conflict of interest rules found in Model Rules 1.11 and 1.12. In addition to these specific lawyer code provisions, lawyers who work for governmental units also are subject to federal and state statutes and regulations that govern their conduct. Violating these regulations can result in a criminal penalty, one you will want to avoid should you join the ever increasing ranks of lawyers and judges employed by federal, state, county, or local governments. Comment [1] to Model Rule 1.11 expressly refers to this other law. Model Rule 1.12 generally parallels Rule 1.11, and together with the Code of Judicial Conduct, forms the primary source of rules that regulate the conduct of judges, arbitrators, and mediators.

Federal Provisions

Federal law, like Model Rule 1.11, regulates the conduct of both current and former government lawyers. Current government lawyers in all three branches of government are subject to the federal conflict of interest statute, which provides that federal employees may not accept payments or gifts or act as agents or lawyers for private parties in a "particular matter" in which the United States has an interest.[1] Officers and employees of the executive branch are subject to additional provisions concerning personal conflicts of interest.[2] Specific conflict of interest rules also apply to lawyers who serve as trustees in bankruptcy courts.[3] Some agencies add additional requirements that govern who can practice before that agency.[4] Some lawyers, such as special prosecutors, also are subject to particular agency regulations.[5]

Former government employees are governed by the Ethics in Government Act, which contains several restrictions that are more strict than those found in the professional codes.[6] Violations of all of these provisions are felonies, punishable with fines and imprisonment for up to five years.[7] Courts have used the elements of these statutes as the basis for granting disqualification motions.[8] State disciplinary agencies also have relied on these provisions in cases of professional discipline.[9] Like Model Rule 1.11, these statutes governing government employees are sometimes referred to as "revolving door rules," a phrase which refers to the practice of

1. 18 U.S.C. §§203, 205 (2000). Members of Congress also are prohibited from practicing in the Court of Federal Claims or the Court of Appeals for the Federal Circuit. 18 U.S.C. §204.
2. 18 U.S.C. §§208, 209 (2000).
3. 18 U.S.C. §154 (2000) imposes criminal liability on trustee and others for certain personal conflicts of interest. Lawyers hired by the trustee also are subject to 11 U.S.C. §327, which creates standards for disinterested representation. *See* Lawrence P. King, ed., *Collier on Bankruptcy* §§8.02, 8.03 (15th ed., Matthew Bender 2000).
4. *See, e.g.*, Practice Before the Internal Revenue Service, 31 C.F.R. §10.25 (1990) (Practice by Partners of Government Employees) and §10.26 (Practice by Former Government Employees, Their Partners and Their Associates).
5. For a discussion of how these regulations impacted on the work of Kenneth Starr, *see* David Halperin, *Ethics Breakthrough or Ethics Breakdown? Kenneth Starr's Dual Roles as Private Practitioner and Public Prosecutor*, 15 Geo. J. Leg. Ethics 231 (2002).
6. 18 U.S.C. §207 (2000). *See* Thomas D. Morgan, *Appropriate Limits on Participation by a Former Agency Official in Matters Before the Agency*, 1980 Duke L.J. 1 (discussing the history of the Ethics in Government Act).
7. 18 U.S.C. §216 (2000).
8. *See, e.g.*, In re Restaurant Dev. of P.R., Inc., 128 B.R. 498 (Bankr. D. P.R. 1991); Kessenich v. Commodity Futures Trading Commn., 684 F.2d 88 (D.C. Cir. 1982).
9. *See, e.g.*, Disc. Counsel v. Eilberg, 441 A.2d 1193 (Pa. 1982) (lawyer who violated 18 U.S.C. §203(a) suspended from practice for five years).

lawyers who move back and forth between government service and private practice. The goal of both sets of rules is to prevent potential abuses, such as use of confidential governmental information or the risk that a lawyer might misuse a government position to benefit herself in later private practice. Most relevant is 18 U.S.C. §207, which contains three provisions that stringently regulate the conduct of former government lawyers.

The first provision permanently prohibits appearances and communications with any government agency, department, or court in particular matters where the person participated "personally and substantially" while a government employee.[10] The consent of the agency is not a defense (as it would be in Model Rule 1.11). As long as the former employee made the communication "with the intent to influence" the government on behalf of another person in a matter in which she formerly participated, the crime is complete. Thus, filing an amicus brief on behalf of a private client that urged a federal court to adopt the government's position would violate this rule, as long as the former government lawyer personally and substantially participated in the same case while in government employment. On the other hand, expert testimony on behalf of the government may be exempt.[11]

The second provision creates a two-year restriction on communication or appearance with any governmental agency, court, or department on behalf of another party in connection with particular matters under that person's official responsibility before she left the government.[12] For example, a high-level employee of the Internal Revenue Service who retired and started a tax service violated this provision when he attended meetings with an IRS officer and three taxpayers whose tax collection had been his responsibility prior to retirement.[13] The third creates a one-year prohibition on certain senior governmental personnel from appearing before or communicating with, the governmental agency for which they worked.[14]

State Provisions

The majority of states also have enacted ethics laws that restrict the practice of both current and former lawyers and other governmental employees.[15] Like federal lawyers, state lawyers are subject to both these ethics statutes and the relevant professional code.[16] State provisions generally parallel those in the federal law and Model Rule 1.11. For example, many include bans on appearances or representation before the lawyer's former agency for a period of time.[17] Many states also bar

---

10. 18 U.S.C. §207(a)(1) (2000).
11. 18 U.S.C. §207(j)(6) (2000); EEOC v. Exxon Corp., 202 F.3d 755 (5th Cir. 2000).
12. 18 U.S.C. §207(a)(2) (2000).
13. United States v. Coleman, 805 F.2d 474 (3d Cir. 1986).
14. 18 U.S.C. §207(c).
15. *See, e.g.,* National Conference of State Legislators, *The State of State Legislative Ethics* (2002); Rachel E. Boehm, Student Author, *Caught in the Revolving Door: A State Lawyer's Guide to Post-Employment Restrictions,* 15 Rev. Litig. 525, 532 n.26 (1996), citing statutes in 30 states.
16. *See, e.g.,* P.J.S. v. Penn. St. Ethics Comm., 723 A.2d 174 (Pa. 1999) (lawyer who served as part-time city solicitor subject to both state ethics laws and state lawyer code). These provisions have withstood constitutional attack. *See, e.g.,* Midboe v. Commn. on Ethics for Pub. Employees, 646 S.2d 351 (La. 1994) (Code of Governmental Ethics for public servants was not unconstitutional as applied to lawyer because the legislature was not regulating law practice in general). *Cf.* Shaulis v. Penn. St. Ethics Commn., 833 A.2d 123 (Pa. 2003) (Public Official and Employee Ethics Act violated separation of powers because it specifically targeted lawyers who were former government employees).
17. *See, e.g.,* Cal. Govt. Code §87406(d)(1) (one-year ban on acting as an attorney for any person before the agency that formerly employed the lawyer); N.Y. Pub. Off. Law §73(8)(a)(i) (2002) (two-year ban on appearing or practicing before state agency that formerly employed the person in any matter).

representation in matters in which the former government lawyer participated personally and substantially.[18] A few jurisdictions regulate additional matters as well, such as prohibiting former lawyers from accepting employment with entities that are subject to regulation by their former agency employer or with those that do business with the state.[19] State law also parallels federal law in targeting former employees of particular agencies or commissions.[20] Despite these similarities, each state has enacted its own special mix of prohibitions, often in response to a particular political embarrassment.[21]

Judges

Many of the federal and state statutes discussed above apply only to executive or legislative branch employees. While serving in a judicial capacity, judges are subject to the Code of Judicial Conduct adopted by the highest court in that jurisdiction. Nearly every state has created a judicial disciplinary commission by constitutional amendment or statute empowered to discipline sitting judges. In the federal courts, Article III judges can only be removed from office by impeachment, a seldom-used remedy. However, the Chief Judge of a circuit can empanel investigative committees and impose some sanctions, such as censure.[22] In addition, federal statutes prohibit the practice of law by judges[23] and create standards for disqualification.[24]

Those who leave the bench are subject to the lawyer code provisions in the jurisdiction where they are licensed to practice, such as Model Rule 1.12, and occasionally to court rules that regulate their subsequent practice. For example, United States Supreme Court Rules prevent law clerks from participating in any case before the Court for two years after they leave government service.[25] Model Rule 1.12 regulates the conduct of former arbitrators and mediators as well as that of former judges. Lawyers who serve in these capacities also may be subject to more stringent standards from state law or the code of ethics of a private organization, such as the American Arbitration Association or The Society of Professionals in Dispute Resolution.[26]

All of this legal regulation demands careful attention, especially to several details that many of these rules share. First, each rule makes the role of the government employee relevant to its reach. Second, many of these rules also define the lawyer's role after leaving government service. Finally, each rule creates a distinctive penalty. Some create criminal penalties, others administrative remedies, such as loss of a government contract or benefit.[27] Federal and state governments have

---

18. *See, e.g.*, Ark. Code §19-11-709(b)(1) (2001) (permanent disqualification); Ind. Code §4-2-6-11(d) (one year).
19. Boehm, *supra* note 15, at 535.
20. *See, e.g.*, Ohio Rev. Code §102.03(2) (2002) (regulating practice of former commissioners and attorney examiners of the public utilities commission); Tex. Water Code §26.0283 (2002) (regulating assistance by former employees of the Texas Natural Resource Conservation Commission); Or. Rev. Stat. §244.045(2) (2001) (regulating former deputy and assistant attorneys general).
21. *See, e.g.*, Robert C. Newman, *New York's New Ethics Law: Turning the Tide on Corruption,* 16 Hofstra L. Rev. 319 (1988).
22. 28 U.S.C. §372 (2000).
23. 28 U.S.C. §454 (2000).
24. 28 U.S.C. §144 (2000) (bias or prejudice of a judge); §455 (2000) (disqualification).
25. U.S. Sup. Ct. R. 7 (2003); *see also* John Paul Jones, *Some Ethical Considerations for Judicial Clerks*, 4 Geo. J. Leg. Ethics 771 (1991).
26. *See* Model Rule 1.12, Comment [2]; Model Rule 2.4, Comment [2].
27. *E.g.*, Tex. Water Code, *supra* note 20, provides that the Texas Water Commission "shall deny an application . . . for a permit" if a former employee provides assistance to the applicant.

found these additional remedies necessary to curb specific abuses of the public trust. Courts also have used these provisions as a guide to other relief, such as disqualification. Wise government lawyers need to remain aware of both professional code provisions and other state and federal law to fully understand their obligations.

I. Imputed Conflicts

Problems

6-28. Martyn & Fox agrees to staff a hot line for the local legal services project every Tuesday. One Tuesday a Martyn & Fox associate received a phone call from an individual who has been the subject of predatory lending by The Dollar Store. Without seeing any documents, the associate gave the woman advice about possible remedies and only learned upon returning to the firm that Big Bank, Martyn & Fox's largest client, owns The Dollar Store. Is Martyn & Fox in trouble?

6-29. Martyn & Fox is in a ten-day countdown to trial when one of its associates darkens Fox's door to announce that she is leaving the firm on Friday. When Fox recovers from the shock of losing his right arm in the case on such short notice, the associate tells him that she will be joining the firm on the other side of the case, but not to worry—she'll be screened. What should Martyn & Fox do?

6-30. Martyn & Fox signs a joint defense agreement with a law firm representing a co-defendant of Martyn & Fox's client. Plaintiff succeeds in getting the other law firm disqualified because plaintiff is the other firm's former client. What happens to Martyn & Fox?

Consider: Model Rules 1.0(c), 1.7, 1.9, 1.10, 1.16, 6.3, 6.5
Model Code DR 4-101, 5-101(D)
RLGL §124

Kala v. Aluminum Smelting & Refining Company, Inc.

688 N.E.2d 258 (Ohio 1998)

Plaintiff-appellee, Sher S. Kala, retained attorney Michael Pearson and the law firm of Spangenberg, Shibley & Liber ("Spangenberg") to represent him in a lawsuit against appellant Aluminum Smelting & Refining Co., Inc. ("Aluminum Smelting"), his former employer. In the 1993 lawsuit, Kala alleged, inter alia, that Aluminum Smelting had wrongfully terminated his employment on the basis of age. Richard C. Hubbard III of the law firm of Duvin, Cahn & Hutton ("Duvin") represented the appellant.

. . . The case went to trial in September 1995, resulting in a directed verdict for Aluminum Smelting.

On behalf of Kala, Pearson filed an appeal on October 20, 1995. Pearson stayed in contact with Kala during the appeal and participated in settlement discussions with Kala in preparation for a prehearing settlement conference with the Eighth District Court of Appeals on November 13, 1995, according to Kala's brief in the Supreme Court. Kala had numerous conversations with Pearson during the litigation in which Kala relied on the fact that his conversations were confidential. Kala does not contend that Pearson has ever disclosed any confidences that Kala entrusted to him.

It is undisputed that, on January 8, 1996, after he had obtained an extension of time for filing Kala's brief, Pearson announced his intention to leave the Spangenberg law firm and to join Duvin. In a memo to all Duvin attorneys on January 16, 1996, Steven Aronoff, an attorney with Duvin, asked the attorneys to make him aware of any cases which they were handling against the Spangenberg law firm so that Duvin could institute a "Chinese wall" prior to Pearson's joining the Duvin firm. A memo to the file from Steven Aronoff noted that Duvin was sending the trial file to an off-site storage location, and when an attorney requested it, the trial file would be sent back to the office and the requesting attorney would be required to sign for the file. In addition, the entire appellate file was maintained in Hubbard's office and was accessible to Duvin attorneys only through him.

On January 19, 1996, Aronoff sent a letter to attorney Peter Weinberger at the Spangenberg firm regarding the steps taken to insulate Pearson from any contact with the pending appeal. The letter informed the Spangenberg firm that Pearson had not discussed with his new firm any of his substantive legal work or any confidential client information learned while at the Spangenberg firm, and had been instructed not to do so in the future. In addition, it stated, all of the attorneys at Duvin had been instructed not to discuss with Pearson any aspect of cases pending in the Spangenberg office or to share any documents or other information concerning those cases. Further, the letter assured the Spangenberg law firm that all concerned were mindful of and intended to abide by all of the ethical considerations relevant to the transition. In addition, Aronoff noted that Duvin had canvassed its attorneys in order to identify any cases in which there may have been a substantial relationship between the subject matter of Spangenberg's representation during Pearson's tenure there and Duvin's current clients, including any active cases. The letter also stated, "We will institute further procedures" to protect client disclosures.

On January 22, 1996, Pearson voluntarily left the Spangenberg firm to accept a position of associate attorney with Duvin. On January 29, 1996, Pearson stated in an affidavit that he agreed to abide by all ethical and professional requirements in his transition from Spangenberg to Duvin. Further, he stated that he would not discuss the substantive work he did while at Spangenberg that involved client confidences. Pearson stated that he had not spoken with any member of Duvin about such matters. In addition, he noted that in regard to the Kala case, he had not discussed any substantive issues regarding that case with anyone at Duvin, nor had anyone at Duvin tried to discuss those matters with him. He also noted that Lee Hutton, a partner at Duvin, had specifically instructed him not to discuss these issues with any member or associate or staff or client of Duvin.

On April 12, 1996, after Kala requested several extensions to file his appellate brief, Kala filed a motion to disqualify Duvin, alleging a conflict of interest. On May 10, 1996, the court, without opinion, ordered the disqualification of Duvin....

LUNDBERG STRATTON, J.

The issue before the court is whether a law firm should be automatically disqualified from representing a party when an attorney leaves his or her former employment with a firm representing a party and joins the law firm representing the opposing party, or whether that law firm may overcome any presumption of shared confidences by instituting effective screening mechanisms. Although this issue has been dealt with in many other jurisdictions, this is a case of first impression for Ohio. To fairly decide this issue, we must consider the Disciplinary Rules and Ethical Considerations in the Ohio Code of Professional Responsibility, competing public policy interests, and the guidance provided by federal case law. . . .

II. ETHICAL PRINCIPLES

As a starting principle, a court has inherent authority to supervise members of the bar appearing before it; this necessarily includes the power to disqualify counsel in specific cases.

A fundamental principle in the attorney-client relationship is that the attorney shall maintain the confidentiality of any information learned during the attorney-client relationship. A client must have the utmost confidence in his or her attorney if the client is to feel free to divulge all matters related to the case to his or her attorney. . . .

The obligation of an attorney to preserve the confidences and secrets of the client continues even after the termination of the attorney's employment.[1] . . .

When an attorney leaves his or her former employment and becomes employed by a firm representing an opposing party, a presumption arises that the attorney takes with him or her any confidences gained in the former relationship and shares those confidences with the new firm. This is known as the presumption of shared confidences. Some courts have held that such a change of employment results in an irrebuttable presumption of shared confidences that necessitates the disqualification of the attorney (primary disqualification) and the entire new firm (imputed disqualification).

III. CLIENT'S RIGHT TO CHOOSE COUNSEL

Balanced against the former client's interest in preventing a breach of confidence is the public policy interest in permitting the opposing party's continued representation by counsel of his or her choice. Disqualification interferes with a client's right to choose counsel. . . .

This issue has become increasingly important as the practice of law has changed. A review of the historical development of disqualification issues reveals the early conflicts created by the clash of the above principles.

IV. HISTORY OF MOTIONS TO DISQUALIFY

Many of the early disqualification cases arose out of charges of conflict of interest where government attorneys left the public service and went into private practice. Early courts struggled with the need to fashion a rule that would preserve the confidences of the government client yet not discourage able attorneys from entering public service through fear of being locked forever into government service, unable to change positions. As the Court of Appeals for the Seventh Circuit noted:

---

1. In its response to the motion to disqualify, filed on April 22, 1996, Duvin stated:

> "The appellate brief filed by Plaintiff-Appellant raises a few errors alleged to have occurred, but any 'confidences' or trial strategies are irrelevant to those matters. In view of the fact that the trial of these issues has been concluded, it is clear that any issue of client confidences is long since passed."

However, we fail to see, particularly when a directed verdict at trial is the matter on appeal, how the issue of client confidences has "long since passed." A successful appeal demands an intimate knowledge of the facts of the case and requires ongoing representation. In addition, if the appeal is successful and the directed verdict is overturned, this matter would return to the trial court for a new trial.

"If past employment in government results in the disqualification of future employers from representing some of their long-term clients, it seems clearly possible that government attorneys will be regarded as 'Typhoid Marys.' Many talented lawyers, in turn, may be unwilling to spend a period in government service, if that service makes them unattractive or risky for large law firms to hire." LaSalle Natl. Bank v. Lake Cty., 703 F.2d 252, 258 (7th Cir. 1983).

As more and more private attorneys also began changing firms, motions to disqualify under the irrebuttable presumption of shared confidences increased, and inequities and abuses also began to surface. While some of these motions to disqualify were legitimate and necessary, such motions were also often misused to harass an opponent, disrupt the opponent's case, or to gain a tactical advantage, and therefore were viewed with increasing caution....

As a result of the changing legal profession, federal courts and the ABA Model Rules of Professional Conduct began allowing the use of various mechanisms to isolate an attorney who had transferred employment. Although originally applied only to government attorneys, these mechanisms have now been extended to situations involving transfers of private counsel as well.[3]

V. DEVELOPMENT OF STANDARDS FOR DISQUALIFICATION

Several federal courts in addressing both primary and imputed disqualification have devised a three-part test to determine whether disqualification is proper when one attorney leaves a firm and joins another firm representing an opposing party. We believe this test adequately covers many different scenarios and will give the courts of Ohio guidance on disqualification issues.

First, a court must determine whether a substantial relationship exists between prior and present representations. If there is no substantial relationship, then no ethical problem exists. For example, when an attorney had represented a client in a trademark infringement case, the Court of Appeals for the Sixth Circuit denied disqualification in a later unrelated civil RICO case. Dana Corp. v. Blue Cross & Blue Shield Mut. of N. Ohio, 900 F.2d 882 (6th Cir. 1990).

Second, if a substantial relationship is found between the current matter and the prior matter, the court must examine whether the attorney shared in the confidences and representation of the prior matter. There is a presumption that such confidences would also be shared among members of the prior firm, but that presumption may be rebutted. Schiessle v. Stephens, 717 F.2d 417 (7th Cir. 1983) (attorney denied contact with case and prior client; challenging firm established by affidavit that attorney did have contact with the case and clients; presumption not rebutted).

If the presumption of shared confidences within the prior firm is rebutted by such evidence, then there is again no need for primary disqualification, as there are no confidences to be shared. However, if that presumption is not rebutted, and the attorney does or is presumed to possess client confidences,

3. The American Law Institute's latest pronouncement on this issue now states:

"Imputation . . . does not restrict an affiliated lawyer with respect to a former client conflict . . . , when there is no reasonably apparent risk that confidential information of the former client will be used with material adverse effect on the former client because . . . the personally prohibited lawyer is subject to screening measures adequate to eliminate involvement by that lawyer in representation." *Restatement of the Law Governing Lawyers*, Section 204.

However, the American Bar Association still has not extended such recommendations to the private sector.

primary disqualification results, and a presumption of shared confidences arises between the attorney and the members of the attorney's new firm. The issue then is whether a presumption of shared confidences will also disqualify the entire new firm (imputed disqualification). Kala implies that this presumption should be irrebuttable and that once an attorney, particularly one as involved in the case as Pearson was, moves to opposing counsel's firm, no steps can be taken to restore confidence so as to overcome the appearance of impropriety; the entire firm must be disqualified.

Some courts have taken this approach. New Jersey has refused to adopt the rebuttable-presumption approach, finding that there is no way to overcome the appearance of impropriety in a "side-switching attorney" case. Cardona v. Gen. Motors Corp., 942 F. Supp. 968, 976-977 (D.N.J. 1996). The New Jersey courts cite the impossibility of proving when a breach has been made, as those lawyers within the new firm are least likely to divulge such information. Judge Orlofsky in *Cardona* explained:

> "At the heart of every 'side-switching attorney' case is the suspicion that by changing sides, the attorney has breached a duty of fidelity and loyalty to a former client, a client who had freely shared with the attorney secrets and confidences with the expectation that they would be disclosed to no one else. It is for this reason that the 'appearance of impropriety doctrine' was adopted to protect the public, our profession, and those it serves. In short, this much maligned doctrine exists to engender, protect and preserve the trust and confidence of clients." 942 F. Supp. at 975.

On the other hand, with the realities of modern-day practice, . . . such a hard-and-fast rule works an unfair hardship also. Ultimately, one must have faith in the integrity of members of the legal profession to honor their professional oath to uphold the Code of Professional Responsibility, safeguarded by the precautions required to rebut the presumption of shared confidences. . . . If used properly, the process of screening attorneys who possess client confidences from other members of a firm can preserve those confidences while avoiding the use of the motion to disqualify as a device to gain a tactical advantage. Therefore, we believe that the fairer rule in balancing the interests of the parties and the public is to allow the presumption of shared confidences with members of the new firm to be rebutted.

Thus, the third part of the test on disqualification is whether the presumption of shared confidences with the new firm has been rebutted by evidence that a "Chinese wall" has been erected so as to preserve the confidences of the client.[6] The Chinese wall is the specific institutional screening mechanisms that will prevent the flow of confidential information from the quarantined attorney to other members of the law firm.

Factors to be considered in deciding whether an effective screen has been created are whether the law firm is sufficiently large and whether the structural divisions of the firm are sufficiently separate so as to minimize contact between the quarantined attorney and the others, the likelihood of

---

6. "Chinese wall" has become the legal term to describe a "procedure which permits an attorney involved in an earlier adverse role to be screened from other attorneys in the firm so as to prevent disqualification of the entire law firm simply because one member of firm previously represented a client who is now an adversary of the client currently represented by the firm." Black's Law Dictionary (6 ed., Rev. 1990) 240. This term refers historically to the Great Wall of China, which served ancient Chinese emperors as a barrier to invasion. Wolfram, *Modern Legal Ethics* (1986), Section 7.64. Ironically, however, the Great Wall of China was of limited military value. The concept is also referred to in cases and commentary as "screening devices," "ethical screens," or "institutional mechanisms for screening."

contact between the quarantined attorney and the specific attorneys responsible for the current representation, the existence of safeguards or procedures which prevent the quarantined attorney from access to relevant files or other information relevant to the present litigation, prohibited access to files and other information on the case, locked case files with keys distributed to a select few, secret codes necessary to access pertinent information on electronic hardware, instructions given to all members of a new firm regarding the ban on exchange of information, and the prohibition of the sharing of fees derived from such litigation.

A very strict standard of proof must be applied to the rebuttal of this presumption of shared confidences, however, and any doubts as to the existence of an asserted conflict of interest must be resolved in favor of disqualification in order to dispel any appearance of impropriety.

Some courts have held that unrebutted affidavits attesting to a Chinese wall are sufficient to prevent disqualification. However, we reject such a bright-line test, as the court should maintain discretion to weigh issues of credibility. The court should be free to assess the reputation of an attorney and law firm for integrity and honesty. . . .

If applied properly, screening mechanisms to insulate a quarantined attorney from the rest of the firm can protect client confidences while allowing for attorney mobility and the right of a client to choose counsel.

VI. ADDITIONAL FACTORS TO CONSIDER IN MOTIONS TO DISQUALIFY

In addition to the screening devices, there are other important factors to be considered by the trial court. First, the screening devices must be employed as soon as the disqualifying event occurs. Very few cases address how early the disqualifying event occurs . . . , although all cases agree that the screens must be in place when the attorney joins the firm. Instituting screens after a motion to disqualify is too late. Accordingly, a court must weigh the timeliness of the screening devices.

A second factor to consider is the hardship that a client would incur in obtaining new counsel if a motion to disqualify is granted. Hardship may be more of an issue if a conflict arose after a transfer. However, hardship may not carry much weight in a "side-switching" case. Ironically, where an attorney switches sides and joins an opposing counsel's firm, the attorney has de facto deprived his or her first client of the attorney of that client's choice, namely himself or herself. If the attorney has been lead counsel, other counsel in the firm must spend time and effort to take over the lead. If no one remaining in the prior firm is able to handle the matter, or if the attorney was a sole practitioner, the former client must seek out new counsel and incur the burden and expense created by the switch. In this scenario, the departing attorney has created a competing hardship for his or her former client, and the claim by the new firm of hardship created by its own doing in accepting the new attorney into the firm may no longer be persuasive. These are matters that should be left to the trier of fact to weigh.

In addition, a law firm contemplating hiring counsel who had been directly involved on the opposing side also has a duty to disclose to its own client that such a hiring may place the firm in conflict and could result in disqualification. The law firm may have to subordinate its desire to augment its staff against its duties to its client and avoid placing the firm's interests above the client's interests.

Finally, the court should hold an evidentiary hearing on a motion to disqualify and must issue findings of fact if requested based on the evidence presented. Because a request for disqualification implies a charge of unethical conduct, the challenged firm must be given an opportunity to defend not only its relationship with the client, but also its good name, reputation and ethical standards. . . .

VII. THE REBUTTABLE-PRESUMPTION TEST FOR MOTIONS TO DISQUALIFY

In conclusion, we hold that in ruling on a motion for disqualification of either an individual (primary disqualification) or the entire firm (imputed disqualification) when an attorney has left a law firm and joined a firm representing the opposing party, a court must hold an evidentiary hearing and issue findings of fact using a three-part analysis:

(1) Is there a substantial relationship between the matter at issue and the matter of the former firm's prior representation;

(2) If there is a substantial relationship between these matters, is the presumption of shared confidences within the former firm rebutted by evidence that the attorney had no personal contact with or knowledge of the related matter; and

(3) If the attorney did have personal contact with or knowledge of the related matter, did the new law firm erect adequate and timely screens to rebut a presumption of shared confidences with the new firm so as to avoid imputed disqualification?

VIII. APPLICATION OF TEST TO THIS CASE

Under the facts of this case, Pearson clearly met the substantial-relationship test and possessed client confidences, as he was the lead attorney on Kala's lawsuit. Thus, the first two parts of the test require disqualification of Pearson and raise a presumption in favor of disqualification of Duvin. No one disputes that Pearson, himself, cannot work further on the case.

Therefore, we must determine whether the entire firm should be disqualified under the third part of the analysis, imputed disqualification. . . .

Kala retained Pearson and the Spangenberg firm in 1993 as his attorneys. From 1993 through 1995, Kala trusted Pearson, relied upon him as his attorney, and disclosed all matters pertaining to his case involving his former employer, Aluminum Smelting. Pearson proceeded to file an appeal after the directed verdict and apparently even participated in a settlement conference with the Eighth District Court of Appeals on November 13, 1995. On January 8, 1996, Pearson obtained a continuance to file Kala's appellate brief. On January 22, 1996, Pearson left the Spangenberg firm and joined the Duvin firm, which was representing Aluminum Smelting and had been throughout the prior proceedings with Kala. The only conclusion that can be reached from the record is that Pearson was negotiating with Duvin while still actively representing Kala without disclosing to Kala his negotiations. . . .

. . . [N]othing that the Duvin firm could have done would have had any effect on Kala's perception that his personal attorney had abandoned him with all of his shared confidences and joined the firm representing his adversary while the case was still pending. No steps of any kind could possibly replace the trust and confidence that Kala had in his attorney or in the legal system if such representation is permitted. This is the classic "side-switching attorney" case.

FLIP-FLOPPER!

We find that under this set of egregious facts, . . . that the attempts made by Duvin to erect a Chinese wall were insufficient. . . . Accordingly, we affirm the disqualification ruling of the court of appeals.

Judgment affirmed.

The Law Governing Lawyers: *Do Screens Work?*

Kala sheds light on the increasingly common use of law firm screens to avoid imputed disqualification. These screens originated as a condition of client or former client informed consent to a conflict, and then became available to former government lawyers by case law and lawyer code provisions. Today, lawyers in private firms also seek screens with the consent of their clients or former clients, and when that consent is not forthcoming, seek the blessing of a court or code provision to avoid disqualification or discipline. The majority of jurisdictions do not allow screens without client or former client informed consent. The dozen or so that do, like Ohio in *Kala,* have made them available to law firms only in former client cases. Recent debates about the subject boil down to one key factor: Do screens work?

Screening Provisions

Every jurisdiction allows screens in some situations. When a lawyer code provision makes a conflict consentable, the client can condition her consent on a screen that protects the rest of the firm from the tainted lawyer.[1] *Kala* indicates that jurisdictions also agree that screens are appropriate when lawyers leave governmental service.[2] The argument that created this first exception to consent was that lawyers in public service should not be barred from finding employment with those most likely to hire them: law firms adverse to the government. The government also was viewed as a different kind of client that could be asked to live with screens as a tradeoff for encouraging the best lawyers to undertake public service.

Experience with screens in these two situations soon led to arguments that private lawyers also should be able to avail themselves of screening, both to promote their own job mobility, and to protect their current clients from disqualification motions. At this point, three approaches emerged. The vast majority of courts reject involuntary screening except for former government lawyers.[3] *Kala* represents the other end of the spectrum, allowing involuntary screens in all former client cases except those that involve "side-switching"; that is, a lawyer's move to the opposing party's law firm while the case is pending. The third approach, adopted by the Restatement of the Law Governing Lawyers, allows screens only where "any confidential client information communicated to the personally prohibited lawyer is unlikely to be significant in the subsequent matter."[4] This concept also allows screens in the case where prospective clients share confidential information, as long as the lawyer takes reasonable measures to avoid exposure to too much disqualifying information.[5]

---

1. *E.g.,* Model Rules 1.7, 1.8, 1.9.
2. *E.g.,* Model Rules 1.11, 1.12.
3. *See, e.g.,* Cardona v. Gen. Motors Corp., 942 F. Supp. 968 (D.N.J. 1996); Elan Transdermal Ltd. v. Cygnus Therapeutic Sys., 809 F. Supp. 1383 (N.D. Cal. 1992).
4. *Restatement (Third) The Law Governing Lawyers* §124 (2000).
5. *Id.* at §15(2); Model Rule 1.18(d).

The Policy Debate

Kala focuses on the main policy debate. It upholds involuntary screens in former client cases, where the new law firm erected an "adequate and timely screen."[6] Presumably, this means that the screen was established at a time and in a manner that prevented any communication of information from the migrating lawyer to the new firm. Larger firms should have an easier time separating a screened lawyer from others in the firm, as long as they also institute procedures that preclude revenue sharing and access to documents.[7] Even then, in side-switching cases like *Kala,* where the lawyer negotiates with the new law firm for a time before moving, too much time, contact, and potential shifts in loyalty have already occurred to prevent this from happening. Courts that allow involuntary screens agree with the Ohio Court on this point, uniformly rejecting them in side-switching cases.[8]

The Restatement also focuses on the significance of the information and the timing and adequacy of the screen. It finds screening appropriate only where the information possessed by the migrating lawyer is insignificant, that is, peripheral, or not very valuable in the subsequent matter.[9] Even then, the screen must prevent the confidential information from leaking into the new firm. In other words, the screened lawyer cannot know much, and what she does know should not be material. Even then, the screen should prevent all of this confidential information from ever being disseminated.[10]

The vast majority of jurisdictions reject involuntary screens absent client informed consent.[11] These courts are not willing to decide on a case-by-case basis whether a screen will adequately protect the confidential information because they believe the former client should decide whether the information is significant and whether to trust the new firm's screening mechanisms.

The most recent debate about screens occurred during consideration of the Ethics 2000 proposals. The commission proposed amendments to Model Rule 1.10 much like the rule in *Kala,* but without the side-switching limitation. In explaining this proposal, one commission member wrote:

> The commission dismissed concerns that firms cannot be counted on to administer screens effectively, that former clients will have not ability to police screening arrangements, and that confidences will inevitably be disclosed inadvertently in certain practice

---

6. Courts that generally approve of screens for lawyers also approve of them for other employees, such as secretaries and paralegals. *See, e.g.,* Green v. Toledo Hosp., 764 N.E.2d 979 (Ohio 2002).

7. The vast majority of cases involving former client conflicts have occurred in firms of 50 or more lawyers. *See* Susan R. Martyn, *Visions of the Eternal Law Firm: The Future of Law Firm Screens,* 45 S.C. L. Rev. 937, 942 (1994).

8. *See, e.g.,* Lennartson v. Anoka-Hennepin Ind. School Dist. No. 11, 662 N.W.2d 125 (Minn. 2003); Doe v. Perry Community School Dist., 650 N.W.2d 594 (Iowa 2002); Clinard v. Blackwood, 46 S.W.3d 177 (Tenn. 2001); Commonwealth v. Maricle, 10 S.W.3d 117 (Ky. 1999) (despite Rule 1.11, no screen allowed where lead counsel for the prosecution joined firm that represented defendant after negotiating employment for more than two months while the case was pending); Kassis v. Teacher's Ins. & Annuity Assn., 717 N.E.2d 674 (N.Y. 1999).

9. *Restatement (Third) The Law Governing Lawyers* §124, Comment d(i) (2000).

10. *See, e.g.,* Carbo Ceramics, Inc. v. Norton-Alcoa Proppants, 155 F.R.D. 158 (N.D. Tex. 1994).

11. *See, e.g.,* Towne Dev. v. Superior Ct., 842 P.2d 1377 (Ariz. App. 1992). These courts apply the same rules to other law firm employees. *See, e.g.,* Zimmerman v. Mahaska Bottling Co., 19 P.3d 784 (Kan. 2001) (screen not allowed for secretary who overheard conversations about the same matter at former law firm); In re American Home Products Corp., 985 S.W.2d 68 (Tex. 1998) (disqualification ordered where law firm assigned legal assistant to work on the same case she had previously researched for the other side).

> settings. But the commission heard no evidence to suggest that these objections have a factual basis in the experience of jurisdictions that permit screening.
>
> The commission's decision to propose a general screening rule initially seemed a leap of faith. But our confidence mounts that we are doing the right thing.[12]

The ABA House of Delegates rejected this proposal, and embraced the majority rule rejecting screens in private practice without client consent.[13] Whether you agree or disagree with this result, the quoted language vividly conveys the debate. Those in favor of screening believe that it works and that lawyers can be trusted to implement adequate screens.[14] Those who oppose involuntary screens would leave that call to the affected client or former client, not to the law firm seeking to avoid disqualification.[15]

The Evidence

Very little empirical evidence exists about whether screens are properly erected and maintained. The Ethics 2000 Commission heard oral testimony from grievance administrators in jurisdictions with screening rules,[16] who said they had received no complaints from former clients about breaches in screens. One published empirical study and several cases suggest another possibility: although most lawyers want to act appropriately, screens will never be completely effective. Further, when breaches do occur, they are very difficult for affected clients to discover.

In the only published empirical study about law firm screens, Professor Pizzimenti sent a lengthy questionnaire to large law firms in four states that allowed nonconsensual screening.[17] She found that most were generally aware of the relevant law governing conflicts of interest, but more than half incorrectly assumed that they were free to evaluate the need for a screen on a case-by-case basis, even where their local rules restrained law firm discretion.[18] The study also examined the potential for breaches of law firm screens. With respect to maintaining screens, only 35 percent of the firms had any written policy statement on the topic, and none had developed any policy about sanctions for a breach of a screen.[19] Many did not notify the opposing party about the screen, depriving that party of any opportunity to police it.[20] In short, this study concluded that the majority of firms took conflicts

---

12. Margaret C. Love, *Screening Lawyers from Conflicts*, 87 ABA J. 61 (May 2001).
13. *See* Model Rule 1.10. You should know that both of the authors of this book dissented from the Ethics 2000 Commission's recommendation and led the fight to defeat the screening proposal.
14. *See, e.g.*, Nemours Found. v. Gilbane, 632 F. Supp. 418, 428 (D. Del. 1986) (members of the legal profession should be credited with "a certain level of integrity").
15. *See, e.g.*, Cardona v. Gen. Motors Corp., 942 F. Supp. 968, 977-978 (D.N.J. 1996) ("In the end there is little but the self-serving assurance of the screening-lawyer foxes that they will carefully guard the screened-lawyer chickens." quoting Charles W. Wolfram, *Modern Legal Ethics* 402 (West 1986)).
16. *See, e.g.*, Ill. R. Prof. Conduct 1.10(b)(2), 1.10(e); Mich. R. Prof. Conduct 1.10(b); Minn. R. Prof. Conduct 1.10(b)(11); Or. DR 5-105(I); Pa. R. Prof. Conduct 1.10(b)(1)(2); Wash. R. Prof. Conduct 1.10(b).
17. Lee A. Pizzimenti, *Screen Verite: Do Rules About Ethical Screens Reflect the Truth About Real-Life Law Firm Practice?*, 52 U. Miami L. Rev. 305 (1997). Prof. Pizzimenti received responses from about 20 percent, or 30 law firms.
18. *Id.* at 327.
19. *Id.* at 329.
20. *Id.* When asked whether other firms would inform them of a breach in a screen, half did not answer, but 62 percent of those who did answered "no." All agreed that that a screen at another law firm could be breached without their firm detecting it, although some breaches, such as document sharing would be easier to detect than others. Observations about the character or reputation of parties or experts were viewed as the most difficult to detect. *Id.* at 332.

seriously, but that they "were hampered by flawed conflicts detection, flawed systems for maintaining screens and to some extent, an adversarial rather than fiduciary analysis of screen issues."[21]

We have already encountered several cases in these materials that may support these conclusions. In a previous note, we discussed whether Jones Day erected an appropriate screen in *ACC* and whether the former government lawyer involved intentionally breached that screen.[22] In *Maritrans,* we encountered a client that agreed to a screen because it believed this was the only way to prevent its lawyers from representing more of its competitors, especially Bouchard. The screen allowed Messina (the lawyer most familiar with Maritrans) to continue to represent four smaller New York–based competitors, but not Bouchard. Messina then conducted joint negotiations on behalf of the New York–based firms and Bouchard in spite of the screen agreement.[23] Messina also "parked" Bouchard with another lawyer outside the law firm in response to the screen. However, without telling Maritrans, he proceeded to negotiate with that same lawyer to join Pepper Hamilton as a partner. A month later, Pepper dropped Maritrans as a client, and a few weeks after that, welcomed this outside lawyer into the firm as a partner, bringing with him Bouchard, the very client the screen was designed to exclude.[24]

Kala represents a case where the court saw so much potential for inadvertent breach of a screen, that it would not allow it.[25] The fact that the opposing party's lawyers had contact before they announced the job change meant that they also had the opportunity to share information and influence client loyalty in the case. Another case that illustrates a similar problem of inadvertence involved a lawyer who left a law firm that represented GM in lemon law cases.[26] When he switched to a plaintiff's firm, the firm erected a screen to prevent him from having any involvement in GM lemon law cases. The screen included elaborate procedures, which the firm generally followed. Despite these precautions, the screened lawyer signed a settlement agreement on a GM lemon law case on one occasion, and several retainer letters for new clients against GM. When confronted by the court with this information, the firm's senior partner replied that there was no excuse for this lapse. The next day, he changed his position, arguing that that there had been no breach of the screen because the client's interests demanded immediate attention. However, he did admit to "a violation of our firm administrative policy with regard to the segregation of cases."[27] The court had no time for these justifications and disqualified the firm, suggesting that the five-person firm was too small for a screen in the first place and finding that the implemented screen was inadequate to prevent leaks.[28]

---

21. *Id.* at 333.
22. *See* Lawyer's Roles: The Instrumental Lawyer and the Limits of the Law, *supra* p.202.
23. We do not mean that Pepper Hamilton disclosed or used confidential information against Maritrans; but recall that the court found that, notwithstanding Pepper's agreement in the consent screen it established, "for all intents and purposes" it represented Bouchard, which breached the agreement.
24. An earlier case found a blatant breach of an attempted screen in a simultaneous representation case. *See* Westinghouse Elec. Corp. v. Kerr-McGee Corp., 580 F.2d 1311 (7th Cir. 1978).
25. *See also* Prince Jefri Bolkiah v. KPMG, 2 A.C. 222 (H.L. 1999).
26. Steel v. Gen. Motors Corp., 912 F. Supp. 724 (D.N.J. 1995).
27. *Id.* at 731-732.
28. *Id.* at 744.

Clearer Rules

Professor Pizzimenti concluded her study with this observation: "The truth about screens is that lawyers attempting to do the right thing need guidance, and lawyers attempting to cheat need to know that the consequences are not worth the risk. Clearer screen rules and predictable sanctions could go a long way to resolve these problems."[29]

The Revised Model Rules of Professional Conduct recognize the need for clearer screening rules by creating new rule 1.0(k), which defines "screened" as "isolation of a lawyer from any participation in a matter through the timely imposition of procedures within a firm that are reasonably adequate under the circumstances to protect information that the isolated lawyer is obligated to protect under these Rules or other law."[30] The rules that allow screening for former government lawyers and judges, arbitrators, and mediators also include two other requirements imposed by most courts: the screened lawyer may not receive any revenue from the case, and the firm must notify the former government agency or other parties of the screen.[31]

Even if all screens could be timely implemented and carefully maintained, these examples also show how they can cause huge administrative difficulties. A jurisdiction like Ohio that allows screens also encourages them to proliferate. This is especially true for large law firms that easily could have hundreds of screens, each one generating the need to notify affected parties, segregate files, prevent communication, and preclude revenue sharing. Keeping track of these details requires a great deal of skill. Some firms may assign the screened lawyer primary responsibility for maintaining the integrity of the screen. Even then, the immediate needs of clients may lead a lawyer to breach a screen as occurred in *Steel.*[32] Further, the screened lawyer cannot prevent all attempts by other firm lawyers who may seek the information.

This review of the evidence about the implementation of law firm screens suggests that we do not yet know whether one empirical study of a decade ago and a few anecdotal examples of breach indicate a more widespread problem or aberrations that stand out from otherwise exemplary conduct. We do, however, know three things. First, clients and lawyers can negotiate for screens as an additional potential safeguard in all cases of consentable conflicts. They also can bargain for the administrative procedures necessary to implementing and maintaining the screen. Second, in the vast majority of jurisdictions, without client consent involuntary screens are allowed only for former government lawyers, judges, arbitrators, and mediators. *Kala* illustrates that a few jurisdictions, by professional code or case law, also allow screens for former client conflicts.[33] In these cases, all courts require timely and adequate implementation of the screen, and do not allow them where the risk of breach is high, such as side switching in pending litigation. Third, monitoring established screens is essential to protect the integrity of the former client's confidences, but difficult to measure. Examples like *ACC, Maritrans,* and *Steel* illustrate that a

29. Pizzimenti, *supra* note 17, at 350.
30. Model Rule 1.0(k).
31. Model Rule 1.11 (former government officers and employees); Rule 1.12 (former judges, arbitrators, and mediators). It is interesting that the revenue requirement was not mentioned in the screen in *Maritrans,* and the court also found the lack of such a guarantee troubling in *Steel, supra* note 26.
32. *See* note 26, *supra.*
33. *See* notes 8 and 16, *supra.*

breach can be quite serious, whether intentional or inadvertent.[34] One empirical study also indicates that breaches are difficult to detect. Ultimately, screening procedures are no substitute for judgments about integrity and likelihood of inadvertent disclosure, both of which will rarely be known to a client unless voluntarily disclosed.

Beyond individual client protection, lawyers who favor screens ultimately will have to convince courts that the risk of breach falls far short of the need to protect current clients' choices of lawyers and the freedom of lawyers to move from job to job. One thing is certain. You must know both the conflicts rules and the provisions about screening if you are to have any hope of convincing a client to consent to a screen or a court to accept an involuntary substitute.

Lawrence J. Fox

Legal Tender: A Lawyer's Guide to Handling Professional Dilemmas

122-125 (ABA 1995)

My Lawyer Switched Sides; Don't Worry, There's a Screen

The litigation department breakfasts always seemed to be scheduled for the wrong day of the week. Just when the key deposition loomed with its 10:00 A.M. start, the chairman insisted everyone meet at 7:30 in the tired windowless conference room on 13, the one with the boring duck prints that were always askew. Obligations and self-interest overcame the need for last-minute deposition preparations. After all, associate reviews were just around the corner. She wondered, as she raced to be on time, why she had ever bothered to switch firms. It was true: they weren't all identical; they were just the same. They made you feel the same—tired and overworked—and the paycheck was delivered with the same heavy resentment. They made you feel the same anxiety that you would not meet the firm's billable hour "targets," the euphemism employed by the chair of each firm to describe her 2,200 hour quota. She had to find a better way, she thought, as she slumped resignedly into the well-worn conference room chair. How many hours had she spent in this room? In these meetings? Being bored?

Barely listening, she maintained her studied attentive pose, one she had mastered to get her through those interminable depositions. She would follow her usual rule: make an attempt at one cogent remark, but otherwise remain silent. Talking at meetings like this could only hurt her chances for partnership (as if she cared), and no one ever made partner because of her "performance" at departmental meetings. Wait, look alert, pick your moment, and then get out as soon as possible.

The conversation turned to privileged documents: something about whether you could withhold internal corporate memos in document discovery on the grounds of privilege when they were addressed to multiple executives as well as in-house general counsel. Her mind wandered back to the practice of one of her clients at the old firm. Suddenly sensing this anecdotal tidbit as "her" moment, she shared with the assembled group, "When I was at Bryans & Putnam, one of our clients, City Trust Company, had a bright line rule: so long as the document had counsel's name or initials on it anywhere—as writer, addressee, copied in or later sent the

---

34. For example, Pepper Hamilton eventually settled with Maritrans for $3 million. *See* James L. Kelley, *Lawyers Crossing Lines* 79 (Carolina Academic Press 2001).

document—they deemed it privileged. It made it real easy to decide which documents to withhold."

Several minutes later, as the discussion rejected her formulation as far too broad, even unprofessional, it suddenly occurred to her. Of course! The firm had litigation against City Trust Company, she was "screened" from that litigation (she had prepared some early interrogatories for City Trust) and she had suddenly revealed a City Trust confidence to everyone. Panic replaced boredom; nausea gripped her. What should she do? What would her firm colleagues do? Was her career going up in smoke before her eyes? She had broken her trust; she hadn't intended to, she hadn't been thinking. It was just a passing remark. She rose shakily, mumbled an apology and hurried to the ladies' room.

Her mind raced back to her first thoughts about leaving her old firm. The headhunter had called and indicated how easy it was to place a young associate practicing in Pennsylvania, one of the few states that provided for screening of private lawyers when they switched firms. It made looking for a job so much simpler. She did not have to worry about whether the possible new employers had cases against her old clients. If the headhunter found a firm that liked her, she could just accept the job without worrying about potential conflicts. If any were discovered, the Pennsylvania rules would simply require that she be screened from those matters.

She felt comfortable with that arrangement. She knew how she viewed client confidences—she would never share them. In fact, it gave her great pride to think of herself as a lawyer of integrity, one who could be trusted with confidential information. Indeed it was one of the things that drove her husband crazy—the way she always knew the best secrets weeks before he would hear about it at a cocktail party or read it in the newspaper. She even felt flattered when, after the two matters from which she had to be screened were identified, the chairman of her new firm's professional responsibility committee said to her that the firm was not going to take any elaborate measures to screen her because the firm had a long tradition of placing substantial trust in their associates.

But now! What could she do? Maybe she shouldn't do anything. If she talked to anyone at her new firm that would just emphasize the importance of her disclosure. Would her new firm then have to resign from handling the City Trust matters? One of them involved Pegasus Construction Company, her new firm's largest litigation client. And did she have to tell City Trust? Or anyone at Bryans & Putnam? So many questions! No one to turn to. She was spinning with concerns. It was too much to handle. She would leave early—it would be her first pre-8:00 P.M. departure in weeks—and maybe she could persuade her husband that dinner at the new Thai restaurant on South Street would be in order . . . she needed a chance to clear her head, to regroup.

The next day dawned early and bright—the kind of day that gave June such a good reputation. The dinner had been close to perfect, perhaps a tad too much wine. And while she hated to admit it, it may have been the wine that permitted her to see the situation clearly.

There was no doubting her mistake; she shouldn't have blurted out those remarks at the meeting the day before, but it was only after the dinner that she recalled how upset she had been originally when she learned that City Trust took this position on the privilege. She recalled with clarity how it had offended her at the time, how surprised she was that the partners at old Bryans & Putnam had so blithely accepted the client's notion of privilege. So was there really anything wrong with what she had said? If City Trust's position were defensible . . . maybe she had an obligation to tell someone, maybe her new firm would be obliged to resign. But since it was her view that City Trust was wrong, there really was no harm. If her colleagues who worked on City Trust matters at her new firm used her information to press a little harder for documents that City Trust withheld on the ground of privilege, it would be for the courts to decide who was right. And it wasn't like she had shared confidential facts about the case.

As she contemplated all of this, she couldn't really tell whether it was the weather, the Cabernet Sauvignon, or the chicken satay that had induced this new sense of calm; the problems of yesterday had been put to rest and, particularly pleasing, she had handled the entire matter herself. Off she went to work with a new lightness in her step, not unlike the way she felt the day she learned she had passed the bar exam. Maybe she would go for partner after all.

Practice Pointers: *Implementing a Conflicts Control System*

This chapter illustrates the need to identify and properly respond to a wide variety of potential conflicts of interest. Model Rule 5.1 further requires that law firm partners and those with similar managerial authority "make reasonable efforts to ensure that the firm has in effect measures giving reasonable assurance that all lawyers in the firm conform to the Rules of Professional Conduct." A law firm will not be able to identify or avoid conflicts unless it collects information that will reveal them. To this end, the firm needs to establish, maintain, and continually update a system of accurate information.[1] As soon as this information reveals the presence of a potential conflict, the firm will be in a position to respond by understanding the nature of the conflict and the sources of legal regulation that govern it.

Building a Data Base

Current law regulates personal, concurrent, third person, and former client conflicts and requires precise identification of the client, nature of the matter, and the lawyers who will work on the case. Model Rules 1.8(h), 1.10, 1.11, and 1.12 generally impute the conflict of one lawyer to others in the firm.[2] These aspects of the law governing lawyer conflicts of interest should shape similar categories of information that are entered in the conflicts checking database of every law practice.

Personal Conflicts: Law Firm Lawyers File A separate entry should be made in the law firm lawyers file for each lawyer in the law firm. Each entry in the law firm's database should include three distinct pieces of information:

- The name of each lawyer;
- A list of material interests (property, business, and financial) owned by that lawyer; and
- Substantial property, business, or financial interests of persons in that lawyer's household.

1. New York *requires* law firms to implement such a system. *See* N.Y. DR 5-105(E).
2. Rule 1.10(a) exempts prohibitions "based on a personal interest of the prohibited lawyer" if the personal interest "does not present a significant risk of materially limiting the representation of the client by the remaining lawyers in the firm."

Concurrent and Third Person Conflicts: Current Client File Each entry for current clients should include at least four elements:

- Identification of each current client. Subsidiaries, parents, or other affiliates, and control persons (key officers and employees) of entity clients as well as all changes or variations in corporate or personal name should be carefully described;[3]
- A description of the subject matter of the client representation, including the identities (with changes when they occur) of actual and potential opposing parties;
- Any third persons or entities, such as insurers, who are paying for or are direct beneficiaries of the representation; and
- The names of all law firm lawyers working on the matter.

Former Client Conflicts: Former Clients File Each entry for former clients should also include three elements:

- Accurate identification of the client, including subsidiaries, parents, or other affiliates and control persons of entity clients as well as changes or variations in personal or corporate name;
- Subject matter of the representation, including the identities (with changes when relevant) of related and opposing parties; and
- The names of lawyers who worked on the matter.

Since former client conflicts can be generated not only by past law firm representation but also by the past employment of law firm personnel, it is essential to include the three elements listed above (client identification, subject matter, lawyers) for all of the following:

- All former clients of the firm;
- All former clients of lawyers joining the firm;
- All former clients of current law firm paralegals, secretaries, investigators, and related paraprofessionals; and
- All former clients of paraprofessionals joining the firm.

Using the Data Base

Lawyers never should rely on their memory as a substitute for a conflicts check. Instead, conflicts should be monitored by timely entries into the database, and by timely use of the database to search for relevant matches. Once the initial database has been established, new data should be added before any new client matter is opened by the firm, as well as at any time new personnel join the firm. Law firm lawyers also should be notified about new client matters through interoffice memoranda. This procedure both initiates and backs up a centralized data base search and entry.

A new client file should not be opened, and no time should be billed to the client by the firm until at least four steps have been completed:

3. Commercial services make this information available to law firms.

1. The prospective client's identifying information has been run through the law firm's database;
2. A written conflicts memo has been circulated throughout the firm;
3. The responsible lawyer has indicated in writing either that no matches were found, or if they were, that they indicate no conflict or a consentable conflict for which consent has been obtained; and
4. A neutral person has reviewed any information, matches, and explanatory memo.

Any information about changes in client identity, opposing parties, or lawyers working on the file should be entered on the day the change occurs or the firm becomes aware of it. Entries should be moved from the current client file to the former client file list whenever the firm concludes its representation in a client matter. When potential conflicts are detected, lawyers need a list of each lawyer code provision that governs each category of conflicts in the jurisdiction(s) where their lawyers are admitted to practice, such as the one on the first two pages of this chapter.

Identifying and Responding to Personal Conflicts

To identify and respond to personal conflicts:

- Search for any matches between the current client file and the law firm lawyers file.
- If any occur, does the client's interest potentially differ from an interest of any lawyer in the firm?
- If so, is the conflict consentable in your jurisdiction?
- If so, has the client's informed consent been obtained in writing to allow the lawyer or the firm to continue with the representation?

Identifying and Responding to Current Client Conflicts

Concurrent client conflicts can occur because of the interests of third persons or the interests of another client.

To identify and respond to current client conflicts:

- Search for any third persons who pay for the representation in the current client file.
- If any occur, seek the consent of the current client to the representation.
- Search for any matches between clients within the current client file.
- If any occur, does the firm represent conflicting or potentially differing interests?
- If so, are they consentable conflicts in your jurisdiction?
- Has informed consent of all affected clients been obtained in writing?
- If not, client consent should be sought, or the firm should withdraw from the representation of the client that last retained the firm (the "hot potato" doctrine).
- If the firm completes a matter, withdraws from any representation, or is discharged by a client, the entry for that client should be moved from the current client file to the former client file.

Identifying and Responding to Conflicts Between Former Clients and Current Clients

For conflicts between former and current clients:

- Search for any matches between the former client file and the current client file.
- If they occur, does the firm represent any current clients whose interests are materially adverse to those of any former clients?
- If so, identify the lawyers or other staff and the clients matters involved in both the current and former representations.
- Are the matters substantially related in your jurisdiction?
- If so, was the prior representation peripheral?
- If not, has the former client's informed consent been obtained in writing?
- If the former client will not consent, are screens available to vitiate this kind of conflict in your jurisdiction?
- If so, establish an adequate screening mechanism.
- If your firm continues the current representation either because of former client consent or a screen, seek consent from the current client as well.

Integrating a Conflicts Control System into Law Firm Management

Law firms should establish a committee or designate a partner with responsibility to implement and use the conflicts control system. Once a committee or partner is identified as having responsibility for monitoring conflicts within the firm, all conflicts detection and avoidance practices should be made routine by written policies and procedures that require compliance by all law firm personnel. When potential conflicts are discovered, the partner or committee should have the authority to decide how to respond. Law firm policy should include the requirement that any member of a law firm ethics committee potentially involved in any conflict be disqualified from considering its resolution. The partner or committee in charge of conflicts should also make clear that deviations from the firm policy are serious concerns and will result in appropriate penalties.

Following these procedures will not prevent conflicts, but they will put you in a position to know about them and respond appropriately. The law governing lawyers makes clear that failure to discover a conflict is no defense to discipline, disqualification, fee forfeiture, and other client remedies.

Chapter 7

Fees and Client Property

The materials in this chapter represent a very small sample of an enormous body of law that governs the fees lawyers can contract for and collect from their clients. Disputes over fees are common, and occur for at least three reasons. First, some lawyers who do a good job of explaining the basis of the fee and who keep more than adequate records of the time they have expended on the matter nevertheless face clients who are unhappy with the lawyer or the result in their case, or are otherwise unwilling to pay for the representation. Second, most lawyers do not intentionally overcharge, but may fail to explain the fee so that clients are unpleasantly taken by surprise when they later receive the bill. Third, some lawyers overcharge clients, and some do so fraudulently.

Although it may appear that lawyers are free to bargain with clients at arms length regarding fees before they enter into a client-lawyer relationship, notions of fiduciary duty in the law governing lawyers in fact limit the freedom of lawyers to contract for and collect fees. Fee agreements nearly always involve some degree of conflict of interest, because a lawyer's personal financial interest potentially conflicts with the client's representation. As we have seen in prior chapters, the remedy for this potential conflict in loyalty is consultation, communication, and informed consent. For fees, as for other conflicts, the greater the potential for conflict, the greater the legal regulation provided to curtail it.

The loyalty based conflict of interest rules discussed in the last chapter apply only after a lawyer has agreed to represent a client. Model Rule 1.5 nevertheless imposes several fiduciary-like requirements in the context of precontractual fee negotiations, such as obligations to communicate the basis of the fee, limitations on the propriety of certain fee arrangements, and the general requirement that fees are subject to an objective standard of reasonableness. This chapter explores these obligations in the context of hourly, contingent, statutory and flat fees, as well as the lawyer's fiduciary obligation to handle client funds and property.

A. Hourly Fees

Problems

7-1. Martyn flies to San Francisco for a client that pays full hourly rates for travel. If during a six-hour flight, Martyn works on another client's matters for four hours, may she bill two clients a total of ten hours? What if the work on the plane was *pro bono*?

7-2. May Martyn & Fox charge clients $2/page for all incoming and outgoing faxes? What about billing clients $200/hour for contract lawyers whose agency charges us $150?

Consider: Model Rule 1.5
Model Code DR 2-106

ABA Formal Opinion 93-379

American Bar Association Standing Committee on Ethics and Professional Responsibility

BILLING FOR PROFESSIONAL FEES, DISBURSEMENTS AND OTHER EXPENSES

Consistent with the Model Rules of Professional Conduct, a lawyer must disclose to a client the basis on which the client is to be billed for both professional time and any other charges. Absent a contrary understanding, any invoice for professional services should fairly reflect the basis on which the client's charges have been determined. In matters where the client has agreed to have the fee determined with reference to the time expended by the lawyer, a lawyer may not bill more time than she actually spends on the matter, except to the extent that she rounds up to minimum time periods (such as one-quarter or one-tenth of an hour). . . .

It is a common perception that pressure on lawyers to bill a minimum number of hours and on law firms to maintain or improve profits may have led some lawyers to engage in problematic billing practices. These include charges to more than one client for the same work or the same hours, surcharges on services contracted with outside vendors, and charges beyond reasonable costs for in-house services like photocopying and computer searches. Moreover, the bases on which these charges are to be assessed often are not disclosed in advance or are disguised in cryptic invoices so that the client does not fully understand exactly what costs are being charged to him.

The Model Rules of Professional Conduct provide important principles applicable to the billing of clients, principles which, if followed, would ameliorate many of the problems noted above. The Committee has decided to address several practices that are the subject of frequent inquiry, with the goal of helping the profession adhere to its ethical obligations to its clients despite economic pressures.

The first set of practices involves billing more than one client for the same hours spent. In one illustrative situation, a lawyer finds it possible to schedule court appearances for three clients on the same day. He spends a total of four hours at the courthouse, the amount of time he would have spent on behalf of each client had it not been for the fortuitous circumstance that all three cases were scheduled on the same day. May he bill each of the three clients, who otherwise understand that they will be billed on the basis of time spent, for the four hours he spent on them collectively? In another scenario, a lawyer is flying cross-country to attend a deposition on behalf of one client, expending travel time she would ordinarily bill to that client. If she decides not to watch the movie or read her novel, but to work instead on drafting a motion for another client, may she charge both clients, each of whom agreed to hourly billing, for the time during which she was traveling on behalf of one and drafting a document on behalf of the other? A third situation involves research on a particular topic for one client that later turns out to be relevant to an inquiry from a second client. May the firm bill the second client, who agreed to be charged on the basis of time spent on his case, the same amount for the recycled work product that it charged the first client?

The second set of practices involve billing for expenses and disbursements, and is exemplified by the situation in which a firm contracts for the expert witness services of an economist at an hourly rate of $200. May the firm bill the client for the expert's time at the rate of $250 per hour? Similarly, may the firm add a surcharge to the cost of computer-assisted research if the per-minute total charged by the computer company does not include the cost of purchasing the computers or staffing their operation? . . .

Professional Obligations Regarding the Reasonableness of Fees

Implicit in the Model Rules and their antecedents is the notion that the attorney-client relationship is not necessarily one of equals, that it is built on trust, and that the client is encouraged to be dependent on the lawyer, who is dealing with matters of great moment to the client. The client should only be charged a reasonable fee for the legal services performed. Rule 1.5 explicitly addresses the reasonableness of legal fees. The rule deals not only with the determination of a reasonable hourly rate, but also with total cost to the client. The Comment to the rules states, for example, that "[a] lawyer should not exploit a fee arrangement based primarily on hourly charges by using wasteful procedures." The goal should be solely to compensate the lawyer fully for time reasonably expended, an approach that if followed will not take advantage of the client. . . .

The lawyer's conduct should be such as to promote the client's trust of the lawyer and of the legal profession. . . . An unreasonable limitation on the hours a lawyer may spend on a client should be avoided as a threat to the lawyer's ability to fulfill her obligation under Model Rule 1.1 to "provide competent representation to a client." . . .

On the other hand, the lawyer who has agreed to bill on the basis of hours expended does not fulfill her ethical duty if she bills the client for more time than she actually spent on the client's behalf. In addressing the hypotheticals regarding (a) simultaneous appearance on behalf of three clients, (b) the airplane flight on behalf of one client while working on another client's matters and (c) recycled work product, it is helpful to consider these questions, not from the perspective of what a client could be forced to pay, but rather from the perspective of what the lawyer actually earned. A lawyer who spends four hours of time on behalf of three clients has not earned twelve billable hours. A lawyer who flies for six hours for one client, while working for five hours on behalf of another, has not earned eleven billable hours. A lawyer who is able to reuse old work product has not re-earned the hours previously billed and compensated when the work product was first generated. Rather than looking to profit from the fortuity of coincidental scheduling, the desire to get work done rather than watch a movie, or the luck of being asked the identical question twice, the lawyer who has agreed to bill solely on the basis of time spent is obliged to pass the benefits of these economies on to the client. The practice of billing several clients for the same time or work product, since it results in the earning of an unreasonable fee, therefore is contrary to the mandate of . . . Model Rule 1.5.

Moreover, continuous toil on or over-staffing a project for the purpose of churning out hours is also not properly considered "earning" one's fees. One job of a lawyer is to expedite the legal process. Model Rule 3.2. . . . A lawyer should take as much time as is reasonably required to complete a project, and should certainly never be motivated by anything other than the best interests of the client when determining how to staff or how much time to spend on any particular project.

It goes without saying that a lawyer who has undertaken to bill on an hourly basis is never justified in charging a client for hours not actually expended. If a lawyer has agreed to charge the client on this basis and it turns out that the lawyer is particularly efficient in accomplishing a given result, it nonetheless will not be permissible to charge the client for more hours than were actually expended on the matter. When that basis for billing the client has been agreed to, the economies associated with the result must inure to the benefit of the client, not give rise to an opportunity to bill a client phantom hours. This is not to say that the lawyer who agreed to hourly compensation is not free, with full disclosure, to suggest additional compensation because of a particularly efficient or outstanding result, or because the lawyer was able to reuse prior work product on the client's behalf. The point here is that fee enhancement cannot be accomplished simply by presenting the client with a statement reflecting more billable hours than were actually expended. On the other hand, if a matter turns out to be more difficult to accomplish than first anticipated and more hours are required than were originally estimated, the lawyer is fully entitled (though not required) to bill those hours unless the client agreement turned the original estimate into a cap on the fees to be charged.

Charges Other than Professional Fees

In addition to charging clients fees for professional services, lawyers typically charge their clients for certain additional items which are often referred to variously as disbursements, out-of-pocket expenses or additional charges. . . . [W]e believe that the reasonableness standard explicitly applicable to fees under Rule 1.5(a) should be applicable to these charges as well. . . .

First, which items are properly subject to additional charges? Second, to what extent, if at all, may clients be charged for more than actual out-of-pocket disbursements? Third, on what basis may clients be charged for the provision of in-house services? . . .

A. *General Overhead*

When a client has engaged a lawyer to provide professional services for a fee (whether calculated on the basis of the number of hours expended, a flat fee, a contingent percentage of the amount recovered or otherwise) the client would be justifiably disturbed if the lawyer submitted a bill to the client which included, beyond the professional fee, additional charges for general office overhead. In the absence of disclosure to the client in advance of the engagement to the contrary, the client should reasonably expect that the lawyer's cost in maintaining a library, securing malpractice insurance, renting of office space, purchasing utilities and the like would be subsumed within the charges the lawyer is making for professional services.

B. *Disbursements*

At the beginning of the engagement lawyers typically tell their clients that they will be charged for disbursements. When that term is used clients justifiably should expect that the lawyer will be passing on to the client those actual payments of funds made by the lawyer on the client's behalf. Thus, if the lawyer hires a court stenographer to transcribe a deposition, the client can reasonably expect to be billed as a disbursement the amount the lawyer pays to the court reporting service. Similarly, if the lawyer flies to Los Angeles for the client, the client can reasonably expect to be billed as a disbursement the amount of the airfare, taxicabs, meals and hotel room.

It is the view of the Committee that, in the absence of disclosure to the contrary, it would be improper if the lawyer assessed a surcharge on these disbursements over and above the amount actually incurred unless the lawyer herself incurred additional expenses beyond the actual cost of the disbursement item. In the same regard, if a lawyer receives a discounted rate from a third party provider, it would be improper if she did not pass along the benefit of the discount to her client rather than charge the client the full rate and reserve the profit to herself. Clients quite properly could view these practices as an attempt to create additional undisclosed profit centers when the client had been told he would be billed for disbursements.

C. In-House Provision of Services

Perhaps the most difficult issue is the handling of charges to clients for the provision of in-house services... [such as] charges for photocopying, computer research, on-site meals, deliveries and other similar items. Like professional fees, it seems clear that lawyers may pass on reasonable charges for these services. Thus, in the view of the committee, the lawyer and the client may agree in advance that, for example, photocopying will be charged at $.15 per page, or messenger services will be provided at $5.00 per mile. However, the question arises what may be charged to the client, in the absence of a specific agreement to the contrary, when the client has simply been told that costs for these items will be charged to the client. We conclude that under those circumstances the lawyer is obliged to charge the client no more than the direct cost associated with the service (i.e., the actual cost of making a copy on the photocopy machine) plus a reasonable allocation of overhead expenses directly associated with the provision of the service (e.g., the salary of a photocopy machine operator).

. . . Any reasonable calculation of direct costs as well as any reasonable allocation of related overhead should pass ethical muster. On the other hand, in the absence of an agreement to the contrary, it is impermissible for a lawyer to create an additional source of profit for the law firm beyond that which is contained in the provision of professional services themselves. The lawyer's stock in trade is the sale of legal services, not photocopy paper, tuna fish sandwiches, computer time or messenger services.

Matter of Fordham

668 N.E.2d 816 (Mass. 1996)

O'Connor, J.

This is an appeal from the Board of Bar Overseers' (board's) dismissal of a petition for discipline filed by bar counsel against attorney Laurence S. Fordham...

We summarize the hearing committee's findings. On March 4, 1989, the Acton police department arrested Timothy, then twenty-one years old, and charged him with OUI, operating a motor vehicle after suspension, speeding, and operating an unregistered motor vehicle. At the time of the arrest, the police discovered a partially full quart of vodka in the vehicle. After failing a field sobriety test, Timothy was taken to the Acton police station where he submitted to two breathalyzer tests which registered .10 and .12 respectively.

Subsequent to Timothy's arraignment, he and his father, Laurence Clark (Clark) consulted with three lawyers, who offered to represent Timothy for fees between $3,000 and $10,000. Shortly after the arrest, Clark went to Fordham's home to service an alarm system which he had installed several years before. While there, Clark discussed Timothy's arrest with Fordham's wife who invited Clark to discuss the case with Fordham. Fordham then met with Clark and Timothy.

At this meeting, Timothy described the incidents leading to his arrest and the charges against him. Fordham, whom the hearing committee described as a "very experienced senior trial attorney with impressive credentials," told Clark and Timothy that he had never represented a client in a driving while under the influence case or in any criminal matter, and he had never tried a case in the District Court. The hearing committee found that "Fordham explained that although he lacked experience in this area, he was a knowledgeable and hard-working attorney and that he believed he could competently represent Timothy. Fordham described himself as efficient and economic in the use of [his] time....

"Towards the end of the meeting, Fordham told the Clarks that he worked on [a] time charge basis and that he billed monthly ... In other words, Fordham would calculate the amount of hours he and others in the firm worked on a matter each month and multiply it by the respective hourly rates. He also told the Clarks that he would engage others in his firm to prepare the case. Clark had indicated that he would pay Timothy's legal fees." After the meeting, Clark hired Fordham to represent Timothy.

According to the hearing committee's findings, Fordham filed four pretrial motions on Timothy's behalf, two of which were allowed. One motion, entitled "Motion in Limine to Suppress Results of Breathalyzer Tests," was based on the theory that, although two breathalyzer tests were exactly .02 apart, they were not "within" .02 of one another as the regulations require. The hearing committee characterized the motion and its rationale as "a creative, if not novel, approach to suppression of breathalyzer results."... [T]he trial, which was before a judge without jury, was held on October 10 and October 19, 1989. The judge found Timothy not guilty of driving while under the influence.

Fordham sent ... bills to Clark... [that] totaled $50,022.25, reflecting 227 hours of billed time, 153 hours of which were expended by Fordham and seventy-four of which were his associates' time. Clark did not pay the first two bills when they became due and expressed to Fordham his concern about their amount. Clark paid Fordham $10,000 on June 20, 1989. At that time, Fordham assured Clark that most of the work had been completed "other than taking [the case] to trial." Clark did not make any subsequent payments. Fordham requested Clark to sign a promissory note evidencing his debt to Fordham and, on October 7, 1989, Clark did so. In the October 13, 1989, bill, Fordham added a charge of $5,000 as a "retroactive increase" in fees. On November 7, 1989, after the case was completed, Fordham sent Clark a bill for $15,000.

Bar counsel and Fordham have stipulated that all the work billed by Fordham was actually done and that Fordham and his associates spent the time they claim to have spent. They also have stipulated that Fordham acted conscientiously, diligently, and in good faith in representing Timothy and in his billing in this case.

. . . Although the hearing committee determined that Fordham "spent a large number of hours on [the] matter, in essence learning from scratch what others . . . already know," . . . [it] reasoned that even if the number of hours Fordham "spent [were] wholly out of proportion" to the number of hours that a lawyer with experience in the trying of OUI cases would require, the committee was not required to conclude that the fee based on time spent was "clearly excessive." It was enough, the hearing committee concluded, that Clark instructed Fordham to pursue the case to trial, Fordham did so zealously and, as stipulated, Fordham spent the hours he billed in good faith and diligence. We disagree.

Four witnesses testified before the hearing committee as experts on OUI cases. One of the experts, testifying on behalf of bar counsel, opined that "the amount of time spent in this case is clearly excessive." He testified that there were no unusual circumstances in the OUI charge against Timothy and that it was a "standard operating under the influence case." The witness did agree that Fordham's argument for suppression of the breathalyzer test results, which was successful, was novel and would have justified additional time and labor. He also acknowledged that the acquittal was a good result; even with the suppression of the breathalyzer tests, he testified, the chances of an acquittal would have been "not likely at a bench trial." The witness estimated that it would have been necessary, for thorough preparation of the case including the novel breathalyzer suppression argument, to have billed twenty to thirty hours for preparation, not including trial time.

A second expert, testifying on behalf of bar counsel, expressed his belief that the issues presented in this case were not particularly difficult, nor novel, and that "the degree of skill required to defend a case such as this . . . was not that high." He did recognize, however, that the theory that Fordham utilized to suppress the breathalyzer tests was impressive and one of which he had previously never heard. Nonetheless, the witness concluded that "clearly there is no way that [he] could justify these kind of hours to do this kind of work." . . .

An expert called by Fordham testified that the facts of Timothy's case presented a challenge and that without the suppression of the breathalyzer test results it would have been "an almost impossible situation in terms of prevailing on the trier of fact." He further stated that, based on the particulars in Timothy's case, he believed that Fordham's hours were not excessive and, in fact, he, the witness, would have spent a comparable amount of time. The witness later admitted, however, that within the past five years, the OUI cases which he had brought to trial required no more than a total of forty billed hours, which encompassed all preparation and court appearances. He explained that, although he had not charged more than forty hours to prepare an OUI case, in comparison to Fordham's more than 200 expended hours, Fordham nonetheless had spent a reasonable number of hours on the case in light of the continuance and the subsequent need to reprepare, as well as the "very ingenious" breathalyzer suppression argument, and the Clarks' insistence on trial. In addition, the witness testified that, although the field sobriety test, breathalyzer tests, and the presence of a half-empty liquor bottle in the car placed Fordham at a serious disadvantage in being able to prevail on the OUI charge, those circumstances were not unusual and in fact agreed that they were "normal circumstances."

The fourth expert witness, called by Fordham, testified that she believed the case was "extremely tough" and that the breathalyzer suppression theory was novel. She testified that, although the time and labor consumed on the case was more than usual in defending an OUI charge, the hours were not excessive. They were not excessive, she explained, because the case was particularly difficult due to the "stakes [and] the evidence." She conceded, however, that legal issues in defending OUI charges are "pretty standard" and that the issues presented in this case were not unusual....

In considering whether a fee is "clearly excessive" within the meaning of S.J.C. Rule 3:07, DR 2-106(B), the first factor to be considered pursuant to that rule is "the novelty and difficulty of the questions involved, and the skill requisite to perform the legal service properly." That standard is similar to the familiar standard of reasonableness traditionally applied in civil fee disputes. Based on the testimony of the four experts, the number of hours devoted to Timothy's OUI case by Fordham and his associates was substantially in excess of the hours that a prudent experienced lawyer would have spent. According to the evidence, the number of hours spent was several times the amount of time any of the witnesses had ever spent on a similar case. We are not unmindful of the novel and successful motion to suppress the breathalyzer test results, but that effort cannot justify a $50,000 fee in a type of case in which the usual fee is less than one-third of that amount.

The board determined that "because [Fordham] had never tried an OUI case or appeared in the district court, [Fordham] spent over 200 hours preparing the case, in part to educate himself in the relevant substantive law and court procedures." Fordham's inexperience in criminal defense work and OUI cases in particular cannot justify the extraordinarily high fee. It cannot be that an inexperienced lawyer is entitled to charge three or four times as much as an experienced lawyer for the same service. A client "should not be expected to pay for the education of a lawyer when he spends excessive amounts of time on tasks which, with reasonable experience, become matters of routine."...

DR 2-106(B) provides that the third factor to be considered in ascertaining the reasonableness of the fee is its comparability to "the fee customarily charged in the locality for similar legal services." The hearing committee made no finding as to the comparability of Fordham's fee with the fees customarily charged in the locality for similar services. However, one of bar counsel's expert witnesses testified that he had never heard of a fee in excess of $15,000 to defend a first OUI charge, and the customary flat fee in an OUI case, including trial, "runs from $1,000 to $7,500." Bar counsel's other expert testified that he had never heard of a fee in excess of $10,000 for a bench trial. In his view, the customary charge for a case similar to Timothy's would vary between $1,500 and $5,000. One of Fordham's experts testified that she considered a $40,000 or $50,000 fee for defending an OUI charge "unusual and certainly higher by far than any I've ever seen before." The witness had never charged a fee of more than $3,500 for representing a client at a bench trial to defend a first offense OUI charge. She further testified that she believed an "average OUI in the bench session is two thousand [dollars] and sometimes less."...

Although finding that Fordham's fee was "much higher than the fee charged by many attorneys with more experience litigating driving under the influence cases," the hearing committee nevertheless determined that the fee charged by Fordham was not clearly excessive because Clark "went into the relationship with Fordham with open eyes," [and] Fordham's fee fell within a "safe harbor."...

The finding that Clark had entered into the fee agreement "with open eyes" was based on the finding that Clark hired Fordham after being fully apprised that he lacked any type of experience in defending an OUI charge and after interviewing other lawyers who were experts in defending OUI charges.... It is also significant, however, that the hearing committee found that "despite Fordham's disclaimers concerning his experience, Clark did not appear to have understood in any real sense the implications of choosing Fordham to represent Timothy. Fordham did not give Clark any estimate of the total expected fee or the number of $200 hours that would be required." The express finding of the hearing committee that Clark "did not appear to have understood in any real sense the implications of choosing Fordham to represent Timothy" directly militates against the finding that Clark entered into the agreement "with open eyes."

That brings us to the hearing committee's finding that Fordham's fee fell within a "safe harbor." The hearing committee reasoned that as long as an agreement existed between a client and an attorney to bill a reasonable rate multiplied by the number of hours actually worked, the attorney's fee was within a "safe harbor" and thus protected from a challenge that the fee was clearly excessive....

The "safe harbor" formula would not be an appropriate rationale in this case because the amount of time Fordham spent to educate himself and represent Timothy was clearly excessive despite his good faith and diligence. Disciplinary Rule 2-106(B)'s mandate that "[a] fee is clearly excessive when, after a review of the facts, a lawyer of ordinary prudence, experienced in the area of the law involved, would be left with a definite and firm conviction that the fee is substantially in excess of a reasonable fee," creates explicitly an objective standard by which attorneys' fees are to be judged. We are not persuaded by Fordham's argument that "unless it can be shown that the 'excessive' work for which the attorney has charged goes beyond mere matters of professional judgment and can be proven, either directly or by reasonable inference, to have involved dishonesty, bad faith or overreaching of the client, no case for discipline has been established." Disciplinary Rule 2-106 plainly does not require an inquiry into whether the clearly excessive fee was charged to the client under fraudulent circumstances, and we shall not write such a meaning into the disciplinary rule.

Finally, bar counsel challenges the hearing committee's finding that "if Clark objected to the numbers of hours being spent by Fordham, he could have spoken up with some force when he began receiving bills." Bar counsel notes, and we agree, that "the test as stated in the DR 2-106(A) is whether the fee 'charged' is clearly excessive, not whether the fee is accepted as valid or acquiesced in by the client." Therefore, we conclude that the hearing committee and the board erred in not concluding that Fordham's fee was clearly excessive....

... In addition, nothing contained within the disciplinary rule nor within any pertinent case law indicates in any manner that a clearly excessive fee does not warrant discipline whenever the time spent during the representation was spent in good faith. The fact that this court has not previously had occasion to discipline an attorney in the circumstances of this case does not suggest that the imposition of discipline in this case offends due process.

In charging a clearly excessive fee, Fordham departed substantially from the obligation of professional responsibility that he owed to his client. The ABA Model Standards for Imposing Lawyer Sanctions §7.3 (1992) endorses a public reprimand as the appropriate sanction for charging a clearly excessive fee. We deem such a sanction appropriate in this case. Accordingly, a judgment is to be entered in the county court imposing a public censure....

B. Contingent Fees

Problems

7-3. Martyn & Fox entered into a one-third contingent fee agreement with Client, who has been seriously injured by Drunk Driver. Two weeks later, after we have spent about 10 hours on the case, Drunk Driver's insurer offered the policy limits of $150,000. Client threatens to file a disciplinary complaint unless we agree to reduce our fee to $5,000 ($500/hour). What should we do?

7-4. Massachusetts hired Martyn & Fox to sue the tobacco companies at a time when the suit seemed hopeless. The fee agreement, signed for Massachusetts by the Attorney General, called for a 25 percent contingent fee. Two years later, as part of an overall settlement with 40 states, Massachusetts was awarded $8.3 billion. Should Martyn & Fox collect $2.075 billion?

7-5. Martyn & Fox's client is sued for $10 million to be trebled as part of an alleged antitrust conspiracy among drug companies. May Martyn & Fox negotiate a fee agreement that would award the firm 25 percent of everything the client saves below $30 million?

7-6. Martyn & Fox routinely refers medical malpractice actions to Hastie & Moore, in exchange for one fourth of Hastie & Moore's 40 percent contingent fee. Fox just discovered that Hastie & Moore has not paid us our share after settling the last two cases we referred. What should we do?

Consider: Model Rule 1.5
Model Code DR 2-106, 2-107

ABA Formal Opinion 94-389

American Bar Association Standing Committee on Ethics and Professional Responsibility

CONTINGENT FEES

A. *Introduction . . .*

In the opinion of the Committee, the charging of a contingent fee, in personal injury and in all other permissible types of litigation, as well as in numerous non-litigation matters, does not violate ethical standards as long as the fee is appropriate in the circumstances and reasonable in amount, and as long as the client has been fully advised of the availability of alternative fee arrangements. . . .

B. *Contingent Fees Are Employed in Multiple Situations*

It should be recognized at the outset that when we address contingent fees we are talking about a wide variety of situations. Contingent fees are no longer, if ever they were, limited to personal injury cases. Nor are contingent fees limited to suits involving tortious conduct. Contingent fees are now commonly offered to plaintiff-clients in collections, civil rights, securities and anti-trust class actions, real estate tax appeals and even patent litigation.

Nor is this compensation arrangement limited to plaintiffs. In this Committee's recent Formal Opinion 93-373, the Committee considered the ethical issues raised by the increasingly employed so-called "reverse contingent fees," in which defendants hire lawyers who will be compensated by an agreed upon percentage of the amount the client saves. The Committee concluded that as long as the fee arrangement reached between the lawyer and client realistically estimates the exposure of the defendant client, such a fee is consistent with the Model Rules.

Moreover, contingent fees are not limited to litigation practice. Fees in the mergers and acquisitions arena are often either partially or totally dependent on the consummation of a takeover or successful resistance of such a takeover. Additionally, fees on public offerings are often tied to whether the stocks or bonds come to market and to the amount generated in the offering. Banks are also hiring lawyers to handle loan transactions in which the fee for the bank's lawyers is dependent in whole or part on the consummation of the loan.

The use of contingent fees in these areas, for plaintiffs and defendants, impecunious and affluent alike, reflects the desire of clients to tie a lawyer's compensation to her performance and to give the lawyer incentives to improve returns to the client. The trend also may reflect a growing dissatisfaction with hourly rate billing. Because of the growing importance and widespread use of contingent fees, the Committee will first address in detail the factors that should be considered before a lawyer and client enter into such a fee arrangement, and then address the specific questions occasioning this opinion.

C. *The Decision by the Client to Enter Into a Contingent Fee Agreement Must Be an Informed One*

Nothing in the Model Rules expressly prohibits a lawyer from entering into a contingent fee agreement with any client. Nevertheless, the lawyer must recognize that not all matters are appropriate for a contingent fee. For example, Model Rule 1.5(d) makes it clear that a contingent fee may never be agreed to, charged or collected in a criminal matter or divorce proceeding. More to the point, in Informal Opinion 86-1521 this Committee concluded that, "when there is any doubt whether a contingent fee is consistent with the client's best interest," and the client is able to pay a reasonable fixed fee, the lawyer "must offer the client the *opportunity* to engage counsel on a reasonable fixed fee basis before entering into a contingent fee arrangement." (Emphasis added.)...

In other words, regardless of whether the lawyer, the prospective client, or both, are initially inclined towards a contingent fee, the nature (and details) of the compensation arrangement should be fully discussed by the lawyer and client before any final agreement is reached.

The extent of the discussion, of course, will depend on whether it is the lawyer or the client who initiated the idea of proceeding with the contingent fee arrangement, the lawyer's prior dealings with the client (including whether there has been any prior contingent fee arrangement), and the experience and sophistication of the client with respect to litigation and other legal matters. Among the factors that should be considered and discussed are the following:

a. The likelihood of success;
b. The likely amount of recovery or savings, if the case is successful;
c. The possibility of an award of exemplary or multiple damages and how that will affect the fee;

d. The attitude and prior practices of the other side with respect to settlement;
e. The likelihood of, or any anticipated difficulties in, collecting any judgement;
f. The availability of alternative dispute resolution as a means of achieving an earlier conclusion to the matter;
g. The amount of time that is likely to be invested by the lawyer;
h. The likely amount of the fee if the matter is handled on a non-contingent basis;
i. The client's ability and willingness to pay a non-contingent fee;
j. The percentage of any recovery that the lawyer would receive as a contingent fee and whether that percentage will be fixed or on a sliding scale;
k. Whether the lawyer's fees would be recoverable by the client by reason of statute or common law rule;
l. Whether the jurisdiction in which the claim will be pursued has any rules or guidelines for contingent fees; and
m. How expenses of the litigation are to be handled....

E. *In a Case in Which Liability Is Clear and Some Recovery Is Certain, a Fee Based on a Percentage of the Recovery Can Be Ethically Proper...*

...[E]ven in cases where there is no risk of non-recovery, and the lawyer and client are certain that liability is clear and will be conceded, a fee arrangement contingent on the amount recovered may nonetheless be reasonable. As the increasing popularity of reverse contingent fees demonstrates, for almost all cases there is a range of possible recoveries. Since the amount of the recovery will be largely determined by the lawyer's knowledge, skill, experience and time expended, both the defendant and the plaintiff may best be served by a contingency fee arrangement that ties the lawyer's fee to the amount recovered.

Also, an early settlement offer is often prompted by the defendant's recognition of the ability of the plaintiff's lawyer fairly and accurately to value the case and to proceed effectively through trial and appeals if necessary. There is no ethical reason why the lawyer is not entitled to an appropriate consideration for this value that his engagement has brought to the case, even though it results in an early resolution.

Given the foregoing, the Committee concludes that as a general proposition contingent fees are appropriate and ethical in situations where liability is certain and some recovery is likely.

That having been said, there may nonetheless be special situations in which a contingent fee may not be appropriate. For example, if in a particular instance a lawyer was reasonably confident that as soon as the case was filed the defendant would offer an amount that the client would accept, it might be that the only appropriate fee would be one based on the lawyer's time spent on the case since, from the information known to the lawyer, there was little risk of non-recovery and the lawyer's efforts would have brought little value to the client's recovery.[15] And even if, in such circumstances, after a full discussion, it were agreed between lawyer and client that a contingent fee was appropriate, the fee arrangement should recognize the likelihood of an early favorable result by providing for a significantly smaller

15. Similar reasoning has led many courts to find that it is inappropriate to charge a contingent fee in cases involving first party insurance benefits where there is no risk of non-recovery and the lawyer merely submits the claim on behalf of the client. But courts have also found that contingent fees may be appropriate in these types of cases, if the lawyer performs additional services relating to the recovery by the client. *See* In re Doyle, 581 N.E.2d 669 (Ill. 1991).

percentage recovery if the anticipated offer is received and accepted than if the case must go forward through discovery, trial and appeal.[16]...

H. *The Contingent Fee Arrangement Must Be Reasonable*

In addition to the requirement that a fee be appropriate, Model Rule 1.5 requires that the fee, whether based on an hourly rate, a contingent percentage or some other basis, "shall be reasonable."...

We stress that the lawyer should take all these factors into account in evaluating every case. *See* ABA Formal Opinion 329 (1972). For this reason, a lawyer who always charges the same percentage of recovery regardless of the particulars of a case should consider whether he is charging a fee that is, in an ethical context, a reasonable one....

As with the question of appropriateness, the mere fact that liability may be clear and that some recovery is likely does not per se make any given contingent fee unreasonable. It is important to keep in mind that the reasonableness as well as the appropriateness of a fee arrangement necessarily must be judged at the time it is entered into. All contingent fee agreements carry certain risks: the risk that the case will require substantially more work than the lawyer anticipated; the risk that there will be no judgment, or only an unenforceable one; the risk of changes in the law; the risk that the client will dismiss the lawyer; and the risk that the client will require the lawyer to reject what the lawyer considers a good settlement or otherwise to continue the proceedings much further than in the lawyer's judgment they should be pursued. If a lawyer accepts a given risk—for example, the risk posed by the fact that the opposing party has a reputation for being intransigent in its approach to settlement—and offers a fee contract reflecting that risk, which is accepted by a fully informed client, the lawyer should not be required as a matter of ethics to give up the benefit of the agreement because the opposing party, to everyone's surprise, offers an early settlement that is acceptable to the client.... By the same token, a later development that increases the risk to the lawyer—for example, a statutorily imposed cap on liability, the loss of a summary judgment motion everyone expected to win, or the need to take three times the number of depositions originally anticipated—should not permit the lawyer to demand a new, more generous fee arrangement.[22]

I. *The Percentage of a Contingent Fee May as an Ethical Matter Be Increased on the Basis of How Far the Lawyer Must Proceed in Prosecuting the Case*

The Committee has also been asked whether it is ethical for a lawyer and client to enter into a fee agreement that provides for higher contingent fees after specific

16. A recognition of the amount of additional work required to take a case through trial and appeals is reflected by several states which cap percentage fees in certain types of cases but allow the percentage charged to rise after certain milestones, i.e., 25% if settled before trial, 33 1/2% if tried. *See* N.J. Ct. R. 1.27 (C)(f) (limiting fees in tort cases involving minors). States have also mandated differing percentages depending on the amount recovered. *See* N.Y. Jud. L. §474-A (McKinneys 1994 Supp.); Conn. Gen. St. Ann. §52-251(c) (1991)....

22. *See, e.g.*, Chase v. Gilbert, 499 A.2d 1203 (D.C. 1985) (a lawyer cannot modify a fee agreement even if he ends up performing significantly more services than were contemplated when agreement was entered into). Because reasonableness is judged at the time the contract is entered into, there is nothing necessarily unethical about charging a contingent fee on the portion of any recovery that is equal to an early settlement offer....

benchmarks, for example, 25% if the case settles within six months and 33% after trial. The higher contingent fee at advanced stages of the matter is meant to compensate the lawyer for the additional time and labor necessary in the case. As demonstrated in the factors set forth in Model Rule 1.5(a) set out above, the time and labor involved in a matter are among the reasonable bases for setting a fee. Therefore, it is the Committee's opinion that such a fee agreement is ethical as long as the overall fee is appropriate and reasonable. *See, e.g.*, Phila. Bar Assoc. Ethics Opinion 93-11 (approving such a fee arrangement).

J. The Percentage of a Contingent Fee May Increase with the Amount of the Recovery

Finally, the Committee has been asked whether it is ethical for a lawyer to enter into a fee agreement that provides for a higher percentage fee as the amount of the recovery goes up or the amount of the savings increases: for example, 15% on the first $100,000 recovered or saved, 20% on the next hundred thousand, and 25% on everything thereafter. Such an arrangement on its face runs contrary to what several states have mandated in terms of reducing the percentage recovery as the amount recovered rises.... Nonetheless, as a matter of ethics, the Committee is of the view that a percentage that increases with the amount of the recovery can be permissible. Model Rule 1.5(a) refers, in connection with the reasonableness of a fee, to "results obtained," and the "ability of the lawyer or lawyers performing the services" as factors that may be considered. Since a higher recovery would, by definition, reflect the first of these factors and, in all likelihood, reflect the other as well, the Committee is of the view that such a fee agreement is ethical, so long as the matter for which the fee is charged is appropriate and the amount of the fee is reasonable. Indeed, many would say that this form of contingent fee agreement more closely rewards the effort and ability the lawyer brings to the engagement than does a straight percentage fee arrangement, since everyone would agree that it is the last dollars, not the first dollars, of recovery that require the greatest effort and/or ability on the part of the lawyer. It may be that any lawyer would have been able to achieve a $100,000 verdict for a given plaintiff's injuries, but that only the most skilled would have been able to secure a $500,000 award plus an additional sum for exemplary damages....

C. Statutory Fees

Problem

7-7. Martyn & Fox agrees to a one-third contingent fee contract with Client and spends 2,000 hours on Client's federal civil rights action alleging police brutality against Local Municipality, resulting in injunctive relief and a jury verdict of $21,000. What fee will we receive? What if Local Municipality offers to settle for injunctive relief in exchange for Client's agreement not to seek statutory attorney fees?

Consider: Model Rule 1.5
Model Code DR 2-106

Gisbrecht v. Barnhart

535 U.S. 789 (2002)

Justice GINSBURG delivered the opinion of the Court.

This case concerns the fees that may be awarded attorneys who successfully represent Social Security benefits claimants in court. . . .

Congress, we conclude, designed §406(b) to control, not to displace, fee agreements between Social Security benefits claimants and their counsel. Because the decision before us for review rests on lodestar calculations and rejects the primacy of lawful attorney-client fee agreements, we reverse the judgment below and remand for recalculation of counsel fees payable from the claimants' past-due benefits.

I

A

Fees for representation of individuals claiming Social Security old-age, survivor, or disability benefits, both at the administrative level and in court, are governed by prescriptions Congress originated in 1965. . . .

For proceedings in court, Congress provided for fees on rendition of "a judgment favorable to a claimant." The Commissioner has interpreted §406(b) to "prohibit a lawyer from charging fees when there is no award of back benefits."

As part of its judgment, a court may allow "a reasonable fee . . . not in excess of 25 percent of the . . . past-due benefits" awarded to the claimant. The fee is payable "out of, and not in addition to, the amount of [the] past-due benefits." Because benefits amounts figuring in the fee calculation are limited to those past due, attorneys may not gain additional fees based on a claimant's continuing entitlement to benefits.

The prescriptions set out in §§406(a) and (b) establish the exclusive regime for obtaining fees for successful representation of Social Security benefits claimants. Collecting or even demanding from the client anything more than the authorized allocation of past-due benefits is a criminal offense.

In many cases, as in the instant case, the Equal Access to Justice Act (EAJA), enacted in 1980, effectively increases the portion of past-due benefits the successful Social Security claimant may pocket. 28 U.S.C. §2412. Under EAJA, a party prevailing against the United States in court, including a successful Social Security benefits claimant, may be awarded fees payable by the United States if the Government's position in the litigation was not "substantially justified." EAJA fees are determined not by a percent of the amount recovered, but by the "time expended" and the attorney's "[hourly] rate," capped in the mine run of cases at $125 per hour.[4]

Congress harmonized fees payable by the Government under EAJA with fees payable under §406(b) out of the claimant's past-due Social Security benefits in this manner: Fee awards may be made under both prescriptions, but the claimant's attorney must "refund to the claimant the amount of the smaller fee." Act of Aug. 5, 1985, Pub. L. 99-80, §3, 99 Stat. 186. Thus, an EAJA award offsets an award under Section 406(b), so that the [amount of the total

4. A higher fee may be awarded if "the court determines that an increase in the cost of living or a special factor, such as the limited availability of qualified attorneys for the proceeding involved, justifies a higher fee." 28 U.S.C. §2412(d)(2)(A)(ii).

past-due benefits the claimant actually receives] will be increased by the . . . EAJA award up to the point the claimant receives 100 percent of the past-due benefits.

B

[Petitioners all agreed to standard 25 percent contingency fee agreements and all prevailed in seeking Social Security disability benefits under Title II of the Social Security Act. Each petitioner also successfully sought attorneys' fees payable by the United States under EAJA. Gisbrecht was awarded $28,366 in past-due benefits and $3,339.11 in attorneys' fees payable by the United States under the EAJA. His lawyer accordingly requested §406(b) fees of 25 percent or $7091.50, with an EAJA offset of $3,339.11, resulting in a total of $3,752.39 from Gisbrecht's recovery.]

Following Circuit precedent, the District Court in each case declined to give effect to the attorney-client fee agreement. Instead, the court employed for the §406(b) fee calculation a "lodestar" method, under which the number of hours reasonably devoted to each case was multiplied by a reasonable hourly fee. This method yielded as §406(b) fees $3,135 from Gisbrecht's recovery [which was completely offset by his EAJA award of $3,339.11]. The three claimants appealed.[6] . . .

We granted certiorari in view of the division among the Circuits on the appropriate method of calculating fees under §406(b). . . .

II

Beginning with the text, §406(b)'s words, "a reasonable fee . . . not in excess of 25 percent of . . . the past-due benefits," read in isolation, could be construed to allow either the Ninth Circuit's lodestar approach or petitioners' position that the attorney-client fee agreement ordinarily should control, if not "in excess of 25 percent." The provision instructs "a reasonable fee," which could be measured by a lodestar calculation. But §406(b)'s language does not exclude contingent-fee contracts that produce fees no higher than the 25 percent ceiling. Such contracts are the most common fee arrangement between attorneys and Social Security claimants. . . .

The lodestar method has its roots in accounting practices adopted in the 1940's to allow attorneys and firms to determine whether fees charged were sufficient to cover overhead and generate suitable profits. W. Ross, *The Honest Hour: The Ethics of Time-Based Billing by Attorneys* 16 (1996). An American Bar Association (ABA) report, published in 1958, observed that attorneys' earnings had failed to keep pace with the rate of inflation; the report urged attorneys to record the hours spent on each case in order to ensure that fees ultimately charged afforded reasonable compensation for counsels' efforts. *See* Special Committee on Economics of Law Practice, *The 1958 Lawyer and His 1938 Dollar* 9-10 (reprint 1959).

Hourly records initially provided only an internal accounting check. The fees actually charged might be determined under any number of methods: the annual retainer; the fee-for-service method; the "eyeball" method, under which the attorney estimated an annual fee for regular clients; or the contingent-fee method, recognized by this Court in Stanton v. Embrey, 93 U.S. 548, 556

6. Although the claimants were named as the appellants below, and are named as petitioners here, the real parties in interest are their attorneys, who seek to obtain higher fee awards under §406(b). For convenience, we nonetheless refer to claimants as petitioners. . . .

(1877), and formally approved by the ABA in 1908. As it became standard accounting practice to record hours spent on a client's matter, attorneys increasingly realized that billing by hours devoted to a case was administratively convenient; moreover, as an objective measure of a lawyer's labor, hourly billing was readily impartable to the client. By the early 1970's, the practice of hourly billing had become widespread.

The federal courts did not swiftly settle on hourly rates as the overriding criterion for attorney's fee awards. In 1974, for example, the Fifth Circuit issued an influential opinion holding that, in setting fees under Title VII of the Civil Rights Act of 1964, 42 U.S.C. §2000e-5(k) (1970 ed.), courts should consider not only the number of hours devoted to a case but also 11 other factors. Johnson v. Georgia Highway Express, Inc., 488 F.2d 714, 717-719 (1974). The lodestar method did not gain a firm foothold until the mid-1970's, and achieved dominance in the federal courts only after this Court's decisions in Hensley v. Eckerhart, 461 U.S. 424 (1983), Blum v. Stenson, 465 U.S. 886 (1984), and Pennsylvania v. Delaware Valley Citizens' Council for Clean Air, 478 U.S. 546 (1986).

Since that time, "the 'lodestar' figure has, as its name suggests, become the guiding light of our fee-shifting jurisprudence." Burlington v. Dague, 505 U.S. 557, 562 (1992) (relying on *Hensley, Blum,* and *Delaware Valley* to apply lodestar method to fee determination under Solid Waste Disposal Act, §7002(e), 42 U.S.C. §6972(e), and Clean Water Act, §505(d), 33 U.S.C. §1365(d), and noting prior application of lodestar method to Civil Rights Attorney's Fees Awards Act of 1976, 42 U.S.C. §1988; Title VII of Civil Rights Act of 1964, 42 U.S.C. §2000e-5(k); and Clean Air Act, 42 U.S.C. §7604(d)).... Thus, the lodestar method today holds sway in federal-court adjudication of disputes over the amount of fees properly shifted to the loser in the litigation.

Fees shifted to the losing party, however, are not at issue here. Unlike 42 U.S.C. §1988 and EAJA, 42 U.S.C. §406(b) does not authorize the prevailing party to recover fees from the losing party. Section 406(b) is of another genre: It authorizes fees payable from the successful party's recovery. Several statutes governing suits against the United States similarly provide that fees may be paid from the plaintiff's recovery.... Characteristically in cases of the kind we confront, attorneys and clients enter into contingent-fee agreements "specifying that the fee will be 25 percent of any past-due benefits to which the claimant becomes entitled."

Contingent fees, though problematic, particularly when not exposed to court review, are common in the United States in many settings. Such fees, perhaps most visible in tort litigation, are also used in, e.g., patent litigation, real estate tax appeals, mergers and acquisitions, and public offerings. *See* ABA Formal Opinion 94-389 (1994). Traditionally and today, "the marketplace for Social Security representation operates largely on a contingency fee basis."

Before 1965, the Social Security Act imposed no limits on contingent-fee agreements drawn by counsel and signed by benefits claimants. In formulating the 1965 Social Security Act amendments that included §406(b), Congress recognized that "attorneys have upon occasion charged ... inordinately large fees for representing claimants [in court]. Arrangements yielding exorbitant fees, the Senate Report observed, reserved for the lawyer one-third to one-half of the accrued benefits. Congress was mindful, too, that the longer the litigation persisted, the greater the build-up of past-due benefits and, correspondingly, of legal fees awardable from those benefits if the claimant prevailed.

Attending to these realities, Congress provided for "a reasonable fee, not in excess of 25 percent of accrued benefits" as part of the court's judgment, and further specified that "no other fee would be payable." Violation of the "reasonable fee" or "25 percent of accrued benefits" limitation was made subject to the same penalties as those applicable for charging a fee larger than the amount approved by the Commissioner for services at the administrative level—a fine of up to $500, one year's imprisonment, or both. "To assure the payment of the fee allowed by the court," Congress authorized the agency "to certify the amount of the fee to the attorney out of the amount of the accrued benefits."

Congress thus sought to protect claimants against "inordinately large fees" and also to ensure that attorneys representing successful claimants would not risk "nonpayment of [appropriate] fees." But nothing in the text or history of §406(b) reveals a "design to prohibit or discourage attorneys and claimants from entering into contingent fee agreements."...

It is also unlikely that Congress, legislating in 1965, and providing for a contingent fee tied to a 25 percent of past-due benefits boundary, intended to install a lodestar method courts did not develop until some years later. Furthermore, we again emphasize, the lodestar method was designed to govern imposition of fees on the losing party. In such cases, nothing prevents the attorney for the prevailing party from gaining additional fees, pursuant to contract, from his own client. *See* Venegas v. Mitchell, 495 U.S. 82, 89(1990) ("[None] of our cases has indicated that [42 U.S.C.] §1988... protects plaintiffs from having to pay what they have contracted to pay, even though their contractual liability is greater than the statutory award that they may collect from losing opponents. Indeed, depriving plaintiffs of the option of promising to pay more than the statutory fee if that is necessary to secure counsel of their choice would not further §1988's general purpose of enabling such plaintiffs . . . to secure competent counsel."). By contrast, §406(b) governs the total fee a claimant's attorney may receive for court representation; any endeavor by the claimant's attorney to gain more than that fee, or to charge the claimant a noncontingent fee, is a criminal offense.

Most plausibly read, we conclude, §406(b) does not displace contingent-fee agreements as the primary means by which fees are set for successfully representing Social Security benefits claimants in court. Rather, §406(b) calls for court review of such arrangements as an independent check, to assure that they yield reasonable results in particular cases. Congress has provided one boundary line: Agreements are unenforceable to the extent that they provide for fees exceeding 25 percent of the past-due benefits. Within the 25 percent boundary, as petitioners in this case acknowledge, the attorney for the successful claimant must show that the fee sought is reasonable for the services rendered.[17]

Courts that approach fee determinations by looking first to the contingent-fee agreement, then testing it for reasonableness, have appropriately reduced the attorney's recovery based on the character of the representation and the results the representative achieved. *See, e.g.*, Lewis v. Secretary of Health and Human Servs., 707 F.2d 246, 249-250 (6th Cir. 1983) (instructing reduced fee

17. Specifically, petitioners maintain that "although section 406(b) permits an attorney to base a fee application on a contingent fee agreement with the claimant, the statute does not create any presumption in favor of the agreed upon amount. To the contrary, because section 406(b) requires an affirmative judicial finding that the fee allowed is 'reasonable,' the attorney bears the burden of persuasion that the statutory requirement has been satisfied."

when representation is substandard). If the attorney is responsible for delay, for example, a reduction is in order so that the attorney will not profit from the accumulation of benefits during the pendency of the case in court. If the benefits are large in comparison to the amount of time counsel spent on the case, a downward adjustment is similarly in order. In this regard, the court may require the claimant's attorney to submit, not as a basis for satellite litigation, but as an aid to the court's assessment of the reasonableness of the fee yielded by the fee agreement, a record of the hours spent representing the claimant and a statement of the lawyer's normal hourly billing charge for noncontingent-fee cases. Judges of our district courts are accustomed to making reasonableness determinations in a wide variety of contexts, and their assessments in such matters, in the event of an appeal, ordinarily qualify for highly respectful review. . . .

The courts below erroneously read §406(b) to override customary attorney-client contingent-fee agreements. We hold that §406(b) does not displace contingent-fee agreements within the statutory ceiling; instead, §406(b) instructs courts to review for reasonableness fees yielded by those agreements. Accordingly, we reverse the judgment of the Court of Appeals for the Ninth Circuit and remand the case for further proceedings consistent with this opinion. . . .

Justice SCALIA, dissenting.

. . . In my view, the only possible way to give uniform meaning to the statute's "reasonable fee" provision is to understand it as referring to the fair value of the work actually performed, which we have held is best reflected by the lodestar. . . .

I conclude that a "reasonable fee" means not the reasonableness of the agreed-upon contingent fee, but a reasonable recompense for the work actually done. We have held that this is best calculated by applying the lodestar, which focuses on the quality and amount of the legal work performed, and "provides an objective basis on which to . . . estimate . . . the value of a lawyer's services." . . .

Practice Pointers: *Fee Agreements*

The materials in this chapter demonstrate that the reasonableness requirement in Model Rule 1.5 applies to every kind of lawyer fee.[1] Statutes, case law, administrative regulation, and court rules all assume that lawyers may bargain for fees, but only within limits. When those limits are exceeded, lawyers will not be able to collect the fee they bargained for, and may be subject to professional discipline as well.[2]

Legal Regulation of Lawyer's Fees

Although professional discipline is not common in fee cases, Matter of Fordham illustrates that it is possible whenever expert witnesses will testify that a fee is unreasonable.[3] Statutes and regulations also control the amount of the fee in an increasing numbers of cases.[4] Some, like the social security act provisions in Gisbrecht v.

1. *Restatement (Third) The Law Governing Lawyers* §34 (2000).
2. *See, e.g.*, Robert L. Rossi, *Attorneys' Fees* (2d ed., Thomson 1995).
3. *See* Dale R. Agthe, *Attorney's Charging Excessive Fee as Ground for Disciplinary Action,* 11 A.L.R.4th 133 (1982).
4. *See* Rossi, *supra* note 2, at Chapter 10.

Barnhart, directly control the amount and calculation of the fee. Others, such as the federal Equal Access to Justice Act, discussed in *Gisbrecht,* provide for fee shifting, that is, the statute specifically entitles a prevailing plaintiff to recover "reasonable fees and expenses of attorneys" directly from an unsuccessful defendant.[5]

Fee-shifting provisions typically are found in statutes that encourage private attorneys general to assist in enforcing a statutory policy, such as securities, antitrust, environmental, and civil rights laws.[6] A large body of federal law has addressed the calculation of a reasonable attorney's fee under these provisions, culminating in Burlington v. Dague, where the Supreme Court held that recovery of reasonable fees under federal fee-shifting statutes requires a lodestar method of calculation, (reasonable hourly rate times reasonable number of hours expended) and does not allow for any contingency enhancement beyond the lodestar amount.[7]

Every state has similar statutes and regulations that control lawyer's fees, both in certain kinds of representations such as worker's compensation, or by providing for fee shifting in statutory actions such as consumer or securities fraud.[8] Each jurisdiction has developed its own jurisprudence about the definition of a "reasonable attorney's fee" under these statutes. Some courts allow for contingency fees or contingency enhancements in addition to a lodestar amount. Others mirror federal jurisprudence, relying solely on lodestars. Beyond these specific statutes, many states now limit the amount of all contingent fees, providing that a lawyer who charges more than the regulated amount will be deemed to have charged an unreasonable fee within the meaning of Model Rule 1.5.[9] Violations of these provisions not only subject a lawyer to discipline, but also create the basis for the client to argue that the fee contract is illegal and therefore unenforceable.[10]

Judicial control of lawyer's fees apart from statutory provisions such as those discussed in *Gisbrecht* also has become more common in the past few decades. Although judges have no general power to regulate the amount of a fee,[11] fee disputes increasingly come before courts in a number of ways.[12] Most common are suits by

---

5. Recall that the EAJA also allows the United States to avoid fees by showing that its position in the litigation was "substantially justified," a provision not commonly found in most fee-shifting statutes.

6. For a list of federal statutes with fee shifting provisions, *see* John W. Toothman & William G. Ross, *Legal Fees: Law and Management* 351-407 (Carolina Academic Press 2003).

7. Burlington v. Dague, 505 U.S. 557 (1992).

8. *See, e.g.,* Roa v. Lodi Med. Group, 695 P.2d 164 (Cal. 1985) (citing representative statutes); Rossi, *supra* note 2, §§11:79-11:87.

9. *E.g.,* N.J. Ct. R. 1:21-7 (2002); N.Y. Jud. L. §474a (2002); Fla. R. Prof. Conduct 1.5(f) (2002). Some states also require a prescribed closing statement that regulates the calculation of the contingent fee. *See, e.g.,* Ohio Rev. Code §4705.15 (2002).

10. *See, e.g.,* Fourchon Docks, Inc. v. Milchem Inc., 849 F.2d 1561 (5th Cir. 1988) (limiting a liquidated damages clause of $216,000 for lawyer's fees in a lease to a reasonable fee of $57,750); Starkey, Kelly, Blaney & White v. Estate of Nicholaysen, 796 A.2d 238 (N.J. 2002) (oral contingent fee contract not enforceable, but recovery allowed in quantum meruit); White v. McBride, 937 S.W.2d 796 (Tenn. 1996) (lawyer who charged excessive contingent fee loses both contractual rights and quantum meruit recovery); American Home Assurance Co. v. Golomb, 606 N.E.2d 793 (Ill. App. 1992) (lawyer who charged fee in excess of that allowed by state statute in medical malpractice cases barred from recovering any fee, including quantum meruit). *Cf.* Winkler v. Keane, 7 F.3d 304 (2d Cir. 1993) (lawyer's use of an illegal contingent fee in a criminal case was not grounds for reversing conviction for ineffective assistance of counsel absent actual prejudice to the defendant).

11. Gagnon v. Shoblom, 565 N.E.2d 775 (Mass. 1991) (trial judge has no power to raise issue of excessive fee *sua sponte*).

12. *See, e.g.,* Jane Massey Draper, *Excessiveness or Inadequacy of Attorney's Fees in Matters Involving Commercial and General Business Activities,* 23 A.L.R.5th 241 (1994); Jane Massey Draper, *Excessiveness or Adequacy of Attorneys' Fees in Domestic Relations Cases,* 17 A.L.R.5th 366 (1994); John E. Theuman, *Excessiveness or Adequacy of Attorneys' Fees in Matters Involving Real Estate—Modern Cases,* 10 A.L.R.5th 448 (1993).

lawyers to recover unpaid fees. Clients also may sue to claim refunds or disgorgement of fees already paid. Model Rule 1.6(b)(5) recognizes the right of a lawyer to use confidential information to bring such a suit, and many lawyers successfully recover sums from clients who unjustly refuse to pay. On the other hand, one constant problem with fee suits is procedural: any invocation of the court's jurisdiction may result in a counterclaim for other behavior the client might not otherwise have contested. For example, clients have raised claims about sexual misconduct in the context of a fee suit, and counterclaims for malpractice also are common.[13]

Courts also have jurisdiction to consider the reasonableness of the fee because of other obligations. For example, lawyers who serve as fiduciaries are subject to the power of a probate court to examine and approve expenditures against an estate.[14] In cases that involve juveniles or other persons who lack legal capacity, courts have a similar responsibility to approve fees as part of their *parens patriae* power to protect the ward.[15] In class actions, court approval is required for fees that come from any common fund generated by settlement or judgment.[16] Bankruptcy proceedings also require judicial approval of lawyer's fees because of the court's supervision over the costs of administering the estate.[17]

All of this legal regulation means that many fees routinely are reviewed by courts or are subject to explicit legal regulation by statute or court rule. Beyond this specific oversight, any fee also can come to a court's attention by virtue of a suit to recover a promised or already paid fee. Many jurisdictions have established fee arbitration systems to promote alternatives to formal lawsuits.[18] Like the judges called on in lawsuits to decide when fees are payable or refundable, the arbitrators who rule or make recommendations in these cases also rely on the factors set forth in Model Rule 1.5.

Fee Agreements

The best way to avoid fee disputes is to communicate the basis or rate of the fee and the client's responsibility for costs and expenses in a written document. Model Rule 1.5(c) already requires written contingent fees agreements, which all but a few jurisdictions have implemented without much difficulty. In addition, ten jurisdictions currently require that *all* fee agreements be reduced to a writing.[19] In spite of

13. *See, e.g.*, Barbara A. v. John G., 193 Cal. Rptr. 422 (Cal. App. 1983); McDaniel v. Gile, 281 Cal. Rptr. 242 (Cal. App. 1991); Ronald E. Mallen & Jeffrey M. Smith, *Legal Malpractice* §15.9 (5th ed., West 2000).
14. Rossi, *supra* note 2, §§11:39-11:60.
15. *E.g.*, Hoffert v. General Motors Corp., 656 F.2d 161 (5th Cir. 1981) (upholding trial court's reduction of 40 percent contingent fee contract for a minor to 20 percent of the recovery). Recall that in Spaulding v. Zimmerman, *supra* p.161, the court relied on this same *parens patriae* power to justify reopening the judgment under the Minnesota equivalent of Fed. R. Civ. P. 60.
16. *E.g.*, Lealao v. Beneficial California, Inc., 97 Cal. Rptr. 2d 797 (Cal. App. 2000) (trial court had discretion to adjust lodestar in successful $14 million consumer class action by applying a multiplier where necessary to insure that the fee awarded would be within the range of fees freely negotiated in the legal marketplace in comparable litigation); Bowling v. Pfizer, Inc., 922 F. Supp. 1261, 1283 (S.D. Ohio 1996), *aff'd*, 132 F.3d 98 (6th Cir. 1998) (lawyer's fee in successful and valuable class action reduced by 2/3 because work was "not even remotely commensurate" with the amount requested). For a discussion of particular applications of this doctrine, *see* Rossi, *supra* note 2, at Chapter 6.
17. *See, e.g.*, Watkins v. Sedberry, 261 U.S. 571 (1923); Rossi, *supra* note 2, at §§10:10-10:15.
18. *See, e.g.*, ABA Model Rules for Fee Arbitration (1995); Fla. Bar Reg. Rule 14-5 (2002). *See also* Disc. Counsel v. McCord, 770 N.E.2d 571 (Ohio 2002) (lawyer who failed to return fee following an arbitration award to his client suspended for six months for conduct prejudicial to the administration of justice); Guralnick v. N.J. S. Ct., 747 F. Supp. 1109 (D.N.J. 1990), *aff'd*, 961 F.2d 209 (3d Cir. 1992) (N.J. system of compulsory binding arbitration for lawyer-client fee disputes not unconstitutional).
19. Alaska R. Prof. Conduct 1.5(b) (2003) (over $500); Cal. Bus. & Prof. Code §6147 (2003); Colo. R. Prof. Conduct 1.5(b) (2003); Conn. R. Prof. Conduct 1.5(b) (2003); D.C. R. Prof. Conduct 1.5(b) (2003);

this growing trend toward written fee agreements, the ABA has twice refused to amend Model Rule 1.5(b) to require a written communication of every fee.[20]

Yet, the cases in this chapter make clear that fee agreements do produce misunderstandings and for that reason are increasingly subject to overt regulation. One recent case upheld a jury verdict of breach of fiduciary duty against a lawyer who failed to reduce a fee agreement to writing after his client requested a written document. The lack of documentation cost the lawyer all but $11,000 of the $100,000 fee to which he claimed entitlement.[21]

A written fee agreement also gives clients and lawyers the opportunity to consider alternative fee structures. This chapter focuses primarily on the common fee arrangements: hourly, contingent, and flat fees. Lawyers and clients are becoming increasingly creative in creating other options. Some adopt blended hourly fees, where the client pays a set rate regardless of which lawyer performs the work. Others prefer retainer plus fees, which supplement monthly retainers with an hourly fee when the lawyer works more than an agreed upon number of hours per month. Task-based fees, which break or unbundle a representation into different legal tasks, such as complaint drafting, negotiation, or interrogatories also are becoming more common, along with work-unit fees, which allocate flat fees by a client-determined unit such as number of lots sold.[22]

Finally, fee disputes are not uncommon, and written documents not only may avoid them but also clarify the respective rights of both client and lawyer if they do occur. Thus, while it is possible that you may practice in an area of law where fee contracts are not overtly regulated, the best practice nonetheless is to provide your clients with a written document that communicates both "the scope of the representation and the basis or rate of the fee and expenses for which the client will be responsible."[23] The effort you invest in providing such a writing will more than be repaid in client understanding and goodwill, and if necessary, in forming the basis for the resolution of a fee dispute.

Fee Collection

Of course, lawyers not only must provide clients with clear fee agreements, but also abide by their provisions in charging and collecting their fees, and provide clarifications where necessary.[24] Lawyers who amend fee contracts after the representation has commenced are subject to the law of undue influence designed to enforce their fiduciary obligations to clients. This means that changes to initial agreements are subject to general conflict of interest rules and voidable by the client.[25]

N.J. R. Prof. Conduct 1.5(b) (2003); N.Y. DR 2-106(c)(2)(ii) (domestic relations matters); Pa. R. Prof. Conduct 1.5(b) (2003); R.I. R. Prof. Conduct 1.5(b) (2003); Utah R. Prof. Conduct 1.5(b) (2003) (over $750).

20. The ABA House of Delegates defeated both the Kutak Commission proposal in 1983 and the Ethics 2000 proposal in 2001 that would have required a written communication to the client about the scope of the representation and the basis or rate of the fee. Recall that the House of Delegates recently opted for a writing requirement for conflicts waivers. *See* Practice Pointers: Written Consents to Conflicts of Interest, *supra* p.322. Can you make a principled distinction between these outcomes?

21. Frazier v. Boyle, 206 F.R.D. 480 (E.D. Wis. 2002).

22. *ABA Panelists Look into Whys and Hows of Moving to Different Fee Arrangements*, 18 ABA/BNA Lawyers' Manual on Prof. Conduct 485 (2002).

23. Model Rule 1.5(b).

24. Cox's Case, 813 A.2d 429 (N.H. 2002) (lawyer who failed to respond to client's request for accounting data reprimanded for violating MR 1.4 and 1.15(b)).

25. Brown & Sturm v. Frederick Road Ltd. Partn., 768 A.2d 62 (Md. Ct. Spec. App. 2001); Mallen & Smith, *supra* note 13.

Lawyers who execute otherwise valid fee contracts also engage in what ABA Opinion 93-379 called "problematic billing practices." Unfortunately, some of these practices include fraud. For example, Professor Lerman has documented the practices of 16 well-respected lawyers who engaged in blatant billing and expense fraud.[26] Another survey finds that more subtle deception, ranging from performing unnecessary work and "estimating" billable hours to deliberately padding bills or expenses, occurs more than occasionally.[27] Of course, if deliberate, these practices constitute fraud,[28] and if done repeatedly, mail or wire fraud under state and federal criminal statutes.[29] We have seen that a clear and serious violation of a lawyer's duty to a client also constitutes grounds for total or partial fee forfeiture.[30] Further, sloppy or negligent billing that does not accurately reflect the agreement or the time spent may be grounds for a breach of contract, malpractice, or breach of fiduciary duty claim.[31] State consumer fraud laws also have been used against lawyers who engage in deceptive billing practices.[32]

Lawyers and law firms must monitor the accuracy of fee billings to prevent both intentional and inadvertent wrongdoing. The power of clients to discharge lawyers at any time discussed in the next two cases, *Rosenberg* and *Sather,* means that regardless of the nature of the fee agreement, every lawyer must keep records of time actually spent on each matter to be able to establish the alternative basis for quantum meruit recovery. Billing systems should include efficient and nearly simultaneous recording of time. Good record keeping also serves to document adherence to contractual terms, and provides the basis for lawyers to recover fees against clients who refuse to honor their own obligations. In law firms, no lawyer should have carte blanche to send out any bill he or she wishes.[33] Lawyers who lose their fees or are subject to damages in civil actions usually bind their law firms as well. Model Rule 5.1 also makes supervisory lawyers responsible for violations by other lawyers in their firms.

---

26. Lisa G. Lerman, *Blue-Chip Bilking: Regulation of Billing and Expense Fraud by Lawyers,* 12 Geo. J. Legal Ethics 205 (1999). For example, one judge described the practices of one of these lawyers as "almost fictional," because they included nearly $100,000 billed for services that were never performed, nearly $500,000 for work done by paralegals that was actually performed by secretaries and a receptionist, and $66,000 for legal research that cost the firm $395. His partners helped cover up the fraud when complaints were made. *Id.* at 238. *See also* Dresser Indus. v. Digges, 1989 U.S. Dist. LEXIS 17396. Because the conduct was fraudulent, a later case determined that the law firm's insurer had no contractual obligation to pay the judgment the client obtained against the firm. St. Paul Fire & Marine Ins. Co. v. Dresser Indus., 1992 U.S. App. LEXIS 18561 (4th Cir.). The lawyer pled guilty to one count of mail fraud and was sentenced to 30 months in prison, and ordered to pay $1 million in restitution to the client and a $30,000 fine. Lerman, *supra,* at 264.

27. *See* William G. Ross, *The Honest Hour: The Ethics of Time-based Billing by Attorneys* 23-38 (Carolina Academic Press 1996); Lisa G. Lerman, *Lying to Clients,* 138 U. Penn. L. Rev. 659, 705 (1990). The bill padding was accomplished by billing for hours not actually worked, or by "premium billing," which adds lump sums to a bill based on the lawyer's subjective determination of its value. *Id.* at 709-715.

28. *See, e.g.,* Ratcliff v. Boydell, 674 S.2d 272 (La. App. 1996) (lawyer who misrepresented amount of client's annuity at settlement to increase his contingent fee and later sued client for defamation and malicious prosecution liable for fraud, intentional infliction of emotional distress, and abuse of process); Cantu v. Butron, 921 S.W.2d 344 (Tex. App. 1996) (lawyers who increased fee from 40 to 45 percent liable for fraud and breach of fiduciary duty, including punitive damages).

29. Lerman, *supra* note 26, at 263-271 (detailing criminal prosecutions of nine lawyers for billing fraud); *id.* at 282-287 (detailing civil penalties in 16 cases of billing fraud).

30. *E.g., Golomb, supra* note 10 (total fee forfeiture of illegal fee that violated state statute); Limits of the Law: Loss of Fee or Other Benefits, *supra* p.**291**.

31. *See, e.g.,* Lerman, *supra* note 27, at 696-698; Cripe v. Leiter, 703 N.E.2d 100 (Ill. 1998) (citing cases).

32. Lerman, *supra* note 27, at 698-699.

33. Ross, *supra* note 27, at 249-260.

To sum up: lawyers have every right to be compensated for their work, as long as the compensation is reasonable. To protect yourself, and increase your chances of avoiding or winning a fee dispute, you should reduce fee agreements to a writing or include them in written retainer agreements,[34] and you should keep accurate records of the time you spend on each client matter. The time these tasks take will more than repay you in client goodwill,[35] and eventual recovery of adequate compensation.

D. Fees on Termination

Problem

7-8. Martyn & Fox agrees to defend Client's breach of contract action for a flat fee of $20,000. Six months later, after extensive discovery, Client fires us, saying, "I just like the lawyers down the block better," and demands a refund of $15,000. What should Martyn & Fox do? Does it matter if we've already spent $25,000 in time on the matter?

Consider: Model Rules 1.5, 1.15
RLGL §40

Rosenberg v. Levin

409 So. 2d 1016 (Fla. 1982)

... OVERTON, J.

... The issue to be decided concerns the proper basis for compensating an attorney discharged without cause by his client after he has performed substantial legal services under a valid contract of employment....

We hold that a lawyer discharged without cause is entitled to the reasonable value of his services on the basis of quantum meruit, but recovery is limited to the maximum fee set in the contract entered into for those services. We have concluded that without this limitation, the client would be penalized for the discharge and the lawyer would receive more than he bargained for in his initial contract....

The facts of this case reflect the following. Levin hired Rosenberg and Pomerantz to perform legal services pursuant to a letter agreement which provided for a $10,000 fixed fee, plus a contingent fee equal to fifty percent of all amounts recovered in excess of $600,000. Levin later discharged Rosenberg and Pomerantz without cause before the legal controversy was resolved and subsequently settled the matter for a net recovery of $500,000. Rosenberg and Pomerantz sued for fees based on a "quantum meruit" evaluation of their services. After lengthy testimony, the trial judge concluded that quantum meruit was indeed the appropriate basis for compensation and awarded Rosenberg and Pomerantz

34. *See* Practice Pointers: Engagement, Nonengagement, and Disengagement Letters, *supra* p.79.
35. *See, e.g.*, Avi Azrieli, *Your Lawyer on a Short Leash: A Survivor's Guide to Dealing with Lawyers* 125-138 (Bridge St. 1997).

$55,000. The district court also agreed that quantum meruit was the appropriate basis for recovery but lowered the amount awarded to $10,000, stating that recovery could in no event exceed the amount which the attorneys would have received under their contract if not prematurely discharged.

The issue submitted to us for resolution is whether the terms of an attorney employment contract limit the attorney's quantum meruit recovery to the fee set out in the contract....

There are two conflicting interests involved in the determination of the issue presented in this type of attorney-client dispute. The first is the need of the client to have confidence in the integrity and ability of his attorney and, therefore, the need for the client to have the ability to discharge his attorney when he loses that necessary confidence in the attorney. The second is the attorney's right to adequate compensation for work performed. To address these conflicting interests, we must consider three distinct rules.

CONTRACT RULE

The traditional contract rule adopted by a number of jurisdictions holds that an attorney discharged without cause may recover damages for breach of contract under traditional contract principles. The measure of damages is usually the full contract price, although some courts deduct a fair allowance for services and expenses not expended by the discharged attorney in performing the balance of the contract. *E.g.*, Bockman v. Rorex, 208 S.W.2d 991 (Ark. 1948) (fixed fee contract); Tonn v. Reuter, 95 N.W.2d 261 (Wis. 1959). Some jurisdictions following the contract rule also permit an alternative recovery based on quantum meruit so that an attorney can elect between recovery based on the contract or the reasonable value of the performed services. *E.g.*, In re Downs, 363 S.W.2d 679 (Mo. 1963); French v. Cunningham, 49 N.E. 797 (Ind. 1898).

Support for the traditional contract theory is based on: (1) the full contract price is arguably the most rational measure of damages since it reflects the value that the parties placed on the services; (2) charging the full fee prevents the client from profiting from his own breach of contract; and (3) the contract rule is said to avoid the difficult problem of setting a value on an attorney's partially completed legal work.

QUANTUM MERUIT RULE

To avoid restricting a client's freedom to discharge his attorney, a number of jurisdictions in recent years have held that an attorney discharged without cause can recover only the reasonable value services rendered prior to discharge.... This rule was first announced in Martin v. Camp, 114 N.E. 46 (N.Y. 1916), where the New York Court of Appeals held that a discharged attorney could not sue his client for damages for breach of contract unless the attorney had completed performance of the contract. The New York court established quantum meruit recovery for the attorney on the theory that the client does not breach the contract by discharging the attorney. Rather, the court reasoned, there is an implied condition in every attorney-client contract that the client may discharge the attorney at any time with or without cause. With this right as part of the contract, traditional contract principles are applied to allow quantum meruit recovery on the basis of services performed to date. Under the New York rule, the attorney's cause of action accrues immediately upon his discharge by the client, under the reasoning that it is unfair to make the attorney's right to compensation dependent on the performance of a successor over whom he has no control.

The California Supreme Court, in Fracasse v. Brent, 494 P.2d 9 (Cal. 1972), also adopted a quantum meruit rule. That court carefully analyzed those factors which distinguish the attorney-client relationship from other employment situations and concluded that a discharged attorney should be limited to a quantum meruit recovery in order to strike a proper balance between the client's right to discharge his attorney without undue restriction and the attorney's right to fair compensation for work performed. The *Fracasse* court sought both to provide clients greater freedom in substituting counsel and to promote confidence in the legal profession while protecting society's interest in the attorney-client relationship.

Contrary to the New York rule, however, the California court also held that an attorney's cause of action for quantum meruit does not accrue until the happening of the contingency, that is, the client's recovery. If no recovery is forthcoming, the attorney is denied compensation. The California court offered two reasons in support of its position. First, the result obtained and the amount involved, two important factors in determining the reasonableness of a fee, cannot be ascertained until the occurrence of the contingency. Second, the client may be of limited means and it would be unduly burdensome to force him to pay a fee if there was no recovery. The court stated that: "(S)ince the attorney agreed initially to take his chances on recovering any fee whatever, we believe that the fact that the success of the litigation is no longer under his control is insufficient to justify imposing a new and more onerous burden on the client."

QUANTUM MERUIT RULE LIMITED BY THE CONTRACT PRICE

The third rule is an extension of the second that limits quantum meruit recovery to the maximum fee set in the contract. This limitation is believed necessary to provide client freedom to substitute attorneys without economic penalty. Without such a limitation, a client's right to discharge an attorney may be illusory and the client may in effect be penalized for exercising a right.

The Tennessee Court of Appeals, in Chambliss, Bahner & Crawford v. Luther, 531 S.W.2d 108 (Tenn. App. 1975), expressed the need for limitation on quantum meruit recovery, stating: "It would seem to us that the better rule is that because a client has the unqualified right to discharge his attorney, fees in such cases should be limited to the value of the services rendered or the contract price, whichever is less." In rejecting the argument that quantum meruit should be the basis for the recovery even though it exceeds the contract fee, that court said:

> To adopt the rule advanced by Plaintiff would, in our view, encourage attorneys less keenly aware of their professional responsibilities than Attorney Chambliss, . . . to induce clients to lose confidence in them in cases where the reasonable value of their services has exceeded the original fee and thereby, upon being discharged, reap a greater benefit than that for which they had bargained.

Other authorities also support this position.

CONCLUSION

. . . It is our opinion that it is in the best interest of clients and the legal profession as a whole that we adopt the modified quantum meruit rule which limits recovery to the maximum amount of the contract fee in all premature discharge cases involving both fixed and contingency employment contracts. The attorney-client relationship is one of special trust and confidence. The client must rely entirely on the good faith efforts of the attorney in representing his interests. This reliance requires that the client have complete confidence in the integrity and ability of the attorney and that absolute fairness and candor characterize all dealings between them. These considerations dictate that clients be given greater freedom to change legal representatives than might be tolerated in other employment relationships. We approve the philosophy that there is an overriding need to allow clients freedom to substitute attorneys without economic penalty as a means of accomplishing the broad objective of fostering public confidence in the legal profession. Failure to limit quantum meruit recovery defeats the policy against penalizing the client for exercising his right to discharge. However, attorneys should not be penalized either and should have the opportunity to recover for services performed.

Accordingly, we hold that an attorney employed under a valid contract who is discharged without cause before the contingency has occurred or before the client's matters have concluded can recover only the reasonable value of his services rendered prior to discharge, limited by the maximum contract fee. We reject both the traditional contract rule and the quantum meruit rule that allow recovery in excess of the maximum contract price because both have a chilling effect on the client's power to discharge an attorney. Under the contract rule in a contingent fee situation, both the discharged attorney and the second attorney may receive a substantial percentage of the client's final recovery. Under the unlimited quantum meruit rule, it is possible, as the instant case illustrates, for the attorney to receive a fee greater than he bargained for under the terms of his contract. Both these results are unacceptable to us.

We further follow the California view that in contingency fee cases, the cause of action for quantum meruit arises only upon the successful occurrence of the contingency. If the client fails in his recovery, the discharged attorney will similarly fail and recover nothing.... There should, of course, be a presumption of regularity and competence in the performance of the services by a successor attorney.

In computing the reasonable value of the discharged attorney's services, the trial court can consider the totality of the circumstances surrounding the professional relationship between the attorney and client. Factors such as time, the recovery sought, the skill demanded, the results obtained, and the attorney-client contract itself will necessarily be relevant considerations.

We conclude that this approach creates the best balance between the desirable right of the client to discharge his attorney and the right of an attorney to reasonable compensation for his services.... We find the district court of appeal was correct in limiting the quantum meruit award to the contract price, and its decision is approved....

In re Sather

3 P.3d 403 (Colo. 2000)

En Banc ...

Justice Bender delivered the Opinion of the Court.

I. INTRODUCTION

In this attorney regulation proceeding, we address the conduct of the attorney-respondent, Larry D. Sather, who spent and failed to place into a trust account $20,000 he received as a "non-refundable" advance fee for a civil case. Because Sather treated these funds as his own property before earning the fee, Sather's conduct violated Colo. RPC 1.15(a). Sather labeled the $20,000 fee "non-refundable" even though he knew that the fee was subject to refund under certain circumstances, thereby violating Colo. RPC 8.4(c). After being discharged by his client, Sather failed to return all of the unearned portion of the $20,000 promptly, in violation of Colo. RPC 1.16(d).

In this original proceeding, we hold that an attorney earns fees by conferring a benefit on or performing a legal service for the client. Thus, under Colo. RPC 1.15 an attorney cannot treat advance fees as property of the attorney and must segregate all advance fees by placing them into a trust account until such time as the fees are earned.... An attorney cannot label advance fees "non-refundable" because it misleads the client and risks impermissibly burdening the client's right to discharge his attorney, in violation of Colo. RPC 8.4(c) and 1.16(d).

Because we have not previously explained that all advance fees, including "lump-sum" fees and "flat fees," must be placed into trust accounts and withdrawn only as the attorney performs services or confers benefits on the client, we do not impose a sanction on Sather for his violation of Colo. RPC 1.15(a). However, we agree with the hearing board that Sather be disciplined for violating Colo. RPC 1.16(d) and 8.4(c). Because Sather knowingly mishandled client funds and knowingly deceived a client, and in light of Sather's disciplinary history, we suspend Larry D. Sather for six months....

II. FACTS AND PROCEDURAL BACKGROUND

The hearing board found the following facts were established by clear and convincing evidence. Sather agreed to represent Franklin Perez in a lawsuit against the Colorado State Patrol and certain individual troopers. Perez alleged that the troopers violated his civil rights during a traffic stop on December 7, 1995. Almost a year after the stop, on November 15, 1996, Sather and Perez entered into a written agreement for legal services, captioned "Minimum Fee Contract." Sather drafted the agreement, the terms of which required Perez to pay Sather $20,000 plus costs to represent Perez in the case against the State Patrol. Sather testified that he had never charged this large an amount as a flat fee in a civil case.

The contract referred to the $20,000 alternatively as a "minimum fee," a "non-refundable fee," and a "flat fee." The contract stated that Perez understood his obligation to pay this fee "regardless of the number of hours attorneys devote to [his] legal matter" and that no portion of the fee would be refunded "regardless of the time or effort involved or the result obtained." The contract acknowledged Perez's right to discharge Sather as his attorney, but the contract informed Perez that in no circumstance would any of the funds paid be refunded:

> IN ALL EVENTS, NO REFUND SHALL BE MADE OF ANY PORTION OF THE MINIMUM FEE PAID, REGARDLESS OF THE AMOUNT OF TIME EXPENDED BY THE FIRM.
>
> The client has been advised that this is an agreed flat fee contract. The client acknowledges that the minimum flat fee is the agreed upon amount of $20,000, regardless of the time or effort involved or the result obtained.

Thus, the contract stipulated that Perez pay Sather $20,000 for his legal services; that he pay all legal costs incurred by Sather in the case; and that no funds would be refundable after Perez paid Sather the flat fee of $20,000.[3]

Perez paid Sather $5,000 of the minimum fee on November 17, 1996.

3. In contrast to the contract's language, Sather testified that he knew that the fees were subject to refund and that he "never treated the fees as non-refundable."

He paid the remaining $15,000 on December 16th. Sather spent the $5,000 soon after receiving the money. Sather kept the second payment of $15,000 for approximately one month before spending these funds. Sather did not place any of these funds in his trust account before spending them. Sather testified that he spent Perez's $20,000 because he believed he earned the fees upon receipt. Sather stated that while he could not cite a specific rule for this opinion, he thought it was a common practice in the legal community to treat flat fees as being earned on receipt.

Less than a month after agreeing to represent Perez, on December 6, 1996, Sather filed suit in Denver District Court on behalf of Perez against the State Patrol and three troopers. In addition to claims for tort and civil rights injuries, the complaint included a claim for attorney's fees. The Attorney General's Office, which represented the State Patrol and three troopers, negotiated with Sather and offered Perez a $6,000 settlement, which Perez refused. Sather then requested an extension of time to respond to a pretrial motion, which the court granted.

On April 21, 1997, in a matter unrelated to the Perez case, this court suspended Sather from the practice of law for thirty days, effective May 21, 1997. *See* People v. Sather, 936 P.2d 576, 579 (Colo. 1997). As required, Sather notified Perez of his suspension and Perez responded on May 23, requesting an accounting of the hours Sather worked on his case. Perez requested that Sather provide the accounting by May 30, but Sather replied that he would be unable to provide this information until the third week of June. Thereafter, on June 4, 1997, Perez faxed Sather notice discharging him from his case because of the suspension.

Acting pro se, Perez received an extension of time to file a response to the State Patrol's motion after informing the court that he was seeking replacement counsel to handle the case. Then, on August 21, 1997, Perez wrote a letter to the Attorney General's Office, accepting the offer of $6,000 to settle all of his claims against the State Patrol and the troopers....

Sather provided the accounting requested by Perez on June 27, 1997. Sather claimed that his fees, his paralegal assistant's fees, costs and expenses in Perez's case as of the date of discharge totaled $6,923.64. At that time, Sather acknowledged that he should refund $13,076.36, the balance of the $20,000 paid by Perez.

Despite acknowledging his duty to return the unearned $13,076.36 to Perez, Sather did not refund any money to Perez because at the time of discharge he had spent Perez's funds. On September 3, 1997—three months after Perez discharged him—Sather paid Perez $3,000. Sather paid the remaining $10,076.36 on November 2, 1997. The hearing board found that this delay prejudiced Perez because he did not have access to his funds for almost five months.

At the time Sather and Perez entered into the flat fee agreement, Sather was involved in personal bankruptcy proceedings. Sather filed a Chapter 7 bankruptcy proceeding in U.S. Bankruptcy Court in March 1995, over a year before agreeing to represent Perez. Sather later converted this case to a Chapter 13 proceeding, and then attempted to reconvert the case to a Chapter 7 filing. At the time of the hearing, the bankruptcy case was still pending. During the representation, Sather never told Perez that he had declared bankruptcy. After discharging Sather, Perez hired an attorney to pursue a claim against Sather in the bankruptcy proceeding for a refund of the fees ($6,923.64) Sather charged for work on Perez's suit.

Much later, in June 1998, Perez and Sather agreed to an arbitration by the Colorado Bar Association concerning the amount of fees charged by Sather for his work. The arbitrator awarded Perez $2,100.00, which represented the cost to Perez to bring the arbitration action. The arbitrator did not award Perez any recovery of the fees Sather charged for work performed. Shortly before the hearing in this case, on November 17, 1998, Sather paid Perez the award....

III. DISCUSSION . . .

A. Colo. RPC 1.15 Requires Segregation of Attorney and Client Property

Initially, we address Colo. RPC 1.15(a), which requires that an attorney keep client funds separate from the attorney's own property....

In addition to this subsection of the rule, Colo. RPC 1.15(f)(1) . . . requires that an attorney maintain client funds submitted to the attorney as advance fees in a separate trust account until the attorney earns the fees.... Thus, Colo. RPC 1.15(a) and (f) indicate that an attorney has an obligation to keep clients' funds separate from his own, and that advance fees remain the property of the client until such time as the fees are "earned."

The rule requiring that an attorney segregate funds advanced by the client from the attorney's own funds serves important interests. As a fiduciary to the client, one of an attorney's primary responsibilities is to safeguard the interests and property of the client over which the attorney has control. *See Restatement (Third) of the Law Governing Lawyers* §56 cmt. (b) (Proposed Final Draft No. 1 1996) [hereinafter Draft Restatement]. Requiring the attorney to segregate all client funds—including advance fees—from the attorney's own accounts unless and until the funds become the attorney's property protects the client's property from the attorney's creditors and from misuse by the attorney. Thus, Colo. RPC 1.15(a) and (f) further the attorney's fiduciary obligation to protect client property.

In addition to protecting client property, requiring an attorney to keep advance fees in trust until they are earned protects the client's right to discharge an attorney. Upon discharge, the attorney must return all unearned fees in a timely manner, even though the attorney may be entitled to quantum meruit recovery for the services that the attorney rendered and for costs incurred on behalf of the client.

If an attorney suggests to a client that any pre-paid or advance funds are "non-refundable" or constitute the attorney's property regardless of how much or how little work the attorney performs for the client, then the client may fear loss of the funds and may refrain from exercising his right to discharge the attorney....

B. An Attorney Earns Fees by Conferring a Benefit on or Providing a Service for the Client

... When a client pays an attorney before the attorney provides legal services, the crucial issue becomes whether funds are "earned on receipt" and may be treated as the attorney's property, or whether the fees are unearned, in which case the funds must be segregated in a trust account under Colo. RPC 1.15. As one publication aptly framed this dilemma:

> The basic question is, Whose money is it? If it's the client's money in whole or in part, it is subject to the trust account requirements. If it is the lawyer's money, placing it into a trust account would violate the anti-commingling rule. ABA/BNA *Lawyers' Manual on Professional Conduct* 45:109 (1993).

We hold that an attorney earns fees only by conferring a benefit on or performing a legal service for the client.

Unless the attorney provides some benefit or service in exchange for the fee, the attorney has not earned any fees and, with a possible exception in very limited circumstances, the attorney cannot treat advance fees as her property.

Funds given by clients to attorneys as advance fees or retainers benefit attorneys and clients. Some forms of advance fees or retainers appropriately compensate an attorney when the fee is paid because the attorney makes commitments to the client that benefit the client immediately. Such an arrangement is termed a "general retainer" or "engagement retainer," and these retainers typically compensate an attorney for agreeing to take a case, which requires the attorney to commit his time to the client's case and causes the attorney to forego other potential employment opportunities as a result of time commitments or conflicts. Although an attorney usually earns an engagement retainer by agreeing to take the client's case, an attorney can also earn a fee charged as an engagement retainer by placing the client's work at the top of the attorney's priority list. Or the client may pay an engagement retainer merely to prevent the attorney from being available to represent an opposing party. In all of these instances, the attorney is providing some benefit to the client in exchange for the engagement retainer fee.

In contrast to engagement retainers, a client may advance funds—often referred to as "advance fees," "special retainers," "lump sum fees," or "flat fees"—to pay for specified legal services to be performed by the attorney and to cover future costs. We note that unless the fee agreement expressly states that a fee is an engagement retainer and explains how the fee is earned upon receipt, we will presume that any advance fee is a deposit from which an attorney will be paid for specified legal services.

Advance fees present an attractive option for both the client and the attorney. Like engagement retainers, advance fees allow clients to secure their choice of counsel. Additionally, some forms of advance fees, e.g., "lump sums" or "flat fees," benefit the client by establishing before representation the maximum amount of fees that the client must pay.... So long as the fees are reasonable, such arrangements do not violate ethical rules governing attorney fees.

Advance fees benefit the attorney because the attorney can secure payment for future legal services, eliminating the risk of non-payment after the attorney does the work.... Attorneys often deduct costs from advance payments as they incur the costs, similar to the manner in which they deduct their fees as they are earned. Advance fees represent an alternative method of obtaining legal assistance that accommodates legitimate needs of both clients and attorneys, and by this opinion we do not intend to discourage these fee arrangements provided the fee agreements comply with the ethical principles discussed in this case....

C. "Non-refundable" Fees

Having discussed the ethical principle requiring that attorneys maintain in trust all advance fees until the attorney earns the fees, we address Sather's characterization of his fee as "non-refundable." Because fees are always subject to refund under certain conditions, labeling a fee "non-refundable" misleads the client and may deter a client from exercising their rights to refunds of unearned fees under Colo. 1.16(d). Thus, we hold that attorneys cannot enter into "non-refundable" retainer or fee agreements....

In the limited circumstances in which an attorney earns fees before performing any legal services (i.e., engagement retainers) or where an attorney and client agree that the attorney can treat advance fees as the attorney's property before the attorney earns the fees by supplying a benefit or performing a service, the fee agreement must clearly explain the basis for this arrangement and explain how the client's rights are protected by the arrangement. In either of these situations, however, an attorney's fees are always subject to refund if excessive or unearned, and an attorney cannot communicate otherwise to a client....

general/ engagement retainer

IV. DISCIPLINE OF ATTORNEY-RESPONDENT SATHER ...

...[W]e agree with the board's conclusion that Sather violated Colo. RPC 1.16(d) by only partially repaying Perez's advance fee three months after being discharged and paying the balance of the refund five months after being discharged.... A discharged attorney must refund unearned fees in a timely fashion and failure to do so is a violation of Colo. RPC 1.16(d). Upon discharge, Sather acknowledged his obligation to return the unearned portion of the $20,000 to Perez, and Sather eventually returned the entire unearned amount of $13,076.36. Perez claimed that he was unable to retain alternate counsel because he did not have access to those funds after he discharged Sather, and the board concluded that his inability to use those funds caused harm to Perez. Because Sather only partially returned the unearned fees three months after being discharged and did not return the remainder of the unearned fees until five months after being discharged, we agree with the board that his conduct violated Colo. RPC 1.16(d).

We also agree with the board's determination that Sather violated Colo. 8.4(c) by materially misrepresenting to Perez the nature of the fee he paid. Colo. RPC 8.4(c) prohibits attorneys from engaging in conduct that involves "dishonesty, fraud, deceit, or misrepresentation." The fee agreement Sather drafted clearly expressed that the $20,000 was non-refundable, irrespective of the number of hours Sather spent on the case, and that "*In All Events, No Refund Shall Be Made Of Any Portion*" of the $20,000. (Emphasis in original.) Despite this strong language of the contract he drafted, Sather testified that he understood his ethical obligation to return any unearned portion of the fees in the event of discharge. We approve of the board's finding that Sather knowingly used misleading language to describe the fee arrangement and knowingly made a material misrepresentation to his client concerning the $20,000 advance fee. Thus, we accept the board's finding that Sather's conduct involved dishonesty, deceit, fraud and misrepresentation in violation of Colo. RPC 8.4(c)....

Practice Pointers: *Trust Fund Management*

The Colorado Supreme Court disciplined lawyer Sather for failing to repay his client's advance fee after being discharged and for materially misrepresenting the nature of the fee as "nonrefundable." Lawyers like those in *Rosenberg* who are prematurely discharged without cause also may be forced to repay some or all of their client's previous payments. *Sather* represents the view shared by nearly every jurisdiction: knowing violations of rules that require segregation of client funds will result in severe discipline, even when client's interests are not otherwise compromised.[1]

1. *See, e.g.,* Douglas' Case, 809 A.2d 755 (N.H. 2002) (lawyer who improperly withdrew funds from client trust account in the "startlingly erroneous" belief that withdrawal was proper suspended from practice

Until the turn of the twentieth century, lawyers commonly commingled their client's funds with their own. Stock market crashes in both England and America led to a reexamination of professional accounting requirements, and eventually to the requirement in the 1908 ABA Canons of Professional Ethics that lawyers could not commingle client funds with lawyer operating accounts.[2]

The Code of Professional Responsibility tightened this obligation in DR 9-102, by requiring clear separation of client funds in "one or more identifiable bank accounts" and complete record keeping that would enable a lawyer to "render appropriate accounts to his client."[3] It also provided that any funds belonging to both lawyer and client be deposited in the client trust account. Any portion of the disputed amount must remain in the trust account until the dispute was resolved. Model Rule 1.15, discussed in *Sather*, also mandates separation of client and lawyer funds, record keeping, and the retention of any disputed fees or funds in the trust account.[4] Rule 1.15(e) further requires that the lawyer must "promptly distribute all portions of the property as to which the interests are not in dispute."

Yet, in spite of these requirements, so many clients have been the victims of lawyers who have "borrowed" or stolen client funds that many jurisdictions have adopted additional specific rules that govern trust account management.[5] By 1976, nearly every jurisdiction had created a client protection fund, financed by assessments on all lawyers, which reimburses clients who have been the victims of lawyer theft.

In addition, some jurisdictions require that lawyers keep specific records recommended by the ABA Model Rule on Financial Recordkeeping. Fourteen jurisdictions require a ledger for each client showing the source of all funds deposited, the name and description of payees, and the amount of all deposits and payments.[6] Ten further require that lawyers maintain journals, which record receipts and disbursements from all law practice bank accounts.[7] Others require that banks notify disciplinary authorities of any overdrafts in a trust account.[8] A few even require audits of trust accounts.[9]

---

for six months); Atty. Grievance Commn. v. Hayes, 789 A.2d 119 (Md. 2002) (lawyer who operated practice for 30 years using only a trust account suspended for 90 days for commingling and misusing funds despite otherwise spotless record); In re Reynolds, 39 P.3d 136 (N.M. 2002) (neither lawyer's consent to discipline for misappropriating checks nor his cooperation with disciplinary authorities were sufficient to show that he was fit to be automatically reinstated).

2. ABA Canons of Prof. Ethics, Canon 11 Dealing with Trust Property (1908).

3. ABA Model Code of Prof. Resp., DR 9-102(A) and (B)(3) (1969).

4. Model Rule 1.15(a) also applies to funds held for third parties. *See* Atty. Grievance Commn. v. Clark, 767 A.2d 865 (Md. 2001) (lawyer who repeatedly failed to pay state income withholding taxes violated Rule 1.15 by failing to remit money that belonged to the state).

5. Lawyers also have been disciplined for negligently failing to pay third parties with valid legal rights to client funds. *See, e.g.*, St. ex rel. Okla. Bar Assn. v. Taylor, 71 P.3d 18 (Okla. 2003) (lawyer who failed to understand applicable law regarding the distribution of client funds to third-party medical providers publicly reprimanded).

6. Ariz. A. Ct. R. 43(d)(2); Cal. R. Prof. Conduct 4-100(C); Colo. R. Prof. Conduct 1.15(g); Conn. R. Super. Ct. Gen. §2-27(b); Fla. Bar R. 5-1.2; Haw. R. Prof. Conduct 1.15(g); Ind. Admis. & Disc. R. 23, §29(a); Minn. Law. Prof. Resp. Bd. Op. 9 (1999); N.J. R. Prof. Conduct 1.15; N.J. R. Gen. Application 1:21-6(c), Ct. R. 1:21(6); N.Y. DR 9-102(D); Or. DR 9-101(C)(3); R.I. R. Prof. Conduct 1.16(a); Vt. R. Prof. Conduct 1.15A(a); Va. R. Prof. Conduct 1.15(e).

7. Cal., Colo., Conn., Haw., Ind., Minn., N.J., N.Y., R.I., Va.

8. *See, e.g.*, Fla. Bar R. 5-1.2(c)(4); Ind. Admis. & Disc. R. 23, §29(b); Mass. R. Prof. Conduct 1.15(f).

9. *See, e.g.*, N.J. R. Gen. Application 1:21-6(h); Vt. R. Prof. Conduct 1.15A(b). For a compilation of the ABA Model Rules governing these subjects, *see* American Bar Association, Model Rules for Client Protection (1999).

To meet the requirement of a separate account for client funds, most lawyers today establish an IOLTA or Interest on Lawyer Trust Account with a local bank. All client funds that cannot earn net interest are kept in this account, and the interest is paid to a central fund that is used to fund legal services for those unable to pay.[10] Local rules additionally may require that some client funds, such as those that are significant in size or held for a long period of time or those for trusts or estates, be kept in another separate account where the interest accrues to that client.

How do lawyers avoid inadvertent breach of these trust account obligations? First, just as law firms should not allow any one lawyer carte blanche in billing clients, law firms also should make at least two lawyers responsible for administration of law firm trust accounts.[11] Second, all trust accounts should adhere to certain fundamental rules designed to prevent inadvertent breaches. Jay Foonberg has written an entire book on the subject, and summarizes his advice in what he calls "The Ten Commandments of Good Trust Accounts."[12]

- Rule 1: Have a trust account.
- Rule 2: Never let anyone else sign your trust account.
- Rule 3: Obtain and understand your IOLTA (Interest on Lawyers' Trust Account) rules.
- Rule 4: Immediately notify the client every time something is added to the client's account balance and every time something is taken from the account balance.
- Rule 5: Unearned fees and unexpended costs belong in the trust account until earned or spent.
- Rule 6: Do not commingle your funds with the client funds in the trust account.
- Rule 7: Be sure you understand the exact nature of the item deposited or credited to the trust account.
- Rule 8: Reconcile the bank trust account monthly.
- Rule 9: Reconcile and examine the individual client trust account balances monthly, and do not delay giving the clients their money.
- Rule 10: Be alert to third party claims.

In addition, Foonberg recommends that all lawyers maintain specific records required by the ABA Model Rule on Financial Recordkeeping and a growing number of jurisdictions. Most important is a journal, which records all deposits, checks, dates, and amounts, and explains each item, and a client ledger, or running balance by client of all checks, disbursements, dates, amounts, and explanations.[13] Lawyers and law firms also should keep all bank statements and records, and copies of each month's or quarter's reconciliation of the lawyer's accounts with the bank's statements.

Easy access to client funds continues to tempt lawyers. If history is any guide, you should expect increasing regulation of your bookkeeping practices to prevent further loss to clients.

---

10. In Brown v. Legal Found. of Wash., 123 S. Ct. 1406 (2003), the Supreme Court upheld the constitutionality of state IOLTA programs as long as client funds held in the accounts do not earn net interest for the client.

11. *See Reynolds, supra* note 1, at 142, where the court recommends allocation of responsibility to at least two lawyers within a law firm. *See also* In re Bailey, 821 A.2d 851 (Del. 2002) (managing partner of a law firm has enhanced duties to ensure the firm's obligation to comply with its record keeping obligations under the Rules of Prof. Conduct).

12. Jay G. Foonberg, *The ABA Guide to Lawyer Trust Accounts* 97-100 (1996).

13. Jay G. Foonberg, *How to Start and Build a Law Practice* 491-496 (ABA Law Practice Management Section, Law Student Division 1999).

Chapter 8

Terminating the Relationship

Just as no fiduciary duties attach until a lawyer agrees to represent a client, so also do most, but not all fiduciary duties, end when a lawyer completes a client matter. In Chapter 6, we identified specific rules that govern conflicts of interest concerning former clients. In Chapter 7, we saw that the lawyer's fee agreement may be invalidated when a client fires a lawyer. In this chapter, we review the various ways a client representation can end, including termination by the client and withdrawal from the matter by the lawyer. We also focus here on situations where the client's activity may force a lawyer to resign, and whether a lawyer faced with such a circumstance can seek any remedy.

Problems

8-1. Martyn & Fox has been suing Colossus on behalf of its client, Magna Industries, for three years. Then Colossus' assets are purchased by Excelsior Enterprises, a client of Martyn & Fox. Must Martyn & Fox resign? May Martyn & Fox resign?

8-2. Martyn & Fox has been handling a litigation matter for a client for several years. Last September, the client stopped paying Martyn & Fox's bills, and has given one excuse after another. May Martyn & Fox resign?

8-3. Due to FDA regulations, Martyn thinks her corporate client must disclose the receipt of a shipment of defective kidney dialysis machines because they could put some patients at risk by not adequately cleansing their blood. Client refuses, saying, "We'll resell them to Short Co.—they care more about price than quality." May (must) Martyn resign? What if Martyn is inside counsel to the corporation?

Consider: Model Rules 1.2, 1.6, 1.7, 1.16
Model Code DR 2-110

Gilles v. Wiley, Malehorn & Sirota

783 A.2d 756 (N.J. App. 2001)

PRESSLER, P.J.A.D.

Plaintiff Denise Gilles appeals from a summary judgment dismissing her legal malpractice complaint against defendants, the law firm of Wiley, Malehorn & Sirota, and its partner, Arthur L. Raynes, who had represented her. The gravamen of her complaint is that Raynes, voluntarily and without good cause attributable to her, terminated the representation without adequately protecting her against the running of the statute of limitations, thus causing her to lose her medical malpractice cause of action. . . .

. . . Plaintiff's asserted medical malpractice cause had its genesis in a colonoscopy she underwent on February 26, 1996, to determine the cause of occult bleeding. . . . The gravamen of the asserted medical malpractice was that the physician who performed the . . . colonoscopy perforated her colon, requiring her to undergo an emergency surgical repair that day. During her week-long hospital stay following the surgery, she developed a right hydropneumothorax that retarded her recovery. She apparently did, however, fully recover.

Persuaded by advice she had received from a physician family member that the perforation resulting in the emergency surgery was caused by malpractice, she consulted Raynes in early April 1996. . . .

. . . At Raynes's instruction, plaintiff obtained and delivered to him the relevant medical records. Raynes explained to her that before suit could be commenced, he would need a report from a medical expert opining that she had been the victim of malpractice. Accordingly, he sought an opinion from a forensic gastroenterologist, Dr. Andrew Lo of Beth Israel Medical Center in New York, who reported to him that he believed there had not been malpractice. By letter dated March 24, 1997, Raynes advised plaintiff of Dr. Lo's opinion but added that:

> Let me make clear that the above opinions on your care are those of Dr. Lo, and not of this office. We are willing to pursue your case further. However, in order to make this case viable, we will need to find an expert witness who can testify authoritatively that the care you received did not meet acceptable medical standards. If we do proceed with your case, we will need to lay out additional monies to potential witnesses in order to find one who agrees that you have received substandard treatment. This means that you will incur several hundred more dollars of expenses.

The letter concluded with Raynes's request that plaintiff telephone him to "discuss this further and decide whether you want us to continue to search for an independent expert." Plaintiff communicated her desire to proceed and agreed to pay the expenses involved.

A little over three months later, Raynes received a report dated July 3, 1997, from Dr. Lawrence B. Stein, a board-certified gastroenterologist, who opined that . . . [The medical technique used] . . . "greatly increased the likelihood of creating a colonic perforation and is a deviation from acceptable medical practice." Raynes mailed a copy of Dr. Stein's report to plaintiff on July 18, 1997, under cover of letter simply referring to it and making no further comment thereon.

On October 20, 1997, Raynes wrote to plaintiff again complaining that she had not yet paid the $1,204 she had been billed to cover expenses. The letter noted that the last payment he had received from her was the previous May. He then went on to say that:

> I understand that you want us to continue representing you in this matter; if that has changed, please advise us accordingly. In any event, you must reimburse us for the monies we have disbursed in working on your case thus far, as well as any expenses which may result from future work on your case. We cannot continue as your attorneys unless you fulfill that responsibility.
>
> I would ask that you pay us in full by no later than October 31, 1997. If we do not receive payment from you by that time, we may reconsider our representation of you in this matter. . . .

Although there was some dispute as to when that $1,204 was paid and as to just what the installment arrangements, if any, had been, Raynes agreed in his deposition testimony that by the beginning of January 1998 the balance due had been reduced to something just under $125.

Despite the favorable report from Dr. Stein, Raynes did not file a medical malpractice complaint. Some six months had gone by after his receipt of that report, when, on January 6, 1998, Raynes wrote the following letter to plaintiff:

> This is to advise that our firm has taken a new direction, away from most plaintiffs' malpractice cases. I therefore need to tell you that we will not be in a position to file suit on your behalf.
>
> The work that we have done for you, in obtaining a report from a reputable expert, Dr. Stein, will be useful to you with your next attorney. I enclose a copy of that report for you. Your next attorney will know to obtain the required affidavit from Dr. Stein.
>
> You have two years from the incident of malpractice to file suit. This should afford you sufficient time to obtain another attorney. Failure to file suit within the two year period will likely result in your losing your right to sue. I suggest that you contact another attorney immediately to protect your rights.
>
> There are numerous attorneys who handle medical malpractice cases. I recommend Tom Chesson of Porzio, Bromberg and Newman, whose telephone number is (973) 538-4006, or Adrian Karp, whose telephone number is (973) 267-7787.
>
> We have not charged you at all for our legal time. We have only charged you for reimbursement to us of our expenses.
>
> Best of luck to you.

Several comments must be made about that letter. First, at his deposition, Raynes explained that the firm had had some financially negative experience with contingent fee cases and while some were retained and some new ones being undertaken, they were not regarded as a desirable type of business. He then went on to explain that plaintiff's case was not as good—presumably in terms of damages—as he had originally thought and that Dr. Stein's report was not as strong as he had hoped for. He also suggested that plaintiff's failure to make prompt payment of the bill for expenses played a part in his decision to terminate the representation, although this had not been expressed to her and although her balance at the time of the termination was relatively insignificant.

In any event, the letter, which referred to the two-year statute of limitations but did not expressly state the date on which it would expire, came as a complete surprise to plaintiff, who, as she testified, was away on a trip when it was sent and did not believe that she actually received it until the end of January 1998. She did not, upon its receipt, immediately attempt to communicate with another lawyer, either one of the lawyers mentioned by Raynes or anyone else. As she testified on her deposition, she thought that if Raynes were sending her to another lawyer, then he should have made the referral himself and that in any event, she was so upset when she did receive his letter that she was unable to mobilize herself to take further steps although she did see another lawyer after the statute ran, some three or four weeks later. . . .

. . . Plaintiff asserts that Raynes breached his duty to her by unreasonably terminating the attorney-client relationship so soon before the running of the statute of limitations and without adequately protecting her interests in preserving her cause of action.

The Rules of Professional Conduct (R.P.C.s) speak to termination of the representation. And while we recognize that a cause of action for malpractice cannot be based exclusively on the asserted breach of an R.P.C., nevertheless it is clear that the R.P.C.s may be relied on as prescribing the requisite standard of care and the scope of the attorney's duty to the client. . . .

[The court cites Model Rule 1.16(b)(1) and (d).] The issue then, as we view it, is whether in the totality of the circumstances, Raynes's withdrawal, considering both the manner in which it was done and its timing, was accomplished without "material adverse effect" on plaintiff's interests in that it was attended by those steps "reasonably practicable" to protect her interests.

The trial judge concluded that Raynes had, beyond any question of material fact, acted reasonably. The sole basis of that conclusion was our decision in Fraser v. Bovino, 721 A.2d 20 (N.J. App. 1998), in which we held that in the circumstances there an attorney's termination of the attorney-client relationship "several weeks" before the statute of limitations had run was reasonable in that it afforded plaintiff adequate time to obtain another lawyer. We did not, however, in *Fraser* establish a bright-line rule that a withdrawal several weeks before the running of the statute of limitations is reasonable as a matter of law. We reached that conclusion there based on the operative facts in that case including the plaintiff's sophistication as a business man having regular dealings with lawyers, including such dealings with respect to the basic transactions in controversy; his having failed to raise the issue of possible litigation with defendant attorney until five years and nine months of the six-year statute of limitations had elapsed; and the brief period, some three months, during which the defendant-lawyer reviewed and studied the file. We note further that the defendant-lawyer there had denied that he had ever undertaken the representation.

Clearly the determination of reasonableness is ordinarily circumstantially dependent, and we are satisfied that a finder of fact would be justified in finding from the circumstances here that the timing and method of withdrawal were not reasonable. The facts here are very different from those in *Fraser*. Here, unlike *Fraser*, there was never a disavowal during a twenty-one month period of representation that Raynes represented plaintiff. As he said in his deposition, "I was her lawyer." For a six-month period he had all the information he needed not only to commence an action but also to have reached the conclusion that he eventually did reach respecting the probable unprofitability of the representation, a conclusion that evidently was the primary reason for the withdrawal. Plaintiff, on the other hand, was an unsophisticated lay person unaccustomed to legal dealings. The letter of termination, moreover, while it referred to the two-year statute of limitations and "suggested" plaintiff contact another lawyer immediately, did not specify the critical date. Finally, a fact-finder could also conclude that the period of time left to plaintiff before the statute of limitations had run was unreasonably short, particularly in view of the preceding six-month period following Raynes's receipt of Dr. Stein's favorable report. In this regard, we note that medical malpractice cases are ordinarily difficult representations and are not lightly or casually undertaken by serious and responsible lawyers. It is by no means clear that plaintiff could have obtained a new lawyer who, in three weeks, would have been able to review her file, make the necessary evaluations, and agree to file a complaint, particularly after knowing that her previous lawyer, who had represented her for twenty-one months, had suddenly declined to continue. After all, it apparently took Raynes six months after having reviewed the medical records and experts' reports to decide that he was no longer interested. Finally, and most significantly, a finder of fact could have found that Raynes failed to take those steps "reasonably practicable" to protect her interests, a matter we address hereafter.

Plaintiff supported her resistance to the summary judgment motion by submission of a report from an expert, a member of the bar of this State. The report opined that defendant, after his almost two years of representation, should not have terminated the relationship by a letter sent by ordinary mail but rather should have explained the situation and its imperatives to the client or, at the least, sent her his withdrawal by certified mail both to assure its timely receipt and to impress upon her the urgency of the situation. He also opined that considering the late withdrawal, reasonable steps to protect her interests would have required him to prepare for her a pro se complaint which she could have filed to avoid the danger of the statute running. . . .

The point, of course, is that plaintiff perceived herself as having been abandoned by defendant too late in the day to enable her to protect herself, and we do not regard that perception as prima facie unreasonable. We addressed the issue of abandonment in Kriegsman v. Kriegsman, 375 A.2d 1253 (N.J. App. 1977). Although we were there dealing with an attorney's motion for leave to withdraw from a matter already in litigation, what we said there is equally apt to an attorney's pre-litigation obligations. Thus, in affirming the denial of that motion, we started from the premise that "when a firm accepts a retainer to conduct a legal proceeding, it impliedly agrees to prosecute the matter to a conclusion. The firm is not at liberty to abandon the case without justifiable or reasonable cause, or the consent of its client." . . . [O]ur rationale in *Kriegsman* remains as relevant today as it was then in defining the attorney's duty. As we explained:

> We are not unmindful of the fact that the Rose firm has performed substantial legal services for plaintiff and clearly is entitled to reasonable compensation therefor. Nevertheless, an attorney has certain obligations and duties to a client once representation is undertaken. These obligations do not evaporate because the case becomes more complicated or the work more arduous or the retainer not as profitable as first contemplated or imagined. . . .

Whether Raynes's withdrawal afforded plaintiff a reasonable opportunity in the circumstances to protect her cause of action was, in our view, at least a question of fact precluding summary judgment dismissing the complaint. . . .

Crews v. Buckman Laboratories International, Inc.

78 S.W.3d 852 (Tenn. 2002)

William M. Barker, J. . . .

The sole issue in this case is whether an in-house lawyer can bring a common-law claim for retaliatory discharge when she was terminated for reporting that her employer's general counsel was engaged in the unauthorized practice of law. The trial court dismissed the plaintiff's complaint for failure to state a claim, and the dismissal was affirmed by the Court of Appeals. We hold that in-house counsel may bring a common-law action for retaliatory discharge resulting from counsel's compliance with a provision of the Code of Professional Responsibility that represents a clear and definitive statement of public policy. . . .

According to the allegations of the complaint, the plaintiff was hired by Buckman in 1995 as associate general counsel in its legal department, and while working in this capacity, she reported to Buckman's General Counsel, Ms. Katherine Buckman Davis. Sometime in 1996, the plaintiff discovered that Ms. Davis, who "held herself out as a licensed attorney," did not possess a license to practice law in the State of Tennessee. The plaintiff became concerned that Ms. Davis was engaged in the unauthorized practice of law, and she discussed her suspicions with a member of Buckman's Board of Directors.[1]

Ms. Davis eventually took and passed the bar exam, but the plaintiff learned some time later that Ms. Davis had yet to complete the requirements for licensure by taking the Muti-State Professional Responsibility Examination. The plaintiff informed Buckman officials of the continuing problem, and she advised them on how best to proceed. On June 17, 1999, Ms. Davis allegedly entered the plaintiff's office, yelling that she was frustrated with the plaintiff's actions. The plaintiff responded that she also was frustrated with the situation, to which Ms. Davis remarked that "maybe [the plaintiff] should just leave." The plaintiff declined to leave, and she later received a below-average raise for the first time during her tenure at Buckman, despite having been told earlier by Ms. Davis that she was "doing a good job in position of Associate Counsel."

In August, the plaintiff sought legal advice concerning her ethical obligations, and based on this advice, she informed the Board of Law Examiners of Ms. Davis's situation. The Board later issued a show-cause order asking Ms. Davis to clarify certain facts in her bar application. Upon receipt of the order, Ms. Davis demanded to know from the plaintiff what information the Board possessed in its application file. The plaintiff stated that she knew nothing of the file, and she told Ms. Davis that her actions were threatening and inappropriate. Ms. Davis then apologized, but she immediately proceeded to schedule the plaintiff's performance review.

The plaintiff then informed Mr. Buckman and the Vice-President of Human Resources that "the situation [had become] untenable and that she could not function under those

---

1. This Director then requested an opinion from the Board of Professional Responsibility based on a hypothetical scenario mirroring the situation at Buckman. The Board replied that a person without a Tennessee law license may not be employed as general counsel in this state and that the failure to have such a license constitutes the unauthorized practice of law.

circumstances." They agreed that the plaintiff should be immediately transferred to a position away from Ms. Davis's supervision and that she should eventually leave the company altogether within six to nine months. However, while the plaintiff was "in the midst of working out the new arrangement," Ms. Davis informed her that her services would no longer be needed. More specifically, Ms. Davis told her that "since [the plaintiff] had given her notice of resignation, it was logically best to end the Plaintiff's association with Buckman." Although the plaintiff denied that she had resigned, her computer was confiscated; she was placed on personal leave; and she was given a notice of termination.

On April 10, 2000, the plaintiff filed suit against Buckman in the Shelby County Circuit Court, alleging a common-law action for retaliatory discharge in violation of public policy. . . .

IN-HOUSE COUNSEL AND THE TORT OF RETALIATORY DISCHARGE

Tennessee has long adhered to the employment-at-will doctrine in employment relationships not established or formalized by a contract for a definite term. Under this "employment at will" doctrine, both the employer and the employee are generally permitted, with certain exceptions, to terminate the employment relationship "at any time for good cause, bad cause, or no cause.". . .

However, an employer's ability to discharge at-will employees was significantly tempered by our recognition in Clanton v. Cain-Sloan Co., 677 S.W.2d 441 (Tenn. 1984), of a cause of action for retaliatory discharge. Since that time, we have further recognized that an at-will employee "generally may not be discharged for attempting to exercise a statutory or constitutional right, or for any other reason which violates a clear public policy which is evidenced by an unambiguous constitutional, statutory, or regulatory provision." Therefore, in contrast to the purposes typically justifying the employment-at-will doctrine, an action for retaliatory discharge recognizes "that, in limited circumstances, certain well-defined, unambiguous principles of public policy confer upon employees implicit rights which must not be circumscribed or chilled by the potential of termination.". . .

DECISIONS OF OTHER STATES RELATING TO DISCHARGE IN VIOLATION OF PUBLIC POLICY

Several jurisdictions have grappled with how to balance the competing interests involved in these types of cases. Although the rationales often differed, most of the earlier cases on this subject held that a lawyer could not bring a retaliatory discharge action based upon the lawyer's adherence to his or her ethical duties. *See, e.g.*, Willy v. Coastal Corp., 647 F. Supp. 116 (S.D. Tex. 1986); McGonagle v. Union Fid. Corp., 556 A.2d 878 (Pa. Super. Ct. 1989); Herbster v. North Am. Co. for Life & Health Ins., 501 N.E.2d 343 (Ill. App. Ct. 1986). This line of cases culminated in Balla v. Gambro, Inc., 584 N.E.2d 104 (Ill. 1991), in which the Illinois Supreme Court reviewed the other cases and set forth several rationales why in-house counsel should not be permitted to assert an action for retaliatory discharge. These rationales included (1) that because "in-house counsel do not have a choice of whether to follow their ethical obligations as attorneys licensed to practice law," lawyers do not need an action for retaliatory discharge to encourage them to abide by their ethical duties; and (2) that recognizing such an action would affect the foundation of trust in attorney-client relationships, which would then make employers "naturally hesitant to rely upon in-house counsel for advice regarding [the employer's] potentially questionable conduct."

In more recent years, however, other states have permitted a lawyer, under limited circumstances, to pursue a claim of retaliatory discharge based upon termination in violation of public policy. The principal case permitting such an action is General Dynamics Corp. v. Rose, 876 P.2d 487 (Cal. 1994), in which the California Supreme Court rejected the views held by *Balla* and others and established an analytical framework permitting a lawyer to sue for retaliatory discharge. According to this framework, a lawyer is generally permitted to assert a retaliatory discharge action if the lawyer is discharged for following a mandatory ethical duty or engaging in conduct that would give rise to an action by a non-lawyer employee. However, the General Dynamics Court cautioned that the lawyer bringing the action could not rely upon confidential information to establish the claim and that any unsuccessful lawyer breaching his or her duty of confidentiality was subject to disciplinary sanctions.

Following California's lead, the Supreme Judicial Court of Massachusetts has also permitted in-house counsel to assert a limited retaliatory discharge action. In GTE Products Corp. v. Stewart, 653 N.E.2d 161 (Mass. 1995), the court questioned why the employee's status as an attorney should preclude an action: "It thus seems bizarre that a lawyer employee, who has affirmative duties concerning the administration of justice, should be denied redress for discharge resulting from trying to carry out those very duties." However, while the *Stewart* Court permitted a limited retaliatory discharge action based upon a lawyer's refusal to violate "explicit and unequivocal statutory or ethical norms," it also restricted the scope of such an action to that in which "the claim can be proved without any violation of the attorney's obligation to respect client confidences and secrets."

Finally, and most recently, the Montana Supreme Court also held that in-house counsel should be permitted to bring retaliatory discharge actions when necessary to protect public policy. In Burkhart v. Semitool, Inc., 5 P.3d 103 (Mont. 2000), the court discussed the rationales in favor of adopting such an action and noted that while clients have a right to discharge counsel at any time and for any reason, this right does not necessarily apply to in-house counsel. Instead, the court reasoned that "by making his or her attorney an employee, [the employer] has avoided the traditional attorney-client relationship and granted the attorney protections that do not apply to independent contractors, but do apply to employees. . . ." Moreover, unlike the previous cases recognizing such an action, the *Burkhart* Court permitted lawyers to disclose the employer's confidential information to the extent necessary to establish a retaliatory discharge claim.

REJECTION OF THE RATIONALES ADVANCED BY *BALLA* AND OTHER CASES

Considering these two general approaches to retaliatory discharge actions based upon termination in violation of public policy, we generally agree with the approaches taken by the courts in *General Dynamics*, *Stewart*, and *Burkhart*. The very purpose of recognizing an employee's action for retaliatory discharge in violation of public policy is to encourage the employee to protect the public interest, and it seems anomalous to protect only non-lawyer employees under these circumstances. Indeed, as cases in similar contexts show, in-house counsel do not generally forfeit employment protections provided to other employees merely because of their status or duties as a lawyer.[2]

Moreover, we must reject the rationales typically set forth by *Balla* and the Court of Appeals in this case to generally deny lawyers the ability to pursue retaliatory discharge actions. *Balla*'s principal rationale was that recognition of a retaliatory discharge action was not necessary to protect the public interest so long as lawyers were required to follow a code of ethics. . . .

. . . It is true that counsel in this case was under a mandatory duty to not aid a non-lawyer in the unauthorized practice of law, *see* Tenn. Sup. Ct. R. 8, DR 3-101(A), Model Rule 5.5(b), and the intermediate court was also correct that lawyers do not have the option of disregarding the commandments of the Disciplinary Rules. . . .

Ultimately, sole reliance on the mere presence of the ethical rules to protect important public policies gives too little weight to the actual presence of ecsonomic pressures designed to tempt in-house counsel into subordinating ethical standards to corporate misconduct. Unlike lawyers possessing a multiple client base, in-house counsel are dependent upon only one client for their livelihood. As the *General Dynamics* Court acknowledged, the economic fate of in-house attorneys is tied directly to a single employer, at whose sufferance they serve. Thus, from an economic standpoint, the dependence of in-house counsel is indistinguishable from that of other corporate managers or senior executives who also owe their livelihoods, career goals and satisfaction to a single organizational employer.

The pressure to conform to corporate misconduct at the expense of one's entire livelihood, therefore, presents some risk that ethical standards could be disregarded. Like other non-lawyer employees, an in-house lawyer is dependent upon the corporation for his or her sole income, benefits, and pensions; the lawyer is often governed by the corporation's personnel policies and employees' handbooks; and the lawyer is subject to raises and promotions as determined by the corporation. In addition, the lawyer's hours of employment and nature of work are usually determined by the corporation. To the extent that these realities are ignored, the analysis here cannot hope to present an accurate picture of modern in-house practice. . . .

We also reject *Balla*'s reasoning that recognition of a retaliatory discharge action under these circumstances would have a chilling effect upon the attorney-client relationship and would impair the trust between an attorney and his or her client. This rationale appears to be premised on one key assumption: the employer desires to act contrary to public policy and expects the lawyer to further that conduct in violation of the lawyer's ethical duties. We are simply unwilling to presume that employers as a class operate with so nefarious a motive, and we recognize that when employers seek legal advice from in-house counsel, they usually do so with the intent to comply with the law.

2. For example, courts have permitted in-house lawyers to sue for age and race discrimination in violation of federal law, Stinneford v. Spiegel Inc., 845 F. Supp. 1243, 1245-47 (N.D. Ill. 1994); Golightly-Howell v. Oil, Chem. & Atomic Workers Intl. Union, 806 F. Supp. 921, 924 (D. Colo. 1992); to sue for protections under a state "whistleblower" statute, Parker v. M & T Chemicals, Inc., 566 A.2d 215, 220 (N.J. App. 1989); to sue for breach of express and implied employment contracts, Chyten v. Lawrence & Howell Invs., 46 Cal. Rptr. 2d 459, 464-65 (Cal. App. 1993); Nordling v. Northern State Power Co., 478 N.W.2d 498, 502 (Minn. 1991); and to sue based on implied covenants of good faith and fair dealing, *Golightly-Howell*, 806 F. Supp. at 924.

Moreover, employers of in-house counsel should be aware that the lawyer is bound by the Code of Professional Responsibility, and that the lawyer may ethically reveal client confidences and secrets in many cases. Therefore, with respect to the employer's willingness to seek the advice of the lawyer for legally questionable conduct, the nature of the relationship should not be further diminished by the remote possibility of a retaliatory discharge suit. In fact, "there should be no discernible impact on the attorney-client relationship [by recognition of a retaliatory discharge action], unless the employer expects his counsel to blindly follow his mandate in contravention of the lawyer's ethical duty." Therefore, we conclude that little, if any, adverse effect upon the attorney-client relationship will occur if we recognize an action for discharge in violation of public policy.

Finally, we reject *Balla*'s assertion that allowing damages as a remedy for retaliatory discharge would have the effect of shifting to the employer the costs of in-house counsel's adherence to the ethics rules. The very purpose of permitting a claim for retaliatory discharge in violation of public policy is to encourage employers to refrain from conduct that is injurious to the public interest. Because retaliatory discharge actions recognize that it is the employer who is attempting to circumvent clear expressions of public policy, basic principles of equity all but demand that the costs associated with such conduct also be borne by the employer. . . .

. . . Therefore, we hold that a lawyer may generally bring a claim for retaliatory discharge when the lawyer is discharged for abiding by the ethics rules as established by this Court.

PROPER STANDARD TO APPLY IN TENNESSEE

In Tennessee, the elements of a typical common-law retaliatory discharge claim are as follows: (1) that an employment-at-will relationship existed; (2) that the employee was discharged, (3) that the reason for the discharge was that the employee attempted to exercise a statutory or constitutional right, or for any other reason which violates a clear public policy evidenced by an unambiguous constitutional, statutory, or regulatory provision; and (4) that a substantial factor in the employer's decision to discharge the employee was the employee's exercise of protected rights or compliance with clear public policy.

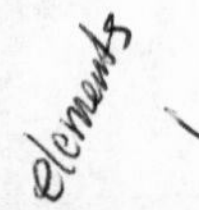

However, as we have noted throughout this opinion, this case does not present the typical retaliatory discharge claim. Consequently, while the special relationship between a lawyer and a client does not categorically prohibit in-house counsel from bringing a retaliatory discharge action, other courts have held that it necessarily shapes the contours of the action when the plaintiff was employed as in-house counsel. For example, the courts in *General Dynamics* and *Stewart* held that a lawyer could pursue a retaliatory discharge claim, but only if the lawyer could do so without breaching the duty of confidentiality. Indeed, the California Supreme Court went so far as to forewarn lawyers that those who revealed confidential information in a retaliatory discharge suit, without a basis for doing so under the ethics rules, would be subject to disciplinary proceedings. . . .

If we perceive any shortcomings in the holdings of *General Dynamics* and *Stewart*, it is that they largely take away with one hand what they appear to give with the other. Although the courts in these cases gave in-house counsel an important right of action, their respective admonitions about preserving client confidentiality appear to stop just short of halting most of these actions at the courthouse door. With little imagination, one could envision cases involving important issues of public concern being denied relief merely because the wrongdoer is protected by the lawyer's duty of confidentiality. Therefore, given that courts have recognized retaliatory discharge actions in order to protect the public interest, this potentially severe limitation strikes us as a curious, if not largely ineffective, measure to achieve that goal.

. . . Unlike Disciplinary Rule 4-101(C), Model Rule 1.6(b)(2) permits a lawyer to reveal "information relating to the representation of a client" when the lawyer reasonably believes such information is necessary "to establish a claim or defense on behalf of the lawyer in a controversy between the lawyer and the client. . . ." Although some commentators have asserted that this provision merely permits lawyers to use confidential information in fee-collection disputes as under the Model Code, the plain language of the Model Rule is clearly more broad than these authorities would presume. In fact, at least one state supreme court has held that this language permits in-house counsel to reveal confidential information in a retaliatory discharge suit, at least to the extent reasonably necessary to establish the claim. *See Burkhart,* 5 P.3d at 1041.

We agree with the approach taken by the Model Rules, and pursuant to our inherent authority to regulate and govern the practice of law in this state, we hereby expressly adopt a new provision . . . [that] parallels the language of Model Rule of Professional Conduct 1.6(b)(2), and we perceive the adoption of a similar standard to be essential in protecting the ability of in-house counsel to effectively assert an action for discharge in violation of public policy. Nevertheless, while in-house counsel may ethically disclose such information to the extent necessary to establish the claim, we emphasize that in-house counsel "must make every effort practicable to avoid unnecessary disclosure of [client confidences and secrets], to limit disclosure to those having the need to know it, and to obtain protective orders or make other arrangements minimizing the risk of disclosure." Model Rule 1.6 Comment 19.

ANALYSIS OF THE COMPLAINT IN THIS CASE

Having found that in-house counsel are not categorically prohibited from maintaining retaliatory discharge actions against their former employers, we now examine whether the plaintiff in this case has stated such a claim in her complaint. As for the first element, the existence of an at-will employment relationship, . . . we will presume that the plaintiff intended to allege an at-will employment relationship. . . .

The next issue, then, is whether the complaint alleges the existence of a "clear public policy which is evidenced by an unambiguous constitutional, statutory, or regulatory provision." To establish this second element, the plaintiff argues that the ethical rules relating to the unauthorized practice of law—such as Disciplinary Rule 3-101(A), which places upon lawyers a mandatory ethical duty "not [to] aid a non-lawyer in the unauthorized practice of law"—are for the protection of the public interest and may serve as the basis for a retaliatory discharge action. We agree. . . .

Although we need not conclude today that every provision of the Code of Professional Responsibility reflects an important public policy, there can be no doubt that the public has a substantial interest in preventing the unauthorized practice of law. As this Court has acknowledged, "the purpose of regulations governing the unauthorized practice of law is . . . to serve the public right to protection against unlearned and unskilled advice in matters relating to the science of the law." Further, the Court of Appeals has recognized that regulations proscribing the unauthorized practice of law are designed to protect "the public from being advised and represented in legal matters by incompetent and unreliable persons over whom the judicial department could exercise little control." As such, we find here the existence of a clear public policy evidenced by the ethical duty not to aid in the unauthorized practice of law.

To be clear, although the plaintiff was not under a mandatory ethical duty to report Ms. Davis's alleged unauthorized practice of law to the Board of Law Examiners, she certainly possessed a permissive duty to report Ms. Davis's conduct.[6] Ethical Consideration 1-3 is clear that "although lawyers should not become self-appointed investigators or judges of applicants for admission, they should report to proper officials all unfavorable information they possess relating to the character or other qualifications of applicants." As such, given the clear expression of this permissive duty, combined with the clear expression of public policy in Disciplinary Rule 3-101(A), we hold that the complaint has sufficiently alleged the existence of a clear public policy evidenced by an unambiguous provision of the Tennessee Code of Professional Responsibility.

Next, we examine whether the complaint has sufficiently alleged that the plaintiff was discharged from her employment with Buckman. With regard to these allegations, we note that the plaintiff has asserted that she was constructively discharged from her position as in-house counsel. . . .

Here, we find that the complaint has fairly raised an allegation that the plaintiff did not voluntarily leave her employment with Buckman. Importantly, after her final encounter with Ms. Davis, the corporation is alleged to have removed the plaintiff's computer; to have placed the plaintiff on temporary leave; and to have given the plaintiff a notice of termination. Under these circumstances, the allegation is fairly raised that a reasonable person would have felt compelled to resign, and we therefore conclude that the plaintiff has sufficiently alleged a termination of employment necessary to state a claim for relief.

Finally, we examine whether the complaint alleges that a substantial factor in Buckman's decision to discharge the plaintiff was her adherence to her ethical duties under the Code of Professional Responsibility. Here, the plaintiff alleges that the sole motivation for the constructive discharge was her adherence to her ethical duties to report the unauthorized practice of law to the Board of Law Examiners. Accordingly, we conclude that the existence of this element has likewise been sufficiently alleged in the complaint and that, consequently, the plaintiff has stated a cause of action for retaliatory discharge in violation of public policy. . . .

Lawyers and Other Professionals: *Wrongful Discharge*

In the last chapter, we saw that an implied condition of every client-lawyer contract is the client's right to discharge the lawyer at any time, for any reason. *Crews*, on the

6. Disciplinary Rule 1-103(A) imposes a mandatory duty to report clear violations of Disciplinary Rule 1-102, which itself prohibits violations of a Disciplinary Rule. However, Rule 1-102 applies only to violations by lawyers, and because Ms. Davis was not yet licensed at the time the plaintiff reported her conduct to the Board of Law Examiners, it appears that the plaintiff's only mandatory duty here was to refrain from furthering Ms. Davis's application for admission to the bar under Disciplinary Rule 1-101(B).

other hand, tells us that one group of lawyers—those who are employees of the client they serve—may have claims similar to those of other employees for wrongful discharge in some circumstances.

L=IC

Employment At Will

Most lawyers are independent contractors. When a client hires a lawyer to perform legal services, the lawyer becomes an agent, but not a servant or employee of the client. As an independent business, the lawyer or law firm provides its own employment terms and benefits. Most lawyers also serve a multiple client base.

After World War II, corporations began to follow the lead of governmental units by hiring more inside lawyers as employees.[1] Unlike lawyers in their own practices, these inside lawyers had only one client and were employees who depended on a corporation or government for benefits and terms of employment. For the most part, they performed legal tasks similar to lawyers in outside practices, but often concentrated on providing advice and counsel to prevent or solve legal issues rather than litigation services after a controversy arose. As the value of these services to large organizations increased, more and more legal work has been moved inside organizations. Today, inside lawyers often manage nearly all of the legal issues that confront the organization, and usually decide when to hire outside lawyers for specific tasks.

During the time this move to inside counsel was developing, courts in most jurisdictions were beginning to develop exceptions to the employment at-will doctrine. Developed in the latter part of the nineteenth century, this doctrine provided that absent contractual agreements to the contrary, both employer and employee were free to terminate the employment relationship at any time.[2] The first exception was created judicially in 1959, when an employee were fired for refusing to commit perjury when his employer ordered him to do so. A California court provided the employee with a cause of action for wrongful discharge, holding that the at-will doctrine was subject to important public policies.[3] This public policy exception has gained wide recognition in the past twenty years.[4] Federal and state whistleblowing statutes create similar rights for employees in both the public and private sectors.[5] Beyond statutory rights, courts also have recognized the rights of employees to sue for breach of express and implied provisions in employment contracts, as well as on the basis of an implied covenant of good faith.[6]

---

1. In 1951, about 3 percent of all lawyers worked directly for private industry, and 10 percent worked for various levels of the government. *See* Reginald Heber Smith, *The Second Statistical Report on The Lawyer of the United States* 2 (ABA 1951). By 1960, 10 percent of all lawyers worked for private industry. Since then, these percentages have remained about the same for both private industry and government lawyers, although the total numbers in each category have risen, from about 28,000 in 1960 to 70,000 in 1995. *See* Clara N. Carson, *The Lawyer Statistical Report: The Legal Profession in 1995*, at 7 (Am. Bar Found. 1999); Barbara A. Curran, *The Lawyer Statistical Report: A Statistical Profile of the U.S. Legal Profession in the 1980s*, at 12 (Am. Bar Found. 1985).
2. Mark A. Rothstein et al., *Employment Law* §8.1 (2d ed., West 1999).
3. Petermann v. Teamsters Local 396, 344 P.2d 25 (Cal. App. 1959).
4. *See* Lionel J. Postic, *Wrongful Termination: A State-by-State Survey* (BNA 1994).
5. *See* Daniel P. Westman, *Whistleblowing: The Law of Retaliatory Discharge* (BNA 1991).
6. *See* Rothstein, *supra* note 2, at §§8.2-8.6.

Public Policy

The public policy exception recognizes that employers are not free to fire employees because they report or refuse to engage in illegal activity, exercise a statutory or constitutional right, or perform a duty required by law. All three of these categories of public policy exceptions were implicated in *Crews*.

Both common law and statutes protect whistleblowers who threaten to report, refuse to be part of, or report unlawful activity. Some states construe this exception narrowly, limiting it to facts such as *Petermann*, where the employer instructs the employee to commit an illegal act that is criminal.[7] Others extend it to tortious acts as well,[8] and some grant the cause of action to employees who refuse to commit a violation of administrative regulations.[9] Jurisdictions differ on whether the unlawful activity must relate to public health and safety, and whether the employee must actually report the activity outside the organization.[10] In *Crews*, the court found that although not every provision of the lawyer's code might reflect an important public policy, refusing to assist in the unauthorized practice of law certainly qualified.

Statutes and case law also recognize that employees who exercise a statutory right, such as the right to seek worker's compensation for a workplace injury, also are protected from retaliatory discharge.[11] Crews alleged, and the Tennessee Supreme Court agreed, that she had a right to report her supervisor's conduct.

Finally, many courts and statutes create a public policy exception for the performance of a public duty. *Crews* points out that the plaintiff was under no such obligation to report her supervisor's conduct, because the latter was not yet a lawyer subject to the state professional code. Similarly, very few public reporting obligations create mandatory duties. Nevertheless, the courts have not hesitated to protect employees who were fired because they were called to jury service, or insisted on obeying a subpoena, or reported child or elder abuse.[12]

Professional Code Violations

Many courts have recognized that refusal to violate a professional ethics code may qualify as an important public policy.[13] These courts agree with *Crews* that not all professional codes provisions qualify as important public policies, either because they may lack a clear mandate to act or because they may have been created to serve primarily the profession's own interests rather than the public's.[14]

For example, a physician who disagreed with her drug company employer's decision to proceed with testing a new drug in children and elderly people alleged that her participation would violate the Hippocratic Oath. The New Jersey Supreme Court recognized a potential cause of action in her situation, but held that she could

---

7. *See, e.g.*, Sabine Pilot Service v. Hauck, 687 S.W.2d 733 (Tex. 1985).
8. *See, e.g.*, Delaney v. Taco Time Intl. Inc., 681 P.2d 114 (Or. 1984) (potential defamation).
9. *See, e.g.*, Minn. Stat. §181.932 (2003); N.Y. Lab. Law §740 (2003); Tenn. Code §50-1-304 (2003).
10. Rothstein, *supra* note 2, at §§8.10-8.11.
11. *See* Theresa Ludwig Kruk, *Recovery for Discharge from Employment in Retaliation for Filing Workers' Compensation Claim*, 32 A.L.R.4th 1221 (1984).
12. Rothstein, *supra* note 2, at §8.13.
13. *See* Genna H. Rosten, *Wrongful Discharge Based on Public Policy Derived from Professional Ethics Codes*, 52 A.L.R.5th 405 (1997).
14. *E.g.*, Warthen v. Toms River Community Meml. Hosp., 488 A.2d 229 (N.J. App. 1985) (provision in nurse's code of ethics, excusing nurses from administering treatment if personally opposed to the delivery of care protected nurses, not the public, and was therefore not a mandate of public policy).

not prevail because she did not allege any violation of federal or state law or of any specific provision of the AMA Principles of Medical Ethics.[15] Similarly, ethical code provisions that rest on the judgment of professionals do not constitute a clear mandate of public policy unless they require a specific action.[16] On the other hand, a pharmacist who alleged that state regulations would be violated if he were forced to close a pharmacy on a holiday stated a cause of action.[17] The same is true of an accountant who alleged that he was terminated for objecting to an employer's accounting practices because they misrepresented facts in contravention of a specific provision in the State Board of Accountancy Rules of Professional Conduct.[18]

Crews agrees with these decisions, finding that first, the unauthorized practice rules were intended to protect the public, and second, that they provided a permissive duty combined with a clear public policy. Other courts also have found clear public policies in lawyer professional codes, including Model Rule 1.2(d)'s prohibition against counseling or assisting fraudulent client conduct,[19] Ethical Considerations which entitle citizens to consult with lawyers,[20] Model Rules 3.3 and 3.4 that prohibit the submission of false evidence,[21] and Model Rules 1.5, 7.1, and 8.4(c), which prohibit fraudulent billing.[22]

Discharge

The plaintiff in a wrongful discharge case must prove not only that she sought to vindicate an important public policy, but also that she was fired for doing so. When an employee like Ms. Crews resigns or quits her job, the implication is that the employer did not discharge her. The Tennessee court recognizes the doctrine of constructive discharge in her situation, where facts indicate that the plaintiff did not voluntarily leave her job, but felt compelled to resign because of the employer's actions. Most courts agree with *Crews* that intolerable employment conditions created by the employer, which essentially force the employee to quit, constitute constructive discharge. On the other hand, single instances of demotion, unfavorable performance reviews, or dissatisfaction with assignments are not enough.[23]

---

15. Pierce v. Ortho Pharm. Corp., 417 A.2d 506 (N.J. 1980).
16. *E.g.,* Lay v. St. Louis Helicopter Airways, 869 S.W.2d 172 (Mo. App. 1993) (Code of Ethics of Helicopter Assn. Intl. requirement that pilots use their "best judgment" was not a clear mandate of public policy); Birthisel v. Tri-Cities Health Servs. Corp., 424 S.E.2d 606 (W. Va. 1992) (provisions in social worker's administrative regulations which stated that a social worker should act in accordance with the highest standards of professional integrity, and that social worker's primary responsibility was to clients were not "substantial public policies" that provided specific guidance to social workers).
17. Kalman v. Grand Union Co., 443 A.2d 728 (N.J. App. 1982).
18. Rocky Mountain Hosp. & Med. Services v. Mariani, 916 P.2d 519 (Colo. 1996).
19. O'Brien v. Stolt-Nielsen Trans. Group, Ltd., 2003 Conn. Super. LEXIS 1763; Burkhart v. Semitool, Inc., 5 P.3d 1031 (Mont. 2000) (refusing to prepare fraudulent patent applications); Shearin v. E. F. Hutton Group, 652 A.2d 578 (Del. Ch. Ct. 1994) (refusing to be part of material misrepresentations to banks and securities regulators); Parker v. M & T Chemicals, Inc., 566 A.2d 215 (N.J. Super. 1989) (objecting to "unlawful and fraudulent conduct" of client).
20. Thompto v. Coborn's Inc., 871 F. Supp. 1097 (N.D. Iowa 1994) (nonlawyer employee fired when she threatened to consult with a lawyer).
21. Paralegal v. Lawyer, 783 F. Supp. 230 (E.D. Pa. 1992) (paralegal fired for notifying her employer's lawyer that her employer submitted false evidence).
22. Brown v. Hammond, 810 F. Supp. 644 (E.D. Pa. 1993).
23. *See, e.g.,* GTE Products Corp. v. Stewart, 653 N.E.2d 161 (1995) (inside counsel who quit his job not constructively discharged because conditions under which he would have been forced to work were not so intolerable that a reasonable person would have felt compelled to resign).

Are Lawyers Different?

When lawyer employees initially sought court recognition of a wrongful discharge cause of action, courts reasoned that the right of clients to fire lawyers at any time should trump any contrary employment law doctrine. *Crews* illustrates how several state courts over the past decade have moved away from that notion and have begun to emphasize the similarity between lawyer-employees and other employees protected by the wrongful discharge doctrine.

With respect to confidentiality, *Crews* applies the self-defense exception to client confidentiality in the Tennessee lawyer code to justify the disclosure necessary to establish a cause of action.[24] Recognizing such an exception parallels the situation of other employees who also have confidentiality obligations as a matter of common law fiduciary duty.[25] When these employees become whistleblowers, they are permitted to use some of this sensitive information to prove that they had a good faith belief that their employer was engaged in wrongful activity.[26] The ABA Ethics committee recently reached the same result for lawyers, finding that wrongful discharge actions by inside counsel fall within the meaning of the term "claim" in Model Rule 1.6(b)(5) and that in pursuing such a claim "the lawyer must limit disclosure of confidential client information to the extent reasonably possible."[27]

Of course, the real policy debate in all of the lawyer cases is whether the right of clients to fire lawyers should override other employment protections. *Crews* begins by pointing out that inside counsel do not forfeit other statutory employment rights simply because they are lawyers. Other professionals along with lawyers have long been accorded rights under a myriad of these provisions.[28] Once a court recognizes that a lawyer employee may sue her employer for race, age, or gender discrimination, the public policy in other employment law, such as federal and state whistleblower statutes, becomes equally easy to follow.[29]

---

24. The California court in *General Dynamics* similarly relied on the statutory exceptions to the attorney-client privilege found in its evidence code to provide the basis for a cause of action. General Dynamics v. Superior Court, 876 P.2d 487, 503 (Cal. 1994). A subsequent California court ruled that a lawyer who seeks legal advice about whether to bring a wrongful discharge suit may disclose relevant facts to her own lawyer, including employer confidences and privileged communications. Fox Searchlight Pictures, Inc. v. Paladino, 106 Cal. Rptr. 2d 906 (Cal. App. 2001).

25. For example, the common law duty not to divulge trade secrets can be remedied by injunctive relief by the organization. *See, e.g.,* Webcraft Technologies v. McCaw, 674 F. Supp. 1039 (S.D.N.Y. 1997).

26. *See* Westman, *supra* note 5, at 22-44.

27. ABA Formal Op. 01-424; *see also* Spratley v. St. Farm Mut. Auto Ins. Co., 78 P.3d 603 (Utah 2003) (insurer's inside counsel lawyers who alleged that they quit their employment because insurer required them to violate ethical duties to insureds could disclose matters relating to their representation of insurer, but not insureds, to prove their claim for wrongful discharge).

28. *See, e.g.,* Sonja A. Soehnel, *Sex Discrimination in Employment Against Female Attorney in Violation of Federal Civil Rights Law—Federal Cases,* 81 L. Ed. 2d 894 (1999); Gregory G. Sarno, *Liability Under Racketeer Influenced and Corrupt Organization Act (RICO) (18 U.S.C. §§1961-68) for Retaliation Against Employee for Disclosing or Refusing to Commit Wrongful Act,* 100 A.L.R. Fed. 66 (1990); Daniel A. Klein, *Whistleblowers' Protection Under Energy Reorganization Act (42 USCA §5851),* 79 A.L.R. Fed. 631 (1986).

29. *See, e.g.,* In re Newark, 788 A.2d 776 (N.J. App. 2002) (unionization of nonmanagerial lawyers employed by city permitted under state public employment law). Federal and state whistleblower statutes provide protection mainly for public sector employees who disclose illegal acts of their government employers. Some also protect private sector employee from retaliation. *See* Rothstein, *supra* note 2, at §8.17. A number of cases have raised the question whether federal statutes that include antiretaliation provisions preempt state law. *See, e.g.,* Gregory G. Sarno, *Federal Pre-Emption of Whistleblower's State-Law Action for Wrongful Retaliation,* 99 A.L.R. Fed. 775 (1990).

The last vestige of the employment-at-will doctrine concerns lawyers like Crews, who have no statutory or contractual cause of action against their employers. Their claims raise the issue of the relationship between the lawyer codes and employment law, which may incorporate other conflicting public policies. *Crews* indicates that the early cases, such as Balla v. Gambro,[30] rejected any cause of action for wrongful discharge by lawyer-employees, even where another professional employee, such as an engineer, would be granted a cause of action if fired for making the same disclosure. These courts reasoned that a lawyer who discovers that a client insists on pursuing illegal activity must either convince the client to stop or leave the employment. If disclosure was allowed or required by lawyer codes to prevent harm to others, lawyers could disclose, but they were not free to use the same client confidences to create a cause of action against their employer.

These decisions stressed the need for organizations to trust their lawyers, the need for confidentiality to foster that trust, and the social value of encouraging organizations to seek legal advice. Recognizing a cause of action for wrongful discharge ultimately would lead organizations to avoid sharing information about sensitive or questionable activity with their legal staff. This avoidance would in turn erase opportunities for inside lawyers to counsel their clients about better means of complying with legal requirements.

Crews represents the opposite point of view: that conduct giving rise to a cause of action by other organizational employees also ought to extend to a cause of action for wrongful discharge by lawyer-employees. The client remains free to discharge the lawyer, but may have to suffer a monetary penalty for punishing lawyers who refuse to violate clear mandates in their professional rules. Inside counsel are more like other employees than they are like other lawyers, because they depend on their one client/employer for their livelihood. Expecting inside lawyers to adhere to professional codes in the face of the economic pressure of losing their job undervalues lawyer professionalism, as well as the important public policy in other law that these lawyers help implement. Allowing such a cause of action also deters the employer that seeks to engage in clearly unlawful activity.

One thing is certain. Competent lawyering requires any lawyer who disagrees with a decision by corporate management first to determine the basis for the disagreement. The lawyer or other professional who can articulate a clear public policy, embodied in a specific statute, regulation, professional code, or constitutional provision should communicate that policy to responsible decisionmakers. If at that point the professional loses her job, she will have created a record that her discharge was caused by her insistence that the organization not violate the articulated public policy.

Whether a court will recognize such a cause of action for lawyers depends on that court's view of the realities of the role of inside counsel. Those who see organizations as reliant on legal advice and worry about the pressure to conform will agree with the rationale in *Crews*. Those who wish to promote more open communication with inside counsel may be willing to risk the economic pressures on such lawyers and hope that the threat of professional discipline will adequately protect the public interest. Ultimately, the best result will be a function not only of the equities in a particular case, but also the incentives those equities create in the ongoing relationship between inside counsel and their clients.

30. 584 N.E.2d 104 (Ill. 1991).

Part III

Lawyers and Justice: The Limits of Advocacy

Chapter 9

The Limits of the Law

A. Introduction

Problem

9-1. How do you advise Martyn & Fox's client who just told us that an otherwise perfectly legal $10,000 political contribution to the Republican Party will guarantee issuance of a building permit six months sooner, saving our client hundreds of thousands of dollars? What if our client asks us to buy five of the ten $1000 tickets to the County Lincoln Day Dinner necessary to complete the transaction?

Consider: Model Rules 1.2(d), 8.4
Model Code DR 1-102, 7-102(A)(7)
18 U.S.C. §201

The Limits of the Law: *A Reprise*

Up to this point in these materials, we have been traversing the ethical minefield of fiduciary duty. We have examined the contours of the four "C's": competence, communication, confidentiality, and (avoiding) conflicts of interest. Along the way, we have come across a number of legal constraints that impose equally important limits on a lawyer's fiduciary duty or advocacy on behalf of a client.

These legal responses create additional minefields waiting for the lawyer who is unaware of their existence or unclear about their relevance in a given case. In previous notes and cases, we have identified some of these limits of the law that restrain unfettered client allegiance. We have encountered both lawyer and client fraud and criminal conduct, court orders that require or limit lawyer advocacy, procedural requirements that require disclosure of information, and federal and state conflict of interest statutes that limit the advocacy of former government lawyers.

This chapter sheds light on additional examples of these legal limits on client advocacy that may ensnare an unenlightened lawyer. Before turning to these new examples, we pause first to identify the bodies of law that create these restraints. We have already encountered at least eight distinct kinds of legal constraints that can limit a lawyer's advocacy on behalf of a client:

1. The **law of tort**, such as the law of **fraud** that created a duty to a third party in Greycas v. Proud, or the law of negligence, which potentially can create a duty to third parties in a *Tarasoff*-like case, as discussed in Hawkins v. King County.
2. The law of **evidence**, which can create exceptions to confidentiality enforced through court orders, like the crime-fraud exception to the attorney-client privilege, discussed in Purcell v. District Attorney and United States v. Chen.
3. **Court orders**, issued pursuant to the **inherent power** of a court, that can require a lawyer to provide representation, as discussed in Bothwell v. Republic Tobacco, enjoin a lawyer from further representation, as occurred in Maritrans GP Inc. v. Pepper, Hamilton & Sheetz, disqualify a lawyer whose representation will taint the trial, as in Kanaga v. Gannett Co., and Kala v. Aluminum Smelting & Refining Co., provide for contempt if a lawyer refuses to obey an order, as occurred in In re Original Grand Jury Investigation, or impose sanctions against lawyers who disregard their obligations of candor to the court, as occurred in United States v. Shaffer Equipment Co.
4. Rules of **civil procedure**, such as Rule 60(b), which provided the basis for relief against an opposing party in Spaulding v. Zimmerman.
5. Civil and criminal provisions in state and federal **securities law**, such as the provisions that afforded relief to third parties in Meyerhofer v. Empire Fire & Marine Ins. Co. and In re American Continental Corporation/Lincoln Savings & Loan Securities Litigation.
6. General **criminal statutes**, such as the prohibition against criminal impersonation, which created a limit on the lawyer's advocacy in People v. Casey, or the prohibition against obstruction of justice, which was not transgressed by the lawyers in People v. Belge. We encountered similar criminal laws that limit the practice of former government lawyers in an earlier note.
7. The provisions of **insurance law**, which enforce contractual duties to insured persons, such as the law of bad faith discussed in Wolpaw v. General Accident Insurance Co.
8. Rules of **mediation**, which required limits on subsequent advocacy in Poly Software Intl. v. Su.

All of this generally applicable law served as the basis for limiting what a lawyer was able to do on behalf of a client. Each legal provision also created substantial penalties or other ramifications for the lawyers unaware of the relevant limit.

In some instances, the lawyer or law firm involved paid substantial damages to third parties or a court for violating relevant legal prohibitions. In *Greycas* for example, the court upheld a judgment against an opposing party's lawyer for $833,760. Even more daunting was the result in *ACC*, where the law firm eventually settled the bondholder's claims for $24 million and the government's claims for $51 million, $20 million of which was paid personally by law firm partners. You might also recall that the government lawyers in *Shaffer Equipment* were ordered to pay personal sanctions of $2,000 each.

Two of the cases listed above also illustrate that a lawyer who ignores a relevant limit on advocacy often buys that client extended future litigation. The insurance company that hired the lawyers in *Spaulding* probably was not happy to have to relitigate its exposure, and may actually have ended up paying more than if it initially had disclosed the fact of Spaulding's injury. Contrast the lawyer in *Meyerhofer* who tried to change several clients' conduct before they violated federal securities laws.

The law firm fired him, only to subject itself and its clients to subsequent securities liability.

In other cases such as *Casey*, the lawyer's violation of a criminal statute resulted in discipline for an indictable offense. On the other hand, acceding to the appropriate limit on advocacy resulted in quashing the criminal indictment in *Belge*.

And finally, consider the consequence to the lawyers in *Kanaga, Poly Software,* and *Kala*. Although it may have been worth their time to litigate the question of whether they or their law firms could represent a client against a former client, all of these cases resulted in eventual disqualification.

The additional legal limits discussed in the following materials also create the potential for criminal, civil, disciplinary, or procedural sanctions. We begin by considering the effect of a federal anti-money-laundering statute on the practice of criminal defense lawyers. Next we consider a variety of procedural rules and inherent powers that provide the basis for monetary sanctions against lawyers who file frivolous lawsuits or evade discovery obligations. We then turn to consider limitations imposed on lawyers by laws that prohibit bias, such as civil rights provisions and the ADA. Near the end of the chapter, we focus on additional professional rules that prohibit or limit communication with represented and unrepresented persons, judges, and jurors. Finally, we examine the scope and application of professional code provisions that prohibit lawyers from appearing as witnesses in clients' cases.

Taken together, these requirements remind lawyers that neither they nor their clients are exempt from legal requirements that may create limitations on client advocacy. Legal limits on client loyalty also can create affirmative duties to third parties, such as the obligation to disclose client confidential information.

Two recent examples add to this list of limitations on advocacy. The first involves the Sarbanes-Oxley Act,[1] in which Congress directed the Securities and Exchange Commission to draft rules requiring lawyers who represent public companies "to report evidence of a material violation of securities law" to those within the corporate family. The regulations require such a lawyer to report both securities violations as well as breaches of fiduciary duty to the board of directors.[2] Lawyers who violate the rule face disbarment from SEC practice; that is, they would lose their ability to prepare documents or otherwise appear before the SEC. The Sarbanes duty applies to both inside and outside lawyers who represent the company in any matter[3] and is triggered by a lawyer's "reasonable belief" that such wrongdoing has occurred or is about to happen.

The second example flows from the USA Patriot Act, passed after 9-11 to respond to terrorist activities. One goal of the law was to strengthen the previously existing Financial Action Task Force on Money Laundering (FATF), an intergovernmental body designed to promote national and international policies to combat money laundering. A new undertaking of this group, called the "Gatekeeper Initiative," is directed at professionals including lawyers, whose clients transact domestic and international financial transactions and business. Should this initiative become law, lawyers could be required to submit Suspicious Transaction

1. 15 U.S.C. §7201 *et seq.* (2003).
2. 17 C.F.R. Part 205, 68 Fed. Reg. 6296 (2-6-03). Proposed regulations also provide that if the board fails to act, the lawyer must quit and disaffirm any documents previously submitted to the SEC, the so-called noisy withdrawal provision. 17 C.F.R. Part 205, 68 Fed. Reg. 6324 (2-5-03).
3. We commented on these provisions earlier in The Limits of the Law: Client Fraud, *supra* p.196 and Lawyers' Roles: The Instrumental Lawyer and the Limits of the Law, *supra* p.202.

Reports (now required of financial institutions)[4] regarding client activities and would be prohibited from telling their clients they had done so. In some countries, such obligations already apply to lawyers who manage client money or who assist in the planning or execution of transactions for clients concerning any financial or real estate transaction.

The ABA House of Delegates recently recommended that requiring lawyers who receive or transfer funds on behalf of clients "to verify the identity of clients, maintain records on domestic and international transactions, and develop training programs that would help attorneys identify potential money laundering schemes" was appropriate.[5] The same group strongly opposed the so-called tip off provisions, which would require lawyers to submit Suspicious Transaction Reports to government authorities based on a mere suspicion that the funds involved in the client's transaction stemmed from illegal activity, and would prevent lawyers from telling their clients they had done so.

Proposals like these are not likely to end the debate about the appropriate scope of client loyalty. We probably should be most wary of these efforts when the government seeks to make lawyers agents of its law enforcement efforts. On the other hand, we probably should welcome limits on advocacy when they seek to provide a fair and accessible justice system.

B. Reporting Requirements

Problem

9-2. Martyn & Fox's client in a criminal matter brings an $11,000 cash retainer to the office. He reminds Fox that he does not want the fact that he retained us or his identity disclosed unless he is indicted. Do we have any problem meeting this request?

Consider: Model Rules 1.6, 8.4
Model Code DR 4-101

Gerald B. Lefcourt, P.C. v. United States

125 F.3d 79 (2d Cir. 1997), cert. denied, *524 U.S. 937 (1998)*

WALKER, Circuit Judge:

Plaintiff-appellant Gerald B. Lefcourt, P.C. ("Lefcourt" or "the law firm") appeals from the May 16, 1996 judgment entered in the United States District Court for the Southern District of New York (Robert P. Patterson, Jr., District Judge), granting the United States' motion for summary judgment and denying plaintiff's cross-motion for summary judgment in plaintiff's tax refund action. In so doing, the district court affirmed the imposition of a

4. 31 U.S.C. §5318(g) (2000).
5. ABA Task Force on Gatekeeper Regulation and the Profession, *Comments of the ABA Task Force on Gatekeeper Regulation and the Profession on the Financial Action Task Force Consultation Paper dated May 30, 2002*, at 10 (2002).

$25,000 penalty by the Internal Revenue Service ("IRS") on the ground that Lefcourt had intentionally failed to comply with certain reporting requirements set forth in 26 U.S.C. §6050I and that the law firm had not established "reasonable cause" for doing so.

Lefcourt has advanced a number of reasons for failing to file the information required by §6050I, all of which are animated by a concern for the sensitive relationship that exists between attorney and client. We recognize the importance of this privilege and the impulse of attorneys to defend it vigorously, as Lefcourt has done here. However, for the following reasons, we affirm the judgment of the district court.

BACKGROUND

Title 26, section 6050I, of the United States Code requires "any person . . . engaged in a trade or business" who "in the course of such trade or business, receives more than $10,000 in cash . . ." to report to the IRS the person from whom the cash was received, the amount of cash received, the date and nature of the transaction, and "such other information as the Secretary may prescribe." Form 8300 is the form used to report such a transaction.

During the summer of 1993, Lefcourt, a law firm specializing in criminal defense work, undertook the representation of a client facing federal drug and money laundering charges. The client paid Lefcourt over $10,000 in cash for legal services. On July 9, 1993, the law firm submitted a Form 8300 to the IRS, stating that it had received in excess of $10,000, and particularizing the date of the payment. The firm, however, deliberately omitted the payor's name. In doing so, Gerald Lefcourt, the law firm's name partner, attached to the Form 8300 an affidavit asserting that revealing the client-identifying information called for by §6050I would prejudice the interests of a client whom the law firm was actively representing and that the confidentiality of the information was protected by the Fifth and Sixth Amendments of the Constitution and by the Lawyers' Code of Professional Responsibility.

On December 14, 1993, the IRS served the law firm with a Notice of Proposed Penalties under 26 U.S.C. §6721(e), which allows for the imposition of a penalty where "intentional disregard" of §6050I's reporting requirements is established. Over the following four months, Lefcourt initiated numerous correspondences with the IRS to request a conference with the IRS's Office of Appeals concerning the proposed penalty, and to explain the basis for its failure to provide the name of its client on the Form 8300. The overtures resulted in an apparently unsuccessful pre-settlement conference between Lefcourt and the IRS on April 12, 1994: on August 8, 1994 the IRS assessed the law firm a $25,000 penalty pursuant to §6721.

In September of 1994, the law firm paid the full amount of the assessed penalty and, on that date, claimed a refund for the same amount. The following day, the IRS notified Lefcourt that no refund would be granted. On December 6, 1994, Lefcourt brought this refund action in the district court pursuant to 28 U.S.C. §1346(a)(1).

In May 1995, while the case was pending before the district court, the law firm filed an amended Form 8300 that provided the name of the client that had previously been omitted from the form that was filed on July 9, 1993. . . .

I. INTENTIONAL DISREGARD

We first turn to the question of whether, by declining to provide its client's name as called for by Form

8300, the law firm acted with "intentional disregard" of §6050I's filing requirements. . . .

. . . When a party is deemed to have failed to file the information required by §6050I because of "intentional disregard of the filing requirement," the Internal Revenue Code provides that the party shall be fined the greater of $25,000 or the amount of cash received in the transaction. *See* 26 U.S.C. §6721(e)(2)(C). Title 26, section 301.6721-1(f)(2)(ii), of the Code of Federal Regulations indicates that "a failure is due to intentional disregard if it is a knowing or willful . . . failure to include correct information." . . .

. . . Lefcourt takes the position that under §6721, a good faith belief in the legality of one's conduct—even where that belief later proves to be mistaken or unreasonable—precludes a finding of intentional disregard. Put another way, Lefcourt argues that one must be aware of the law's requirements in order to disregard them, and thus, a subjective good faith belief that one's conduct is lawful precludes the imposition of the penalty. Lefcourt suggests that Congress chose to adopt this heightened "bad faith" requirement because the penalties provided for by the statute are severe. . . .

Section 6721 does not use the term "willful"; it uses the term "intentional disregard." But 26 C.F.R. §301.6721-1(f)(2)(ii) defines "intentional disregard" as synonymous with "willfulness." Thus, in our view, the "intentional disregard" set forth in §6721's penalty provision means conduct that is willful, a term which in this context requires only that a party act voluntarily in withholding requested information, rather than accidentally or unconsciously. Once it is determined, as it was here, that the failure to disclose client-identifying information was done purposefully, rather than inadvertently, it is irrelevant that the filer may have believed he was legally justified in withholding such information. The only question that remains is whether the law required its disclosure.

As it is uncontested that Lefcourt was aware that Form 8300 asked for its client's identity and nonetheless chose to refuse to provide the name, there is no dispute that Lefcourt acted voluntarily. We thus agree with the district court that, as a matter of law, Lefcourt's failure to disclose the client-identifying information was willful and in "intentional disregard" of the law firm's obligation.

II. MANDATORY WAIVER

Lefcourt argues that even if the law firm acted with intentional disregard of §6050I's reporting requirements, it was entitled to the automatic penalty waiver under 26 U.S.C. §6724. That section sets forth the waiver rules that apply to the penalties for failure to comply with certain IRS reporting requirements. It provides that "no penalty shall be imposed under this part with respect to any failure if it is shown that such failure is due to reasonable cause and not to willful neglect." . . . The burden of showing reasonable cause is on the party seeking the waiver. We hold that Lefcourt was not entitled to the waiver because the law firm failed to establish that it had an objectively reasonable argument for failing to disclose its client's identity. . . .

. . . Thus the appropriate inquiry in this case is whether the law firm's decision to withhold client-identifying information was consistent with the standard of care that a reasonably prudent attorney would use under the circumstances in the course of his or her business.

Preliminarily, we acknowledge that a reasonable attorney carefully attends to the attorney-client privilege. Not only is the attorney bound to do so under the various codes of professional responsibility that govern the practice of law, but also, to many attorneys, the privilege between attorney and client "is essential to enhancing frank and complete communication between attorney and client, which, in turn, promotes compliance with the law and facilitates the administration of justice." Yet the attorney-client privilege, however important to our system of justice, is not a license for an attorney to act "unreasonably" in willfully failing to comply with clear federal law. . . .

Lefcourt argued to the IRS and to the district court that under Second Circuit law the attorney-client privilege protects an attorney from disclosing the client-identifying information required under §6050I in certain "special circumstances." The law firm contended that it did not submit the required information principally because it believed that a special circumstance might be found to exist where the completed Form 8300 would provide the government with evidence of its client's unexplained wealth—evidence that could incriminate the client in the same proceedings for which the client had retained the law firm. Lefcourt also referred to the fact that disclosure of the client's identity might lead eventually to Lefcourt's being called as a witness against the client, which would in turn result in the law firm's disqualification.

Our assessment of the reasonableness of the law firm's claimed "special circumstances" begins with United States v. Goldberger & Dubin, P.C., 935 F.2d 501 (2d Cir. 1991). In *Goldberger*, . . . the attorneys argued that §6050I's reporting requirements were unconstitutional and violative of the attorney-client privilege. We rejected both claims and affirmed the district court's order directing disclosure of the client-identifying information.

With respect to the attorney-client privilege, we held that "absent special circumstances . . . the identification in Form 8300 of respondents' clients who make substantial cash payments is not a disclosure of privileged information." Thus, we suggested that although a client's identity is generally not privileged, there might be "special circumstances" where such information would be protected from disclosure. . . .

As a general rule, a client's identity and fee information are not privileged. *See* In re Grand Jury Subpoena Served Upon John Doe, Esq., 781 F.2d 238, 247 (2d Cir. 1989) (en banc). Although the court in *Goldberger* did not elaborate on the meaning of the special circumstances exception to the rule, it offered some guidance as to what might and what might not constitute such a circumstance. Significant to this case, the court expressly rejected the essence of Lefcourt's claim when it stated that the "asserted possibility" that a client may be incriminated by disclosure does not constitute a special circumstance.

In so doing, the court cited In re Grand Jury Subpoena Duces Tecum Served Upon Gerald L. Shargel, 742 F.2d 61 (2d Cir. 1984), which involved a defense attorney's appeal of a district court order denying a motion to quash a subpoena issued by a grand jury that sought to compel the attorney to produce records of money he had received from several clients who had been indicted for RICO violations. The government in *Shargel* admitted that the grand jury wanted the information as possible evidence that the defendants possessed unexplained wealth. Shargel argued that disclosure of the information would violate the attorney-client privilege by incriminating his clients in the RICO case. The court unequivocally rejected this "incrimination rationale" that Lefcourt now claims provided a reasonable basis for its own noncompliance. . . .

Goldberger and *Shargel*, read together, squarely reject the principal argument put forward by Lefcourt here: that possible or even likely client incrimination constitutes a special circumstance justifying nondisclosure. *See also Doe,* 781 F.2d at 247-48 (compelled disclosure of client identity and fee information that is incriminating evidence of unexplained wealth does not, "absent special circumstances," violate the attorney-client privilege).

Lefcourt attempts to avoid the force of *Goldberger* and *Shargel* by arguing that its case presents a unique twist on the incrimination rationale because the incrimination would have occurred in the very case for which the funds triggering the obligation to file a Form 8300 were expended as legal fees. . . .[5]

The foregoing argument by Lefcourt has been characterized by courts as the "legal advice exception," which holds client-identifying information privileged "where there is a strong probability that disclosure would implicate the client in the very criminal activity for which legal advice is sought." However, this exception (which has been described by [the Tenth Circuit] as "questionable validity,") has never once been accepted in this circuit. . . .

Thus the law is clear, and was so when Lefcourt refused to file its completed Form 8300: to the extent that the legal advice exception exists in any jurisdiction, it plainly is not recognized as a special circumstance in this circuit. . . .

Lefcourt next argues that incrimination in the very case for which the attorney was retained implicates (or could reasonably be thought to implicate) the so-called "direct linkage" special circumstance that this court mentioned in *Goldberger,* 935 F.2d at 505. If there is such an exception in this circuit outside of the Fifth Amendment context—a matter we do not decide—it must be derived from Marchetti v. United States, 390 U.S. 39, 48-49 (1968), a case where the Supreme Court held that the Fifth Amendment privilege against self-incrimination was a defense in a prosecution for failing to register as a gambler under the IRS's wagering tax provisions where the "direct and unmistakable consequence" of registration would be to implicate the party registering in the crime of gambling. The present case does not remotely resemble the facts of *Marchetti*, a case in which disclosure of the information provided the proof necessary to convict the filer of the crime of gambling—where the statutory filing requirement produced, in effect, a compelled confession of criminal activity. Here, in contrast, the client was not compelled to pay the law firm in cash, but rather did so voluntarily. *See Goldberger,* 935 F.2d at 504 ("To avoid disclosure under section 6050-I, they need only pay counsel in some manner other than with cash. The choice is theirs."). Furthermore, the disclosure that a client consulted an attorney and paid that attorney in cash, although probative of unexplained wealth, does not link the defendant to a crime in the manner required by *Marchetti.* Rather, "seeking legal advice is as much a first step in demonstrating innocence as it is an admission of guilt." And, most significantly, we have explicitly rejected claims of attorney-client privilege where disclosure of fee information might provide the government with evidence of unexplained wealth in a criminal case. . . .

In sum, we conclude that Lefcourt had no reasonable basis for failing to

5. In fact, *Shargel* arguably presents a worse case from a client's perspective than that presented here: in *Shargel,* there was no doubt that the information would be used against Shargel's clients, as that was the very purpose for which the grand jury sought it. In the present case, the information was sought by the IRS pursuant to a general reporting requirement. Whether the IRS would forward it to the U.S. Attorney for prosecutorial purposed was not a certainty.

provide the information required by §6050I under the facts presented here. Although the contours of the special circumstance exception have not been exhaustively developed, no doubt due to the fact special circumstances are seldom found to exist, it is clear that there is no special circumstance in this circuit simply because the provision of client-identifying information could prejudice the client in the case for which legal fees are paid. . . . We believe that this legal principle is firmly established and was so when the incomplete Form 8300 was filed. Thus we conclude that Lefcourt did not exercise the "standard of care that a reasonably prudent person would use under the circumstances in the course of its business in determining its filing obligations" in asserting otherwise. 26 C.F.R. §303.6724-1(d)(i).

We therefore agree with the district court that Lefcourt has not established "reasonable cause" for its willful noncompliance with §6050I. . . .

C. Frivolous Claims

Problem

9-3. Martyn & Fox filed a lawsuit against Chemco one week before the statute of limitations ran on behalf of three children born with birth defects, alleging that the birth defects were caused in utero by their mother's exposure to poisonous chemicals Chemco emitted into the air near their homes. Ten months later, Martyn & Fox consulted an expert for the first time, who told them there was no way to prove that Chemco's chemicals caused the birth defects in question. Martyn & Fox then voluntarily dismissed the claim, after Chemco had spent thousands of dollars on its own experts. Is Martyn & Fox in trouble?

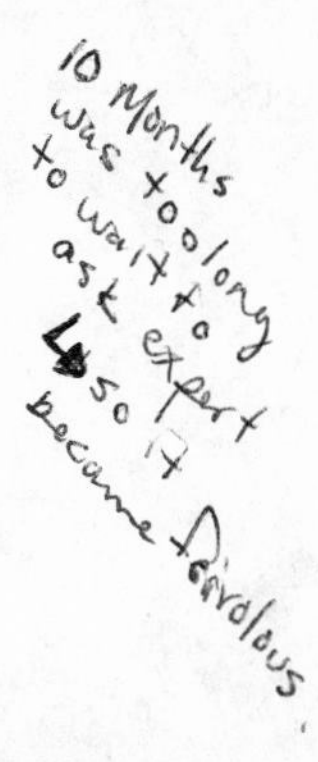

Consider: Model Rules 3.1, 3.4
Model Code DR 7-102(A)(1)
Federal Rule of Civil Procedure 11

Christian v. Mattel, Inc.

286 F.3d 1118 (9th Cir. 2002)

McKeown, Circuit Judge:

It is difficult to imagine that the Barbie doll, so perfect in her sculpture and presentation, and so comfortable in every setting, from "California girl" to "Chief Executive Officer Barbie," could spawn such acrimonious litigation and such egregious conduct on the part of her challenger. In her wildest dreams, Barbie could not have imagined herself in the middle of Rule 11 proceedings. But the intersection of copyrights on Barbie sculptures and the scope of Rule 11 is precisely what defines this case.

James Hicks appeals from a district court order requiring him, pursuant to Federal Rule of Civil Procedure 11, to pay Mattel, Inc. $501,565 in attorneys' fees that it incurred in defending against what the district court determined to be a frivolous action. Hicks brought suit on behalf of Harry Christian, claiming that Mattel's Barbie dolls infringed Christian's Claudene doll sculpture copyright. In its sanctions orders, the district court found that Hicks should have discovered prior to commencing the civil action that Mattel's dolls could not have infringed Christian's copyright because, among other things, the Mattel dolls had been created well prior to the Claudene doll and the Mattel dolls had clearly visible copyright notices on their heads. After determining that Hicks had behaved "boorishly" during discovery and had a lengthy rap sheet of prior litigation misconduct, the district court imposed sanctions.

We hold that the district court did not abuse its discretion in determining that the complaint filed by Hicks was frivolous under Rule 11. In parsing the language of the district court's sanctions orders, however, we cannot determine with any degree of certainty whether the district court grounded its Rule 11 decision on Hicks' misconduct that occurred outside the pleadings, such as in oral argument, at a meeting of counsel, and at a key deposition. This is an important distinction because Rule 11 sanctions are limited to misconduct regarding signed pleadings, motions, and other filings. Fed. R. Civ. P. 11. Consequently, we vacate the district court's orders and remand for further proceedings consistent with this opinion. In so doing, we do not condone Hicks' conduct or suggest that the district court did not have a firm basis for awarding sanctions. Indeed, the district court undertook a careful and exhaustive examination of the facts and the legal underpinnings of the copyright challenge. Rather, the remand is to assure that any Rule 11 sanctions are grounded in conduct covered by Rule 11 and to ensure adequate findings for the sizeable fee award.

BACKGROUND

I. PRIOR LITIGATION BETWEEN MATTEL AND CDC

Mattel is a toy company that is perhaps best recognized as the manufacturer of the world-famous Barbie doll. Since Barbie's creation in 1959, Mattel has outfitted her in fashions and accessories that have evolved over time. In perhaps the most classic embodiment, Barbie is depicted as a slender-figured doll with long blonde hair and blue eyes. Mattel has sought to protect its intellectual property by registering various Barbie-related copyrights, including copyrights protecting the doll's head sculpture. Mattel has vigorously litigated against putative infringers.

In 1990, Claudene Christian, then an undergraduate student at the University of Southern California ("USC"), decided to create and market a collegiate cheerleader doll. The doll, which the parties refer to throughout their papers as "Claudene," had blonde hair and blue eyes and was outfitted to resemble a USC cheerleader.

Mattel soon learned about the Claudene doll . . . [and] commenced a federal court action in 1997 in which it . . . alleged that CDC infringed various of Mattel's copyrights. At the time, Claudene Christian was president of CDC and Harry Christian was listed as co-founder of the company and chief financial officer. CDC retained Hicks as its counsel. After the court dismissed CDC's multiple counterclaims, the case was settled. Mattel released CDC from any copyright infringement liability in exchange for, among other things, a stipulation that Mattel was free to challenge CDC's alleged copyright of the Claudene doll should CDC "or any successor in interest" challenge Mattel's right to market its Barbie dolls.

II. THE PRESENT ACTION

Seizing on a loophole in the parties' settlement agreement, within weeks of the agreement, Harry Christian, who was not a signatory to the agreement, retained Hicks as his counsel and filed a federal court action against Mattel. In the complaint, which Hicks signed, Christian alleged that Mattel obtained a copy of the copyrighted Claudene doll in 1996, the year of its creation, and then infringed its overall appearance, including its face paint, by developing a new Barbie line called "Cool Blue" that was substantially similar to Claudene. Christian sought damages in the amount of $2.4 billion and various forms of injunctive relief. In an apparent effort to demonstrate that the action was not a sham, Claudene Christian and CDC were also named as defendants. . . .

Two months after the complaint was filed, Mattel moved for summary judgment. In support of its motion, Mattel proffered evidence that the Cool Blue Barbie doll contained a 1991 copyright notice on the back of its head, indicating that it predated Claudene's head sculpture copyright by approximately six years. Mattel therefore argued that Cool Blue Barbie could not as a matter of law infringe Claudene's head sculpture copyright. . . .

At a follow-up counsel meeting required by a local rule, Mattel's counsel attempted to convince Hicks that his complaint was frivolous. During the videotaped meeting, they presented Hicks with copies of various Barbie dolls that not only had been created prior to 1996 (the date of Claudene's creation), but also had copyright designations on their heads that pre-dated Claudene's creation. Additionally, Mattel's counsel noted that the face paint on some of the earlier-created Barbie dolls was virtually identical to that used on Claudene. Hicks declined Mattel's invitation to inspect the dolls and, later during the meeting, hurled them in disgust from a conference table.

Having been unsuccessful in convincing Hicks to dismiss Christian's action voluntarily, Mattel served Hicks with a motion for Rule 11 sanctions. In its motion papers, Mattel argued, among other things, that Hicks had signed and filed a frivolous complaint based on a legally meritless theory that Mattel's prior-created head sculptures infringed Claudene's 1997 copyright. Hicks declined to withdraw the complaint during the 21-day safe harbor period provided by Rule 11, and Mattel filed its motion.

Seemingly unfazed by Mattel's Rule 11 motion, Hicks proceeded with the litigation and filed a motion pursuant to Federal Rule of Civil Procedure 56(f) to obtain additional discovery. . . . The district court summarily denied the motion. . . .

Hicks then began filing additional papers that were characterized by frequency and volume. Following official completion of the summary judgment briefing schedule, Hicks filed what was styled as a "supplemental opposition." In those papers, Christian asserted for the first time that the head sculpture of Mattel's CEO Barbie (which was created in 1998) infringed Christian's copyright in the Claudene doll. He did not, however, move for leave to amend the complaint.

Hicks later filed additional papers alleging that several additional Barbie dolls infringed the Claudene sculpture. . . . [N]o motion for leave to amend the complaint was filed. . . .

III. THE DISTRICT COURT'S ORDERS

The district court granted Mattel's motions for summary judgment and Rule 11 sanctions. The court ruled that Mattel did not infringe the 1997 Claudene copyright because it could not possibly have accessed the Claudene doll at the time it created the head sculptures of the Cool Blue (copyrighted in 1991). . . .

Having rejected Hicks' reasons for eschewing a fees award, the district court made the following observations and findings:

> The court has considered whether an award of monetary sanctions less than the fees actually incurred would represent an appropriate sanction. The court has concluded that it would not. There is no dispute that Mr. Hicks was directly responsible for filing and pursuing this frivolous suit. Nor is there any dispute that the fees sought were actually incurred and paid. *Moreover, the court is satisfied from the documentation provided by Mattel's counsel that the fees incurred were reasonable.* While recognizing the significant burden this award imposes, the court has concluded that in light of Mr. Hicks' failure to respond to lesser sanctions and his continuing disregard for the most basic rules governing an attorney's professional conduct, the costs of his unacceptable behavior should fall squarely on him. Finally, while the court may reimburse an adverse party for expenses incurred in disposing of frivolous litigation, it can never compensate the judicial system for the time spent to dispose of an action that should never have been brought. The court can only hope that a sanction of this size will, at last, put a stop to Mr. Hicks' continuing pattern of abuse.

Emphasis added. . . .

> The court is satisfied that the other attorneys' fees Mattel has claimed are both reasonable and proximately caused by Mr. Hicks' pursuit of this frivolous action. [T]he Court *grants* Mattel its attorneys' fees in the amount of $501,565.00.

Original emphasis.

DISCUSSION. . .

II. IMPOSITION OF RULE 11 SANCTIONS. . .

A. General Rule 11 Principles

Filing a complaint in federal court is no trifling undertaking. An attorney's signature on a complaint is tantamount to a warranty that the complaint is well grounded in fact and "existing law" (or proposes a good faith extension of the existing law) and that it is not filed for an improper purpose.

Rule 11 provides in pertinent part:

> (a) Signature. Every pleading, written motion, and other paper shall be signed by at least one attorney of record in the attorney's individual name. . . .
>
> (b) Representations to Court. By presenting to the court (whether by signing, filing, submitting, or later advocating) a pleading, written motion, or other paper, an attorney or unrepresented party is certifying to the best of the person's knowledge, information, and belief, formed after an inquiry reasonable under the circumstances . . .
>
> (2) the claims, defenses, and other legal contentions therein are warranted by existing law or by a nonfrivolous argument for the extension, modification, or reversal of existing law or the establishment of new law;
>
> (3) the allegations and other factual contentions have evidentiary support or, if specifically so identified, are likely to have evidentiary support after a reasonable opportunity for further investigation or discovery[.]

The attorney has a duty prior to filing a complaint not only to conduct a reasonable factual investigation, but also to perform adequate legal research that confirms whether the theoretical underpinnings of the complaint are "warranted by existing law or a good faith argument for an extension, modification or reversal of existing law." Golden Eagle Distrib. Corp. v. Burroughs Corp., 801 F.2d 1531, 1537 (9th Cir. 1986). One of the fundamental purposes of Rule 11 is to "reduce frivolous claims, defenses or motions and to deter costly meritless maneuvers, . . . [thereby] avoiding delay and unnecessary expense in litigation." Nonetheless, a finding of significant delay or expense is not required under Rule 11. Where, as here, the complaint is the primary focus of Rule 11 proceedings, a district court must conduct a two-prong inquiry to determine (1) whether the complaint is legally or factually "baseless" from an objective perspective, and (2) if the attorney has conducted "a reasonable and competent inquiry" before signing and filing it.

B. The District Court's Findings Regarding the Meritless Claim

1. *Did Hicks Have an Adequate Legal or Factual Basis for Filing the Complaint?*

Hicks filed a single claim of copyright infringement against Mattel. The complaint charges that the Cool Blue Barbie infringed the copyright in the Claudene doll head. . . . Hicks cannot seriously dispute the district court's conclusions that, assuming the applicability of the doctrine of prior creation, Christian's complaint was legally and factually frivolous.

Indeed, as a matter of copyright law, it is well established that a prior-created work cannot infringe a later-created one. *See* Grubb v. KMS Patriots, L.P., 88 F.3d 1, 5 (1st Cir. 1996) (noting that "prior creation renders any conclusion of access or inference of copying illogical.").

Copyright infringement requires proof that a plaintiff owns a valid copyright in the work and that the defendant copied the work. . . . By simple logic, it is impossible to copy something that does not exist. Thus, if Mattel created its doll sculptures before CDC created Claudene in 1994, it is factually and legally impossible for Mattel to be an infringer.

The record of creation is telling and conclusive. The Cool Blue Barbie doll uses the Neptune's Daughter doll head which was created in 1991, some six years before the Claudene doll. . . . Hicks should have been well aware of the prior creation, not to mention that the copyright notice (including date of creation) appears prominently on the back of the dolls' heads. . . .

Consequently, in the face of undisputed evidence concerning the prior-creation of the Barbie dolls, the district court did not abuse its discretion by ruling that the complaint was frivolous.

2. *Did Hicks Conduct an Adequate Factual Investigation?*

The district court concluded that Hicks "filed a case without factual foundation." Hicks, having argued unsuccessfully that his failure to perform even minimal due diligence was irrelevant as a matter of copyright law, does not contest that he would have been able to discover the copyright information simply by examining the doll heads. Instead he argues that the district court did not understand certain "complex" issues. Simply saying so does not make it so. The district court well understood the legal and factual background of the case. It was Hicks' absence of investigation, not the district court's absence of analysis, that brought about his downfall.

The district court did not abuse its discretion in concluding that Hicks' failure to investigate fell below the requisite standard established by Rule 11.

III. THE DISTRICT COURT'S ADDITIONAL FINDINGS REGARDING MISCONDUCT

Hicks argues that even if the district court were justified in sanctioning him under Rule 11 based on Christian's complaint and the follow-on motions, its conclusion was tainted because it impermissibly considered other misconduct that cannot be sanctioned under Rule 11, such as discovery abuses, misstatements made during oral argument, and conduct in other litigation.

Hicks' argument has merit. While Rule 11 permits the district court to sanction an attorney for conduct regarding "pleadings, written motions, and other papers" that have been signed and filed in a given case, Fed. R. Civ. P. 11(a), it does not authorize sanctions for, among other things, discovery abuses or misstatements made to the court during an oral presentation. . . .

In its January 5, 2000, order, the district court cited multiple bases for its Rule 11 findings. . . .

In connection with the conclusion on boorish behavior, the court cited Hicks' conduct ("tossing Barbie dolls off a table") at a meeting of counsel and his interruption of a deposition following a damaging admission by his client. The charge of misrepresentation of facts was based on a statement made at oral argument that he had never seen a particular catalogue while a videotape of exhibit inspections showed him" leisurely thumbing through the catalogue." Hicks' conflicting representations in pleadings as to the identity of allegedly infringing Barbie dolls was an additional example of misrepresentation noted by the court. Finally, the court determined that Hicks made misrepresentations in his briefs concerning the law of joint authorship in the copyright context. . . .

. . . Further, in determining that monetary sanctions were appropriate, the district court considered Hicks' "failure to respond to lesser sanctions" imposed in earlier actions and his "continuing disregard for the most basic rules governing an attorneys' professional conduct."

The orders clearly demonstrate that the district court decided, at least in part, to sanction Hicks because he signed and filed a factually and legally meritless complaint and for misrepresentations in subsequent briefing. But the orders, coupled with the supporting examples, also strongly suggest that the court considered extra-pleadings conduct as a basis for Rule 11 sanctions. Although the court also referenced conduct in related litigation, it is unlikely that the court based its order on such conduct because Hicks had already been sanctioned for violating local rules in the context of the related litigation and the court noted that fact.

The laundry list of Hicks' outlandish conduct is a long one and raises serious questions as to his respect for the judicial process. Nonetheless, Rule 11 sanctions are limited to "papers" signed in violation of the rule. Conduct in depositions, discovery meetings of counsel, oral representations at hearings, and behavior in prior proceedings do not fall within the ambit of Rule 11. Because we do not know for certain whether the district court granted Mattel's Rule 11 motion as a result of an impermissible intertwining of its conclusion about the complaint's frivolity and Hicks' extrinsic misconduct, we must vacate the district court's Rule 11 orders.

We decline Mattel's suggestion that the district court's sanctions orders could be supported in their entirety under the court's inherent authority. To impose sanctions under its inherent authority, the district court must "make an explicit finding [which it did not do here] that counsel's conduct constituted or was tantamount to bad faith." We acknowledge that the district court has a broad array of sanctions options at its disposal: Rule 11, 28 U.S.C. §1927,[11] and the court's inherent authority. Each of these sanctions alternatives has its own particular requirements, and it is important that the grounds be separately articulated to assure that the conduct at issue falls within the scope of the sanctions remedy. . . . On remand, the district court will have an opportunity to delineate the factual and legal basis for its sanctions orders.

IV. THE DISTRICT COURT'S DECISION TO AWARD ATTORNEYS' FEES

Hicks raises various challenges to the quantum of attorneys' fees. Because we are vacating the district court's Rule 11 orders on other legal grounds, we express no opinion at this stage about the particular reasonableness of any of the fees the district court elected to award Mattel. We do, however, encourage the district court on remand to ensure that the time spent by Mattel's attorneys was reasonably and appropriately spent in relation to both the patent frivolousness of Christian's complaint and the services directly caused by the sanctionable conduct.[12] *See* Fed. R. Civ. P. 11, advisory committee notes, 1993 Amendments, Subdivisions (b) and (c) (noting that attorneys' fees may only be awarded under Rule 11 for those "services directly and unavoidably caused" by the sanctionable conduct).

CONCLUSION

We vacate the district court's Rule 11 orders and remand for further proceedings consistent with this opinion. . . .

D. Discovery Abuse

Problem

9-4. An associate at Martyn & Fox believes the firm must produce certain damaging documents in a product liability case, which virtually concede our client's liability in the matter. Fox insists they not be produced because the documents came from the client's subsidiary in Germany, and it would be burdensome to search the German subsidiary's warehouse. "Let's just object to producing any of the subsidiary's documents," Fox instructs the associate. May the associate accept direction from Fox, the experienced partner? What if documents from the subsidiary have not been requested?

Consider: Model Rules 3.2, 3.4, 5.2
Model Code DR 7-106(A) and (C), 7-109(A)
Federal Rules of Civil Procedure 26, 37

---

11. Section 1927 provides for imposition of "excess costs, expenses, and attorneys' fees" on counsel who "multiplies the proceedings in any case unreasonably and vexatiously."

12. For example, because the action was frivolous on its face, why would Mattel's attorneys need to spend 700 hours ($173,151.50 in fees) for the summary judgment motion and response? Although Hicks clearly complicated the proceedings through multiple filings, Mattel's theory and approach was stunningly simple and required little explication: (1) Mattel's Barbie dolls and face paint were prior copyright creations that could not infringe the after-created Claudene doll and (2) Christian was neither a contributor to nor owner of the copyright. This is not to say that Hicks' defense of the motion necessarily called for a timid response, but neither does it compel a bazooka approach.

In re Tutu Wells Contamination Litigation

120 F.3d 368 (3d Cir. 1997)

BECKER, Circuit Judge.

This is an appeal from an order of the district court imposing heavy sanctions upon a law firm, several of its partners, and its client for discovery violations in connection with a large environmental lawsuit. The client, Esso, is charged in the underlying complaint with having "poisoned the wells" in the Estate Tutu area in the eastern end of St. Thomas by releasing from the Esso Tutu service station petroleum hydrocarbons and chlorinated hydrocarbons into the Tutu aquifer which supplies drinking water to much of the east end of the island. The discovery abuse primarily involves the alleged suppression by Esso's former counsel in the litigation, the San Juan, Puerto Rico law firm of Goldman, Antonetti, Ferraiuoli & Axtmayer, of a report by Jose Agrelot, a professional engineer, summarizing the results of soil and liquid tests he had performed at the Esso Tutu site in December 1989. The suppression of this report is claimed to have dramatically increased the discovery time and expense for other parties in connection with their prosecution of the case. . . .

What specially marks this case is the character and magnitude of the sanctions imposed. Eschewing the auspices of Fed. R. Civ. P. 37, which authorizes sanctions for failure to make disclosure or cooperate in discovery, the district court imposed the challenged sanctions under its inherent power. The sanction imposed on the lawyers was suspension from practice in the District Court of the Virgin Islands: Jose Cepeda and Francis Torres for three years, and Eugenio Romero for one year.[4] The sanction imposed upon Esso was the payment of $750,000 to a "Community Service Sanction Account" to be utilized to fund construction of a halfway house on St. Thomas, the training of inmates, and renovation of the St. Thomas Criminal Justice Complex. The sanction imposed upon Goldman Antonetti was the payment of $250,000 to the Community Service Sanction Account (for the same purpose), and the sum of $120,000 as counsel fees and costs ($30,000 incurred by each of four moving parties for time they spent in connection with the sanctions proceedings themselves). Esso was similarly assessed a sanction of $30,000 to be paid to each of four other movants, but Esso has paid that sum and does not challenge it on this appeal.

Goldman Antonetti, its three named partners, and Esso appeal the sanctions imposed against them on a variety of grounds. . . .

I. FACTS AND PROCEDURAL HISTORY

A. Background and Overview

In the summer of 1987, a water well owner noticed the smell of gasoline emanating from his well. He contacted local environmental officials who, with the help of the federal government, began an investigation into possible contamination of the Tutu aquifer. Investigators discovered the presence of gasoline and chlorinated organics in the aquifer. Government officials thereafter closed many of the wells.

Sanctions

4. Romero and Torres were admitted to practice before the court *pro hac vice*. There is some dispute as to whether Cepeda was technically admitted. . . .

The discovery of the contamination led to a number of private lawsuits. Detailed explication of the anatomy of the various suits is unnecessary; it is sufficient to note that the private litigation seeks to assign responsibility for the contamination between and among a number of possible contaminators, including but not limited to two automobile service stations, an automobile dealer, a shopping plaza, a dry cleaner, and a former textile plant. That private litigation also includes claims for contribution under CERCLA. The parties in the litigation include both possible contaminators and businesses and landowners allegedly harmed by the contamination. The law firm of Goldman, Antonetti, Ferraiuoli & Axtmayer ("Goldman Antonetti") represented Esso for much of the period in question but no longer does so.

Discovery began in 1989. During this discovery, Esso and Goldman Antonetti employed practices the district court found to be sanctionable. In its three opinions regarding the sanctions, the district court grouped the discovery violations into three categories. First, the court found that Esso and its attorneys engaged in a strategy that kept the various other parties in the litigation from obtaining needed information in a timely fashion. . . . Without delving into the specifics of individual abuses, the court noted that Esso and Goldman Antonetti met many discovery requests with legal tactics intended to delay, oppress, or harass their opponents. Often, Esso and Goldman Antonetti would refuse to turn over requested documents until forced to do so by court order. According to the court, the level of judicial involvement in the discovery process was consequently unusually high, requiring the court unnecessarily to devote significant resources to resolving ordinary discovery disputes.

Second, the court focused on the handling of the so-called Agrelot memorandum. In December 1989, Soil Tech, a company that specializes in environmental analyses of soil, took samples from the soil at the Esso Tutu Service Station ("ETSS") and from liquid in a holding tank at ETSS. Soil Tech sent those samples to the Environmental Testing and Certification Corp. ("ETC") for analysis. ETC returned the results of the investigation to Soil Tech shortly thereafter. The results revealed some contamination. Jose Agrelot, President of Soil Tech, received the preliminary results and summarized them in a memorandum, which he forwarded to Goldman Antonetti in anticipation of a meeting in January 1990. ETC produced the final results of the testing shortly after the meeting had occurred. Agrelot testified that he discussed the memorandum with attorneys at Goldman Antonetti, including Jose Cepeda and Francis Torres. . . .

Although for the most part the Agrelot memorandum merely summarized the information contained in the ETC findings, the memorandum did include a map pinpointing the locations of the soil borings from which the tested soil was taken. It appears from the record that, without the Agrelot memorandum, someone examining the ETC data could not determine with precision the location of the borings. The record does, however, give some indication that there is enough information in the ETC supporting data that was made available to determine that the ETC analyzed soil from ETSS rather than from some other location above the Tutu aquifer. Esso and its attorneys produced the full ETC report on which the Agrelot memorandum was based.

However, neither Esso, Goldman Antonetti, nor Soil Tech turned over the Agrelot memorandum during discovery until October 1993. Prior to that time, various parties had specifically requested all reports generated from soil and groundwater testing in the Tutu area, but the responses to such requests, either signed by or reviewed by Esso employees or Goldman Antonetti attorneys, made no mention of the Agrelot memorandum. The reasons for this omission are not clear. Lawyers from Goldman Antonetti testified that the Agrelot memorandum had been indexed incorrectly in their computer database; Agrelot himself testified that the memorandum had been labeled incorrectly and therefore misfiled in his office. The district court found that the failure to produce the Agrelot memorandum was intentional. . . . At all events, only after Agrelot had searched his files in the fall of 1993 to assist Esso in negotiating a case management order did he find the memorandum and turn it over to Esso, who revealed it to its new counsel Archer & Greiner. It was Archer & Greiner that finally notified the other parties of its existence.

The third category of violations occurred in connection with an attempted inspection underneath the surface of the ETSS site. In particular, the plaintiffs wished to determine whether an underground storage tank was located on the site, and also to trace the pipes leading out of the oil/water separator located on the site. The parties refer to this aspect of the discovery as the "anomaly investigation." In May, 1992, the plaintiffs employed ground penetrating radar ("GPR") to examine the area beneath the ETSS. The GPR turned up an anomalous shadow in the corner of the site, possibly indicating the presence of an underground storage tank. Esso claimed that the GPR produced a false result because of interference from overhead power lines or from a reinforcing bar in a nearby retaining wall. The magistrate judge ultimately ordered an excavation of the site to determine once and for all if such a tank existed. It did not.

Excavation of the site was to occur in accordance with the magistrate judge's order. However, according to the district court, Esso failed to comply with this order. . . . This failure led to months of wrangling among the parties and between Esso and the court until Esso finally conducted the investigation to the satisfaction of the court, nearly 10 months after the investigation was scheduled to be completed. . . .

II. SUSPENSIONS OF ATTORNEYS CEPEDA, ROMERO, AND TORRES . . .

Cepeda, Romero, and Torres submit that their suspensions cannot stand because the district court did not afford them particularized notice of the form of the sanctions they faced. They had no way of knowing, they contend, that the possibility of suspension as a sanction existed. Therefore, they conclude, their right to due process was infringed. . . .

In considering the suspension of an attorney as a sanction, courts must provide the attorney with due process. Although the precise contours of the process that is due varies given the particular context, "the fundamental requirements of due process—notice and an opportunity to respond—must be afforded before any sanction is imposed." Similarly, prior to the suspension of an attorney from practicing before the District Court of the Virgin Islands because of misconduct as defined by local rule, an attorney must be provided "notice and an opportunity to be heard." D.V.I. R. 83.2(b)(4)(A).

The party against whom sanctions are being considered is entitled to notice of the legal rule on which the sanctions would be based, the reasons for the sanctions, and the form of the potential sanctions. . . .

In the present case, neither Cepeda, Romero, nor Torres received particularized notice that the court was contemplating suspending them from practicing law as a sanction. . . . As far as we can tell, the possibility of suspension arose for the first time in the court's third and final published opinion on the matter, when the court actually imposed the suspensions. Neither did the parties moving for sanctions seek suspension; their papers before the district court sought only monetary sanctions and dismissal. . . .

. . . Put differently, had Cepeda, Romero, and Torres been on notice that they faced suspension, they doubtless would have utilized their opportunity to be heard to raise different matters. As it happened, because of the lack of notice, the attorneys' opportunity to be heard was less than meaningful; they were not given the appropriate opportunity to present relevant defenses to the penalties which they were ultimately assessed. . . . Because their rights to due process were violated, we will vacate that portion of the order on appeal suspending them from practice in the District Court of the Virgin Islands.

III. THE COMMUNITY SERVICE SANCTION . . .

As previously noted, the district court employed its inherent powers to sanction Esso and Goldman Antonetti. A threshold question, then, might be whether the court's resort to the inherent powers, in lieu of the rule-based and statute-based sanctions—e.g., Fed. R. Civ. P. 11, 16, and 37, or 28 U.S.C. §1927—was appropriate.[13] We need not reach this question, however. As we shall discuss more fully below, the court had no authority under its inherent powers to impose the type of sanction it did.

The Supreme Court has furnished us with at least a partial list of a court's inherent powers. Employing its inherent powers, a court can control admission to its bar, discipline attorneys, punish for contempt, vacate its own judgment upon a finding of fraud, bar a criminal defendant from a courtroom for disruptive behavior, dismiss a suit on forum non conveniens grounds or for failure to prosecute, and assess attorney's fees. *See* Chambers v. NASCO, Inc., 501 U.S. 32 (1991).

In addition to those mentioned by the Supreme Court, other inherent powers include the power to fine, to disqualify counsel, to preclude claims or defenses, and to limit a litigant's future access to the courts. With these many bows in their sanctioning quivers, courts have frequently invoked their inherent powers "to regulate the conduct of the members of the bar as well as to provide tools for docket management."

Notwithstanding the variety of tools available to a court under its inherent powers, we believe that an order directing a party to the litigation to remit funds to a third party is outside the scope of a court's inherent powers. We begin our analysis by noting that "because of their very potency, inherent powers must be exercised with restraint and discretion." *Chambers*, 501 U.S. at 44. That "inherent powers are shielded from direct democratic controls" makes this exercise of restraint and discretion even more important. Roadway Express, Inc. v. Piper, 447 U.S. 752, 764 (1980). . . .

13. In Chambers v. NASCO, Inc., 501 U.S. 32 (1991), the Supreme Court discussed at length the inherent powers of a court to sanction and their relationship to rule-based and statute-based powers to sanction, e.g., Rule 11, Rule 16, Rule 37, and §1927. To oversimplify somewhat, the Court held that the existence of rule-based or statute-based powers does not preclude a court's employing its inherent powers. The Court observed, but apparently did not require, that normally a court should look first to those rule-based or statute-based powers before turning to its inherent powers, reserving the inherent powers for instances in which the rule-based or statute-based powers are not "up to the task."

. . . [I]nherent powers fall into three distinct categories: powers arising from Article III, powers arising from the nature of the court, and powers arising from historical notions of the courts of equity.

No matter where one places their origin, it is clear that the power exercised in this case cannot be derived from a court's inherent powers. The district court's actions are essentially legislative in nature. Although we recognize that the line between a judicial act and legislative act is difficult to fix with certainty, the district court's sanction here falls on the legislative side of whatever line we may draw. The court ordered the reallocation of resources from private entities to an agency of the public sector not a party in the case. It chose from whom the resources would be taken and to whom the resources would redound, without regard to the anatomy of the case before it. In so doing, the court ventured well beyond the case and controversy before it.

We do not find persuasive the argument that a court's inherent powers include the wielding of what is essentially a legislative power. We believe that it is not in the nature of courts of justice normally to engage in the redistribution of wealth to parties outside of the litigation. We find nothing in Article III that allows for such a power. Further, we do not believe that such a power is necessary for the efficient functioning of a court. Fines made payable to the court would do just as well in ensuring that parties do not interfere with that functioning. From the standpoint of the sanctioned party, the disciplining effect of a fine made payable to the court is no different from the disciplining effect of a sanction made payable to some third party; the sanctioned party is out of pocket the same amount either way. Finally, we have been directed to no historical evidence demonstrating that courts of equity had this power, and given that the inherent powers must be exercised with restraint, we see no reason to permit this power now. . . .

We appreciate the sense of outrage that motivated the district court's decision to impose the community service sanction. The contamination of the Tutu aquifer was tragic, and the delay in determining responsibility for that contamination is doubtless frustrating. The community service sanction, at least on its face, is attractive because it seeks to punish those who have caused, at least in part, that delay and assist those who might have been harmed by the contamination. In that sense, the district court's actions were admirable. However, a court does not always do well by doing good. Though we applaud the district court's motives, we are constrained to find fault with its remedy.

In sum, we hold that the district court's inherent powers cannot support the imposition of the community service sanction.[18]

IV. MONETARY SANCTIONS . . .

Was the Monetary Sanction Appropriate?[21] . . .

Goldman Antonetti argues that the district court impermissibly awarded sanctions based on the costs and

18. Moreover, we have serious doubts that one could plausibly argue that Congress provided the courts—by statute or by rule—the power to impose the type of sanction imposed here. In order to provide such power, we believe three criteria must be satisfied: (1) this must be a power that Congress can constitutionally delegate to a coordinate branch; (2) Congress must clearly indicate its intent to delegate this power; and (3) Congress must provide intelligible principles to guide the courts in the exercise of this power. None of these criteria is satisfied here.

21. The analysis that follows in the text does not make a distinction between inherent powers sanctions and statute-based or rule-based sanctions. In respects relevant to our discussion, the sanctioning tools are the same.

expenses arising from the sanctions proceedings themselves. In the firm's submission, such an award constitutes improper fee shifting. We disagree. It is beyond dispute that attorney's fees are, in certain circumstances, properly awarded as a sanction. . . . The time, effort, and resources expended in bringing sanctionable conduct to light would have been unnecessary had the sanctionable conduct never occurred. These costs are as much a harm to a party in the litigation as is the delay in the litigation or the substantive prejudice caused by the conduct. If we exclude from a possible award the costs of sanctions proceedings, we would undermine the compensatory goal of a sanctions award.

Further, if a party is aware ex ante that the costs he incurs in exposing sanctionable conduct will never be recouped, that party may decide to forgo a sanctions proceeding altogether. . . . In doing so, however, that party might allow otherwise sanctionable conduct to go unaddressed. In such cases, the deterrent goal of a sanction award has been lost; parties who know that the likelihood of facing a sanction proceeding are low may engage in sanctionable conduct more often. . . .

In addition, in 1993, Rule 11 was amended to add language that would allow sanctions for the costs associated with presenting or opposing a motion for Rule 11 sanctions. . . .

Goldman Antonetti is correct in pointing out that the district court did not identify with specificity many of the acts that caused it to infer that Esso and Goldman Antonetti were engaged in a pattern of delay. The court did, however, make extensive findings as to the Agrelot memorandum and the anomaly investigation. With respect to both of those matters, the district court's findings were not unreasonable. The undisputed fact is that the Agrelot memorandum did not surface until well after discovery had begun and until well after parties to the litigation had made repeated requests that clearly covered the document.

Goldman Antonetti advances a plausible explanation for why the Agrelot memorandum was produced so late in the litigation. It is certainly possible that no attorney from Goldman Antonetti knew of the Agrelot memorandum until it was found in October 1993, notwithstanding testimony to the contrary; it is equally possible that the Agrelot memorandum was misfiled by both Soil Tech and by Goldman Antonetti. That is not to say, however, that the court's findings, which are based on an inference that Goldman Antonetti intentionally withheld the Agrelot memorandum, are unreasonable. There is evidence in the record that Goldman Antonetti attorneys knew of the memorandum's existence. Those same attorneys responded to the discovery requests covering such memorandum, and yet the document was not produced.

With respect to the anomaly investigation, our analysis is similar. Goldman Antonetti relies on a report by a magistrate judge concluding that the firm's actions during the investigation amounted to nothing more than zealous advocacy in representation of its clients and therefore did not warrant sanctions. The firm submits that the district court had no basis to disagree with the magistrate judge's conclusions. However, the district court in that instance did not owe the magistrate judge any deference. Further, the undisputed evidence makes it clear that it was not unreasonable for the district court to conclude that the delays in the investigation were willful and in bad faith. The investigation began late, was aborted prematurely because of the failure of the parties to arrive with appropriate equipment, and was not completed for many months.

Goldman Antonetti's next argument—that the failure to produce the Agrelot memorandum caused no harm to the other parties in the litigation—suffers the same fate. The firm here stresses that it produced the entire ETC report, of which the Agrelot memorandum was merely a summary. If, Goldman Antonetti questions, a full report has been produced, how can the failure to produce a summary of the report cause any harm to a party that can easily summarize the report for itself? The firm has a good point, but it does not mean that the district court's conclusion was contrary to reason. The ETC report was both complex and voluminous. Examining it required significant costs. A summary prepared by an expert would have reduced these costs and identified the problems that could only have been discovered by imposing a considerable burden on those examining the report for the first time. We concede, as did the district court, that the summary, timely produced, might have provided the parties to the litigation with less assistance than they claim. Still, it would have provided assistance, and that is the crux of the harm caused by the failure of Esso and Goldman Antonetti to produce the Agrelot memorandum. . . .

In sum, we are satisfied that the district court did not abuse its discretion in concluding that Goldman Antonetti is subject to some form of sanction and that $120,000 was an appropriate sanction. . . .

Having held that the discovery violations caused harm, the court examined the papers these parties submitted that purported to describe the extent of that harm. The court believed that the papers "suffered from two shortcomings." First, the papers did not adequately categorize the claimed harm within the framework the court had created for addressing the sanctionable conduct. The court found it difficult to determine whether the moving parties were seeking costs and expenses from (1) discovery violations related to the search for evidence of contamination at ETSS; (2) the failure to disclose the Agrelot memo; or (3) the sanctions proceedings themselves, the three broad areas into which the court held sanctionable conduct fell. Second, the court faulted the parties for their general failure to provide it with documentation "that adequately and efficiently explained to the court how those expenses could be justified as a sanction."

These shortcomings led the court to award only a portion of the sanctions sought. The court declined to scrutinize the voluminous submissions of the parties in order to perform the categorization it had requested the parties to perform. Instead, the court simply denied the award of sanctions arising from (1) discovery violations related to the search for evidence of contamination at ETSS; and (2) the failure to disclose the Agrelot memo. The court did, however, award sanctions arising from the sanctions proceedings themselves. The court set a uniform level of sanction award based on L'Henri's request. The court did so because it believed that L'Henri's request was clear, well supported, and, in all, "unassailable.". . .

We believe that the district court was well within its discretion to deny the requested sanctions based upon the parties' submissions. . . .

. . . Although a court is free to do so, it is not incumbent upon a district court to devote its own valuable time, energy, and resources to remedy the shortcomings of movants' submissions if that assistance falls short. Nor will we require the court to do so here. We thus do not believe the district court abused its discretion in refusing to award sanctions based on the submissions of the movants. . . .

According to the court, L'Henri's counsel, Nancy D'Anna, submitted well-reasoned, thoroughly researched, and adequately documented material to the court throughout the sanctions proceedings. What is more, the court continued, L'Henri produced such material efficiently and relatively cheaply. In deciding to base the uniform level of sanction on L'Henri's request, the district court implicitly found that each party could have produced similarly well-reasoned, thorough, and adequately documented material for no greater cost than that incurred by L'Henri. We believe that it is not an abuse of discretion for the district court to assume that all parties can produce work of L'Henri's quality for approximately the same cost.

In sum, we believe the district court acted within its discretion in awarding only a portion of the monetary sanctions sought by the moving parties. . . .

E. Bias

Problem

9-5. Martyn is furious with opposing counsel, who happens to be one of the most highly regarded male lawyers in town. In the course of a recent deposition, this lawyer referred to Martyn as "office help," and repeatedly called her "sweetheart," "dear," and raised his voice to drown her out, which required Martyn to stop talking until he was finished and then inquire if she could be heard. What do you advise?

Consider: Model Rules 4.4, 8.4
Model Code DR 7-101

In re Charges of Unprofessional Conduct Contained in Panel Case No. 15976

653 N.W.2d 452 (Minn. 2002)

Per Curiam.

Respondent represented a disabled plaintiff in a personal-injury action. During the jury trial, respondent moved for a mistrial advocating on behalf of his client that the presence of the court's severely disabled law clerk diminished his client's ability to receive a fair trial. At the conclusion of trial, respondent moved for a new trial, once again objecting to the presence of the law clerk in the courtroom. Judge Franklin J. Knoll (complainant) filed a complaint with the Office of Lawyers Professional Responsibility (OLPR) asserting that respondent's conduct violated the Minnesota Rules of Professional Conduct. . . .

Respondent's client sustained serious permanent physical injuries that disabled him when a school bus hit and ran over him with a rear tire while he was riding a bicycle in South Minneapolis. The accident crushed his pelvis, and left him in a coma for approximately 1 month. By the time of trial, the client was able to walk with the assistance of a cane. Before the accident, the client was employed as a checker and bagger at a grocery store and as a greeter at a restaurant. His employment background consisted of similar unskilled and physical labor positions. At trial, the client asserted that his permanent injuries prevented him from performing physical-labor-type jobs and that he did not qualify educationally or intellectually for other types of employment. Therefore, he sought damages for future loss of wages and future diminished earning capacity.

Complainant presided over the personal-injury action and assigned one of his two law clerks to assist with the action. The clerk assigned by complainant to assist in this case is physically disabled. He is paralyzed from his mouth down and has difficulty breathing and speaking. He performed his duties as a law clerk with the assistance of a large wheelchair, respirator and full-time attendant. The disabled clerk was present in the courtroom at the outset of the personal-injury trial, assisted with jury selection, and remained in the courtroom throughout the trial.

On the first day of trial, respondent's client expressed reservations about his ability to receive a fair trial grounded on the fact that if the disabled law clerk continued to work in the courtroom, the jury would compare the clerk who was more severely disabled yet able to work, to himself, who was less severely disabled and claiming an inability to work. Later that same day respondent made an oral motion outside the presence of the jury, "for a mistrial and another panel of jurors without your law clerk present or in the alternative that this case be assigned to another judge." Respondent gave the following explanation for his motion:

> I will be asking the jury to award future loss of wages, future diminished earning capacity. I do not believe a jury when they look at the comparison with your law clerk, who's obviously gainfully employed, working in the courtroom under great handicap and great duress, will be able to award anything to my client under those circumstances.

Respondent stated that he brought the motion with "great reluctance" and acknowledged that the motion was "outrageous and distasteful for the court." He did not support his motion with any legal authority. Stating that the motion was "un-American," complainant denied the motion.

The jury found in favor of the defendant on the issue of liability. Subsequently, respondent brought a written motion for a new trial. Respondent asserted the presence of the disabled clerk in the courtroom as one basis for the motion. Respondent again stated that his objection to the clerk's presence in the courtroom was made with "the greatest reluctance," but he argued that the jury would compare the disabilities of the law clerk with the injuries of his client. Again, respondent failed to cite any legal authority in support of his position. . . .

. . . The Panel found that respondent violated Rule 8.4(d) by bringing the written motion for a new trial. We have concluded that similar race-based misconduct violates Rule 8.4(d). In re Panel File 98-26, 597 N.W.2d 563 (Minn. 1999).

In In re Panel File 98-26, we issued an admonition to a prosecutor for making a motion to exclude a public defender from participating in a trial based solely on his race. After accepting a position as a special assistant county attorney, the prosecutor was assigned to take over the prosecution of an African-American male charged with two counts of felony robbery of a Caucasian couple. The prosecutor previously assigned to the case left a memorandum in the case file explaining that the public defender felt race was an issue in the case and planned to recruit an

African-American public defender to try the case. Subsequently, the prosecutor brought a motion in limine requesting:

> An Order from this Court prohibiting counsel for the defendant to have a person of color as co-counsel for the sole purpose of playing upon the emotions of the jury.

Two workdays after filing the motion, the prosecutor realized the gravity of her mistake, withdrew the motion, and apologized to both public defenders. She also implemented measures to prevent reoccurrence of the misconduct. . . .

On review, we rejected the Panel's determination that the prosecutor's conduct was "non-serious" and unequivocally held that race-based misconduct is inherently serious. Moreover, we emphasized that race-based misconduct committed by an officer of the court is especially destructive because it "undermine[s] confidence in our system of justice [and] erode[s] the very foundation upon which justice is based.". . .

In In re Panel File 98-26, we emphasized that race should never be used as a basis for limiting an attorney's participation in a court proceeding. We extend this holding to encompass situations where disability is used to limit a court employee's participation in a court proceeding. Neither race nor disability should be used as a means of limiting participation in our courts. Minnesota has adopted legislation prohibiting discrimination against individuals with disabilities. *See* Minnesota Human Rights Act (MHRA), Minn. Stat. §§363.01-363.20 (2000). The MHRA prohibits discrimination against individuals with disabilities in employment, housing, public accommodations, public services and education; the MHRA also prohibits race-based discrimination in these same areas. . . . Therefore, we conclude that the Panel's determination that respondent violated Rule 8.4(d) is not clearly erroneous. . . .

The circumstances of this case support the Panel's determination that respondent's misconduct was an isolated incident. Respondent made two arguments during the same trial that related to the same issue. There were no other incidents of misconduct. . . .

. . . A disabled court employee has a right to perform his job in the courtroom. But here we have the perceived rights of two disabled persons potentially in conflict with one another. Respondent's client also suffers from a disability. Respondent's client was concerned that the jury would compare the law clerk's more severe disability with his less severe disability and that comparison would unduly influence the jury to decide against him on his claims and deprive him of a fair trial. Ironically, the concern of respondent's client, as argued by respondent, was not that the law clerk's disability prevented him from capably performing his job, but that the law clerk's demonstrated capability would diminish the client's disability claim. Respondent's motion can be viewed as an inappropriate attempt to address the respective rights of two disabled persons, rather than elevating the rights of one over the rights of another. If respondent was concerned that the jury might make improper comparisons, respondent could have addressed those concerns during voir dire. Nonetheless, when viewed in context, we conclude that the Panel did not act arbitrarily, capriciously or unreasonably by finding that respondent's conduct in this particular situation was non-serious.

Any discriminatory effect from the motion was indirect because respondent did not exercise any authority or control over the disabled clerk. In contrast, the prosecutor in In re Panel File 98-26 misused the power of the state by interfering with a defendant's right to counsel in seeking to prevent the public defender from representing the defendant based solely on the public defender's race. Taking into consideration the unique circumstances of this case, we conclude that the Panel did not act arbitrarily, Capriciously, or unreasonably by issuing an amended admonition to respondent. . . .

F. Communication with Represented Persons

Problems

9-6. Negotiations have been going on for months. Then Martyn receives a call from the potential buyer. "With my lawyer involved, we'll never reach agreement. Let's talk—just you and me." What if buyer announces, "I fired my lawyer"?

9-7. Martyn & Fox's client is totally frustrated. "I'll bet our settlement offers are not even being passed on to the plaintiff by that shyster lawyer of his. Why don't you just call the plaintiff up yourself and tell him our latest?" What if the client simply asks us to write the lawyer on the other side, with a copy to the plaintiff? What if our client asks us to write a letter for the client to send to the plaintiff?

9-8 Martyn & Fox's client has a petition for a variance pending. Client tells Fox, "I think if you meet with the Zoning Board Chairman and explain our position, the hearing will go a lot better. That's what the Democratic committeeman told me." What may Fox do?

9-9. An Assistant U.S. Attorney gets a call from a defendant whose trial is now scheduled in six weeks. "I can't stand it," defendant exclaims, "That guy [from Martyn & Fox] the company hired to represent me couldn't care less about my case. All he wants is to make sure the company gets off scot-free. Can't we talk? I'll meet you at Local Pub at 11:00 P.M. OK?"

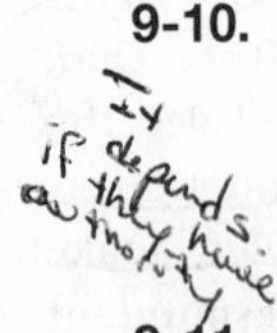

9-10. Martyn & Fox has been representing a corporate client in an SEC investigation, a fact known to the SEC. One Saturday morning, Fox gets a panicked telephone call from our client's sales manager. The cause: Justice Department lawyers visited at least ten brokers employed by our client this morning. What should Fox do?

9-11. Can Martyn & Fox send a memorandum to all our client's corporate employees directing them not to talk to anyone from the Justice Department?

9-12. The trial is a week away. Can Martyn visit with the other side's expert witness? How about a former employee of the party on the other side? What if the employee was separately represented at her deposition?

9-13. Martyn & Fox's client, an activist vegetarian group, thinks that a national chain is using beef tallow in processing its French fries. They believe the only way to prove this is to get someone hired to work at the national chain's French fry processing center. They ask Martyn & Fox if we will get one of our paralegals to apply for employment at the plant. What should we say?

Consider: Model Rules 4.1, 4.2, 4.3, 5.3
Model Code DR 7-104
RLGL §§99-103

Messing, Rudavsky & Weliky, P.C. v. President & Fellows of Harvard College

764 N.E.2d 825 (Mass. 2002)

COWIN, J.

The law firm of Messing, Rudavsky & Weliky, P.C. (MR&W), appeals from an order of the Superior Court sanctioning the firm for violations of Mass. R. Prof. C. 4.2, and its predecessor, S.J.C. Rule 3:07, Canon 7, DR 7-104(A)(1). Both versions of the rule prohibit attorneys from communicating with a represented party in the absence of that party's attorney. This appeal raises the issue whether, and to what extent, the rule prohibits an attorney from speaking ex parte to the employees of an organization represented by counsel. A judge in the Superior Court interpreted the rule to prohibit communication with any employee whose statements could be used as admissions against the organization pursuant to Fed. R. Evid. 801(d)(2)(D), and sanctioned MR&W for its ethical breach. We vacate the order and remand for entry of an order denying the motion for sanctions. . . .

. . . From the stipulated facts, we distill the following. In August of 1997, MR&W filed a complaint against President and Fellows of Harvard College (Harvard) with the Massachusetts Commission Against Discrimination (commission) on behalf of its client, Kathleen Stanford. Stanford, a sergeant with the Harvard University police department (HUPD), alleged that Harvard and its police chief, Francis Riley, discriminated against her on the basis of gender and in reprisal for earlier complaints of discrimination. MR&W represented Stanford, and Harvard was represented before the commission by in-house counsel, and thereafter by a Boston law firm. Following the institution of the suit, MR&W communicated ex parte with five employees of the HUPD: two lieutenants, two patrol officers, and a dispatcher. Although the two lieutenants had some supervisory authority over Stanford, it was not claimed that any of the five employees were involved in the alleged discrimination or retaliation against her or exercised management authority with respect to the alleged discriminatory or retaliatory acts.

In response to a motion by Harvard, the commission ruled that MR&W's ex parte contacts with all five employees violated rule 4.2, but declined to issue sanctions for these violations. MR&W removed the case to the Superior Court, where Harvard filed a motion seeking sanctions for the same violations of rule 4.2 on which the commission had previously ruled. The Superior Court judge then issued a memorandum of decision and order holding that MR&W violated the rule with respect to all five employees, prohibiting MR&W from using the affidavits it had procured during the interviews, and awarding Harvard the attorney's fees and costs it had expended in litigating the motion, in a later order calculated as $94,418.14.[3]. . .

. . . [The Court cites DR 7-104(A)(1) and Model Rule 4.2.]

The rule has been justified generally as "preserving the mediating role of counsel on behalf of their clients . . . protecting clients from overreaching by counsel for adverse interests," and "protecting the attorney-client relationship."

3. Harvard claimed fees of $152,255.96. The judge reduced this amount after deducting fees incurred in the proceedings before the commission, and subtracting a portion of the billing rate as excessive.

Neither version of the rule explicitly addresses the scope of the prohibition when the represented person is an organization. When the represented person is an individual, there is no difficulty determining when an attorney has violated the rule; the represented person is easily identifiable. In the case of an organization, however, identifying the protected class is more complicated.

Because an organization acts only through its employees, the rule must extend to some of these employees. However, most courts have rejected the position that the rule automatically prevents an attorney from speaking with all employees of a represented organization. . . .

The comment to rule 4.2 provides guidance in the case of a represented organization. Because both versions of the rule prohibit essentially the same conduct, the comment is instructive (although not controlling) in determining the scope of both the old and new versions of the rule.

According to comment [4] to rule 4.2, an attorney may not speak ex parte to three categories of employees: (1) "persons having managerial responsibility on behalf of the organization with regard to the subject of the representation"; (2) persons "whose act or omission in connection with that matter may be imputed to the organization for purposes of civil or criminal liability"; and (3) persons "whose statement may constitute an admission on the part of the organization."

. . . The [Superior Court] judge held that all five employees interviewed by MR&W were within the third category of the comment. He reached this result by concluding that the phrase "admission" in the comment refers to statements admissible in court under the admissions exception to the rule against hearsay. The Commonwealth's version of this rule was defined in Ruszcyk v. Secretary of Pub. Safety, 517 N.E.2d 152 (Mass. 1988), where we held that a court may admit a "statement by [the party's] agent or servant concerning a matter within the scope of [the] agency or employment, made during the existence of the relationship." *Id.* at 420, quoting Proposed Mass. R. Evid. 801(d)(2)(D). This rule is identical to Fed. R. Evid. 801(d)(2)(D). Because the comment includes any employee whose statement may constitute an admission, this interpretation would prohibit an attorney from contacting any current employees of an organization to discuss any subject within the scope of their employment. This is, as the Superior Court judge admitted, a rule that is "strikingly protective of corporations regarding employee interviews.". . .

Some jurisdictions have adopted the broad reading of the rule endorsed by the judge in this case. *See, e.g.,* Weibrecht v. Southern Ill. Transfer, Inc., 241 F.3d 875 (7th Cir. 2001); Cole v. Appalachian Power Co., 903 F. Supp. 975 (S.D. W. Va. 1995); Brown v. St. Joseph County, 148 F.R.D. 246, 254 (N.D. Ind. 1993). Courts reaching this result do so because, like the Superior Court, they read the word "admission" in the third category of the comment as a reference to Fed. R. Evid. 801(d)(2)(D) and any corresponding State rule of evidence. This rule forbids contact with practically all employees because "virtually every employee may conceivably make admissions binding on his or her employer." However, some of the courts that have adopted this interpretation have expressed reservations. *See* Pratt v. National R.R. Passenger Corp., 54 F. Supp. 2d 78, 80 (D. Mass. 1999).

At the other end of the spectrum, a small number of jurisdictions have interpreted the rule narrowly so as to allow an attorney for the opposing party to contact most employees of a represented organization. These courts construe the rule to restrict contact with only those employees in the organization's "control group," defined as those employees in the uppermost echelon of the organization's management. *See* Johnson v. Cadillac Plastic Group, Inc., 930 F. Supp. 1437, 1442 (D. Colo. 1996); Fair Automotive Repair, Inc. v. Car-X Serv. Sys., Inc., 471 N.E.2d 554 (Ill. App. 1984) (applying rule only to "top management persons who had the responsibility of making final decisions"); Wright v. Group Health Hosp., 691 P.2d 564 (Wash. 1984) (applying rule only to "those employees who have the legal authority to 'bind' the corporation in a legal evidentiary sense, i.e., those employees who have 'speaking authority' for the corporation").

Other jurisdictions have adopted yet a third test that, while allowing for some ex parte contacts with a represented organization's employees, still maintains some protection of the organization. The Court of Appeals of New York articulated such a rule in Niesig v. Team I, 558 N.E.2d 1030 (N.Y. 1990), rejecting an approach that ties the rule to Fed. R. Evid. 801(d)(2)(D). Instead, the court defined a represented person to include "employees whose acts or omissions in the matter under inquiry are binding on the corporation . . . or imputed to the corporation for purposes of its liability, or employees implementing the advice of counsel." Other jurisdictions have subsequently adopted the *Niesig* test. *See, e.g.*, Weider Sports Equip. Co. v. Fitness First, Inc., 912 F. Supp. 502 (D. Utah 1996); Branham v. Norfolk & W. R.R., 151 F.R.D. 67, 70-71 (S.D. W. Va. 1993); State v. CIBA-GEIGY Corp., 589 A.2d 180 (N.J. Super. 1991); Dent v. Kaufman, 185 W. Va. 171, 406 S.E.2d 68 (1991); Strawser v. Exxon Co., U.S.A., 843 P.2d 613 (Wyo. 1992). In addition, the Restatement (Third) of the Law Governing Lawyers endorses this rule. See *Restatement (Third) of Law Governing Lawyers* §100 Reporter's Note comment e, at 98 (1998).

. . . We adopt a test similar to that proposed in Niesig v. Team I, *supra*. Although the comment's reference to persons "whose statement may constitute an admission on the part of the organization" was most likely intended as a reference to Fed. R. Evid. 801(d)(2)(D), this interpretation would effectively prohibit the questioning of all employees who can offer information helpful to the litigation. We reject the comment as overly protective of the organization and too restrictive of an opposing attorney's ability to contact and interview employees of an adversary organization.

We instead interpret the rule to ban contact only with those employees who have the authority to "commit the organization to a position regarding the subject matter of representation." *Restatement (Third) of Law Governing Lawyers, supra* at §100 comment e. *See also* Ethics 2000 Commission Draft for Public Comment Model Rule 4.2 Reporter's Explanation of Changes (Feb. 21, 2000) (recommending deletion of the third category of the comment). The employees with whom contact is prohibited are those with "speaking authority" for the corporation who "have managing authority sufficient to give them the right to speak for, and bind, the corporation." Employees who can commit the organization are those with authority to make decisions about the course of the litigation, such as when to initiate suit, and when to settle a pending case. *See Restatement (Third) of the Law Governing Lawyers, supra at* §100 comment e, at 93 (employees who have the power to make binding evidentiary admissions are "analogous to . . . persons who possess[] power to settle a dispute on behalf of the organization"). We recognize that this test is a retrenchment from the broad prohibition on employee contact endorsed by the comment.

This interpretation, when read in conjunction with the other two categories of the comment, would prohibit ex parte contact only with those employees who exercise managerial responsibility in the matter, who are alleged to have committed the wrongful acts at issue in the litigation, or who have authority on behalf of the corporation to make decisions about the course of the litigation. This result is substantially the same as the *Niesig* test because it "prohibits direct communication . . . 'with those officials . . . who have the legal power to bind the corporation in the matter or who are responsible for implementing the advice of the corporation's lawyer . . . or whose own interests are directly at stake in a representation."

Our test is consistent with the purposes of the rule, which are not to "protect a corporate party from the revelation of prejudicial facts," but to protect the attorney-client relationship and prevent clients from making ill-advised statements without the counsel of their attorney. Prohibiting contact with all employees of a represented organization restricts informal contacts far more than is necessary to achieve these purposes. The purposes of the rule are best served when it prohibits communication with those employees closely identified with the organization in the dispute. The interests of the organization are adequately protected by preventing contact with those employees empowered to make litigation decisions, and those employees whose actions or omissions are at issue in the case. We reject the "control group" test, which includes only the most senior management, as insufficient to protect the "principles motivating [Rule 4.2]." The test we adopt protects an organizational party against improper advances and influence by an attorney, while still promoting access to relevant facts. The Superior Court's interpretation of the rule would grant an advantage to corporate litigants over nonorganizational parties. It grants an unwarranted benefit to organizations to require that a party always seek prior judicial approval to conduct informal interviews with witnesses to an event when the opposing party happens to be an organization and the events at issue occurred at the workplace.

While our interpretation of the rule may reduce the protection available to organizations provided by the attorney-client privilege, it allows a litigant to obtain more meaningful disclosure of the truth by conducting informal interviews with certain employees of an opposing organization. Our interpretation does not jeopardize legitimate organizational interests because it continues to disallow contacts with those members of the organization who are so closely tied with the organization or the events at issue that it would be unfair to interview them without the presence of the organization's counsel. Fairness to the organization does not require the presence of an attorney every time an employee may make a statement admissible in evidence against his or her employer. The public policy of promoting efficient discovery is better advanced by adopting a rule which favors the revelation of the truth by making it more difficult for an organization to prevent the disclosure of relevant evidence. . . .

Our decision may initially result in some increased litigation to define exactly which employees fall within the bounds of the rule. Although "a bright-line rule" in the form of a "control group" test or a blanket ban on all employee interviews would be easier to apply, the rule we adopt is, as discussed above, fair, and will allow for ex parte interviews without prior counsel's permission when an employee clearly falls outside of the rule's scope.

. . . The five Harvard employees interviewed by MR&W do not fall within the third category of the comment as we have construed it. As employees of the HUPD, they are not involved in directing the litigation at bar or authorizing the organization to make binding admissions. In fact, Harvard does not argue that any of the five employees fit within our definition of this category.

The Harvard employees are also not employees "whose act or omission in connection with that matter may be imputed to the organization for purposes of civil or criminal liability." Stanford's complaint does not name any of these employees as involved in the alleged discrimination. In fact, in an affidavit she states that the two lieutenants "had no role in making any of the decisions that are the subject of my complaint of discrimination and retaliation," and Harvard does not refute this averment. All five employees were mere witnesses to the events that occurred, not active participants.

We must still determine, however, whether any of the interviewed employees have "managerial responsibility on behalf of the organization with regard to the subject of the representation." Although the two patrol officers and the dispatcher were subordinate to Stanford and had no managerial authority, the two lieutenants exercised some supervisory authority over Stanford. However, not all employees with some supervisory power over their coworkers are deemed to have "managerial" responsibility in the sense intended by the comment. "Supervision of a small group of workers would not constitute a managerial position within a corporation."

Even if the two lieutenants are deemed to have managerial responsibility, the Massachusetts version of the comment adds the requirement that the managerial responsibility be in "regard to the subject of the representation." Thus, the comment includes only those employees who have supervisory authority over the events at issue in the litigation. There is no evidence in the record that the lieutenants' managerial decisions were a subject of the litigation. The affidavits of the two lieutenants indicate that they did not complete any evaluations or offer any opinions of Stanford that Chief Riley considered in reaching his decisions.

. . . Because we conclude that rule 4.2 did not prohibit MR&W from contacting and interviewing the five HUPD employees, we vacate the order of the Superior Court judge and remand the case for the entry of an order denying the defendant's motion for sanctions. . . .

G. Communication with Judges and Jurors

In the Matter of Disciplinary Proceedings Against Ragatz

429 N.W.2d 488 (Wis. 1988)

PER CURIAM . . .

In early 1986, Attorney Ragatz, as a member of the Foley and Lardner law firm, undertook to represent the estate of Marie Swerig in a will contest filed in Dane county circuit court by the law firm of Clifford and Relles on behalf of the decedent's son. Soon thereafter, Attorney Ragatz filed an action, entitled Bennin v. Swerig, claiming equitable adjustment with respect to the will contestant's indebtedness to his parents, indebtedness which had been discharged in bankruptcy prior to the commencement of that action. The lawsuit was intended to reduce the amount the son might receive in the event he prevailed in the will contest.

The Clifford and Relles law firm moved to dismiss the equitable adjustment action and have it declared frivolous, thereby entitling its client to payment of costs and attorney fees. Foley and Lardner agreed to dismiss the action but opposed the motion to hold the action frivolous. Oral argument on the frivolousness issue was made to the court, the Honorable Paulette Siebers presiding, and written briefs were then filed. Bennin remained pending in that court when John Aulik succeeded Judge Siebers to the bench. . . .

In late October or early November, 1986, Judge Aulik met Attorney Ragatz by chance and in a brief conversation told him that the judge's law clerk had stated to the judge that *Bennin* might indeed be frivolous. Attorney Ragatz responded to the judge's remarks, maintaining that the law clerk was in error and that the action was not frivolous. Opposing counsel was not present during that conversation or thereafter advised that it had occurred.

Shortly after that conversation, Attorney Ragatz received by mail a document "in the form of a proposed decision in the *Bennin* case" indicating a ruling that the lawsuit was frivolous. Attorney Ragatz had not solicited that document and correctly assumed it had been sent by Judge Aulik.[1]

After Attorney Ragatz ascertained the contents of the document he received from Judge Aulik, he met with Attorney David Reinecke, the attorney in his office who had been assigned to work on *Bennin* under his supervision, and directed him to prepare a response. Attorney Reinecke did so, citing authority and making legal arguments "intended to influence the Court in its decision." Attorney Ragatz reviewed and edited that letter, changing the salutation from "Dear Judge Aulik" to "Dear Jack" and signing it "Tom." Attorney Ragatz also added a paragraph stating that it was unlikely either side would appeal the judge's ruling on the frivolousness issue and pointed out that argument in the will contest was scheduled for November 26, 1986, and a ruling in that case from the bench or shortly after argument was possible. He wrote that, if successful in the will contest, he believed he could reach a compromise in *Bennin*. Attorney Ragatz then had the letter marked "Confidential" and sent to Judge Aulik, but he did not provide opposing counsel with a copy of it. Moreover, Attorney Ragatz did not intend that opposing counsel be aware of the existence or contents of it.

The related will contest was tried to another branch of Dane county circuit court and in late November, 1986, the court ruled in favor of the will proponent, Foley and Lardner's client. . . .

In late January or early February, 1987, Attorney Reinecke initiated contact with the Clifford and Relles law firm attempting to resolve all pending litigation between the parties. By February 4, 1987 Attorney Ragatz himself attempted to pursue settlement negotiations in those matters. At no time during conversations with that law firm did Attorney Ragatz or Attorney Reinecke disclose the fact that ex parte communications had taken place with the judge or that Attorney Ragatz had submitted legal arguments to the judge

---

1. We considered the judge's conduct in this matter in Disc. Proceedings Against Aulik, 429 N.W.2d 759 (Wis. 1988). [Ed. Note: Judge Aulik was suspended from the bench for 90 days for violating a provision substantially the same as current Code of Judicial Conduct Canon 3 B (7).]

in response to the "proposed decision" favoring Attorney Clifford's client.

On February 5, 1987, Attorney Clifford examined the court file in *Bennin* and in it discovered the letter Attorney Ragatz had sent to the judge in November setting forth legal arguments on the frivolousness issue. He asked the judge's clerk for a copy of the letter, but the clerk stated that she could not provide him one without the judge's authorization, as it had been marked "Confidential." The clerk took the letter to the judge, who was elsewhere in the courthouse, relaying Attorney Clifford's request for a copy. Judge Aulik retained the letter, and when the clerk returned to Attorney Clifford without either the letter or a copy, Attorney Clifford went to see the judge. When Attorney Clifford found him, the judge was engaged in a telephone conversation. Unbeknownst to Attorney Clifford, Judge Aulik was telling Attorney Ragatz that Attorney Clifford had found the letter. However, the judge did not tell Attorney Clifford to whom he had been talking or the subject of the conversation.

Attorney Clifford then returned to his office without having obtained a copy of the Ragatz letter, whereupon he called Attorney Ragatz. During the ensuing conversation, Attorney Ragatz did not reveal the fact that the judge had called him and he denied familiarity with the letter, stating that he would attempt to find a copy of it. The next morning, Attorney Ragatz telephoned the judge and suggested that he schedule a conference with counsel. That request was not made through the judge's clerk, nor was it made in a telephone conference call with Attorney Clifford participating. Judge Aulik told Attorney Ragatz in that conversation that he had already determined to schedule such a conference for that morning.

That conference was held in the judge's chambers, at which time Judge Aulik signed and distributed copies of his decision on the frivolousness issue, which was in favor of Attorney Clifford's client. During the conference, Attorney Clifford renewed his request for a copy of the Ragatz letter, but Judge Aulik stated that he was no longer in possession of it and Attorney Ragatz said that he had not yet been able to locate a copy.

During the conference in the judge's chambers, both Attorney Ragatz and Judge Aulik urged Attorney Clifford to settle the pending litigation, as Judge Aulik's decision had not awarded a specific amount of attorney fees to the Clifford firm and that issue remained to be addressed. Attorney Clifford stated that he was not comfortable settling the matter until he had received a copy of the Ragatz letter. A file copy was later found in Attorney Ragatz's office and a copy of it was sent to Attorney Clifford. . . .

. . . The referee considered Attorney Ragatz's letter to be "an advocacy piece" which "could have no possible intended purpose but to influence the outcome of litigation." In the referee's view, whether Attorney Ragatz was successful in having the judge decide the matter in favor of his client or in using his knowledge of the proposed decision to gain a favorable settlement did not alter the wrongfulness of the conduct. While on the basis of the character testimony presented on Attorney Ragatz's behalf the referee expressed a willingness to believe that his misconduct was "out of character," she considered it serious nonetheless.

The referee concluded that, by directing the preparation of the letter on the frivolousness issue and causing it to be sent to the judge without disclosing its contents to opposing counsel, Attorney Ragatz violated SCR 20: 4.4(2), which prohibits a lawyer from engaging in ex parte communications on the merits of a case with a judge before whom that case is pending, with exceptions not here relevant.

We adopt the referee's findings of fact and conclusions of law and accept the recommendation for discipline. It is significant that in neither of the two instances of ex parte communication did Attorney Ragatz bring up the subject of the pending litigation. Rather, he was responding to communication from the judge: in one instance, to remarks concerning the judge's law clerk's conclusion on the frivolousness issue; in the other, to a proposed decision on that issue the judge had sent him, apparently without having sent a copy to opposing counsel. Nevertheless, the proscription against ex parte communications between a lawyer and a judge on the merits of a pending adversary proceeding applied here.

Attorney Ragatz had the duty to either refrain from participating in those communications or provide a copy of his response to opposing counsel. His refusal to do so was a serious breach of his professional responsibilities. He permitted ex parte information from the judge on a contested issue and additional ex parte argument to the judge on that issue to influence the outcome of litigation. In so doing, he acted contrary to the objectives of our court system, a system in which he, as attorney, serves an integral role. In effect, his actions denied one party to that litigation a full and fair hearing on the merits of the controversy.

As it violated a fundamental principle of our justice system, Attorney Ragatz's misconduct warrants severe discipline—a suspension of his license to practice law. In determining the appropriate length of that suspension, we take into account the fact that Attorney Ragatz did not initiate the ex parte communications but, rather, responded to communications initiated by the judge and the fact that this is the first time Attorney Ragatz has been the subject of a disciplinary proceeding.

IT IS ORDERED that the license of Thomas G. Ragatz to practice law in Wisconsin is suspended for a period of 60 days, commencing November 7, 1988. . . .

H. Lawyer as Witness

Problem

9-14. Martyn actively negotiates a business deal for Client with Third Party. Two years later, Third Party sues Client to rescind the deal, alleging that Client committed fraud during the negotiations.

(*a*) Can Martyn defend Client in the rescission action? Does it matter if Client is now terminally ill? Can Martyn do pretrial work only?

(*b*) Can Fox represent Client in the rescission action? Does it matter if Martyn's recollection of the facts might not support Client's position?

(*c*) What if Third Party calls Martyn to the stand during the trial? Can Martyn & Fox continue the representation?

Consider: Model Rule 3.7
Model Code DR 5-101(B), 5-102

Stewart v. Bank of America, N.A.

203 F.R.D. 585 (M.D. Ga. 2001)

OWENS, District Judge.

This matter is before the Court on Defendant's Motion to Disqualify Robert Cork and Patrick Cork as Plaintiff's Counsel. Defendant contends that pursuant to M.D. Ga. L.R. 83.2.1(A), Georgia Rule of Professional Conduct 3.7(a) and American Bar Association Model Rule of Professional Conduct 3.7(a), Robert Cork and Patrick Cork are wrongfully counsel for Plaintiff and necessary, material witnesses in this case. Defendants contend that proper discovery will require the deposition of both attorneys because they were eyewitnesses to and have personal knowledge of the foreclosure transaction and events subsequent thereto that are the subject matter of this litigation. Robert Cork and Patrick Cork contend they should not be disqualified because the situation fits within the exceptions to the ethical rules listed above.

I. DISCUSSION

The local rule of this court, M.D. Ga. L.R. 83.2.1(A), provides that attorneys practicing in this court shall be governed by this Court's local rules, any rules of conduct adopted by the Supreme Court of Georgia and the American Bar Association Model Rules of Professional Conduct. The Georgia Supreme Court and the ABA's Model Rules employ an identical rule that prohibits attorneys from serving in the capacity as both an advocate and a witness. [The court cites Model Rule 3.7 and comments 2 and 4.]

Because the adoption of the ABA version of this rule is relatively new in Georgia, there are few cases directly on point. Therefore, caselaw from other circuits interpreting the ABA Rule 3.7 will be analyzed for guidance in this area. This caselaw is in accord with the comments to the newly adopted Georgia Rule and is thus instructive in the case at bar.

Even before the recent adoption of new rules of professional conduct, it had been the law in this state for some time that the trial judge has the authority and discretion to disqualify counsel attempting to serve as both advocate and witness. In a Seventh Circuit case, the court analyzed an Indiana Rule of Professional Conduct identical to Georgia's Rule 3.7. Hutchinson v. Spanierman, 190 F.3d 815 (7th Cir. 1999), *cert. denied*, 529 U.S. 1068 (2000). In *Hutchinson*, the court of appeals affirmed the disqualification of an attorney because there was sufficient evidence to suggest to the trial judge that the attorney would likely be called as a material witness in the case. The attorney was a witness to several of the conversations the substance of which involved the civil RICO count in the complaint. For that and various other reasons, the court found that the attorney was properly disqualified as counsel. One district court noted that as a rule "once counsel recognizes that opposing counsel is 'likely to be a necessary witness,' a motion to disqualify opposing counsel should be filed." Freeman v. Vicchiarelli, 827 F. Supp. 300, 302 (D.N.J. 1993). That court explained Rule 3.7 does not require an absolute certainty that the attorney will be called as a witness, only that there is a "likelihood" that the attorney will be a necessary witness. Moreover, "once an attorney recognizes that he is 'likely' to be a witness in litigation, he must choose whether he will proceed as advocate or witness; he may not choose both." In *Freeman*, the court noted it was imperative that this take place as soon as possible before the case approaches a trial date.

In another case, the defendant's attorney was disqualified in a breach of contract action between a festival organizer and a merchandiser. World Youth Day, Inc. v. Famous Artists Merchandising Exchange, Inc., 866 F. Supp. 1297 (D. Colo. 1994). The court disqualified the attorney because he was likely to be called as a necessary witness based on the fact that he was the sole negotiator for the merchandiser. The court held that a lawyer is "'necessary' witness if his or her testimony is relevant, material and unobtainable elsewhere." The attorney in that case was "the only individual on [the defendant's] side with first-hand non-privileged knowledge of many relevant and material facts at issue in [that] case." The attorney's testimony was essential in establishing whether a valid and enforceable contract was initially formed and whether it still existed. The court held that a jury would be confused by an advocate also appearing as a witness and "may attribute too much or too little weight to [an attorney's] testimony because of his dual role." Therefore, the attorney was disqualified from acting as defense counsel and from taking or defending all depositions.

In a Title VII wrongful termination case, a court suspended consideration of the disqualification motion until discovery could be completed. Caplan v. Braverman, 876 F. Supp. 710 (E.D. Pa. 1995). The defendants moved for disqualification because plaintiff's attorney was part of a conversation where one of the defendant partners allegedly made admissions damaging to the defendants concerning plaintiff's departure from the firm. Considering the factors from Rule 3.7, the court found that (1) the point on which the attorney at issue would testify was contested, (2) the proposed testimony would not relate to the value of legal services and (3) disqualification was unlikely to work substantial hardship on the plaintiff. However, it could not determine at that time if it was necessary to disqualify plaintiff's counsel. . . . [T]he court noted the plaintiff's contention that her attorney's possibly damaging testimony about the termination could be ruled inadmissible as a statement made in the context of an offer to compromise under F.R.E. 408. The court instructed the attorney to prepare other counsel for the event that he may be disqualified if discovery shows that the attorney would have to testify at trial. The court denied the motion to disqualify without prejudice but noted that even if plaintiff's attorney was later disqualified from acting as plaintiff's advocate at trial, the attorney would not be prohibited from representing the client in pre-trial and post-trial matters.

In the case at bar, it is readily apparent that the rules and caselaw requiring disqualification in a advocate/witness conflict situation are applicable. There is no question that Robert Cork and Patrick Cork are necessary, material eyewitnesses to the several transactions that are the subject matter of this case. It is also clear that the exceptions in Rule 3.7 are not applicable. Specifically, any statements the Plaintiff's attorney would make about the events in question would be based on personal knowledge from their participation therein. Because there is much debate over what happened at the foreclosure sale and thereafter, their statements or testimony would be related to hotly contested issues. Second, the testimony from the attorneys would not relate to the nature and/or value of their legal services rendered in this case. Third, the disqualification of the attorneys would not work any hardship on the Plaintiff at this point. Discovery has not yet taken place, no dispositive motions have been filed and a trial date has not been set. Accordingly, this case has not yet moved to the point where it would be detrimental to the Plaintiff's interests to find substitute counsel. Rather, it is in Plaintiff's best interest for the attorneys to withdraw at this point before the case proceeds any further.

Indeed, if the attorneys were not disqualified at this point, it is very likely that Plaintiff's case would be jeopardized. From the record before the Court, it is obvious that the Plaintiff has precious few witnesses, if any, to relate his side of the story to a jury. The parties dispute whether there were witnesses at the actual foreclosure sale. The Plaintiff's attorneys assert that a deputy sheriff and a lawclerk were present. However, the Defendant contends that there were no witnesses at the foreclosure sale. Consequently, there is more than a mere 'likelihood' that Robert Cork and Patrick Cork will be necessary, material witnesses for the Plaintiff in any trial of this case. As in *World Youth Day*, *supra*, the attorneys were the sole negotiators for the Plaintiff at the foreclosure sale. They are the only ones on Plaintiff's side, other than the Plaintiff, with first-hand knowledge of many relevant and material facts at issue in this case. Therefore, their testimony is essential in establishing whether a valid foreclosure sale actually took place. Any statements they would make at trial regarding the foreclosure or any subsequent, related events would completely confuse a jury because they would attribute too much, or possibly too little, weight to the attorneys' testimony.

Moreover, it is unnecessary to hold the motion to disqualify in abeyance pending discovery as was done in *Caplan*. It is obvious from the pleadings, the motions filed by the parties and the in-chambers conference on August 14, 2001 that it is in the Plaintiff's best interest that Robert Cork and Patrick Cork be removed as Plaintiff's attorneys and substitute counsel found immediately.[2] Therefore, Defendant's Motion to Disqualify Robert Cork and Patrick Cork as Plaintiff's Counsel is granted.

---

2. It must be noted that Robert Cork and Patrick Cork's assertions that this disqualification will harm their reputation as attorneys is unfounded. Rule 3.7 provides that the only possible punishment for proceeding as counsel and a witness in the same case is a public reprimand. This Court's Order removing them from counsel prevents them from violating this rule in the future. Therefore, there will be no harm to their professional reputation.

Part IV

Lawyers and Society: The Profession

Chapter 10

Self-Regulation

Part IV of this book offers us an opportunity to examine additional issues about the structure, function, and regulation of the legal profession itself. In this chapter, we address subjects that raise the question whether the legal professional truly can be considered self-regulating. We begin by looking at restrictions on the ability of lawyers to organize their practices. We then reexamine the inherent powers of courts, this time with a focus on whether the judicial branch can prevent the regulation of lawyers by other branches of government. We move next to consider the impact of federal law on the business practices of lawyers, and end the chapter by considering the current regime of unauthorized practice restrictions that both exclude nonlawyers from legal practice and prevent lawyers from practicing across state boundaries.

A. Restrictions on Practice

Problems

10-1. Martyn & Fox is worried about the firm's new lease obligation. What if we say that "any lawyer who leaves the firm and practices within 100 miles must pay the firm his last year's draw"? "Forfeits his pension"? "Owes the firm 25 percent of all fees generated by former Martyn & Fox clients"?

10-2. Martyn & Fox's manufacturing client is fed up with repetitive product liability suits over allegedly defective forklift trucks brought by one law firm over the last decade. "Tell them we'll settle with their latest client for an extra $100,000, if they promise never to sue us again," CEO tells our lawyer. Is this a great idea?

Consider: Model Rules 1.17, 5.6
Model Code DR 2-108

B. Inherent Power

So far in these materials, we have had at least eight examples of the inherent power of the judicial branch of government:

1. *Bothwell* (inherent power to compel an unwilling lawyer to accept a civil appointment);

2. *Converse* (bar admission);
3. *Attorney U, Busch* (bar discipline);
4. *Chen, Grand Jury* (contempt power);
5. *Shaffer Equipment* (sanctions against lawyers for failing to mitigate client perjury);
6. *In re Rules* (original jurisdiction due to a constitutional mandate to interpret the rules of professional conduct);
7. *Mattel* (sanctions for frivolous lawsuit); and
8. *Tutu Wells* (sanctions for discovery abuse).

These are all examples of *positive* inherent powers, that is, power the judicial branch of government finds necessary to perform its constitutionally required functions.

This chapter begins by examining a different but related facet of the inherent powers doctrine: *negative* inherent powers. When a court exercises a negative inherent power, it finds the judicial branch's constitutional power to regulate the bar sufficiently powerful enough to nullify another branch of government's exercise of the same power. Courts exercise a negative inherent power when they declare a legislative enactment unconstitutional because it infringes on a judicial prerogative.

Problem

10-3. The State Trial Lawyer's Association recently retained Martyn & Fox because it wants to do something about recent tort reform legislation that caps contingent fees in state medical malpractice and worker's compensation actions. What advice should Martyn & Fox give its new client?

Consider: Model Rule 1.5
Model Code DR 2-106

Lloyd v. Fishinger

605 A.2d 1193 (Pa. 1992)

CAPPY, J.

Issue: This case presents an issue involving the constitutional doctrine of separation of powers. Specifically, may the legislature prescribe rules directly affecting the conduct of attorneys in this Commonwealth, when the Pennsylvania Constitution at Article V, Section 10, has expressly delegated the authority to oversee the conduct of lawyers to the judiciary?

The question posed to this Court arises from the efforts of the appellants to dismiss the appellees from acting as their legal counsel in a personal injury action. Ralph Fishinger, the appellant, was seriously injured in a motorcycle accident occurring on June 6, 1987. As a result of the accident Mr. Fishinger underwent amputation of part of one leg, and remained hospitalized for one month. On June 8, 1987, two days after the accident, the appellee, attorney Lloyd arrived at the hospital to discuss a contingent fee agreement with Mr. Fishinger, whereby Mr. Lloyd would provide legal representation for Mr. Fishinger as a result of any claim arising from the accident. Mr. Fishinger signed the agreement at that time. Prior to visiting Mr. Fishinger, attorney Lloyd had been to the

Fishinger home, where he obtained Mrs. Fishinger's signature on the contingent fee agreement, to represent her interests as a result of her husband's accident.

Upon being released from the hospital on July 9, 1987, Mr. Fishinger called attorney Lloyd and told him that his services were not wanted. Attorney Lloyd requested written verification of dismissal. Mr. Fishinger instructed his new counsel to provide written verification. Attorney Lloyd then insisted upon written verification by Mr. and Mrs. Fishinger, who promptly complied with that request. Attorney Lloyd then filed a complaint against the Fishingers in contract to enforce the contingent fee agreement, with an alternative count in equity for quantum meruit.

The Fishingers filed preliminary objections to the complaint alleging the invalidity of the contingent fee agreement on the basis of 42 Pa. C. S. §7101(a)(3), entitled Settlements and other agreements with hospitalized persons, which provides in pertinent part:

> Where a person is injured and confined as a patient to a hospital or sanitarium due to such injuries, no attorney shall, during the first 15 days of the confinement of such patient, enter or attempt to enter into an agreement relating to compensation wholly or partly on a contingent basis with such patient in connection with his injuries. . . .

Article V, Section 10(c) of the Pennsylvania Constitution distinctly delineates the authority of the judiciary, providing in pertinent part:

> The Supreme Court shall have the power to prescribe general rules governing practice, procedure and the conduct of all courts, justices of the peace and all officers serving process or enforcing orders, judgments or decrees of any court or justice of the peace, . . . *and for admission to the bar and to practice law*, and the administration of all courts and supervision of all officers of the judicial branch, if such rules are consistent with this Constitution and neither abridge, enlarge nor modify the substantive rights of any litigant, nor affect the right of the General Assembly to determine the jurisdiction of any court or justice of the peace, nor suspend nor alter any statute of limitation or repose. All laws shall be suspended to the extent that they are inconsistent with rules prescribed under these provisions.

In Wajert v. State Ethics Commission, 420 A.2d 439 (Pa. 1980), this Court made clear that it holds the exclusive power to govern the conduct of attorneys in Pennsylvania. Wajert was a former judge, who, upon leaving the bench in the Court of Common Pleas, sought to resume his legal practice. He was informed by the State Ethics Commission that he would be prohibited from representing any clients before the Court of Common Pleas from which he had resigned for a period of one year. This Court held that the "application of this statute to a former judge constitutes an infringement on the Supreme Court's inherent and exclusive power to govern the conduct of those privileged to practice law in this Commonwealth."

The statute was declared inapplicable to Wajert as a violation of the doctrine of separation of powers. The same statute was held inapplicable, for the same reason, to former attorney employees of the Public Utility Commission in Pennsylvania Public Utility Commission Bar Association v. Thornburgh, 450 A.2d 613 (Pa. 1982).[5]

5. In Maunus v. Commonwealth State Ethics Commission, 544 A.2d 1324 (Pa. 1988), the requirement of the State Ethics Act that public employees file financial disclosure forms was held applicable to attorney public employees and not violative of this Court's authority to govern the conduct of attorneys. The fact that the attorneys had chosen employment within the public domain was found to be the controlling distinction, along with the fact that the requirement was not one already provided within the rules of professional conduct.

In a rather unusual format, this Court crystallized the importance of the doctrine of separation of powers in In re 42 PA. C. S. §1703, 394 A.2d 444 (Pa. 1978). The Legislature had enacted, and the Governor had approved, a provision of the Public Agency Open Meeting Law, which would require this Court to hold sessions open to the public while exercising its rule-making powers. In an open letter to the executive and legislative branches, this Court emphatically expressed its view that provision was unconstitutional:

> While the separation of powers doctrine does not "contemplate total separation of [the] three . . . branches of Government," Buckley v. Valeo, 424 U.S. 1, 104 (1976), the existence of appropriate overlap between branches with respect to some functions of government does not mean that such overlap is appropriate with respect to all functions. The Pennsylvania Constitution grants the judiciary—and the judiciary alone—power over rule-making. . . .

At its original conceptualization, the theory of separation of powers was to prohibit tyranny by creating a system within which no one branch of government would hold all the reins of power. *See, The Federalist* No. 47 (J. Madison). Admittedly, the threat of tyranny is not as active a concern today as it was at the birth of our State and Federal Constitutions. However, the principles upon which we developed three separate branches of government, each with its own field of expertise and dominion, are still to be strictly followed.

The Supreme Court in this Commonwealth is empowered by the Pennsylvania Constitution to govern the conduct of attorneys practicing law within the Commonwealth. In furtherance of that authority, this Court has enacted rules of professional conduct. At present, Rule 7.3 Direct Contact with Prospective Clients, prohibits the actions taken by attorney Lloyd in the instant case. Although Rule 7.3 was not in effect at the relevant time herein, its predecessor, DR 2-103, was in full force and effect, and contained the same prohibition.

In our serious task of overseeing ethical conduct within the bar, this Court is not unaware of the evils involved in direct solicitation of clients by attorneys. Those inherent evils were succinctly summarized by the United States Supreme Court in Ohralik v. Ohio State Bar Association, 436 U.S. 447 (1978):

> The substantive evils of solicitation have been stated over the years in sweeping terms; stirring up litigation, assertion of fraudulent claims, debasing the legal profession, and potential harm to the solicited client in the form of overreaching, overcharging, underrepresentation, and misrepresentation.

The aversion of this Court for the conduct of attorney Lloyd described in this case, however, cannot be a reason to uphold an unconstitutional infringement by the legislature upon the exclusive power and authority of this Court. Rules of conduct disapproving direct solicitation have always been part of this Courts disciplinary focus. As 42 Pa. C. S. §7101(a)(3) is a clear attempt by the legislature to enact rules of conduct in an area exclusively within the province of this Court that section of the statute is unconstitutional. . . .[6]

6. Although we find that the trial court incorrectly granted preliminary objections on the basis of the statute at issue, we make no finding as to whether or not the complaint states a cause of action.

FLAHERTY, J. [Dissenting]

We all agree—the public, the legislature, the bar, and the Supreme Court of Pennsylvania—that the actions of attorney Lloyd were blatantly improper. I therefore believe it was correct for the trial court to dismiss Lloyd's complaint on preliminary objections. . . .

As the plurality points out, the Code of Professional Conduct in effect in 1987 prohibited the actions taken by attorney Lloyd. . . .

I read 42 Pa. C. S. §7101(a)(3) as an amplification of our regulation of attorney conduct set forth in DR 2-103(A), not as a usurpation of our exclusive prerogative of regulating the practice of law.

This court has stated: "We must presume that an Act of the legislature is intended to be constitutional and wherever a legislative act can be preserved from unconstitutionality it must be preserved." I see no compelling need to declare the statute unconstitutional when it is consistent with our regulation of attorney conduct and merely explains our disciplinary rule.

Furthermore, I perceive the thrust of 42 Pa. C. S. §7101(a)(3) to be the protection of the public, not the regulation of the practice of law. We have held that rules of professional conduct applicable to attorneys do not have the force of substantive law but are to be utilized in disciplinary proceedings. The preamble to the current Rules of Professional Conduct expresses this scope of the Rules as follows:

> Violation of a Rule should not give rise to a cause of action nor should it create any presumption that a legal duty has been breached. The Rules are designed to provide guidance to lawyers and to provide a structure for regulating conduct through disciplinary agencies. They are not designed to be a basis for civil liability.

In keeping with that interpretation, a disciplinary rule which prohibits conduct such as attorney Lloyd's would not affect the validity of a contract created in violation of the rule. The statute, on the other hand, clearly establishes that such a contract is against public policy and is therefore void. Thus I view the statute, not as an impermissible intrusion on the power of this court to regulate the practice of law, but as a proper legislative act in the public interest affecting the substantive law of contracts. . . .

C. Advertising and Solicitation

Problems

10-4. Can Martyn & Fox advertise their new phone number as "1-800-HonestL"? What about "1-800-NOTGLTY"?

10-5. Can Martyn & Fox use commercially available email lists to solicit clients for estate planning? Can Fox follow up on email responses with phone calls? Can he follow up using real-time electronic exchanges?

10-6. Can Martyn & Fox email families of a recent accident to inform them of their need for counsel?

10-7. Can Martyn & Fox advertise "Law for You" seminars where Martyn touts the advantage of living trusts? Can Martyn hand out business cards to those who attend the seminars? Advertising brochures?

10-8. Can Martyn ask those who attend the seminar to hire the firm to draft a living trust? Does it matter if the seminar is sponsored by a local not-for-profit organization?

10-9. While visiting her father at a local hospital, Martyn warns the person in the next bed not to sign an insurance settlement form until she speaks to a lawyer. Can Martyn & Fox take the case?

Consider: Model Rules 7.1-7.5
Model Code DR 2-101-2-105

Florida Bar v. Went For It, Inc.

515 U.S. 618 (1995)

Justice O'CONNOR delivered the opinion of the Court.

Rules of the Florida Bar prohibit personal injury lawyers from sending targeted direct-mail solicitations to victims and their relatives for 30 days following an accident or disaster. This case asks us to consider whether such Rules violate the First and Fourteenth Amendments of the Constitution. We hold that in the circumstances presented here, they do not.

I

In 1989, the Florida Bar (Bar) completed a 2-year study of the effects of lawyer advertising on public opinion. After conducting hearings, commissioning surveys, and reviewing extensive public commentary, the Bar determined that several changes to its advertising rules were in order. In late 1990, the Florida Supreme Court adopted the Bar's proposed amendments with some modifications. Two of these amendments are at issue in this case. Rule 4-7.4(b)(1) provides that "[a] lawyer shall not send, or knowingly permit to be sent, . . . a written communication to a prospective client for the purpose of obtaining professional employment if: (A) the written communication concerns an action for personal injury or wrongful death or otherwise relates to an accident or disaster involving the person to whom the communication is addressed or a relative of that person, unless the accident or disaster occurred more than 30 days prior to the mailing of the communication." Rule 4-7.8(a) states that "[a] lawyer shall not accept referrals from a lawyer referral service unless the service: (1) engages in no communication with the public and in no direct contact with prospective clients in a manner that would violate the Rules of Professional Conduct if the communication or contact were made by the lawyer." Together, these rules create a brief 30-day blackout period after an accident during which lawyers may not, directly or indirectly, single out accident victims or their relatives in order to solicit their business.

In March 1992, G. Stewart McHenry and his wholly owned lawyer referral service, Went For It, Inc., filed this action for declaratory and injunctive relief in the United States District Court for the Middle District of Florida challenging Rules 4-7.4(b)(1) and 4-7.8 as violative of the First and Fourteenth Amendments to the Constitution. . . .

The District Court . . . entered summary judgment for the plaintiffs, relying on Bates v. State Bar of Ariz., 433 U.S. 350 (1977), and subsequent cases. The Eleventh Circuit affirmed on similar grounds. . . . We granted certiorari, 512 U.S. 1289 (1994), and now reverse.

II

A

Constitutional protection for attorney advertising, and for commercial speech generally, is of recent vintage. Until the mid-1970's, we adhered to the broad rule laid out in Valentine v. Chrestensen, 316 U.S. 52, 54 (1942), that, while the First Amendment guards against government restriction of speech in most contexts, "the Constitution imposes no such restraint on government as respects purely commercial advertising." In 1976, the Court changed course. In Virginia Bd. of Pharmacy v. Virginia Citizens Consumer Council, Inc., 425 U.S. 748, we invalidated a state statute barring pharmacists from advertising prescription drug prices. At issue was speech that involved the idea that "'I will sell you the X prescription drug at the Y price.'"... Striking the ban as unconstitutional, we rejected the argument that such speech "is so removed from 'any exposition of ideas,' and from 'truth, science, morality, and arts in general, in its diffusion of liberal sentiments on the administration of Government,' that it lacks all protection."

... In Bates v. State Bar of Arizona, *supra,* the Court struck a ban on price advertising for what it deemed "routine" legal services: "the uncontested divorce, the simple adoption, the uncontested personal bankruptcy, the change of name, and the like." Expressing confidence that legal advertising would only be practicable for such simple, standardized services, the Court rejected the State's proffered justifications for regulation.

Nearly two decades of cases have built upon the foundation laid by *Bates.* It is now well established that lawyer advertising is commercial speech and, as such, is accorded a measure of First Amendment protection. *See, e.g.*, Shapero v. Kentucky Bar Assn., 486 U.S. 466, 472 (1988); Zauderer v. Office of Disciplinary Counsel of Supreme Court of Ohio, 471 U.S. 626, 637 (1985); In re R. M. J., 455 U.S. 191, 199 (1982). Such First Amendment protection, of course, is not absolute. We have always been careful to distinguish commercial speech from speech at the First Amendment's core. "'Commercial speech [enjoys] a limited measure of protection, commensurate with its subordinate position in the scale of First Amendment values,' and is subject to 'modes of regulation that might be impermissible in the realm of noncommercial expression.'" Board of Trustees of State Univ. of N.Y. v. Fox, 492 U.S. 469, 477 (1989), quoting Ohralik v. Ohio State Bar Assn., 436 U.S. 447, 456 (1978)....

Mindful of these concerns, we engage in "intermediate" scrutiny of restrictions on commercial speech, analyzing them under the framework set forth in Central Hudson Gas & Elec. Corp. v. Public Serv. Comm'n of N.Y., 447 U.S. 557 (1980). Under *Central Hudson*, the government may freely regulate commercial speech that concerns unlawful activity or is misleading. Commercial speech that falls into neither of those categories, like the advertising at issue here, may be regulated if the government satisfies a test consisting of three related prongs: First, the government must assert a substantial interest in support of its regulation; second, the government must demonstrate that the restriction on commercial speech directly and materially advances that interest; and third, the regulation must be "'narrowly drawn.'"

B

"Unlike rational basis review, the *Central Hudson* standard does not permit us to supplant the precise interests put forward by the State with other suppositions," Edenfield v. Fane, 507 U.S. 761, 768 (1993). The Florida Bar asserts that it has a substantial interest in protecting the privacy and tranquility of personal injury victims and their loved ones against intrusive, unsolicited contact by lawyers. This interest obviously factors into the Bar's paramount (and repeatedly professed) objective of curbing activities that "negatively affect the administration of justice." Because direct mail solicitations in the wake of accidents are perceived by the public as intrusive, the Bar argues, the reputation of the legal profession in the eyes of Floridians has suffered commensurately. The regulation, then, is an effort to protect the flagging reputations of Florida lawyers by preventing them from engaging in conduct that, the Bar maintains, "'is universally regarded as deplorable and beneath common decency because of its intrusion upon the special vulnerability and private grief of victims or their families.'"

We have little trouble crediting the Bar's interest as substantial. . . .

Under *Central Hudson*'s second prong, the State must demonstrate that the challenged regulation "advances the Government's interest 'in a direct and material way.'" . . . That burden, we have explained, "'is not satisfied by mere speculation or conjecture; rather, a governmental body seeking to sustain a restriction on commercial speech must demonstrate that the harms it recites are real and that its restriction will in fact alleviate them to a material degree.'" In *Edenfield*, the Court invalidated a Florida ban on in-person solicitation by certified public accountants (CPA's). We observed that the State Board of Accountancy had "presented no studies that suggest personal solicitation of prospective business clients by CPA's creates the dangers of fraud, overreaching, or compromised independence that the Board claims to fear." Moreover, "the record [did] not disclose any anecdotal evidence, either from Florida or another State, that validated the Board's suppositions." In fact, we concluded that the only evidence in the record tended to "contradict, rather than strengthen, the Board's submissions." Finding nothing in the record to substantiate the State's allegations of harm, we invalidated the regulation.

The direct-mail solicitation regulation before us does not suffer from such infirmities. The Florida Bar submitted a 106-page summary of its 2-year study of lawyer advertising and solicitation to the District Court. That summary contains data—both statistical and anecdotal—supporting the Bar's contentions that the Florida public views direct-mail solicitations in the immediate wake of accidents as an intrusion on privacy that reflects poorly upon the profession. As of June 1989, lawyers mailed 700,000 direct solicitations in Florida annually, 40% of which were aimed at accident victims or their survivors. A survey of Florida adults commissioned by the Bar indicated that Floridians "have negative feelings about those attorneys who use direct mail advertising." Fifty-four percent of the general population surveyed said that contacting persons concerning accidents or similar events is a violation of privacy. A random sampling of persons who received direct-mail advertising from lawyers in 1987 revealed that 45% believed that direct-mail solicitation is "designed to take advantage of gullible or unstable people"; 34% found such tactics "annoying or irritating"; 26% found it "an invasion of your privacy"; and 24% reported that it "made you angry." Significantly, 27% of direct-mail recipients reported that their regard for the legal profession and for the judicial process as a whole was "lower" as a result of receiving the direct mail.

The anecdotal record mustered by the Bar is noteworthy for its breadth and detail. With titles like "Scavenger Lawyers" and "Solicitors Out of Bounds," newspaper editorial pages in Florida have burgeoned with criticism of Florida lawyers who send targeted direct mail to victims shortly after accidents. . . .

In light of this showing . . . we conclude that the Bar has satisfied the

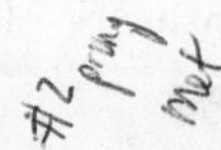

second prong of the *Central Hudson* test. . . .

In reaching a contrary conclusion, the Court of Appeals determined that this case was governed squarely by Shapero v. Kentucky Bar Assn., 486 U.S. 466 (1988). Making no mention of the Bar's study, the court concluded that "'a targeted letter [does not] invade the recipient's privacy any more than does a substantively identical letter mailed at large. The invasion, if any, occurs when the lawyer discovers the recipient's legal affairs, not when he confronts the recipient with the discovery.'" In many cases, the Court of Appeals explained, "this invasion of privacy will involve no more than reading the newspaper."

While some of *Shapero*'s language might be read to support the Court of Appeals' interpretation, *Shapero* differs in several fundamental respects from the case before us. First and foremost, *Shapero*'s treatment of privacy was casual. . . . Second, in contrast to this case, *Shapero* dealt with a broad ban on all direct-mail solicitations, whatever the time frame and whoever the recipient. Finally, the State in *Shapero* assembled no evidence attempting to demonstrate any actual harm caused by targeted direct mail. The Court rejected the State's effort to justify a prophylactic ban on the basis of blanket, untested assertions of undue influence and overreaching. Because the State did not make a privacy-based argument at all, its empirical showing on that issue was similarly infirm. . . .

Here . . . the harm targeted by the Florida Bar cannot be eliminated by a brief journey to the trash can. The purpose of the 30-day targeted direct-mail ban is to forestall the outrage and irritation with the state-licensed legal profession that the practice of direct solicitation only days after accidents has engendered. The Bar is concerned not with citizens' "offense" in the abstract, but with the demonstrable detrimental effects that such "offense" has on the profession it regulates. Moreover, the harm posited by the Bar is as much a function of simple receipt of targeted solicitations within days of accidents as it is a function of the letters' contents. Throwing the letter away shortly after opening it may minimize the latter intrusion, but it does little to combat the former. . . .

Passing to *Central Hudson*'s third prong, we examine the relationship between the Florida Bar's interests and the means chosen to serve them. *See* Board of Trustees of State Univ. of N.Y. v. Fox, 492 U.S. at 480. With respect to this prong, the differences between commercial speech and noncommercial speech are manifest. In *Fox*, we made clear that the "least restrictive means" test has no role in the commercial speech context. "What our decisions require," instead, "is a 'fit' between the legislature's ends and the means chosen to accomplish those ends,' a fit that is not necessarily perfect, but reasonable; that represents not necessarily the single best disposition but one whose scope is 'in proportion to the interest served,' that employs not necessarily the least restrictive means but . . . a means narrowly tailored to achieve the desired objective. . . .

III

Speech by professionals obviously has many dimensions. There are circumstances in which we will accord speech by attorneys on public issues and matters of legal representation the strongest protection our Constitution has to offer. *See, e.g.*, Gentile v. State Bar of Nevada, 501 U.S. 1030 (1991); In re Primus, 436 U.S. 412 (1978). This case, however, concerns pure commercial advertising, for which we have always reserved a lesser degree of protection under the First Amendment. Particularly because the standards and conduct of state-licensed lawyers have traditionally been subject to extensive regulation by the States, it is all the more appropriate that we limit our scrutiny of state regulations to a level commensurate with the "'subordinate position'" of commercial speech in the scale of First Amendment values.

We believe that the Florida Bar's 30-day restriction on targeted direct-mail solicitation of accident victims and their relatives withstands scrutiny under the three-pronged *Central Hudson* test that we have devised for this context. The Bar has substantial interest both in protecting injured Floridians from invasive conduct by lawyers and in preventing the erosion of confidence in the profession that such repeated invasions have engendered. The Bar's proffered study, unrebutted by respondents below, provides evidence indicating that the harms it targets are far from illusory. The palliative devised by the Bar to address these harms is narrow both in scope and in duration. The Constitution, in our view, requires nothing more.

The judgment of the Court of Appeals, accordingly, is *Reversed*.

Justice KENNEDY, with whom Justice STEVENS, Justice SOUTER, and Justice GINSBURG join, Dissenting.

Attorneys who communicate their willingness to assist potential clients are engaged in speech protected by the First and Fourteenth Amendments. That principle has been understood since Bates v. State Bar of Arizona, 433 U.S. 35 (1977). The Court today undercuts this guarantee in an important class of cases and unsettles leading First Amendment precedents, at the expense of those victims most in need of legal assistance. With all respect for the Court, in my view its solicitude for the privacy of victims and its concern for our profession are misplaced and self-defeating, even upon the Court's own premises.

I take it to be uncontroverted that when an accident results in death or injury, it is often urgent at once to investigate the occurrence, identify witnesses, and preserve evidence. Vital interests in speech and expression are, therefore, at stake when by law an attorney cannot direct a letter to the victim or the family explaining this simple fact and offering competent legal assistance. Meanwhile, represented and better informed parties, or parties who have been solicited in ways more sophisticated and indirect, may be at work. Indeed, these parties, either themselves or by their attorneys, investigators, and adjusters, are free to contact the unrepresented persons to gather evidence or offer settlement. This scheme makes little sense. As is often true when the law makes little sense, it is not first principles but their interpretation and application that have gone away.

Although I agree with the Court that the case can be resolved by following the three-part inquiry we have identified to assess restrictions on commercial speech, Central Hudson Gas & Elec. Corp. v. Public Serv. Comm'n of N.Y., 447 U.S. 557, 566 (1980), a preliminary observation is in order. Speech has the capacity to convey complex substance, yielding various insights and interpretations depending upon the identity of the listener or the reader and the context of its transmission. It would oversimplify to say that what we consider here is commercial speech and nothing more, for in many instances the banned communications may be vital to the recipients' right to petition the courts for redress of grievances. The complex nature of expression is one reason why even so-called commercial speech has become an essential part of the public discourse the First Amendment secures. If our commercial speech rules are to control this case, then, it is imperative to apply them with exacting care and fidelity to our precedents, for what is at stake is the suppression of information and knowledge that transcends the financial self-interests of the speaker. . . .

In the face of these difficulties of logic and precedent, the State and the opinion of the Court turn to a second interest: protecting the reputation and dignity of the legal profession. The argument is, it seems fair to say, that all are demeaned by the crass behavior of a few. . . . While disrespect will arise from an unethical or improper practice, the majority begs a most critical question by assuming that direct-mail solicitations constitute such a practice. The fact is, however, that direct solicitation may serve vital purposes and promote the administration of justice, and to the extent the bar seeks to protect lawyers' reputations by preventing them from engaging in speech some deem offensive, the State is doing nothing more (as amicus the Association of Trial Lawyers of America is at least candid enough to admit) than manipulating the public's opinion by suppressing speech that informs us how the legal system works. The disrespect argument thus proceeds from the very assumption it tries to prove, which is to say that solicitations within 30 days serve no legitimate purpose. This, of course, is censorship pure and simple; and censorship is antithetical to the first principles of free expression. . . .

It is telling that the essential thrust of all the material adduced to justify the State's interest is devoted to the reputational concerns of the Bar. It is not at all clear that this regulation advances the interest of protecting persons who are suffering trauma and grief, and we are cited to no material in the record for that claim. . . .

. . . The accident victims who are prejudiced to vindicate the State's purported desire for more dignity in the legal profession will be the very persons who most need legal advice, for they are the victims who, because they lack education, linguistic ability, or familiarity with the legal system, are unable to seek out legal services. *Cf.* Trainmen v. Virginia ex rel. Virginia State Bar, 377 U.S. 1, 3-4 (1964).

The reasonableness of the State's chosen methods for redressing perceived evils can be evaluated, in part, by a commonsense consideration of other possible means of regulation that have not been tried. Here, the Court neglects the fact that this problem is largely self-policing: Potential clients will not hire lawyers who offend them. And even if a person enters into a contract with an attorney and later regrets it, Florida, like some other States, allows clients to rescind certain contracts with attorneys within a stated time after they are executed. *See, e.g.*, Rules Regulating the Florida Bar, Rule 4-1.5 (Statement of Client's Rights) (effective Jan. 1, 1993). . . . The very fact that some 280,000 direct-mail solicitations are sent to accident victims and their survivors in Florida each year is some indication of the efficacy of this device. . . .

It is most ironic that, for the first time since Bates v. State Bar of Arizona, the Court now orders a major retreat from the constitutional guarantees for commercial speech in order to shield its own profession from public criticism. Obscuring the financial aspect of the legal profession from public discussion through direct-mail solicitation, at the expense of the least sophisticated members of society, is not a laudable constitutional goal. There is no authority for the proposition that the Constitution permits the State to promote the public image of the legal profession by suppressing information about the profession's business aspects. If public respect for the profession erodes because solicitation distorts the idea of the law as most lawyers see it, it must be remembered that real progress begins with more rational speech, not less. . . .

Utah State Bar Ethics Advisory Opinion Committee

*Opinion No. 99-04**

General Issue: What are the ethical considerations that govern a lawyer who wishes to conduct legal seminars; provide legal information to groups of retirement-home residents; host open houses; set up information booths at trade shows; participate in Bar-sponsored question-and-answer programs; or make in-person contacts with prospective clients at the request of their friends or relatives?

Summary: This Opinion analyzes and decides a range of related questions that have arisen in connection with lawyers' marketing and solicitation activities. In general, we find that lawyers may make their services known through a variety of methods that do not involve uninvited, one-on-one approaches, discussions or solicitations. On the other hand, where monetary gain is a significant motivation, lawyers may not generally engage in uninvited, direct in-person communications with prospective clients in order to indicate the lawyer's availability to accept professional employment.

Issue No. 1: May a lawyer sponsor and advertise a free seminar on legal issues to be presented in a group setting to members of the public and (i) offer literature or videos discussing the legal topic, either with or without fee, to attendees of the seminar, (ii) give a business card to attendees who request one, and (iii) accept employment to provide legal services to an attendee who initiates a request for professional services?

Opinion: Yes . . .

Rule 7.3(a) prohibits in-person and telephonic communication directed to a specific recipient with whom the lawyer has no family or prior professional relationship soliciting professional employment when a significant motive for the lawyer's doing so is pecuniary gain.

Unlike the rules in some other states, the Utah Rules of Professional Conduct do not define the term "solicit" as this term is used in Rule 7.3(a). We believe that "solicit" in this context means a communication initiated by the lawyer with respect to the lawyer's availability to provide or to accept professional employment.[3] The term "solicit" necessarily includes an offer initiated by the lawyer to provide or to accept professional employment and the unrequested advice or recommendation of the lawyer that the lawyer be engaged to provide professional services.

Rule 7.3 prohibits only solicitations to provide legal services. An invitation to attend a law-related seminar without any communication of the lawyer's availability to accept professional employment is not a solicitation of professional employment. Therefore, a lawyer may invite attendance at a law-related seminar sponsored by the lawyer or by others by telephone or by direct in-person communication, so long as the lawyer does not communicate a message or offer concerning the availability of the lawyer to accept professional employment. If the invitation contains such a message or offer, the invitation must be made by mail and must comply with Rules 7.1, 7.2 and 7.3(b).

A lawyer may appear and make presentations at a law-related seminar provided he does not engage in in-person solicitation prohibited by Rule 7.3(a). Therefore, a

* Ed. Note: Portions of this opinion have been reordered for clarity.

3. *See* Cal. R. Prof. Conduct, Rule 1400(B)(1) ("solicitation" is any communication "concerning the availability or professional employment of a member or law firm in which a significant motive is pecuniary gain").

lawyer may not communicate the lawyer's availability to provide professional employment, offer to provide or accept professional employment or recommend that the lawyer or the lawyer's firm be employed to provide legal services.[7] The lawyer may distribute or offer in person to each attendee of the seminar, with or without fee, literature or video tapes concerning the legal issues addressed at the seminar that may state the lawyer's name, firm affiliation, address and telephone number.[8] Literature or video tapes offered in person to each attendee may not communicate the lawyer's availability to provide or accept professional employment.[9] Therefore, the lawyer's business card, brochures or other endorsements of the lawyer or the lawyer's law firm should not be generally distributed in person to attendees of law-related seminars.[10] If an attendee of a law-related seminar initiates a request to the lawyer to receive literature or video tapes that communicate the lawyer's availability to provide or to accept professional employment, the lawyer may ethically provide such materials to the attendee. Letters and brochures offering the lawyer's legal services may be mailed by the lawyer after the seminar to the attendees of the seminar.[11]

A lawyer may not provide individualized legal advice during the course of a law-related seminar.[12] By doing so, the lawyer would be providing legal services. In response to questions by attendees, the lawyer must endeavor to respond generally so as to create no impression that the lawyer has accepted professional employment on behalf of an attendee. While the lawyer may not initiate a recommendation of the lawyer's engagement by any attendee of the seminar, he may recommend, when appropriate, that an attendee of the seminar consult with a lawyer of the attendee's own choosing.

A lawyer may meet one on one with an attendee of the seminar, when such a contact is initiated by an attendee. In private sessions with attendees, if a request for individualized legal advice is initiated by the attendee, the lawyer may provide individualized legal advice. The lawyer may accept professional employment offered by an attendee of the seminar, either offered privately at the seminar or after the seminar, provided the lawyer has not initiated the offer by engaging in in-person solicitation in violation of Rule 7.3(a).

Some state bar associations have placed additional restrictions on lawyer participants at law-related seminars. The Committee chooses not to adopt these additional restrictions. . . .

---

7. Some state bar associations have allowed lawyers to make generalized statements at law-related seminars regarding their availability to accept professional employment. *See, e.g.*, Ohio St. Bar Assn., Op. 94-13, ABA\BNA Lawyer's Man. on Prof. Conduct 1001:6862 (Dec. 2, 1994); Ariz. St. Bar Assn., Op. 87-23, ABA\BNA Lawyer's Man. on Prof. Conduct 901:1408 (Oct. 26, 1987). Arizona allows lawyer presenters at law-related seminars to offer to provide legal services with or without fee, if no pressure or coercion is exercised upon attendees at the seminar. We do not agree with these opinions. We believe such conduct constitutes in-person solicitation prohibited by Rule 7.3(a).

8. Ill. St. Bar Assn., Op. 96-01, 1996 WL 466449.

9. Mass. St. Bar Assn., Op. 86-3, ABA\BNA Lawyer's Man. on Prof. Conduct 901:4601 (Nov. 25, 1996); L.A. County Bar Assn., Formal Op. 494.

10. The Committee does not believe that Rule 7.3(a) precludes lawyer sponsors or presenters at law-related seminars from leaving business cards, brochures or other literature communicating the lawyer's availability to accept professional employment at tables where these materials may be picked up by any attendee choosing to do so. However, the lawyer may not in any way promote or encourage attendees in person to pick up such written materials.

11. S.C. St. Bar Assn., Op. 97-05, ABA\BNA Lawyer's Man. on Prof. Conduct 1101:7904 (April 1997).

12. Ohio St. Bar Assn., Op. 94-13, ABA\BNA Lawyer's Man. on Prof. Conduct 1001:6862 (Dec. 2, 1994); Ala. State Bar Assn., Op. 87-119, ABA\BNA Lawyer's Man. on Prof. Conduct 901:1032 (Sept. 29, 1987); Pa. St. Bar Assn., Op. 93-42A, ABA\BNA Lawyer's Man. on Prof. Conduct 1001:7326 (June 2, 1993).

Issue No. 3: If a lawyer purchases booth space at a trade show, may the lawyer (i) discuss legal topics one on one with persons who voluntarily visit the lawyer's booth and (ii) accept legal engagements offered by attendees of the trade show who visit the lawyer's booth and engage in one-on-one discussions with the lawyer?

Opinion: Yes, so long as the lawyer complies with the requirements of Rule 7.3(a) and does not engage in in-person solicitation of professional employment. . . .

It is not unethical for a lawyer to purchase booth space at a trade show. So long as advertisements attached to or near the booth space comply with Rules 7.1 and 7.2, it is not unethical for the lawyer to display print advertisements of the lawyer's availability to accept legal employment. This is equivalent to outdoor advertising authorized by Rule 7.2. What distinguishes booth space at a trade show from outdoor advertising is the presence of the lawyer at the booth to engage in one-on-one oral communications with attendees of the trade show.

Other state bar associations are divided on what activities a lawyer at a trade-show booth may ethically engage in. . . .

The Committee believes that visits to a lawyer's trade-show booth should be likened to visits to a lawyer's office during an advertised open house. Non-clients who attend an advertised lawyer open house do not reasonably anticipate that they will be subjected to in-person solicitation of professional employment.[19] For this reason, it is unethical for lawyers to engage in in-person solicitation of such persons.[20] These occasions afford the lawyer the opportunity to meet prospective clients and for prospective clients to meet the lawyer. The lawyer may discuss legal topics with the attendees and may, when the request is initiated by the prospective client, privately provide individualized legal advice.[21]. . .

The Committee believes that the same analysis applies to trade-show booths. The lawyer may get acquainted with those who visit the booth, may discuss legal topics generally and may, when the request is initiated by the prospective client, privately provide individualized legal advice. The lawyer may not initiate in-person communications about the lawyer's availability to accept professional employment. The lawyer may not in person distribute business cards, brochures or other literature communicating the lawyer's availability to accept professional employment unless the person visiting the booth initiates the request for this information. So long as the lawyer does not engage in in-person solicitation in violation of Rule 7.3(a), he is free to accept professional employment offered by those who visit the booth.

Issue No. 4: May a lawyer volunteer to set up a table in a common area of a retirement or senior center in order to meet one on one to discuss legal topics with residents of the center who voluntarily visit the lawyer's table, and may the lawyer accept legal engagements proposed by residents of the center who visit the lawyer's table and voluntarily engage in one-on-one discussions of legal issues with the lawyer?

---

19. This Opinion assumes that the invitation to a lawyer's open house does not specifically invite the public to attend for the purpose of being solicited to provide professional employment to the lawyer. The Committee believes that non-clients who attend an open house in response to an invitation that states that the non-clients will be solicited have, in turn, invited the in-person solicitation. It would, therefore, not be unethical for a lawyer to make an in-person solicitation to such a person.

20. N.C. St. Bar Assn., Op. 146, 1992 WL 753128 (Jan. 15, 1993); Or. St. Bar Assn., Op. 1991-35, 1991 WL 279176 (July, 1991); *see also* R.I. St. Bar Assn., Op. 89-14, ABA\BNA Lawyer's Man. on Prof. Conduct 901:7805 (July 20, 1989) (lawyer may attend social gatherings to meet prospective clients, but may not engage in in-person solicitation).

21. When providing individualized legal advice, the lawyer must comply with all Rules of Professional Conduct, including the conflict-of-interest Rules 1.7, 1.9 and 1.10 and Rule 1.6 concerning client confidences.

Opinion: Yes, so long as the lawyer complies with the requirements of Rule 7.3(a). . . .

The Committee believes that a table set up by a lawyer at a retirement or senior center for the purpose of meeting with residents of the center who voluntarily visit the lawyer's table to discuss legal topics is indistinguishable from a lawyer's open house or a booth set up by a lawyer at a trade show. The analysis of this issue is the same as the analysis of Issue No. 3, and the ethical restraints on the lawyer's conduct are the same as the restraints on a lawyer's holding an open house or setting up a trade-show booth.

Issue No. 5: May a lawyer volunteer to provide one-on-one consultations with residents of a retirement or senior center concerning legal topics, initiate one-on-one in-person communications with residents of the center in their rooms or common areas to discuss their legal questions or concerns, and accept legal engagements proposed by such residents who discuss legal topics one on one with the lawyer?

Opinion: No. . . .

The lawyer's conduct in initiating uninvited communications with residents of the senior center, whether in their rooms or in common areas of the center, is distinguishable from establishing a table in a common area of the senior center. When the lawyer initiates the contact, the resident is subjected to the uninvited presence of the lawyer in a one-on-one encounter. This situation is "fraught with the possibility of undue influence, intimidation and over-reaching."[23] The residents of the senior center are subjected to "the private importuning of a trained advocate, in a direct interpersonal encounter" which was wholly uninvited by the resident. Because the communications are private and oral and not visible or otherwise open to public scrutiny, it is nearly impossible for the lawyer's conduct to be regulated. The potential for abuse inherent in this situation justifies a prophylactic prohibition of the acceptance of legal representation offered by the residents of the senior center under these circumstances, unless the representation is *pro bono*.[25]

It may be argued that such uninvited one-on-one contact to discuss legal topics of interest to the residents of the senior center is not solicitation unless the lawyer communicates his availability to accept legal employment. . . . While the one-on-one communications at the lawyer open house, lawyer trade-show booth and discussion table are also fraught with the danger of undue influence, intimidation and over reaching, and are also private and not open to public scrutiny, they are at least invited communications. . . .

In Shapero v. Kentucky Bar Association, the United States Supreme Court distinguished solicitation by targeted mail from in-person solicitation, stating: "In assessing the potential for over reaching and undue influence, the mode of communication makes all the difference." We agree, but further note that uninvited one-on-one communication is fraught with the most danger of abuse. It is this form of communication to attract professional employment that Rule 7.3(a) was intended to prevent. A lawyer may not accept professional employment resulting from such uninvited one-on-one contacts, unless the representation is solicited and provided on a pro bono basis.

---

23. Rule 7.3 cmt.

25. Ohralik v. Ohio State Bar, 436 U.S. 447 (1978) (prophylactic rule against in-person solicitation does not violate the rights of free expression afforded by the First and Fourteenth Amendments of the United States Constitution even in the absence of a showing of any specific harm to the prospective clients). *Accord* Shapero v. Kentucky Bar Assn., 486 U.S. 466 (1988). If the representations are accepted on a *pro bono* basis, then Rule 7.3(a) would not be applicable. The primary motive of the lawyer would not be pecuniary gain.

Issue No. 6: If a lawyer volunteers to answer questions of members of the public participating in a Utah State Bar-sponsored one-on-one question-and-answer session, such as a Bar-sponsored telethon (in-person telephonic contact) or the Bar-sponsored Tuesday Night Bar (face-to-face contact), may the lawyer provide to a member of the public his name and telephone number during the Bar-sponsored communication and accept professional employment for a fee offered by a member of the public during or after the Bar-sponsored communication?

Opinion: No. . . .

Bar-sponsored telethons and the "Tuesday Night Bar" result in in-person communications by members of the public with lawyers similar to the lawyer open house, trade-show booth and discussion table communications discussed earlier in this Opinion. There is, however, one important distinction. These events are sponsored and advertised to the public by the Bar. Lawyers volunteering to participate in these Bar-sponsored programs are, therefore, subject to the Bar's rules, regulations and policies regarding the program, in addition to the Utah Rules of Professional Conduct.

Each participant in the Tuesday Night Bar Program receives a policy statement which describes the program as being designed to provide preliminary counseling and general legal information and, if appropriate, referral to a lawyer using the Bar's Lawyer Referral Service. The policy statement further states: "[The program] is not intended to create an on-going attorney-client relationship between the participants. . . . Attorneys shall not take clients and\or cases from the Program unless the attorney does so on a pro bono basis." The Bar has also informally indicated it intends to apply a similar policy statement regarding Bar-sponsored telethons. . . .

If there were no Bar policy preventing a lawyer participant from accepting professional employment on a for-fee basis from members of the public with whom the lawyer has made contact during a Bar-sponsored program, the lawyer would be governed by the same limitations as discussed previously in this Opinion with respect to communications at lawyer open houses, trade-show booths and discussion tables.

Issue No. 7: If a relative or close friend of a prospective client requests that the lawyer telephone the prospective client to offer to provide legal representation, is it ethical for the lawyer to telephone the prospective client and to offer to provide legal representation?

Opinion: Generally no, unless the relative or friend of the prospective client requesting the lawyer to make the contact is the agent of the prospective client. . . .

Rule 7.3(a) states in part: "A lawyer may not solicit in person, professional employment from a prospective client with whom the lawyer has no family or prior professional relationship, when a significant motive for the lawyer's doing so is the lawyer's pecuniary gain." Thus, the lawyer may not generally communicate in person with the prospective client and offer to provide legal services, even if the lawyer has been requested by a friend or close relative of a prospective client to make the communication.[27]

27. Norris v. Ala. St. Bar, 582 So. 2d 1034 (Ala. 1991) (lawyer suspended from practice for two years after delivering to a funeral home a funeral wreath and a letter addressed to the widow offering assistance after having received an anonymous telephone call from someone purporting to be a friend of the widow stating that she required legal services and did not have sufficient funds for a funeral wreath); Spence, Payne, Masington & Grossman, P.A. v. Gerson, 483 So. 2d 775 (Fla. App. 1986) (unethical in-person solicitation for a lawyer to send an investigator to obtain a retainer agreement from a widow after receiving a telephone call from a client of the lawyer and a close friend of the widow requesting that the lawyer offer to provide professional services to the widow).

However, if the person requesting the lawyer to contact the prospective client is the prospective client's agent, . . . the in-person contact has been invited by the prospective client. To satisfy this requirement, a lawyer must make an objective, reasonable good-faith determination that the person is actually the agent of the prospective client.

In these circumstances, it would be best for the lawyer to advise the person referring the prospective client that the prospective client should contact the lawyer and request the lawyer's professional services. Otherwise, the lawyer runs the risk that the prospective client's friend or family member is not authorized by the prospective client to request the lawyer's direct in-person communication with the prospective client.

The Limits of the Law: *The Constitution*

In previous notes, we have examined legal restraints that limit a lawyer's advocacy on behalf of a client, such as the law of fraud, crime, court orders and procedural sanctions. *Lloyd, Went For It*, and *Lawline* (in the next section of this chapter) illustrate another legal limit. In all three cases, lawyers claimed that the federal or state constitution created a decisive limit on the law governing lawyers itself. They argued that constitutional provisions protected their advocacy on behalf of clients, and prevented state regulation or limitation of lawyer behavior.

The First Amendment: Lawyer Speech and Prospective Clients

First Amendment challenges figured prominently in the unsuccessful constitutional attacks on state regulation in both *Went For It* and *Lawline*. The results in these cases belie the vitality of the First Amendment as a means of overturning state regulation of lawyer speech. In a series of cases over the past four decades, the Supreme Court has forced the rewriting of traditional rules that prevented advertising and solicitation by applying the First Amendment to lawyer speech. In doing so, the Court has labeled some lawyer speech "political," some "commercial," and some as "unprotected." The following chart categorizes these cases and the current professional rules that these cases have shaped.

FIRST AMENDMENT REGULATION OF LAWYER ADVERTISING AND SOLICITATION

Level of Const. protection	**Traditional First Amendment Protection**	**Commercial Speech (intermediate level scrutiny)**	**Unprotected Speech (no Const. protection)**
Kind of speech	Political speech, speech that seeks access to the courts	Speech that proposes a commercial transaction	Speech that proposes an illegal activity; misleading commercial speech

(continued)

FIRST AMENDMENT REGULATION OF LAWYER ADVERTISING AND SOLICITATION *(continued)*

Governmental interest necessary to justify regulation	Compelling gov. interest; Regulation must be the least restrictive means to promote governmental interest (no prior restraints)	Substantial gov. interest; Speech restriction must directly and materially advance gov. interest and regulation must be narrowly drawn (prior restraints allowed)	Gov. interest presumed; Complete ban allowed
Cases	NAACP v. Button, 371 U.S. 415 (1963) Bhd. of R.R. Trainmen v. Va., 377 U.S. 1 (1964) United Mine Workers v. Ill. St. Bar Assn., 389 U.S. 217 (1967) United Trans. Union v. St. Bar of Mich., 401 U.S. 576 (1971) In re Primus, 436 U.S. 412 (1978)	Bates v. St. Bar. of Ariz., 433 U.S. 350 (1977) In re RMJ, 455 U.S. 191 (1982) Zauderer v. Disc. Counsel of S. Ct. of Ohio, 471 U.S. 626 (1985) Shapero v. Ky. Bar Assn., 486 U.S. 466 (1988) Peel v. Atty. Registration & Disc. Commn., 496 U.S. 91 (1990) Fla. Bar v. Went For It, 515 U.S. 618 (1995)	Ohralik v. Ohio St. Bar Assn., 436 U.S. 447 (1978)
Challenged Rules	MR 7.3; DR 2-103, 2-104	MR 7.1, 7.2, 7.4; DR 2-101, 102, 105	MR 7.3(a); DR 2-103, 104

The left column of the chart includes cases where the Supreme Court has afforded lawyer speech the highest level of First Amendment protection. Here, the Court allows an overbreadth analysis and requires a compelling interest to justify the restriction on speech. In addition, the regulation must be the least restrictive means to promote the governmental interest, and, to prevent chilling fragile First Amendment interests, no prior restraints are allowed.

In *Button*, for example, the court overturned a Virginia antisolicitation regulation that had been applied to prohibit NAACP lawyers from general solicitation of persons to serve as plaintiffs in constitutional challenges by the NAACP to segregated education. The Court held that the regulation violated the NAACP's First and Fourteenth Amendment rights by "unduly inhibiting protected freedoms of expression and association." It characterized the NAACP's litigation activity as "political expression," which "may well be the sole practicable avenue open to a minority to petition for redress of grievances."[1]

1. NAACP v. Button, 371 U.S. 415, 429-430 (1963).

In the next three cases, the court applied the same level of constitutional protection to the activities of labor unions that sought to provide low cost legal services to their members. These decisions culminated with the statement in *United Transportation Union* quoted in *Lawline:* "the common thread running through our decisions in NAACP v. Button, Trainmen, and United Mine Workers is that collective activity undertaken to obtain meaningful access to the courts is a fundamental right within the protection of the First Amendment."[2]

In *Primus*, the Court returned to a distinction it had first made in *Button* between private pecuniary gain and political expression to overturn an attempt by South Carolina to prohibit an ACLU lawyer from soliciting civil rights plaintiffs. The Court found that the ACLU, like the NAACP, used litigation as a "form of political expression," not as a means to resolve private differences. Responding to the state's argument that the ACLU's policy of requesting attorney's fees took the case outside of political expression, the Court found that such a possibility was not sufficient to equate the work of these lawyers "with that group that exist for the primary purpose of financial gain through the recovery of counsel fees."[3]

The middle column of the chart includes a line of cases where commercial rather than political speech is at stake. Here, the speech proposes a purely commercial transaction, such as "I will sell you the X prescription drug at Y price."[4] *Went For It* indicates that the First Amendment also protects commercial speech, but common sense differences between political and commercial speech justify a different level of constitutional scrutiny. Thus, a substantial rather than compelling governmental interest must be shown to uphold the regulation. Further, the regulation need not be the least restrictive means of promoting the governmental interest so long as it directly and materially advances the interest and is narrowly drawn. Prior restraints (such as requiring a bar ethics opinion before releasing an advertisement)[5] are allowed. Further, to prevent fraud, states can require that lawyers add disclaimers to their communications, such as "Advertising Material."[6] Finally, constitutional challenges to professional advertising can be made only as applied to the conduct of the person regulated. An overbreadth analysis is not available to challenge every conceivable application of the regulation because the commercial motive makes such speech likely to recur.[7]

This extensive line of cases means that states cannot completely prohibit advertising, but can regulate it to prevent false, fraudulent, or misleading statements. *RMJ* and *Shapero* made clear that "advertising" includes targeted mail as well as mass media communications. *Peel* addressed claims of certification in a letterhead, holding that states could not categorically ban lawyers from honestly advertising a certification granted by a national organization, but they were free to prevent potentially misleading certifications from private organizations by creating official state specialty designations.[8] In the context of a partial, time based prohibition, *Went For It* adds the protection of personal privacy and, where empirical evidence exists, the reputation of the profession as justifiable state interests.

---

2. United Transp. Union v. St. Bar of Mich., 401 U.S. 576, 585 (1971).
3. In re Primus, 436 U.S. 412, 428, 431 (1978).
4. Va. Pharm. Bd. v. Va. Consumer Council, 425 U.S. 748, 761 (1976).
5. Central Hudson Gas & Elec. Corp. v. Pub. Serv. Commn. of N.Y., 447 U.S. 557, 571 (1980).
6. Model Rule 7.3(c).
7. Bates v. St. Bar of Ariz., 433 U.S. 350, 380-381 (1977).
8. Model Rule 7.4 represents the ABA response to *Peel*.

Despite its extensive application of the First Amendment to lawyer speech, the Supreme Court has characterized one form of lawyer speech—in-person solicitation for pecuniary gain—as unprotected by the First Amendment. The right column of the chart summarizes these decisions, referred to in both *Lloyd* and *Went For It*. When lawyers seek employment by speaking face to face with potential clients, the state may presume harm in order to prevent it. In *Ohralik*, the court upheld a complete ban on in-person solicitation by lawyers, finding that speech was a subordinate part of a purely commercial transaction. Unlike media advertising, the pressure of in-person solicitation often demands an immediate response, not leaving the recipient free to evaluate the speech. The evils of fraud, undue influence, intimidation, and overreaching in such a circumstance can be presumed as so likely to occur that the state can prohibit all in-person solicitation by lawyers to prevent them. No actual injury need be shown to justify a complete ban on speech in this circumstance.[9]

Although it is now clear that the First Amendment applies to lawyer advertising and solicitation, some issues remained unresolved. The Supreme Court has not yet addressed radio and television or email, but the Model Rules include them in the advertising category.[10] On the other hand, because it demands more of an immediate response, real time electronic or telephone contact is included in the ban on in-person solicitation in Model Rule 7.3.[11]

Other First Amendment Issues

The First Amendment has been instrumental in a number of other challenges to regulations of lawyer speech, including restrictions on pretrial publicity, criticism of judges, judicial elections, the use of mandatory bar dues, and gag rules on the litigation activity of legal services lawyers.

Model Rule 3.6, which governs trial publicity, has been rewritten following the Supreme Court's decision in Gentile v. St. Bar of Nevada.[12] There, the Court unanimously upheld the "substantial likelihood of material prejudice" test in the rule as "designed to protect the integrity and fairness of a state's judicial system." At the same time, a majority of the Court found that part of the rule was void for vagueness as applied to Gentile, because its provisions failed to give him adequate warning or principle for determining "when his remarks pass from the safe harbor of the general to the forbidden sea of the elaborated." As a result, the ABA rewrote Model Rule 3.6 in 1994 to eliminate the qualifying terms the Court found misleading and to authorize a lawyer to respond to adverse publicity initiated by others.

Free speech also collides with the integrity and fairness of the judicial system when lawyers criticize judges. Model Rule 8.2 recognizes that judges are public officials by restating the First Amendment standard required in defamation cases: a lawyer can be disciplined only for making a false statement (not opinion) about a judge if he or she knows the statement is false or acts in reckless disregard of the truth.[13] Several courts have held that an isolated incident of rude comment should not be enough to constitute discipline under this or more general provisions such as

9. Ohralik v. Ohio St. Bar Assn., 436 U.S. 447, 466 (1978).
10. Model Rule 7.2.
11. Model Rule 7.3, Fla. St. Bar Assn., Op. A-00-1 (2000).
12. 501 U.S. 1030 (1991).
13. For a discussion of the constitutional application of this rule, *see* In re Shearin, 765 A.2d 930, 937-938 (Del. 2000); In re Palmisano, 70 F.3d 483, 487-488 (7th Cir. 1995); Standing Comm. on Disc. v. Yagman, 55 F.3d 1430, 1438 (9th Cir. 1995).

Model Rule 8.4(d) (conduct prejudicial to the administration of justice).[14] Untrue statements have resulted in discipline, however, where the criticism could have been investigated first, or raised with judicial disciplinary authorities rather than in court proceedings or with the press.[15] Similarly, a number of courts have upheld discipline where lawyers have made repeated untrue derogatory statements about judges.[16]

Most recently, the Supreme Court relied on the First Amendment to overturn a state rule of judicial ethics that prohibited judicial candidates from announcing their views on disputed legal and political issues.[17] The Court found the state prohibition was not narrowly tailored to serve an otherwise legitimate state interest in the impartiality of judges, defined as lack of bias for or against particular parties to particular proceedings.

The First Amendment further has played a role in reining in the power of State Bar Associations who use mandatory dues structures to fund not only admission and discipline, but also to promote political viewpoints with which individual members may disagree. In Keller v. St. Bar of Cal., the Supreme Court held that the State Bar's compulsory dues could only be used to fund activities "justified by the State's interest in regulating the legal profession and improving the quality of legal services."[18] Although the precise line may not be easy to ascertain, ideological activities such as lobbying for or against state legislation or funding state initiatives not reasonably related to these legitimate state goals violates the First Amendment.[19] Subsequent cases have determined that blanket challenges to lobbying efforts cannot be maintained,[20] and that bar dues may fund public relations activities that advance the understanding of law,[21] or *pro bono* legal services to military reservists.[22] Funding for nonideological activities such as office space for state bar employees,[23] or awards to journalists for writing on law-related topics also have been upheld.[24] A state bar also has been allowed to fund a campaign advocating voter approval of two initiatives concerning the merit selection and retention of state judges because it relates to improvement of the function of the judicial system,[25] and to fund lobbying activities concerning the regulation and discipline of lawyers, client trust accounts, and the availability of legal services.[26] The same jurisdiction has refused, however, to allow dues to pay for lobbying on child welfare or family wellness matters.[27]

---

14. *See, e.g.*, In re Snyder, 472 U.S. 634 (1985); St. Bar v. Semann, 508 S.W.2d 429 (Tex. Civ. App. 1974); Justices of Appellate Div. v. Erdmann, 301 N.E.2d 426 (N.Y. 1973).
15. *See, e.g.*, In re Becker, 620 N.E.2d 691 (Ind. 1993); Matter of Holtzman, 577 N.E.2d 30 (N.Y. 1991), *cert. denied*, 502 U.S. 1009 (1991); In re Lacey, 283 N.W.2d 250 (S.D. 1979).
16. *See, e.g.*, Comm. on Legal Ethics of W. Va. v. Farber, 408 S.E.2d 274 (W. Va. 1991), *cert. denied*, 502 U.S. 1073 (1992); St. ex rel. Neb. Bar Assn. v. Michaelis, 316 N.W.2d 46 (Neb. 1982), *cert. denied and appeal dismissed*, 459 U.S. 804 (1982).
17. Republican Party of Minn. v. White, 536 U.S. 765 (2002).
18. 496 U.S. 1, 13-14 (1990).
19. Morrow v. St. Bar of Cal., 188 F.3d 1174 (9th Cir. 1999), *cert. denied*, 528 U.S. 1156 (2000) (requiring membership in State Bar that takes positions on public issues is not unconstitutional so long as members who dissent can obtain a refund of the portion of their mandatory dues used for that purpose).
20. Popejoy v. N.M. Bd. of Bar Commrs., 887 F. Supp. 1422 (D.N.M. 1995).
21. Gardner v. St. Bar of Nev., 284 F. 3d 1040 (9th Cir. 2002).
22. Popejoy, *supra* note 20.
23. *Id.*
24. Thiel v. St. Bar of Wis., 94 F.3d 399 (7th Cir. 1996).
25. Alper v. Fla. Bar, 771 So. 2d 523 (Fla. 2000).
26. Fla. Bar re Schwarz, 552 So. 2d 1094 (Fla. 1989).
27. Fla. Bar re Frankel, 581 So. 2d 1294 (Fla. 1991).

Finally, in Legal Services Corp. v. Velazquez, the Supreme Court invalidated a gag rule that restricted Legal Service Corporation lawyers from challenging existing welfare laws when representing clients seeking welfare benefits.[28] The court held that the LCS Act funded constitutionally protected expression, including welfare representation, and that the restriction on speech was an attempt to "exclude from litigation those arguments and theories Congress finds unacceptable but which by their nature are within the province of the courts to consider."[29] In invalidating the restriction, the Court relied not only on the First Amendment, but also on constitutional separation of powers principles. The legislatively imposed restriction on Legal Services lawyers threatened "serious impairment of the judicial function" because it prohibited "expression upon which the courts must depend for the proper exercise of the judicial power."[30]

Beyond the First Amendment

Other fundamental constitutional provisions have played a role in shaping the legal regulation of lawyers. *Lloyd* illustrates, for example, the state separation of powers doctrine that parallels the federal law relied on in *Velazquez*. We have also seen how the Supreme Court has interpreted the Privileges and Immunities Clause to overturn residency requirements that limit bar admission.[31]

The Supremacy Clause The Supremacy Clause is the focus of litigation when federal law clearly preempts state provisions to the contrary. For example, a lawyer licensed to practice before the United States Patent Office successfully opposed a state's claim that he was engaged in the unauthorized practice of law. The Supreme Court held that the state unauthorized practice law must yield to incompatible federal legislation, and that the Commissioner of Patents was well within his statutory authority to license nonlawyer patent practitioners.[32] The Supremacy Clause also has played a role in several bankruptcy cases where lawyers have discharged debts such as loans or malpractice judgments that later become relevant in bar admission or disciplinary proceedings. Several cases have held that the Supremacy Clause prevents the imposition of conditions on admission or readmission that require a lawyer to repay debts discharged in bankruptcy.[33] On the other hand, some courts have avoided the Supremacy Clause problem by finding that the debt was not the sole cause for the denial of admission,[34] or the repayment was for some purpose other than penalizing the lawyer for discharging a debt, such as protecting the public.[35]

Although Congress has the power to preempt contrary state legislation, it must do so explicitly in order for the Supremacy Clause to apply. So, for example, where the Department of Justice relied on a general federal "housekeeping statute" that authorizes executive department officials to set up offices and file governmental

---

28. 531 U.S. 533 (2001).
29. *Id.* at 546.
30. *Id.* at 545.
31. *See* Lawyers and Other Professionals: Professional Licensure, *supra* p.28.
32. Sperry v. Fla. ex rel. Fla. Bar, 373 U.S. 379 (1963).
33. *See, e.g.*, Cleveland Bar Assn. v. Gay, 763 N.E.2d 585 (Ohio 2002); In re Batali, 657 P.2d 775 (Wash. 1983).
34. In re Gahan, 279 N.W.2d 826 (Minn. 1979).
35. *See, e.g.*, People v. Sullivan, 802 P.2d 1091 (Colo. 1990); Brookman v. St. Bar of Cal., 760 P.2d 1023 (Cal. 1988).

documents to justify a substantive regulation, the Eight Circuit held that the Department lacked "valid statutory authority" to exempt its lawyers from state professional regulation.[36] Shortly thereafter, Congress passed the McDade Amendment, which specifically requires federal prosecutors to abide by state ethics rules.[37]

Due Process In cases where lawyers have been admitted to the bar and have a vested right to practice law, courts impose procedural due process requirements on limitations of the right. *Tutu Wells*, for example, illustrates that courts must afford lawyers procedural due process rights when considering professional discipline. We also considered the contours of these guarantees in detail in Chapter 2.[38] In Chapter 5, we encountered similar due process guarantees when lawyers or others are held in criminal contempt.[39]

In cases where lawyers seek admission, however, courts are much less likely to impose procedural due process guarantees. So, for example, when a lawyer who is not admitted in a jurisdiction seeks leave of a court for admission *pro hac vice*, the Supreme Court has held that a lawyer has no right to appear and need not be afforded any procedural due process if the motion to appear is denied.[40] Some jurisdictions have created more exacting standards that require a judge to provide substantial justifications for refusing *pro hac vice* admission.[41] In criminal cases where the rights of the defendant rather than the interests of the lawyer are at stake, many courts are more likely to require a judge to provide a legitimate reason why the defendant should be deprived of his choice of counsel,[42] but it is enough if the judge provided notice and an opportunity to show cause why the admission should not be allowed.[43]

Constitutional Power and Client Advocacy

It should come as no surprise that the constitution, which provides the framework for all law, also has shaped the law governing lawyers. Other notes in this series entitled "The Limits of the Law" have discussed the boundaries created by general law that limits a lawyer's ability to advocate on behalf of a client. In this note, by contrast, we have seen lawyers who seek to advocate on behalf of their clients by invoking constitutional rights to restrict the application of other general law, such as professional rules, court procedures, or legislative enactments. In pursuing your law practice, you should be alert to other occasions when state or federal constitutional rights may help you promote legitimate client advocacy.

---

36. United States ex rel. O'Keefe v. McDonnell Douglas Corp., 132 F.3d 1252, 1257 (8th Cir. 1998).
37. 28 U.S.C. §530(B) (2000). *See, e.g.*, Model Rule 3.8.
38. *See* Law Governing Lawyers: Professional Discipline, *supra* p.48.
39. The Limits of the Law: Court Orders, *supra* p.144.
40. Leis v. Flynt, 439 U.S. 438 (1979). A California court rule prohibiting *pro hac vice* admission by California residents also has withstood a privileges and immunities challenge, because the state's requirement that residents take and pass the bar examination simply ensures that all residents are treated alike. Paciulan v. George, 229 F.3d 1226 (9th Cir. 2000), *cert. denied*, 531 U.S. 1077 (2001).
41. *See, e.g.*, St. ex rel. H.K. Porter Co. v. White, 386 S.E.2d 25 (W. Va. 1989); Hahn v. Boeing Co., 621 P.2d 1263 (Wash. 1980).
42. *See, e.g.*, Panzardi-Alvarez v. United States, 879 F.2d 975, 980 (1st Cir. 1989); Fuller v. Diesslin, 868 F.2d 604, 607-608 (3d Cir. 1989); *cert. denied sub nom.* Parretti v. Fuller, 493 U.S. 873 (1989); Herrmann v. Summer Plaza Corp., 513 A.2d 1211, 1214 (Conn. 1986).
43. *See, e.g.*, United States v. Collins, 920 F.2d 619 (10th Cir. 1990), *cert. denied*, 500 U.S. 920 (1991).

D. Federal Intervention

Lawline v. American Bar Association

956 F.2d 1378 (7th Cir. 1992), cert. denied, 510 U.S. 992 (1993)

CUMMINGS, Circuit Judge.

This case presents antitrust and constitutional challenges to two legal ethics rules recommended by the American Bar Association and adopted by the Illinois Supreme Court and the United States District Court for the Northern District of Illinois. The disciplinary rules at issue forbid lawyers from assisting laypersons in the unauthorized practice of law (the "unauthorized practice rule") and also forbid lawyers from entering into partnerships with non-lawyers if any of the activities of the partnership consist of the practice of law (the "partnership rule"). Specifically, plaintiffs challenge ethics rules 5.4(b) and 5.5(b) contained in the ABA Model Rules of Professional Responsibility (the "Model Rules"). . . . The Illinois Supreme Court and the Northern District of Illinois have adopted these rules verbatim. . . .

Plaintiffs contend that these two rules violate Sections 1 and 2 of the Sherman Antitrust Act (15 U.S.C. §§1 and 2). Plaintiffs also claim that the adoption of these two rules violates their constitutional right to due process and equal protection, as well as the rights secured them by the First Amendment. As a result of this alleged deprivation of rights, plaintiffs base part of their suit on the Civil Rights Act of 1871 (42 U.S.C. §1983). They seek an award of money damages and a declaratory judgment that the contested rules are unconstitutional.

The district court dismissed plaintiffs' complaint on a Federal Rule of Civil Procedure 12(b)(6) motion for failure to state a claim on which relief can be granted. . . . For the reasons discussed below, we affirm the judgment of the district court.

I

The first amended complaint describes the initial plaintiff, Lawline, as an unincorporated association of lawyers, paralegals and laypersons with its principal office in Chicago. The other three plaintiffs are Thomas Holstein, an Illinois lawyer who is the managing director and supervising attorney of Lawline; LeNore Nelson, a paralegal serving as Lawline's office manager and head paralegal; and Joyce Novak, a Chicagoan described as a general factory worker for Procter and Gamble Co. who received information from Lawline regarding Chapter 7 bankruptcy proceedings.

According to the plaintiffs, Holstein founded Lawline in 1978 to use law students, paralegals and lawyers to answer legal questions from the public without charge over the telephone and to assist them in representing themselves in routine legal matters. Lawline's other stated purposes are to refer members of the public without financial resources to agencies providing legal services and to refer them to young lawyers who charge reduced fees, thus creating a "prototype legal delivery system" subsidized by referral fees. In its ten years of existence, Lawline is said to have answered legal questions for more than 500,000 people, particularly in Illinois, Indiana and Wisconsin, and also nationally through a toll-free telephone number.

Plaintiffs' first amended complaint consists of 109 pages and has 86 pages of exhibits. The complaint names as defendants the American Bar Association ("ABA"), the Illinois State Bar Association ("ISBA"), the Chicago Bar Association ("CBA"), the Justices of the Illinois Supreme Court, the members of its Committee on Professional Responsibility, the members of its Attorney Registration and Disciplinary Commission ("ARDC"), the United States Trustee for the Northern District of Illinois, the United States Trustee's Assistant, and five members of the executive committee of the court below.

The ABA House of Delegates adopted Model Rule 5.4(b) and Rule 5.5(b) in 1983. Plaintiffs allege that the adoption of the two ethics rules at issue was the result of a conspiracy among the ABA House of Delegates, ISBA Delegates, and CBA Delegates to protect traditional law firms and restrain trade. In pursuance of the conspiracy the defendants allegedly agreed to have the three bar associations issue advisory ethics opinions prohibiting non-lawyers from owning financial interests in law firms and prohibiting lawyers from forming partnerships with non-lawyers if any of the activities of the partnership consist of the practice of law. . . .

Plaintiffs further complain that in February 1988, defendants United States Trustee and his assistant reported to the Illinois Supreme Court's Attorney Registration and Disciplinary Commission that non-lawyers at Lawline were giving legal advice to debtors in Chapter 7 bankruptcy proceedings. According to the plaintiffs, this report resulted in an investigation of managing director Holstein. A few months later the United States Trustee filed a motion in a bankruptcy proceeding to enjoin Lawline from engaging in the practice of law in bankruptcy proceedings. He also filed an adversary proceeding against plaintiffs Lawline, Holstein and Nelson in furtherance of the supposed conspiracy.

In their pleadings, plaintiffs assail the partnership rule and the unauthorized practice rule and assert that these provisions resulted from a conspiracy between the courts and the organized bar to monopolize the dissemination of legal advice in violation of the Sherman Act (Count I) and to deprive plaintiffs of their First Amendment rights to freedom of speech and association as well as their rights of due process and equal protection in violation of the 1871 Civil Rights Act (Count II). Count III sought a declaratory judgment that the Northern District and Illinois rules are unconstitutional on their face.

Due to these alleged violations, plaintiffs contend that the defendants harmed Lawline by restricting it and other similar private law referral services from advertising. In addition plaintiffs allege that they were injured because Holstein and Nelson were prevented from forming a business entity to provide low-cost legal services, resulting in lost revenues of $650,000. In their prayers for relief, plaintiffs have sought treble damages, attorney's fees, and an injunction prohibiting the enforcement of the challenged rules and requiring defendants to adopt new rules permitting non-lawyers to own interests in law firms. They have also asked for an order requiring the establishment of a $1,000,000 research institute to promote "the development of inter-professional models for the cost-efficient delivery of legal information" and the "assistance of the general public in pro-se representations." . . .

II

A. Sherman Act Immunity

In the opinion below, Judge Holderman held that all defendants were immune from federal antitrust liability so that Count I was dismissed. We agree.

As to the three bar associations, Eastern Railroad Presidents Conference v. Noerr Motor Freight, Inc., 365 U.S. 127, controls. . . . As the Supreme Court held in *Noerr*, "Where a restraint upon trade or monopolization is the result of valid governmental action, as opposed to private action, no violation of the [Sherman] Act can be made out." It is immaterial that these rules were prompted by the defendant bar associations, because *Noerr* also decided that "the Sherman Act does not prohibit two or more persons from associating together in an attempt to persuade the legislature or the executive [here the judiciary acting in a legislative capacity] to take particular action with respect to the law that would produce a restraint or monopoly." *Id.* It is immaterial too that the bar associations encouraged the adoption of these rules because Allied Tube & Conduit Corp. v. Indian Head, Inc., 486 U.S. 492, 499, decided that "those urging the governmental action enjoy absolute immunity for the anticompetitive restraint."

The plaintiffs also challenge as anti-competitive certain ethical opinions promulgated by the defendant bar associations. However, this Court has held that "when a trade association provides information" (by giving its approval in that case, its disapproval in this case) "but does not constrain others to follow its recommendations, it does not violate the antitrust laws." This is so even where the organization at issue has a towering reputation. Even if the Illinois State Bar Association had issued an opinion that it believed certain types of conduct to be violative of the Illinois Rules of Professional Conduct, that opinion could have no anti-competitive effect unless the Illinois State Supreme Court or the Northern District agreed with the ISBA's assessment. It is Illinois' and the Northern District's promulgation and enforcement of the challenged ethics rules and not private parties' interpretation of those rules that restrains competition. In sum, the three bar associations are immune from the alleged antitrust liability.

The district court also correctly held that the justices of the Illinois Supreme Court,[4] the Attorney Registration and Disciplinary Commission, the Executive Committee of the district court, the United States Trustee and the United States Trustee's Assistant are immune from antitrust liability. The Illinois Supreme Court and the ARDC are protected by the state-action doctrine enunciated in Parker v. Brown, 317 U.S. 341. There the Supreme Court adopted a state-action immunity from the Sherman Act because its legislative history showed no congressional purpose to restrain state action or official action directed by a state. Here the Illinois Supreme Court was acting in a legislative capacity and therefore in the same position as a state legislature, so that the activities in question are exempt from Sherman Act liability. Hoover v. Ronwin, 466 U.S. 558, 568; Bates v. St. Bar of Ariz., 433 U.S. 350, 360. The ARDC serves as an agent of the Illinois Supreme Court; consequently the members of the ARDC also enjoy antitrust immunity.

Similarly, the Executive Committee of the district court is insulated from Sherman Act liability. The members of that committee consist of five federal district court judges who are responsible for supervising and disciplining attorneys practicing before them. Since

4. Our disposition of all counts with respect to the Illinois Supreme Court applies to its agent, the Committee on Professional Responsibility, as well.

they are serving as instrumentalities of the United States, this suit cannot be maintained against them.

The United States Trustee and the Trustee's assistant were also made defendants. Because in their official actions they are federal executive officers (28 U.S.C. §§581-582) and were acting in their official capacities, they also are not liable under the Sherman Act.

As the district judge held, Count I must be dismissed because all the defendants are immune from federal anti-trust liability.

B. Liability under Section 1983 of the Civil Rights Act of 1871

1. *State Action*

In Count II plaintiffs allege that defendants' adoption and enforcement of the disciplinary rules at issue contravene the First Amendment and the Due Process and Equal Protection clauses of the United States Constitution, thus violating Section 1983 of the 1871 Civil Rights Act. In order to establish a viable claim of deprivation of rights under Section 1983, plaintiffs must not only show that their constitutional rights were violated, they must also show that the defendants acted under color of state law. Here the three bar associations have not engaged in state action by formulating the disciplinary rules in question. In concluding that the private bar associations are not state actors for the purpose of Section 1983, this Court relies upon the fact that "the power to prescribe rules governing attorney conduct and to discipline attorneys for violating those rules, rests solely in [the Illinois Supreme Court]." The Illinois Supreme Court has not only adopted its own disciplinary rules, but has also appointed an Attorney Registration and Disciplinary Commission not affiliated with the private bar associations to administer those rules. Similarly, the Northern District exercises exclusive power to regulate attorney conduct within its jurisdiction. *See* United States District Court for the Northern District, General Rules 3.51-3.53 (1991). Consequently, Count II is not viable against the three bar associations.[5] Therefore it becomes necessary to see whether Count II states a claim against the Illinois Supreme Court, the ARDC and the Northern District's Executive Committee. As state actors performing acts in their legislative capacity, these defendants are immune from money damages. S. Ct. of Va. v. Consumers Union, 446 U.S. 719, 731-737 (1961).

2. *Constitutional Challenges*

Due Process and Equal Protection

Plaintiffs also seek a declaratory judgment that the rules in question are unconstitutional as violative of the Due Process Clause and the Equal Protection Clause. Unless a governmental regulation draws a suspect classification or infringes on a fundamental right, the government need only show that its regulation is rationally related to a legitimate state interest. As the district court explained, the two rules in question meet this test because they are designed to safeguard the public, maintain the integrity of the profession, and protect the administration of justice from reproach.

The partnership rule limitation promotes the independence of lawyers

---

5. In addition, the United States Trustee and the Assistant United States Trustee are immune from a §1983 suit because they are federal officers and their actions fall short of establishing a private conspiracy with state officials to deprive plaintiffs of their constitutional rights. *See* Tarkowski v. Robert Bartlett Realty Co., 644 F.2d 1204 (7th Cir. 1980).

by preventing non-lawyers from controlling how lawyers practice law. The regulation attempts to minimize the number of situations in which lawyers will be motivated by economic incentives rather than by their client's best interests. . . . The state's interest in preserving the professional independence of lawyers is an adequate justification for the partnership rule and is within the legitimate interest of the state in governing the legal profession. Goldfarb v. Va. St. Bar, 421 U.S. 773, 792 (noting that States have broad power in regulating professional practice).

. . . Some commentators disagree with government prohibitions against unauthorized practice, *see, e.g.*, Deborah L. Rhode, *Policing the Professional Monopoly: A Constitutional and Empirical Analysis of Unauthorized Practice Problems*, 34 Stan. L. Rev. 1 (1981) (arguing that restraints on lay practice are not necessary to a state's interest in preventing incompetent legal assistance); . . . Milton S. Friedman, *Capitalism and Freedom* (1962) (arguing that licensure invariably leads to monopolistic control by members of an occupation). Although scholars may disagree about the effect of the legal ethics rules, the state may choose any regulations that are rational. When employing the appropriate rational basis test, this Court does not require that the state choose the wisest policy, only that it choose a constitutional one.

In sum, we too conclude that the assailed rules bear a rational relation to proper state goals, thus requiring the dismissal of the equal protection and due process claims.

First Amendment

The plaintiffs also assert that both the unauthorized practice rule and the partnership rule violate their First Amendment rights in violation of Section 1983 of the Civil Rights Act.

The plaintiffs contend that the unauthorized practice rule violates their First Amendment freedom of speech. Plaintiffs have conceded that the states have a right to restrict the practice of law to qualified individuals, thus justifying the unauthorized practice rules provision that lawyers may not assist non-lawyers in the unauthorized practice of law. Any abridgment of the right to free speech is merely the incidental effect of observing an otherwise legitimate regulation. Ohralik v. Ohio St. Bar Assn., 436 U.S. 447, 459, 467-468. Although we uphold the validity of the unauthorized practice rule against facial constitutional attack, we do not speculate as to whether this regulation would be constitutional as applied to particular cases. . . .

Finally, plaintiffs challenge the partnership rule as violative of their First Amendment freedom of association. In support of their claim, plaintiffs cite United Mine Workers v. Ill. St. Bar Assn., 389 U.S. 217. In that case the Supreme Court held that union members had a First Amendment right to collectively employ an attorney. It therefore invalidated an Illinois Supreme Court injunction that prevented the union's conduct as the unauthorized practice of law. In reaching its holding, the Supreme Court rejected the Illinois State Bar Association's argument that allowing a union to employ a lawyer would lead to "baseless litigation and conflicting interests between the association and individual litigants." Although the rationales advanced here in support of the partnership rule are exactly those advanced in the *Mine Workers* case, defendants have inexplicably failed to cite that case. . . .

Although this Court notes that the interests sought to be protected by the state in this case are nearly identical to those advanced in *Mine Workers*, there is an important difference between the two cases. *Mine Workers* does not establish laypersons' right to associate with lawyers in the abstract. Rather it supports the proposition that laypersons have a right to obtain meaningful access to the courts, and to enter into associations with lawyers to effectuate that end. In *Mine Workers* plaintiffs had shown that the association prohibited by the state rule was necessary for the union members in order to realize their right to free speech, petition and assembly. As the Court said in United Transp. Union v. State Bar of Michigan, the common thread in the line of cases that includes *Mine Workers* and NAACP v. Button, 371 U.S. 415, "is that collective activity undertaken to provide meaningful access to the courts is a fundamental right within the protection of the First Amendment." 401 U.S. 576, 585-586. . . .

In this case, however, no such fundamental right is at issue. Plaintiffs have not shown that laypersons will be deprived of meaningful access to the courts if lawyers are unable to form partnerships with laypersons. Thus the heightened scrutiny of the state's justification in *Mine Workers* has not been triggered in this case.

Like the unauthorized practice rule, scholars disagree about the desirability and effect of the partnership rule. Jurisdictions that disagree with restrictions on legal partnerships can change, and at least one jurisdiction already has changed, those rules. *See* Note, *Law Firm Diversification and Affiliations Between Lawyers and Nonlawyer Professionals*, Geo. J. Legal Ethics, Vol. III, No. 4, 885 (1990) (discussing Washington D.C.'s abandonment of the partnership rule). However, this Court is not persuaded that states are constitutionally required to do so.

Since these two rules do not violate the Due Process and Equal Protection clauses or the First Amendment, Count II was properly dismissed. . . .

Judgment of dismissal affirmed.

Lawyers and Other Professionals: *Concluding Thoughts*

We conclude this series of notes that compare the legal regulation of lawyers to that of other professionals by considering the issues addressed in this chapter.

Practice Restrictions

Unlike lawyers, all other professionals are free to enter into employment contracts that create subsequent practice restrictions such as covenants not to compete.[1] They also are free to sell professional practices, which, until recently, lawyers were not. Both of these practice restrictions on lawyers are designed to protect clients' freedom to select the lawyers of their choice. They also promote lawyer mobility.

Model Rule 5.6 states the universal rule that third persons, including other lawyers or opposing parties, may not exact a promise that restricts the lawyer's subsequent practice.[2] "Restrictions on a lawyer's right to practice" include agreements not to practice in a specified geographical area[3] as well as financial penalties imposed on lawyers leaving a practice, even if they otherwise retain the right to

1. *See* ABA Section of Labor and Employment Law, *Covenants Not to Compete: A State-by-State Survey* (Brian M. Malsberger, ed., BNA 1996).
2. *Restatement (Third) The Law Governing Lawyers* §13 (2000).
3. Whiteside v. Griffis & Griffis P.C., 902 S.W.2d 739 (Tex. App. 1995).

practice in the geographical area.[4] They also include agreements not to advertise in a certain geographical area,[5] and denials of deferred compensation (income accrued but not yet distributed).[6]

One court has departed from these proscriptions. In Howard v. Babcock,[7] the California Supreme Court decided that law practices should be treated like other professional businesses. The court recognized "sweeping changes in the practice of law"[8] including a decline in institutional loyalty and the open recognition of commercial concerns, which meant that economic interests of law firms could be protected "as they are in other business enterprises."[9] Specifically, the court held that a liquidated damages clause in a partnership contract constituted a reasonable tax on the departing partner rather than a "restriction" on the right to practice law as long as the amount was proportional to the anticipated damages. Disproportionate amounts would remain unenforceable under the general law regulating liquidated damages clauses as penalties. With respect to clients' rights to select lawyers, the court pointed out that clients in civil cases have no right to counsel, and lawyers have "no duty to take any client who proffers employment."[10]

Similar concerns have motivated Model Rule 1.17, which allows for the sale of part or all of a law practice, including goodwill. Note, however, that this rule builds in client protections similar to those that guarantee client choice of counsel under Rule 5.6. For example, the clients of the selling lawyer must be notified of the sale, and given the choice to retain other counsel.[11] The purchasing lawyer also is prohibited from increasing previously negotiated fee agreements.[12]

Advertising and Solicitation

Earlier in this chapter, we saw that the Supreme Court has applied the First Amendment to state attempts to restrict the advertising and solicitation of lawyers. The Court has not, however, always treated other professional groups or competing state interests in the same manner. For example, in Edenfield v. Fane,[13] the Court found that legitimate commercial speech was suppressed by a state ban on in-person telephone solicitation by certified public accountants. The Court reiterated that the state's interests in preventing fraud and maintaining CPA independence were substantial, but found no facts to support the existence of these dangers in any literature, anecdotal evidence, or in accountant Fane's own conduct. The Court also rejected the contention that the ban was a reasonable time, manner, or place restriction because it did not serve the state's interests in a direct and material way.

Distinguishing lawyers, the Court concluded by finding that the ban also could not be justified as a prophylactic rule, because CPA solicitations in a business

4. *See, e.g.*, Cohen v. Lord, Day & Lord, 550 N.E.2d 410 (N.Y. 1989).
5. Blackburn v. Sweeney, 637 N.E.2d 1340 (Ind. App. 1994). A later antitrust attack on the restriction was upheld as constituting a horizontal restraint of trade that was a per se violation of the Sherman Act. No damages were allowed the departing lawyers, however, because they were a party to the agreement. Blackburn v. Sweeney, 53 F.3d 825 (7th Cir. 1995).
6. Spiegel v. Thomas, Mann & Smith, 811 S.W.2d 528 (Tenn. 1991).
7. 863 P.2d 150 (Cal. 1993).
8. *Id.* at 157.
9. *Id.* at 156.
10. *Id.* at 158.
11. Model Rule 1.17(c).
12. Model Rule 1.17(d).
13. 507 U.S. 761 (1993).

context are "not inherently conducive to overreaching and other forms of misconduct."[14] Lawyers, who are trained in the art of advocacy and persuasion, are not like CPAs, who are trained to be independent and objective. Further, prospective clients of CPAs typically are in business and have more experience than many prospective clients of lawyers, who may be unsophisticated, injured, or distressed laypersons.[15]

Edenfield has been relied on to limit advertising and solicitation restrictions by other professionals. Most recently, the Court invalidated a portion of the Food and Drug Administration Act that prevented pharmacists from advertising compounded drugs.[16] The Court held that even if the ban did directly advance a substantial governmental interest, the government failed to demonstrate that the restrictions were not more extensive than necessary to promote the government's interest. Other decisions have struck down similar bans on advertising and solicitation by accountants,[17] chiropractors,[18] dentists,[19] and real estate brokers.[20]

Lawyers have had much less success arguing that *Edenfield* invalidates restrictions on lawyer advertising and solicitation. Courts have upheld state regulations that required prior review of advertisements,[21] restrictions on the content of advertising specialty designations,[22] and disclaimer requirements in newspaper ads.[23]

Although one court has invalidated a total ban on direct mail advertising to personal injury victims,[24] other courts have refused to extend the logic of *Edenfield* to bans on lawyer in-person telephone solicitation.[25]

Federal Intervention

Lawline illustrates how federal laws apply to lawyers. Other professionals, such as physicians and engineers, also are subject to antitrust and antidiscrimination laws, as well as the Americans with Disabilities Act. Most of these applications raise issues similar to those we have encountered in cases involving lawyers, and most courts resolve them in a manner entirely consistent with the law governing lawyers.

So, for example, the state action immunity created by Parker v. Brown in federal antitrust cases discussed in *Lawline* also applies to anticompetitive regulations imposed by licensing authorities of other professions, as long as their action

---

14. *Id.* at 774.
15. *Id.* at 774.
16. Thompson v. W. States Med. Ctr., 535 U.S. 357 (2002).
17. Ibanez v. Fla. Dept. of Bus. & Prof. Reg., 512 U.S. 136 (1994) (lawyer-accountant could not be prevented by Fla. Bd. of Accountancy from truthfully including "CPA" in her advertisement).
18. Bailey v. Morales, 190 F.3d 320 (5th Cir. 1999) (state regulation that banned in-person and telephone solicitation of personal injury victims unconstitutional as applied to chiropractors); Snell v. Dept. of Prof. Reg., 742 N.E.2d 1282 (Ill. App. 2001) (state regulation that banned written testimonials by patients of medical practitioners violates First Amendment rights of chiropractor).
19. Appeal of Sutfin, 693 A.2d 73 (N.H. 1997) (state may not ban advertisement of "inherently misleading" information without proof that it is likely to deceive the public); *cf.* Simm v. La. St. Bd. of Dentistry, 2002 U.S. Dist. LEXIS 3195 (E.D. La. 2002) (use of an acronym in yellow pages advertising potentially misleading because consumers could be misled about the nature of the credential).
20. Cleveland Area Bd. of Realtors v. City of Euclid, 88 F.3d 382 (6th Cir. 1996) (city ordinance banning use of yard signs unconstitutional because it failed to leave open ample alternative channels for communication).
21. McDevitt v. Disc. Bd. of the S. Ct., 1997 U.S. App. LEXIS 3706 (10th Cir. 1997).
22. Iowa S. Ct. Bd. of Prof. Ethics & Conduct v. Wherry, 569 N.W.2d 822 (Iowa 1997).
23. Walker v. Bd. of Prof. Resp. of the S. Ct. of Tenn., 38 S.W.3d 540 (Tenn. 2001).
24. Revo v. Disc. Bd. of the S. Ct., 106 F.3d 929 (10th Cir. 1997).
25. Falanga v. St. Bar, 150 F.3d 1333 (11th Cir. 1998); Texans Against Censorship v. St. Bar, 888 F. Supp. 1328 (E.D. Tex. 1995). *See also* Desnick v. Dept. of Prof. Reg., 665 N.E.2d 1346 (Ill. 1996) (telephone solicitation scripted by ophthalmologist that targeted elderly persons, offering a free eye exam inherently misleading when tied to physician's in-person solicitation of persons for eye surgery).

constitutes official state authorization of the conduct.[26] On the other hand, the private activity of professionals, including engineers,[27] physicians,[28] and dentists[29] has increasingly become the subject of antitrust regulation in the past few decades. Lawyers have avoided most of this scrutiny by successfully seeking official authorization for their anticompetitive activities.[30] The only exception appears to be Goldfarb v. Va. St. Bar,[31] which held that a state and county bar's minimum fee schedule constituted price fixing under the Sherman Act and was private, rather than official state action, because the state supreme court had neither approved nor required the regulation.

Unauthorized Practice

All professional groups have used professional licensing as a means to limit competition from related professionals.[32] The unauthorized practice committees established by state courts in many jurisdictions have official power to bring legal actions for injunctive relief against laypersons whose practices overlap with that of lawyers. Similarly, state administrative agencies charged with licensing other professional groups also have authority to bring administrative actions against those who engage in the unlicensed practice of that profession. The outcome of these actions depends on the exact definition of the professional practice under the relevant statutes.[33] Professionals threatened by a definition often seek separate licensing to legitimate their practice.[34]

---

26. Earles v. St. Bd. of Certified Pub. Accountants of La., 139 F.3d 1033 (5th Cir.), *cert. denied*, 525 U.S. 982 (1998).

27. Natl. Socy. of Prof. Engineers v. United States, 435 U.S. 679 (1978) (professional society's safety concerns do not justify its ban on competitive bidding that violates the Sherman Act).

28. U.S. Dept. of Justice and FTC, Statements of Antitrust Enforcement Policy in Health Care, 4 Trade Reg. Rep. (CCH) ¶13,153 (Aug. 18, 1996); Ariz. v. Maricopa County Med. Socy., 457 U.S. 332 (1982) (nonprofit corporation that set maximum fee schedules by majority vote of its physician members constituted per se violation of the Sherman Act); Wilk v. Am. Med. Assn., 895 F.2d 352 (7th Cir.), *cert. denied*, 498 U.S. 982 (1990) (AMA's boycott directed at chiropractors constituted an illegal restraint of trade in violation of the Sherman Act).

29. Cal. Dental Assn. v. FTC, 526 U.S. 756 (1999) (FTC jurisdiction extends to nonprofit professional association but anticompetitive effects of association's advertising rules demand thorough enquiry into their effects); FTC v. Ind. Fedn. of Dentists, 476 U.S. 447 (1986) (dentists' anticompetitive actions constitute "unfair method of competition" in violation of §5 of FTC Act).

30. *See, e.g.*, Hoover v. Ronwin, 466 U.S. 558 (1984) (committee on bar admissions established by state supreme court acted as official state actor for purposes of state action immunity under Parker v. Brown); Lender's Serv. v. Dayton Bar Assn., 758 F. Supp. 429 (S.D. Ohio 1991) (private bar association authorized to investigate unauthorized practice of law by board of commissioners established by state supreme court constituted state action); Hass v. Oregon St. Bar, 883 F.2d 1453 (9th Cir. 1989), *cert. denied*, 494 U.S. 1081 (1990) (state bar association's requirement of malpractice insurance was a clearly articulated and firmly expressed state policy that qualified for state action immunity).

31. 421 U.S. 773 (1975).

32. *See, e.g.*, In re Guess, 393 S.E.2d 833 (N.C. 1990) (physician who practiced homeopathic medicine disciplined for engaging in unprofessional conduct); *but see* N.C.G.S. §90-14(6) (2001) ("The Board shall not revoke the license of or deny a license to a person solely because of that person's practice of a therapy that is experimental, nontraditional, or that departs from acceptable and prevailing medical practices unless, by competent evidence, the Board can establish that the treatment has a safety risk greater than the prevailing treatment or that the treatment is generally not effective").

33. *E.g.*, St. Bd. of Nursing v. Ruebke, 913 P.2d 142 (Kan. 1996) (lay midwife not engaged in unauthorized practice of nursing or medicine); Hunter v. St., 676 A.2d 968 (Md. 1996) (lay midwife engaged in unauthorized practice of nursing).

34. *E.g.*, Sermchief v. Gonzales, 660 S.W.2d 683 (Mo. 1983) (legislative revision of nursing practice act immunizes nurse practitioners from charges of unauthorized practice of medicine).

The Future

This series of notes has shown that in fashioning legal rules, courts attempt to treat professional groups consistently. This is especially true where civil relief is at stake, such as in malpractice suits or actions by third parties against professionals. In some situations, such as sexual relationships with clients and wrongful discharge causes of action, other professions have identified the issues and developed professional and legal standards earlier than lawyers. In others, such as informed consent, the law has developed on different legal theories, but with a fair amount of consistency. Overall, professionals are distinguished by their licensing, which excludes others, and by their advanced learning, which requires specialized standards of care. All professional groups recognize that certain public service obligations follow from the privilege of licensure.

We can end where we began. Professionals (a) "profess" a body of knowledge, (b) on behalf of someone else, (c) subject to the standards of that group of colleagues.[35] Licensure, although necessary, is not sufficient to qualify a group for professional status. Professionals are distinguished from technicians by their level of knowledge and required study and their internal professional standards designed to serve the public.

E. Unauthorized Practice

Problems

10-10. In an attempt to expand their practice, Martyn & Fox hope to strike a deal with Doris Davenport, a licensed insurance salesperson. Davenport has her own office in a rural community just over the state line.

- **(*a*)** Can Martyn & Fox provide estate-planning services to clients Davenport refers? Does it matter where the clients live?
- **(*b*)** Can Martyn & Fox provide probate services to clients referred by Davenport? Does it matter where the clients live?
- **(*c*)** Can Martyn & Fox agree to refer its estate planning clients to Davenport in exchange for a 10 percent share of the commission she receives on the sale of each investment? How about if we bring her in-house? If we pay her a salary?
- **(*d*)** Can Martyn & Fox agree to refer its estate planning clients to Davenport in exchange for her referrals of insurance clients to Martyn & Fox for estate planning services?

10-11. Martyn & Fox represents a Norwegian company that has subsidiaries in two distant states. Martyn & Fox lawyers travel to both states to negotiate collective bargaining agreements. Has Martyn & Fox engaged in unauthorized practice? Does it matter if the Norwegian company has an office in Martyn & Fox's state?

Consider: Model Rules 5.4, 5.5, 5.7, 7.2
Model Code Canon 3

---

35. William F. May, *Beleaguered Rulers: The Public Obligation of the Professional* 7 (Westminster John Knox Press 2001).

Birbrower, Montalbano, Condon & Frank P.C. v. Superior Court

949 P.2d 1 (Cal. 1998), cert. denied, *525 U.S. 920 (1998)*

CHIN, J.

Business and Professions Code section 6125 states: "No person shall practice law in California unless the person is an active member of the State Bar. . . . " We must decide whether an out-of-state law firm, not licensed to practice law in this state, violated section 6125 when it performed legal services in California for a California-based client under a fee agreement stipulating that Cali-fornia law would govern all matters in the representation.

Although we are aware of the interstate nature of modern law practice and mindful of the reality that large firms often conduct activities and serve clients in several states, we do not believe these facts excuse law firms from complying with section 6125. Contrary to the Court of Appeal, however, we do not believe the Legislature intended section 6125 to apply to those services an out-of-state firm renders in its home state.

I. BACKGROUND

The facts with respect to the unauthorized practice of law question are essentially undisputed. Birbrower is a professional law corporation incorporated in New York, with its principal place of business in New York. During 1992 and 1993, Birbrower attorneys, defendants Kevin F. Hobbs and Thomas A. Condon (Hobbs and Condon), performed substantial work in California relating to the law firm's representation of ESQ. Neither Hobbs nor Condon has ever been licensed to practice law in California. None of Birbrower's attorneys were licensed to practice law in California during Birbrower's ESQ representation.

ESQ is a California corporation with its principal place of business in Santa Clara County. In July 1992, the parties negotiated and executed the fee agreement in New York, providing that Birbrower would perform legal services for ESQ, including "All matters pertaining to the investigation of and prosecution of all claims and causes of action against Tandem Computers Incorporated [Tandem]." The "claims and causes of action" against Tandem, a Delaware corporation with its principal place of business in Santa Clara County, California, related to a software development and marketing contract between Tandem and ESQ dated March 16, 1990 (Tandem Agreement). The Tandem Agreement stated that "The internal laws of the State of California (irrespective of its choice of law principles) shall govern the validity of this Agreement, the construction of its terms, and the interpretation and enforcement of the rights and duties of the parties hereto." Birbrower asserts, and ESQ disputes, that ESQ knew Birbrower was not licensed to practice law in California.

While representing ESQ, Hobbs and Condon traveled to California on several occasions. . . .

ESQ eventually settled the Tandem dispute, and the matter never went to arbitration. But before the settlement, ESQ and Birbrower modified the contingency fee agreement. The modification changed the fee arrangement from contingency to fixed fee, providing that ESQ would pay Birbrower over $1 million. The original contingency fee arrangement had called for Birbrower to receive "one-third (1\3) of all sums received for the benefit of the Clients . . . whether obtained through settlement, motion practice, hearing, arbitration, or trial by way of judgment, award, settlement, or otherwise. . . ."

In January 1994, ESQ sued Birbrower for legal malpractice and related claims in Santa Clara County Superior Court. Birbrower removed the matter to federal court and filed a counterclaim, which included a claim for attorney fees for the work it performed in both California and New York. The matter was then remanded to the superior court. . . . ESQ argued that by practicing law without a license in California and by failing to associate legal counsel while doing so, Birbrower violated section 6125, rendering the fee agreement unenforceable. . . .

We granted review to determine whether Birbrower's actions and services performed while representing ESQ in California constituted the unauthorized practice of law under section 6125 and, if so, whether a section 6125 violation rendered the fee agreement wholly unenforceable.

II. DISCUSSION

A. The Unauthorized Practice of Law

The California Legislature enacted section 6125 in 1927 as part of the State Bar Act (the Act), a comprehensive scheme regulating the practice of law in the state. . . . Since the Act's passage, the general rule has been that, although persons may represent themselves and their own interests regardless of State Bar membership, no one but an active member of the State Bar may practice law for another person in California. The prohibition against unauthorized law practice is within the state's police power and is designed to ensure that those performing legal services do so competently.

A violation of section 6125 is a misdemeanor. Moreover, "No one may recover compensation for services as an attorney at law in this state unless [the person] was at the time the services were performed a member of The State Bar."

Although the Act did not define the term "practice law," case law explained it as " 'the doing and performing services in a court of justice in any matter depending therein throughout its various stages and in conformity with the adopted rules of procedure.'" (People v. Merchants Protective Corp., 209 P. 363, 365 (Cal. 1922).) *Merchants* included in its definition legal advice and legal instrument and contract preparation, whether or not these subjects were rendered in the course of litigation. . . .

In addition to not defining the term "practice law," the Act also did not define the meaning of "in California." In today's legal practice, questions often arise concerning whether the phrase refers to the nature of the legal services, or restricts the Act's application to those out-of-state attorneys who are physically present in the state.

Section 6125 has generated numerous opinions on the meaning of "practice law" but none on the meaning of "in California." In our view, the practice of law "in California" entails sufficient contact with the California client to render the nature of the legal service a clear legal representation. In addition to a quantitative analysis, we must consider the nature of the unlicensed lawyer's activities in the state. Mere fortuitous or attenuated contacts will not sustain a finding that the unlicensed lawyer practiced law "in California." The primary inquiry is whether the unlicensed lawyer engaged in sufficient activities in the state, or created a continuing relationship with the California client that included legal duties and obligations.

Our definition does not necessarily depend on or require the unlicensed lawyer's physical presence in the state. Physical presence here is one factor we may consider in deciding whether the unlicensed lawyer has violated section 6125, but it is by no means exclusive. For example, one may practice law in the state in violation of section 6125 although not physically present here by advising a California client on California law in connection with a California legal dispute by telephone, fax, computer, or other modern technological means. Conversely, although we decline to provide a comprehensive list of what activities constitute sufficient contact with the state, we do reject the notion that a person automatically practices law "in California" whenever that person practices California law anywhere, or "virtually" enters the state by telephone, fax, e-mail, or satellite. . . .

If we were to carry the dissent's narrow interpretation of the term "practice law" to its logical conclusion, we would effectively limit section 6125's application to those cases in which nonlicensed out-of-state lawyers appeared in a California courtroom without permission. . . .

Exceptions to section 6125 do exist, but are generally limited to allowing out-of-state attorneys to make brief appearances before a state court or tribunal. They are narrowly drawn and strictly interpreted. For example, an out-of-state attorney not licensed to practice in California may be permitted, by consent of a trial judge, to appear in California in a particular pending action.

In addition, with the permission of the California court in which a particular cause is pending, out-of-state counsel may appear before a court as counsel *pro hac vice*. A court will approve a *pro hac vice* application only if the out-of-state attorney is a member in good standing of another state bar and is eligible to practice in any United States court or the highest court in another jurisdiction. The out-of-state attorney must also associate an active member of the California Bar as attorney of record and is subject to the Rules of Professional Conduct of the State Bar.

The Act does not regulate practice before United States courts. Thus, an out-of-state attorney engaged to render services in bankruptcy proceedings was entitled to collect his fee.

Finally, California Rules of Court, rule 988, permits the State Bar to issue registration certificates to foreign legal consultants who may advise on the law of the foreign jurisdiction where they are admitted. These consultants may not, however, appear as attorneys before a California court or judicial officer or otherwise prepare pleadings and instruments in California or give advice on the law of California or any other state or jurisdiction except those where they are admitted.

The Legislature has recognized an exception to section 6125 in international disputes resolved in California under the state's rules for arbitration and conciliation of international commercial disputes. This exception states that in a commercial conciliation in California involving international commercial disputes, "The parties may appear in person or be represented or assisted by any person of their choice. A person assisting or representing a party need not be a member of the legal profession or licensed to practice law in California." (Code Civ. Proc., §1297.351.) Likewise, the Act does not apply to the preparation of or participation in labor negotiations and arbitrations arising under collective bargaining agreements in industries subject to federal law.

B. The Present Case

The undisputed facts here show that neither *Baron*'s definition nor our "sufficient contact" definition of "practice law in California" would excuse Birbrower's extensive practice in this state. Nor would any of the limited statutory exceptions to section 6125 apply to Birbrower's California practice. As the Court of Appeal observed, Birbrower engaged in unauthorized law practice in California on more than a limited basis, and no firm attorney engaged in that practice was an active member of the California State Bar. As noted, in 1992 and 1993, Birbrower attorneys traveled to California to discuss with ESQ and others various matters pertaining to the dispute between ESQ and Tandem. Hobbs and Condon discussed strategy for resolving the dispute and advised ESQ on this strategy. Furthermore, during California meetings with Tandem representatives in August 1992, Hobbs demanded Tandem pay $15 million, and Condon told Tandem he believed damages in the matter would exceed that amount if the parties proceeded to litigation. Also in California, Hobbs met with ESQ for the stated purpose of helping to reach a settlement agreement and to discuss the agreement that was eventually proposed. Birbrower attorneys also traveled to California to initiate arbitration proceedings before the matter was settled. As the Court of Appeal concluded, ". . . the Birbrower firm's in-state activities clearly constituted the [unauthorized] practice of law" in California.

Birbrower contends, however, that section 6125 is not meant to apply to any out-of-state attorneys. Instead, it argues that the statute is intended solely to prevent nonattorneys from practicing law. This contention is without merit because it contravenes the plain language of the statute. Section 6125 clearly states that no person shall practice law in California unless that person is a member of the State Bar. The statute does not differentiate between attorneys or nonattorneys, nor does it excuse a person who is a member of another state bar. . . .

Birbrower next argues that we do not further the statute's intent and purpose—to protect California citizens from incompetent attorneys—by enforcing it against out-of-state attorneys. Birbrower argues that because out-of-state attorneys have been licensed to practice in other jurisdictions, they have already demonstrated sufficient competence to protect California clients. But Birbrower's argument overlooks the obvious fact that other states' laws may differ substantially from California law. Competence in one jurisdiction does not necessarily guarantee competence in another. By applying section 6125 to out-of-state attorneys who engage in the extensive practice of law in California without becoming licensed in our state, we serve the statute's goal of assuring the competence of all attorneys practicing law in this state.

California is not alone in regulating who practices law in its jurisdiction. Many states have substantially similar statutes that serve to protect their citizens from unlicensed attorneys who engage in unauthorized legal practice. Like section 6125, these other state statutes protect local citizens "against the dangers of legal representation and advice given by persons not trained, examined and licensed for such work, whether they be laymen or lawyers from other jurisdictions." (Spivak v. Sachs, 211 N.E.2d 329 (N.Y. 1965).) Whether an attorney is duly admitted in another state and is, in fact, competent to practice in California is irrelevant in the face of section 6125's language and purpose. . . .

Assuming that section 6125 does apply to out-of-state attorneys not licensed here, Birbrower alternatively asks us to create an exception to section 6125 for work incidental to private arbitration or other alternative dispute resolution proceedings. Birbrower points to fundamental differences between private arbitration and legal proceedings, including procedural differences relating to discovery, rules of evidence, compulsory process, cross-examination of witnesses, and other areas. As Birbrower observes, in light of these differences, at least one court has decided that an out-of-state attorney could recover fees for services rendered in an arbitration proceeding. . . . (*See* Williamson v. John D. Quinn Const. Corp., 537 F. Supp. 613, 616 (S.D.N.Y. 1982).)

In *Williamson*, a New Jersey law firm was employed by a client's New York law firm to defend a construction contract arbitration in New York. It sought to recover fees solely related to the arbitration proceedings, even though the attorney who did the work was not licensed in New York, nor was the firm authorized to practice in the state. In allowing the New Jersey firm to recover its arbitration fees, the federal district court concluded that an arbitration tribunal is not a court of record, and its fact-finding process is not similar to a court's process. The court relied on a local state bar report concluding that representing a client in an arbitration was not the unauthorized practice of law. But as amicus curiae the State Bar of California observes, "While in *Williamson* the federal district court did allow the New Jersey attorneys to recover their fees, that decision clearly is distinguishable on its facts. . . . [¶] In the instant case, it is undisputed that none of the time that the New York attorneys spent in California was" spent in arbitration; *Williamson* thus carries limited weight. Birbrower also relies on California's rules for arbitration and conciliation of international commercial disputes for support. . . .

We decline Birbrower's invitation to craft an arbitration exception to section 6125's prohibition of the unlicensed practice of law in this state. Any exception for arbitration is best left to the Legislature, which has the authority to determine qualifications for admission to the State Bar and to decide what constitutes the practice of law. Even though the Legislature has spoken with respect to international arbitration and conciliation, it has not enacted a similar rule for private arbitration proceedings. Of course, private arbitration and other alternative dispute resolution practices are important aspects of our justice system. Section 6125, however, articulates a strong public policy favoring the practice of law in California by licensed State Bar members. In the face of the Legislature's silence, we will not create an arbitration exception under the facts presented. . . .

Finally, Birbrower urges us to adopt an exception to section 6125 based on the unique circumstances of this case. Birbrower notes that "Multistate relationships are a common part of today's society and are to be dealt with in commonsense fashion." In many situations, strict adherence to rules prohibiting the unauthorized practice of law by out-of-state attorneys would be "'grossly impractical and inefficient.'" (Appell v. Reiner, 204 A.2d 146, 148 (N.J. 1964) [strict adherence to rule barring out-of-state lawyers from representing New Jersey residents on New Jersey matters may run against the public interest when case involves inseparable multistate transactions].)

Although, as discussed, we recognize the need to acknowledge and, in certain cases, to accommodate the multistate nature of law practice, the facts here show that Birbrower's extensive activities within California amounted to considerably more than any of our state's recognized exceptions to section 6125 would allow. Accordingly, we reject Birbrower's suggestion that we except the firm from section 6125's rule under the circumstances here.

C. Compensation for Legal Services

Because Birbrower violated section 6125 when it engaged in the unlawful practice of law in California, the Court of Appeal found its fee agreement with ESQ unenforceable in its entirety. Without crediting Birbrower for some services performed in New York, for which fees were generated under the fee agreement, the court reasoned that the agreement was void and unenforceable because it included payment for services rendered to a California client in the state by an unlicensed out-of-state lawyer. The court opined that "When New York counsel decided to accept [the] representation, it should have researched California law, including the law governing the practice of law in this state." The Court of Appeal let stand, however, the trial court's decision to allow Birbrower to pursue its fifth cause of action in quantum meruit.[5] We agree with the Court of Appeal to the extent it barred Birbrower from recovering fees generated under the fee agreement for the unauthorized legal services it performed in California. We disagree with the same court to the extent it implicitly barred Birbrower from recovering fees generated under the fee agreement for the limited legal services the firm performed in New York.

It is a general rule that an attorney is barred from recovering compensation for services rendered in another state where the attorney was not admitted to the bar. The general rule, however, has some recognized exceptions. . . .

Birbrower asserts that even if we agree with the Court of Appeal and find that none of the above exceptions allowing fees for unauthorized California services apply to the firm, it should be permitted to recover fees for those limited services it performed exclusively in New York under the agreement. In short, Birbrower seeks to recover under its contract for those services it performed for ESQ in New York that did not involve the practice of law in California, including fee contract negotiations and some corporate case research. . . .

We agree with Birbrower that it may be able to recover fees under the fee agreement for the limited legal services it performed for ESQ in New York to the extent they did not constitute practicing law in California, even though those services were performed for a California client. Because section 6125 applies to the practice of law in California, it does not, in general, regulate law practice in other states. Thus, although the general rule against compensation to out-of-state attorneys precludes Birbrower's recovery under the fee agreement for its actions in California, the severability doctrine may allow it to receive its New York fees generated under the fee agreement, if we conclude the illegal portions of the agreement pertaining to the practice of law in California may be severed from those parts regarding services Birbrower performed in New York. . . .

Thus, the portion of the fee agreement between Birbrower and ESQ that includes payment for services rendered in New York may be enforceable to the extent that the illegal compensation can be severed from the rest of the agreement. On remand, therefore, the trial court must first resolve the dispute surrounding the parties' fee agreement and determine whether their agreement

5. We observe that ESQ did not seek (and thus the court did not grant) summary adjudication on the Birbrower firm's quantum meruit claim for the reasonable value of services rendered. Birbrower thus still has a cause of action pending in quantum meruit.

conforms to California law. If the parties and the court resolve the fee dispute and determine that one fee agreement is operable and does not violate any state drafting rules, the court may sever the illegal portion of the consideration (the value of the California services) from the rest of the fee agreement. Whether the trial court finds the contingent fee agreement or the fixed fee agreement to be valid, it will determine whether some amount is due under the valid agreement. The trial court must then determine, on evidence the parties present, how much of this sum is attributable to services Birbrower rendered in New York. The parties may then pursue their remaining claims. . . .

Practice Pointers: *Multijurisdictional and Multidisciplinary Practice*

Unauthorized practices rules such as those discussed in *Birbrower* act to restrict lawyers from practicing law in two different ways. First, *Birbrower* illustrates the fact that lawyers risk a number of penalties if they represent clients in a jurisdiction where they are not admitted to practice law. In other words, the unauthorized practice rules combine with Model Rule 5.5(a) to keep lawyers jurisdiction-specific and prevent multijurisdictional practice. At the same time, Model Rule 5.5(b) prevents lawyers from aiding the unauthorized practice of law by laypersons. This rule along with Model Rule 5.4 prevents multidisciplinary practice in most jurisdictions because they prevent lawyers from sharing fees and control with nonlawyers. The restrictions on both multijurisdictional and multidisciplinary practice have been the subject of increasing attack in the past few decades.[1] Understanding the debate can help you avoid professional discipline and other consequences such as the fee forfeiture that occurred in *Birbrower.*

Multijurisdictional Practice

Current restrictions on the unauthorized practice of law originated about a century ago and apply to both non-admitted lawyers and laypersons. In most states, statutes define the restriction and provide for criminal (usually misdemeanor) penalties.[2] Typically, cases define the scope of the restriction, which is commonly enforced through injunctive relief rather than criminal penalty.[3] As both individual and corporate clients have become more mobile, they often want to take a trusted lawyer with them. Individuals may live in several jurisdictions in a given time period and may need legal services in all of them. Many entity clients do business throughout the United States and may wish to concentrate their legal work with only a few firms. Many are impacted by federal as well as state environmental, labor, securities, and antitrust laws.

Birbrower states that many jurisdictions have developed exceptions to the jurisdiction-specific rules that currently exist. It also shows how a law firm can rely on such a safe harbor developed in one jurisdiction to its detriment (such as

1. *See, e.g.*, Deborah H. Rhode, *Policing the Professional Monopoly: A Constitutional and Empirical Analysis of Unauthorized Practice Restrictions*, 34 Stan. L. Rev. 1 (1981).

2. *E.g.*, Cal. Bus. & Prof. Code §6126 (2003); Minn. Stat. §481.02 (2003); N.Y. Jud. L. §478 (2003); Tex. Penal Code §38.123 (2003); Va. Code §54.1-3904 (2003).

3. *See, e.g.*, Disc. Counsel v. Shrode, 766 N.E.2d 597 (Ohio 2002) (nonlawyer enjoined from filing court documents for a corporation as a "statutory agent"); Fla. Bar v. Furman, 376 So. 2d 378 (Fla. 1979) (nonlawyer enjoined from providing legal advice about marriage dissolutions and adoptions).

representation in arbitration matters) because the jurisdiction where it provided legal services will not recognize the same exception. For this reason, a consensus has developed that these allowable instances of multijurisdictional practice should become part of the black letter of a revised uniform Model Rule 5.5, which was recently adopted by the ABA House of Delegates.

These changes carve out two groups of exceptions, which allow some, but not all, multijurisdictional practice. The basic rule remains the same: a lawyer not admitted to practice is not allowed to establish an office or "other systematic and continuous presence" in a jurisdiction where he or she is not admitted to practice. The first group of exceptions all hinge on temporary presence in a jurisdiction to accomplish some specific purpose, such as associating with another lawyer admitted in the jurisdiction, practice reasonably related to a matter where the lawyer is admitted to practice, or alternative dispute resolution proceedings that are reasonably related to practice where the lawyer is admitted. Would these exceptions have legitimated the California practice of the New York lawyers in *Birbrower*? Should they?

The second group of exceptions does not rest on temporary presence, but acknowledges the need for multijurisdictional services to some clients. Thus, entities can hire inside counsel who do not need to be admitted in the jurisdiction where their office is located, and legal services can be provided in any jurisdiction if they are either authorized by federal law[4] or the law of that jurisdiction.

Revised Model Rule 5.5 also recognizes *pro hac vice* admission, reciprocal admission by motion, the licensing of legal consultants, and the temporary practice by foreign lawyers. All of this should go a long way toward creating more clearly defined uniform exceptions. Once such multijurisdictional practice is accepted, however, another jurisdictional issue arises. Jurisdictions where unadmitted lawyers practice on a temporary or otherwise acceptable basis need the power to discipline a lawyer who provides legal services in that jurisdiction. To accomplish this, the ABA amended Model Rule 8.5 to clarify that such jurisdiction exists, and to provide a clearer choice of law provision.[5]

Multidisciplinary Practice

Multidisciplinary practice (MDP) occurs when lawyers and nonlawyers collaborate to provide clients legal and nonlegal services, such as those proposed in *Lawline*. Under current rules, this is perfectly acceptable so long as lawyers and nonlawyers do not share legal fees or work in an organization in which lawyers and nonlawyers share managerial control. In other words, lawyers can hire nonlawyers but cannot be hired by for-profit organizations controlled by nonlawyers.

In 1980, the Kutak Commission recommended that these prohibitions be scuttled in favor of multidisciplinary practice, including the sharing of fees and management control, as long as lawyers in such an enterprise remained free to exercise their independent professional judgment and to adhere to all of their professional obligations under the Model Rules. These amendments were defeated in the House of Delegates, and Model Rule 5.4 retained all of the historic limitations on multidisciplinary practice found in the Model Code.

---

4. *See, e.g.*, In re Desilets, 291 F.3d 925 (6th Cir. 2002) (lawyer licensed to practice in Texas and admitted in a Michigan federal court may practice law in a federal bankruptcy court in Michigan).

5. Several jurisdictions have disciplined non-admitted lawyers. *See, e.g.*, In re Marks, 665 N.W.2d 836 (Wis. 2003); In re Mothershed, 2001 Ariz. LEXIS 63.

In 1998, the ABA established a Multidisciplinary Practice Commission to reexamine these issues. The Commission's recommendations, which would have allowed some fee sharing, were soundly defeated once again in 2000 by the House of Delegates. These events have shifted the focus of reform efforts to the individual states, where some are considering rule changes to allow some form of MDP. These proposals all include some combination of the following changes:[6]

1. Shared ownership or equity interest in the firm with nonlawyers,
2. Ancillary business ownership by lawyers,
3. Strategic alliances (formal affiliations of law firms and other service providers),
4. Specifications that MDP clients be governed by the legal profession's confidentiality and conflict of interest rules,
5. Requirements that nonlawyers in MDPs be members of another licensed profession,
6. Disclosure to clients that reveals the extent of shared ownership or contractual agreement to provide nonlegal services, and
7. Permission from the relevant court to establish an MDP.

States considering MDP reform must face a number of issues. First, empirically, do clients want diversified professional services? Second, if client demand is present, will clients benefit from MDPs? Third, if demand occurs and clients seem happy, what will happen when a client who receives MDP services claims competence, confidentiality, or loyalty obligations from such an integrated firm? Will courts impose lawyers' fiduciary duties if lawyers are members of the firm even if other professionals offer a large part of the service?

New York, for example, has amended its professional code, but has also declared: "Multi-disciplinary practice between lawyers and nonlawyers is incompatible with the core values of the legal profession" and therefore requires "strict division between services provided by lawyers and those provided by nonlawyers."[7] The new rule does allow for business alliances between lawyers and nonlawyers and also mandates that a "Statement of Client's Rights in Cooperative Business Arrangements" be signed by clients to protect them.[8]

As you might expect, lawyers differ tremendously over the answers to these questions. Those who favor change dream of "an unregulated marketplace," where "clients would have the choice of hiring a single firm that provided all of these services or multiple firms that specialized in some subset."[9] One can imagine mental health counselors teamed with divorce lawyers, real estate brokers and title insurance providers with lawyers, or social workers with criminal defense lawyers. Specifically, imagine how clients in complex business transactions might benefit from the services of investment bankers, lawyers, accountants, and other associated consultants, a service they can now receive from many accounting firms.

6. For a more detailed account of current proposals, *see* Robert A. Esperti et al., *Latest Developments on the State of Multidisciplinary Practice*, 29 Est. Plan. 267 (June 2002).
7. N.Y. DR 1-107 (2002).
8. 22 N.Y.C.R.R. Part 1205 (2002). *Cf.* Model Rule 7.2(b)(4).
9. Daniel R. Fischel, *Multidisciplinary Practice*, 55 Bus. Law. 951 (2000).

These proponents for change also argue that it is too late to turn back the clock because law firms already are run like big businesses, and self-interested economic behavior furthers social welfare in a market economy.[10] With respect to confidentiality, they maintain that clients can decide when the attorney-client privilege is important enough not to risk an MDP.[11] With respect to loyalty, MDPs offer a great opportunity to get rid of imputed conflicts rules that restrict law firms from growing to their efficient size.[12] This would mean that MDPs could represent clients with adverse interests as well as those who interests are adverse to former clients of the firm in the same or substantially related matters. Screens "may not work perfectly" but, along with "structural separations," would for the most part protect clients from information sharing.[13] Further, equity markets could be opened to MDPs, which would create a new mechanism for financing litigation.[14] Overall, lawyers should welcome MDPs as a new economic opportunity. If law firms can't compete with a Sears MDP, then their "position is exactly analogous to horse and buggy manufacturers faced with the invention of the automobile."[15]

Those who oppose MDPs could not disagree more.[16] They argue that clients already can get the services they need from independent professionals. It is not too late to stop MDPs because a number of core values already restrain the ability of lawyers to compete in an unregulated market. The social welfare is promoted by lawyer *pro bono* efforts[17] and by the entire law governing lawyers that imposes fiduciary duties on lawyers to assure that client interests curb lawyer economic advantage. Loyalty rules including imputed disqualification mean that lawyers must say "no" to some clients in order to protect the interests of others.[18] Association with other service providers easily could compromise the confidentiality obligations of lawyers because MDPs need shared information among professionals to thrive. Worst of all, MDPs could come to compromise the independent judgment of lawyers in the same way HMOs have come to compromise the independent medical judgment of some physicians. Lawyers may be tempted to cheat on competence if their part of the package is the loss leader that brings in the business but needs to be subordinated to some other service such as the sale of securities or insurance in order to maximize profit.[19]

Law firms should not compete with Sears MDPs because Sears should not be able to practice law. The market does not always provide more consumer choice, but can lead to monopoly power that robs consumers of bargaining power. Witness the former Big 8 accounting firms, which, without limitations on concentration, soon became the Big 5 and, after further losing their way, are now the regulated Final 4.[20] The best way to preserve the core values of the legal profession that protect clients from harm is to prevent the economic association of lawyers with other groups, because such influence will inevitably lead to compromise of clients'

10. *Id.* at 957.
11. *Id.* at 964.
12. *Id.* at 965-967.
13. *Id.* at 966.
14. *Id.* at 968.
15. *Id.* at 972.
16. Lawrence J. Fox, *Dan's World: A Free Enterprise Dream; An Ethics Nightmare*, 55 Bus. Law. 1533 (2000).
17. *Id.* at 1551.
18. *Id.* at 1557-1559.
19. *Id.* at 1546-1547.
20. *Id.* at 1539-1540.

interests. Lawyers have special roles to play in our society and "the forces of the economic model are real."[21] We need more than the market to punish the bad and reward the good. We need black letter rules and effective enforcement to protect the best interests of clients.

The Future

The sheer number of jurisdictions considering some change in unauthorized practice rules may mean that some forms of MDPs will be forthcoming.[22] Although some jurisdictions seem to favor fully integrated MDPs, key issues such as sharing of profits and management control still remain. Ultimately, it remains to be seen whether these new structures will attract both lawyers and clients. MDP regulations that subject other professionals to lawyer codes may be seen as too economically restrictive to those who favor fully integrated MDPs.

Provisions that allow full sharing of profits and management initially may be likely to attract new forms of practice. If MDPs grow and multiply, eventually an aggrieved client will bring a malpractice suit, just as aggrieved clients of lawyers and other professionals do. Or an MDP client may seek some other remedy such as disqualification or injunctive relief against the MDP, or fee forfeiture based on similar claims. At that point, courts will have to decide first, whether the law governing lawyers applies, and if so, whether it also creates remedies against the entire MDP. In truly integrated entities, ordinary agency principles of vicarious liability easily could mean that the entire firm would be subject to the law governing lawyers, and that lawyers in the firm also may be subject to additional legal provisions that govern other professionals with whom they are associated.

A British case offers us a glimpse of the litigation that may ensue. There, an accounting firm hired lawyers to offer prelitigation services in teams with other professionals. They later took on an audit of a matter adverse to the former prelitigation services client in a substantially related matter. The House of Lords applied the substantial relationship test applicable to lawyers in deciding a loyalty dispute, even though the accounting firm argued that such a standard was not required by accounting profession rules for audit matters.[23] The reasonable expectations of the client, who understood that lawyers were part of the prelitigation services team, trumped the accounting firm's assumption that it could define loyalty and confidentiality obligations by the standards of another profession.

Should more cases produce similar results, professionals in MDPs will have to face the prospect that the legal standards governing all professionals in the group provide a wide range of remedies to their clients. MDPs will then need to reassess whether the expanded liability and range of remedies opened to clients of the firm are worth the prospect of increased profits.

---

21. *Id.* at 1564.
22. In Wouters v. Algemene Raad de Nederlandse Orde van Advocaten, 2002 ECR I-1577 (2002), the European Court of Justice of the European Communities upheld a ban on partnerships between lawyers and other professionals adopted by the Bar of the Netherlands. The Court held that despite its restrictive effects on competition, the regulation was "necessary for the proper practice of the legal profession," even though other EU Member States allowed multidisciplinary partnerships.
23. Prince Jefri Bolkiah v. KPMG, 2 A.C. 222, 2 W.L.R. 215 (H.L. 1998).

Chapter 11

Being a Lawyer

In this chapter, we turn our attention to you, asking what kind of a profession you wish to be a part of in the future as well as what kind of person you want to be as you practice law. We begin by returning to a consideration of what it means to be a professional. We then examine lawyer personality and professionalism. We conclude by returning to some examples in this book that may help you find your own way in the world of law practice.

A. Being a Professional

Problems

11-1. Associate tells Fox he has discovered that Martyn has been sending bills to clients charging them for Martyn's services at Martyn's hourly rate for services actually performed by Associate. Fox investigates and tells Associate that in each instance where this occurred, the client was billed either a fixed fee or a uniform hourly rate regardless of which lawyer performed the work, that Martyn will not repeat the conduct because she is now on medication for her depression, and that Fox considers the matter satisfactorily resolved. What should Associate do?

11-2. Fox tells Martyn that he has just been convicted of drunk driving in a distant state. He admits he may have a drinking problem, but tells Martyn not to worry, "I'll handle it myself." What should Martyn do?

Consider: Model Rules 5.1, 5.2, 8.3, 8.4
Model Code DR 1-102, 1-103

Kelly v. Hunton & Williams

1999 U.S. Dist. LEXIS 9139 (E.D.N.Y.)

GLEESON, District Judge:

Peter M. Kelly brought this diversity action against his former employer, the law firm of Hunton & Williams ("H&W"), alleging that H&W breached implied contractual obligations owed him when it terminated his employment with the firm. Specifically, plaintiff claims that H&W forced him to resign and implicitly threatened to withhold a favorable job reference, in order to impede and discourage him from reporting H&W partner Scott Wolas's billing fraud to the Disciplinary Committee. Hunton & Williams moves for summary judgment. The motion is denied.

FACTS . . .

Plaintiff first worked for H&W as a summer associate in the firm's New York City office during the summer of 1989. At the end of that summer, H&W extended him an offer to join the firm as an associate upon his graduation from law school in June 1990. In October 1990, plaintiff began working in H&W's New York office as an associate in the litigation department. . . .

H&W is a large, prestigious law firm. Founded in 1901 in Richmond, Virginia, it now has 650 lawyers in fifteen offices, five of which are overseas. Among its illustrious alumni is Lewis F. Powell, Jr., who left the firm to become an Associate Justice of the Supreme Court of the United States. When plaintiff began with H&W in October 1990, the litigation department in the New York office (which was founded in 1983) consisted of fewer than ten partners and associates. Plaintiff was one of two first-year associates. He worked primarily with Scott Wolas and Franklin Stone, who were partners, and with Christopher Mason, who became a partner in early 1992.

Plaintiff's first-year performance reviews, prepared in June and July of 1991, resulting in favorable ratings but expressed some concern over his not having passed the bar examination. In October 1991, Stone described plaintiff to another H&W partner as "a terrific associate—functioning well above his second year." The following month, when the favorable result of the bar examination was announced, partner Kathy Robb . . . wrote the following on plaintiff's first annual associate evaluation: "Typical 1st year. Strong 'goods.' Apply with vigor to work. Congratulations on passing the bar. Good potential here." Stone wrote: "Peter does excellent work and is a valuable asset to our team. He brings an intelligence and maturity to his work that is rare in a first year associate." Mason wrote: "Peter has good skills, indeed, very good skills in many ways. . . . I also have a good deal of confidence in his work, confidence beyond his first-year level." Plaintiff received the maximum pay raise for his class.

Earlier in 1991, around April or May, plaintiff began suspecting Scott Wolas of billing fraud. Wolas had billed four hours per day over a two-week period for a particular matter, and plaintiff suspected that Wolas had not worked those hours. He shared those suspicions with another litigation associate, Joseph Saltarelli. In June 1991, Saltarelli informed plaintiff that Wolas had billed fictitious hours on a series of matters. Over the next several months, Saltarelli related to plaintiff other instances of Wolas's improper billing.

In November 1991, Saltarelli told plaintiff that Saltarelli was meeting with B. Carey Tolley, III, the managing partner of the firm's New York office, along with Stone, Mason, and Robb to discuss Wolas's billing practices. . . .

Around this time, plaintiff began socializing with Saltarelli and Hal Geary, a litigation associate hired from another firm in 1991. They frequently lunched together and went out after work for drinks or dinner. The other attorneys on plaintiff's floor, including Wolas, Stone, and Mason, were aware of the close association of plaintiff and Saltarelli. For this reason, and because plaintiff was involved in preparing fee applications (and thus had access to

Wolas's billing records), plaintiff asserts that, as early as November 1991, Wolas, Stone, Mason, and Robb knew that plaintiff was aware of Wolas's billing improprieties.

In approximately June of 1992, plaintiff told Mason that Wolas was billing clients for time not worked. Unbeknownst to plaintiff, Mason had been investing heavily (and profitably) through Wolas for nearly two years. In addition to Wolas's status as a "rainmaking" partner at H&W, he solicited investments in his family's liquor business. These so-called investments were actually part of an alleged "Ponzi scheme" Wolas was conducting from his office at H&W. Wolas lent considerable credence to those allegations—in fact, everyone now seems to agree they are true—by absconding in 1995, leaving behind more than 100 investors who claim to have been defrauded of more than $30 million. Mason, however, was not one of the investors who were left holding the bag. To the contrary, he profited enormously from Wolas's scheme; in 1994 alone he earned $2 million. In any event, when plaintiff told him in June 1992 that Wolas was billing for time not worked, Mason responded curtly, telling plaintiff that things are not always what they seem, and that Wolas's billing was not plaintiff's concern.

Before his conversation with Mason about Wolas's billing fraud, plaintiff had not received any substantial negative criticism of his work or work habits. However, shortly after the meeting, Stone began inquiring about plaintiff's whereabouts on mornings when he arrived late to the office. Stone, like Mason, invested heavily with Wolas from 1990 through 1995. In an e-mail to Robb, dated July 24, 1992, Stone wrote that plaintiff's "problems with basic logistics have gotten Scott [Wolas], Chris [Mason] and me pulling our hair out." Robb, like Mason and Stone, had invested substantial sums through Wolas. Four days later, in a July 28, 1992 e-mail to Stone, Wolas, and Mason, Robb mentioned that she had spoken to plaintiff about "his constant tardiness and other inattentions to the administrative aspects of practicing law (e.g., not pursuing finalizing his bar application in a timely fashion)." Robb continued, "I told him that all of you liked him enormously, think he is talented, and view him as having the potential to become an excellent lawyer, but that if he didn't take his inability to get to work consistently seriously, there was a good chance that you were going to boot him out of here."

Meanwhile, after putting Saltarelli off for months, Tolley finally reviewed Wolas's billing records. Tolley refused to approach Wolas for an explanation, but rather told Saltarelli in early August 1992 to raise it directly with Wolas, in a non-accusatory manner, under the guise of asking his help in explaining billing records that might raise questions when cases were settled or fee applications were made to courts. In essence, Tolley told Saltarelli to help Wolas repair billing records that Saltarelli believed were fraudulent.

On September 10, 1992, Robb and Mason spoke further to plaintiff regarding his performance. As a result, plaintiff prepared a memorandum on September 16, 1992, listing ten steps he intended to take to improve his work habits. On November 10, 1992, plaintiff again met with Mason and Robb for his second annual associate evaluation. They informed him that he had received "needs improvement" ratings in several critical categories, that he displayed "poor attention to work" in general. . .

Over the following months, plaintiff, Saltarelli, and Geary encountered additional evidence of Wolas's systematic overbilling of clients. Sensing that Tolley was not going to deal with the problem, they approached James A.

Jones, III, Tolley's predecessor as managing partner, in February of 1993. The three came forward as a group, prompted in part by the advice of a federal district judge whom Geary had served as a law clerk. The judge had further told Geary that he might have an ethical obligation to disclose the billing irregularities to the Disciplinary Committee if appropriate action were not taken by the firm.

Saltarelli, Geary, and plaintiff raised the issue of Wolas's improper billing with Jones in February 1993. Geary brought to Jones documentary evidence of Wolas's fraud, and informed Jones that plaintiff had further evidence of it and was willing to assist the firm in its investigation of the matter. The day following Geary's meeting with Jones, plaintiff met with Tolley to discuss Wolas's billing practices. In the ensuing weeks, plaintiff had additional meetings with Tolley, Jones, and Wolas himself to review Wolas's billing records. In late February, Tolley informed plaintiff that W. Taylor Reveley, the former managing partner of the firm's Richmond office, would be coming to New York to head the investigation into Wolas's billing. . . .

On February 25, 1993, Stone sent an e-mail to Mason and Robb. She stated, "I want to fire Peter Kelly NOW. He missed his deadline: 10:00 a.m. this morning to give me a draft. . . . Then Peter disappeared all day. He just returned and has nothing more for me. . . . I can't stand it anymore. We must get rid of him now." Plaintiff claims that, in fact, he met Stone's deadline, and that he had worked through the previous night to do so.

On March 1, 1993, the day before Reveley was scheduled to interview plaintiff about Wolas's billing activities, Robb and Mason told plaintiff that he had to leave the firm. They gave him a choice: he could (a) be fired immediately, without severance pay or a favorable job reference; or (b) announce his resignation and stay with the firm the next several months, which would gain him a favorable reference. This was not much of a choice. Plaintiff had no other employment lined up and no other source of income. He would face a difficult job search if he could not obtain a favorable reference from H&W. . . . Consequently, plaintiff chose coerced resignation over being fired.

Before coming to New York to conduct his inquiry, Reveley spoke by telephone with Robb, who disparaged plaintiff and Geary. Stone admits that she "might have" told her partners (presumably including Reveley) before the billing investigation that plaintiff had concocted his allegations against Wolas in order to stretch out his employment at H&W. In any event, Reveley promptly rejected the accusing associates' claims. He interviewed them on March 2, 1993. He conducted a "hearing" nine days later. Present were the three accusers, Stone (whom Reveley insisted be present because she was "inextricably relevant" to the hearing), Mason, and Wolas. It was not much of a hearing. Reveley denied the accusing associates access to Wolas's written response to their charges and refused to permit them to question Wolas. Stone and Mason sat silently. They did not disclose their separate, investment-based financial interest in Wolas's continued membership in the firm. Indeed, Mason had invested $12,900 with Wolas the day before the hearing, and had received a $35,000 "return of principal" from him just ten days before that. Stone had received $96,200 in "repayments" from Wolas in the seven weeks before the hearing. Indeed, though Mason, Stone, and Robb were all integrally involved as H&W partners in exonerating Wolas and getting rid of plaintiff—Wolas's accuser—none of them revealed to

Tolley, Reveley, or Jones their involvement as investors in Wolas's scheme. Indeed, if Mason, Stone, and Robb are to be believed, they never even discussed their financial stakes in Wolas among themselves until 1994 at the earliest.

It took Reveley only one day to decide that Wolas had not committed billing fraud, but he waited almost a month to meet with his accusers. On April 7, 1993, Reveley met with plaintiff, Geary, Saltarelli, and Tolley to discuss his findings. He told them that Wolas was a "sloppy pig, not a dirty rat." The three associates responded by presenting Reveley with additional evidence of fraudulent billing by Wolas. Reveley promised to continue his investigation.

On April 13, 1993, Tolley e-mailed Reveley. The subject was whether the firm or the accusing associates had an obligation to report the facts about Wolas's billing to the Disciplinary Committee. The e-mail made explicit reference to Wieder v. Skala, 609 N.E.2d 105 (N.Y. 1992), the December 1992 New York Court of Appeals decision that is discussed *infra*. Tolley opined that the firm's determination that fraud had not been clearly established extinguished the obligation to report not only for the firm, but for the associates as well. He sought Reveley's counsel on how to tell the associates that they had no obligation to report Wolas. On May 6, 1993, Reveley met with the accusing associates separately and told them they had no ethical obligation to take their accusations further. Although he added that each associate had to make that decision for himself, it was clear that anyone taking on Wolas before the Disciplinary Committee would be taking on H&W as well.

Plaintiff left H&W at the end of May 1993, although he remained on the firm's payroll for another month. In seven letters to prospective employers, dated July 27 through September 3, 1993, plaintiff stated that he left the firm "voluntarily." On November 11, 1993, a partner at another firm in New York contacted Stone seeking a job reference for plaintiff. Stone praised plaintiff's substantive abilities but mentioned that a series of personal problems had negatively affected plaintiff's job performance and attendance. According to Stone, the caller told her that plaintiff had mentioned that H&W let him go because he had blown the whistle on a partner's billing irregularities. Stone informed him that plaintiff's departure from H&W stemmed entirely from plaintiff's performance problems.

Unable to secure work in New York, plaintiff moved to Texas in 1994. On February 28, 1994, an attorney placement firm in Houston contacted Stone with regard to plaintiff. According to Stone, she told the placement firm that plaintiff "was very smart and a very good writer, but that he suffered from performance problems and family crises which severely affected his work."

Plaintiff was admitted to the Texas bar in 1994, and was finally admitted to the New York bar in the summer of 1997. On September 29, 1997, he brought this action.

DISCUSSION . . .

Plaintiff concedes that he worked at H&W as an employee-at-will, and that, under New York law, an employer may generally terminate such an employee at any time for any or no reason. He contends that his termination fits within the narrow exception to that rule established by the New York Court of Appeals in Wieder v. Skala, 609 N.E.2d 105 (N.Y. 1992).

In *Wieder*, the court held that even though an associate at a law firm was an at-will employee, he had a valid claim against his firm for breach of contract based on the firm's discharging him for his insistence that the firm comply with the Code of Professional Responsibility by reporting to the Disciplinary Committee the professional misconduct of another associate. The court noted that associates at law firms are not only employees, they are also independent officers of the court, responsible in a broader public sense for their professional obligations. The court further stated that

> in any hiring of an attorney as an associate to practice law with a firm there is implied an understanding so fundamental to the relationship and essential to its purpose as to require no expression: that both the associate and the firm in conducting the practice will do so in accordance with the ethical standards of the profession. Erecting or countenancing disincentives to compliance with the applicable rules of professional conduct . . . would subvert the central professional purpose of [plaintiff's] relationship with the firm—the lawful and ethical practice of law.

As in this case, the particular rule of professional conduct at issue in *Wieder* was DR 1-103(A), which imposes on lawyers a duty to report to the Disciplinary Committee any potential violations of the disciplinary rules that raise a substantial question as to another lawyer's honesty. The court held that the allegation that the firm had placed the associate in the position of having to choose between continued employment and fulfilling this ethical obligation stated a claim for breach of contract based on an "implied-in-law obligation" in the employment relationship. . . .

A. The Availability of a *Wieder* Claim to an Associate Not Yet Admitted to the Bar . . .

At H&W, as in most firms like it, the distinction between associate and partner is everything, but the distinction between admitted junior associate and unadmitted junior associate is gossamer, and the distinction pressed here—between junior associate and "law clerk"—simply does not exist.

It is difficult to conceive of H&W telling its clients what it is now telling me, i.e., that, as far as the firm is concerned, its unadmitted associates are not bound by the disciplinary rules and may knowingly act contrary to them without fear of professional sanction. More difficult still is imagining H&W telling that to the new class of law graduates that joins the firm as unadmitted associates each fall.

In any event, the question whether the *Wieder* cause of action would be extended by New York courts to unadmitted law graduates working as associates in law firms is easily answered. The answer is yes. *Wieder* applies to "any hiring of an attorney as an associate.". . . When H&W hired plaintiff, it paid him as an associate, evaluated him as an associate, and gave him assignments as an associate. The only restrictions he faced as an unadmitted associate were that he could neither sign briefs nor appear in court on behalf of clients. In a big-firm practice, those restrictions have little operational significance.

I reject H&W's contention that an unadmitted associate cannot, because he is unadmitted, face the dilemma of having to choose between continued employment at a firm and compliance with lawyers' disciplinary rules. The state bar may be unable to kick an unadmitted attorney off the roll of attorneys, but it certainly can keep him from getting on it. An associate at a law firm might reasonably believe that his knowing failure to disclose an attorney's fraud would cause the Character and Fitness Committee to recommend the denial of his application for admission to the bar. . . .

. . . Plaintiff was not hired as a paralegal, or to perform administrative tasks. He was hired by H&W for the sole purpose of practicing law. H&W owed him the same implied-in-law obligation it owed its other associates. . . .

Finally, it bears mention that in April 1993, just four months after *Wieder* was decided, H&W itself carefully examined whether the three accusing associates had a duty to report Wolas to the Disciplinary Committee. Mason gathered the relevant materials, including a copy of *Wieder*, and provided them to Tolley, who analyzed them for Reveley. Reveley spoke personally and separately to the three associates. The argument advanced here—that plaintiff, unlike Saltarelli and Geary, was simply a "law clerk" who had no reporting obligation at all—occurred to no one at H&W at the time. This is not because the H&W partners involved are not resourceful lawyers. Rather, it is because the formal, legalistic contention the firm now makes is incompatible with the way associates like Peter Kelly are viewed and expected to act in the real world of big-firm practice.

B. The Other Claimed Limitations on the *Wieder* Cause of Action

The upshot of H&W's other arguments regarding the scope of *Wieder* is surprising. According to H&W, if there is actual fraud at the firm, about which an associate has complained to the firm, the firm can immediately fire the associate in retaliation for complaining and threaten to ruin his future with bad references if he reports the fraud to the Disciplinary Committee. As long as the associate is fired before he threatened to go to the Disciplinary Committee, and if only a favorable reference (i.e., not his job) is conditioned on his continuing violation of DR 1-103(A), H&W asserts that "the *Wieder* case does not create a cause of action in that setting.". . .

First, I do not consider the absence of a threat by plaintiff to go to the disciplinary Committee as raising an open question of New York Law. If a law firm fires an associate in retaliation for reporting a lawyer's misconduct to the firm, its action is inherently coercive and necessarily implies an effort to impede post-termination reporting to the Disciplinary Committee. Thus, a cause of action is available under *Wieder*. The associate's stated intention to go to the disciplinary authorities may be powerful circumstantial evidence of the firm's intent to punish and/or silence him or her, but it is neither dispositive nor necessary to the associate's claim.

H&W's contention that *Wieder* is inapplicable to a law firm's conditioning of a favorable job reference on the attorney's silence arguably raises an open question of New York law, but the question is easily answered. Where, as here, a jury can reasonably infer that a law firm's unfavorable reference can effectively prevent the attorney from obtaining the type of employment he seeks, conditioning a favorable reference on continued silence may properly be found to be "placing him in the position of having to choose between continued employment" and the consequences of failing to comply with DR 1-103(A).

Finally, H&W's reply brief contends that the January 21, 1999 decision of the Appellate Division in Geary v. Hunton & Williams, 684 N.Y.S.2d 207 (A.D. 1999), is "completely dispositive" of this motion. That case held that Geary's breach of contract claim against H&W "was properly rejected on the basis of evidence establishing that defendant terminated plaintiff before plaintiff had raised any concerns about [Wolas's] billing practices with the other partners. A jury could find otherwise here, that is, it could find that the decision to fire plaintiff was made only after he first told Mason about Wolas's billing for time he did not work. . . .

. . . Plaintiff, unlike Geary, claims not only that he was forced to resign in retaliation for blowing the whistle on Wolas, but also that the firm continued to discourage him from reporting Wolas to the Disciplinary Committee even after he was fired. Specifically, plaintiff contends that Reveley's statement to him that he had no ethical responsibility to report Wolas, at a time when Plaintiff sorely needed a favorable reference from the firm, "was designed to create an appearance of compliance with *Wieder* while simultaneously discouraging me from reporting another attorney's professional misconduct to authorities. . . ."

. . . [T]he Appellate Division's decision states that H&W could not have impeded or discouraged Geary's compliance with the obligation he "did not believe he had, did not express an intent to carry out, and did not carry out." Here, there is evidence from which a jury could infer that plaintiff believed he had such an obligation, including the statements by Reveley that explicitly sensitized the accusing associates to their obligation.

In sum, while I recognize that *Wieder* established a narrow exception to New York's at-will employment law, I decline to give it the crabbed construction advanced by H&W. If the jury resolves the disputed issues of facts in plaintiff's favor, it may properly conclude that H&W breached its employment contract with him. . . .

The rest of H&W's arguments in support of its motion rely on purportedly undisputed facts that are anything but undisputed. It contends that it is undisputed that prior to February 1993 plaintiff had never apprised an H&W partner that he believed Wolas had engaged in billing fraud. But plaintiff testified that he told Mason in June or July of 1992 that Wolas was not working all the hours that he was billing. Billing for hours not worked is fraud. H&W further contends that plaintiff indisputably left H&W voluntarily. But plaintiff asserts that he was forced out by the threat that he would be fired without severance pay or a favorable job reference if he did not resign. A jury could conclude that his departure from the firm was not voluntary. That he told subsequent employers or bar examiners otherwise will be fair ground for impeachment at trial, but it does not warrant summary judgment for H&W. H&W contends that it indisputably did not threaten adverse action to plaintiff if he reported Wolas's misconduct to the Disciplinary Committee. While it is true that the H&W partners studied *Wieder* closely during the events in question and made no explicit threat, a rational jury could conclude that H&W fired plaintiff because he had insisted on airing Wolas's fraud, and implicitly conditioned its favorable references to prospective future employers on plaintiff's keeping quiet about that fraud. . . .

Mullison v. People

61 P.3d 504 (Colo. O.P.D.J. 2002)

Opinion issued by a Hearing Board consisting of John E. Hayes and Kathryn S. Lonowski, both members of the bar, and the Presiding Disciplinary Judge Roger L. Keithley. . . .

Michael Dean Mullison took the oath of admission and was admitted to the bar of the State of Colorado on November 1, 1985. The events leading to this attorney's disbarment occurred during a time period in which Mullison developed an addiction to cocaine which increased to a level where it destroyed the attorney's personal and professional life.

After graduating from law school, Mullison practiced in Colorado for one year, then relocated to the State of Washington to work for a firm handling no-contest divorce and bankruptcy matters. While working for the firm, in 1988, Mullison agreed to represent a client "on the side" in a contested divorce. Mullison accepted money from this client outside of his employment, and diverted those funds to his own use for drug purchases. When his employer discovered Mullison's "on the side" representation, Mullison's employment was terminated.

Mullison returned to Colorado with his wife and daughter. He did not inform his wife the true reason for the termination of his employment and continued to conceal his drug use from her. He established a solo practice in Longmont where he handled bankruptcy, domestic relations and civil matters.

The stress of his solo practice exacerbated his use of cocaine. He charged a relatively small flat fee for bankruptcy work and other matters, but routinely used those fees for drug purchases. His practice became a "shell game" in which he would use fees collected from subsequent clients to pay the filing fees required to complete previous clients' work.

During this time, Mullison represented a client, Kathy Rush, and accepted fees and costs from her to file a petition for dissolution of marriage on her behalf. Mullison converted the fees and costs to his own use and never filed the petition. Later, Mullison forged what purported to be a copy of the decree. Another attorney who had been consulted by the client reported his forgery of the decree. Mullison pled guilty to second degree forgery, a class four felony. He admitted to having used the money paid to him for the purchase of drugs.

In another matter a client retained Mullison and paid him to file a personal bankruptcy action. Mullison never filed the bankruptcy petition, although he misrepresented to the client that it had been filed and that the court date had been set. Mullison pled guilty to felony theft for taking the client's money and failing to perform the agreed-upon legal services. In addition to these two specific instances, in eleven separate additional instances in 1989, Mullison failed to perform legal services while accepting and retaining payment for services.

The State of Washington brought criminal charges against Mullison based on his diversion of client funds for his own use. He pled guilty to attempted theft in the second degree, a misdemeanor, and was subsequently suspended by the Washington Supreme Court. . . .

Mullison was immediately suspended from the practice of law in Colorado on November 9, 1989, based on the criminal charges in the State of Washington and Mullison's misconduct following his return to Colorado. Thereafter, as a result of a stipulated sanction of disbarment . . . Mullison was disbarred from the practice of law in the State of Colorado on April 27, 1992. People v. Mullison, 829 P.2d 382 (Colo. 1992).

Mullison finally admitted to his wife and family that he had a serious cocaine addition. He began to realize the extent of his addiction, and that it had resulted in the ruin of his personal and professional life. At the same time, he was relieved that he need no longer lie about his addiction.

On April 13, 1990, after entering a plea of guilty to second degree forgery . . . arising out of Mullison's forgery of a court document in his representation of Kathy Rush, Mullison was sentenced to six years in community corrections and was ordered to pay restitution in the amount of $7,157.00. Mullison was placed in community corrections in the Longmont, Colorado facility and served one hundred and twenty-nine (129) days as a resident of that facility where he received intensive treatment for his addiction to cocaine. In this facility, Mullison was subjected to detoxification, random testing, counseling, and seminars on remaining drug-free. He developed skills to live without the use of drugs.

After being released from the Longmont facility, Mullison was transferred to Larimer County Community Corrections, and was under its supervision until the termination of his sentence on December 9, 1994. While under its supervision, Mullison worked long hours in non-legal positions including delivering milk in the evening and furniture in the daytime. He later obtained paralegal positions. He supported his wife and children, and earned the funds to make full restitution as ordered in both the criminal and disciplinary proceedings.

As part of his sentence, Mullison entered drug treatment in the "New Beginnings" program in Fort Collins, Colorado in 1989, involving weekly meetings, consultation with a caseworker, drug addiction after care, and random drug testing. New Beginnings helped Mullison to change his behavior and thinking and helped him begin to piece his life back together. He was also involved in Narcotics Anonymous on a daily basis from 1989 to 1997. He assisted in establishing a Fort Collins chapter of "Coke Anon" and spoke to college students and school groups about cocaine addiction. As a result of these rehabilitative programs, Mullison came to understand that his cocaine addiction caused him to act dishonestly and exercise extremely poor judgment.

Mullison's family relationship was badly harmed by his cocaine habit and the resulting consequences. During the years following his criminal conviction, Mullison and his wife—also an attorney—separated twice. Following those separations, both Mullison and his wife attended counseling, devoted substantial effort to their relationship, and were able to reestablish the marriage. Mullison has maintained a close relationship to his children, spending a great deal of time with them, coaching basketball teams and attending school events.

In 1991 Mullison, through his wife, sought paralegal employment, [and has worked] as a paralegal in the area of worker's compensation law, personal injury, and social security matters . . . from May 1991 until . . . [the present]. . . . He engages in legal research, maintains client files, prepares forms, contacts clients, performs extensive research and prepares legal briefs under the supervision of [Attorney Regina] Adams. He has been responsible for delivering funds to clients, performing disbursement of payments on cases, and depositing funds in the firm account. Mullison's work with Adams has been exemplary; he is punctual, organized, responsible and demonstrates attention to detail. If readmitted, Adams intends to offer an associate position to Mullison. . . .

The [Colorado Supreme Court] disbarment order also required Mullison to pay restitution to eleven separate clients for a total amount of $3,122. . . . Mullison made all reimbursement payments required . . . [and he] has completed all drug treatment requirements from the Boulder County matters and has scrupulously maintained adherence to a drug-free lifestyle.

Mullison sat for and passed both the May 2002 Colorado Bar Examination and the Multistate Professional Responsibility Exam. He has remained current in the law by regularly reading The Colorado Lawyer, attending legal seminars throughout his period of employment, keeping abreast of the law through reading of case law, ethics opinions and disciplinary cases, and other legal publications.

Mullison candidly acknowledged and admitted that his disbarment for dishonesty and conversion of client funds was justified. He acknowledged the harm that he caused to his clients and the legal profession, and has paid reimbursement to his clients in full. He acknowledged the harm he caused to his wife and family, and is committed to setting an example to his children of the harm that can result from drug use. He forthrightly acknowledged and admitted that his prior conduct was deceptive, that he had, but ignored, opportunities to obtain help with his problems, and that he engaged in "rock bottom conduct."

Mullison is now forty-two years of age, does not suffer from any physical or emotional disorder, and has not used illegal drugs since November 1, 1989.

At the conclusion of the evidence, the People stipulated to Mullison's readmission. . . .

C.R.C.P. 251.29(a) provides:

> Readmission After Disbarment. A disbarred attorney may not apply for readmission until at least eight years after the effective date of the order of disbarment. To be eligible for readmission the attorney must demonstrate the attorney's fitness to practice law and professional competence, and must successfully complete the written examination for admission to the Bar. The attorney must file a petition for readmission, properly verified, . . . [and] the attorney . . . must demonstrate by clear and convincing evidence the attorney's rehabilitation and full compliance with all applicable disciplinary orders and with all provisions of this Chapter. . . .

Imposition of discipline against an attorney includes a determination that some professional or personal shortcoming existed upon which the discipline is premised. The shortcoming may have resulted either from personal deficits or from a combination of personal deficits and professional and/or environmental inadequacies. It necessarily follows that the analysis of rehabilitation should be directed at the professional or moral shortcoming which resulted in the discipline imposed. A prior disbarment based upon felonious conduct requires a close examination of the actual misconduct. In this case, Mullison was disbarred due to the commission of two criminal acts. First, Mullison knowingly caused the falsification of a court document in an effort to hide from the client that he had not performed the work he had been retained to complete. In the second instance of criminal misconduct, Mullison knowingly utilized client funds in order to finance his cocaine habit.

Both of these criminal episodes reveal character deficits present at the time the events transpired. Both episodes and the additional episodes giving rise to the disbarment arose from Mullison's placing his cocaine addiction above his professional responsibilities to his clients. In order to be readmitted to the practice of law, Mullison must establish that those character deficits present at the time of his misconduct have now been removed so as to insure that similar misconduct does not recur.

Mullison has established that he has undergone a fundamental character change. Almost immediately after his convictions, Mullison acknowledged the wrongfulness of his misconduct and began the lengthy process of restructuring his life. During his sentence in community corrections after the initial one hundred and twenty-nine day period, he continuously maintained jobs to support his family and earn the funds necessary to pay restitution. He pursued extensive programs and counseling aimed at rehabilitation and recovery. He has applied these concepts successfully to his routine life for over eleven years. The period of time which has transpired between Mullison's last submission to his addiction and the time of this readmission proceeding, eleven years, is a significant factor. It independently demonstrates that Mullison has developed sufficient character to control his addictions and conform his personal conduct to the standards required by our society.

Mullison has engaged in community service by sharing the story of his professional and personal experiences with college students and school groups, informing them of the hazards of cocaine use. He was dedicated to Narcotics Anonymous and assisted in developing a chapter of "Coke Anon" in Fort Collins. His free time is currently focused on raising his children and coaching them and other children in sports. He has worked hard to overcome his former behavior and win back the trust of those he previously hurt and deceived. In that regard, he has focused on repairing his marital relationship, and providing honesty and guidance to his children by playing an active role in their upbringing.

Mullison has candidly acknowledged, expressed and demonstrated sincere remorse for his conduct. He did not attempt to use his drug addiction as an excuse for his previous behavior but at the same time, he acknowledged that his addiction played a major role underlying the actions leading to his disbarment. . . .

These facts demonstrate by clear and convincing evidence that Mullison no longer entertains the thought of using drugs to alleviate the difficulties in life, and is committed to return to the profession. Because Mullison has demonstrated that change in character, he is rehabilitated. . . .

Substance abuse and/or addiction poses an ever present threat of recurrence. Although the evidence presented is both clear and convincing that Mullison is presently free from substance abuse, the remote possibility of relapse warrants the imposition of conditions upon Mullison's readmission to the practice of law as an added measure of protection to the public. . . .

It is therefore ORDERED:

Mullison's Petition for Readmission is GRANTED;

Mullison shall be subject to not more than fifteen random drug/urinalysis tests during a period of twelve months from the date of this Order. The Office of Attorney Regulation Counsel shall initiate such tests at such times as they may elect. . . .

B. Personality and Professionalism

Martin E.P. Seligman, Paul R. Verkuil & Terry H. Kang*

Why Lawyers Are Unhappy

23 Cardozo L. Rev. 33 (2001)

. . . Introduction

Much attention has been paid recently to the disillusionment among lawyers. The New York City Bar Association, a leader among bar groups, has focused upon the

* Martin Seligman is Robert A. Fox Leadership Professor of Psychology, University of Pennsylvania; Paul Verkuil is Professor, Benjamin N. Cardozo School of Law, Yeshiva University, and Terry Kang, J.D., is an Assistant to Professor Seligman.

lawyer's (especially young associate's) "quality of life." Its Task Force Report cites "unhappiness" among young lawyers and measures its impact. The implication and costs of this unhappiness are significant, as many bright attorneys grow disillusioned and cynical, with diminishing career opportunities. Unhappy associates fail to achieve their full potential at a cost to them, their firms, their clients, and even their families. Invariably many lawyers leave the law firm, and some the practice of law, prematurely, resulting in undesirable turnover, and a loss of talent to the profession.[2]

In this essay we suggest that much of the unhappiness of lawyers can be cured. It stems from three causes: (1) Lawyers are selected for their pessimism (or "prudence") and this generalizes to the rest of their lives; (2) Young associates hold jobs that are characterized by high pressure and low decision latitude, exactly the conditions that promote poor health and poor morale; and (3) American law is to some extent a zero-sum game, and negative emotions flow from zero-sum games. We acknowledge that while the first two causes have well-documented antidotes, the third, the zero-sum nature of law, may be a justifiable aspect of the profession; but even in this case we suggest promising amelioratives. . . .

The unhappiness and discontent of lawyers is well documented[3] and much lamented.[4] Since lawyers are members of a "public profession,"[5] their dysfunction entails societal, as well as personal, costs. Indeed, the creation of law itself is in one sense bound up with the health of judges, lawyers, legislators, and academicians. But remedies for lawyer distress and the collective malaise of the profession are harder to identify. The attempts by lawyer groups, even distinguished ones like the New York City Bar, to address the issues seem self-serving and half hearted—driven more by public relations and economic concerns than objective study. . . .

I. Defining the Unhappiness Problem

Practitioners have increasingly acknowledged that law is a profession in crisis,[13] and the crisis they speak of relates to the widespread disenchantment among even the most talented lawyers.[14]. . .

---

2. *See* Report of the Task Force on Lawyers' Quality of Life, 55 Rec. Assn. B. N.Y. 755, 756 (2000) [hereinafter N.Y. Bar Task Force Report].

3. *See generally* John P. Heinz et al., *Lawyers and Their Discontents: Findings from a Survey of the Chicago Bar*, 74 Ind. L.J. 735 (1999); Patrick J. Schiltz, *On Being a Happy, Healthy, and Ethical Member of an Unhappy, Unhealthy, and Unethical Profession*, 52 Vand. L. Rev. 871 (1999).

4. *See* Anthony T. Kronman, *The Lost Lawyer: Failing Ideals of the Legal Profession* 13 (1993) (lamenting the "demise of the lawyer-statesman ideal"); *see also* Mary Ann Glendon, *A Nation Under Lawyers: How the Crisis in the Legal Profession Is Transforming American Society* (1994) (characterizing lawyers today as contentious litigators rather than impartial advocates).

5. *See* Charles Silver & Frank B. Cross, *What's Not to Like About Being a Lawyer?*, 109 Yale L.J. 1443 (2000) (reviewing Arthur L. Liman, *Lawyer: A Life of Counsel and Controversy* (1998)). The authors, in defending the public nature of private-sector practice, argue that private-sector lawyers make "an enormous economic contribution to social welfare, including the welfare of the poor. . . . [They] help our economy grow, producing jobs and making people's lives better." *Id.* at 1479; *see also* Amiram Elwork, *Stress Management for Lawyers: How to Increase Personal & Professional Satisfaction in the Law* (1997).

13. *See* Carl Horn, *Twelve Steps Toward Personal Fulfillment in Law Practice*, 25 ABA L. Prac. Mgmt. 36 (Oct. 1999).

14. *See* Robert Kurson, *Who's Killing the Great Lawyers of Harvard?*, Esquire, Aug. 2000, at 82. The author, himself a 1990 Harvard Law graduate, describes the trend among his former classmates: "One after another, those who have left law, especially law firms, seem happy. Those who have not are suffering or, worse, resigned. They talk about losing themselves. . . . More vow to leave the law with the next infusion of cash or gumption." *Id.* at 84. *See also* Note, *Making Docile Lawyers: An Essay on the Pacification of Law Students*, 111 Harv. L. Rev. 2027, 2028 (1998) (documenting the "psychological distress that so often accompanies a Harvard Law School education").

In many cases, the problem is not financial. Associates at top firms can earn (with bonuses) up to $200,000 per year in their first year of practice. . . . The recent pay increases at large law firms are themselves partially caused by lawyer dissatisfaction. The euphemistic "retention bonuses" are awarded to ensure that young associates extend their service beyond two or three years. Combating this desire to leave early is among law firms' highest priorities, since they can only recoup their investment in new lawyers over a longer period of time.

In addition to being disenchanted, lawyers are "in remarkably poor health."[19] They are at much greater risk than the general population for depression, heart disease, alcoholism and illegal drug use. For example, researchers at Johns Hopkins University found statistically significant elevations of major depressive disorder ("MDD") in only three of 104 occupations surveyed.[20] When adjusted for socio-demographic factors, lawyers topped the list, suffering from MDD at a rate 3.6 times higher than employed persons generally.[21] The researchers noted the possibility that the work environments in these at-risk professions were conducive to depression. Further, they proposed that lawyers and secretaries—two of the three highest risk groups—have little autonomy and control, a factor that has been implicated in depression. These studies confirm the hypothesis that lawyer unhappiness can lead to serious health and social problems that pose a threat to the legal profession.

Unhappy lawyers not only burden their families. Given their role in a public profession they can also injure their clients by failing to provide adequate representation.[23] Unhappiness and depression are intimately associated with passivity and poor productivity at work. Bar associations have the best data on these costs since lawyers who violate their clients' interests often become disciplinary problems. But formal recognition usually comes late in lawyers' careers, after a long period of unrecognized and unaddressed problematic behavior. By that point, inadequate representation may already have caused irreparable injuries to clients and the legal system. The task, then, is to protect the public against harm by addressing potential problems before they rise to the level of disciplinary offenses.

That said, we must remember that not all lawyers are unhappy or dysfunctional; indeed, many are very happy and highly functional. And some may follow the course of Justice Cardozo, channeling their unhappiness into professional excellence or even perfectionism. . . .

II. Psychological Explanations for Lawyer Unhappiness. . .

A. Pessimism

. . . Pessimism is defined not in the colloquial sense: "seeing the glass as half full or half empty" but rather, as a pessimistic "explanatory style." This is the tendency to interpret the causes of negative events in stable, global and internal

---

19. *See* Schiltz, *supra* note 3, at 873; see also Michael Quinn, *Reality Bites*, Tex. Law., Jan. 31, 2000, at 63 (reviewing Steven Keeva, *Transforming Practices: Finding Joy and Satisfaction in the Legal Life* (1999)).
20. *See* William W. Eaton et al., *Occupations and the Prevalence of Major Depressive Disorder*, 32 J. Occupational Med. 1079, 1081 (1990) (discussing findings based on interviews of 1,200 workers).
21. The other two at-risk occupations are teachers and counselors, with a depressive rate of 2.8; and secretaries, with a rate of 1.9. *Id.* at 1079.
23. *See* John F. Harkness, Jr., *Lawyers Helping Lawyers: A Message of Hope*, 73 Fla. B.J. 10 (Dec. 1999) (reporting that over half the grievances filed against lawyers have addiction or mental disorder as a significant contributing factor).

ways: "It's going to last forever; it's going to undermine everything; it's my own fault."[28] Under this definition, the pessimist will view bad events as unchangeable. The optimist, in contrast, sees setbacks as temporary. That crucial distinction is what connects pessimism to unhappiness.

Research has revealed, predictably, that pessimism is maladaptive in most endeavors: pessimistic life insurance agents make fewer sales attempts, are less productive and persistent, and quit more readily than optimistic agents. Pessimistic undergraduates get lower grades, relative to their SAT's and past academic record, than optimistic students. Pessimistic swimmers have more sub-standard swims and bounce back from poor swims less readily than do optimistic swimmers. Historical research even suggests that pessimistic world leaders take fewer risks and act more passively during political conflicts than their optimistic counterparts. In the context of a military crisis and aggression by an adversary, such passivity can have devastating consequences.

But while pessimists tend to be losers on many fronts, there is one striking exception: pessimists may fare better in law. . . . In sharp contrast to results in other realms of life, law students whose attributional style defined them as "pessimistic" actually fared better than their optimistic peers. Specifically, the pessimists outperformed more optimistic students on traditional measures of achievement, such as grade-point average and law journal success.

These data suggest that what is labeled as pessimism is not a detriment and may even be a virtue for lawyers. Pessimism encompasses certain "positive" dimensions; it contains what we call—in less pejorative terms—"prudence." A prudent perspective, which requires caution, skepticism and "reality-appreciation," may be an asset for law or other skill-based professions. It is certainly a quality that is embraced in legal education. Prudence enables a good lawyer to see snares and catastrophes that might conceivably occur in any given transaction. The ability to anticipate a whole range of problems that non-lawyers do not see is highly adaptive for the practicing lawyer. Indeed clients would be less effectively served if lawyers did not so behave, even though this ability to question occasionally leads to lawyers being labeled as deal breakers or obstructionists.

The qualities that make for a good lawyer, however, may not make for a happy human being. Pessimism is well documented as a major risk factor for unhappiness and depression. Lawyers cannot easily turn off their pessimism (i.e. prudence) when they leave the office. Lawyers who can see acutely how bad things might be for clients are also burdened with the tendency to see how bad things might be for themselves. . . . In this manner, pessimism that might be adaptive in the profession also carries the risk of depression and anxiety in the lawyer's personal life. The challenge is how to remain prudent professionally and yet contain pessimistic tendencies in domains of life outside the office.

B. Low Decision Latitude

. . . Decision latitude refers to the number of choices one has or, as it turns out, one believes one has. Workers in occupations that involve little or no control are at risk for depression and for poor physical health. An important study of the correlation of job conditions with depression and coronary disease used two dimensions:

28. *See* Martin E.P. Seligman, *Helplessness: On Depression, Development, and Death* (2d ed., W.H. Freeman 1992).

(1) job demands and (2) decision latitude. There is one quadrant particularly inimical to health and morale: high job demand combined with low decision latitude. Individuals with jobs in this quadrant had a much higher incidence of coronary disease and depression than individuals in the other three quadrants.

Nurses and secretaries are the usual occupations falling in that quadrant, but in recent years, junior associates at major law firms have been added to the list. These lawyers often confront situations of high pressure combined with low decision latitude. Beyond the intense job demands of law practice, low decision latitude is also a frequently cited problem. Associates often have little voice or control over their work, only limited contact with their superiors, and virtually no client contact. Instead, for at least the first few years of practice, many remain cloistered and isolated in a library (or behind a computer screen), researching and drafting memos.

In these high-pressure, low decision latitude positions, the associates are likely candidates for negative health effects, such as higher rates of heart disease; and for higher divorce rates. These same associates are, not surprisingly, candidates for early departure from law firms [and]. . . many young lawyers who do leave firms early choose alternative legal careers, such as legal aid or assistant district attorney, where the pay is considerably lower but the decision latitude is considerably greater.

III. Remedies for Pessimism and for Low Decision Latitude

There are well-documented antidotes for the difficulty lawyers face because of their pessimism and low decision latitude. As to pessimism, the antidote is to enlist its opposite dimension: optimism. Optimism is the ability to dispute recurrent catastrophic thoughts effectively, and it can be learned. "Flexible optimism" can be taught to both children and adults to enable them to determine how and in what situations one should use optimism and when to use pessimism. The techniques of "learned optimism," can teach lawyers to use optimism in their personal lives, yet maintain an adaptive pessimism in their professional lives. Flexible optimism can be taught in a group setting such as law firms. If firms are willing to experiment, we believe the positive effects on the performance and morale of associates in those firms could be significant.

Learned optimism recommends that individuals employ a "disputing technique" to control their negative emotions. In the disputing technique, the lawyer first learns to identify catastrophic thoughts she has, and the circumstances under which they occur: "I'll never make it to partner," whenever a senior member of the firm fails to return her greeting. Then she learns to treat these thoughts as if they were uttered by a rival for her job, a third person whose mission is to make her life miserable. She then learns to marshal evidence against the catastrophic thoughts, "Even though he didn't smile when I said 'hi' this morning, he praised my brief in the meeting last week. He probably is on my side and was distracted by the big case he has to argue this afternoon." Credible disputing of pessimistic thinking (unlike, say dieting) is self-maintaining because one feels better at the moment one does it.

As to the high pressure-low decision latitude problem, there is a remedy as well. We accept that pressure is an inescapable aspect of law practice. But high pressure itself does not seem to be the problem; rather, it is the combination of high pressure and low decision latitude that causes negative health effects. By modifying this dimension, lawyers can become both more satisfied and more productive. One solution is to tailor a lawyer's day so there is considerably more personal control over work.[52] . . . . Antidotes to associate malaise include more substantive training, mentoring, a voice in management, and earlier client contact—not expensive dinners or Cuban cigars. Those firms who understand the need to make these changes will benefit. Those who do not so respond, who instead simply throw money at the problem, will continue to see associates vote with their feet. . . .

Law firms should discover the particular signature strengths of their associates.[58] Exploiting them could make the difference between a demoralized associate and an energized, productive colleague. A firm can produce higher morale by setting aside five to ten hours of the workweek for "signature strength time," (i.e., a non-routine assignment that uses the signature strengths).[59] Over time, higher morale will translate into higher billing hours.

Some examples may serve to make the point. If an associate's strengths include leadership he or she could be assigned to associate committee work; or if it is social intelligence, he or she could be exposed to clients at an earlier stage. Originality might send an associate to the library to search out a non-obvious theory to an intractable legal problem. That may sound like the kind of duty all associates should assume; however, the idea of signature strengths is that some associates are indeed better suited to library work, and others to different roles at the firm, even though they must all have a commitment to legal analysis.

IV. The Harder Case: Zero vs. Non-Zero Sum Games

A. Zero-Sum Games and Emotion

A zero-sum game is a familiar occurrence. It is an endeavor in which the net result is zero. For every gain by one side, there is a counterbalancing loss by the other. A sports event is a zero-sum game, in that there must be winners and losers. A non-zero-sum game, in contrast, is an endeavor in which there is a net gain. Reading this essay is a positive-sum game: your exposure to new information does not mean someone else has forgotten an equivalent amount of information. Rather, there are gains on both sides: the reader learns something new, the authors disseminate their ideas, and so forth. . . .

B. The Adversary System as a Zero-Sum Game

The adversary process, which lies at the heart of the American system of law, has long been viewed as a classic zero-sum game: in litigation, one side's gain often moves in lockstep with the other side's loss. Lawyers are trained to be aggressive and competitive precisely because they must win the litigation game. This training, because it is fueled by negative emotions, can be a source of lawyer demoralization, even if it fulfills a social function. One problem with the adversarial paradigm,

---

52. Volvo solved a similar problem on its assembly lines in the 1960s by giving its workers the choice of building a whole car in a group, rather than repeatedly building the same part. Similarly, a junior associate might be given a better sense of the whole picture by being introduced to clients, mentored by partners, and involved in transactional discussions.

58. *See* http://www.psych.upenn.edu/seligman for identification of these and other strengths, and a self-test. A law firm can develop an inventory of associate strengths by having associates take tests and assigning duties based on the results. At law schools, the strengths analysis can be used to give students and placement directors a better sense of their career goals.

59. In each of these cases, the five to ten hours an associate devotes to using his or her signature strengths should be considered part of the normal workload, whether or not this time produces billable hours. This is similar to what happens when pro bono hours are calculated into an associate's workweek.

according to leading lawyers like Sol Linowitz, is that "the single-minded drive toward winning the competition . . . will make these young lawyers not only less useful citizens . . . but also less good as lawyers, less sympathetic to other people's troubles, and less valuable to their clients."[64]. . . . By understanding the values of the adversary system in terms of its zero-sum nature, we can assess alternatives that seek to soften competition with cooperation. Modifications to our legal system must be justified both in terms of an individual's well-being, and of our system of justice.

C. The Adversary System as a Social Good . . .

An accepted virtue of the common law, adversarial system of justice is that it leaves more control in the parties (through their attorneys). The civil law, accusatory system, on the other hand, places more control on the judge (or other decision-maker). Since control has a salutary psychological effect, the adversary model is one expression of a satisfactory political system. By placing control in the individual over the state the adversary system reflects deeper values of liberalism and even natural justice. In this way, the lawyer has a central role as a public servant, a preserver of the values inherent in our political structure, even when he or she is seemingly only arguing for a client's self-interest. And since the days of Adam Smith, we have believed that self-interest serves the public interest.

The psychological question is whether adversaries can be competitive without being pessimistic. . . .

This is not just a question of positive psychology. Justice Sandra Day O'Connor has asked why the profession envisions litigation as war.[71] The question is, can lawyers serve the adversary system without generating conflict on a personal level? Civility need not weaken the lawyer's commitment to the adversary system. In fact, a growing number of law schools and law firms now recognize the importance of instilling civility and teaching team-building skills. Under this vision, it may be possible to retain the virtues of adversariness while discarding some of its negative dimensions.

We suggest that controlling the intensity of non-zero behavior, like curbing the effects of pessimism in the earlier examples, can serve as a coping technique with positive health effects. Moreover, our initial description of the litigation experience emphasizes a largely limited, if not misleading, reality. The zero-sum effects of the adversary model, in terms of its "winner-take-all" mentality, usually occur where cases are tried to judgment—a small minority of cases. Where settlements occur, both sides frequently have made wise choices that allow them to claim victory.

Outside of litigation, non-zero expectations can play an even greater role. As Dean Clark has noted, most lawyers are not litigators; rather they are specialists in "normative ordering."[75] The notion of normative ordering suggests a role that fits the lawyer-statesman ideal Dean Kronman seeks to revive. When lawyers assume these roles, cooperation challenges the virtue of competition. For example, Ronald Gilson has argued that business lawyers—the deal-makers—can create value in such a way as to eliminate the zero-sum problem altogether.[76]. . .

---

64. Sol M. Linowitz, *The Betrayed Profession: Lawyering at the End of the Twentieth Century* 107-08 (1994).

71. *See* Sandra Day O'Connor, Speech, *Professionalism*, 78 Or. L. Rev. 385, 388 (1999). The "war" analogy is deeply imbedded in the litigation world, where dealings with other attorneys are described with terms such as "attacked" and "shot down." *Id.*

75. Robert C. Clark, *Why So Many Lawyers: Are They Good or Bad?*, 61 Fordham L. Rev. 275, 281 (1992).

76. *See* Ronald J. Gilson, *Value Creation by Business Lawyers: Legal Skills and Asset Pricing*, 94 Yale L.J. 239, 253-55 (1984) (labeling those lawyers "transaction cost engineers").

V. The Role and Responsibility of Law Schools

Law schools are both a source of the problem and a necessary part of the solution. The Socratic teaching method—employed especially in large, first-year classes—cultivates and encourages adversarial thinking by emphasizing zero-sum situations. The students' adversarial skills are honed by withstanding questioning from skeptical interrogators. In this respect, law school pedagogy differs from that of business schools, where cooperative projects and thinking are the rule in leading MBA programs. Moreover, competition for grades, among a group who self selects law for its pessimistic qualities, adds to the challenges. . . . This relationship of success in classroom performance to the litigation model is rarely explored or explained in legal education. Yet the connections between the Socratic method and the adversary system may well set the stage for the kinds of difficulties law students later face as young associates, as well as their successes. We encourage further study into the relationships among teaching style, grading methods, and the pessimistic tendencies of law students.

The connection between law teaching and the demands of practice might be revealed early in the first year, rather than assumed. Such an explanation may not overcome embarrassing moments in the classroom, but it can provide an objective rationale for an experience that some now find alienating precisely because it seems unnecessary or even gratuitous. At the least, explaining that their education serves certain social purposes gives students the illusion of control and also introduces them to the demands they will face in practice.

The subject of positive psychology and lawyer unhappiness deserves exploration in the academic setting. Offering law students a sense of what the lawyer's life demands can increase the feeling of control over their professional lives. With this background, both academic and career choices can be made on a more intelligent and emotionally satisfying basis. In fact, a survey of student strengths at this stage might have considerable value. Some students have talents for litigation, for example, while others lean in the direction of less confrontational forms of practice. Some have signature strengths of valor and originality, others of social intelligence and fairness. These strengths have a real world dimension: they could be factored into the career placement function at law schools in order to provide a better fit between a first job and the talents of graduating students. . . .

VI. Summary and Next Steps

The pervasive disenchantment among lawyers and the concomitant attrition rate among law firms can be remedied. The solutions will be found not by increasing compensation or perks, but instead by using more valuable, but less tangible rewards. This will require changes in law firm culture—greater emphasis on positive-sum games and cooperation—as well as reforms at three levels: individual, firm-wide, and institutional. At the individual level, lawyers must first recognize that pessimism is maladaptive outside of work. Perhaps they then can learn to apply the techniques of flexible optimism in their private lives. At the law firm level, those members with the most power to effect change should actively participate in creating more decision latitude for junior associates. At the least, partners should create mentoring relationships with junior associates. They should also delegate responsibilities and allocate tasks to junior associates that better speak to their signature strengths, thereby providing more control and decision-making power at an earlier stage in their development.

Third, at the institutional level, bar associations that foster and promote civility among their members are on the right track. Judges and counsel who encourage settlement and direct cases toward mediation may deserve credit for dampening the zero-sum nature of practice. The law schools also play an institutional role. They are the entry point to the profession and help shape the system. By assisting new lawyers to adapt to the demands of practice they can become agents for positive change. The goal is clear if elusive: create a psychologically healthier profession while honoring the essential role of lawyers as client representatives. These need not be incompatible objectives.

. . . We suggest that by decreasing pessimism, increasing decision latitude, and leavening zero-sum games with a cooperative dimension, the practice of law can become healthier and no less profitable. Admittedly, this is a challenging agenda. But even if it cannot be fully realized, we have at least helped answer the question why lawyers are unhappy and we have suggested why they need not be in the future.

Lawyers' Roles: *Finding Your Own Way*

In Chapter 1, we defined legal ethics as the study of what is required for a lawyer to provide a professional service to another. Lawyers' roles are complicated by the fact that the client simultaneously empowers the lawyer to act, and becomes subject to the lawyer's power created by the lawyer's specialized knowledge and ability to access the legal system. Several notes and cases in Chapter 5 commented on lawyers who apparently assumed directive or instrumental roles, which caused them to risk violating legal norms designed to protect clients or the public.[1] At the end of Chapter 5, we pointed out that most lawyers get it right most of the time by zealously representing their clients within the bounds of the law.[2] The cases and materials in the second half of this book illustrate these same themes. Some of the lawyers in these cases acted in directive roles, serving the interests of third persons or their own interests before those of their clients. Others got into trouble by overidentifying with their clients; by seeing themselves as instrumental cogs in the machinery of the legal system.

Directive Self-Servers

Chapter 6 concerning loyalty offered numerous examples of lawyers who breached fiduciary duty by failing to recognize or respond properly to conflicts of interest. These lawyers underidentified with their clients and fell short of providing zealous representation. They neglected the lessons of fiduciary duty that lawyers serve client interests, not their own, another client's or the interests of a third party.[3] Chapter 7 also offered examples of lawyers who placed profit maximization above fiduciary duty to their clients. These lawyers failed to recognize that lawyering is a regulated

1. Lawyers' Roles: The Directive Lawyer and Fiduciary Duty, *supra* p.127; Lawyers' Roles: The Instrumental Lawyer and the Limits of the Law, *supra* p.202.
2. Lawyers' Roles: Zealous Representation Within the Bounds of the Law, *supra* p.245.
3. *See* Maritrans GP Inc. v. Pepper Hamilton & Scheetz, *supra* p.257; Monco v. Janus, *supra* p.266; In re Halverson, *supra* p.271; Burrow v. Arce, *supra* p.285; Universal City Studios v. Reimerdes, *supra* p.296; Matter of Disc. Proc. Against Wildermuth, *supra* p.314; Kanaga v. Gannett Co., *supra* p.336; Kala v. Aluminum Smelting & Refining Co., *supra* p.348.

market, and that clients have absolute rights to discharge them at will.[4] Similarly, *Gilles* in Chapter 8 illustrates a lawyer and law firm that failed to view fiduciary duty from the client's point of view, incorrectly thinking they could abandon the client's case without assuring that the client has ample opportunity to find replacement counsel. In this chapter, *Mullison* offers an extreme example of a directive self-serving lawyer who eventually redeemed himself.

Instrumental Cogs

At the same time, Chapter 9 offered new and serious examples of lawyers who understood their role in largely instrumental terms. These lawyers provided zealous advocacy, but failed to recognize a clear legal limit to their representation of client interests, such as those provided by Federal Rules of Civil Procedure 11 or 26. They overidentified with their clients and suffered sanctions, discipline and disqualification as a result.[5]

Dual Difficulties

Several lawyers in the second half of this book suffered from the excesses of both directive and instrumental role behavior at the same time. For example, the insurance defense firm in *Wolpaw,*[6] like those in *Perez*[7] and *Spaulding,*[8] acted instrumentally toward one potential client, the insurer who hired it and paid the bill, and inappropriately directed the other primary client, the insured, who was equally entitled to representation complete with a full array of fiduciary duties. In serving the insurance company, they breached duties to the insured and at the same time aided the insurer in neglecting its contractual obligations to the insured.

A similar dual difficulty arose in Chapter 9 in *Stewart,* where the court disqualified a lawyer who was a necessary witness in the matter.[9] Initially, the lawyer ignored the limit on advocacy inherent in the lawyer-witness rule by failing to appreciate the court's interest in avoiding the confusion between the role of witness and advocate. At the same time, the lawyer needed as a primary witness also might prejudice the client's case. In disqualifying the lawyer, the court was concerned that the client have enough time to find appropriate substitute counsel who could provide zealous representation without such a personal conflict of interest.

The same duality of role confusion comes through in *Birbrower.*[10] The court there was concerned with protecting the public from unlicensed professionals and made clear that the New York law firm failed to recognize that legal limit on their right to practice law. At the same time, the court characterized the firm's unauthorized practice of law as a breach of a client obligation by granting the affected client a complementary remedy, freedom to avoid its contractual fee. Finally, *Kelly* portrays a lawyer who defrauded both clients and third persons.

---

4. *See* Matter of Fordham, *supra* p.371; Rosenberg v. Levin, *supra* p.390; In re Sather, *supra* p.393.
5. *See* Gerald B. Lefcourt, P.C. v. United States, *supra* p.424; Christian v. Mattel, Inc., *supra* p.429; In re Tutu Wells Contamination Litigation, *supra* p.436; In re Charges of Unprofessional Conduct, *supra* p.443; Matter of Disc. Proceedings Against Ragatz, *supra* p.451.
6. *See* Wolpaw v. Gen. Accident Ins. Co., *supra* p.312.
7. Perez v. Kirk & Carrigan, *supra* p.125.
8. Spaulding v. Zimmerman, *supra* p.161.
9. Stewart v. Bank of America, N.A., *supra* p.454.
10. Birbrower, Montalbano, Condon & Frank P.C. v. Superior Court, *supra* p.494.

Getting It Right

At the end of Chapter 5, we commented that most lawyers avoid both of these extremes by acting as collaborators with their clients.[11] Many of the lawyers in the second half of this book also found the right course. For example, the law firm in A. v. B. sought the discretion to disclose material information learned from one client to another.[12] Note that the lawyers and law firm did not automatically favor one client over another by disclosing, as occurred in *Perez*. Instead, it recognized that some strong policy must justify limiting their fiduciary duty to one client, then sought and won court approval to rely on an explicit confidentiality exception to legitimate the disclosure. The lawyer's recognition of the importance of confidentiality owed a prospective client in *Poly Software* was reflected in the lawyer's efforts to limit initial disclosures, and paid off in freeing the lawyer from disqualification.[13] On the other hand, the opposing lawyer who had served as a mediator for the parties in an earlier related matter was not allowed to represent one of them in later litigation.

Consider further the law firm in *Messing*.[14] After being sanctioned nearly $100,000 for unlawful contact with Harvard employees, the firm had to decide whether to recommend an appeal of such a sanction to its client. Although the client interests (in avoiding additional litigation costs) and the law firm interests in reversing the sanction conflicted, ultimately both client and lawyer interests were vindicated on appeal. The case attracted a number of amicus briefs from other groups including labor unions, which supported the law firm's activity. The court acknowledged the significance of the client interests at stake, but also identified the competing interests in fair access to evidence, concluding that an intermediate legal definition of "represented person" should include some but not all corporate employees. The law firm took some risk in advising its client to appeal the issue, but also no doubt recognized that the lower court's decision was not universally supported by other courts and had negative policy implications both for its client and others in similar circumstances.

Finally, consider the actions of the lawyers who blew the whistle on employers in *Crews* and *Kelly*.[15] Both understood that lawyers in their offices were engaged in violations of the rules of professional conduct, both understood their own obligation to speak up, and both did so, first to supervisors and eventually to others. Each encountered significant economic, personal, and professional incentives not to speak, or to defer to supervisors who told them that the matter was handled. Like the lawyer in *Meyerhofer*,[16] both carefully documented the continuing rule violations, and both suffered the loss of a job as a result. Neither had any assurance that any legal relief would later be available to them for doing the right thing. Yet each persevered.

All of these lawyers got it right. They also realized that the rules of professional conduct allowed them a great deal of professional discretion to do the right thing. We have seen, for example, that lawyers are free to participate in *pro bono* and law reform cases, an option open to lawyers in a case like *Messing* when client financial limitations may otherwise prevent full judicial consideration of an important legal

---

11. *See* Lawyers' Roles: Zealous Representation Within the Bounds of the Law, *supra* p.245.
12. A. v. B., *supra* p.316.
13. Poly Software Intl., Inc. v. Su, *supra* p.338.
14. Messing, Rudavsky & Weliky, P.C. v. President & Fellows of Harvard College, *supra* p.447.
15. Crews v. Buckman Laboratories Intl., Inc., *supra* p.406; Kelly v. Hunton & Williams, *supra* p.505.
16. Meyerhofer v. Empire Fire & Marine Ins. Co., *supra* p.173.

issue. Further, lawyers are free to choose the kind of practice they prefer and to decide which cases to take.[17] Lawyers also can limit the scope of the engagement and have a great deal of discretion to counsel clients about moral as well as legal limits to their conduct. If a client insists on advocacy arguably or clearly outside of legal limits, lawyers also may or must end the representation.[18] Ultimately, lawyers, like all other professionals, have the option of changing jobs, as the lawyers in *Meyerhofer, Crews,* and *Kelly* demonstrate.

These lawyers also recognized that the law itself is not good or evil, but the use they made of it might be.[19] But how did they formulate their chosen course of action? First, each of these lawyers learned from the law of lawyering to avoid the extremes of both instrumental and directive behavior. They avoided instrumental thinking by being aware of the limits of the law and by refusing to "exclude their own personal values from all professional decisionmaking."[20] At the same time, they avoided directive thinking by recalling the dictates of fiduciary duty and by checking their personal beliefs against their professional obligations to represent clients zealously within the bounds of the law. In other words, they relied on both their personal values and their professional obligations "to signal an ethical quandary," and drew on these values to construct a personal goal. In this process, they were continually informed by their responsibilities to clients and the limits of the law to assure them that the action they took was well within the scope of professional discretion "relegated to the lawyer's ungrounded discretion."[21]

Law and Life

In an earlier note, we introduced the idea that lawyers who represent clients zealously within the bounds of the law act as translators or mediators between the private world of clients and the public world of law. The lawyers in these materials who got it right did the same thing for themselves, mediating between their own personal values and the public world of law. They translated the law for themselves, as well as for their clients, and translated their own values into the law they eventually were a part of making. This insight leads us to consider a fuller meaning of the lawyer as translator metaphor, and we defer here to Professor James Boyd White, who created it:

> What I suggest, briefly, is this: that the lawyer is not, as we sometimes think, only a cog in a system of social administration, nor simply a profit-maximizing service provider, but a person who meets, who can learn to meet, the moment at which the language of the law—a language that has justice as its aim—is applied to experience, the moment at which it must confront other languages. . . . The lawyer or judge live constantly at the edge of language, the edge of meaning, where the world can be, must be, imagined anew; to do this well is an enormous achievement; to do it badly, a disaster of real importance, not only for the lawyer or judge but for the social world of which they are a part, including the particular people whose lives they affect. . . .

---

17. *See, e.g.,* Patrick J. Schilt, *On Being a Happy, Healthy, and Ethical Member of an Unhappy, Unhealthy, and Unethical Profession,* 52 Vand. L. Rev. 871 (1999).
18. *See* Nathan M. Crystal, *Developing a Philosophy of Lawyering,* 14 Notre Dame J.L. Ethics & Pub. Policy 75 (2000).
19. Fred C. Zacharias, *Five Lessons for Practicing Law in the Interests of Justice,* 70 Fordham L. Rev. 1939 (2002).
20. Bruce A. Green, *The Role of Personal Values in Professional Decisionmaking,* 11 Geo. J. Legal Ethics 19, 56 (1997).
21. *Id.*

I might sum it up in this way: Of course the lawyer usually knows more than his client about the law, and in some sense has thus already thought about the issue his client presents; but there is always, or almost always, something new and distinctive and problematic about what the client brings him that requires further thought, and often thought of a deep and uncertain kind. . . .

One way to think about the law, in fact, is as an intervention into a world that works largely in nonlegal terms, and for the most part well enough, but that has now suffered a crisis or breakdown calling for its help. . . .

In each case we begin with the life of the world that precedes the lawyer's involvement, where the parties are competent at shaping their own existences; there is then an event that leads one, then the other, to go to a lawyer; there then ensues a lot of activity, mainly in language—followed by an action, or a refusal to act, by the court or by the lawyers in negotiation, and a return to the world of ordinary life, either changed by what has happened, or unchanged. It thus always is—or should be—a question for the lawyer what relation exists or can exist between the language of the law, the language in which he talks and functions, and the experience and life of the world. . . .

[T]he lawyer must perpetually face the relation between legal language and other languages—other ways of representing the situation or the actors in it, other ways of imagining human motive and experience, other ways of shaping the future. In the courtroom and negotiation alike other languages and voices are regularly translated into the law, always with some distortion, sometimes to good effect, sometimes to bad. Sometimes the law itself changes as a result, but in the end it systematically excludes voices, narratives, languages—ways of thinking and talking that it finds irrelevant to its concerns or of which it does not approve. It is thus a constant question for the lawyer how to manage the relation between law and other languages. . . .

Think for example what it would be like to have someone come to you and describe the collapse of a commercial deal, perhaps a partnership or a long-term contract, for which he had once had great hopes, but which has now proven a disaster. How completely could you capture in your own mind what happened in the world, what its significance was, and how would you think about what ought to happen next? How adequate do you suppose the legal language of partnerships or contracts would be to this situation? The language of accounting or economic theory? What place would the voices of languages of the parties, or of outside experts on technical issues, have in what you said or did? This set of questions could be asked about virtually any case—a divorce, an accident, a crime—and they are present not only when the law looks back on past experience, as it does here, but when it tries to shape experience for the future, by drafting a partnership agreement, for example, or a prenuptial contract, or a divorce settlement. . . .

The law is among other things a system for attracting our attention to difficult questions, and holding it there; for stimulating thought of a disciplined and often creative kind, and feelings too, especially . . . the desire for justice that is called into existence by the questions the case presents, by the contrasting views of the lawyers on each side, and by our own inner sense of the reality and importance of what is at stake. The process of legal thought simultaneously resists simplicity and appeals to the side of us that wants to imagine the world, and ourselves and others within it, in a coherent way. A case is a bright moment, at which we have the opportunity to face at once the language we are given to use and the particulars of the case before us, and in both directions we are drawn into real struggles of mind and imagination. The object of law is justice; but the law teaches us, over and over again, that we do not have unmediated access to the pure idea of justice in the heavens, which we can apply directly and with confidence, but rather live in a world in which everything has to be thought about, argued out, and reimagined afresh. It is a lesson in the difficulty of imagining the world, and the self and others within it, in such a way as to make possible coherent speech and meaningful action.[22]

---

22. James Boyd White, *The Edge of Meaning* 223-226, 250-251 (U. Chi. Press 2001).

Your Way

Of course, you may not agree with all Professor White has to say, or with our characterization of the lawyers in this book. At the very least, we hope that these materials illustrate for you the wide latitude you will have in practice to establish your own role with clients, as well as the clear dangers you will face if you err too far on either end of the spectrum.

Like some of the lawyers in this book, you can choose a somewhat simplistic but psychologically comfortable role, which tends to emphasize instrumental behavior. You may even delight in thinking of yourself as a hired gun, serving the autonomous interests of each client. You may overidentify with your clients, turning into a "business servant"[23] or become cynical about your client's motives, assuming that most clients do not want to be fair and assisting them in getting away with what they can.

Or, like other lawyers in this book, perhaps you prefer to think of yourself more as a directive lawyer who finds security not in psychological identification with clients but who prefers distance from their needs; a lawyer who runs a business. You may decide that profit is what led you to law school, and that the pursuit of profit will determine what kind of cases you target, what level of service each client gets, and how you bill.

You also might choose parts of each of these conceptions of a lawyer's role. As a profit maximizer, you may decide to accept any case if it pays, but prefer not to think of yourself as a hired gun who identifies too closely with (some) client interests. As a directive lawyer who knows best, you may assume that every client's best interest requires you to focus solely on the client's financial, liberty, or security interests. You may also assume that every client wants you to use your skills instrumentally to achieve the result you presume they seek. In other words, depersonalizing clients also can lead to instrumental behavior, just as an instrumental view of the law and the legal system can lead lawyers to act as authorities who impose their own view of the appropriate outcome on a client.

The materials in this book demonstrate that the law governing lawyers has responded to both of these extremes with concrete incentives that steer lawyers away from the minefields of violating fiduciary duty and exceeding the bounds of legitimate advocacy. If you favor or tend toward an instrumental role, you need to be especially alert to the limits of the law that apply to your own conduct as well as that of your client. The lawyers in this book who evaded those limits suffered liability for fraud and malpractice, sanctions for violations of procedural rules, criminal liability, disqualification and professional discipline. If you favor or tend toward a directive role, you will be wise to recall the lawyers in this book who ignored fiduciary duty and suffered malpractice liability, disqualification, loss of a fee or contractual benefit, and professional discipline.

Ultimately, these legal rules spring from and dictate ethics: how we ought to respond to those we chose to serve.[24] They require concrete action, not just intent or thought. They also prod you to assess risk realistically. Beyond understanding these rules and assessing the obligations they create, however, the materials in this

---

23. Russell G. Pearce, *The Professional Paradigm Shift: Why Discarding Professional Ideology Will Improve the Conduct and Reputation of the Bar,* 70 N.Y.U. L. Rev. 1229 (1995).

24. *See, e.g.,* Anthony E. Cook, *Forward: Towards a Postmodern Ethics of Service,* 81 Geo. L.J. 2457 (1993).

chapter also ask you to consider how your life as a lawyer will influence the living of the rest of your life and how the rest of your life will influence your practice of law. Most people and most lawyers want to reconcile their personal values with their professional life. To do so requires continuing dialogue between your personal beliefs and your professional practice.[25] Just as representing clients well requires translation of their personal beliefs into the professional language of the law and translation of the moral fabric of legal rules to your client's situation, so also does your sense of self require continuing translation of your professional to your personal self and back again.

In the end, if you hope to develop the ability to serve clients' interests well, to invent and articulate plans for them, or to grease the bearings of social justice by translating their stories into the language of the law, you will need to develop and maintain the ability to mediate between the ordinary world of everyday life and the legal system.[26] If you want to find guidance for the exercise of your own professional discretion, you also will need to mediate between your personal self and the legal world you work in.[27] As you do this, we wish you the blessing of a life that allows you to integrate your personal and professional self. The lawyers able to discover this connection will be most capable of practicing what they advise their clients: moving on with their lives, perhaps with a renewed sense of vision, influenced both by the ordinary world and the lessons of law that support it.

---

25. *See* George W. Kaufman, *The Lawyers' Guide to Balancing Life and Work: Taking the Stress Out of Success* (ABA 1999).
26. *See* Lawrence S. Krieger, *What We're Not Telling Law Students—and Lawyers—That They Really Need to Know: Some Thoughts-in-Action Toward Revitalizing the Profession from Its Roots,* 13 J. of Law & Health 1 (1998-1999).
27. *See, e.g.,* Joseph Allegretti, *Lawyers, Client, and Covenant: A Religious Perspective on Legal Practice and Ethics,* 66 Fordham L. Rev. 1101 (1998).

Appendix

Researching the Law Governing Lawyers

A. Research Problems

Select one of the following problems as the basis for your research following the guidelines in this appendix:

A-1. Martyn & Fox has decided to open a new office in the jurisdiction where you intend to practice law. Select any problem in this book, and research the answer to that problem in that jurisdiction.

A-2. Interview a practicing lawyer, asking him or her to identify an ethics issue he or she has faced in practice. Research the answer to the lawyer's problem in the jurisdiction where that lawyer practices, or in the jurisdiction where you intend to practice law.

A-3. Videotape a legal ethics problem presented in a movie or television program. Research the answer to that problem in the jurisdiction where the lawyers in the program practice law or in the jurisdiction where you intend to practice.

B. Finding the Law Governing Lawyers

The materials in this book demonstrate that the law governing lawyers stems from a number of sources and has some distinctive features in each jurisdiction. Lawyers searching for a concrete resolution of a legal ethics issue need to find jurisdiction-specific law, but also will discover that many jurisdictions have not yet addressed many issues. This Appendix is intended to help you find the relevant sources you will need to provide answers to issues about lawyer conduct that you and fellow lawyers can rely on. To do this, you will need to identify issues, learn some advanced research techniques, and evaluate the materials you discover to know whether to pursue additional research in other jurisdictions.

Identifying Issues, Rules, and Remedies

This course should help you identify issues in professional responsibility. It also should familiarize you with sections of the professional rules that speak to general obligations of lawyers, such as competence, confidentiality, conflicts of interest, or duties to the court. When a problem involving the conduct of lawyers arises, the first step in solving it is to define the issues. You may immediately discover some, such as confidentiality or loyalty, and you may immediately recognize the relevance of specific professional rules, such as Model Rule 1.6 or 1.7. Whether or not this occurs, be open to the possibility that additional professional rules or legal remedies also may be relevant to your inquiry.

Regardless of whether or not you initially identify any issues when you first think about a problem in professional responsibility, you can benefit by consulting several general research resources that will help you identify issues and relevant law. These resources are listed below.

1. **ABA, Annotated Model Rules of Professional Conduct** (5th ed. 2003)

   Content and Organization: Organized by Model Rule Number, this series of case annotations provides helpful examples of representative court and ethics opinions as well as selected citations to secondary authorities. New Editions are published every few years.

   Special Features: Two tables at the end of the volume provide parallel tables between the ABA Model Code and the ABA Model Rule provisions.

2. **ABA/BNA Lawyers' Manual on Professional Conduct** (2003)
   3 Volumes, monthly updates.

   Content and Organization: This resource is divided into three different volumes. The first, called the "Manual," is organized by topics that generally follow the order of the Model Rules. Each topic begins with a short "practice guide," followed by "background" and "application" sections. Bibliographies follow each topic. Although the entire volume covers the scope of the entire law governing lawyers, special sections also focus on types of practice and malpractice. The second series of volumes includes full text of ABA and some state ethics opinions. Other state opinions are described in annotations. The third loose-leaf volume contains "Current Reports," and an index to these reports, which are both published every two weeks.

   Special Features: The current reports are the most complete recent updates to case law, rules changes and ethics opinions. Each issue includes cites to Internet sources and ABA contacts that can assist your research. The Manual includes both a topical and case index.

3. **Geoffrey C. Hazard, Jr. & W. William Hodes, The Law of Lawyering** (3d ed., Aspen 2001)
   2 Volumes, yearly updates.

   Content and Organization: This loose-leaf service is organized by topics, which follow the order of the Model Rules of Professional Conduct. The treatise reflects latest developments in the law of lawyering, including citations to the Restatement, ethics opinions and case law. The authors discuss multiple remedies, including malpractice, disqualification, discipline, and fee forfeiture.

   Special Features: Each section includes illustrations that apply the law governing lawyers to concrete situations. The Appendix in Vol. II includes the text of the ABA Model Rules and the black letter of the Restatement.

4. **Restatement (Third) The Law Governing Lawyers** (American Law Institute 2000)
   2 Volumes, yearly case citation updates.

   Content and Organization: The Restatement is organized by topic, and covers most issues addressed by professional codes, with the exception of advertising and solicitation. It addresses issues of civil liability, the attorney-client privilege and work product doctrine in depth.

   Special Features: Each restatement section is followed by a Reporter's Note, which includes citations to relevant primary and secondary authority. A Table of Codes, Rules and Standards at the end of Volume II includes restatement citations to professional code sections, individual state professional rules, other restatements, and the model penal code.

5. **Charles W. Wolfram, Modern Legal Ethics** (West 1987)

   Content and Organization: This hornbook is organized by topics and covers all the issues. It is especially helpful for historical development of the professional code provisions and case law.

   Special Features: Each section includes preformulated computer searches to locate case law. Appendices include parallel tables between the ABA Canons, ABA Model Code, and ABA Model Rules.

6. Web sites that contain ethics information are listed at:
   htttp://home.wlu.edu/~wendelb/ethlinks.htm

   Content and Organization: This website offers links to legal ethics locations. Updated periodically.

   Special Features: When using web cites, be careful to note the dates when the database was last updated. Many web cites are maintained by volunteer lawyers who may not have been as thorough as your own research.

If you have no idea where to begin your research, check the table of contents or index of one of these resources.[1] Hornbooks or treatises about the law of professional responsibility also exist in many individual jurisdictions. This is another place to start your research. Always note the publication date of every resource you consult, because nearly every jurisdiction has recently revised some or all of its professional rules. Law review articles and ALR annotations also address a wide variety of issues about lawyer conduct. You may find one or several directly on point.

Finding Relevant Professional Rules

Once you identify issues, you should consider whether any professional rules address them. Of course, if the issue is professional discipline, the professional rules directly apply. If the issue involves other remedies, such as disqualification or malpractice, we have seen that the professional rules also speak to the underlying

1. The Restatement also is available on Westlaw, under the topic "Legal Ethics and Professional Responsibility."

legal ethics issue, and often guide court decisions concerning other remedies. For this reason, you will need to identify the relevant professional code rules in your jurisdiction once you have targeted the relevant issues. Of course, some issues, such as the attorney-client privilege or work product doctrine, might be resolved without citations to professional code provisions. Be careful, however, that the privilege issue does not overlap with the professional rules governing confidentiality or vice versa.

Because the judicial branch of government regulates lawyers, most lawyer professional rules are found in volumes of state or federal court rules. These court rules often may be found in a separate volume in a set of annotated statutes. A few jurisdictions such as California regulate the bar through both statutes and court rules.

Professional rules governing lawyers are also easy to find on line. On LEXIS or Westlaw, go to your state's court rules file ("XXRule" on LEXIS, "XXRules" on Westlaw).[2] Westlaw additionally provides a topical database in "Legal Ethics and Professional Responsibility that contains files which include "state rules of professional conduct" and leads you directly to the "XXRules" menu. In the federal courts, search the relevant circuit rules file with a search such as "discipline."[3] Each circuit's rule imposes slightly different standards, but they usually defer to some extent to individual state rules.[4] Federal district court local trial rules also can be searched on line. District courts usually provide for reciprocal discipline and discipline following a felony conviction, and further impose the state court rules of the jurisdiction in which they sit.[5] Each court has added some distinctive nuances, however, which make finding local rules imperative.[6]

Once you find the court rules volume or file, search by rule number or text of a rule. If you do not know the relevant rules, go back to the last section and identify issues first. You may be surprised to find that your jurisdiction's rule contains distinctive language or provisions not found in the ABA Model Rules. This occurs with some frequency, so never rely on the Model Rules (or Model Code) provisions alone.

Once you have found your jurisdiction's current professional rules, recall that most jurisdictions have adopted some version of the Model Rules of Professional Conduct during the past twenty years. If you wish to find all of the relevant law on point, you will therefore need to be aware of previous Model Code of Professional Responsibility provisions. Although very little case law developed before the Model Code, to find all relevant law, you also may need to travel back to your jurisdiction's version of the Canons of Professional Ethics, adopted before 1970. Most juristrictions also have relied on two different iterations of the CJC. The chart below lists this general historical development. Parallel citation tables between the Model Rules, Model Code, and Canons can

---

2. "XX" is the state's two letter postal abbreviation.
3. U.S.C.S. Tax Ct. R. 201 (2003) (ABA Model Rules govern lawyer conduct).
4. *E.g.*, 4th Cir. Local R. 46(g)(1)(c) (2003) (rules of professional conduct where lawyer maintains principal office); 11th Cir. Appx. R. 1 (2003) (ABA Model Rules and rules of professional conduct where lawyer is licensed to practice if not inconsistent with ABA Model Rules).
5. *E.g.*, N.D. Cal. U.S.D.C. Civil L.R. 11-7 (2003); C.D. Cal. U.S.D.C. Civil L.R. 83-3.1.2 (2003); U.S.D.C. N.D. Tex. L. Cr. R. 57.8 (2003).
6. *E.g.*, N.D. Cal. U.S.D.C. Civil L.R. 11-6 (b) (2003) ("attorney" includes law corporations and partnerships); N.Y. U.S.D.C. Rule 83.4(j) (2003) (ABA Code of Professional Responsibility applies to lawyer conduct).

be found in most standard reference works and often in the history of each professional rule itself.

PROFESSIONAL RULES GOVERNING LAWYER CONDUCT

I. LAWYERS:

A. Disciplinary Rules:

1. ABA **Canons** of Professional Ethics (1908-1969)
2. ABA **Model Code of Professional Responsibility** (1969-1983)

   Adopted by 47 jurisdictions and D.C.; superseded in most by Model Rules of Professional Conduct
3. ABA **Model Rules of Professional Conduct** (1983-2000)

   Adopted by 45+ jurisdictions and D.C. Exceptions include: California, Iowa, Maine, Nebraska, and Ohio. (Oregon and New York have retained the Model Code format, but have adopted the substance of some of the Model Rules.)
4. **Ethics 2000** Commission (1997-2002)
   http://www.abanet.org/cpr/ethics2k.html

   In February 2002 and August 2003, the ABA House of Delegates adopted nearly all of the revisions recommended by the Ethics 2000 Commission. The current revised ABA Model Rules are published in The Center for Professional Responsibility's Edition of the Model Rule of Professional Conduct, or can be found at the website listed above.

B. General Law:

Restatement of the Law (Third) **The Law Governing Lawyers** (2000)

II. JUDGES:

A. ABA Code of Judicial Conduct (1972)

B. ABA Model Code of Judicial Conduct (1990)

Finding Case Law

Once you have identified the relevant professional rules, you can begin to search for cases that apply, construe, or provide remedies for violations of these provisions. Most instances of professional discipline result in written court opinions, which are easily found in annotated volumes of court rules or online by searching using a rule cite or text. At this point, be sure to search for cases construing parallel provisions from earlier professional codes, such as the Code of Professional Responsibility. Shepard's also maintains a volume that collects citations to Code of Professional

Responsibility and Model Rules provisions, Code of Judicial Conduct provisions, and ethics opinions.[7]

Other remedies also can be found in your search, but may require a search by remedy, such as disqualification, fee forfeiture, or the like.[8] Of course, you may be assisted in understanding your jurisdiction's view of these remedies by reference to other topical resources. For example, a hornbook on Criminal Procedure can help in understanding ineffective assistance of counsel, just as a treatise on evidence can assist you in understanding the finer points of the attorney-client privilege or work product doctrine.

You also may choose to begin your search with cases you have discovered in a secondary source. In particular, you should be aware that a number of courts in the past dozen years have cited and relied on provisions of the Restatement of the Law Governing Lawyers. Many of these courts cited to preliminary drafts of the Restatement, which may cause some confusion, because the numbering system of these drafts was amended when the final version of the document was completed. The chart below indicates these changes in numbers. If you decide to search by Restatement section number, be aware that you should include both the old and new number in your search. If you search for a restatement provision online, try "law governing lawyers" and the section numbers, or "law governing lawyers" and the general topic for which you are looking. You also can search the text of the Restatement on Westlaw. Be careful, however, to select the database that includes the final restatement, not the tentative drafts.

RESTATEMENT OF THE LAW, THIRD, THE LAW GOVERNING LAWYERS
CONVERSION TABLE

OLD = tentative and final drafts (1988-1998)
NEW = final restatement sections (2000)

OLD #	NEW #	OLD #	NEW #	OLD #	NEW #	OLD #	NEW #
1-8	**1-8**	53	**41**	124	**74**	167	**107**
10	**9**	54	**42**	125	**75**	168	**108**
11	**10**	55	**43**	126	**76**	169	**109**
12	**11**	56	**44**	127	**77**	170	**110**
13	**12**	57	**45**	128	**78**	171	**111**
14	**13**	58	**46**	129	**79**	172	**112**
26	**14**	59	**47**	130	**80**	173	**113**
27	**15**	70 (71)	**48**	131	**81**	174	**114**
28	**16**	71	**49**	132	**82**	175	**115**
29	**17**	72	**50**	133	**83**	176	**116**

(continued)

7. *See* Shephard's Professional and Judicial Conduct Citations.

8. Recall that a list of these remedies can be found in *Restatement (Third) The Law Governing Lawyers* §6 (2000).

RESTATEMENT OF THE LAW, THIRD, THE LAW GOVERNING LAWYERS CONVERSION TABLE (continued)

29A	**18**	73	**51**	134A	**84**	177	**117**
30	**19**	74	**52**	134B	**85**	178	**118**
31	**20**	75	**53**	135	**86**	179	**119**
32	**21**	76	**54**	136	**87**	180	**120**
33	**22**	76A	**55**	137	**88**	201	**121**
34	**23**	77	**56**	138	**89**	202	**122**
35	**24**	78	**57**	139	**90**	203	**123**
37	**25**	79	**58**	140	**91**	204	**124**
38	**26**	111	**59**	141	**92**	206	**125**
39	**27**	112	**60**	142	**93**	207	**126**
40	**28**	113	**61**	151	**94**	208	**127**
41	**29**	114	**62**	152	**95**	209	**128**
42	**30**	115	**63**	155	**96**	210	**129**
43	**31**	116	**64**	156	**97**	211	**130**
44	**32**	117	**65**	157	**98**	212	**131**
45	**33**	117A	**66**	158	**99**	213	**132**
46	**34**	117B	**67**	159	**100**	214	**133**
47	**35**	118	**68**	161	**101**	215	**134**
48	**36**	119	**69**	162	**102**	216	**135**
49	**37**	120	**70**	163	**103**		
50	**38**	121	**71**	164	**104**		
51	**39**	122	**72**	165	**105**		
52	**40**	123	**73**	166	**106**		

Finding Ethics Opinions

We have seen throughout these materials that both the American Bar Association and state and local bars have ethics committees that answer individual questions about the application of their rules to a proposed course of conduct. These committees address many issues before they ever reach a court. For that reason, you should also check your jurisdictions ethics opinions for useful insight. Although these opinions do not bind courts, the latter are very reluctant to discipline a lawyer who complies with an ethics committee's advice. At the same time, if you find an ethics opinion, be sure to search your jurisdiction's cases to see whether it has been addressed, approved, or disapproved by the court.

Ethics opinions are most easily accessed online. Most state bar associations have websites for their members, which often include full text of at least recent ethics opinions.[9] Many states also publish these opinions in state or local bar journals. Both LEXIS and Westlaw have ethics opinions online. Your jurisdiction may be on one or the other, or both. ABA ethics opinions can be found in both places. Here, the topical approach works well. For LEXIS, click on "Ethics," for Westlaw, "Legal Ethics and Professional Responsibility." The menus that follow will list the jurisdictions included in that service.

9. Acess to many of these cites can be obtained through FindLaw, www.findlaw.com., using the topic "ethics and professional responsibility."

Identifying Majority and Minority Viewpoints

Research resources such as those listed on pages 532-533 will help you put your jurisdiction's rules and cases in perspective. Many courts have found the Restatement especially helpful. These resources also will help you understand the way most courts have handled an issue if your court has not yet addressed it. Before you decide to cite a decision, be sure that the cases you look at construe professional rules provisions similar to the ones in your jurisdiction.

Your Results

You have learned enough in this course to give you a good start in finding the law governing lawyers. This note should help you with the finer points of locating all of the relevant law. If you find no authority in your jurisdiction, or want to inquire whether the authority you have found may be distinguishable from the situation you or your firm faces, you should consider asking a local or state bar for an ethics opinion.[10] Many organizations, including disciplinary counsel in many states, also offer ethics hotlines to answer your questions or get you started on finding an answer. Remember that Model Rule 1.6(b)(4), if adopted in your jurisdiction, also allows use of client confidences reasonably necessary "to secure legal advice about the lawyer's compliance with these Rules." With these resources, you should be able to identify ethics issues in practice and find the answers you need to practice responsibly.

C. Written Assignment

Goals:

Your ultimate goal should be to produce a paper sufficiently informative that a lawyer could rely on your advice in practice.

1. To do this, you will need to select a problem, identify issues, learn some advanced research techniques, and use and improve your analytical and writing ability.
2. Your grade will be based on the quality of your research, organization, use of authority, analysis, and writing.

Writing and Analysis Outline:

1. Use an interoffice research memo format. Direct the memo to the senior partner in Martyn & Fox who asked you for advice.
2. Begin by describing the facts of the problem you have selected. Next, discuss the relevant law in the following order:
   A. The professional rules that govern in your jurisdiction.
   B. The case law in your jurisdiction.
   C. Any state or ABA ethics opinions that address the issue.
   D. The rules, case law, and other authorities in other jurisdictions. Here, you should focus on whether and how your jurisdiction's result is consistent with the rules and case law in most other jurisdictions. You will find

10. *See, e.g.,* In re Request for Instructions from Disc. Counsel, 610 A.2d 15 (R.I. 1992).

any or all of the Research Resources listed above helpful in this section of your analysis. In particular, you *must* cite to the Restatement if it addresses your topic.

Overall Requirements:

1. *Length:* Your paper should be about 10 double spaced pages including footnotes, which should be used for citations to authorities. Footnotes can appear at the bottom of each page, or at the end of the paper.
2. *Citations:* Use the ALWD, bluebook, or local rules for citation form. When referring to primary source material (statutes, cases, court rules, etc.) always go to the material itself. Do not rely on quotations from other authors.
3. *Plagiarism:* When you quote, paraphrase, rely on or are influenced by someone else's ideas, cite that author. Ideas taken from another source, even if expressed in your own words, also must be cited to avoid misrepresenting the work as your own. As a rule, if you are in doubt, footnote the material.

Table of Cases

Bold indicates principal cases.

Table of Model Rules, Restatements, and Other Regulations

ABA Model Rules of Professional Conduct

ABA Model Code

State Rules, Statutes, and Ethics Opinions

Restatements

Restatement (Third) The Law Governing Lawyers

Restatement of Agency

Miscellaneous

Index